Accounting
for Life Insurance Companies

Accounting

for Life Insurance Companies

CHARLES L. VAN HOUSE, Sr., F.L.M.I.
Member American Academy of Actuaries
Senior Vice President, Administration
Coastal States Life Insurance Company

W. ROGERS HAMMOND, D.B.A., C.P.A.
Dean of Graduate Studies
School of Business Administration
Georgia State College

Published for LIFE OFFICE MANAGEMENT ASSOCIATION
100 Colony Square, Atlanta, Georgia   30361
By RICHARD D. IRWIN, INC., Homewood, Illinois

13 14 15 16 17 18 K 5 4

Library of Congress Catalog Card No. 78-86860
Printed in the United States of America

Preface

This textbook covers the fundamentals of double-entry bookkeeping and presents the principles and many of the practices of life insurance accounting.

Chapters 2 through 5 are devoted to the fundamentals of double-entry bookkeeping. The student who has no previous knowledge of accounting should thoroughly learn these fundamentals before progressing to subsequent chapters. A person trained in accounting may begin at Chapter 6, but it is suggested that he review the summaries of accounting principles included at the end of the previous four chapters. Chapters 6 and 7 cover machines which are used to perform most accounting operations in a modern life insurance company.

The main portion of the book discusses typical accounting processes used in connection with each insurance function within the more common lines of business. Details of annual statements as prescribed by regulatory authorities are included at the end of many of the chapters. In the last two chapters, special features of the U.S. and Canadian annual statement forms are presented. This information is included to provide a continuous and total picture of the life insurance accounting process for the benefit of managerial, financial, actuarial, and accounting personnel. Others will find these two chapters helpful as reference material.

The authors have assumed the student has a general knowledge of the life insurance business and understands the terminology commonly used by persons employed in the life insurance industry.

This book could not have been written without the assistance and suggestions of many well-qualified persons within the life insurance industry. LOMA committees and staff members reviewed several versions of the manuscript and made many valuable suggestions. Officials of companies were most generous in supplying forms and information. To all of these persons the authors extend their most grateful appreciation.

Special credit is due to M. G. Roy Wallace of Loyal Protective Life; Ralph E. Edwards of Baltimore Life; Dr. Kenneth Black, Jr., of Georgia State College; W. Wallace of Confederation Life Association; and William J. Fox of the Canadian Department of Insurance, each of whom made many valuable suggestions.

To the review committee appointed by the LOMA Educational Council and to members of the LOMA staff—particularly John R. Crane, F.L.M.I., and Mrs. Dorothy Fast—much credit is due for extensive aid with the final editing. These persons, of course, bear no responsibility for any deficiencies which may remain in the completed work.

Finally, the authors express their appreciation to Mrs. Lalla Eve, who patiently and expertly typed and retyped many revisions of the manuscript during its formative and review stages, and to Mr. C. H. Poindexter, president of Coastal States Life, who permitted use of company facilities and employee time in preparation of the manuscript.

Atlanta, Georgia   CHARLES L. VAN HOUSE, SR.
October, 1969   W. ROGERS HAMMOND

Table of Contents

1. **Introduction to Accounting** **1**

Usefulness of Accounting Knowledge: *Personal Uses. Business Uses.*
Functions of Accounting: *Basis for Administrative Decisions. Basis
for Credit Determination. Means of Measuring Efficiency. Protection against Fraud. Source of Information.*

2. **Fundamentals of General Accounting** **7**

Forms of Business Ownership. Basic Terminology and the Accounting Equation: *Basic Terminology. The Accounting Equation.* Analyzing Transactions. Accounts. The Ledger. The Journal. Trial
Balance. The Accounting Cycle. Double-Entry and Single-Entry
Bookkeeping: *Double-Entry Bookkeeping. Single-Entry Bookkeeping.* Summary of Accounting Principles.

3. **Accounting for Changes in Surplus** **27**

Changes in the Capital Element. Income and Expense Transactions.
Dividends to Stockholders. Nominal Accounts. Closing the Books:
Closing Entries Illustrated. After-Closing Trial Balance. Review of
Steps in Closing the Books. Statement of Surplus. Time Elements in
Accounting. The Cash and Accrual Basis of Accounting. Adjust-
ments at the End of the Accounting Period: *Unearned Income. Pre-
paid Expense. Accrued Income. Accrued Expense.* Summary of Ac-
counting Principles.

4. **Sales, Inventories, and Working Papers** **49**

Merchandise Operations: *Sales. Purchases. Inventory.* Gross Profit
on Sales. Entries in the Inventory Account. Working Papers: *Prep-
aration of the Working Papers. Adjusting Entries in the Working
Papers. Illustration of Specific Adjustments. Adjusted Balance
Method. Reversal and Reentry Method. Inventory.* Summary of
Accounting Principles.

5. **Miscellaneous Accounting Topics** **72**

Fixed Assets: *Acquisition of Fixed Assets. Depreciation.* Cash: *Imprest System for Petty Cash. Bank Statement Reconciliations. Alter-*

nate Form of Reconciliation. Special Journals. Control Accounts and Subsidiary Ledgers. Chart of Accounts. Summary of Accounting Principles.

6. **Machine Accounting** **99**

Advantages of Machine Methods. Types of Accounting Machines: *Conventional Bookkeeping Machines. Repetitive-Data Processing Equipment*. Terminology Used in Machine Accounting. Input and Storage Media: *Punched Cards. Punched Paper Tape. Magnetic Tape*. Machine Record Files: *Master or Status Files. Transaction or Detail Files. Summary File*. Accounting Controls. Audit Trail.

7. **Accounting Machine Functions** **120**

Conventional Bookkeeping Machines. Unit Record Equipment. Computers: *Mass Storage Devices*.

8. **Introduction to Life Insurance Accounting** **135**

Commercial versus Life Insurance Accounting: *Why is Life Accounting Different?* Annual Statement Forms. Accounting Differences: *Why Cash Basis Accounting? Nonledger Assets and Nonledger Liabilities. Admitted and Nonadmitted Assets. Balance Account*. Summary of Life Insurance Accounting Principles.

9. **Composition of the Annual Statement** **150**

Balance Sheet: *Asset Classifications and Schedules. Liability Classifications. Policy Reserves. Amounts Held on Deposit. Claims Incurred but Not Yet Paid. Dividend Liabilities. Accrued Costs (Other than Claims). Unearned Income. Amounts Temporarily Held for Disposition. Miscellaneous Liabilities. Special Reserves Classed as Liabilities. Capital and Surplus. Capital Stock*. Summary of Operations. Analysis of Operations. Surplus Account. Summary of Life Insurance Accounting Fundamentals.

10. **Accounting for Investments (Part One)** **167**

Accounting for Investment Principal. Accounting for Investment Income. Bond Accounting: *Accrued Bond Interest. Bond Discount and Premium*. Accounting for Stock Owned. Mandatory Securities Valuation Reserve. Mortgage Loans.

11. **Accounting for Investments (Part Two)** **189**

Policy Loans. Real Estate. Other Investments. Gross and Net Investment Income. U.S. Annual Statement Aspects: *Capital Gains and Losses Exhibit*. Canadian Annual Statement Aspects: *Capital Gains and Losses*. Summary of Accounting for Life Insurance Company Investments.

12. Premium Accounting—General **210**

Premium Accounting Systems. Objectives of Premium Accounting. Premium Conditions. Premium Liabilities. Premium Entries. Premium Collection Process and Control: *Item Control. Dollar Control. Typical Premium Control Process.* U.S. Annual Statement Aspects: *Premium Exhibit. Schedule T. Increase in Loading. Miscellaneous.* Canadian Annual Statement Aspects: *Premium Exhibits. Miscellaneous.* Summary of Premium Accounting Fundamentals.

13. Accounting for Agents' Commissions **237**

Objectives of Commission Accounting. Commission Records. Agent's Account Entries: *Commission Entries. Payments to Agents. Taxes on Commission Earnings. Miscellaneous Charges. Remitting Nets.* U.S. Annual Statement Aspects. Canadian Annual Statement Aspects. Summary of Commission Accounting Fundamentals.

14. Individual Premium and Commission Accounting **254**

Characteristics of the Individual System: *Premium Payment Flexibility. Commission Systems.* Policy Status Records: *Policy Record Card. Other Records.* Premium Billing and Control Processes: *Premium Notices and Related Transaction Records. Preparing Notices and Related Accounting Records. Controlling Initial Premiums. Controlling Suspense Accounts.* Processing Individual Premium Payments: *Payment Handling in the Branch Office. Depositing and Remitting Premiums to the Home Office. Processing Payments in the Home Office.* Premium Accounts and Entries in Individual Premium Systems: *Account Titles. Premium Entries.* Controlling, Calculating, and Accounting for Commissions. Special Monthly Payment Systems: *Preauthorized Checks (PAC). Postdated Checks. Government Allotment. Salary Allotment.* Reinsurance Premiums. Year-End Processes.

15. Debit Insurance Accounting **284**

Agency Accounting Functions: *The Debit Agent. The Staff Manager. District Office Cashiers.* Control of Debit Collection: *Advance and Arrears System. Cash Premium Accounting System.* Accounting Records: *Master Policy Record.* Ordinary Premium Collections on the Debit. Commission Payment Systems: *Times Commission System. Commission and Conservation System. Debit Commission Leveling Plans.* Home Office Accounting Processes. Year-End Matters.

16. Group Premium and Commission Accounting Systems **308**

Group Markets and Coverages. Standard Group Characteristics. Employee Group: *Employee Contributions. Employee Classification. Accounting Records.* Employer Group Billing. Premium Reports and Entries. Group Commissions. Experience Refunds. Association Group. Creditor and Credit Union Group Insurance: *Outstanding Balance Plan. Single Premium Plan.* Year-End Matters.

17. Policy Benefit Settlements **327**

Amounts Left on Deposit with the Company: *Ledger Liability Process. The Nonledger Liability Process.* Policy Dividends: *Dividend Payment Options. Dividend Records.* Dividend Entries: *Dividends Paid in Cash. Dividends Applied to Pay Premiums. Other Entries.* Disbursement of Dividends Held under an Option. Nonforfeiture Options: *Cash Surrenders. Reduced Paid-Up and Extended Term Insurance.* U.S. Annual Statement Aspects. Canadian Annual Statement Aspects. Summary of Life Insurance Deposit Dividend and Nonforfeiture Accounting Fundamentals.

18. Claim and Contract Settlement **349**

Death Claims. Matured Endowments. Health Insurance Claims: *Disability Claims. Medical Expense Claims. Indemnity Claims.* Reinsurance Benefit Entries. Claim Records and Controls. Claim Liabilities. Claim Ratios: *Calculating Claim Ratios. Other Observations concerning Cash and Incurred Ratios. Use of Claim Ratios.* Supplementary Contracts and Annuities: *Supplementary Contracts WOLC. Supplemental Contracts WLC. Annuities. Records and Payment Control. Liability for Supplementary Contracts.* U.S. Annual Statement Aspects. Canadian Annual Statement Aspects. Summary of Life Insurance Claim Accounting.

19. Expense and Taxes **382**

Accounting Entries and Payment Control: *Payments for Salaries and Related Taxes. Purchase of Supplies, Furniture, and Equipment. Agents' Balances Charged Off.* Liability for Expenses and Taxes: *Liability Incurred at Time of Order. Liability Incurred Subsequent to the Order Date. Continually Accruing Expenses. Adjusting Expenses and Taxes.* Expense Reporting. Responsibility Reports: *Budget Supervision. Budget Procedures.* Functional Cost Analysis: *Use of Functional Costs. Calculating Functional Costs.* Presentation of Expenses and Taxes in Annual Statements: *Allocation of Expenses to Major Lines of Business.* Types of Expenses: *Rent. Salaries and Wages. Employee Benefits. Professional Service Fees and Expenses. Miscellaneous Expenses. Group Service and Administration Fees. Agency Conferences Other Than Local Meetings. Agency Expense Allowance. Agents' Balances Charged Off. Real Estate Expenses. Investment Expenses Not Included Elsewhere.* Taxes, Licenses, and Fees: *Liabilities for Expenses and Taxes.* Canadian Annual Statement Aspects. Summary of Expense Accounting Fundamentals.

20.   Special U.S. Annual Statement Exhibits and Reports **414**

Asset Exhibit (Exhibit 13): *Non-Ledger Assets. Assets Not Admitted.* Liabilities. Reconciliation of Ledger Assets (Exhibit 12): *Reconciliation Process. Relationship of Balance Account to Reconciliation of Ledger Assets. Description of Items in the Reconciliation of Ledger Assets.* Analysis of Nonadmitted Assets and Related Items (Exhibit 14): *Prepaid Expenses. Company's Stock Owned. Loans and Amounts Receivable Not Adequately Secured.* Surplus Account. Analysis of Operations: *Supplementary Contracts. Insurance Cost and Expense Items.* Interpreting the Analysis of Operations: *Allocation of Investment Income. Distribution of Income and Expense Items by Lines of Business. Effect of Consolidating Income and Costs by Sublines. Effect of New Business on Operating Gains. Effect of Capital and Surplus and Investment Effectiveness on Operating Gains. Value of the Analysis of Operations.* Schedule H— Accident and Health Exhibit.

21.   Special Canadian Annual Statement Reports **448**

Fund Accounting: *Summary of Funds and Amounts Owing by the Company. Reconciliation of Funds.* Reconciliation of Surplus. Revenue Account and Related Analyses: *Columnar Arrangement. Terminology Differences. Settlement Contracts and Amounts on Deposit. Pension and Insurance Funds. Interfund Transfers. Other Items in the Revenue Account and the Analyses.*

Glossary **479**

Answers to Problems **489**

Index **499**

Chapter 1

Introduction to Accounting

USEFULNESS OF ACCOUNTING KNOWLEDGE

Accounting is a vital and necessary tool in the sound management of every business organization. This book will acquaint the student with the broad scope of accounting and will provide him with an understanding of the concepts and methods of this fundamental business process.

The principal focus of the book is on accounting in life insurance companies. The student is first introduced to general accounting procedures, however, since these are basic to an understanding of the nature of life insurance accounting.

Personal Uses

The daily life of nearly every adult is filled with financial problems with which he can cope more easily if he understands accounting processes. Actually, most people do some accounting in the handling of their personal affairs.

Income taxes, for example, are a major concern to all. The proper preparation of personal tax returns requires record keeping, including maintaining a record of dollars contributed to churches and charities, dollars paid in interest and taxes, dollars paid for medical care, and dollars paid for many other items.

Many people invest money as part of a retirement plan or for other reasons. In connection with personal investments, there are many accounting-related problems. For instance, when investments are sold, the gain or loss resulting from the sale must be determined and reported for income tax purposes. In order to determine this gain or loss, accurate records must be maintained from date of purchase to date of sale. Fur-

1

thermore, during the period of ownership, earnings on most types of investment must be reported annually for income tax purposes.

An individual who never expects to become an executive may get along satisfactorily in our society with only a slight understanding of accounting principles. However, any person who expects to have managerial responsibilities will find a sound knowledge of accounting extremely helpful and in some cases absolutely necessary.

Business Uses

Each year thousands of business firms are established by individuals who are competent in their respective fields, but each year many of these firms are forced to close their doors. The reasons for their poor performance are many and varied, but an important cause is the lack of an adequate accounting system which would have provided management with the necessary financial data for wiser decisions.

Knowledge of the financial aspects of a business are needed by a manager to operate the business successfully. These aspects include (1) the primary sources of income; (2) the amount of money available for purchase of merchandise or raw materials; (3) the amount of expenditures necessary to produce and sell the product; (4) a reasonable expectation of profit measured as a percentage of the investment in the business; and (5) the amount of money available for expansion of the business or for dividend payment to owners.

A good accounting system is the primary source of financial information about a business. Unless management knows the present financial status of the business and which business activities create profits or cause losses, it is forced to base decisions on intuition or guess. Intuition is far less reliable than the scientific method of basing decisions on facts provided by a good accounting system and by other objective and quantitative means, such as statistical analysis.

Some might assume that all a company needs to do in order to operate profitably is to buy when it has funds and set a selling price that is higher than the cost of merchandise or raw materials. The truth is not so simple. Many costs, such as rent and the manager's salary, cannot be attributed to a single transaction. Other costs, such as selling costs, are difficult to predict unless records of similar costs in the past are available.

Moreover, credit is involved in most transactions. Both retailing and manufacturing businesses, for example, incur indebtedness in acquiring goods. Usually this indebtedness is short term, i.e., the amount is payable by the 10th of the following month; but frequently the indebtedness is for longer periods. Also, sales are made to customers on credit. Records must be established covering the amounts receivable or payable and the amounts of settlements when they are actually received or paid.

Whenever credit is involved in business transactions, the flow of cash in and out of a business is not directly related, as far as time is concerned, to the volume of business done. Neither is the flow of cash a satisfactory index to earnings or profits. Management must rely on accounting records to determine whether cash received must be applied to reduce the organization's own indebtedness, or if it may be applied to purchase additional merchandise, or paid out to the owners as a return on their investment.

FUNCTIONS OF ACCOUNTING

The examples in the preceding section indicate that accounting is a necessary tool in administering the affairs of a business firm. More specifically, accounting serves the following useful functions:

1. It is a basis for administrative decisions.
2. It is a basis for credit determination.
3. It is a means of measuring efficiency.
4. It is a protection against fraud.
5. It is a source of information for tax reports, business surveys, and governmental supervision.

Basis for Administrative Decisions

Administrative decisions of a financial nature must be based on (1) the present status of the business, such as the amount of cash available, the value of property owned by the business, and the amount of indebtedness; and (2) the financial results (profit or loss) of past operations.

There are two types of decisions which management must make concerning future operations: (1) decisions relating to immediate future operations and (2) decisions relating to long-range planning.

Immediate Future Operations. The decisions required for the immediate future are many and varied. Examples of this type of decision include whether or not to hire additional personnel, whether to buy additional equipment, whether to buy additional merchandise for sale, and whether it is advisable to borrow short-term money.

More specifically, in order to make a decision on whether the firm should employ additional personnel, answers are needed to many questions: Has the income of the business risen sufficiently to justify such an additional expense? If not, can income be increased as a result of adding new personnel or can a reduction be made in other expenses that will offset the expense of such additional personnel? If the answers to these questions are "no," then management knows that it has little recourse other than to try to make more effective use of present personnel. Unless profits of the business can be expected to increase or new staff is needed to maintain current profits, there can be little justification for hiring additional employees.

In deciding whether or not to buy new equipment, the following questions should be asked: Have the activity of the business and its orders from customers increased sufficiently to indicate that present equipment is now or soon will become overloaded? Have maintenance costs of old equipment become so excessive as to make replacement more economical? Will the purchase of the new equipment result in increased production and increased income which will offset its cost?

If the firm is short of cash to pay current bills or to purchase new merchandise, a decision must be made as to whether it should borrow funds to make these payments. Can the firm reasonably anticipate that amounts owed to it will be received in time to meet the payments on any new indebtedness? Are sales increasing sufficiently to provide funds for the repayment of the indebtedness? Can any new indebtedness be expected to produce greater income and, as a result, greater profits? Has the company realized sufficient profits in its past operations to justify borrowing money to buy more merchandise?

Long-Range Planning. If a company is planning to embark on a long-term expansion program, there are a number of pertinent questions to which the accounting records may provide answers:

Are the present earnings of the company sufficient to attract additional capital from outside sources? Are there sufficient funds so that if the expected increase in new business from the expansion is not realized, the company will be able to continue satisfactory operations? Are funds already invested in the business sufficient to pay for the expansion, or must new debt be incurred?

These are just a few of the many questions faced almost daily by management. Good accounting records provide the information on which to base knowledgeable decisions. They enable management to make analyses by showing the past performance of a business and the strong and weak points of its financial structure and condition.

Basis for Credit Determination

Most business firms on occasion borrow from banks or other lending institutions to pay their bills. Merchandise purchased in large volume is usually purchased on credit. Selling firms often are not willing or are unable to extend credit for as long as it may take the buyer to sell the merchandise. To get bank loans to meet this type of debt, the buying firm must be able to convince the bank that it will be able, in turn, to make its payments to the bank.

Financial statements are reviewed by lending institutions to determine whether a company is handling its funds wisely and to determine how and when the company will be able to repay money borrowed. These financial statements can be prepared accurately only from a good accounting system. Among other things, they show the amount of money invested in the business, the cash on hand for payment of debts, amounts receivable, and debts payable. They also show past earnings and thus indicate the quality of management.

Most business firms grant credit to their own customers. When a customer requests new credit, it is necessary to know whether the customer has paid his obligations promptly in the past. It is not sufficient to know only the amount he owes at the present time. The credit manager of a company must therefore have readily available to him accounting records with reference to each customer which he can analyze to determine whether it would be wise to extend new credit.

Means of Measuring Efficiency

A sound accounting system helps to determine the operating efficiency of individuals, processes, and departments (or other subdivisions) of the business. As a business expands, it is necessary to delegate responsibilities to more people and to create more departments or branches for effective operation and control of the business. Accounting records can be analyzed and special reports prepared to show the relative efficiency of each of these departments and to tell management where corrective action should be taken to improve the effectiveness of operations. Often it is practical in order to prepare these reports to maintain the accounting system in such a way that money received and money spent by each department is accounted for separately. Separate reports may be consolidated into a single report for all departments.

Similar techniques can be used to determine the more profitable lines of a business so that unprofitable lines may either be discontinued or made profitable and profitable activities may be expanded.

Protection against Fraud

In a good accounting system, provision is made for an internal check of the handling of funds and other property to prevent irregularities such as fraud and embezzlement. This is accomplished both through the accounting system itself and through periodic audit of the accounts. An audit can be made easily and at minimum cost if the accounting system is properly designed.

Source of Information

Federal, state, or local governments levy taxes upon the income, the property, the payroll, and the sales of most businesses. Accounting records are the primary source of data for the computation of the amounts of these taxes.

Income taxes imposed by state and federal governments are the most important taxes for most businesses. The tax forms require each company to show the sources and amounts of its income and the amounts of various expenditures involved in earning the income.

Both federal and state governments impose taxes upon business payrolls, such as federal taxes for social security. State and local governments levy taxes upon sales and in the life insurance business upon premium income. State and local governments also assess taxes on the property owned by business firms.

Regulatory authorities rely to a great extent on accounting statements and supplementary reports to determine whether or not a company is complying with the laws. Life insurance companies are subject to laws and other forms of government regulation which restrict or limit investment of their funds and regulate insurance operations in other ways. Life insurance company accounting procedures are set up to comply with these regulatory requirements. Such regulation in the United States is the responsibility of state insurance departments. In Canada, it is the responsibility of federal and provincial insurance departments.

QUESTIONS

1. Name two areas of an individual's financial affairs which require that financial records be kept.

2. What four financial aspects of company operations should be understood by management?

3. What is the primary source of financial information about a firm?

4. Give five uses for or purposes served by accounting in a business firm.

5. Give four common examples of matters about which management decisions must be made for (*a*) the immediate future and (*b*) long-range financial planning.

6. How are accounting records used for credit determination?

7. How can accounting be used to measure efficiency?

Chapter 2

Fundamentals of General Accounting

FORMS OF BUSINESS OWNERSHIP

The three most common forms of business ownership are the single proprietorship, the partnership, and the corporation. Insurance companies are organized as corporations of either the stock or the mutual type.

This book is concerned only with the corporate form of ownership. In this presentation of the fundamentals of general accounting, it will be assumed that the accounting entity is a corporation owned by stockholders.[1] Anyone who understands accounting for corporations can very easily and quickly learn the few special aspects of accounting for the other forms of ownership.

A corporation is an entity legally separate from its owners, just as one man is a separate entity from another man. The corporation and its owners are separate accounting entities as well as separate legal entities. This is true even if one person owns *all* of the stock of the corporation. Corporate accounting is concerned with the financial affairs of the corporation *only* and not with the personal financial affairs of the owners of the corporation.

_____

[1] The material presented applies to mutual life insurance companies as well, except that relating to stock ownership.

BASIC TERMINOLOGY AND THE ACCOUNTING EQUATION

Basic Terminology

Accounting may be defined as the art of analyzing, recording, classifying, summarizing, interpreting, and reporting the financial activities of a corporation. Accounting is, therefore, involved in every transaction and event which can be expressed in terms of money which affects the corporation. Accounting may also include some nonfinancial activities in preparing financial statements, but these considerations involve advanced accounting and are not treated in this book.

Three basic terms must be learned as the first step in understanding accounting. These three terms are:

1. *Assets:* anything of value owned by the business. Common examples of assets are cash, debts owed *to* the corporation, buildings, land, and automobiles.

2. *Liabilities:* debts owed *by* the business. A liability is a claim against the assets of the business.

3. *Capital:* the owners' interest, or equity, in the assets. The owners of a corporation are its *stockholders* or *shareholders.* (Two other terms, *stockholders' equity* or *net worth*, are more commonly used in general accounting, but capital is the term traditionally used in life insurance accounting.) In the accounting sense, *capital* is the *net worth* of the business, i.e., cash and other property owned by the business less amounts owed by the business—or more simply, the assets of the business less its liabilities.

The capital and the liabilities represent general interests in, or claims against, *all* of the assets of the corporation. The stockholders and most creditors have no claim against *specific* assets.[2] If the business were to be liquidated, the corporation's debts would have to be paid before the stockholders could realize anything from the corporate assets.

The Accounting Equation

If a corporation had no liabilities, the dollar amount of the capital (stockholders' equity) would be equal to the dollar total of all the assets. This relationship can be expressed as a very simple equation:

$$\text{Total Assets} = \text{Total Capital}$$

If the corporation has liabilities, the capital is equal to the assets minus the amount of the creditors' claims (debts), thus:

$$\text{Total Assets} - \text{Total Liabilities} = \text{Total Capital}$$

---

[2] *Secured* creditors are a special case which is considered in a later chapter.

or simply,

Assets − Liabilities = Capital (or Net Worth)

This equation may be expressed in a different form with the liabilities moved across the equals symbol to the other side of the equation (transposed).[3] When this transposition is done, the equation becomes:

Assets = Liabilities + Capital

In this form, the equation shows that the total of all interests in (capital) and claims to (liabilities) the assets of the corporation is equal to the total assets of the corporation.

The three portions of this accounting equation—assets, liabilities, and capital—frequently are referred to as the *elements* of the equation. This equation is the basis of the financial statement which is called the *balance sheet.*

A balance sheet presents the financial condition of the corporation as of a specific date; and for this reason, the balance sheet is often called the *statement of financial condition.* The financial condition of the corporation as of a specific day is shown on the balance sheet by listing (usually on the left side of a page) all of the assets owned by the corporation on that date and listing (usually on the right side) all of its liabilities and capital.[4] The dollar totals of the two lists must be equal since, as we have just seen, Assets = Liabilities + Capital.

A balance sheet with the usual headings is shown in Figure 2–1. A few

Figure 2–1

X CORPORATION
Balance Sheet
December 31, 19__

ASSETS		LIABILITIES	
Cash......................	$ 4,000.00	Accounts Payable............	$ 3,000.00
Building...................	100,000.00	Mortgage Payable...........	47,000.00
		CAPITAL	
		Capital Stock...............	50,000.00
		Surplus....................	4,000.00
		Total Liabilities and	
Total Assets...........	$104,000.00	Capital..............	$104,000.00

items are included under the headings to illustrate that the dollar total of the assets and the dollar total of the liabilities and capital agree or balance. Note that capital has been divided into two items, capital stock and

---

[3] Transposing and changing signs is easy to see in a simple numerical illustration. If $5 - 2 = 3$, then $5 = 3 + 2$.

[4] This form of statement is called the "account form." If the assets section is listed above the other section, the statement is in the "report form." A form of this type is shown later in this chapter.

surplus. (There are several types of surplus which will be discussed later.) When *surplus* is used without being qualified, it represents the amounts earned and retained by the company as capital (increases in capital resulting from operating the business), as contrasted with capital stock, which represents the amounts invested by owners.

ANALYZING TRANSACTIONS

Events within the corporation and transactions between the corporation and its owners as well as transactions between the corporation and outsiders (other corporations, governments, individuals, etc.) affect the elements of the basic accounting equation: Assets = Liabilities + Capital. When one element of the equation changes, there must be a change in one or both of the other elements (or an offsetting change in the same element) so that the equation stays in balance. Every financial transaction of the corporation results in two changes within the equation.

A transaction or change may occur which affects only one element of the equation. For example, if the company buys an automobile, one asset (cash) is exchanged for another asset (automobile). Since this transaction does not change the *total* assets, liabilities and capital remain unchanged. Nevertheless, two changes did occur: an increase in one asset and a decrease in another asset.

It should be possible now to analyze transactions and see how they affect the elements of the equation. Several common transactions and their effect on the equation are:

1. The owners make an initial investment in the corporation by purchasing stock for $10,000.

Both assets and capital increase by $10,000, the amount invested. The corporation now has an asset, cash, which it did not have before the transaction. The owners' equity, capital, is equal to their initial investment. The equation is $10,000 (A) = $10,000 (C).

2. Office furniture is purchased for $2,000 cash.

One asset, cash, is reduced and another asset, office furniture, is acquired.[5] This is an increase and an equal decrease within one element of the equation. The total of assets does not change. Capital is not affected by the transaction, and no liabilities have yet been incurred. Therefore, the amounts of the elements of the equation remain unchanged. The equation is still $10,000 (A) = $10,000 (C).

3. A typewriter is purchased for $300, but it is to be paid for later.

The corporation now has an additional asset. Its total assets increase by the price of the typewriter, and liabilities are increased by the same amount since there is now a debt of that amount owed to the seller. The equation is now $10,300 (A) = $300 (L) + $10,000 (C).

---

[5] At this stage it is assumed that the value of an asset is equal to its cost and the terms are used interchangeably.

4. The corporation renders a service to a customer for which it receives a fee of $4,000 in cash.

The asset cash increases by the amount of $4,000 received, and since liabilities are not involved, capital must increase by $4,000 in order to keep the equation in balance. The equation now is $14,300 (A) = $300 (L) + $14,000 (C).

The effect of the transaction on the accounting equation would have been the same if the corporation had received no cash at this time for the service. The $4,000 increase in assets would have resulted from the corporation having a new asset in the form of an *account receivable* (that is, a debt owed to the corporation by the customer). The increase in capital (C) would be the same in either case. This example demonstrates that capital increases whenever a business renders a service for which it makes a charge.

5*a*. The corporation receives a license to operate in the city and issues a check for $1,000 to pay for the license.

Assets decrease by the $1,000 paid out and capital decreases by the same amount. The equation is now $13,300 (A) = $300 (L) + $13,000 (C).

5*b*. Had the license not been paid for at once, a new liability in the form of an *account payable* (that is, a debt owed by the corporation) would have resulted. This would increase liabilities by $1,000, while assets would not change. The increase in the corporation's liabilities from $300 to $1,300 would cause capital to decrease from $14,000 to $13,000, even though the bill has not yet been paid. The equation (in example 4) would then become $14,300 (A) = $1,300 (L) + $13,000 (C).

6. The corporation gives a $300 note payable to the seller of the typewriter in transaction 3. A *note payable* is a written promise to pay a certain sum on demand or at a fixed or determinable future time; payment of interest may or may not be part of the promise.

Here one form of debt is exchanged for another. Therefore, total liabilities do not change, nor do the other elements of the equation.

ACCOUNTS

In a going corporation, the accounting procedure starts from the balance sheet at the beginning of an accounting period (which may be a year, a month, or any other time period). Transactions which occur during the period are systematically classified and recorded. From these figures, the balance sheet at the end of the period is obtained. Other useful records of the operations of the period are also obtained.

The basic formal accounting unit is the account. An *account* is a record of all financial transactions within a desired classification. Each element of the accounting equation is subdivided by establishing a separate account for each kind of asset, for each type of liability, and for each of the various aspects of capital. Accounts are therefore classified into three major groups in accordance with the elements of the accounting equation: (1) asset accounts, (2) liability accounts, and (3) capital accounts.

Accounts may be recorded in a manner which is suitable for the particular company. This may be on a simple sheet of paper, on a card, or as invisible markings on a magnetic tape or disk. The essential feature of an account, whatever its form, is that it provides a place for recording all the financial information and changes concerning the specific asset, liability, or capital item represented by the account.

A standard form of an account (see Figure 2–2) is simply a sheet

Figure 2–2

Cash

Debit				Credit			
Date	*Explanation*	*Folio*	*Amount*	*Date*	*Explanation*	*Folio*	*Amount*
19__ Jan. 7		12	10,000.00	19__ Jan. 9		14	2,000.00

of paper with a horizontal line near the top on which the title of the account is written, and with a vertical line down the center which divides the sheet into a left side, known as the *debit* side, and a right side, known as the *credit* side. On each side there are vertical columns for dates, explanation, dollar amounts, and *folio references*. A folio reference is a page reference to the source of the information recorded on each horizontal line.

Information is seldom entered in the Explanation column. This column is used only if a detailed analysis of entries is required later. For example, notes receivable may be entered in an account by that title, with the name of the maker of the note written in the Explanation column. When the balance sheet is prepared, a list of unpaid notes can then be made from information in the Explanation column of the notes receivable account.

For instructional purposes a skeleton form of an account is used. This form is called a *T-account*. A T-account for the asset cash is

Cash

One side of a T-account is used to write (enter) the amount of each increase in the account. The other side is used to enter the amount of each decrease.

Two special terms are used in accounting to identify the left and right sides of accounts. These terms are (1) *to debit,* which means "to make an entry on the left side of the account" and (2) *to credit,* which means "to make an entry on the right side of an account." Debit is abbreviated, "Dr." and credit "Cr." (Note that the standard abbreviation for debit contains the letter "r" which does not appear in the word.)

Every financial transaction affects at least two accounts. For example: the purchase of equipment results in an increase in the asset equipment and a decrease in the asset cash; a payment on a note owed results in a reduction in the asset cash and in a reduction in the liability notes payable.

For every transaction, debit entries (those entered in the left side of an account) *must always be equal to credit entries* (those entered in the right side of an account). This standard method of recording financial transactions is referred to as *double-entry bookkeeping.* Use of this method prevents oversights that might otherwise occur, provides an effective means for preventing errors in recording amounts, and provides a means for locating errors in the amount of entries before financial statements are prepared.

The advantages of double-entry bookkeeping are derived from two facts: (1) each financial transaction affects at least two accounts and (2) the accounting equation must remain in balance at all times.

In order to maintain this equality, accounts represented by the *left* side of the accounting equation, the asset accounts, are increased by an entry to the *left* (debit) side of the account; and accounts represented by the *right* (credit) side of the accounting equation, the liability and capital accounts, are increased by an entry to the *right* (credit) side of the account.

Conversely, asset accounts are decreased by entries to the credit side, and liability and capital accounts are decreased by entries to the debit side.

These facts can be depicted on T-account forms as follows:

Assets		=	Liabilities		+	Capital	
Dr. Increase	Cr. Decrease		Dr. Decrease	Cr. Increase		Dr. Decrease	Cr. Increase

A reexamination of some of the example transactions used to illustrate the effects of transactions on the accounting equation will demonstrate the use of equal debit and credit entries.

When the owners invested $10,000 in the business, assets and capital each increased by that amount. If T-accounts are used to represent the elements of the accounting equation, the two entries can be shown as follows:

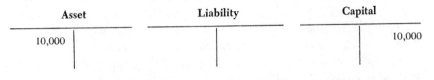

Asset	Liability	Capital
10,000		10,000

The asset account increased by $10,000, which is entered as a debit to that account. Credit entries must equal debit entries, so an increase in capital of $10,000 is entered as a credit in the capital account.

A typewriter worth $300 is purchased and will be paid for later. After the entries, the accounts appear as follows:

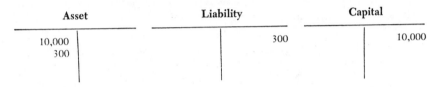

Asset	Liability	Capital
10,000	300	10,000
300		

The company now has assets of $10,000 cash and $300 worth of office equipment. The $300 increase in an asset is a debit. Debit entries must equal credit entries, so the increase in liability is entered as a credit, thereby properly showing the increase in a liability, the $300 debt.

One more transaction will demonstrate the posting of decreases to accounts on the two sides of the accounting equation. Assume a check for $300 is issued in payment for the typewriter. When this is recorded in the accounts they appear as follows:

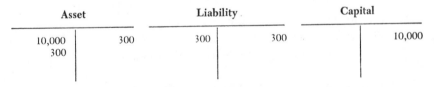

Asset		Liability		Capital
10,000	300	300	300	10,000
300				

The asset was decreased by the amount of the check. This decrease in an asset is recorded as a credit. Since debits must equal credits, the entry to the liability account must be a debit for $300. The debit entry results in the liability account being decreased by $300, which reflects the actual situation when the payment is made.

To recapitulate:

Asset accounts are increased by debits and decreased by credits.

Liability accounts and capital accounts are increased by credits and decreased by debits.

The difference between the total of the debits and the total of the credits in a particular account is called the *balance* of that account. If the total debits exceed the total credits, the account has a *debit balance*. If the total credits exceed the total debits, the account has a *credit balance*. For example, in the T-accounts used to demonstrate debit and credit entries, the asset account now has a debit balance of $10,000 (representing $9,700 cash and $300 worth of equipment), the liability account has a balance of zero, and the capital account has a credit balance of $10,000.

Asset accounts usually have debit balances, and liability and capital accounts usually have credit balances, but there can occasionally be exceptions.[6]

It is usually desirable to use a number of accounts within each element of the accounting equation. In the above example, the assets of $10,000 actually consist of $9,700 cash and $300 worth of equipment. If two accounts had been used, one for cash and one for equipment, the amount of each type of asset could have been shown separately.

The classification and entry of transactions already used as examples are given in the following section in order to emphasize the continued equality of debits and credits, as well as to illustrate the use of a number of separate accounts within each of the three elements of the accounting equation. New entries to T-accounts below are shown in italics.

1. The owners make an initial investment of $10,000 by buying stock in the corporation.

The increase in the asset cash requires a debit to an account called Cash. (Increases in asset accounts are represented by debit entries.)

The increase in the owners' equity requires a credit to the capital account called Capital Stock. (Increases in capital accounts are represented by credit entries.) Capital Stock is one of several accounts within the capital element and is used to record the owners' equity that has resulted from the purchase of stock by the owners.

Expressed in T-accounts, this entry is:

Cash	Capital Stock
10,000	*10,000*

2. Office furniture costing $2,000 is purchased for cash.

The increase in the asset office furniture requires a debit to an account by that name. (Increase in asset accounts are represented by debits.)

---

[6] For example, an Account Receivable account may have a credit balance if for some reason it is overpaid.

The decrease in the asset cash requires a credit to the Cash account. (Decreases in assets are represented by credits.)

This entry recorded in T-accounts is:

Office Furniture		Cash	
2,000		10,000	2,000

3. A typewriter is purchased on account and will be paid for later. The cost is $300, and the seller is J. C. Evans.

The increase in assets as a result of the purchase of a typewriter requires a debit to an account which is typically called Office Equipment.

A liability has been created (the amount owed to J. C. Evans) and an increase to a liability is here recorded as a credit to an account entitled A/P—J. C. Evans (A/P may be used to designate this as an account payable, a fact which would not be clear simply from Evans' name on the account.)

Office Equipment		A/P—J. C. Evans	
300			300

> Note: The typewriter in transaction 3 and the office furniture in transaction 2 might both be recorded in an account entitled Office Furniture and Equipment if we wished to combine them. The determination of just what accounts to create in order to give management the best information for its decision making is an important accounting decision and will be discussed in a later chapter.

4. The corporation renders a service to a customer, T. R. Abrams, for which it receives a fee of $4,000 in cash.

The increase in the asset cash requires a debit to the Cash account. (Remember two entries have already been recorded in the Cash account.) An equal credit entry is required to keep the accounting equation in balance. The liability of the company has not changed, so a $4,000 credit entry must be made to a capital account. (Capital accounts are increased by credit entries.)

The Capital Stock account is not used because its purpose is to reflect the owners' initial investment. Instead, another capital account, called Surplus,[7] is used. In this account, changes in capital which result from the

---

[7] Surplus is the traditional name of this account, but in general business accounting the term *Retained Earnings* is now more commonly used. Surplus, however, continues in wide use by insurance companies and is used throughout this book.

operations of the business are recorded. (Later we will further subdivide the Surplus account, but it will serve for now to use just one surplus account.)

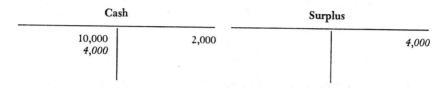

Cash		Surplus	
10,000	2,000		4,000
4,000			

If this fee of $4,000 had not been received in cash but was now owed to the corporation, the entry to Surplus would be exactly the same, but the debit would be to an asset account titled *A/R—T. R. Abrams*. The A/R stands for account receivable.

This fee represents *income* to the company. Income is defined as a value received or earned in the normal course of business. An income transaction increases the capital element of the accounting equation.

5. The corporation issues a check for $1,000 to the city for a license to operate in the city.

The $1,000 decrease in cash requires a credit entry of that amount to the asset account, Cash.

The cost of the license decreases capital and requires a debit to the capital account, Surplus. This debit entry reduces capital by $1,000 and keeps the accounting equation in balance. (Capital accounts are decreased by debit entries.)

Cash		Surplus	
10,000	2,000	1,000	4,000
4,000	1,000		

This payment represents an *expense* to the company. Expense is defined as a value used or consumed in the normal course of business. An expense transaction decreases the capital element of the accounting equation.

6. The corporation gives a note payable[8] to J. C. Evans in payment of the amount owed to him for the typewriter purchased in transaction 3. The transaction represents a decrease in one liability and an increase in another.

The decrease in the liability account *A/P—J. C. Evans* requires a debit to that account. A new liability account, *Notes Payable*, is established for

---

[8] A note payable is a written promise to pay a certain sum on demand or at a fixed or determinable future time.

recording the new type of liability. The increase in the liability notes payable, requires an equal credit to this new liability.

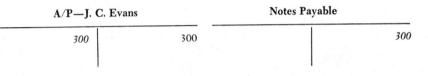

A/P—J. C. Evans		Notes Payable
300	300	*300*

The debit to Evans' account brings its balance to zero, which is correct since the corporation owes him nothing more as an *account payable*. He is owed the $300 on the *note* which was given to him in payment of the account. The promissory note bears his name, but it is common accounting practice to show all notes payable in one account and not separately by the name of the creditor as is done in the case of accounts payable.

THE LEDGER

All of the accounts together constitute the *ledger*. The accounts which compose the ledger may be bound together so that the ledger is a book. The accounts may also be kept in a loose-leaf binder, may be separate cards in a file drawer, or may exist in some other form.

THE JOURNAL

In actual practice it would be inconvenient to make entries directly to the ledger accounts. Furthermore, if this were done, it would be difficult to reconstruct any series of transactions as they occurred in time. The solution to this problem lies in the use of a *journal*.[9] A journal is sometimes called a book of original entry because in it each transaction is recorded for the first time. This recording is called a *journal entry*.

The transactions entered in the journal are transferred to the accounts in the ledger. This transfer process is known as *posting* to the accounts or *posting* the ledger. The posting process rearranges transactions from chronological sequence to account sequence.

The *journal* is a chronological record of transactions as they occur, expressed in debits and credits. A simple journal entry shows the date, the account to be debited, the account to be credited, the dollar amount of the debit and of the credit, and a brief explanation of the transaction. Later in this text, compound entries will be presented. These are entries which have multiple debits or credits.

The form of a general journal and of journal entries is illustrated in

---

[9] There are several types of journals, all of which fit this definition. The *general* journal is the type discussed in this chapter. Several *special* journals are introduced in later chapters.

Figure 2–3, using the transactions in the previous section, now with dates added. (Note the format of the entries in Figure 2–3. Explanations will be omitted in subsequent illustrations in this text to simplify the presentation of material.)

The *Ledger Folio column* is used when journal entries are *posted* (entered) to accounts in the ledger. The numbers in the Ledger Folio columns in Figure 2–3 indicate that these journal entries have already

Figure 2–3. Example of General Journal Form
JOURNAL

Date 19__	Account Titles and Explanations	Ledger Folio	Debit	Credit
Mar. 1	Cash.................................	1	10,000.00	
	Capital Stock.......................	25		10,000.00
	Sold capital stock for cash.			
2	Office Furniture......................	5	2,000.00	
	Cash.............................	1		2,000.00
	Purchased office furniture for cash.			
3	Office Equipment.	6	300.00	
	A/P—J. C. Evans...................	3		300.00
	Purchased a typewriter on account.			
4	Cash................................	1	4,000.00	
	Surplus...........................	26		4,000.00
	Received a cash fee for services rendered.			
5	Surplus..............................	26	1,000.00	
	Cash.............................	1		1,000.00
	Paid license fee in cash.			
6	A/P—J. C. Evans.....................	3	300.00	
	Notes Payable......................	4		300.00
	Gave a promissory note to J. C. Evans in payment of our account.			

been posted. The numbers are ledger page numbers or account numbers which in accounting practice are recorded only after the item has been posted.

The debits, credits, and explanations of the entries in Figure 2–3 appear in various indentations. This is by intention, not by accident. Titles of accounts and amounts to be credited to an account are normally written under and slightly to the right of titles and amounts to be debited to an account. The explanation portion of the entry may be written in several positions. The two most common positions are (1) that shown in Figure 2–3 and (2) further indented from the position used for credited accounts, as follows:

```
Cash (the account debited)....................................10,000
        Capital Stock (the account credited).......................        10,000
        Sold capital stock for cash.
```

Notice that in each journal entry the amount of the debit equals the amount of the credit and that debit amounts are entered in a separate column from credit amounts. The equality of debits and credits can be proven by adding the two columns in the journal and comparing totals. This reduces the possibility of posting an entry that is out of balance, i.e., with debits not equal to credits.

Journal entries may be posted to the accounts in the ledger immediately, daily, or whenever convenient for the particular organization.

TRIAL BALANCE

A *trial balance* is a list of all accounts in the ledger and their balances on a specific date. If the total of all debit balances and the total of all credit balances in the list are equal, the trial balance is in balance. The trial balance has several purposes. The following two are especially important:

1. If the trial balance does balance, this shows that debit transactions equal credit transactions in the journal and the ledger and that amounts were correctly posted from the journal to the ledger. If the trial balance does *not* balance, there are one or more errors in the journal or ledger. However, it is important to understand that there may be errors even though the trial balance does balance. The trial balance will often balance if there are compensating errors, if there are errors in designating the accounts to be debited or credited, or if entries with correct debits or credits are posted to the wrong accounts.

2. The trial balance is a convenient source from which to prepare work sheets which are used to construct the balance sheet and other financial statements.

If the six entries from the journal in Figure 2–3 were posted to ledger accounts, the result in the T-account form would be (the balance of the accounts are shown in small italics):

Cash			A/P—J. C. Evans	
10,000	2,000		300	300
4,000	1,000			*0*
(Balance) *11,000*				

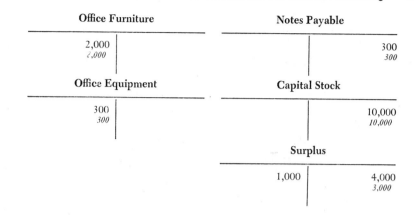

The three T-accounts on the left are asset accounts. Note that they have debit balances. The first two T-accounts on the right are liability accounts and the remaining two are capital accounts. Note that those on the right have credit balances, except the account payable, which is now zero balanced.

The trial balance of this ledger is:

Cash	$11,000.00	
Office Furniture	2,000.00	
Office Equipment	300.00	
Notes Payable		$ 300.00
Capital Stock		10,000.00
Surplus		3,000.00
	$13,300.00	$13,300.00

A balance sheet prepared from the trial balance in the preceding section is shown in Figure 2–4. Usually, the balance sheet and other

Figure 2–4

X CORPORATION
Balance Sheet
March ___, 19__

ASSETS		LIABILITIES	
Cash	$11,000.00	Notes Payable	$ 300.00
Office Furniture	2,000.00	Total Liabilities	$ 300.00
Office Equipment	300.00	CAPITAL	
		Capital Stock.....$10,000.00	
		Surplus.......... 3,000.00	
		Total Capital..	13,000.00
Total Assets	$13,300.00	Total Liabilities and Capital...	$13,300.00

statements are prepared by the use of work sheets, as will be explained in a later chapter. When there are only a few items in a trial balance, however, the balance sheet may be prepared directly from the trial balance. Note that Assets equal Liabilities plus Capital, or $A = L + C$, and that a double ruling is used below a final total.

Balance sheets of financial enterprises, such as insurance companies, banks, and savings and loan associations, are often published in the news

Figure 2–5

THE XYZ INSURANCE COMPANY
Balance Sheet
December 31, 19___

ASSETS

Cash on hand and in banks	$ 1,386,303.29
Stocks and bonds:	
United States Treasury	3,515,392.82
State, county, and municipal	5,881,365.51
Corporate bonds	492,495.47
Preferred and common stocks	1,539,280.50
First-mortgage loans on real estate	4,665,604.62
Collateral loans	2,725.00
Policy loans	674,396.62
Home office lot and building	1,243,348.93
Other real estate	15,620.38
Interest due and accrued	83,188.95
Net due and deferred premiums	733,357.07
Total	$20,233,079.16

LIABILITIES

Policy reserves	$18,212,995.38
Claim reserves	78,049.71
Premiums paid in advance	317,657.50
Mandatory securities valuation reserve	36,577.41
Reserve for taxes	82,958.73
Other liabilities	98,734.95

FUNDS FOR FURTHER PROTECTION OF POLICYOWNERS

Capital	444,192.50
Surplus	961,912.98
Total	$20,233,079.16

media. The published statements often are presented in less detail than the statements required for managerial use. Even so, the published financial statements are informative. The published balance sheet of an insurance company is presented in Figure 2–5. Some of the terminology of insurance statements differs from that of a general business statement, but the concept of the balance sheet is the same. The differences will be discussed in later chapters. Note that in Figure 2–5 the capital section is described as "Funds for Further Protection of Policyowners." This is often the case with insurance company financial statements. On this balance sheet liabilities and capital are listed below assets. This form of balance sheet is known as a "report form."

THE ACCOUNTING CYCLE

The basic *accounting cycle*[10] has now been explained. It consists of five basic steps:

1. Analyzing transactions
2. Journalizing transactions
3. Posting to the ledger accounts
4. Preparing a trial balance of the ledger
5. Preparing financial statements

There are several other phases of the full accounting cycle. These are presented in subsequent chapters.

DOUBLE-ENTRY AND SINGLE-ENTRY BOOKKEEPING

It is appropriate here to make a few general observations about two basic methods of bookkeeping which may be employed in accounting. The *method* of bookkeeping is a major tool in accomplishing the task known as accounting.

Double-Entry Bookkeeping

The double-entry method of bookkeeping presented up to this point is a systematic process based directly upon, and flowing logically from, the basic accounting equation.

The conceptual structure of the double-entry method permits much flexibility in adapting an accounting system to the special needs of individual enterprises or industries. If the double-entry systems of different companies were compared, literally hundreds of differences in detail would be found.

A properly designed double-entry system records in a meaningful and systematic way every transaction which can be expressed in terms of money. The basic system may be expanded indefinitely by adding new accounts and by subdividing existing accounts as a company grows in size.

The double-entry system can be used for the smallest of businesses, even for personal recordkeeping; and it is used in all large and complex accounting systems.

---

[10] Also called the bookkeeping cycle.

Single-Entry Bookkeeping

Although the double-entry method is the most practical accounting system in use today, it is, of course, possible to keep accurate records of financial matters without using the double-entry method. It is customary to identify any bookkeeping system which is less than completely double entry as *single entry*. There is no generally accepted definition of single-entry bookkeeping.

It is sometimes said that single-entry bookkeeping is primarily concerned with accounting for incoming and outgoing cash, essentially as a person does by entries on his checkbook stubs. Single-entry bookkeeping might also cover most assets and liabilities, especially accounts receivable.

If single-entry records are supported by sufficient information from various commercial documents, invoices, receipts, etc., it may be possible to prepare financial statements *similar* to those which result from a double-entry system. This is done in part by supplementing whatever information the records contain by using the inventory process for assets, liabilities, and other things not in the records. This *inventory* process is a very important one, especially in life insurance accounting, and it will be covered later in detail.

The principle of *equality of debits and credits* basic to the double-entry system and the *trial balance* used in the system provide a simple control of accuracy and completeness that is not present in a single-entry system.

SUMMARY OF ACCOUNTING PRINCIPLES

The accounting principles set out in this chapter are very basic and are a foundation for expanded accounting knowledge in later chapters. It is suggested that the student memorize these principles. They are as follows:

Assets are anything of value owned by a business.

Liabilities are amounts owed by a business.

Capital is the *owner's equity* in the assets of a business, or the *net worth* of the business.

The accounting equation is $A = L + C$.

A *balance sheet* is a listing of all asset, liability, and capital items of a business as of a specific date.

An *account* is a record of all financial transactions of a desired classification. It includes dates, explanation space, amount, and journal folio references. Debit entries are shown to the left of a center line, and credit entries to the right.

Asset accounts are increased by debit entries and decreased by credit entries.

Liability and capital accounts are increased by credit entries and decreased by debit entries.

Every financial transaction must be recorded showing *equal debit and credit entries*.

A *ledger* is a complete set of accounts.

A *journal* is a record of transactions in chronological order, showing dates, accounts to be debited and credited, debit and credit amounts, and miscellaneous supplemental information.

A *trial balance* is a listing of all account balances in the ledger as of a particular day. Its purpose is to check accuracy in the journal and the ledger, but it does not prove that amounts were posted to the proper accounts.

QUESTIONS

1. What are the most common forms of business ownership?
2. Define accounting.
3. Define assets, liabilities, and capital.
4. In general accounting, what terms are used to describe capital?
5. Give the basic accounting equation and explain the relationship of its elements.
6. Describe a balance sheet. Why does it balance? What is another name for this statement?
7. Give the five steps in the basic accounting or bookkeeping cycle.
8. In the equation $A = L + C$, explain the possible effect on L and/or C, if A increases. If A decreases.
9. Why is the journal called a book of original entry?
10. What are the rules for debiting and crediting asset accounts? Liability accounts? Capital accounts?
11. What are the essential characteristics of an account regardless of its physical form?
12. Why is the method of bookkeeping described in this chapter called double entry?
13. How is a trial balance prepared? Why should a trial balance balance?
14. If a trial balance balances, does this mean that the journal and ledger are correct? If not, what types of errors may be present?

PROBLEM

Prepare journal entries in general journal form for each of the following transactions, post them to T-accounts, and prepare a trial balance. (All refer to the same company.)

a) A corporation sold 1,000 shares of its stock on April 1 at $10 per share.

b) The company bought an automobile for $2,000 cash on April 2.

c) The company rendered a service to a customer for a fee of $500 on April 4 but did not receive cash.

d) The company paid a clerk's salary of $150 on April 8.

e) The company bought an automobile at a price of $2,200 on April 9, but paid only $700 in cash at this time and gave the seller a promissory note for the remainder.

f) The company received on April 10 $200 in cash as part payment for service rendered April 4.

(The student may check his work on this problem and those in subsequent chapters by referring to answers in the Answers to Problems section at the back of the book.)

Chapter 3

Accounting for Changes in Surplus

CHANGES IN THE CAPITAL ELEMENT

Most financial transactions in a business corporation affect the capital element of the accounting equation. Usually money received for a service is income, which is an increase in capital, and money disbursed is expense, which is a decrease in capital.

Before learning more about the special phases of income and expense accounting, it is necessary to examine the capital element more closely and also the relationship of income and expense transactions to this element.

Changes in the stockholders' equity which result from the issue of stock by a corporation are recorded in the *Capital Stock* account.

In the typical stock life insurance company ledger there is usually one Capital Stock account. In other corporations there may be several such accounts, each representing a particular type of stock sold. In a stock life insurance company the Capital Stock and Surplus accounts together reflect the status of the stockholders' equity.

In a mutual life insurance company there is no Capital Stock account since there are no stockholders. A mutual company is owned by policyowners and not by stockholders. Therefore, only a Surplus account is used to reflect the policyowners' equity.

The Capital Stock account may remain unchanged for years. If one stockholder sells some of his stock to another person, no accounting entry is made on the corporate books. This is because the company does not receive or disburse money and is not a party to the transaction.

When offering additional corporate stock for sale, a corporation may

27

sell stock to its present stockholders or to the public through stockbrokers. In either case, an entry is made to increase the balance of the Capital Stock account.

In most corporations, including life insurance companies, there are several surplus accounts. However, only one of these is used to record the usual type of changes in surplus. The others are special-purpose accounts and will be discussed later in this book.

The Surplus account is increased primarily by earnings realized from the operations of the corporate business (income less expenses) and is primarily decreased by payment of dividends to stockholders. Surplus is also decreased by losses from operations, and it may be increased or decreased by transactions and circumstances which are not a part of the normal business operations. Examples of changes in surplus arising from sources other than the operations of the business are a gain or loss from the sale of an asset used in the business or from the sale of a security held as an investment. Other types of surplus changes will be covered in more detail in later chapters. At this point it is necessary only to realize that such changes do occur and are not classed as either income or expense transactions.

If each transaction that affected surplus were posted to the Surplus account, the entries would so clutter the account that the only useful information it could provide would be its balance. Instead, these changes are recorded in many accounts and the balances are transferred to the Surplus account at the end of the accounting period.

This chapter presents the accounts in which changes in surplus are recorded and the process by which these changes are eventually transferred to the Surplus account. Income and expense transactions are presented first.

INCOME AND EXPENSE TRANSACTIONS

Companies operate to make a profit. Profit is the excess of income over expense. From a management viewpoint, the decrease in capital resulting from an expense is only temporary and is intended to be returned to surplus eventually in the form of income. For example, money spent for a salary should be returned in the form of income realized from service rendered by the employee to a customer. Similarly, money paid for rent provides a place of business in which the company can render service to others and thereby realize income from the services rendered. So that money will be spent wisely and carefully, expenses are analyzed in detail through the use of various expense accounts in the ledger.

Business transactions which affect an income or an expense account are classed as income or expense transactions. Such transactions usually affect an asset or liability account as well. For example, when cash is received for a service, the transaction is classed as an income transaction.

When money is expended, it is an expense transaction. A thorough understanding of the transactions which follow is basic to all phases of life insurance accounting.

An *income* transaction is one in which, in the normal course of business, a value is received or earned, thus increasing the capital element of the accounting equation.

An *expense* transaction is one in which in the normal course of business a value is disbursed or consumed which decreases the capital element of the accounting equation.

The income and expense transactions described in the preceding chapter were examples of business transactions which involve surplus.

These transactions, as handled in Chapter 2, will now be examined more closely.

For example, the income transaction in which the corporation rendered service for a cash fee of $4,000 was recorded by the following journal entry:

```
Cash...................................................4,000.00
     Surplus..........................................          4,000.00
```

The expense transaction in which the corporation paid a license fee of $1,000 in cash to the city was recorded by the following journal entry:

```
Surplus...............................................1,000.00
     Cash............................................          1,000.00
```

Such income and expense transactions, as well as other changes in surplus, could be recorded directly in the Surplus account as shown by the two sample entries. There are, however, very practical reasons for handling them differently.

A corporation may have thousands of transactions involving income during a month or a year and possibly as many others involving expense. To effectively operate, management must have specific and detailed information about income and expenses. This information must include many different sources of income and the total amount of each type of income transaction which occurred during the accounting period. Similarly, information is needed as to many different types of expense and the total amount of each type.

The need for detailed information about income and expense can be satisfied by subdividing the Surplus account into a number of separate accounts, one for each type of income and one for each type of expense. The decision as to which income and expense accounts are needed by a particular business is part of the systems-design function of the accountant.

Assume for the moment that only one income account and one expense account are to be created. The purpose of each account is to receive entries which otherwise would have to be made directly to the Surplus account. The new Income account can receive those entries reflecting income. Without this account, the entries would be made as credits to Surplus. Similarly, the new Expense account can receive those entries reflecting expenses. Without this account, the entries would be made as debits to Surplus. The advantage of using income and expense accounts rather than a single surplus account will become more apparent as we proceed.

The two transactions presented earlier in this chapter may now be reexamined. First, the corporation rendered service for a cash fee of $4,000. The journal entry is:

Cash...4,000.00
    Income...   4,000.00

The debit to Cash represents an increase in the asset account, Cash. The credit to Income represents an increase in capital which is recorded in the Income account rather than directly to Surplus.

The expense transaction in which the corporation paid a license fee of $1,000 cash to the city may now be recorded by the journal entry:

Expense...1,000.00
    Cash..   1,000.00

The debit to Expense represents a temporary decrease in capital which is recorded in the Expense account rather than directly in Surplus. The credit to Cash represents a decrease in the asset account, Cash.

If several income and expense accounts were being created, the income account in the first entry might be entitled *Service Fee Income* and the expense account in the second entry might be called *City License Expense.*

Income accounts are credited for income received because entries to such accounts increase the capital element of the accounting equation. Expense accounts are debited when expenses are recorded because they decrease the capital element. By their nature, therefore, income accounts generally have credit balances and expense accounts generally have debit balances.

The trial balance, which is simply a list of the balances of all the ledger accounts, usually shows a credit balance in each of the income accounts and a debit balance in each of the expense accounts. With this information, it is possible to prepare the second major financial statement, the *income statement.* This statement is also called the *revenue statement,* the *profit and loss statement,* the *income and expense statement,* or the *revenue and expense statement.* In United States life insurance companies, it is called the *summary of operations.*[1]

An *income and expense statement* based on the two transactions for which journal entries were given above is presented in Figure 3–1. Note that the heading of this statement gives the name of the company, the title of the statement, and the period covered by the statement.

---

[1] The Canadian term is *revenue account.*

Figure 3-1
X CORPORATION
Statement of Income and Expense
For the Month of March, 19—

Service fee income	$4,000.00
Less: City license expense	1,000.00
Net Income	$3,000.00

Net income is defined as the excess of operating income over operating expense.

If the expenses had been greater than the income, the last line would have shown net loss rather than net income. *Net loss* is defined as the excess of operating expense over operating income.

Although dollar signs or marks are not used in the T-account, journal, or ledger, they are used in the financial statements. A dollar sign is placed beside the first figure in a column of figures and beside the first figure below an underline. If several income and expense items are shown, the income items and expense items are grouped and totaled separately. Each item may represent a number of account balances from the ledger.

A life insurance company summary of operations is presented in Figure 3-2. (Life insurance terminology will be discussed later.) Note the similarity between the two statements.

Figure 3-2
MODEL LIFE INSURANCE COMPANY
Summary of Operations
For Year Ending December 31, 19—

INCOME

Premiums earned	$15,653,275
Policy proceeds left with company	342,614
Net investment income	3,074,334
Total	$19,070,223

COST OF OPERATIONS

Death benefits and other benefits incurred	$ 6,771,463
Dividends paid to policyowners	331,689
Increase in actuarial reserve	3,825,532
Commissions	2,886,712
Agency expenses	1,048,546
General operating expenses	2,181,980
Taxes, licenses, and fees	492,836
Change in loading, due and deferred premiums	61,112
Total	$17,599,870

NET GAIN from operations before federal income tax	$ 1,470,353
Federal income tax incurred	516,289
NET INCOME after federal income tax	$ 954,064

DIVIDENDS TO STOCKHOLDERS

Another type of transaction which affects the Surplus account is the declaration and payment of dividends to stockholders.

The payment of dividends in cash gives the stockholders some of the earnings of the corporation. Payment of these dividends is not considered an expense in the usual sense of the word, but a special type of surplus decrease.

When the stockholders are given a dividend in cash, the balance of Surplus is reduced by the amount of the dividend. If the entry were made directly to Surplus, the payment of a total of $500 in dividends would be recorded by the following entry:

```
Surplus.....................................................500.00
     Cash.................................................         500.00
```

The same reason which makes separate income and expense accounts advisable makes it more practical to establish a Dividends account to receive the debit part of the transaction:

```
Dividends...................................................500.00
     Cash.................................................         500.00
```

The debit to the Dividends account represents a decrease in capital, which is recorded in the Dividends account rather than directly in Surplus.

Dividends to stockholders may also be paid in the form of additional shares of stock in the company. In such a case, the debit is still to the Dividends account but the credit is now to the Capital Stock account.

The entry is:

```
Dividends...................................................500.00
     Capital Stock........................................         500.00
```

This increases one portion of the capital element, Capital Stock, and indirectly decreases another portion, Surplus.

NOMINAL ACCOUNTS

The new Dividend account and expense and income accounts, as well as any other accounts in which surplus changes are recorded, are called *nominal* accounts; that is, accounts "in name only." Asset, liability, and some capital accounts are called *real* accounts.

The use of nominal accounts facilitates the preparation of income and expense statements and other statements reflecting surplus changes. Account balances in nominal accounts at the end of the accounting period show the amount of each type of surplus change that has occurred during the period.

Nominal accounts are brought to a zero balance at the end of each accounting period by transferring their balances to the Surplus account. This transfer process is called *closing the books*. Nominal accounts start anew with a zero balance at the beginning of each accounting period whereas real accounts have a balance continuously.

CLOSING THE BOOKS

Ordinarily, *closing the books* occurs at the end of each accounting year, although it may be done more often. Only the nominal accounts are closed. Real accounts are not involved in the closing process.

The objectives of the closing process are:

1. To bring the balance of each of the nominal accounts to zero, and

2. To bring the balance of the Surplus account to the amount at which it would have been if all the income, expense, and other surplus change entries (such as the dividend entry) had been made directly to Surplus during the accounting period.

Both objectives of the closing process could be accomplished by a series of *closing entries* which transferred the balance of each of the nominal accounts to Surplus. It is the practice, however, to take an intermediate step in the case of the income and expense accounts.

The balance of each income and each expense account is first transferred (or closed) to an account called the *Income and Expense Summary*.[2]

After each income and expense account is closed and the balance transferred to the Income and Expense Summary account, the balance of this summary account is transferred to Surplus. The Dividends account is closed by transferring its balance directly to Surplus.

When the closing journal entries are posted or transferred to the ledger, the only accounts left with a balance are the asset, liability, capital stock, and surplus accounts.

Closing Entries Illustrated

Assume that the ledger accounts had balances at the end of the accounting year as shown in the T-accounts in Figure 3–3. (Only the balances, not the entries, are shown.) No entries are made to Surplus during the year, so the balance in that account on the last day of the year before the closing entries are posted is the same as on the first day of the year.

The income accounts will be closed first. There is only one income account, Fee Income. The closing journal entry which is required to

---

[2] The traditional name for this summary account is *Profit and Loss Summary*.

Figure 3–3

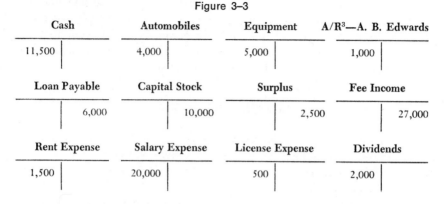

Cash	Automobiles	Equipment	A/R[3]—A. B. Edwards
11,500	4,000	5,000	1,000

Loan Payable	Capital Stock	Surplus	Fee Income
6,000	10,000	2,500	27,000

Rent Expense	Salary Expense	License Expense	Dividends
1,500	20,000	500	2,000

bring the balance of the Fee Income account to zero and to transfer its present balance to the new Income and Expense Summary account is a debit to the Fee Income account and a credit to the I & E Summary (Income and Expense Summary) account.

Fee Income..27,000
    I & E Summary..   27,000

When this entry is posted, the T-accounts involved would then show:

Fee Income		I & E Summary
27.000	27,000	27,000

Note that the credit balance of Fee Income prior to closing is now a credit balance in I & E Summary. The Fee Income account has been decreased to a zero by a debit entry, and the I & E Summary account has been increased by a credit entry. In effect, the credit balance of the Fee Income account has been transferred to the I & E Summary account.

The expense accounts are *Rent Expense, Salary Expense,* and *License Expense.* Closing entries for these accounts can be made as a series of simple entries (one debit and one credit) or as one *compound entry.* A compound entry is one involving more entries than one debit and one credit entry. However, total debits *must* be equal to total credits. As a compound entry, the closing entry would be:

I & E Summary......................................22,000.00
    Rent Expense....................................   1,500.00
    Salary Expense..................................   20,000.00
    License Expense.................................   500.00

The debit ($22,000) to I & E Summary is the total of the credits to the several expense accounts. The expense accounts are now balanced at zero,

---

[3] Accounts Receivable.

and their previous debit balances have been transferred to the I & E Summary account. After posting, this account appears as follows:

I & E Summary

22,000	27,000

The $5,000 balance in the I & E Summary account is the net income that will be shown on an income and expense statement for the accounting period.

The I & E Summary account is now closed by transferring its balance to Surplus. A debit to I & E Summary account and a credit to the Surplus account is made. The entry is:

```
I & E Summary.........................................5,000.00
   Surplus.............................................      5,000.00
```

This entry zero balances the I & E Summary account and transfers its balance ($5,000 net income from operations) to the Surplus account.

The Dividends account is closed directly to Surplus by debiting Surplus and crediting Dividends. The entry is:

```
Surplus................................................2,000.00
   Dividends...........................................      2,000.00
```

When the two entries just given are posted, each nominal account will be zero balanced and all account balances in which surplus changes were recorded will have been transferred to the Surplus account. After these closing entries are posted, the accounts appear as follows (note that the Surplus account prior to closing had a $2,500 balance carried forward from the last period):

I & E Summary		Surplus		Dividends	
22,000	27,000		2,500	2,000	2,000
5,000		2,000	5,000		
27,000	27,000	2,000	7,500	2,000	2,000

The new after-closing balance of Surplus is $5,500.

Accounts are ruled after the books are closed in a manner similar to that shown. The debits and credits in each nominal account are totaled to prove the account is zero balanced, and a double rule is placed below the totals. Asset, liability, and capital accounts are not closed because they are not zero balanced by closing entries.

AFTER-CLOSING TRIAL BALANCE

A trial balance should be prepared from the ledger after the closing entries are posted. The purpose is to check that no error has been introduced in the closing process. The after-closing (or post-closing) trial balance of the accounts in the ledger in Figure 3–3 after the closing entries have been made, would be:

Cash	$11,500.00	
Automobiles	4,000.00	
Equipment	5,000.00	
A/R—Edwards	1,000.00	
Loan payable		$ 6,000.00
Capital stock		10,000.00
Surplus		5,500.00
	$21,500.00	$21,500.00

These accounts are used in preparing the balance sheet. Those with debit balances are assets, and those with credit balances are liabilities and capital.

REVIEW OF STEPS IN CLOSING THE BOOKS

The steps in closing the books are:

1. Prepare a trial balance of the ledger accounts as of the last day of the period.
2. *a*) Make a closing journal entry transferring the balance of each income account to the I & E Summary account.
   b) Make a closing journal entry transferring the balance of each expense account to the I & E Summary account.
   c) Make a closing journal entry transferring the balance of the I & E Summary to Surplus.
   d) Make a closing journal entry transferring the balance of the Dividends account to Surplus.
3. Post the closing journal entries to the ledger and rule the closed accounts.
4. Prepare an after-closing trial balance of the ledger.

Figure 3–4 is an example of a closed income account showing the usual

Figure 3–4

Fee Income

19__ Dec.	31	To I & E Summary	13	27,000.00	19__ Jan.	5		1	3,000.00
					Mar.	11		4	12,000.00
					Sept.	23		7	11,000.00
					Dec.	30		12	1,000.00
				27,000.00					27,000.00

method of ruling such accounts. (Closing entries are dated as of the last day of the period.) This account is now ready to receive entries for the next period as though it were a new account.

The entries on the credit side of the account were made during the accounting period as fee income was recorded.

STATEMENT OF SURPLUS

In addition to the balance sheet and statement of income and expense, a third financial statement is usually prepared, the statement of surplus. The heading of this statement includes the name of the company, the title of the statement, and the period covered by the statement.

A simple statement of surplus is presented in Figure 3–5. This state-

Figure 3–5

X CORPORATION
Statement of Surplus
For the Year Ending 19__

Surplus, January 1, 19__	$2,500.00
Net income for the year	5,000.00
	$7,500.00
Dividends	2,000.00
Surplus, December 31, 19__	$5,500.00

ment shows changes in surplus during the accounting period. All income and expense account balances are reflected by a single amount, the net income (or net loss) as reported on the income and expense statement. All the other figures are from account balances just prior to closing the books.

The first item in the statement of surplus is the balance in the Surplus account on the first day of the accounting period. To this beginning balance is added the net income for the period and any other increases in surplus that resulted from sources other than normal business operations. From the total of these two items is subtracted any dividends paid during the period and any other decreases in surplus. If there had been a net loss, it would have been subtracted in this section of the statement. The resulting figure is the balance of Surplus on the *last* day of the period. This is, of course, the same as the surplus balance on the balance sheet of the last day of the period.

If for the year there were a net loss greater in amount than the opening balance of Surplus on the first day of the year, the Surplus account would show a debit balance at the end of the year. A deficit would then exist. A *deficit* is, by definition, a *debit balance in Surplus*. This condition seldom, if ever, occurs in a profitable business enterprise.

If a deficit does occur, the amount of deficit is usually shown in parentheses on the balance sheet and statement of surplus. For example, in Figure 3–5 a deficit balance would have been shown ($5,500).

TIME ELEMENTS IN ACCOUNTING

Four time elements are used in accounting. These are:

1. Accounting period
2. Date of recording
3. Date due or date payable
4. Period earned or period incurred

An *accounting period* is the period at the end of which the books are closed and financial statements prepared. It may be a month, a quarter year, a full year, or any selected other period of time. However, financial statements may be prepared at any time during an accounting period without the necessity of closing the books.

The accounting period is frequently referred to as the fiscal period. This is usually a period of 12 months, but it need not coincide with a calendar year. A 12-month fiscal period ending on December 31 is usually referred to as a calendar year. A period ending at any other time of the year is simply known as a fiscal period. In life insurance companies the accounting period is the calendar year; therefore, examples in this book are usually based on the calendar year, even though the word period is used in discussing general accounting.

The *date of recording* is the date the transaction is recorded in a journal. If cash is received or paid out, the date of its receipt or its payment is the proper date for recording the transaction. If an amount becomes due or payable, the date of recording may be the date the amount was first recognized as being due or payable, even though cash was not received or paid at that time. This text uses the word *due* in connection with income to mean income receivable and uses the word *payable* in connection with expense payable. However, life insurance annual statement blanks frequently use the word *due* in both senses. Therefore, caution must be used in interpreting the meaning of this word.

Date due or date payable are specific points in time. For example, if interest covering the past six months is due on the first of February, then February 1 is the *date due* for the lender and the *date payable* for the borrower.

The *period earned* is the period to which an amount of income is applicable, and the *period incurred* is the period to which an amount of expense is applicable. For example, if interest for the past six months is $180 and is due on February 1 of the current year, then one sixth of $180 ($30) of interest income was earned by the creditor in January of the current calendar year and five sixths of $180 ($150) was earned in the last five months of the preceding calendar year. The debtor would have incurred $30 of interest expense in the current calendar year and would have incurred $150 of interest expense in the previous year.

THE CASH AND ACCRUAL BASIS OF ACCOUNTING

The fundamental assumption of the *cash basis* of accounting is that income and expense transactions are recorded in, and are recognized as being applicable to, the accounting period in which the cash is received or disbursed. For example, if $180 of interest income became due in February and is received and recorded in March, the full $180 is recognized as income for the month of March.

The cash basis of accounting is rarely used in firms of large size. The accrual basis is far more common, and it generally gives more valid results.

The fundamental assumption of the *accrual* (or revenue) *basis* of accounting is that income and expense transactions are recognized as being applicable to the accounting period in which the income is earned or the expense is incurred.

In accounting on an accrual basis, the date on which income or expense is recorded has no effect on the amount earned or incurred within an accounting period. In the example, the $30 interest earned by the creditor in the current accounting period is recognized as income for the current year, regardless of the year in which it is recorded. Similarly the $150 is recognized as earned income for the preceding year, regardless of the year in which it is recorded.

The method for adjusting to an accrual basis—i.e., adjusting the recorded amount to the earned or incurred amount—is explained in the following section.

ADJUSTMENTS AT THE END OF THE ACCOUNTING PERIOD

When accrual basis statements are prepared, a number of adjustments in account balances must be made at the end of the period, either on the books or on supplemental papers, in order to match income and expense items to the period in which they are earned or incurred. These adjustments are necessary because (1) income may have been recorded but not yet earned, (2) expense may have been recorded but not incurred, (3) income may have been earned but not recorded, and (4) expense may have been incurred but not yet recorded.

To adjust an account balance so that it properly shows earned income or incurred expense, it is necessary to transfer out of the account those amounts recorded in the period which were not applicable to that period. Amounts applicable to the period but not yet recorded must be recorded in the account.

The process of adjusting income and expense accounts to the accrual basis requires the use of special asset and liability accounts established for this purpose and for this purpose alone. The following illustrations show that the initial recording may be made in full to the appropriate asset or liability account; then at the end of the accounting period, the portion earned or incurred during that accounting period is transferred to the related income or expense account.

The accounting period in which income and expense were *recorded* and the time when they actually became due or payable determines the adjustment required to change the recorded amount to the amount actually earned or incurred. In the example involving $180 of interest, the amount earned in the current year is $30, regardless of when the $180 was recorded on the books as income. If the interest was recorded in the current year, $150 must be transferred out of the Interest Income account. However, if the recording took place last year, $30 must be transferred into the Interest Income account this year.

The following examples will clarify the process of making adjusting entries to arrive at earned or incurred account balances and will introduce the asset and liability accounts which are established for use in the adjusting process.

Unearned Income

Unearned income is income which has been received and recorded but not yet earned. Accounts established for the purpose of recording unearned income are liability accounts because they reflect the value or service to be delivered at a later date, i.e., a service owed.

There are two methods for recording and adjusting income to the accrual basis. The first, referred to as the standard method, is widely used in commercial accounting. By this method, income is initially recorded in unearned income accounts if the amount is largely applicable to other accounting periods. At the end of the accounting period, the earned portion of the income is transferred to the income account.

The second method, referred to as a cash basis, is more commonly used in life insurance companies, although both may be used in a single company. By the cash basis method, the amount received is initially recorded in an income account at time of receipt. At the end of the accounting period, the unearned portion is transferred to the unearned income account.

The standard method is simpler to explain and will make clear the theory of adjusting account balances to accrual basis amounts. An example of this method is the accounting a publishing company might use in recording subscription income.

A publisher received $12 on July 1 this year for a two-year subscription to a magazine. The entry is a debit to Cash to show its increase and a credit to the Unearned Subscription Income account to show the liability for services to be rendered. The entry is:

```
Cash.......................................................12.00
    Unearned Subscription Income.............................        12.00
```

The liability amount reflects the price of services to be delivered. The cost of printing, mailing, and delivering the magazines will not be incurred until later, at which time it will become proper to recognize a portion of this liability as income. By the end of this year when six months of the two years have passed, the publisher will have earned one fourth of the $12, or $3. An adjusting entry is needed to transfer $3 earned income from the liability account, Unearned Subscription Income, to the income account, Subscription Income. A debit to Unearned Subscription Income decreases this liability. A credit to Subscription Income records the income earned. The entry is:

```
Unearned Subscription Income..................................3.00
    Subscription Income.......................................        3.00
```

In T-accounts, these two entries would appear (assuming no other entries to these accounts) as follows:

Cash	Unearned Subscription Income		Subscription Income
12.00	3.00	12.00	3.00

At the end of the accounting period, the Subscription Income account is closed to the I & E Summary account and the Unearned Subscription Income account appears in the liabilities section of the balance sheet.

If the insurance company method is used, the initial entry is:

```
Cash.......................................................12.00
    Subscription Income......................................        12.00
```

At the end of the year the adjusting entry is:

```
Subscription Income.........................................9.00
    Unearned Subscription Income.............................        9.00
```

When these entries are posted, the account balances are the same as when the standard method is used. The closing process is, therefore, the same.

Prepaid Expense

Prepaid expense is an expense which has been paid and recorded but not yet fully incurred. Accounts established to record prepaid expense are asset accounts because they show the value of services to be received in the future, i.e., services receivable. An example of prepaid expense is a property insurance premium which must be paid in advance.

As in the case of unearned income, there are two methods for recording and adjusting expense to the accrual basis, the standard method and the cash basis or insurance company method. The standard method is explained first because it is the commonly accepted method for adjusting account balances to the accrual basis.

Assume that the XYZ Company purchases on January 1 a three-year property insurance policy with the full premium of $450 paid at the time of purchase. The entry on the XYZ Company's books is a debit to the Unexpired Insurance account to reflect the asset value for services receivable (insurance protection). The credit to Cash shows the decrease in this asset. The entry is:

```
Unexpired Insurance.......................................450.00
    Cash.................................................          450.00
```

As the protection period passes, the portion of the premium which applied to that period becomes an expense to the company and the asset unexpired insurance is reduced accordingly.

At the end of this year, one third of the three-year policy period will have expired. The expense for the period is $150 (⅓ of $450). The adjusting entry is a debit to the Insurance Expense account in order to record the expense for that portion of the paid premium which provided coverage during this year and a credit to the Unexpired Insurance account to reduce this asset account balance to the new balance of $300. The entry is:

```
Insurance Expense.........................................150.00
    Unexpired Insurance..................................          150.00
```

At the end of the accounting period the Insurance Expense account is closed to the I & E Summary account. The Unexpired Insurance account, with its debit balance of $300, appears in the asset section of the balance sheet.

If a life insurance company purchased this property insurance, the entire amount paid would usually be recorded as an expense at the time of payment. The entry to do this is:

```
Insurance Expense.........................................450.00
    Cash.................................................          450.00
```

Prepaid expenses such as Insurance Expense are not recognized as valid assets in a life insurance company statement submitted to regulatory authorities. Therefore, no adjusting entry is made. When the books are closed, the full amount in the Insurance Expense account, in this case $450, is transferred to the I&E Summary account. The reason for this unusual treatment will be explained in a later chapter.

Accrued Income

Accrued income is income which has been earned but which has not yet been received. Accounts established to record accrued income at the end of the accounting period are asset accounts because they reflect amounts receivable, i.e., values owned.

There is only one method for recording accrued income at the end of the accounting period. The entry is a debit to the accrued income account to record the increase in asset value and a credit to the income account to record income not previously recorded.

A common example of an accrued income item is found in adjusting interest on a loan receivable. Assume that the corporation made a loan for which it receives interest of $50 on March 31 and on September 30 each year. When the interest is received on September 30 for the March–September period, Cash is debited and the Interest Income account is credited in an equal amount to record the income. The entry is:

```
Cash...............................................................50.00
     Interest Income.........................................          50.00
```

The company accounting period ends on December 31. An adjusting entry is needed as of that date to record interest earned between September 30 and December 31, but not yet recorded as income. The adjusting entry is:

```
Accrued Interest Receivable....................................25.00
     Interest Income.........................................          25.00
```

The Interest Income account is, of course, closed to I & E Summary account. The Accrued Interest Receivable account appears on the balance sheet as an asset.

In the following year when the interest payment is received on March 31, either of two methods might be used:

The first method is to record a portion of the amount received so as to make the balance zero in the accrued income account (Accrued Interest Receivable) and to record the remainder in an income account. This method is practical only in small companies.

When this first method is used, the receipt of the $50 interest payment in March of the following year is recorded as follows:

```
Cash...............................................................50.00
     Accrued Interest Receivable...........................          25.00
     Interest Income.........................................          25.00
```

This entry zero balances the asset account, Accrued Interest Receivable and records the interest earned in the current period in the Interest Income account.

The second method, widely used in life insurance companies, is to let the balance in accrued income accounts remain "as is" throughout the year and credit all amounts received during the year to the income accounts. At the end of the year, the accrued income accounts are brought to a zero balance by transferring their old balances to the related income accounts. New adjusting entries are then made for the end of the current year. This method will be referred to as the *reversal and reentry* method.

Under the reversal and reentry method, the entry to record the payment received in March is:

```
Cash.................................................50.00
    Interest Income.......  ...............................        50.00
```

Now let us assume a new loan is made late in the year on which the interest is $50 annually. No interest was due on this second loan during the year, but the accrued interest at the end of the year is $10. Two $50 payments were received on the old loan.

The entry to reverse the adjusting entry at the end of the previous year is:

```
Interest Income.......................................25.00
    Accrued Interest Receivable..............................        25.00
```

The adjusting entry at the end of this year to record the accrued interest on both the old and new loans is:

```
Accrued Interest Receivable...................................35.00
    Interest Income...........................................        35.00
```

The $35 is the sum of $25 accrued interest at the end of the year on the old loan and $10 on the new loan. After the two $50 amounts were received and posted and the two adjusting entries were posted, the Interest Income account appears as follows:

Interest Income

25.00	50.00
	50.00
	35.00

The balance of the account is $110, the amount of interest *earned* during the year ($100 on the old loan and $10 on the new loan).

Accrued Expense

An *accrued expense* is any expense which has been incurred but is not yet paid or recorded on the books. Accrued expense accounts are established at the end of the accounting period. These are liability accounts because they show the cost of services received but not paid for, i.e., amounts owed.

As in the case of accrued income, there is only one method for recording this adjustment, but there are two methods for recording expense in the following accounting period.

The loan which was used in the example on accrued income can be used to illustrate accrued expense adjusting entries. Assume, however, that the company is now the borrower instead of the lender, and therefore is paying interest rather than receiving it. When the interest is paid in September, the entry is a debit to Interest Expense to record the interest cost for March through September and a credit to Cash. The entry is:

```
Interest Expense.................................................50.00
    Cash.......................................................        50.00
```

At the end of the year the adjusting entry is a debit to Interest Expense to record this cost for the last three months of the year and a credit to Accrued Interest Payable to record the liability for the amount of interest owed. The entry is:

```
Interest Expense.................................................25.00
    Accrued Interest Payable...................................        25.00
```

Even though a $50 interest payment will not actually become payable until the following March, one half of the interest was incurred during the current year and should be set up on the books as payable at the end of the accounting period. The Interest Expense account is then closed to the I & E Summary account and the Accrued Interest Payable account is shown on the balance sheet as a current liability. When the company actually pays the interest on March 31 of the next year, the entry is:

```
Interest Expense.................................................25.00
Accrued Interest Payable.........................................25.00
    Cash.......................................................        50.00
```

The debit to Interest Expense records the cost of the interest for the current year. The debit to Accrued Interest Payable zero balances this liability account.

A company may choose to record this entire payment as expense and at the end of the accounting period reverse the previous year's adjusting entry and make a new one for the end of the current year.

Whichever method is used for recording amounts received in the subsequent year, after the adjustments are made, the balance of the Interest Expense account must show the interest expense incurred. Likewise, the balance of the Accrued Interest Payable account must show the interest liability incurred but unpaid as of the end of the year.

Note that adjusting entries are made in connection with income and expense accounts but that they always affect asset and liability accounts also. These adjustments establish temporary asset and liability accounts, i.e., accrued and prepaid, which appear on the balance sheet of a corporation using accrual basis accounting. Adjusting entries of this type are not made in the preparation of financial statements where a cash basis method of accounting is used. Accrued items, therefore, do not appear on a cash basis balance sheet.

Adjusting entries are made in the journal and then posted to the ledger. An *adjusted trial balance* is then prepared to test the accuracy of the posting of the adjusting entries.

The adjusting entries may be determined first on working papers before they are made in the journal. How working papers are prepared is discussed in the next chapter.[4]

SUMMARY OF ACCOUNTING PRINCIPLES

The basic principles of accounting for changes in surplus have been covered in this chapter. These principles are:

An *income* transaction is one in which a value is received or earned in the normal course of business and which *increases* the capital element of the accounting equation.

An *expense* transaction is one in which a value is disbursed or consumed in the normal course of business and which *decreases* the capital element of the accounting equation.

Nominal accounts are temporary accounts which are closed into the Surplus account at the end of the accounting period. They include income, expense, dividend, and other accounts in which changes in surplus may be recorded.

Real accounts are those which appear on the balance sheet after books are closed. They include asset, liability, and capital accounts.

Income accounts are credited for income received and normally have credit balances.

Expense accounts are debited for expenses paid and normally have debit balances.

A *statement of income and expense* shows the income received, expenses paid, and net income from operations during a stated period of time.

Net income is the excess of operating income over expenses.

Net loss is the excess, if any, of expenses over operating income.

Dividends paid to stockholders are treated as deductions from surplus and not as an expense.

Income and expense accounts are closed into the Income and Expense Summary account which is then closed into the Surplus account.

---

[4] Most life insurance companies use cash basis accounting throughout the year but prepare the annual statement required by insurance departments on an accrual basis. Accrual adjustments made for this purpose are not posted to ledger accounts.

An *after-closing trial balance* is prepared by listing balances of real accounts after the books are closed. Its purpose is to prove that no error was introduced during the closing process.

Cash basis accounting is recording and recognizing income and expense transactions as being applicable to the period in which they are received or disbursed.

Accrual basis accounting recognizes income and expense items as being applicable to the period in which the income is earned or the expense incurred.

Adjusting to the accrual basis creates special asset accounts known as *Prepaid Expense* and *Accrued Income* accounts and special liability accounts known as *Accrued Expense* and *Unearned Income* accounts.

QUESTIONS

1. If a stockholder in the XY Corporation sells his stock to someone else, what financial accounts in the corporate books are affected, if any?
2. Define income transactions.
3. Define expense transactions.
4. Why do we need separate income and expense accounts if the entries in these accounts could be made directly in the Surplus account?
5. What are four other titles by which a statement of income and expense might be known?
6. Alongside which figures should dollar marks be placed on financial statements?
7. Define and give examples of *nominal* accounts and of *real* accounts. On which financial statements do nominal accounts appear?
8. What are the two objectives of the process called "closing the books"?
9. What is the traditional name of the account which is now commonly called the Income and Expense Summary?
10. How does an after-closing trial balance differ from a trial balance before the books are closed?
11. What are the steps in closing the books?
12. The balance of which account appears on both the statement of surplus and the balance sheet?
13. Define the term "deficit."
14. Describe four general situations which require adjusting entries at the end of the accounting period.
15. Define unearned income, prepaid expense, accrued income, and accrued expense.

16. Give one example of each of the four items in question 15. (Do not use the examples given in this chapter.)
17. Why must adjusting entries be made before the closing entries?
18. Why should an account entitled Unexpired Insurance appear on the balance sheet rather than on the income and expense statement?

PROBLEM

Prepare journal entries for the following transactions, post to T-accounts, prepare an adjusted trial balance, an income and expense statement, closing entries at the end of the month, and a post-closing trial balance. Assume that on January 1st the account balances in Service, Inc., were as follows:

Cash....................................	$ 8,000.00	
Notes receivable........................	2,100.00	
Prepaid insurance.......................	55.00	
Accrued interest income.................	78.00	
Accounts payable........................		$ 211.00
Accrued salaries........................		325.00
Accrued rent............................		37.00
Prepaid service income..................		185.00
Capital.................................		500.00
Surplus.................................		8,975.00
	$10,233.00	$10,233.00

The ledger also includes these accounts which were closed at the end of the previous month: Service Income, Interest Income, Rent Expense, Insurance Expense, and Salary Expense.

   a) On January 10, a service was rendered to a customer who gave the company a note for $450, payable in 90 days at 6 percent interest.
   b) On January 15, the company paid the manager his monthly salary of $650.
   c) On January 16, an agreement was made to render a service to a customer for $1,000; this amount was received in cash.
   d) On January 22, the rent of $100 per month was paid.
   e) On January 28, the note receivable of $2,100 was paid in full together with interest of $100.

As of the end of the month, make adjusting entries so that all income accounts reflect earned income and all expense accounts reflect incurred expense. Use the standard method of making adjusting entries. At the end of the month, the manager determines that unexpired insurance is now $45, accrued interest income is $1.50, accrued salaries are $346, accrued rent is $37, and prepaid service income is $515.

Chapter 4

Sales, Inventories, and Working Papers

MERCHANDISE OPERATIONS

Life insurance companies do not sell physical goods or merchandise. However, a knowledge of the principles and practices used in accounting for sales of merchandise and for the cost of making those sales is helpful to the student of life insurance accounting.

The manager of a business which sells merchandise must know both the dollar amount of sales and the cost of making the sales, including the cost of the merchandise sold. He uses this knowledge to calculate the profit on past sales and as a guide to establishing prices in the future.

In a sale, the capital element of the accounting equation is increased by the difference between the amount of the sale and the cost of the sale. For example, if merchandise which cost $75 is sold for $100, the capital element of the equation is increased by $25 ($100 − $75).

In accounting for this increase in capital, sales are treated as income and cost of sales is treated as expense. Accounting for income from sales is the simpler process to understand and is discussed first.

SALES

A sale is recorded as income for the full dollar amount of the sale when the transaction occurs.

When a sale of merchandise is made for $100 cash, the journal entry is:

Cash...100.00
    Sales... 100.00

The entry to the Sales account is a credit, reflecting an ultimate increase in Surplus.

If the sale is not for cash, an asset account, Accounts Receivable, is established in the name of the person or organization who owes the money, showing the amount he owes. This account is debited to reflect an increase in the asset accounts receivable. The entry is:

```
Accounts Receivable—ABC Company........................100.00
    Sales................................................        100.00
```

The Sales account, like all other income accounts, is closed at the end of the period to the Income and Expense (I & E) Summary. At the end of the period, the journal entry to close the Sales account, assuming it has a $1,500 credit balance, is:

```
Sales...................................................1,500.00
    I & E Summary......................................        1,500.00
```

The debit entry to the Sales account brings this account to a zero balance and transfers its balance to the I & E Summary account.

For a merchandising operation, only sales of merchandise are recorded in the Sales account. On these transactions the business hopes to realize a profit and thereby increase its net worth.

Purchases

The cost of merchandise purchased for resale is recorded as expense when the merchandise is purchased. Accounting for this item is similar to that for other expenses, but there are differences in the process used at the end of the accounting period.

The debit entry for a $900 cash purchase is made to an account called *Purchases*. This debit represents a decrease in capital equal to the cost of the merchandise purchased. The credit is to Cash.

The entry is:

```
Purchases................................................900.00
    Cash................................................        900.00
```

The entry for a purchase on credit from the XYZ Company requires the establishment of a liability account, Accounts Payable, with the name of the person owed. The debit is to Purchases and the credit is to an Accounts Payable account, thereby increasing the liabilities by the amount owed.

If at the end of the period, the Purchases account has, for example, a debit balance of $900, it is closed to the I & E Summary account by the following entry:

```
I & E Summary............................................900.00
    Purchases...........................................        900.00
```

The credit entry to the Purchases account brings it to a zero balance.

Only purchases of merchandise are recorded in the Purchases account. Purchases of items for use, such as furniture and equipment, are debited to asset accounts as they are bought and are not recorded as expenses.[1]

Inventory

It is especially important to understand a procedure which may be called the *inventory process*. Many insurance company balance sheet items are determined by techniques similar to the inventory process discussed here.

The value of merchandise on hand on the first day of the period is called *beginning inventory* and that which is on hand the last day of the period is called *ending inventory*. The ending inventory of any period is the beginning inventory of the next period; and, of course, the beginning inventory of this period is the ending inventory of the preceding period.

The dollar amount of the ending inventory may be determined by counting each type of item on hand the last day of the period and multiplying by the cost of each item. There are other methods of valuing inventory, but we will consider only this *cost* method.

Merchandise inventory is an asset, but it is recorded on the books only at the end of the accounting period. There are two reasons: (1) in most companies it is not practical to make an entry (at cost) to an inventory account in the ledger as merchandise is sold, and (2) the recording of merchandise inventory at the end of the accounting period facilitates determining the cost of sales and the *gross profit* on sales. Gross profit on sales is the excess of the total sales price of all merchandise sold during the accounting period over the total cost of the merchandise sold.

The impracticality of recording the cost of merchandise sold on an item by item basis may be seen in the operation of a drugstore. Many items may have relatively small values, and drugs used in prescriptions may be poured in small quantities from large bottles. The cost of measuring and recording the cost of each of these items at the time of sale would be excessive. Even if it were practical to keep a record of these costs, over a period of time, some items of merchandise might deteriorate, be damaged, or be stolen. The value of these lost items could not be deducted from the Inventory account balance until the merchandise in stock was counted and such losses detected. Therefore, since the counting and valuing process at the end of the period is necessary in any event, accounting for changes as they occur is unnecessary.

The counting and valuing of each item of merchandise on hand as of a

---

[1] The sale and purchase of assets other than merchandise are discussed in Chapter 5 in the section "Fixed Assets."

specific date is known as *taking an inventory* and is a part of the inventory process.

A simple example will demonstrate how the cost of merchandise sold is determined. If the owner of the business had on hand at the beginning of the period 10 items of merchandise each costing $100 and he purchased during the period 25 more at the same cost, he obviously had available for sale 35 items which cost in total, $3,500. If he had 7 items on hand at the end of the period, he assumes that he sold 28 items which cost $2,800 ($3,500 − $700). Stated in another way, the inventory at the beginning of the period ($1,000) plus purchases ($2,500) less the inventory at the end of the period ($700) gives the cost of merchandise sold ($2,800). The result is the true cost of merchandise sold, which includes the cost of items damaged, deteriorated, or stolen during the accounting period.

Before discussing the entries for recording inventory on the books, it will be useful to examine the format for showing in the statement of income and expense the cost of goods sold and the gross profit on sales.

GROSS PROFIT ON SALES

Gross profit on sales is the excess of the total sales price of all merchandise sold during the accounting period over the total cost of that merchandise. Since the amount of each sale is credited to the Sales account, the balance of that account at the end of the period is considered to be the total sales price of all goods sold during the period.

When there is no inventory at either the beginning or the end of the period, the cost of goods sold is the cost of the goods purchased, which is shown by the balance in the Purchases account at the end of the period. If, for example, the balance of the Sales account at the end of the period is $25,000, the balance of the Purchases account is $15,000, and there was no merchandise on hand either at the beginning or at the end of the period, the gross profit on sales is simply the sales less the purchases.

```
Sales...................... $25,000.00
Less cost of goods sold:
    Purchases................  15,000.00
Gross Profit............... $10,000.00
```

With the appropriate heading and dollar marks added, the information just presented can be the first part of a merchandise company's statement of income and expense.

The several examples which follow illustrate the statement form for calculating gross profit on sales where there are inventories.

Assume that a company had sales of $30,000, no beginning inventory, purchases of $28,000, and an ending inventory of $5,000. The cost of goods sold in this case is the cost of goods bought during the period less the cost of those still unsold at the end of the period. The calculation is:

Sales.................................		$30,000.00
Less cost of goods sold:		
Purchases...........................	$28,000.00	
Less ending inventory..................	5,000.00	23,000.00
Gross Profit on Sales....................		$ 7,000.00

Now, assume the following facts: sales, $50,000; purchases, $30,000; beginning inventory, $25,000; and ending inventory, $20,000. In this case the cost of goods sold is the cost of those in the beginning inventory plus the cost of those purchased during the period (the total of the two is the cost of goods which could have been sold) less the cost of those still unsold (the ending inventory). The determination of gross profit on sales in this case is:

Sales......................................		$50,000.00
Less cost of goods sold:		
Beginning inventory....................	$25,000.00	
Purchases.............................	30,000.00	
Cost of goods available for sale...........	$55,000.00	
Ending inventory......................	20,000.00	
Cost of goods sold.................		35,000.00
Gross Profit on Sales.....................		$15,000.00

If the expenses of the period are subtracted from the gross profit on sales, the difference is the *net profit* on sales for the period.

ENTRIES IN THE INVENTORY ACCOUNT

In the examples showing entries for sales and purchase transactions, no entry was made to the Inventory account. Two entries, and no more, are made to this account. These are made on the last day of the accounting period as a part of closing the books.

Since no entries are made to the Inventory account during the period, the balance in that account on the last day of the period will be the same as it was on the first day. Therefore, when the trial balance is prepared at the end of the period, the balance of the Inventory account which appears in that trial balance is the beginning inventory. The first inventory entry closes the Inventory account and transfers its balance to the I & E Summary. (Remember, the Inventory account balance is the beginning inventory.) Using the figures in the illustration above, the entry is:

I & E Summary..	25,000.00	
Inventory..		25,000.00

The credit to the Inventory account zero balances this account so that it may be closed and the debit to I & E Summary account transfers the beginning inventory balance to the I & E Summary account.

The second inventory entry actually records the new *ending* inventory amount in the Inventory account.

The entry is:

```
Inventory.............................................20,000.00
    I & E Summary.....................................            20,000.00
```

The effect of this entry is to place the ending inventory, an asset, on the books so that it will appear on the balance sheet. Since the preceding entry zero balanced the Inventory account, the $20,000 debit to the account becomes the new Inventory account balance. This balance then appears on the after-closing trial balance and on the balance sheet for the end of the year. It is also, of course, the beginning inventory for the following year.

When these entries are posted to the ledger and the Sales and Purchases accounts are closed by transferring their balances to the I & E Summary account, T-accounts appear as follows (remember the balance in the Inventory account before entering the inventory entries was the beginning inventory):

Inventory		Purchases		Sales		I & E Summary	
25,000	25,000	30,000	30,000	50,000	50,000	25,000	20,000
						30,000	50,000
20,000							
20,000							*15,000*

Note that the balance of the I & E Summary account at this point is the gross profit on sales and that the Inventory account now has the correct opening balance for the next period.

Now that the accounts particularly concerned with merchandise operations have been discussed, we can examine the preparation of working papers.

WORKING PAPERS

Earlier examples of trial balances given in Chapters 2 and 3 contained very few accounts. Actual trial balances may list twenty, fifty, or hundreds of account balances. It would be very difficult to prepare financial statements directly from such complex trial balances. It would also be hazardous to make adjusting entries and closing entries in such cases without some control procedure to assure that these entries are complete and correct before they are posted.

Both the preparation of adjusting and closing entries and the preparation of statements are facilitated by the use of a form which is called a *working paper.* When more than one sheet is required, the set of sheets is referred to as working papers or work sheets.

A working paper is a multicolumned form which may have 4, 6, 12, or more pairs of money columns. A typical financial statement working paper (Figure 4–1) has six pairs of columns. Note that the first pair of columns in Figure 4–1 is intended to show the trial balance; the next pair, the adjusting entries; and the next pair, the adjusted trial balance which is an extension of the first two pairs. The last three pairs will contain the figures that will be shown in the three principal financial statements, namely the balance sheet, statement of income and expense, and the

Figure 4–1

Working Paper
A.B.C. COMPANY
For the Period Ending--

ACCOUNT TITLE	TRIAL BALANCE	ADJUSTMENTS	ADJUSTED TRIAL BALANCE	INCOME AND EXPENSE	SURPLUS	BALANCE SHEET

surplus statement. *Each of the figures entered in the adjusted trial balance will be extended into one, and only one, of the financial statement columns.*

There are several advantages to using working papers:

1. The adjusting entries can be made first in the Adjustments columns, and these columns totaled and balanced;
2. The figures required for the preparation of the financial statements are gathered in a convenient manner;
3. To reduce the possibility of error, the working papers can be balanced before the statements are prepared;
4. If the books are to be closed, the required adjusting and closing entries can be prepared by referring to the working papers; and
5. Statements can be prepared without closing the books.

Perhaps the most valuable advantage of the working papers is the last one listed. It is not uncommon for statements to be prepared monthly, whereas books are usually closed annually.

Most life insurance accountants rely exclusively on working papers for preparing the many exhibits and schedules in the annual statement blank.

Preparation of the Working Papers

The process of preparing working papers can best be understood by considering the simplest case first. The following discussion describes the

Figure 4–2

Working Paper
A.B.C. COMPANY
For the Year Ending December 31, 19--

ACCOUNT TITLE	TRIAL BALANCE		INCOME & EXPENSE		SURPLUS		BALANCE SHEET	
Cash	1,000.-							
A/R-T.R. Milby	1,500.-							
Automobiles	12,000.-							
A/P-AC. Bilke		500.-						
Capital stock		10,000.-						
Surplus		3,000.-						
Sales		45,000.-						
Purchases	28,000.-							
Rent expense	2,400.-							
Salary expense	12,000.-							
Property taxes	500.-							
Dividends	1,100.-							
	58,500.-	58,500.-						

working papers for a company which keeps books on a cash basis so that no end-of-the-period adjustments are required. The use of adjusting entries in working papers is presented in a later section of this chapter.

Each working paper should have a heading which gives the name of the company, the title of the working paper, and the period of time it covers.

The pairs of money columns are then titled. (See Figure 4–2.) In the case we are considering, no adjustments are required, so the headings for the pairs of columns are: Trial Balance, Income and Expense, Surplus, and Balance Sheet. In the first pair of columns (one debit and one credit), the account balances are recorded directly from the ledger. There is also one pair of columns for each of the three principal financial statements. When the working paper is complete, all of the figures needed to prepare each of the financial statements will appear in the pair of columns headed with the title of that statement.

After the trial balance has been recorded in the Trial Balance columns, the working paper is as shown in Figure 4–2. To simplify the illustration assume that there is no inventory at either the beginning or end of the period.

The next step in the preparation of the working papers is to extend each of the figures in the trial balance to the appropriate statement

Figure 4–3

Working Paper
A.B.C. COMPANY
For the Year Ending December 31, 19--

ACCOUNT TITLE	TRIAL BALANCE		INCOME & EXPENSE		SURPLUS		BALANCE SHEET	
Cash	1,000.-						1,000.-	
A/R-T.R. Milby	1,500.-						1,500.-	
Automobiles	12,000.-						12,000.-	
A/P-A.C. Bilke		500.-						500.-
Capital stock		10,000.-						10,000.-
Surplus		3,000.-				3,000.-		
Sales		45,000.-						
Purchases	28,000.-							
Rent expense	2,400.-							
Salary expense	12,000.-							
Property taxes	500.-							
Dividends	1,100.-							
	58,500.-	58,500.-						

columns. It is best to start with the first item in the trial balance, then the second, and so on down the trial balance. The first account balance, for example, is usually *Cash*. The amount shown for cash in the trial balance is extended to the debit column of the Balance Sheet columns. (See Figure 4–3.) Each item in the debit column of the Trial Balance must be extended to a debit column, and each item in the credit column of the Trial Balance must be extended to a credit column in one of the three sets of statement columns.

Continue working down the Trial Balance column through the asset, liability, and the capital stock accounts, all of which are, of course, extended to the Balance Sheet columns.

The next item in the trial balance is Surplus. Remember that no entries are made to the Surplus account during the accounting period. The balance of the Surplus account in the trial balance is, therefore, the beginning balance of that account. The beginning balance of Surplus is not extended to the Balance Sheet columns because the surplus amount on the balance sheet must be the amount of surplus at the end of the year. The beginning Surplus balance (a credit item) is, instead, extended into the credit side of the Surplus columns.

The next accounts in the trial balance are the income and expense accounts. These balances are extended, debit for debit and credit for

Figure 4–4

Working Paper
A.B.C. COMPANY
For the Year Ending December 31, 19--

ACCOUNT TITLE	TRIAL BALANCE		INCOME & EXPENSE		SURPLUS		BALANCE SHEET	
Cash	1,000.-						1,000.-	
A/R-T.R. Milby	1,500.-						1,500.-	
Automobiles	12,000.-						12,000.-	
A/P-A.C. Bilke		500.-						500.-
Capital stock		10,000.-						10,000.-
Surplus		3,000.-				3,000.-		
Sales		45,000.-		45,000.-				
Purchases	28,000.-		28,000.-					
Rent expense	2,400.-		2,400.-					
Salary expense	12,000.-		12,000.-					
Property taxes	500.-		500.-					
Dividends	1,100.-				1,100.-			
	58,500.-	58,500.-						

credit, to the Income and Expense columns. The Dividends account balance is not an income or expense item but a decrease in surplus. It is, therefore, extended as a debit to the Surplus columns. The working papers after these extensions are shown in Figure 4–4.

The next step is to determine the net gain or net loss from operating the business. This is the difference between the total of the debit column and the total of the credit column of the Income and Expense columns. If the credit column (income) has the greater total, the difference in totals is, of course, the *net income* or *net gain* of the period. (See Figure 4–5.) If the debit column has a greater total, the difference is a *net loss*.

A new line is added on the working paper and identified as "Net Income." If there is a net gain, as shown in Figure 4–5, the amount of net gain is entered on this line in the debit column of Income and Expense and in the credit column of Surplus. If there had been a net loss, the debits and credits shown on the new line would have been reversed. In either event the total of the debit column of Income and Expense is made equal to the total of the credit column. These totals are recorded and the columns double-ruled.

Column differences (balances) are transferred from one set of columns to another by equal debit and credit entries. Notice in Figure 4–5 that the net income is transferred from the Income and Expense columns with a

Figure 4–5

Working Paper
A.B.C. COMPANY
For the Year Ending December 31, 19--

ACCOUNT TITLE	TRIAL BALANCE		INCOME & EXPENSE		SURPLUS		BALANCE SHEET	
Cash	1,000.-						1,000.-	
A/R-T.R. Milby	1,500.-						1,500.-	
Automobiles	12,000.-						12,000.-	
A/P-A.C. Bilke		500.-						500.-
Capital stock		10,000.-						10,000.-
Surplus		3,000.-				3,000.-		
Sales		45,000.-		45,000.-				
Purchases	28,000.-		28,000.-					
Rent expense	2,400.-		2,400.-					
Salary expense	12,000.-		12,000.-					
Property taxes	500.-		500.-					
Dividends	1,100.-				1,100.-			
	58,500.-	58,500.-						
Net Income			2,100.-			2,100.-		
			45,000.-	45,000.-				

debit entry and is transferred into the Surplus columns with a credit entry.

In effect the transfer to the Surplus columns accomplishes the same result on the working papers as the closing entry made in the journal accomplishes when the balance of the I & E Summary account is transferred to the Surplus account in the ledger. In fact, the working papers are the source of information for making this closing entry. The working paper at this stage is as shown in Figure 4–5.

The Surplus columns now contain all of the items which will appear in the statement of surplus. As may be seen in Figure 4–5, there are now three figures in the Surplus columns. These figures are: the beginning balance of Surplus; the balance of the Dividends account; and the net income figure just discussed. The totals of the debit and of the credit columns of Surplus should be determined, and the difference entered in the column which has the smaller total. As shown in Figure 4–6, this amount is written on a line below that of the totals of the Income and Expense columns. The word "Surplus" is written on this line in the Account Title column.

The difference between the debit and credit columns of Surplus will be the same as the balance of Surplus account at the end of the period after

Figure 4–6

Working Paper
A.B.C. COMPANY
For the Year Ending December 31, 19—

ACCOUNT TITLE	TRIAL BALANCE		INCOME & EXPENSE		SURPLUS		BALANCE SHEET·	
Cash	1,000.-						1,000.-	
A/R-T.R. Milby	1,500.-						1,500.-	
Automobiles	12,000.-						12,000.-	
A/P-A.C. Bilke		500.-						500.-
Capital stock		10,000.-						10,000.-
Surplus		3,000.-				3,000.-		
Sales		45,000.-		45,000.-				
Purchases	28,000.-		28,000.-					
Rent expense	2,400.-		2,400.-					
Salary expense	12,000.-		12,000.-					
Property taxes	500.-		500.-					
Dividends	1,100.-				1,100.-			
	58,500.-	58,500.-						
Net Income			2,100.-				2,100.-	
			45,000.-	45,000.-				
Surplus 12/31/--						4,000.-		4,000.-
					5,100.-	5,100.-	14,500.-	14,500.-

the books are closed. Unless there is a deficit, this difference will be in the debit Surplus column. The difference is transferred to the credit column of the Balance Sheet columns so that there is now an equal debit and credit on this line. If there is a deficit, the figure will, of course, be entered in the credit Surplus column and debit Balance Sheet column.

The account balances shown in the Surplus columns are each closed into the Surplus account in the ledger by means of closing entries in the journal. The Surplus account balance will be current after these entries have been made.

The Balance Sheet columns of the working papers now reflect all of the account balances as they will appear on the balance sheet. The Surplus columns and the Balance Sheet columns should be totaled next. If the work has been done correctly, the total of each debit column on the working papers will be equal to the total of the corresponding credit column. The completed working paper is shown in Figure 4–6.

For the data shown in Figure 4–6, another method could have been used to enter totals in the Income and Expense column and the Surplus column before recording the difference in debits and credits on the "Net Income" and "Surplus" lines. The columns could have been ruled and then the difference entered. The column totals would then have appeared as follows:

	Income and Expense		*Surplus*		*Balance Sheet*	
	Dr.	Cr.	Dr.	Cr.	Dr.	Cr.
Net Income......	42,900.00 2,100.00	45,000.00		2,100.00		
	45,000.00	45,000.00	1,100.00	5,100.00		
Surplus 12/31....			4,000.00			4,000.00
			5,100.00	5,100.00	14,500.00	14,500.00

If the Balance Sheet columns do not balance, then the entire procedure must be reviewed step by step until the error or errors are located. The steps should, however, be taken in reverse order; that is, the last step completed should be examined first. The last step determining the totals of the Balance Sheet columns should be rechecked first, and so on backward, step by step, to the trial balance itself if necessary.

Adjusting Entries in the Working Papers

In the more realistic case where end of the period adjusting entries are required, the working papers become somewhat more complex but of even greater usefulness. Working papers with at least six pairs of columns are needed when adjustments are made.

The first pair of money columns are still for the trial balance. The second pair are headed Adjustments, and the third pair Adjusted Trial Balance. (See Figure 4–7.) The headings and sequence of the statement columns which follow the Adjusted Trial Balance remain the same: Income and Expense; Surplus; and Balance Sheet. The technique for handling each of the types of end-of-period adjustments are given in the sections which follow this one. When each adjustment has been made, as shown in those sections, the Adjustments columns are totaled and the amounts entered on the working papers. The total of debit and credit columns must be equal before other steps are taken.

After the Adjustments columns are in balance, the items in the Trial

Figure 4–7. Accrued Expense

THE A.B.C. COMPANY
Working Paper
For the Month Ended December 31, 19--

ACCOUNT TITLE	TRIAL BALANCE		ADJUSTMENTS		ADJUSTED TRIAL BALANCE	
Wages expense	1,200.00		(a)1,000.00		2,200.00	
	250,000.00	250,000.00				
Accrued wages payable				(a)1,000.00		1,000.00
			4,700.00	4,700.00	253,400.00	253,400.00

(a) Accrued wages.

Figure 4–8. Accrued Income

THE A.B.C. COMPANY
Working Paper
For the Month Ended December 31, 19--

ACCOUNT TITLE	TRIAL BALANCE		ADJUSTMENTS		ADJUSTED TRIAL BALANCE	
Rental income		1,000.00		(b) 300.00		1,300.00
	250,000.00	250,000.00				
Accrued rent receivable			(b) 300.00		300.00	
			4,700.00	4,700.00	253,400.00	253,400.00

(b) Accrued rent.

Figure 4–9. Prepaid Expense

THE A.B.C. COMPANY
Working Paper
For the Month Ended December 31, 19--

ACCOUNT TITLE	TRIAL BALANCE		ADJUSTMENTS		ADJUSTED TRIAL BALANCE	
Unexpired property insurance	1,500.00			(c) 500.00	1,000.00	
	250,000.00	250,000.00				
Insurance expense			(c) 500.00		500.00	
			4,700.00	4,700.00	253,400.00	253,400.00

(c) Insurance expired.

Figure 4–10. Unearned Income

THE A.B.C. COMPANY
Working Paper
For the Month Ended December 31, 19--

ACCOUNT TITLE	TRIAL BALANCE		ADJUSTMENTS		ADJUSTED TRIAL BALANCE	
Unearned rental income		1,800.00	(d) 800.00			1,000.00
Rental income		900.00		(d) 800.00		1,700.00
	250,000.00	250,000.00	4,700.00	4,700.00	253,400.00	253,400.00

(d) Rental Income.

Balance and those in the Adjustments columns must be combined and entered in the Adjusted Trial Balance columns. The procedure for doing this is to go down the trial balance, extending each adjusted item in it to the Adjusted Trial Balance column. (See Figures 4–7, 4–8, 4–9, and 4–10.) Any account with a debit balance in the trial balance is entered in the Adjusted Trial Balance column as a debit. When there is a figure in the Adjustments columns on the same line with an item in the Trial Balance column, the two figures on that line must be added (if both are debits) and the sum entered on the same line in the Adjusted Trial Balance column. If one is a debit and the other a credit, the difference must be entered on that line in the proper column in the Adjusted Trial Balance.

If any new accounts are used in making the adjusting entries, their titles are written on the working papers in the lines below the totals of the Trial Balance column. The amounts of these items will first appear in the Adjustments columns and will then be extended to the Adjusted Trial Balance columns.

After all extensions to the Adjusted Trial Balance columns have been made, the totals of its two columns are entered on the working papers. The two column totals must, of course, be equal.

Illustration of Specific Adjustments

In the sections which follow four common types of end-of-period adjustments and the process of recording changes in inventory are illustrated in partial working papers.

Before describing how adjustments are made on working papers, it will be helpful to examine the following features on the working papers shown in Figures 4–7 through 4–10. Only the parts of each working paper affected by a specific adjustment are shown in each illustration. The column totals are shown to demonstrate the location of new account titles necessitated by the adjusting entries on the working papers. The letters (*a*), (*b*), etc., are used to help keep track of adjustments when several are involved. For example, an (*a*) is assigned to a debit and to its equal credit in the first adjustment, (*b*) to those in the second adjustment, and so on. Usually a notation of the reason for the adjustment is made by its reference letter either in the lower section of the working paper or on another sheet. The extensions of the amounts to the Adjusted Trial Balance columns would not, in fact, be made until after all adjustments are complete and the Adjustments columns balanced. The extensions are shown in the illustrations merely to give a fuller picture of the adjustments on the working papers.[2]

---

[2] These examples of specific adjustments and the figures illustrating them are from W. Rogers Hammond, *How to Solve Introductory Accounting Problems* (Englewood Cliffs, N.J.: Prentice-Hall, Inc., 1959), by permission.

In making entries in the Adjustments columns on the working papers, the accountant should be constantly aware of the principal purpose of these two columns. To prevent errors, they are designed to be used as a preliminary step in making adjusting entries on the company books and in preparing accrual basis financial statements. However, if statements are prepared at times other than the end of the accounting period, working papers may be used to prepare statements even though entries will not be recorded on the books. The amounts and account titles must be the same as though adjusting entries were to be entered on the books, and each adjustment entered on the working papers must have an equal debit and credit.

There are two acceptable methods used for making adjusting entries. Both produce the same result in the Adjusted Trial Balance column. The most common method used in general commercial accounting will be referred to here as the *adjusted balance method*. The second, more commonly used in insurance company working papers, will be referred to here as the *reversal and reentry method*. The adjusted balance method will be demonstrated on working papers first because it is simpler to grasp. The second method will then be demonstrated and explained.

Adjusted Balance Method

Accrued Expense. Suppose that $1,000 wages for the last half of this month are by company policy to be paid on the fifth day of next month and that the balance of the Wage Expense account at the end of this month is $1,200.

The unpaid wages of $1,000 have been incurred. They represent an expense for wages which has been incurred in this period and not yet charged to the expense account. They also are a debt and, therefore, a liability. The debit is to the expense account, Wages Expense, and the credit is to a liability account, Accrued Wages Payable. The adjusting entry for this situation is indicated by (*a*) in Figure 4–7.

Accrued Income. Assume that we rent certain property to tenants for $1,300 per month. All of the leases except one provide that the rent for each month is due at the end of each month. The lease of the other tenant provides that the monthly rent ($300) is payable on the first of the following month.

This rental income, $300, was earned but not yet recorded. It is an asset because it represents a value owned. Therefore, the debit is to an asset, accrued rent receivable. The credit entry is to the Rental Income account to record the income earned but which has not yet been recorded on the books. The adjusting entry to record the correct accrual basis income is indicated by (*b*) in Figure 4–8.

Prepaid Expense. Assume that the balance of the Unexpired Insurance account at the end of the month is $1,500. You learn that $500 of this amount was for coverage which applied to the previous month. The asset account Unexpired Insurance is credited $500 in order to reduce this account balance to its asset value at the end of the month. The equal debit is, of course, to the expense account Insurance Expense to record the expense for insurance coverage actually applicable to the month. The adjusting entry to record the proper accrual basis income is indicated by (*c*) in Figure 4–9.

Unearned Income. Assume that the company has received rent in advance and that the Unearned Rental Income account in which it has been recorded has a balance at the end of the month of $1,800.

The Unearned Rental Income account is a liability because it represents a service which is owed and has not yet been rendered. The $1,800 credit balance in the Trial Balance columns was the balance at the end of the previous month. Investigation reveals that $800 of the Unearned Rental Income has been earned during the month just ended.

Since this $800 of Unearned Rental Income was earned during the month, a credit entry to the Rental Income account is required to record the income earned. A debit of the same amount to the liability account Unearned Rental Income reduces its balance to $1,000, the remaining liability amount. The *Rental Income* account has a balance of $900. The credit entry increases the Rental Income balance to the earned amount of $1,700. The entry to transfer the earned portion from the Unearned Rental Income account to the Rental Income account is indicated by (*d*) in Figure 4–10.

To sum up, with respect to the adjusted balance method: If there is a balance in an unearned income or accrued expense account at the beginning of a month, the adjusting entry is made in the amount required to bring the balance to the correct end-of-the-month amount.

Suppose that unpaid wages at the beginning of the month were $1,000 and at the end of the month were $1,100, an increase of $100. The $1,000 in wages incurred during the previous month were paid in the current month and recorded in the Wages Expense account at time of payment. The adjusting entry at the end of the month is a $100 debit to Wages Expense and a $100 credit to Accrued Wages Payable. This entry brings the Wages Expense account balance up to the incurred amount of $1,100 for the month, and the $100 credit to the Accrued Wages Payable account brings its balance up to the correct end-of-the-month liability amount.

Suppose that accrued rent receivable is $250 at the beginning of the month and $200 at the end of the month, a decrease of $50. The adjusting entry at the end of the month is a $50 debit to the Rental Income account and a $50 credit to the Accrued Rent Receivable account. This entry adjusts the balance of the Rental Income account to the amount earned and adjusts the balance of the Accrued Rent Receivable account to the correct amount at the end of the month.

Reversal and Reentry Method

Under the reversal and reentry method, the full balance of the special adjustment asset or liability accounts at the beginning of the period are transferred to the related expense or income accounts. This is, in effect, a reversal of the adjustment made at the end of the previous accounting period and zero balances this asset or liability account. A new entry is then made by either debiting the full asset value at the end of the accounting period to the related asset account or crediting the full liability amount at the end of the period to the related liability account. The opposite debit or credit is made in each case to the related expense or income account.

In the "Unexpired insurance" example shown in Figure 4–9, there was a debit balance of $1,500 in the Trial Balance columns reflecting the asset value of this item at the beginning of the period. The adjustments under the reversal and reentry method would consist of (1) a reversal (credit) of the $1,500 on the Unexpired insurance line of the working papers with an equal debit on the "Insurance expense" line and (2) an entry of the new $1,000 balance (debit) on the "Unexpired insurance" line with the equal credit on the "Insurance expense" line.

The working paper appears as follows[3] (cents are omitted for brevity):

	Trial Balance		Adjustments		Adjusted Trial Balance	
	Dr.	Cr.	Dr.	Cr.	Dr.	Cr.
Unexpired insurance........	1,500		(*m*) 1,000	(*c*) 1,500	1,000	
Insurance expense..........			(*c*) 1,500	(*m*) 1,000	500	

(*c*) Unexpired insurance beginning.
(*m*) Unexpired insurance ending.

Note that the *effect* of this adjustment on the Adjusted Trial Balance is the same as shown in Figure 4–9. This demonstrates that both the adjusted balance and the reversal and reentry methods produce the same results.

In Figure 4–10, there was a beginning liability of $1,800 in the Unearned Rental Income account. This amount is transferred to the Rental Income account by a debit to Unearned Rental Income, which zero balances this account, and by a credit to Rental Income (entry *d*). The end-of-period liability of $1,000 must be recorded by a credit to the

---

[3] An extract from the working papers is used here for the sake of simplicity since the manner in which adjustments are entered on working papers has already been explained.

liability account Unearned Rental Income and by a debit to Rental Income (entry *n*).

The working papers appear as follows (cents are omitted for brevity):

	Trial Balance		Adjustments		Adjusted Trial Balance	
	Dr.	Cr.	Dr.	Cr.	Dr.	Cr.
Unearned rental income......		1,800	(*d*) 1,800	(*n*) 1,000		1,000
Rental income.............		900	(*n*) 1,000	(*d*) 1,800		1,700

Note that the difference between the debits and credits in the Adjustments columns on the line for Unearned Rental Income is a net debit of $800, exactly the amount shown in Figure 4–10. Similarly, the difference on the "Rental income" line in the Adjustments columns is a net credit of $800, exactly the amount shown in Figure 4–10. The Adjusted Trial Balance amounts are also the same as in Figure 4–10.

If adjusting entries are recorded on the books monthly in order to prepare financial statements each month, the adjusted balance method is the simpler of the two. However, if adjusting entries are recorded annually or not recorded on the books at any time, as is the case in most United States life insurance companies,[4] the reversal and reentry method is the simpler.

Inventory

In this textbook the process for adjusting inventory balances differs from that used in the adjusting entries just explained. The principal difference is that the change in inventory amounts between the beginning and end of the period is not made in the Adjustment columns but is made in the Income and Expense columns and in the Balance Sheet columns.

The beginning inventory balance, an asset, appears as a debit in the Trial Balance columns. See Figure 4–11. This amount is extended to the debit side of the Adjusted Trial Balance column and then to the debit side of the Income and Expense column. See Figure 4–12. The new inventory amount ($2,000 in Figure 4–12) is then entered on the "Inventory" line as a debit in the Balance Sheet columns and as a credit in the Income and Expense columns.

The journal entries to change the balance of the Inventory account in

---

[4] The adjusting process used by life insurance companies will be explained in a later chapter.

Figure 4–11. Beginning Inventory

THE A.B.C. COMPANY
Working Paper
For the Month Ended December 31, 19--

ACCOUNT TITLE	TRIAL BALANCE		ADJUSTMENTS		ADJUSTED TRIAL BALANCE	
Inventory	1,500.00				1,500.00	
	250,000.00	250,000.00				

the ledger are: (1) The old inventory balance is closed or transferred into the I & E Summary by a debit to the I & E Summary and by a credit entry to the Inventory account. (2) The new inventory is recorded by a debit to the Inventory account and by a credit to the I & E Summary account.

Figure 4–12. Ending Inventory

THE A.B.C. COMPANY
Working Paper
For the Month Ended December 31, 19--

ACCOUNT TITLE	ADJUSTED TRIAL BALANCE		INCOME & EXPENSE		BALANCE SHEET	
Inventory	1,500.00		1,500.00	2,000.00	2,000.00	

Posting these entries to an I & E Summary T-account, using the figures shown in Figure 4–12, should confirm the entries indicated by the working papers.

SUMMARY OF ACCOUNTING PRINCIPLES

A sale of merchandise is recorded as income.

Merchandise purchased for sale is recorded as expense.

Sales, Purchases, and *Inventory* balances (beginning inventory only) are closed into the *I & E Summary* account.

The ending inventory balance is recorded on the books by debiting the *Inventory* account and crediting the *I & E Summary* account. This balance is recorded on the working papers as a debit in the *Balance Sheet* columns and a credit in the *Income and Expense* columns.

Both beginning and ending inventories are shown in an *income and expense statement.*

A *working paper* is a multicolumned form used to facilitate preparation of the three principal financial statements (balance sheet, income and expense statement, and statement of surplus); and to prepare adjusting and closing entries before recording them on the books.

Adjustments on working papers must have equal debit and credit entries.

Each item in the Trial Balance columns is extended on the working papers to the Adjusted Trial Balance columns and then to one of the three sets of financial statement columns.

The difference between debit and credit Income and Expense columns is transferred (not extended) to the Surplus columns of working papers.

The difference between debit and credit Surplus columns is transferred to the Balance Sheet columns.

Adjusting entries recorded on the books at the end of an accounting period must be the same as the adjustments entered on the working papers.

QUESTIONS

1. Give the journal entry for the sale of merchandise for $100 in cash and the entry for the purchase of merchandise costing $75.
2. Calculate the gross profit on sales if total sales for the period were $75,000; purchases, $55,000; beginning inventory, $20,000; and ending inventory, $15,000.
3. Give the end-of-period entries for the inventories in question 2 above.
4. What are some of the advantages of the use of working papers?
5. Give the steps in the preparation of the working papers.

6. Why is the net income (or net loss) figure entered in two sets of columns in the working papers?

7. It would be possible to combine the items in the Trial Balance and those in the Adjustment columns and extend the results directly to the Financial Statement columns. Why is it useful to have the Adjusted Trial Balance columns in the working papers?

PROBLEM

Prepare a working paper from which the ABC Service Company may prepare accrual basis financial statements. The trial balance at the end of December was as follows:

Cash	$ 7,000.00	
Accounts Receivable	2,100.00	
Inventory	4,000.00	
Notes Receivable	1,500.00	
Office Supplies on Hand	700.00	
Unexpired Insurance	1,017.00	
Interest Income Due and Accrued	300.00	
Accounts Payable		$ 250.00
Notes Payable		1,000.00
Accrued Salaries Payable		400.00
Accrued Rent Payable		256.00
Interest Expense Accrued		17.00
Unearned Service Income		2,100.00
Sales		25,000.00
Service Income		5,000.00
Interest Income		300.00
Purchases	15,000.00	
Rent Expense	1,200.00	
Salary Expense	7,500.00	
Dividends Paid	300.00	
Capital		1,000.00
Surplus		5,294.00
	$40,617.00	$40,617.00

The ledger includes an Office Supplies Used account and an Insurance Expense account which were closed at the end of the previous accounting period and are now zero balanced.

The manager finds that at the end of the accounting period there is a merchandise inventory of $6,500 on hand, unused office supplies which cost $500, unexpired insurance of $500, and $150 interest accrued on notes receivable. There is also $1,200 of unearned service income, $300 is rent payable, $400 in salaries is payable, and $34 of interest has accrued on a note payable.

A working paper showing Adjusted Trial Balance columns, Income and Expense columns, Surplus columns, and Balance Sheet columns is included in the Answers to the Problem so that the student may check his work.

Chapter 5

Miscellaneous Accounting Topics

This chapter is concerned with fixed assets and depreciation; the imprest cash system and bank reconciliations; special journals, special ledgers, and control accounts; and the chart of accounts. These topics, along with those in the earlier chapters, do not exhaust the full breadth of general accounting but they serve the purposes for which the first part of this book is intended. These purposes include an introduction to the principles of general accounting, which must be learned before the more specialized phases of life insurance accounting can be properly understood, and to discuss accounting techniques common to all corporations.

FIXED ASSETS

Fixed assets are assets which are used in the operations of the business and which have a useful life of more than one year; and which are acquired primarily for use rather than resale. Examples of fixed assets are buildings, automobiles, office furniture, and equipment. In contrast, the following are not classified as fixed assets: cash, investments, and office supplies.

Acquisition of Fixed Assets

Fixed assets are recorded at cost when acquired. Thus, if office furniture or equipment costing $6,000 is bought for cash, the journal entry is:

Office Furniture and Equipment..............................6,000.00
    Cash...   6,000.00

As time passes and the furniture or equipment is used, its value decreases. The value shown on the books must be decreased accordingly. An approximation of the amount of decrease each year is recorded as an expense because the cost is gradually consumed in the operations of the business. The initial cost of this furniture or equipment is not usually treated as an expense in the year of purchase since it will continue to be used for several years.[1] The method by which a portion of the cost of fixed assets is charged to the proper accounting periods is discussed in the next section.

Depreciation

The method used to spread the cost of fixed assets over the years of their useful life is called the *depreciation process*. That part of the cost which is allocated to an accounting period is called *depreciation expense* for that period.

The simplest and one of the most widely used of the several methods of calculating depreciation expense is called the *straight-line* method. Under the straight-line method, an estimate is made of the *salvage* or *scrap* value, that is, the value that the asset is expected to have at the end of its useful life. This salvage value is subtracted from the cost of the asset to determine the *depreciation base*. The dollar amount of the depreciation base is then divided by the number of years of anticipated useful life to find the annual depreciation expense.

Assume that the $6,000 of office furniture and equipment mentioned earlier was bought on January 1 this year, that its useful life to this company will be five years, and that at the end of five years it can be sold for an estimated salvage value of $2,000. The depreciation expense for one year on this asset is determined as follows:

Cost	$6,000.00
Less salvage value	2,000.00
Depreciation base	$4,000.00
Divided by 5 years	5
Depreciation Expense per Year	$ 800.00

Most of the other methods of calculating depreciation[2] are similar in concept and differ from the straight-line method primarily in the amount of depreciation treated as an expense during the early years of ownership

---

[1] Canadian life insurance companies treat the cost of most furniture and equipment items as an expense in the year of purchase. The reasons are discussed in a later chapter.

[2] These methods are not explained here since they do not affect the bookkeeping process.

as compared with later years. The bookkeeping process is the same regardless of the method used to calculate the expense.

Salvage values must be estimated carefully so that the value at time of disposal is close to the value remaining on the books. Otherwise, the cost of depreciation recorded in each year will be incorrect.

It is useful to retain the original cost on the books and to accumulate depreciation in a separate account during the useful life of the fixed asset. This account is called *Accumulated Depreciation* or *Reserve for Depreciation*, followed by the name of the asset to which it is applicable.

The depreciation entry is made at the end of the accounting period, along with the other adjusting entries. In the case of the office furniture and equipment, the entry on December 31 this year is a debit to the expense account *Depreciation Expense—F & E* and a credit to the account *Accumulated Depreciation—F & E.*

```
Depreciation Expense—F & E.............................800.00
   Accumulated Depreciation—F & E.......................    800.00
```

Like all other expense accounts, the depreciation expense account is closed to the Income and Expense (I & E) Summary account at the end of the accounting period and is shown as an expense on the income and expense statement.

The Accumulated Depreciation account always has a credit balance. It is not closed at the end of each year because it is, in effect, a reduction in the fixed asset account to which it relates. It is listed in the trial balance immediately after this fixed asset account and frequently appears on the balance sheet below the principal account, as shown in the following excerpt:

```
Fixed Assets:
   Furniture and equipment...................$6,000.00
   Less: Accumulated depreciation............   800.00    $5,200.00
```

The difference between the balance of the fixed asset account and the balance of the related accumulated depreciation account ($5,200) is called the *book value* of the asset.

A depreciation entry is made at the end of each accounting period so that at the end of the useful life of the asset, the book value will be equal to the salvage value. In the example, the Accumulated Depreciation account would show a $4,000 credit balance at the end of five years. The book value then would be $6,000 − $4,000, or $2,000, which is also the expected salvage value.

If this furniture and equipment is sold at the end of its useful life for the originally estimated salvage value of $2,000, the entry is:

```
Cash........................................................2,000.00
Accumulated Depreciation—F & E........................4,000.00
   Furniture and Equipment..............................    6,000.00
```

This entry removes this asset and its related accumulated depreciation account from the company's books. In the example, the asset was recorded at time of purchase as a $6,000 debit. A $6,000 credit entry at time of sale, in effect, zero balances the account with reference to this particular item of equipment. (In practice, there will be a number of other items of furniture or equipment in the account, so a balance representing the cost of other items will remain.) Similarly, the debit to Accumulated Depreciation zero balances that account with reference to this particular asset item.[3]

When a fixed asset is sold, it rarely brings exactly the amount originally estimated to be its salvage value. If furniture and equipment is sold for more than the book value, there is a gain to the company for the difference between the sales price and the book value. To record this gain, a new account is required which is called *Gain on Disposal of Fixed Assets.*

If the item used in the example is sold at the end of five years for $2,500, the entry is:

```
Cash................................................2,500.00
Accumulated Depreciation—F & E......................4,000.00
     Furniture and Equipment.............................          6,000.00
     Gain on Disposal of Fixed Assets....................           500.00
```

Note that the debit to Accumulated Depreciation—F & E and credit to Furniture and Equipment is the same as it was when the book value and sale value were equal since the entry must remove the fixed asset and its accumulated depreciation from the books. This is true regardless of the amount of gain or loss. The gain is recorded with a credit and represents an increase in surplus.

If the sales price is less than the book value, there is a loss equal to the difference between book and sales price. The account required to record the loss is called *Loss on Disposal of Fixed Assets.*

If the asset sold for $1,800, the entry is:

```
Cash................................................1,800.00
Accumulated Depreciation—F & E......................4,000.00
Loss on Disposal of Fixed Assets....................  200.00
     Furniture and Equipment.............................          6,000.00
```

The loss causes a decrease in surplus, so it is recorded with a debit.

The equipment might have been sold at any time. Regardless of the time of sale or the amount received, the gain or loss is determined by the difference between book value and sales price at time of sale.

The book value is subject to a partial year's adjustment for depreciation not yet recorded in the year of sale. If the equipment is sold on June 30

---

[3] Techniques used in coordinating the depreciation accounting for hundreds of fixed asset items are not included in this book because this information is not fundamental to understanding general or life insurance accounting.

for $2,500 at the end of four and one-half years, two entries are required —one to record the depreciation for the current year to the date of sale and another to record the sale.

The entry to record one half of a year's depreciation is a debit to Depreciation Expense—F & E for $400 and a credit to Accumulated Depreciation—F & E for $400.

The sale entry is the same as previously shown, except for amounts. The amounts are determined as follows: After the half-year entry just made, the balance shown in the Accumulated Depreciation—F & E account is $3,600 ($800 × 4 years) + $400. The book value is $2,400 ($6,000 cost − $3,600), and the gain is $100 ($2,500 sales price − $2,400 book value).

The account in which a gain or loss on sale of a fixed asset is recorded is a subdivision of the Surplus account and is, therefore, a nominal account. Such an account is not, however, treated as an income or expense account since it does not arise out of the ordinary operations of the business. Gains or losses of this type are considered nonoperating changes in Surplus. At the end of the accounting period, the balance of the account in which the gain or loss on the disposal of fixed assets is recorded is closed directly to the Surplus account. On the working papers, the amount is not entered in the Income and Expense columns but is extended to the Surplus columns.

CASH

Two aspects of handling cash are discussed in this section: The first is the technique for making very small cash disbursements. The second is the procedure for reconciling the company's bank balance at the end of the month.

Imprest System for Petty Cash

Proper control of cash requires that all cash receipts be deposited in the bank daily and that all disbursements be made only by properly authorized checks. Yet there are often small disbursements for which it would be inconvenient and uneconomical to issue checks. For these small disbursements it is the common practice to maintain a *petty* (small) *cash fund*. The *imprest system* is a closely controlled method of operating a petty cash fund.

Under the imprest system one person is designated as petty cash custodian and is responsible for the fund. A dollar amount is decided upon as the size of the fund, perhaps $100, and an initial check is written to give the custodian that amount. The journal entry for this check is a debit to the new asset account, *Petty Cash*, and a credit to Cash. The entry is:

```
Petty Cash................................................100.00
    Cash...............................................        100.00
```

The custodian is then in a position to make small payments in cash as circumstances may require. The money is kept in a locked box, usually called a *petty cash box*. When the custodian makes a cash payment, a *petty cash voucher* or receipt is filled out which shows the amount paid and the reason for the payment.

The amount of petty cash on hand and petty cash vouchers must at all times be equal to $100. When the fund nears depletion (e.g., when only $25 cash remains), the custodian requests a check to bring the fund up to its original balance. The reimbursement check is given to him in return for his paid vouchers or receipts.

The entry to record the reimbursement is a debit to the various expense accounts represented by the receipts and a credit to Cash. No debit or credit is made to Petty Cash in the reimbursement transaction. As a result, the Petty Cash account balance in this example will remain at $100 unless it is decided to change the size of the petty cash fund.

Suppose a reimbursement check is based upon several vouchers for deliveries in the amount of $52 and for postage amounting to $23. The reimbursement entry is:

```
Delivery Expense.............................................52.00
Postage......................................................23.00
    Cash...................................................        75.00
```

This brings the petty cash fund back up to $100 on hand.

When a petty cash fund is kept under the imprest system, any cash received as income must not be placed in the same petty cash box. This is so because if an error occurs, it would be impossible to determine whether the excess or shortage in cash is due to faulty recording of income, failure to get a receipt for an expenditure, carelessness in making change, or stealing. Some of the control effects of an imprest cash system can be achieved by use of cash registers. Since these are rarely used in life companies, they will not be discussed here.

Bank Statement Reconciliations

The balance in the company bank account as shown by the monthly statement from the bank is seldom the same amount as that shown by the balance of the Cash (or Bank) account in the company's ledger. There are several reasons for this difference. The principal one is the difference between dates on which checks or deposits are entered on the company's books and the dates on which they are paid or recorded in the company's account on the bank's records. The process of determining each of the items which enter into this difference is called *reconciling the bank account.* The actual or correct balance is often different from both the bank's figure and that shown in the company ledger.

The basic idea of the reconciliation process appears again in slightly different form in several of the reports included in the annual statements which life insurance companies file with regulatory authorities. It is doubly important, therefore, to understand this basic procedural technique.

There are several forms in which the bank reconciliation may be made. The form presented in the following illustrations is in common usage and has been selected because of two advantages explained in the discussion of the examples.

1. *Outstanding checks.* In this case the only cause of difference between the bank and the books is outstanding checks. Outstanding checks are checks which have been recorded on the books and issued by the company, but which have not yet reached the bank on which they are drawn and are therefore not listed on the bank statement nor reflected in the bank balance.

DUFORE COMPANY*

Bank Reconciliation

June 30, 19—

Balance per bank statement.....$790.00		Balance per Co. books.........$560.00
Less Outstanding checks:		
No. Amt.		
183......$150.00		
201...... 80.00	230.00	
Adjusted bank balance........$560.00		Adjusted book balance........$560.00

* The heading will be omitted from later reconciliations in this chapter.

The outstanding checks are listed by check number and amount. It is sometimes advisable also to list the date of each outstanding check.

The outstanding checks are subtracted from the bank statement figure because they have been issued and the holders have a claim against the bank account for them. These checks have already reduced the Cash account on the company books and that balance is, therefore, correct as it stands.

2. *Bank charges.* In this case there is an outstanding $50 check, No. 135, and the bank has deducted a $1 service charge about which the company had no previous notice. The balance on the bank statement is $569 ($570 minus the $1 service charge).

Balance per bank statement.....$569.00	Balance per Co. books.........$520.00
Less: Outstanding check	
No. 135................. 50.00	Less: Bank charge............. 1.00
Adjusted bank balance........$519.00	Adjusted book balance........$519.00

The $1 bank charge has been deducted by the bank from its balance and must also be deducted from our Cash balance. The bank charge is an expense and must be recorded in our books with a debit entry. The credit to Cash records on our books the decrease in bank account. The journal entry is:

```
Bank Service Charges............................................1.00
    Cash......................................................       1.00
    To record bank charges for the month of _____.
```

3. *Deposit-in-transit.* A deposit-in-transit is a deposit we made in the bank and recorded on our books but which did not reach the bank in time for inclusion on the statement.

Balance per bank statement.......$300.00	Balance per books..............$750.00
Add: Deposit-in-transit.......... 450.00	
Adjusted bank balance..........$750.00	Adjusted book balance...........$750.00

When making the reconciliation, a deposit-in-transit must be added to the balance shown on the bank side of the reconciliation because the deposit has already been recorded as an increase in the book figure. The bank's balance will increase by the amount of this deposit as soon as the deposit is processed by the bank.

4. *Collection of a note by the bank for the company.* The company may give notes receivable to the bank for collection. If the bank collects the note, the bank will send notification of the collection of the note along with the bank statement and will credit the proceeds to the company account. Assume that the amount of the note is $390 and $10 interest was due:

Balance per bank statement.......$900.00*	Balance per Co. books............$500.00
	Add: Proceeds of note collected... 400.00
Adjusted bank balance..........$900.00	Adjusted book balance..........$900.00

* Includes $400 proceeds of note collection.

A journal entry must be made to record the receipt of the cash proceeds of the note collected, and to reduce the balance of the asset account Notes Receivable by the amount of the note which is no longer receivable. The interest received is income. The entry is:

```
Cash.............................................................400.00
    Notes Receivable......................................       390.00
    Interest Income.......................................       10.00
    Collection of note.
```

5. *Bank errors.* Sometimes the bank will make an error, such as charging a check of another corporation to our account or failing to record a deposit:

Balance per bank statement.......$300.00	Balance per Co. books..........$450.00
Add: Check of XY Co. charged	
to us in error................. 150.00	
Adjusted bank balance..........$450.00	Adjusted book balance..........$450.00

The bank figure was understated because of this error. The bank must, of course, be notified; however, the company's book figures are correct and no adjusting entry is required.

6. *Deposit of bad check.* If we deposit a check from one of our customers and the check is not paid by the bank because of insufficient funds in the customer's account, the bank may return it with the statement:

Balance per bank statement.......$420.00	Balance per Co. books..........$550.00
	Less: X.Y.Z. Co. check charged
	back for insufficient funds...... 130.00
Adjusted bank balance..........$420.00	Adjusted book balance..........$420.00

Like all items which affect the book side of the reconciliation, this requires a journal entry. It is:

```
A/R—X.Y.Z. Co.........................................130.00
    Cash..............................................        130.00
        To record X.Y.Z. Co. check returned by bank.
```

The entry reestablishes the asset A/R—X.Y.Z. Co. and decreases the Cash account of the company books by the amount the account was reduced by the bank because of the returned check.

7. *Company book errors.* The company may have recorded a check erroneously in the book. Suppose check No. 193 for car expense was written for $113 (the correct amount) but was recorded by the company accountant as $131.

Balance per bank statement.......$790.00	Balance per Co. book..........$772.00
	Add: Check No. 193 for $113
	erroneously recorded as $131... 18.00
Adjusted bank balance..........$790.00	Adjusted book balance..........$790.00

This was a company error, so a correcting journal entry is required. It is:

```
Cash...................................................18.00
    Car Expense........................................        18.00
        To correct Ck. 193—$113 recorded in error.
```

Note that the bank reconciliation process caused this error to be located. This error would not have been located through the trial balance because there were compensating errors in the debit and credit amounts.

8. Several items may account for the difference between the book and the bank balances:

Balance per bank statement.......$400.00			Balance per Co. books...........$ 71.00	
Add:			Add: Proceeds of note collected... 400.00	
Deposit-in-transit....$200.00				471.00
XY Co. check				
charged to us..... 125.00	325.00			
	725.00			
Less: Outstanding check No. 91... 275.00			Less:	
			Bank charge.........$ 1.00	
			A.B.C. Co. check	
			returned unpaid.... 20.00	21.00
Adjusted bank balance..........$450.00			Adjusted book balance..........$450.00	

Journal entries are required for the three errors on the book (right) side of the reconciliation. None are required for the error and for the outstanding check on the bank statement (left) side.

The process for reconciling a bank account consists of the following steps:

a) Compare the amounts of all checks paid by the bank with the amounts recorded in the journal. List any discrepancies in either the book or bank columns. Place a mark on the journal after each check paid to show that it has been verified.

b) List all outstanding checks (those recorded on the books but not yet paid by the bank). These are the items not marked as having been paid by the bank.

c) Compare the amounts of all deposits recorded in the journal with those shown on the bank statement by placing a mark in the journal after each deposit which appears on the bank statement. List discrepancies in either the book or bank columns (depending upon which is wrong).

d) List all charges made by the bank but not recorded on the books.

e) List all deposits in transit. (Amounts not yet credited to our bank account but which have been recorded on the books.)

f) Complete the bank reconciliation form. If the two sides do not balance, the reconciling process must be repeated until the missing item or items are found and the reconciliation balanced.

g) Make correcting bookkeeping entries.

Alternate Form of Reconciliation

Another form of bank reconciliation starts with the bank balance. To the bank balance figure deposits-in-transit and bank charges are added, and outstanding checks are subtracted. Book and bank errors, and transactions not yet recorded, are added or subtracted, depending on how each item affects the bank's figure. Under this method, all amounts are entered in a single column. If the adjusted bank balance is not the same as the Cash account book balance, the difference must be located.

The advantage of the form of reconciliation used in the first illustrations (not the alternate) is twofold: (1) it produces an adjusted bank balance equal to an adjusted or correct book balance and (2) it isolates the items on the book side that require entries in the books. No correcting entry is required for any item on the bank side.

A separate reconciliation must, of course, be prepared for each bank account maintained by the company.

SPECIAL JOURNALS

The journal used for all entries up to this point is the *general journal.* As described previously, the recording of a transaction in this general journal requires writing the date, the name of the account debited, the amount debited, the name of the account credited, the amount credited, and an explanation of the entry. The next step is posting each debit and each credit to the ledger.

Journalizing and posting can be rather time consuming, even for small businesses. Journalizing and posting in this way each sales transaction of a large department store, or the receipt of each premium by a large life insurance company becomes impractical if not impossible.

The solution lies, in part, in the use of special journals. A special journal is one designed to be the book of original entry for all entries of *a particular type;* for example, all sales on account.

Usually a special journal has several special-purpose columns. Each column is headed with the name of an account in the company's ledger. In addition, there is usually a debit and a credit column for entries for which there is no appropriate special column.

By use of a special journal, the bookkeeper need enter a transaction on one line only. If the amount can be recorded in one of the special columns, he is freed from the necessity for writing the name of the account in each succeeding transaction. If the special column represents sales, for example, the *total* of this column is posted as a credit to the Sales account in the ledger, thereby eliminating the need for posting each of the sales transactions, one by one, to this account.

All of the fundamentals of a general journal are retained in a special journal. It will be recalled that these are dates, folio number, accounts to be debited and credited, the amount of each debit and credit, and, if desired, an explanation of the entry.

Since a sales journal usually reflects only credit sales, much of the common information, which would be repeated in entry after entry in a general journal entry, is unnecessary. All that is needed is the date, the name of the customer, and the amount of the sale. Since every entry in this journal is a credit sale, the title of the journal is adequate explanation. The amount need not be written twice since every amount is a debit to an account receivable and when summarized a credit to the Sales account.

The customer's name identifies the account receivable so the amount on the line with his name can be posted to his account receivable.

Account numbers are assigned to all general ledger accounts to facilitate posting. The number of an account usually is written below the total figure of the column to show that this total has been posted to that account. Account numbers are not used for accounts receivable accounts because usually they are filed alphabetically and are not numbered. In the Folio column of the journal, a check mark instead of a number is used to indicate accounts receivable posting has been completed.

The reduction in effort and in time spent in journalizing and in posting by the use of a sales journal is apparent. Most special journals have several special columns and two or more general-purpose columns.

The exact design of a special journal depends upon the needs of the corporation. If there are hundreds of sales each day, a sales journal for recording sales will be used. If the sales are made on credit, the sales journal will include a column for all debits to accounts receivable accounts. If there are hundreds of purchases each day, a special purchases journal will be used and a column provided for all credits to accounts payable.

Special journals may be designed for any type of transaction which occurs frequently and where there is a common basic debit or credit entry. Thus, there are purchases journals, cash receipts journals, cash disbursements journals, and others. In an insurance company, special journals may be used for premiums received, mortgage payments received, policy settlements, general expenses, and other special purposes.

As has been mentioned, in a special journal there may be many special columns, each representing an account in the general ledger. This technique of journal design may be seen in the simple cash receipts journal illustrated in Figure 5–1. In this journal, three special columns are used to facilitate the journalizing and posting of various credits. A general-purpose credit column is also included.

The figures in the first money column show cash amounts of money received. This special column, of course, is for debits to the Cash account only. These debits are not posted individually but only the total ($3,850) is posted as a debit to the Cash account.

The second money column is for amounts received as payments on accounts receivable. Each amount in this column is posted as a credit to an account receivable.

The third money column is for amounts received from cash sales. This column represents a single account in the general ledger so only one posting, the total, is made as a credit to the Sales account. The number in parentheses is placed beneath the total to indicate that the posting has been made to that account.

The fourth money column is for amounts received for any other reason. This fourth column is frequently called a General Ledger column, and each item in it must be posted individually to an account in the general ledger. These postings are, of course, credits. However, many special journals also include a General Ledger debit column in order to accommodate compound entries.

Figure 5–1

CASH RECEIPTS JOURNAL

DATE	ACCOUNT CREDITED	EXPLANATION	DEBIT CASH	FOLIO	CREDIT ACCTS. REC.	CREDIT CASH SALES	CREDIT G. LEDGER ACCT.	CREDIT G. LEDGER AMT.
19__ Jan 2	R.C Daws	Collection	150.00	✓	150.00			
3	Notes receivable	Received payment	400.00				3	400.00
3	Sales	Cash sales	100.00			100.00		
4	W.A. Wall	Collection	200.00	✓	200.00			
31	Sales	Cash sale	160.00			160.00		
			3,850.00		350.00	3,100.00		400.00
			(1)		(4)	(41)		

A life insurance company, for example, might receive a check for $90 to cover a premium of $100 less a policy dividend of $10. The policy dividend is an expense and will require a debit entry. The cash premium journal must, therefore, either have a debit column called *Dividends Applied to Premiums* or a General Ledger debit column to record the amount and a column for the name of the account to be debited.

Amounts must be posted individually as credits to the general ledger accounts indicated by numbers in the column headed Account. Some special journals use account numbers instead of names. The use of account numbers makes for greater efficiency where there are a large number of accounts. When account numbers are used, the Account Credited column may be eliminated. In this cash receipts journal, the Account Credited column is needed to identify the individual accounts receivable to be credited. In the interest of efficiency, explanations are usually omitted from special journals except for out-of-the-ordinary transactions. They are shown in Figure 5–1 to facilitate understanding. A check mark is placed in the Folio column to indicate that the account receivable posting has been completed.

A cash disbursements journal (which may be called a check register) has one General Ledger column and often has as many as 15 or 20 special columns, one for each of the most active disbursement accounts. Its principal advantage is considerable saving in time and effort since cumulative column totals may be carried forward from page to page for as long as a month. The ledger account balances then may be brought up-to-date with a single posting for each special journal column. Every item in the General Ledger column must, of course, be posted individually.

When a special journal is used, the details of entries that would otherwise be found in the ledger are available only in the special journal. This presents no great handicap, since this information is rarely needed until an audit is made, and it is then as accessible in the journal as it would have been in the ledger.

CONTROL ACCOUNTS AND SUBSIDIARY LEDGERS

A general ledger which contains a great number of accounts becomes difficult to cope with in the posting process. In a large department store, for example, there may be thousands of individual accounts receivable and hundreds of individual accounts payable. In a life insurance company there may be hundreds of accounts with agents and many accounts with banks.

To simplify posting one large ledger, all individual accounts receivable can be kept in a separate ledger called an *accounts receivable subsidiary ledger*. These individual accounts are replaced by one account in the general ledger called the *Accounts Receivable control* account.

A *control account* is an account in the general ledger with a balance equal to the total of all account balances in a subsidiary ledger. If the credit balances in a subsidiary ledger, for example, total $1,005, and the debit balances total $5, the control account balance must have a $1,000 credit balance ($1,005 credits − $5 debits).

To maintain this equality between control account and subsidiary ledger, each transaction affecting an account in the subsidiary ledger must be posted in both ledgers. This is done by posting individual transactions in the subsidiary ledger and a summary of the transactions in the control account. A special journal is commonly used to summarize hundreds of debits or credits for posting to a control account.

If a $1,200 total in the Sales column of a sales journal is posted as a debit to the Accounts Receivable control account (as well as a credit to

Sales), this total debit will necessarily equal the separate debits posted from this journal to the individual accounts in the subsidiary ledger. Likewise, if the total ($350) of the Accounts Receivable column of the cash receipts journal (Figure 5–1) is posted as a credit to Accounts Receivable control account, this total credit must equal the separate credits posted from this journal to the individual accounts receivable. It follows that the balance of the Accounts Receivable control account would if there are no errors be equal to the total of the balances of the individual accounts in the subsidiary ledger.

To illustrate, assume that R. C. Daws and W. A. Wall owed $250 each to our company, we had a $400 note receivable due in January and $1,000 in the bank. These beginning balances are indicated by the symbol # in the following T-accounts. After posting the totals of the sales journal and cash receipts journals, the general ledger accounts appear as follows:

Cash		Accounts Receivable Control		Notes Receivable		Sales
# 1,000		# 500	350	# 400	400	1,200
3,850		1,200				3,100
4,850		*1,350*				*4,300*

The account balances after posting are shown in italics.

Note that only five postings of column totals were required, plus one additional posting from the "General Ledger" or "Other" column; yet there were many individual transactions. There could have been hundreds of individual transactions requiring only five column total postings, plus the credits in the "General Ledger" column of the cash receipts journal.

After the six transactions affecting the individual accounts in the accounts receivable ledger are posted, the accounts appear as follows:

R. C. Daws		W. A. Wall		A. B. Jones
# 250	150	# 250	200	500
100		*50*		*500*

C. D. Green		E. G. Hall		C. R. Merit
100		200		400
100		*200*		*400*

At the end of the month the accounts receivable bookkeeper will prepare a *schedule of accounts receivable* listing each individual account receivable and its balance. The schedule also shows the total of these individual balances. This total must be the same as the balance of the

Accounts Receivable control account. If the two do not agree, the error or errors must be located and corrected.

Schedule of Accounts Receivable
January 19__

R. C. Daws	$ 100
C. D. Green	100
E. J. Hall	200
A. B. Jones	500
C. R. Merit	400
W. A. Wall	50
Total	$1,350

Note that the total of the subsidiary accounts receivable ledger, as shown above, equals the balance of the control account shown on page 88.

A similar control account can be established for accounts payable, for investments owned, for loans made, or for any other group of accounts which are similar in nature. The control account technique builds greater accuracy into the accounting system since it creates internally balancing parts within that system.

This technique can be applied to many phases of life insurance accounting. For example, a control account system is usually used for accounts with agents, accounts with banks, and other investment accounts. A control account might also be used for a cafeteria or printing department operating within the company.

The major advantage of using special journals and subsidiary ledgers is the saving in time and effort required to make journal entries and to post transactions. However, there are other advantages. Their use spreads the accounting responsibility among a number of people. For example, one person might be assigned the responsibility for preparing a particular journal or posting a particular ledger. Each special journal and each subsidiary ledger can be balanced independently, providing a means for checking accuracy and locating errors more easily.

If only one ledger were used, only one person at a time could post to the accounts because all the accounts must be available to him. However, if accounts receivable and accounts payable subsidiary ledgers are used, one person can be assigned to posting each one and a third person to posting the general ledger. The person responsible for the accounts receivable ledger would post primarily from the sales journal and cash receipts journal. The person responsible for the accounts payable ledger would post primarily from the purchases journal and cash disbursements journal. The person responsible for the general ledger would post from all journals, but the entries from the special journals would require very little of his time.

CHART OF ACCOUNTS

The specific accounts required in one business differ from those needed in another and are determined by the size of the business, the nature of its operations, and the kind of information required by management and by regulatory and tax agencies.

A list of all the accounts is called a *chart of accounts*. The sequence of the accounts is generally the order in which they appear on the financial statements, with the balance sheet first, then the statement of surplus, and then the income and expense statement.

In all large companies a system of code numbers is devised for the accounts. The code number identifies the classification of the account to anyone who is familiar with the company's code system.

If a list of the present accounts were made in statement order and the accounts were numbered starting with cash as number 1 and moving on down the list in arithmetical sequence, the accounts would be coded. This method, however, does not identify the classification of an account, and new accounts cannot be easily inserted in a systematic grouping.

A good code system must identify the classification of each of the accounts and must be flexible to permit growth or other changes. A five-digit numerical code can serve in most situations. The first digit identifies the major classification of the accounts as suggested by the following:

1	Assets
2	Liabilities
3	Stockholders equity
4, 5, & 6	Income
7, 8, & 9	Expenses

The second digit is for the subclassification of the account. A partial list might be:

11	Current assets
12	Fixed assets
21	Current liabilities
22	Long-term liabilities
31	Capital stock
41	Sales
51	Financial income
61	Other income
71	Cost of goods sold
72	Selling expenses
81	General expenses
82	Financial expenses
91	Other expenses

The third digit identifies a group of similar accounts. Thus cash accounts of all types might be coded 111. The fourth digit then can identify specific accounts within the group designated by the third digit. For example, Cash on Hand might be 1111; Petty Cash, 1112; First National Bank, 1113; and City National Bank, 1114. The same detailed coding can be continued throughout an almost unlimited number and variety of accounts.

There are many methods of coding, but the one discussed demonstrates the basic nature of coding. One other numerical coding system is illustrated in the chart of accounts for the Model Life Insurance Company shown at the end of this chapter. That chart will be useful for reference in reading later chapters. Good coding is worthwhile in every case, but is perhaps particularly valuable when electronic machines are used.

SUMMARY OF ACCOUNTING PRINCIPLES

Fixed assets consist of property which has a useful life of more than one year, is used in the operations of the business, and was acquired primarily for use rather than sale.

Salvage or *scrap value* is the amount a fixed asset is expected to sell for at the end of its useful life.

Depreciation base is the difference between cost and salvage value.

Depreciation expense is the portion of the cost of a fixed asset that is allocated to one particular accounting period.

Cost of fixed assets is carried in an account until the asset is sold. Amounts charged to depreciation expense are credited to, and accumulated in, an account called *Accumulated Depreciation* until the asset is sold. Then both accounts are zero balanced. Any difference in sales price and book value (cost less accumulated depreciation) is treated as a nonoperating change in surplus.

In the *imprest cash system,* a custodian is responsible for a fixed sum of money with which to pay small bills. Receipts or vouchers for money disbursed, plus cash on hand, must always equal the fixed sum called a *petty cash fund.* Accounting entries for the disbursements are made when a check is written to replenish the petty cash fund.

Bank reconciliation is a process whereby the Cash account on a company's books is reconciled with the company's account on the bank's books. It proves the accuracy of entries made to the Cash account during the month and provides a basis for detecting bookkeeping errors, bank errors, and bank charges or credits not recorded on the company's books.

A *special journal* is a book of original entry designed for recording all entries of a particular type, such as all credit sales. A special column is provided for debit or credit transactions which are frequently repeated. Only the total of each column is posted to the general ledger. Most special journals have general-purpose columns for entries which do not occur often enough to be assigned a column and that must be posted individually to the general ledger.

A *subsidiary ledger* is a group of accounts maintained separately from the general ledger but represented in that ledger by a single account known as a *control account*. Special journals are used to facilitate posting to subsidiary ledgers and control accounts.

A *chart of accounts* is a list of the accounts in the general ledger showing account titles and account numbers arranged in statement sequence. A typical statement sequence is balance sheet, statement of surplus, and income and expense statement.

QUESTIONS

1. Define fixed assets.

2. What is the depreciation process and what is meant by the term depreciation expense?

3. If an asset originally cost $10,000 and now has an accumulated depreciation of $7,000, what is the book value of the asset?

4. Give the entry if the asset in question 3 were sold for $2,500.

5. What is a control account?

6. What are some of the advantages of using special journals? Give some examples to illustrate your answer. What relationship exists, if any, between the following:

   a) Special journal and subsidiary ledger?
   b) Control account and subsidiary ledger?
   c) Subsidiary ledger and general ledger?

7. Why is the imprest system for petty cash better than merely keeping some of the payments which may come to the company on hand to use as petty cash?

8. The petty cash custodian has receipts amounting to $32 for postage he has paid. He has had no other disbursements. He has asked for a reimbursement to bring his fund up to its full balance of $50. What journal entry is required? When should the entry be made?

9. What are some of the common reasons why the balance on the bank statement may be different from the balance of the ledger account for cash in the bank involved?

10. What are the disadvantages of a code system for accounts which simply starts with the first account as No. 1 and numbers the accounts in arithmetical sequence?

PROBLEMS

1. Reconcile a bank account at the end of March and show the correcting entries where the following conditions exist: (*a*) bank statement

balance, $1,050; (*b*) Cash account balance, $994.40; (*c*) cash entries and bank statements as follows (Check No. 104 was issued for rent):

Entries in Cash Disbursement Journal			*Bank Statement* Checks Paid		
Date	*Check No.*	*Amount*	*Date*	*Check No.*	*Amount*
3/1	100	$ 16.00	2/28	98	$ 75.00
3/3	101	110.00	3/5	102	5.00
3/5	102	5.00	3/15	104	53.00
3/10	103	14.00	3/1	100	16.00
3/15	104	35.00	3/25	107	3.00
3/18	105	6.00	3/20	106	11.00
3/20	106	11.00	3/18	105	6.00
3/25	107	3.00	3/28	Service chg.	3.20
3/28	108	22.00			

Deposits in Cash Receipts Journal		*Deposits Received by Bank*	
3/5	$100.00	3/1	$ 78.00
3/15	105.00	3/6	100.00
3/31	69.20	3/17	105.00

2. The premium income journal of a life insurance company appears as follows:

Date	*Policy Number*	*Name*	*Premium*	*Agent Number*	*Commission*
5/1	1238	Jones	$105.00	16	$10.50
5/2	4832	Smith	35.00	25	1.75
5/3	9645	Abercr.	7.50	3	3.75
5/6	2189	Becken	28.00	42	2.10
5/7	4356	Miller	72.10	25	3.61
			$247.60		$21.71

All premiums were received in cash and all commissions, which are expenses, are credited to agents' accounts in a subsidiary ledger. The disbursements journal has a column for the Agents' Ledger control account. It shows two payments, one to agent number 25 for $4.25, and another to agent 16 for $8.31. At the beginning of May, agents' accounts showed credit balances as follows:

Agent No. 3.....................$ 5.25
            16..................... 8.30
            25..................... 4.25
            42..................... 4.75
      Total.......................$22.55

Assume the Cash account had a $1,000 balance and the Surplus account a $977.45 balance at the beginning of May. Record the beginning balances in T-account form and post the transactions to the agents' subsidiary ledger and general ledger. Prepare a trial balance and schedule of balances in the agents' ledger at the end of the month.

The schedule and trial balance are shown in the Answers to Problems so that you may check your work.

MODEL LIFE INSURANCE COMPANY
CHART OF ACCOUNTS

Note: The hundreds position digit of account numbers are assigned according to operating departments and approximate line-of-business. Tens and units position digits are assigned in the sequence of annual statement items, and numbers to right of decimal are desired subdivisions of annual statement items.

Premium Accounts

Title (Add Line of Business)	Industrial	Ordinary	Annuity	Group	Ind. Health
Prems., 1st Yr. Par		201.0	301.0	...	...
Prems., 1st Yr. Non-Par		201.1	301.1	401.1	...
Prems., 1st Yr. Life Reins. Pd		202.0	...	...	...
Prems., 1st Yr. A.D.B. Reins. Pd		202.1	...	...	...
Prems., 1st Yr. Dis. Reins. Pd		202.2	...	...	...
Prems., Single, Par		203.0	303.0	...	...
Prems., Single, Non-Par		203.1	303.1	...	...
Prems., Single, Non-Tax		203.2	...	...	...
Prems., Single, Cr. Life		...	...	403.3	...
Prems., Renewal, Par		204.0	304.0	...	...
Prems., Renewal, Non-Par		204.1	304.1	404.1	...
Prems., Credit Life, OSB		...	...	404.2	...
Prems., Weekly Debit	104.0	...	...	...	...
Prems., Monthly Debit	104.1	...	...	...	...
Prems., Renewal, Life Reins. Pd		205.0	...	...	...
Prems., Renewal ADB Reins. Pd		205.1	...	...	...
Prems., Renewal, Dis Reins. Pd		205.2	...	...	...
Prems., Reins. Dividend Rec'd		205.3	...	...	...
Prems., Health, 1st Yr. Acc		...	...	406.0	506.0
Prems., Health, 1st Yr. Dis		...	...	406.1	506.1
Prems., Health, 1st Yr. HMS		...	...	406.2	506.2
Prems., Health, 1st Yr. Fran		...	...	...	506.3
Prems., Health, Renewal, Acc		...	...	407.0	507.0
Prems., Health, Renewal, Dis		...	...	407.1	507.1
Prems., Health, Renewal, HMS		...	...	407.2	507.2
Prems., Health Renewal, Fran		...	...	...	507.3
Cons. Supp. C. with L/C		208.0	...	...	...
Div. Accs. to Non-F. Options		208.1	...	...	...
Cons. Supp. C. without L/C		209.0	...	...	...
Div. Deposits Rec'd		210.0	...	...	...

Claim, Dividend, and Commission Accounts

	Account Numbers				
Title (*Add Line of Business*)	Industrial	Ordinary	Annuity	Group	Ind. Health
Death Claims Pd., Par...............		220.0	...	420.0	...
Death Claims Pd., Non-Par...........	120.1	220.1	...	420.1	...
Death Claims Reins. Rec'd...........	...	221.0	...	...	...
ADB Claims Pd.....................	120.2	220.2	...	420.2	...
ADB Claims Reins. Rec'd............	...	221.1	...	...	...
Matured Ends. Pd..................	122.0	222.0	...	422.0	...
Coupons Pd........................	...	222.1	...	...	...
Annuity Ben. Pd...................	...	...	323.0	...	...
Dis. Inc. Claims Pd.................	...	224.0	...	...	...
Dis. W.P. Claims Pd................	124.1	224.1	...	...	...
Dis. Reins. Rec'd...................	...	225.0	...	...	...
Surrenders Pd......................	126.0	226.0	326.0	...	...
Group Conversions..................	...	227.0	...	427.0	...
Health Ben. Pd. Acc................	...	...	...	...	528.0
Health Ben. Pd. Dis................	...	...	...	...	528.1
Health Ben. Pd. HMS...............	...	...	...	...	528.2
Health Ben. Pd. Fran...............	...	...	...	...	528.3
Int. Pd. on Pol. & C. Funds.........	...	229.0	...	...	...
Pd. on Supp. C. with L/C...........	...	230.0	...	...	...
Pd. on Supp. C. without L/C........	...	231.0	...	...	...
Div. Accs. Pd......................	...	232.0	...	...	...
Pol. Divs. Pd......................	...	233.0	...	...	...
Pol. Divs. to Prems................	...	233.1	...	...	...
Pol. Divs. to Pd-Up Adds...........	...	233.2	...	...	...
Pol. Divs. Left on Deposit...........	...	233.3	...	...	...
Comms. Life 1st Yr., Par............	...	234.0	334.0	...	...
Comms. Life 1st Yr., Non-Par........	...	234.1	334.1	434.1	...
Comms. Life Sing. Prem., Par........	...	235.0	335.0	...	...
Comms. Life Sing. Prem., Non-Par.....	...	235.1	335.1	...	...
Comms. Life Sing. Prem., Cr. Life.......	...	...	...	...	535 2
Comms. Life Ren., Par..............	...	236.0	336.0	...	...
Comms. Life Ren., Non-Par..........	...	236.1	336.1	436.0	536.0
Comms., Cr. Life OSB...............	...	...	...	436.1	...
Comms., Weekly Debit..............	136.0	...	...	...	...
Comms., Monthly Debit.............	136.1	...	...	...	...
Comms., Health, 1st Yr.............	...	...	...	437.0	537.0
Comms., Health, Ren...............	...	...	...	438.0	538.0

Expense and Tax Accounts

Title (Add Line of Business)	Account Numbers						
	Industrial	Ordinary	Annuity	Group	Health	Investment	General
Rent, Home Office	140.0	240.0	340.0	440.0	540.0	840.0	940.0
Rent, Branch offices	140.1	240.1	340.1	440.1	540.1	840.1	
Salaries, Home Office	141.0	241.0	341.0	441.0	541.0	841.0	941.0
Salaries, Agents	141.1	241.1		441.1	541.1		
Salaries, Field Superv	141.2	241.2	341.2	441.2	541.2		
Salaries, Br. Office	141.3	241.3	341.3	441.3	541.3	841.3	
Employee Benefits	142.0	242.0	342.0	442.0	542.0	842.0	942.0
Cafeteria Income							942.1
Cafeteria, Salaries							942.2
Cafeteria, Food							942.3
Cafeteria, Other Costs							942.4
Agent Benefits	143.0	243.0	343.0	443.0	543.0		
Gifts & Donations							944.0
Legal Exp., Excl. Claims	145.0	245.0	345.0	445.0	545.0	845.0	945.0
Medical Fees	146.0	246.0	346.0	446.0	546.0		
Insp. of Risks	147.0	247.0	347.0	447.0	547.0		
Canc. Fees—Agts		247.1	347.1		547.1		
Consultants Fees		248.0	348.0	448.0	548.0		948.0
Claim Expense Incl. Legal	149.0	249.0	349.0	449.0	549.0		
Travel Expense, H. O.	150.0	250.0	350.0	450.0	550.0	850.0	950.0
Travel Expense, Agents	150.1	250.1	350.1	450.1	550.1		
Travel Expense, Field Superv	150.2	250.2	350.2	450.2	550.2		
Advertising	151.0	251.0	351.0	451.0	551.0		951.0
Postage & Express	152.0	252.0	352.0	452.0	552.0	852.0	952.0
Tele. & Tele.	152.1	252.1	352.1	452.1	552.1	852.1	952.1
Printing Purchased	153.0	253.0	353.0	453.0	553.0	853.0	953.0
Print Dept. Income							953.1
Print Dept. Salaries							953.2
Print Dept. Supplies							953.3

Expense and Tax Accounts—Continued

Title (Add Line of Business)	Account Numbers						
	Industrial	Ordinary	Annuity	Group	Health	Investment	General
Print Dept. Depr. F. & E.	...	...	...	...	...	...	953.4
Print Dept. Other Costs	...	...	...	...	...	...	953.5
Depr. F. & E. H.O.	154.0	254.0	354.0	454.0	554.0	854.0	954.0
Depr. F. & E. Br. Offices	154.1	254.1	354.1	454.1	554.1	...	...
Rental of Equip.	...	...	...	...	...	...	955.0
Books, Newsp. & Periodicals	156.0	256.0	356.0	456.0	556.0	856.0	956.0
Bureau Dues & Assessments	157.0	257.0	357.0	457.0	557.0	857.0	957.0
Insurance exc. Real Est.	158.0	258.0	358.0	458.0	558.0	...	958.0
Collection & Exchange	159.0	259.0	359.0	459.0	559.0	859.0	...
Supplies & Service, H.O.	160.0	260.0	360.0	460.0	560.0	860.0	960.0
Supplies & Service, Br.O.	160.1	260.1	360.1	460.1	560.1	...	...
Sundry Expense	161.0	261.0	361.0	461.0	561.0	861.0	961.0
Agency Allowances	162.0	262.0	362.0	462.0	562.0	...	...
Agts. Bals. Chgd. Off.	...	263.0	...	...	563.0	...	...
Agency Conf., Nonlocal	164.0	264.0	364.0	464.0	564.0	...	...
Stockholder Service	...	...	...	...	...	...	965.0
Real Est. Exp.	...	...	...	...	...	866.0	...
Real Est. Taxes	...	...	...	...	...	867.0	...
State Ins. Dept. Lic. & Fees	168.0	268.0	368.0	468.0	568.0	...	968.0
Prem. Taxes	169.0	269.0	369.0	469.0	569.0	...	...
U. C. Taxes	170.0	270.0	370.0	470.0	570.0	870.0	970.0
Other State Taxes	171.0	271.0	371.0	471.0	571.0	871.0	971.0
F.I.C.A. Tax	172.0	272.0	372.0	472.0	572.0	872.0	972.0
Other Taxes	173.0	273.0	373.0	473.0	573.0	873.0	973.0
Fed. Inc. Tax, Cap. Gains	...	...	...	...	...	874.0	...
Fed. Inc. Tax, Operations	175.0	275.0	375.0	475.0	575.0	875.0	...
Stockholder Divs.—Cash	...	...	...	...	...	...	979.0
Stockholder Divs.—Stock	...	...	...	...	...	...	979.1

Investment Income, Gain, and Loss Accounts

Title	Account Number
Int. Income, Bonds	811.0
Dividends Rec'd, Stock	812.0
Dividends Rec'd, Sav. & L. Shares	812.1
Int. Income, Mortgages	813.0
Rent Income, Home Office	814.0
Rent Income, Foreclosed R.E.	814.1
Rent Income, Investment R.E.	814.2
Int. Income, Pol. Loan, Ord.	815.0
Int. Income, Pol. Loan, MDO	815.1
Int. Income, Pol. Loan, Annuities	815.2
Int. Income, Prem. Notes	815.3
Int. Income, Delinquent Prems.	815.4
Int. Income, Bank Deposits	816.0
Int. Income, Agents' Bals.	817.0
Profit, Sale of Bonds	818.0
Profit, Sale of Stocks	818.1
Profit, Sale of Mort. Loans	818.2
Incr. Book-Value, Bonds	819.0
Incr. Book-Value, Stocks	819.1
Loss, Sale of Bonds	876.0
Loss, Sale of Stocks	876.1
Loss, Sale of Mort. Loans	876.2
Depreciation, Real Estate	877.0
Decr., Book-Value, Bonds	878.0
Decr., Book-Value, Stocks	878.1

Asset and Liability Accounts

Title	Account Number
Bonds	880.0
Stocks, Preferred	881.0
Stocks, Common	881.1
Stocks, Savings & Loan	881.2
Mortgage Loans, First	882.0
Mortgage Loans, Other	882.1
Real Estate, Home Office	883.0
Real Estate, Foreclosed	883.1
Real Estate, Investment	883.2
Policy Loans, Ord.	884.0
Policy Loans, MDO	884.1
Policy Loans, Annuities	884.2
Premium Notes	885.0
Collateral Loans	886.0
Petty Cash	887.0
Bank Control Acct.	887.1
Agents' Control Acct.	988.0
Accounts Receivable	989.0
Furniture & Equipment	990.0
Accumulated Depreciation, Furniture & Equipment	990.1
Prem. Deposit Acct—Ord.	291.0
Income Taxes Withheld	991.0
FICA Taxes Withheld	991.1
Retirement Deductions	991.2
Mortgage Escrow	891.3
Misc. Payroll Deductions	991.4

Asset and Liability Accounts—Continued

Title	Account Number
Suspense, First Year Ord.	292.0
Suspense, Other Ord.	292.1
Suspense, Annuity	392.0
Suspense, First Year Health	592.0
Suspense, Other Health	592.1
Suspense, Group	492.0
Suspense, Investment	892.0
Suspense, General	992.0
Clearing Account	993.0
Balance Account	999.0

Chapter 6

Machine Accounting

Most life insurance companies use machines to prepare journals, post ledgers, and to do other record-keeping work. In fact, the majority of accounting tasks in a typical life insurance company are handled by machine. Therefore, some knowledge of accounting machines and of mechanized accounting systems is desirable as a sound base for the study of insurance accounting practices and procedures.

As a company grows in size and the volume of accounting transactions increases, many changes take place in the accounting system. At first, a simple set of manual (pen and ink) entry books will suffice. Then subsidiary journals and ledgers are adopted to minimize clerical effort and to enable more people to participate in the accounting function. Finally, partial or full mechanization of accounting processes is established in order to reduce the cost per unit of data handled, to provide accounting information faster, and to reduce the possibility of error. The type of equipment used will also change from time to time because increasing volume will justify the higher cost of faster and more efficient equipment.

Although many of the newer types of accounting machines are extremely complex internally, their essential functions are not difficult to understand. Machine accounting systems follow the same principles which apply to manual systems. Additional controls are required to prevent errors because when large volumes of data are handled, errors are very difficult to locate.

Introductory phases of machine accounting and a general description of machine accounting processes are presented in this chapter. More specific descriptions of accounting machine functions are presented in Chapter 7.

ADVANTAGES OF MACHINE METHODS

Machine methods have four general advantages over manual methods: (1) Accounting tasks can be performed much more rapidly. (2) Records are neater and more legible. (3) Greater accuracy can be achieved through controls built into the machines and designed into the systems used. (4) A large volume of data can be handled more economically. These advantages are especially apparent when data must be reused to prepare supplemental reports and statistical analyses of transactions.

The advantages of machine use are partially offset by the relatively high cost of machines and the high degree of skill required to design machine-accounting systems for maximum efficiency. There is also a lack of flexibility in adjusting to special conditions which may arise from time to time. In fact, the complexity of the equipment and the resulting high cost of making changes are factors that must be considered when deciding whether or not to mechanize a phase of the company's operations.

TYPES OF ACCOUNTING MACHINES

A great variety of mechanical equipment is used in life insurance accounting. This equipment cannot be classified precisely, but for study and discussion purposes a useful broad classification is:

1. Conventional bookkeeping machines
2. Unit record equipment
3. Computer systems

There are no standardized titles for machines used in accounting processes because this equipment is constantly being changed and improved. A classification or title that is satisfactory today may not be appropriate tomorrow. Titles and definitions used in this book were appropriate when this book was written and should be accepted to facilitate understanding of the subject matter.

The conventional bookkeeping machine classification covers machines which are operated as independent units and which are designed primarily to process manually entered data. The other two classifications cover sets or configurations of machines which are designed to accept data in machine-readable form as well as manually entered data. Once data is recorded in machine-readable form, it can be reused many times in subsequent data processing. Therefore, the latter two classifications might be described as repetitive-data processing equipment.

Conventional Bookkeeping Machines

Unlike repetitive-data processing equipment, a conventional bookkeeping machine is not dependent upon a number of companion pieces of equipment to perform accounting functions. It journalizes and posts accounting entries simultaneously through a direct keyboard entry process.

Bookkeeping machines are equipped with a keyboard similar to that of a typewriter, or with a group of symbol keys and one or more sets of numerical keys. The operator depresses one key at a time to enter alphabetical or numerical information. The carriage of the machine moves so that the operator may enter dates, account titles, account numbers, and explanatory information. Amounts may be entered in any one of the several columns of a journal page. The machine automatically accumulates totals for each column and usually *crossfoots*, that is, adds and subtracts across each horizontal line of figures. Crossfooting is an excellent control measure to prove that debits and credits on each line are equal and to prevent errors in calculating new ledger balances after each posting.

The adding and subtracting function of these machines is performed in *registers*. A register is a built-in accumulator or adding device. There may be as few as four or more than a dozen registers in one bookkeeping machine so that several column totals can be accumulated simultaneously. At least one register is used for crossfooting.

The crossfooting feature of a bookkeeping machine makes it possible to use *proofing* systems to prevent errors in recording ledger balances and also to insure that debits equal credits in journal entries. Ledger balance proofing is accomplished by carrying an extra balance figure on the ledger card known as a verification proof balance. This must be a figure that bears some relationship to the current account balance, such as double the balance, or the sum of balances if there are several balances on one card. Whenever the account balance is entered on the machine and the proof balance is adjusted and subtracted, the result must be zero to prove that the operator picked up the account balance correctly. Other, more reliable, methods of proofing are more complex, but the principle of arriving at a zero difference to prove balances is used in each of them.

A common method of preventing errors is to use a *control total* based on an adding machine tape of amounts recorded on documents. When this is done prior to journalizing and posting, the appropriate total on the bookkeeping machine's continuous sheet is compared with the total on the adding machine tape after all the work is done. If the totals do not agree, the operator must compare the entries on the continuous sheet to the items on the adding machine tape to detect errors.

When a bookkeeping machine is changed to perform a different type of work, e.g., changed from recording mortgage installments received to recording dividends received, the operator must make an adjustment on the machine or substitute a different control device. A control device is one which causes the machine to do such things as shift to a new column, add, subtract, or perform other functions automatically. When a change in a control device (called a program change) is required, it is usually necessary to call in a specialist employee of the manufacturer.

Figure 6–1.   Punched Card

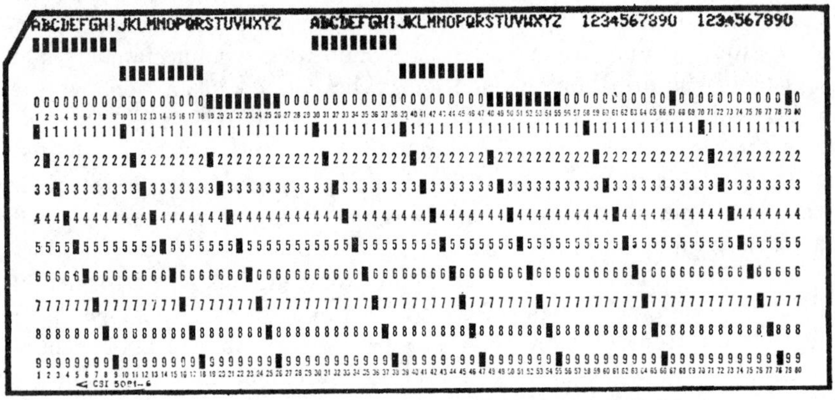

Figure 6–2.   Punched Paper Tape

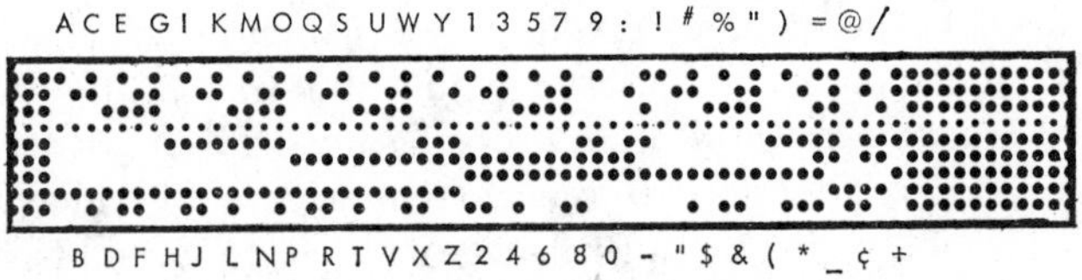

It is possible to retain (i.e., store) data in these machines, but only to the extent of register totals. Usually, information must be manually reentered each time it is needed. It is possible however, to equip many of these machines with devices to capture data in punched cards or paper tape (see Figures 6–1 and 6–2) for later use by other types of equipment. Some will even read data from punched cards, but at a much slower rate than most data processing equipment. Some also have multiplying and dividing capabilities.

Conventional bookkeeping machine processes vary according to particular machine models and the design of the company data processing systems. However, all machines of this type are similar with respect to simultaneous journalizing, posting, and proofing systems. Maximum efficiency is achieved if journal processing and ledger posting are done on a daily basis. A new account balance is shown for each posting.

Bookkeeping machines can be used very effectively with agency ledger accounting, payroll records, investments, expense disbursements, claim payments, and general ledger posting. They may also be used for check writing, combining check preparation, posting, and journalizing into one step.

The principal uses of these machines are in operations which (1) require account balances daily, (2) involve the handling of information of a nonrepetitive nature, and (3) are of too small a volume to justify the higher initial cost of faster and more elaborate equipment.

Despite the obvious advantages of bookkeeping machines over hand methods in large-volume accounting processes, they lack the flexibility and speed of unit record and computer systems.

Repetitive-Data Processing Equipment

Data may be defined as a group of items of information. In a literal sense, data processing equipment can be as simple a device as a pencil or pen. In the machine accounting sense, data is more appropriately defined as a large volume of alphabetic and numeric information.

The term *repetitive-data processing equipment* is used here to describe a set or configuration of machines capable of rapidly processing large volumes of data in machine-readable form for the purpose of preparing accounting and statistical reports. These machines also can print a number of miscellaneous symbols such as +, −, CR, etc. For convenience these machines are referred to more simply as data processing machines or data processing equipment.

To be *machine readable*, data must usually be converted to holes punched in cards or paper tape, or to magnetic dots on surfaces capable of being magnetized. Some data processing machines can "*read*" typewritten characters with special characteristics.

The fact that data processing equipment can process data in machine-readable form makes this equipment especially useful in situations where the same basic data must be reused many times. Only one initial manual typing into a machine-readable form is required. Records can thereafter be reused repeatedly or reproduced partially or totally by machines with or without changes. These features result in significant savings for insurance companies because most insurance transactions are repetitive in nature.

A typical set of closely related insurance transactions are found in the billing and accounting involved in the processing of premium payments on a policy. Assume that a policyowner is paying premiums of $10 monthly. In the following process, note the number of times policy number, premium, name, address, and due date are reused. In billing for the current premium, all of the data except due date is probably the same as last month and can be reused without change. If the policyowner does not pay immediately, all of the billing data is reused to prepare a late notice or lapse notice. If he does make the payment, the policy number, premium, name, and due date are reused to prepare a premium list to be used as a premium journal. The commission amount payable to the agent is calculated on the $10 premium, and the policyowner's policy number and name are reused to prepare a commission listing and journal entry for the commission payable. At the end of the month the premium data and address is reused to prepare a premium summary by states for premium tax purposes.

The high cost of using data processing equipment makes it desirable to extract as much information as possible in each machine operation. As a result, machine-prepared reports or listings used for preparing accounting entries may not be recognized by the novice bookkeeper as either journal or ledger because these reports may include much related statistical information and may not *show* equal debits and credits. When used for accounting entries, reports must contain most of the elements of a journal or ledger, such as dates, amounts, and descriptive data on each transaction. However, data need not be listed in a debit equals credit form on a report used as a journal if the bookkeeper shows the equal debit and credit amounts in a summary included on or attached to the list. For example, if the report is for premiums, the balancing amount will be the cash received which may be represented by an adding machine tape attached or a copy of a deposit ticket showing a total equal to that on the machine-prepared premium report.

Data processing equipment can process a journal, ledger, or supplementary report more effectively if done in one operation after the end of the accounting period. Many companies use computer systems to update ledger balances on a daily basis but make less frequent listing of entries. Monthly listing of entries is more economical than daily listing and provides a ledger page which shows all entries to an account during the month.

Before learning about machine accounting processes in more detail, it is desirable to know (1) the meaning of the more common terms used in data processing, (2) the nature and types of media used to record data in machine-readable form, and (3) the classification of machine process records and files.

TERMINOLOGY USED IN MACHINE ACCOUNTING

Unit record equipment is a phrase commonly used to refer to machines designed to read data in the form of holes punched in cards and which use electromechanical means to perform such operations as sorting cards and calculating and summarizing data contained in cards. Other terms used when referring to this equipment are (1) punched card machines and (2) electric accounting machines (EAM). Neither term is adequately descriptive, however, since they can also be used to describe other machines. Each unit record machine is usually controlled and operated independently, but several machines are usually required to prepare a list or report.

Computer system, computer, and *electronic data processing equipment* are phrases commonly used to describe a set of interconnected machines which use electronic circuits and magnetism for reading, sorting, computing, processing, and storing data in machine-readable form. Computers will "read" data in many forms, such as holes punched in cards or paper tape or as magnetized dots (bits) on specially treated plastic tape or discs (known as magnetic tape and magnetic discs). Computer input can also result from directly connected typing devices. Some computer systems, however, will accept data in only one or two forms, depending upon the design of the equipment and system.

Computer systems are controlled by a set of detailed instructions known as a program, which may be internally stored in a *central processor.* Computers have the ability not only to store a complex set of processing instructions but also to accept and store large volumes of data internally for reference or use as required. The portion of the central processor where this data is stored is known as the *memory.* This ability to internally retain complex instructions and reference data makes it possible to perform many tasks not possible or practical with other equipment.

A *character* is a numerical digit, letter of the alphabet, or special symbol that is used to represent data.

As used in machine accounting, a *record* is a group of related facts which is treated as a unit. It may be about a particular item, person, or transaction but must be in a physical form which can be read and processed by machines. Computer records vary in length, and records of 1,000 characters are not unusual.

A *unit record* contains sufficient data about its subject to permit use of the record independently of other records. A punched card, containing a maximum of 80 or 90 characters of data, is the most common form of unit record.

A *consolidated function record* is one that contains all data available on a particular policy, agent, investment, or other classification of data. It is normally used only with a computer and is a master record, i.e., one which may be used as a data source for all subsequent data processing. For example, a consolidated function record on a policy may provide data for premium billing, premium accounting, insurance statistics by agency and state, and policy liability at the end of the calendar year.

A *file* is a complete set of related records which are treated as a unit, such as a premium billing file.

On line is used to indicate that a machine or device is connected to and under direct control of the central processor.

Off line is used to indicate the device is not so controlled and is being operated independently of the central processor.

Input is used to describe (*a*) data that is to be processed and (*b*) the medium on which data to be processed is recorded. Examples of input media are magnetic tape, magnetic discs, punched cards, punched paper tape, magnetic ink printed on paper (known as Magnetic Ink Character Recognition [MICR] when used on bank checks), and light-sensitive symbols printed in a special type and referred to as optical character recognition (or OCR) when used with special reading devices.

Output refers to the result or product of a machine operation. Output may be produced in the form of a magnetic record file, punched cards or tapes, printing on paper (known as hard copy), visual display on a video-type screen, or in other forms. Any file or report produced may be referred to as output.

Storage is a general term used in data processing to cover any means of retaining data in a machine-readable form. Storage can be described as internal or external and as on line and off line.

Internal storage refers to the memory portion of the central processor. The program is retained in memory during each job while other data is continuously moved in and out of memory to or from other forms of storage.

External storage is used to refer to files not on line and therefore not immediately accessible to the equipment, such as magnetic tape reels on racks near the machine or punched cards.

On-line or *direct access storage* refers to files that are in units under the direct control of the central processor. Any record in this type of storage is accessible to the computer within a fraction of a second, but not as quickly as data stored internally. Devices which provide on-line storage may be referred to as *mass storage* media and are discussed more fully in Chapter 7.

Data coding may be defined as a technique for condensing data by assigning numbers, letters, or symbols to represent more lengthy descriptions or titles. Coding may be considered in two classes: (1) data coding and (2) program coding. Program coding refers to codes used to instruct the computer. This type of coding has no direct bearing on accounting processes and will not be discussed in this book.

Data coding is used for more efficient machine processing and to standardize data designations. When making reports, this standardization provides a simple means for a meaningful, orderly, and useful presentation of items and amounts having the same or similar classification. A code may be alphabetical or numerical. Numeric codes can be processed more quickly by many unit record machines and by some computers, so they are more frequently used. A third type of code, the symbol code, is infrequently used.

The simplest type of data coding system is the assignment of numbers in sequence to items on a list. The items should be in a logical sequence, such as a list of customers in alphabetical or geographical order. When this technique is used, gaps must be left in the coding structure so that new items may be inserted without making the numerical sequence inaccurate. The coding structure may be designed so that it can be expanded by use of decimals. (See Model Life's Chart of Accounts in Chapter 5.) Another system is the assigning of codes by family of items or general classification, such as: life insurance and health insurance; issues, lapses, and reinstatements.

The use of codes does not mean that a person reading a report must familiarize himself with the coding structure. Reports prepared by unit record equipment usually show data in coded form, as do many computer-prepared reports. However, reports prepared by a computer *may* be decoded, i.e., with descriptions or words replacing the codes. Forms may be preprinted to include descriptive captions and titles or with code interpretations along the margins so the data can be understood easily by people who are not familiar with the code symbols.

A *check digit* is an extra digit used to minimize errors in transcribing an identification number such as a policy number. If an incorrect number or check digit is transmitted within the data processing system, an error will be signaled. The check digit is devised to detect the most common human copying errors such as dropping or transposing digits.

There are a number of methods for calculating check digits, one of which produces a check digit of 4 for the number 324.

When using this check digit the number is punched for entry in the computer as 324-4. If a part of the number is transposed so that it reads 234-4 or 342-4 or if any digit is dropped, the method of calculating the check digit will produce a figure other than 4 and will signal an error.

The check digit system is not foolproof, but the probability of failing to catch an error is slight. A computer multiplies so rapidly that there is no noticeable delay because of the check digit calculation.

INPUT AND STORAGE MEDIA

The several media for the input of data to a computer include punched cards, punched paper tape, and magnetic tape. These media are also used for storing data outside the computer and for reentering it. They are, therefore, also off-line storage media.

Punched Cards

The punched card is the most common medium used by life insurance companies for initially entering data into repetitive-data processing equipment, and it is the most common medium for entering *and storing* data in connection with unit record equipment. Large computer-centered data processing systems rarely use cards for storing data because cards require much more storage space for a given volume of data than other storage media and cannot be read into a computer as rapidly as other media. Small computer systems, however, frequently use punched cards instead of magnetic tape for both input and storage because of the simpler and less expensive equipment which can be used.

A punched card for general use must be a standard size, 7.375 inches long by 3.25 inches wide and 0.007 inches thick. Shorter cards may also be accepted by some machines. Data is recorded in the form of holes which are punched in specific locations. The machines "read" these punched holes.

Each card normally contains sufficient data to make the card an independent unit of information. Thus, a card used to journalize a premium payment must cover amount, date due, date paid, policy number, state, agent commission, and any other information in order to process the payment without reference to any other source. Cards can be processed in sets, in which case a record may consist of several cards, but each card must carry certain identifying information common to both cards so that data in it can be combined with other parts of the record.

The punched card in general use has 80 vertical columns placed from left to right along the length of the card (see Figure 6–1), permitting the recording of 80 characters of alphabetic or numeric data on one card. There are 12 punching positions in each of these columns. A character of numerical data (the digits 0–9) is recorded by one hole punched in a column. To record one alphabetical character, two holes are punched, one of which must be in one of the top three rows and is called a zone punch.

Eighty characters might seem to be a very limited amount of information, but good coding techniques enable one card to contain a considerable amount of information. Coding also permits faster processing of data because less sorting time is required when cards must be rearranged. For example, if nine alphabetical characters can be coded into a three-digit numerical code, the card can be sorted in one sixth the time required for sorting the same information in uncoded form.

As an example of how much information can be put into an 80-column card, consider that a well-designed and well-coded agent's statistical card can contain the—

1. Policy number
2. Occupation of policyowner
3. Policyowner's city and state
4. Age of policyowner
5. Agent
6. General agent
7. Territory
8. Month, day, and year of policy issue
9. Initial premium status (prepaid or payable on delivery of the policy)
10. Amount of insurance
11. Mode of premium payment
12. Amount of annual premium.
13. Amount of mode premium
14. Type of business
15. Plan of insurance
16. Number of other policies in force on the insured
17. First-year commission rate for agent and general agent
18. Renewal commission rate for agent and general agent
19. Agent's contest points earned

It should be noted that all the above information can be put into the 80-column card and still not use columns 74 through 80, which can be reserved for termination information. It should also be noted that there are other card forms in use. One type permits entry of 90 characters of data and uses a different hole punching arrangement. There are also special-use cards that are shorter than the one described.

An understanding of *how* coding enables such condensation of data may be gained by realizing one fact: much alphabetical data can be represented by a numerical code. Thus, the second item in the foregoing list—occupation of policyowner—need not consume 10–20 columns of space as would be necessary if occupations were spelled out. Instead, a 2-digit code number is used, allowing for identification of up to 99 occupations or categories of occupations. The company could arbitrarily assign "01" for "professional" and define what specific occupations were included in that category—e.g., doctors, lawyers, schoolteachers, etc. The code "02," "03," and "04" could represent three levels of office clerical occupations; 05 could be office machine operators; 06 could be factory machine operators, etc. Likewise agents' names, territories, and other items could all be represented by numerical codes.

The term *field* is used to refer to a group of columns that contain one item of information. However, a field may require just one column. Each field must be allocated as many columns as are required to hold the maximum data that may be recorded in it. For example, if premium amounts may be as much as $9,999.99, then the field for this data must be six columns. Column space need not be provided for dollar signs or punctuation.

In life insurance companies, data punched on cards may be categorized as (1) card identification data, such as policy number or account number; (2) file identification data, such as the premium due file; (3) classification data to be used in sorting and analyzing, such as policy issue date, state, or plan of insurance; (4) quantitative data to be summarized, such as the amount of insurance or the amount of premium; and (5) record data, such as date of transaction, name and address, or descriptive information about the account represented by the card. All or a part of this data can be *printed on* the cards if they are to be visually read in manual handling.

Policy numbers, for example, can be printed on the cards. Aside from printing data on a card, other visual means of card identification are used to help in the administration of card record files. Special corner cuts, colored card stock, and colored stripes printed on the cards are examples. If a card with a special corner cut is placed in a file of cards with a different corner cut, it can be spotted easily. A card with a different color marking can also be quickly spotted by machine operators. Data must be punched into the designated fields and coded correctly if it is to be sorted or totaled correctly. For example, if a card for state 01 is coded 10, this item would be summarized into the wrong state's totals. A more serious error could occur if the 1 were punched in the wrong column. To avoid this type of error, cards are usually machine-verified for accuracy. Methods of doing this are discussed in Chapter 7.

There are several advantages to punched card data processing: (1) If records must be manually handled, card files are easy to use because data can be printed on them and cards may be selected as needed. (2) Errors on punched cards are more easily detected and more easily corrected than errors on any other type of input media; it is relatively simple to substitute a new card for the incorrect one. (3) Punched cards can be sorted without using computer time. However, sorting of punched cards is done only on small jobs; with large-volume jobs, on-line sorting of data in magnetic storage media is much faster and less subject to human error.

The principal disadvantages in the use of cards instead of other computer input and storage media are: (1) One or more cards in a file may be extracted or mislaid, impairing the completeness and accuracy of the file. (2) Cards are more subject to malfunction caused by improper conditions of moisture, or temperature and other causes. (3) Sorting cards is monotonous work, even when done with machines, so operator carelessness must be guarded against. (4) Storage space required for cards is much greater than that required for either magnetic tape or paper tape. (5) Input and output speed is relatively slow. (6) Repeating identification data on each card requires more key-punching.

Punched Paper Tape

Punched paper tape is a continuous strip of paper one inch or less in width used to record data in the form of punched holes. It is similar to teletype tape. As with a punched card, various arrangements of holes in a "column" running across the width of the tape represent alphabetical or numerical characters. Most paper tapes used with computers are eight-channel tapes, which means that there is a possibility of punching eight holes across the tape width. See Figure 6–2. Tapes of fewer or more channels are also in use.

Paper tape is usually punched automatically as a by-product of a typing or other machine operation. For example, when an operator types a check to pay a policy claim, a paper tape for use in the preparation of journal and ledger entries can be created simultaneously. A second method of preparing paper tape is by use of a specially equipped adding machine (called an add-punch) that records numerical data and adds amounts, simultaneously punching a tape. A third automatic method of preparing paper tape is the use of a reader-punch attached to a computer.

Machines that punch paper tape are often equipped with devices that calculate check digits for the purpose of detecting errors in policy numbers or account numbers before they are read into a computer.

The principal advantage of paper tape over punched cards as an initial input medium is that tape can be more readily punched as a by-product of other machine processes. There are machines which produce punched cards as a by-product, but these are less frequently used. The limited data capacity of punched cards and the need for identifying data in each card are limitations not encountered with paper tape. When an *add-punch* is used to prepare paper tape, the total of the adding machine tape can be compared with the total of checks being deposited in the bank to prove the accuracy of amounts being entered in the computer. Short record identifications can also be shown on the adding machine tape and punched into the paper tape for computer input.

Other advantages of paper tape are a given amount of data can be stored in less space than is required for punched cards, and it may be used more economically than magnetic tape for transmitting moderate amounts of data over conventional telephone and telegraph lines, including inter-city lines.

Paper tape is rarely the best medium for output. However, if the volume of data is small and the data must be stored for long periods of time, paper tape may be best because it is less costly than magnetic tape and requires less space than punched cards.

Major disadvantages to paper tape as compared to punched cards are (1) the difficulty encountered in finding and correcting errors and (2) data cannot be sorted unless it is first transferred to another medium.

Locating errors by visual verification is possible by examining what was typed, such as a bank check or policy issue record. If the typed document is correct, the tape that was punched automatically in the same operation usually is correct. Machines similar in operation to those used for verifying data in punched cards are available for verifying data in paper tapes.

The tape correction process is simple only if the mistake is caught during the initial typing. The operator merely blocks out the incorrect data (see delete portion of Figure 6–2) and repunches the correct data into the next section of the tape.

If errors are detected after the typing is completed and the record is part of a long continuous tape, it is impractical to locate the record for correction because most operators cannot easily read and interpret the holes visually. However, if the operator is able to locate the error, it is possible to reproduce the correct portion of the record on a new tape, cut out the first record, and splice in the new one. However, this is a cumbersome procedure. The preferred method of correction is retyping the record with a code instructing the computer to substitute the correct record for the incorrect one.

Magnetic Tape

Magnetic tape may be described as a long, continuous ribbon or tape of plastic material coated with a substance which can be magnetized. It is similar in appearance to the tape used for recording dictation and music, but it is of a much higher quality than that used in the typical home recorder. The tape is magnetized in tiny spots called *bits*. The combination of bits across the width of the tape constitutes a code that causes the machine to recognize a single number, letter, or other character. The machine code is similar to that used for paper tape except that magnetic bits are used instead of punched holes and the characters are placed much closer together. Several hundred characters can be entered on one inch of tape.

Magnetic tape is the most commonly used medium for externally storing data for later reentry to a computer. Data can be read from magnetic tape much faster than from punched cards or punched paper tape. Many factors contribute to this greater speed. The two principal factors are the compactness or density of data stored on the tape and the high speed at which it can be passed through and read by the equipment.

Magnetic tape is wound on reels which hold many hundreds of feet of tape and consequently millions of characters. The amount of data that may be stored on one reel varies, but one reel of tape can usually hold as much data as 40 or more file drawers of punched cards.

Each time data on a magnetic tape is changed, the entire tape is rewritten onto a new tape with the changes inserted. The old tapes are saved for a reasonable period so that if any data is lost during a process, it can be reconstructed by reprocessing former tape files. This system gives protection against both operator error and machine malfunction. Many other error controls are built into the tape-reading devices so that data is rarely lost as a result of tape or machine malfunction.

Tapes may be stored for years without losing the records stored on them and may be reused hundreds of times. Old data is automatically *erased* as new data is being recorded on a tape that is being reused.

The principal disadvantage of magnetic tape when compared to other storage media is the high cost of equipment required to read it. Other disadvantages are (1) it usually is necessary to make supplemental use of cards or paper tape as initial input media and (2) extreme caution must be used to prevent data on tapes from being accidentally or maliciously destroyed.

In addition to the off-line storage media discussed in this section, there are several types of on-line storage such as magnetic discs, drums, and films. These are discussed in Chapter 7.

MACHINE RECORD FILES

A group or set of related records is called a *file*. All files related to accounting transactions performed on machines may be classified into one of the following categories:

1. *Master* or *status* files
2. *Transaction* or *detail* files
3. *Summary* files

Punched card records and files can usually be classified into one of these categories. When magnetic tape or other electronic storage media are used for record storage, the characteristics of two or more categories may be combined into one.

Master or Status Files

A *master* record is a basic record which reflects current status for a unit of filed information such as a policy contract, an agency account, or a ledger account. It is used to answer inquiries and as a data source for preparing transaction records. A file of master records is, of course, known as a master file.

There may be one master record for premium billing and accounting, another pertaining to policy dividend notices and accounting, and still another for policy liability valuation. Each of these special operations is referred to as a *function*. A single master record that combines all of the data that might have been contained in a number of special purpose records is known as a *consolidated function record*, and a group of consolidated function records is a *consolidated function file*.

The three principal uses for master files are (1) to provide current status such as status of a policy or of an account with an agent; (2) to provide analysis or summary data, such as the amount of claims paid on a policy or life insurance in force by agent; and (3) to provide basic data that is reproduced in new records, such as *transaction records*. This latter use is discussed in the next section of this chapter.

Transaction or Detail Files

A *transaction* record is one created for temporary use. It may be used in controlling a transaction that is expected to occur, in recording it when it does occur, and in analyzing transactions after they occur. A file of transaction records is a *transaction file*, frequently also called a *detail file*. Such a file may be maintained in three sections: (*a*) a pending file, (*b*) a current transaction file, and (*c*) a history file.

A transaction file can first be used to prepare premium notices. It then becomes a pending transaction file. As premiums are paid, the file is used to produce premium and commission listings which provide details that support journal entries. Then the file can be used to update the premium paid to date in the master file. Later, information in this file is used as historical data that is analyzed for premium tax and other purposes.

Data processing transactions may be either accounting transactions which affect financial income or expenditure, or file maintenance transactions which change the status of a record, such as a decrease or increase in the amount of insurance shown on a master record. A file maintenance transaction record is initiated by a manual process, such as keypunching. Additional data is usually added by machine from other sources such as premium rates stored on magnetic files. The new transaction record is then used by the computer to (1) create a new master record, (2) produce statistical reports, and (3) record accounting transactions.

Each record in the transaction file is prepared primarily to process a single transaction, such as a premium receipt or a dividend payment. A transaction file is frequently kept on punched cards even when magnetic tape is available because cards can be read easily, manually extracted for processing, and moved to the next section of the file after the processing is completed.

Summary File

A *summary file* is maintained to accumulate amount totals. The purpose of this type of file is to spread throughout the accounting period the work of obtaining end-of-accounting-cycle totals. The file is built up by summarizing transactions each day, week, or month into a set of summary records. Or, the summary file may be continuously updated so that at the end of a period the totals in the file are final totals for the period. The file may also be used to accumulate separate subtotals for parts of the accounting period. These can later be summarized into final totals.

A summary file is often used to summarize general ledger account balances during a month. Good work scheduling requires that the work load be spread over the month. This is accomplished by sorting and summarizing transaction cards by account number from time to time during the month, listing the transactions by account, and storing the totals in summary records. Subsequently, only the summary records need be totaled and listed to obtain the trial balance.

Summary files may also be used effectively for many statistical and accounting analyses such as summarizing premium collections by states for premium tax purposes, or summarizing claims paid by plan of insurance or by age. The summary process is often used with valuation files from which the policy reserve liability is calculated at the end of the year.

Summary files are not used as often with computers as with unit record equipment. Transactions stored on magnetic tape can be summarized so rapidly that the summary procedure is not so necessary. However, the number of tapes available for storage of past transactions may sometimes be limited so that a summary file may be useful.

Sometimes totals may be included as part of a master record file when it is maintained on magnetic tape. This practice is common with agents' accounts and agents' production totals, and it lessens the need for special summary files.

ACCOUNTING CONTROLS

Accounting controls are procedures used to insure mathematical accuracy of reports and records. The use of a control account in a general ledger to prove the accuracy of accounts in a subsidiary ledger is one form of accounting control. Others which have been mentioned in this chapter are proofing and pre-adding amounts to be posted (discussed in connection with conventional bookkeeping machines) and check digits discussed in the section on terminology.

It is more economical to locate errors at the earliest possible moment than it is to search for and correct them after reports have been completed. In fact, without accounting controls the accountant may not know that an error has occurred until it is called to his attention by some other circumstance. Then many hours may be lost trying to locate similar errors and in rerunning reports.

One of the machine accounting controls most frequently used is a control total to prove that all records have been processed. A control total is a predetermined grand total of all amounts or quantities to be processed. Control totals can be used to insure the (1) accuracy of numerical data in the individual records, (2) completeness of the file being processed, and (3) proper control over and functioning of the machines used to prepare the reports.

One of the simpler methods of establishing a control total is by the use of a *register*. If totals of a group of documents, such as premium notices, etc., are recorded on the register, along with document numbers and dates, a control total may be produced by adding the amounts on the register. Cards are then prepared for each item on each document. These cards are listed and summarized by document number and a grand total obtained. If the total from the register and the grand total on the summary list do not agree, an error is indicated. Then the incorrect card can be located by comparing document totals on the register with document totals on the list.

A register is also used to maintain a *dollar control*. A dollar control is a type of control total which is continuously updated for changes made in a file. Once a control total is obtained for the file of records, it can be adjusted for new records added to and old records removed from the file by listing and summarizing the former control total and the changes on a machine. This list then becomes a register showing the items added to or deleted from the file, with a new adjusted dollar control amount.

Files can also be controlled by what are known as *hash totals*. This phrase is used to describe a control total made by adding numbers or codes to obtain a total which has no significance other than as a control figure.

Another simple but effective type of control total is an item count. Items to be punched are counted and verified against the number of cards processed in a machine operation. If an item count is updated for changes in a file, the file is said to be under *item control*.

Once control totals are established, the file can be sorted in many different classifications and totals prepared for each such classification. The summary of amounts for all classifications must be equal to the control total each time to prove accuracy. If during one of these sortings and subsequent totaling, the control amount is not reached, the operator must determine whether (1) records are missing and need to be returned to the file; (2) the machine was improperly set up; (3) or the machine malfunctioned. When the difficulty is located and corrected, the reports can be rerun with the assurance that they will be in line with the control figures.

AUDIT TRAIL

An *audit trail* is created by recording financial transactions in sufficient detail and in such a way that an auditor can trace any particular transaction from the originating document to the ledger account. Audit trail might also mean that an auditor can reconstruct all of the transactions in a particular account or with a particular agent or policyholder during a particular period of time. When manual bookkeeping methods are used, the traditional procedures provide a clear audit trail by use of dates, folio columns, subsidiary journal postings, etc.

With computers, the need for an audit trail must not be overlooked in planning for efficient data handling. Computer time is so expensive that some systems designers tend to think of print-outs of details required to provide an audit trail as a waste of valuable machine time and paper. Internal controls provide a much higher degree of accuracy than ever before achieved in accounting operations, but even so the fiduciary nature of the insurance business makes it imperative in some situations that a recorded trail of transactions be left for auditors and insurance examiners.

The National Association of Insurance Commissioners has established requirements to be incorporated in computer systems. The following are edited passages from the *NAIC Examiner's Handbook:*

Data entering the accounting system as input, including transactions, should either be printed out in appropriate sequence, or be available for print-out in appropriate sequence, to allow checking back to source data underlying that input, and to allow tracing transactions from input to result.

The insurer must provide records for the examiners of the detail files through a prior print-out, or by the ability to print out at request of the examiners.

Adequate facilities and procedures for record retention should be provided to assure the safe and proper storage of printed listings, reports, and applicable supporting documentation.

A common method of providing an audit trail from the originating document to a ledger account is to make detailed lists of transactions and record the total in a control register. Only list totals and dates are posted to the ledger account. An auditor can examine the register to prove that the detail on the lists produces the amounts entered on the ledger account or accounts.

A method sometimes used to reconstruct transactions relating to a single policyholder or agent is to print out all transactions as they occur and to include on the print-out the date of the preceding transaction. Thus, it is possible to trace transactions for a period of time by first obtaining the date of the last transaction and from it locate the date of the next preceding transaction which in turn will show the date of the next preceding transaction, etc., back as far in time as the auditor needs to make his review. If numerous transactions are processed on a given date, batch numbers may also be assigned to facilitate locating a particular transaction on that date.

Accounting by exception is a method of providing an audit trail by a process which eliminates much detailed listing of separate records. The normal accounting procedure is to record each transaction as it occurs. This is direct or positive accounting and is by far the most common method used. There are situations, however, in which exception accounting and exception control are desirable. For example, a register or dollar control is established by listing and totaling all premiums due on a particular day for a particular group of insured persons. Each time their premiums become due or are paid, a list of additions or deletions is prepared covering changes which occurred between billing dates. The net effect of such changes is used to adjust the in-force total. This in-force total is the amount billed, and when the payment is received, it is the amount recorded in the journal. The record of changes must be recorded with, or bound to, the original list to insure permanency of the audit trail.

Under the exception method the audit trail is as clear as though all of the items had been relisted each time. The method reduces the amount of detail that must be recorded and is commonly used in accounting for group insurance and industrial insurance premiums.

QUESTIONS

1. What are the principal advantages of machine methods over manual methods for performing accounting functions?

2. Describe a conventional bookkeeping machine. How can the operator adjust the machine for a different accounting task? How is the machine adjusted to handle a task not previously performed? What two accounting operations can be performed simultaneously while writing checks on such machines?

3. Describe two processes to prevent errors when bookkeeping entries are made through use of conventional bookkeeping machines.

4. What is meant by the following data processing terms: input, output, hard copy, on-line storage, off-line storage, memory, data coding?

5. Name the two principal types of repetitive-data processing equipment. What type of accounting tasks do they perform more efficiently than conventional bookkeeping machines? Compare each of the two types of repetitive-data processing equipment to conventional bookkeeping machines in the following areas: method of adapting machine to new tasks, control of machine functions on routine jobs, and for most efficient preparation of accounting reports.

6. Compare unit record equipment with data processing equipment in the following areas: control of machines, length of and type of records that can be machine read, and speed of operation.

7. What are the two principal coding classifications? Give two reasons for coding data. Name three of the more commonly used data coding systems.

8. Under what conditions are punched cards desirable for storing data as compared to paper tape and magnetic tape? What are the limitations of punched cards as compared to magnetic tape and paper tape? Paper tape is desirable as an input medium under what conditions? What are its limitations?

9. Describe briefly the nature of and a few typical uses for a master file, transaction file, and summary file. What is meant by "consolidated function file"?

10. Briefly describe the following control methods and how they are used: register or dollar control, item count, and hash total.

11. What is meant by "audit trail"? How is an audit trail provided under a manual accounting system? How is it provided under a machine system? How is it provided under accounting by exception?

Chapter 7

Accounting Machine Functions

Large life insurance companies do accounting with computer systems but usually have other types of equipment available for small jobs. Many small companies rely on less costly unit record equipment and conventional bookkeeping machines. An understanding of the specific functions of these machines will facilitate understanding of typical life insurance accounting practices.

CONVENTIONAL BOOKKEEPING MACHINES

The functions of the conventional bookkeeping machine were discussed in general terms in Chapter 6. A more detailed description of the simultaneous writing, journalizing, and posting of payroll checks, a typical bookkeeping-machine process, is presented here to illustrate the use of these machines and of the proofing system.

The operator inserts in the machine a continuous roll of paper with carbon copies. A roll of chemically treated paper that produces copies without the need for carbon paper may be used instead. All accounting transactions are recorded on this paper, which then serves as a journal. (See Figure 7–1.)

For each employee to be paid, the operator inserts the payroll record card in front of the journal sheet. The first blank line of the card is placed to coincide with the next blank line on the journal. The payroll card records a history of payments to an employee along with earnings year-to-date and several other totals or balances. For purposes of illustration, assume that the card shows a previous earnings balance of $4,500, previous FICA tax deductions of $180, total withholding tax deductions of $500,

Figure 7-1. Payroll Journal, Ledger, and Check

PAYROLL JOURNAL

NO. PROOF	EARNINGS	TOTALS TO DATE FEDERAL W/H TAX	STATE W/H TAX	F.I.C.A.	PROOF	DATE	HOURS REGULAR	HOURS O'TIME	EARNINGS REGULAR	EARNINGS O'TIME	GROSS	FEDERAL W/H TAX	STATE W/H TAX	F.I.C.A.	RETIRE-MENT	OASI-CO F.C.U.	GROUP INS.	CONTRI-BUTIONS	MISC. CODE	MISC. AMOUNT	NET PAY	EMPLOYEE'S NAME	DATE	CHECK NUMBER	AMOUNT OF CHECK
00	747.50	113.50	12.06	32.89	613.17	MAR 28	25.00		50.00		50.00	7.50	.71	2.20							39.59	JOHN DOE	MAR 28	88621	39.59
00	797.50	121.00	12.77	35.09	654.18	MAR 28	40.00		84.50		84.50	11.00	.53	3.72							48.87	PETE SMITH	MAR 28	88622	48.87
00	241.54	31.00	1.37	10.63	201.28	MAR 28	40.00	3.00	76.00	8.55	84.55	11.00	.53	3.72	1.60	9.09	2.00	3-28-68	1	7.69	69.30	JOHN BROWN	MAR 28	88623	69.30

POSTED BY _____   SHEET NO. _____

EMPLOYEE EARNINGS RECORD

TAX CODE 142.010

NAME John Brown
STREET 200 Pleasant St.
CITY Atlanta, Georgia 30300
RATE
DATE

S.S. NO. 000-00-0000
DATE OF BIRTH
NATURE OF WORK
REASON TERMINATED

MARITAL STATUS
DATE EMPLOYED
DATE TERMINATED

STANDARD DEDUCTIONS

EARNINGS	TOTALS TO DATE FEDERAL W/H TAX	STATE W/H TAX	F.I.C.A.	PROOF	DATE	HOURS REGULAR	HOURS O'TIME	EARNINGS REGULAR	EARNINGS O'TIME	GROSS	FEDERAL W/H TAX	STATE W/H TAX	F.I.C.A.	RETIRE-MENT	OASI-CO F.C.U.	GROUP INS.	CHARITY CONTRIB.	MISC. CODE	MISC. AMOUNT	NET PAY
74.58 T	9.30 T	.35 T	3.28 T	62.35 #	FEB 29	39.25		74.58		74.58 S	9.30	.35	3.28							61.65 S
156.99 T	20.00 T	.84 T	6.91 T	130.92 #	MAR 21	40.00	2.25	76.00	6.41	82.41 S	10.70	.49	3.63							67.59 S
241.54 T	31.00 T	1.37 T	10.63 T	201.28 #	MAR 28	40.00	3.00	76.00	8.55	84.55 S	11.00	.53	3.72							69.30 S

142.010

Coastal States Life Insurance Company
1459 Peachtree Street N. E.
Atlanta, Georgia 30309

No. 88623

Form 71-026

DATE	HOURS REGULAR	HOURS O'TIME	EARNINGS REGULAR	EARNINGS O'TIME	GROSS	FEDERAL W/H TAX	STATE W/H TAX	F.I.C.A.	RETIRE-MENT	OASI-CO F.C.U.	GROUP INS.	CONTROL BOTTOMS	CHARITY CONTRIB.	MISC. CODE	MISC. AMOUNT	NET PAY
MAR 28 68	40.00	3.00	76.00	8.55	84.55	11.00	.53	3.72								69.30 S

PLEASE DETACH AND RETAIN THIS STATEMENT
IT IS A RECORD OF YOUR EARNINGS AND DEDUCTIONS AS
REPORTED TO THE FEDERAL AND STATE GOVERNMENTS.

MISCELLANEOUS CODE:
1-SALARY SAVINGS INS.
2-DISABILITY INS.
3-OLDLINE INS.
4-GOVT. BONDS

Coastal States Life Insurance Company
No. 88623
1459 Peachtree Street N. E.
Atlanta, Georgia 30309

DATE   MAR 28 68

CHECK NUMBER 88,623   AMOUNT 69.30

SPECIMEN

PAY TO THE ORDER OF   JOHN BROWN

THE CITIZENS AND SOUTHERN NATIONAL BANK
PERIMETER POINT OFFICE
ATLANTA, GEORGIA

⑈⑆⑆⑄⑊⑆⑆⑆⑌⑈ ⑆⑊⑍ ⑈⑇ ⑏⑊⑈⑈⑆

and a proof balance of $5,180. This proof balance is a sum of the other balances.

The operator enters the several balances from the card to the journal sheet. The machine automatically subtracts these balances from the proof balance to give a zero total. The result must be zero to insure that all balances have been entered correctly. Otherwise, the balances must be cleared and reentered.

A blank payroll check with a sheet of carbon behind it is now inserted in front of the record card. The spaces for data on the check and stub are arranged so as to coincide with the various columns on the journal sheet and payroll record card. The single data line of the check is placed over the first blank line on the journal page and the record card. The amount of salary this week is $84.55. Deductions are FICA tax, $3.72; withholding taxes, $11.53; and group insurance premium $5. The operator types these figures on the check stub. Meanwhile, the crossfooting feature of the machine automatically calculates a net pay of $64.30 insuring that debits equal credits. The $84.55 salary is a debit to an expense account, the deductions are credits to liability accounts, and the net pay is a credit to the bank account representing *Cash*.

The operator then types the check number and name of payee. The current date and net payment are automatically entered on the check, which is then removed from the machine. All of the check information was recorded simultaneously on the payroll record card and on the journal by means of carbon impressions. At the same time the amount of salary, tax deductions, and net pay were added to the employee account balances being temporarily stored in the machine. The new balances, plus a new proof balance, are automatically calculated by the machine and printed on the record card, which is then removed from the machine. The total pay, the various deductions, and the net pay are automatically added into the registers, and the journal page is automatically moved up one line.

The process is then repeated for other paychecks. After all paychecks are written, the registers are subtotaled and printed on the journal sheet. A control card is then inserted in front of the journal sheet. This card is similar to the individual record cards except that it carries summary amounts only. The previous balances on the control card are entered, and a proof taken. The machine automatically adds these balances to the amounts in the registers, arriving at new balances, to be used as control totals later when tax reports are prepared.

The operator depresses a key to clear the registers. This causes the new balances to be recorded automatically on the control card and on the journal by means of carbon impressions. The control card and journal are then removed from the machine, and the journal totals are posted to the proper accounts in the general ledger. If several salary accounts are affected, the checks might be written in separate batches with a master card for each.

A general ledger account card could have been inserted in the machine in the same manner as the payroll record. The result would have been a ledger card posting simultaneously with the making of the journal entry.

UNIT RECORD EQUIPMENT

Unit record equipment machine processes are simpler and more uniform than those of computers. Computers vary considerably in their capabilities, so discussion of their use in accounting areas must be very general. Some of the basic unit record machines, such as the key punch, will probably be used for many years to come for the purpose of supplementing computer operations.

Unit record machines were designed originally to process punched cards. Collectively, they were called *punched card equipment*. This description is no longer sufficient because most computers also are capable of utilizing punched cards in data processing operations. There are also unit record machines that process punched paper tape. Since these are seldom used by life insurance companies this discussion will deal with the most widely used media, the equipment that processes punched cards.

Most computations and other functions of unit record equipment are performed electromechanically. Each machine usually operates independently of other machines and performs only one or two card-oriented functions, such as punching, sorting, merging, reproducing, summarizing, calculating, and printing. A number of different machines, therefore, are required to prepare a single report.

Most unit record machines are controlled by wired panels known as *plug boards*. These boards are wired by the operators, and when it becomes necessary to make a change in a job or process, they are rewired by them. Boards may be used time after time for a job without being rewired. Switches are also provided so that one plug board may be used for two or more jobs where the card format and report arrangement are similar. The ease with which changes can be made from one task to another makes unit record equipment simple to adjust for scheduled and preplanned work applications.

Tabulator

The basic unit record machine is known simply as an accounting machine. These machines were known many years ago as *tabulators* because at that time they could process only numerical information. They can now process alphabetic data and various symbols but are still widely referred to as tabulators, a practice that will be used in this book to prevent possible confusion with other accounting machines.

A tabulator has limited data storage capacity. This capacity consists primarily of the ability to store amounts and totals in summary registers and the ability to retain data from one card long enough to compare it with data on the next card. It processes one card completely before it processes the next. The tabulator reads punched cards, accumulates totals, and prints data at speeds measured in hundreds of cards per minute. It prints data at the same speed at which it processes cards. Its functions are usually limited to printing, adding and subtracting numeric data, and comparing and printing both numeric and alphabetic data.

The listing and summarizing capability of this machine makes it especially useful where volumes of data must be listed from cards and totaled, as in the case of preparing a list of premiums to be journalized or a list of commissions to be credited to an agent's account.

Tabulators can compare classification codes in two cards. This comparing ability enables the machine to determine when all cards in one classification have been processed and to print totals for the classification. This capability is useful in summarizing items by account number, premiums by state, or other analyses required from a file of cards.

A cross-adding feature that can balance each line of data is not built into tabulators as it is on conventional bookkeeping machines. Totals may be cross-added manually or by special wiring of the machine's control panel to prove that all debit columns equal all credit columns or that a gross figure less deductions equals a net figure. There are auxiliary machines which accomplish this task more effectively.

The list-printing ability of the machines is rarely utilized to prepare journals with dates and equal debits and credits, but it is used frequently to prepare lists from which journal entries may be made. If punched cards are used to prepare a journal, a separate card is required for each debit and each credit. Use of separate cards permits sorting them into account-number order for the purpose of printing a ledger, an operation equivalent to posting a ledger.

Ledger sheets may be prepared on unit record equipment but are seldom prepared daily. If a ledger sheet is desired, the pertinent cards are usually held until the account listing is needed. They are then sorted into account number order and merged with cards containing the old balances. They are then listed, amounts are summarized, and new balances are printed by the tabulator. The lists then constitute ledger sheets. This technique is used often for maintaining agents' ledgers.

Key Punch. The function of the key punch is to punch holes in precise locations on cards. Each card is automatically fed into the first punching position, moved to subsequent columns, and ejected. The operator uses a keyboard similar to that of a typewriter. The process is quite fast when data has been precoded. The rate of production depends upon the skill of the operator, the legibility of the source document, and, of course, the number of holes to be punched. Typical rates might vary between 150 and 800 cards per hour.

Many key punches print data on the top line of the card as the card is punched. This process is known as interpreting. It facilitates error detection and eliminates the need for a *separate* interpretation process. Some data managers prefer not to have this feature so that key punch operators will rely on the feel or touch of the keyboard and, presumably, be able to punch faster.

The key punch is also capable of reproducing one punched card from another, in whole or in part. Thus, data common to a group of cards (such as a date) may be punched into the first card of the group and then duplicated into the rest of the cards in that group. This feature of the machine also facilitates producing a replacement card when an error is made in punching. The machine rapidly reproduces one column at a time but is not fast enough for major card-reproduction jobs.

All key punches are equipped with devices that are "programed" to cause the machine to automatically skip fields and move to the next punching position when a portion of the card is not to be used. This field-skipping feature and automatic ejection of completed cards speeds punching. These features also assist the operator in detecting off-column punches because the machine *will not go* into one of these automatic functions unless the field before the function is completely punched, or it *may go* into an automatic function *too soon* if too many columns have been punched.

Cards may be punched by machines other than the key punch, often as a by-product of another function.

Sorter. The sorter is used to arrange cards into any desired order. This machine is of critical importance in handling punched cards. The facility for analyzing data would be lost if it were not possible to arrange cards mechanically.

The sorter is one of the simplest of all data processing machines. There are several models of sorters, but a description of one of the most frequently used types will explain how it operates. It sorts on one column at a time, placing each card into one of 13 pockets. Ten of these represent the 10 digits of the decimal system, two represent zone digits that are used in alphabetic codes, and the third, known as the reject pocket, is for cards which have no data in the column being sorted.

The sorter is simple to control. The operator moves a selector on the machine to the column on which he wishes to sort. By sorting one column at a time, moving from right to left, many columns of data can be placed in the desired sequence.

An example of sorter use might be the arranging of a file of transaction records into account number sequence. Cards representing the transactions are sorted on the account number field. The numbers are then in ascending sequence and can be listed and summarized in this order. Grouping items, such as premiums received according to states, can also be done with the sorter so that separate totals for each group can then be added on the tabulator.

Verifier. The function of the verifier is to detect errors in punching. This machine is similar in design to a key punch. The verifier operator repeats the typing operations of the key punch operator on the same cards, but the verifier detects erroneous punches without punching new holes. Once a hole is punched in the card, the hole cannot move or be moved. A correct punch will never become an error and an error will never correct itself. The first protection against error is a good operator, but even the best operator makes occasional errors.

When the verifier operator depresses a different key from the one depressed by the key punch operator who made the card originally, the card stops its automatic movement until the operator determines whether there is an actual error or whether the wrong key on the verifier has been depressed. The card is notched by the verifier machine *on the end* of the card if it is correct. If there is an error or more than one error, the notches are *in the column*(s) which have errors. The correction process entails making a new card, verifying it, and destroying the incorrect one.

Interpreter. This machine reads the data punched in a card and prints this data in one or two lines in any desired sequence along the top edge of the card. Interpreted cards are easier to handle in procedures where they must be selected manually, since the operators can read them easily. A specialized *interpreter* is available which can print on any part of the card. It can be used to write checks on punched card forms.

A typical use for interpreted cards is found in a premium collection process where a prepunched card is selected by a cashier from a pending file and used to prepare a journal list.

Reproducer. This machine can reproduce all or any part of an entire file of cards (known as reproducing) or it can automatically punch into all of the cards in a group (known as *gang-punching*) information which is common to that group.

An application of this machine is in premium notice preparation prior to the due date. The proper premium billing cards are selected from the master file. These cards are then partially reproduced into blank cards which become a pending transaction file. The due date of the premium is then gang-punched into each card. Cards are selected from the file as each premium is paid. Each day the date paid is gang-punched into the appropriate transaction cards which are then used in journal preparation. Most reproducers can also be used as summary punches.

Summary Punch. A summary punch machine is connected to the tabulator by cable and automatically punches into new cards totals which have been accumulated in the tabulator for a particular group of cards or classification of data, along with classification codes. This is accomplished as the tabulator is listing or tabulating so that the process eliminates keypunching of summary cards and the human errors which might result from such manual keypunching.

One application is general ledger preparation. Transaction cards might be listed each day in account order and a summary card punched. At the end of the month, the daily balance summary cards are combined with cards containing the beginning account balances. These are listed and summary-punched to obtain cards containing new account balances. From these an updated trial balance is prepared by machine. This machine process is also useful for accumulating statistical summaries of transactions, such as premiums paid by state.

Collator. This machine can merge two separate files of cards which are in a particular sequence (alphabetical or numerical) into one deck in the same sequence. This machine can also select from a file all cards which contain certain common information, such as all business in a particular state or all business written by a particular agent. It also can compare two files of cards to ascertain that there are matching cards in each, or select those that do or do not match. It can also be used to sequence-check a file of cards to prove they are in consecutive order. This machine is much faster than a sorter for selecting cards or merging two files in the same sequence. The sequence-checking feature is very useful in insuring the correct sequencing of a long list being prepared from cards.

One application of the collator is to use transaction cards to select name and address cards for use in addressing premium notices. The collator can then merge the name and address cards with the proper premium transaction card, and after the notices are run, it can separate the name and address cards from the due cards, and, finally, merge the address cards back into the original address file in the original sequence.

Calculator. A unit record calculator can perform addition, subtraction, multiplication, and division on data in cards and automatically punch the answers into the original or the following card. Common uses are in payroll and commission applications. It can also be used to crossfoot a single card to prove that several parts equal the whole.

Mark Reading Machine. These machines read marks which have been placed in precise positions on paper or cards. When the marks are made with a high graphite content pencil, data can be automatically punched into cards by electrical contact with those marks. A somewhat similar machine can read *normal* pencil markings and punch data into cards on the basis of light recognition. These machines are useful for preparing data which may change data already in machine records. One example is the making of changes in premium amounts and modes of payment. The amount and code for the mode of the new premium are marked on a blank card or on a card that has been partially punched. This machine then automatically punches the new data. This card and the old master record are processed to prepare a new updated master record. Cards of this type also can be marked to show the number of premiums paid and fed into either unit record equipment or a computer to update the payment record. Other than to visually verify the accuracy of the payment, manual intervention is not necessary.

COMPUTERS

The modern computer is the result of using modern electronic knowledge to improve unit record equipment. Computers have not caused the older form of data processing equipment to become obsolete because the cost of operating computers is generally much greater.

The first computers used in the life insurance industry were large calculating or computing machines. The input and output capability was limited. Models were later developed which were capable of processing large volumes of input and output, but these were not economically practical for smaller companies. Recently, computer models have been introduced to handle moderate volumes of data at costs that compare favorably with the cost of unit record equipment.

The phrase *computer system* more aptly describes any particular set of electronic data processing machines than does the single word, *computer*. This is so because several machines are required to make the simplest computation or prepare the simplest form of report and because the configuration of equipment varies from one system to another. No one machine can function independently, but a system may consist of as few as two machines or as many as 20, 30, or more.

Many consecutive operations can be performed automatically by computers in one continuous process, whereas many separate machine operations are required on unit record equipment. The accuracy, speed, and ability of computers to calculate and to use and reuse previously recorded data in later transactions provide the basis for revised accounting systems which result in substantial savings in clerical costs.

Important physical characteristics of computers which are not inherent in a system which utilizes unit record equipment are (1) capacity to store internally large volumes of data, (2) instantaneous manipulation of data by electronic means, and (3) central and coordinated program control of machines. These characteristics result in the following primary advantages over unit record equipment: (1) ability to process records which are much longer than the 80 or 90 columns of space available on a punched card, (2) greater accuracy because of checks which can be performed on the data processed by a computer, (3) faster production of reports which may contain more analytical data than those produced by punched card systems, and (4) ability to handle more intricate processing instructions.

Although computers are referred to as electronic data processing equipment, they are not completely electronic as the title might indicate. There are many electromechanical devices used to supplement computers. The paper feed, for example, and printing mechanisms which produce finished reports, are electromechanical. The central processor, however, is completely electronic, which means that all calculating, comparing, adding, subtracting, and other data manipulation is done with electricity and magnetism. Calculating speeds of computers are measured in millionths of a second (microseconds) and in billionths of a second (nanoseconds). Generally, larger computers process data faster than do smaller ones.

The *central processor* is the main unit of a computer. It has two principal functions, one of which is to *store in memory* data and instructions (which tell the processor and attached equipment what to do and when to do it). The second function of the central processor is to perform various arithmetical functions. The processor adds, subtracts, multiplies, divides, and compares at extremely high rates of speed. The combination of storage and comparing capabilities in the central processor make it possible to sort records rapidly into any desired order and to compare new data with standard data in order to determine its accuracy or validity.

The capacity of memory to store data is measured in thousands of characters with the letter k usually representing 1,000. For example, a 65k memory will store 65,000 characters or a 250k memory 250,000 characters. Additional storage capacity may be available in mass storage devices which supplement the main memory unit. Capacity of memory may also be measured in *bytes* or *words*.

Control of electronic equipment is achieved by the program which is internally stored in the memory of the central processor. A program is a set of instructions used to direct operation of the central processor. A computer can do only what it is specifically instructed to do.

Programs must be in *machine language*, that is, in coding which a machine can read and process in order to be usable in computer systems. Programs are usually written initially in a condensed special form known as *programer language*. This special language is translated by the computer into machine language by use of special translator programs. A very simple program might first be described somewhat as follows:

1. Read a punched card into memory area A.
2. Compare data in memory area A with data in area B.

3. Is data in A equal to or greater than data in B? If yes, add A to data in area C.
4. If A is less than B, subtract A from B and add the difference to data in area D.
5. Print data from area A and area B.
6. Read next card and repeat the above process.

Each step of the sample program just given would in practice be coded so that only a relatively few characters or symbols would be needed to describe each step.

The various machines in an electronic data processing installation remain connected to the central processor since each unit is largely dependent on the central processor for instructions. The printer, for example, will not print or roll the paper to the next line until the processor instructs it to do so.

Frequently two computers of different sizes are used together. The larger one would normally process magnetic tapes much faster than the smaller one and have a larger memory, permitting it to handle larger amounts of data. It is used, therefore, for processing data on magnetic tapes; and the smaller computer is used to print the desired report. The smaller computer is then said to be operating off line, even though the smaller computer has its own central processor.

The *printer* is an important part of every modern business computer. It receives data from the central processor and prints finished reports on continuous forms or sheets of paper at a speed that can with some models exceed 1,000 lines per minute. Unlike a tabulator, a printer cannot calculate. It is completely dependent on the central processor, even when no computations are being performed.

Magnetic tapes are processed by machines known as *tape drives*. Tape drives read data from the magnetic tape and transmit it to the central processor. The central processor, through a program, instructs the tape drive in such matters as when to read another record into the processor, when to stop, and when to record revised information onto another tape. In many applications which use magnetic tapes for input, one or more tape drives read data while one or more other drives concurrently record revised or extracted data. A single tape drive might be used if a report is being printed and no other processing is required.

A *console* is usually attached to the central processor and is used to enable operators to communicate with and control the computer. Although the principal method of controlling a computer is through a program stored in the central processor, there are conditions under which operator control is required or desirable. The console is the unit "with all the buttons and flashing lights." Some consoles are equipped with a typewriter keyboard with which the operator can insert special instructions, such as date of the report, or with which he can make *inquiries* into the computer.

If the computer stops due to invalid data or an error in a program, the operator can cause a record or a part of the program in the machine to print out on a character-at-a-time basis instead of a line-at-a-time as in the case of a printer. This permits the making of corrections without changing forms on the printer or otherwise interrupting a job in process. Among computers, the capability of consoles varies so that some provide a greater degree of operator control than others.

A *remote inquiry station* is a machine which provides contact with a computer located elsewhere. Such a device may be located in a different room or even in a different city. A remote inquiry station may be similar in appearance and operation to a console typewriter or it may resemble a television set. The latter type is also known as a *visual display terminal*. Some remote inquiry stations can be used to change data in a record and to cause the computer to make calculations, such as determining a policy cash value. In the insurance industry these stations may be used by branch offices in communication with the home office to request and report policy status.

Figure 7–2

A B C D O P 1 2 3 4 0

An *optical scanner* or *optical character reader* is a machine which reads data that has been printed in letters or numbers having a standard size and configuration. Such a machine can convert data into machine language thereby avoiding manual key punching. A special style of type is used to prevent confusion between the letter "O" and the zero digit, and between the letter "I" and the number "1." See Figure 7–2. Computer printers can be equipped with this type style so that output documents prepared on the printer can later be used as input.

The capability of a scanner to read documents is particularly useful in connection with premium notices. The notices can be prepared on the printer and mailed to the policyowner. When the notice is returned with the premium payment, it can be used as input to prepare a journal entry and signal the computer to calculate a commission for the agent.

The principal advantage of an *optical scanner* is its ability to accept, as input, forms which are completely legible to the general public. For the company, this capability eliminates the need for punching cards to serve as input and the cost of pulling prepunched cards from a pending file for use as computer input. For the policyowner, this capability eliminates the annoyance of punched cards which are sometimes used as notices and returned to the company for use as input. (Policyowners are requested not to fold, mutilate, or spindle cards.)

The principal disadvantage of an optical scanner is its high cost. A very large volume of documents must be processed to justify this cost.

Mass Storage Devices

Data stored on magnetic tape or punched cards is available only during periods when the records are being processed. Only one record can be processed at a time, and for efficient handling, all records must be processed in the same sequence as they are stored in file. If status of a policy or other record is needed immediately, it is necessary to examine lists which have been printed periodically by the computer. This method is much too slow and tedious to be practical in any but emergency situations. Many insurance companies find delays of this type objectionable, especially when policyowners call for the information by phone. This kind of delay can be avoided by computer systems that use mass storage devices.

Most medium-sized and large computers are equipped with mass storage devices which remain on line at all times. Millions and even billions of characters of data can be stored in this manner. Mass storage devices are also referred to by such terms as *direct access devices* and *random access devices*. Storage media in this category include data cells, drums, and disc packs. The mass storage devices of each manufacturer differ slightly, but the methods of storing and retrieving data are similar.

Data may be selected from any portion of the file *at random* without processing the entire file. This is true regardless of file sequence. In other words, the operator has *direct* and almost immediate *access* to each of the records stored on the device.

One advanced phase of direct access processing is known as *real time* capability. This term describes the ability of a computer to process immediately, in the order received, inquiries or instructions from remote inquiry stations. Usually this is done while the computer is processing magnetic tapes in connection with an unrelated program. The latter process may be delayed slightly while the inquiries are processed, but the machine operates so fast that usually the delay is not noticeable.

A typical use of real-time computers in the life insurance industry is to supply immediate policy status or loan values to branch offices; or making record changes, such as an address change, in branch offices. These branches must be equipped with remote inquiry stations. Airlines use this type of equipment for handling flight reservations and cancellations.

Most mass storage devices use either plastic cards coated with a material that can be magnetized or revolving discs similar in appearance to phonograph records. Data stored on these media can be changed or retrieved and printed out in a fraction of a second.

Devices which use plastic cards select the required card from a magazine, pass it over a reading head, and print out the data on a special typewriter or show it on a visual display terminal. The card is then automatically refiled. The disc type machine has arms which travel over the rapidly revolving discs and select the data desired for "reading."

Some computers are equipped so that the direct access storage media such as discs can be removed and stored off line. This type of equipment provides some of the advantages of mass storage at less cost than equipment with real-time capability.

Mass-storage devices are usually used in addition to magnetic tape drives because they provide several special advantages such as the ability to—

1. Put data into or extract data from a file on a random basis rather than accumulate transactions into batches. Batched work is necessary for the efficient processing of files stored on magnetic tape. Typical uses for this ability are random-posting of ledger accounts and instantly answering requests for policy status.

2. Store large amounts of reference data which can be quickly accessed and used by a program. An illustration of such mass storage is the storing of premium rate tables which can then be used by the computer to instantly determine the correct premium for new policies that are being issued. Another illustration is the storage of tables of height and weight information which can be used by the machine in making comparisons in simplified underwriting of life insurance applications. The machine compares data given on the application to tables of maximum heights and weights for standard insurance, minimum amounts of insurance, minimum premium acceptable, and other factors. Tape drives may be used for this purpose, but only at infrequent intervals such as once per day.

3. Store supplemental programs that can be quickly transferred to the computer's main memory unit whenever required. This capability permits use of a greater portion of the memory for data and less for program storage.

Limitations of mass storage devices when compared to tape processing are (1) a slower speed when processing data serially and (2) a higher cost per character of data stored. However, with new developments, the cost is being reduced and speed increased so that it is probable that in the near future, most computers in insurance companies will have real-time capabilities.

QUESTIONS

1. What three accounting functions are handled simultaneously by a conventional bookkeeping machine? What does a proof balance verify? How can an operator prove that new balances on ledger cards are

correct? How is the amount determined that is posted to ledger accounts, such as a salary expense account?

2. What type of control device is used on a unit record machine? What is the data storing capability of a tabulator? What is the function of reproducers, summary punches, collators, and calculators?

3. Describe a key-punching process. To what extent can a key punch be used to reproduce cards? What features help the operator obtain accuracy and punch data in the correct columns? How is the verifier used to detect errors? What is the function of an interpreter? Of a mark reading machine?

4. Describe the sorting process as done by unit record equipment. Why is this process an important step in preparing a report?

5. What processing advantages do computers have over unit record equipment? What physical characteristics produce these advantages? What are the functions of the central processor? How is a computer controlled?

6. What is the difference between machine language and program language? How is each used? What is meant by real time? What special devices are required in connection with a real-time computer?

7. Briefly describe the function of each of the following electronic data processing machines: printer, tape drive, console, remote inquiry station, optical scanner, card reader-punch, mass storage devices.

Chapter 8

Introduction to Life Insurance Accounting

COMMERCIAL VERSUS LIFE INSURANCE ACCOUNTING

Basic accounting principles apply to companies of all types. However, the nature of the product and special reporting requirements of the particular industry determine to a great extent the accounting practices adopted. This is particularly true of the life insurance industry where accounting practices in some respects are different from those of other industries. To facilitate discussion of these differences, the expression *life accounting* is used here as a general term to mean accounting as practiced within the life insurance industry. *Commercial accounting* is used to mean accounting as practiced outside the industry.

Life companies use double-entry bookkeeping in journalizing financial transactions as they occur and in posting them from journals to ledger accounts. In fact, the fundamental principles of commercial accounting are used generally in life accounting. The differences exist primarily in methods used for recording liabilities and in the procedure used at the end of the calendar year for preparing financial statements.

It is important to understand why and where these differences exist before studying life accounting practices in detail. To avoid confusion, students who have studied commercial accounting or who have prepared adjusting and closing entries or financial statements in other than life insurance accounting should especially note these differences and the reasons for them.

Life accounting practices are standardized to a considerable extent by Annual Statement forms required by regulatory authorities, but account-

135

ing practices still may vary among companies. This is so because (1) some accountants have brought into the industry many practices that are closer to those commonly used in commercial accounting and (2) the needs for financial data in one company may be considerably different from those of another company. The type of mechanical equipment used is also a contributing factor.

In this book a near-standard method of insurance accounting as practiced in the United States and Canada is presented. There are some differences in the methods used in the two countries, primarily because of differences in Annual Statement requirements.

Why Is Life Accounting Different?

The special characteristics of life accounting may be traced to two principal sources: (1) the nature of the life insurance business and (2) government regulation. To a considerable degree the two sources are interrelated.

The nature of the life insurance business might be described as the acceptance of mortality risks on a long-term basis. The typical life company also accepts disability, annuity, and other long-term risks which have many of the same characteristics as mortality risks from an accounting standpoint.

Life insurance companies must guarantee premium rates for the entire insurance period even though the cost of insuring the risk may increase with the passing of time. To accomplish this, amounts must be set aside each year from premiums received on long-term risk business to assure the company's ability to pay claims in later years when claim costs may exceed premiums received. These amounts are liabilities and are known as *policy reserves.*

Policy reserves continuously change with the passing of time. It is the practice to determine policy reserve amounts and many other insurance liabilities only when a financial statement is being prepared and to record the amounts directly on the statement without recording them in the books. Since these liabilities are not carried on the books, they are commonly referred to as nonledger liabilities.

A reason for governmental regulation is that mortality risks cannot be measured exactly, especially on a long-term basis. There is a need to safeguard public interest by ascertaining that amounts set aside will be adequate to meet future obligations. Most states have laws which prescribe valuation standards for measuring the extent of these obligations and which regulate investments. Careful measurement of liabilities is of little help if the assets have been dissipated.

Annual Statement forms have been adopted to provide information to regulatory authorities in a uniform manner. These authorities must determine whether a company is being managed in the interests of policyowners and whether a company is legally solvent (able to meet current and future obligations). The Annual Statement also provides information for the company's federal income tax returns, and a copy is filed with the tax return.

Information similar in form to that included in a company's Annual Statement is reported each year to the board of directors of the company. Most companies also publish condensed data from the Annual Statement, in a form called the *Annual Report,* for stockholders, policyowners, and the public.

If we know the final objectives to be attained, the methods used to attain them are easier to understand. It is useful, therefore, to study the nature of the Annual Statement before examining the accounting details and methods used to produce this complex document.

ANNUAL STATEMENT FORMS

Government authorities determine the exact Annual Statement form to be used, although the needs of management undoubtedly affect its design. Accounting practices are developed in each company to facilitate completion of this statement as well as to meet the special internal needs of management.

Taken as a whole, the life insurance Annual Statement contains a mass of data extracted from the company's accounting and statistical records. The Annual Statement includes a balance sheet, a statement of income and expense, a surplus statement, and many supporting exhibits, schedules, and supplemental questionnaires and reports.

The Annual Statement forms required in the United States and Canada are very similar in structure. These forms, therefore, are presented together in this chapter.

Each company must file a copy of its Annual Statement shortly after the end of each year with regulatory authorities in the states or provinces in which the company is licensed to do business. Companies licensed in both the United States and Canada must file separate forms in each country.

In the United States, state regulation of the insurance business as far as accounting is concerned is reflected in the official Annual Statement form prescribed by the National Association of Insurance Commissioners (NAIC). The *basic* format of the Annual Statement has remained unchanged since 1951, although some changes have been made each year since.

Whenever the terms *Annual Statement, U.S. Annual Statement,* or *the Statement* are used in this book, they refer to the official NAIC form. Other terms are also used by insurance company officials in referring to it, including the *Association Annual Statement* (from the National Association of Insurance Commissioners), the *Convention Blank*, and the *Blue Statement* (from the traditional color of its cover).

There are a number of Annual Statement forms required of life insurance companies licensed in Canada. Most Canadian companies are registered under the Canadian and British Insurance Companies Act and are required to file an annual statement in a form prescribed by the Department of Insurance of the Dominion of Canada. These companies also file a simpler form with the insurance departments in provinces in which they are licensed. A company licensed only within its home province files a form similar to the federal form, but with the Insurance Department of its home province.

A British, United States, or other foreign company operating in Canada must file an Annual Statement form which covers only its Canadian business.

Life companies which sell health insurance in Canada are also required to file a casualty insurance company form[1] relating to this portion of their business.

Many Canadian companies are licensed to do business in one or more states of the United States. They are required to use the official NAIC form and to file Annual Statements with each of the states in which they are licensed.

Whenever the *Canadian Annual Statement* is mentioned in this book, the reference is to the life form prescribed by the Department of Insurance of the Dominion of Canada for use by Canadian companies registered under the Canadian and British Insurance Companies Act and identified as Form Ins. 54.

ACCOUNTING DIFFERENCES

Two of the basic facts of life accounting which distinguish it from commercial accounting are (1) normally, accounting entries are not made until cash transactions take place, and (2) assets are valued on a more conservative basis than that normally used in commercial accounting.

These unusual features of life accounting will be more completely discussed under the headings of (1) Why Cash Basis Accounting? (2) Nonledger Assets and Nonledger Liabilities, (3) Admitted and Nonadmitted Assets, and (4) Balance Account.

First, however, it is necessary to define terms that are useful in discussing the various phases of life insurance accounting.

The statement of income and expense in a life insurance company will be referred to in general as the *operating statement*. In the U.S. Annual

---

[1] Reference herein to a Canadian casualty form applies to Form INS-53 entitled Annual Statement Required from Canadian Companies Registered or Licensed to Transact the Business of Insurance Other than Life Insurance in Canada.

Statement blank, the operating statement is known as the *summary of operations* and will hereafter be referred to by that title. The equivalent statement in the Canadian Annual Statement blank is called the *revenue account*.

A distinction is made in the remainder of this book between insurance *costs* and *expenses*. *Insurance costs* will be used in a broad sense to describe all deductions from income (including expenses) to obtain net income, which is called *net gain from operations* in the *summary of operations*. (See line 33, page 4, in the blank.) The net income of the revenue account of the Canadian Annual Statement is called the *balance*. *Expense* will be used in a limited sense to describe controllable costs such as salaries, rent, printing, etc. Claim payments and increases in policy reserves are examples of insurance costs other than expenses. The distinction will become more apparent in later chapters.

The statement of surplus will be referred to by that title, or as the *surplus* statement when it is discussed in a general sense. The term used in the U.S. Statement blank is *surplus account*. The equivalent Canadian statement is called the *reconciliation of surplus*.

It is assumed that the reader is familiar with commonly used insurance terms. A glossary is included at the end of this book, however, for the benefit of those who desire a specific definition of an important insurance or accounting term.

Account titles must be adequately descriptive of items posted in the accounts. These titles generally follow Annual Statement terminology but may vary considerably from company to company. "Single Premiums to Purchase Paid-Up Additions," for example, would be equally descriptive if phrased in any one of the following ways:

Premiums, Single, PUA
Premiums, Single, Nontaxable
Single Premiums to Purchase Insurance Options

A chart of accounts is included in the Appendix to show a general classification of accounts in U.S. Annual Statement sequence. However, these account titles are not used in this book when other word arrangements seem more appropriate. For example, "Single Premiums" is used rather than "Premiums, Single." Abbreviations have been avoided except when account titles would otherwise be quite long, such as "Considerations for Supplementary Contracts Without Life Contingencies." In a typical company, account titles are shortened as much as possible while still providing an adequate description.

Why Cash Basis Accounting?

In commercial accounting an entry is made when income becomes receivable, as in the case of a sale on credit, and when expense becomes payable, as in the case of merchandise purchased on credit. In contrast, almost without exception, life insurance companies make a bookkeeping entry only when a cash transaction occurs.

Most life insurance companies maintain their ledgers on a cash basis, but prepare financial statements on an accrual basis. This is done by entering adjustments from the cash to the accrual basis on working papers, but not in the accounts of the general ledger. This method is referred to as cash basis accounting, but is actually a modification of the cash basis. In true cash basis accounting, financial statements are not prepared on the accrual basis.

This form of cash basis accounting is less detailed than complete accrual or revenue basis accounting if financial statements are prepared only once each year. It is less efficient when more frequent statements are desired. Most commercial enterprises use the accrual basis and there is a developing trend in life insurance companies toward its use. Three principal reasons why many life insurance companies prefer the cash basis are:

1. *A life insurance company does business on a cash basis.* In general it does not buy or sell on credit. The company is a financial institution with funds to invest and it is easy to retain sufficient funds on hand to pay amounts owed promptly.

Insurance premiums are payable in cash, and credit is not extended to policyowners, except by specific agreement. The policyowner has the option to pay but has no legal liability to do so. It is *not correct*, therefore, to record a premium as income at the time it becomes due. It is also *simpler* to record premium income when it is actually received.

Investment income is legally collectible and usually has been earned when the due date arrives. Recording it as income at that time is justified. Premium income, however, is the more important type of income, both as to amount received and volume of transactions. The accounting process is based, therefore, on the conditions which surround the collection and recording of premium income. As a result, entries are usually made only when money is received.

2. *Certain exhibits in the U.S. Annual Statement require showing cash basis account balances.* Most income and expense account balances are entered on a cash basis in the exhibits of the U.S. Annual Statement. The exhibit totals are then adjusted to produce accrual basis figures. Cash basis figures must also be shown in a special asset exhibit and in an exhibit entitled "Reconciliation of Ledger Assets." This latter exhibit shows cash basis income, costs, and other items which change surplus. The preparation of each of these exhibits is simplified if the ledger account balances show cash basis figures.

In the Canadian Statement, account balances are initially entered to the various exhibits on an accrual (revenue) basis. The totals of the exhibits are then entered in either the *balance sheet* or *revenue account*, whichever is appropriate. Cash basis figures are not shown, with the result that a Canadian company writing business only in Canada might make adjustments in its ledger as well as on working papers without complicating the preparation of the Canadian Statement forms.

The Canadian Statement does not include a *reconciliation of ledger assets,* the exhibit of the U.S. Annual Statement which more or less forces the use of cash basis accounting in U.S. companies.

3. *Use of cash basis ledgers speeds closing of the books at the end of the year and reopening them for the new year.*

In a commercial concern it may be necessary to value merchandise or raw material on hand at the end of the accounting period, but this usually only requires a few days. Assets and liabilities are entered on the ledger because they are usually fixed in amount and the amounts do not change unless a cash transaction takes place. For example, when merchandise is purchased on credit, a liability of a fixed amount is created. When a payment is made, the liability is reduced by the exact amount of the payment. To determine the total liability, it is necessary only to examine the account balance. The trial balance is usually prepared within a few days after the end of the period, and statements are prepared shortly thereafter.

In a life insurance company, the process is more time consuming. Policy reserves, the most significant liability classification in a life insurance company, are not fixed in amount but are constantly changing.

Policy reserves are valued by a process similar to that used for valuing the inventory of merchandise or raw materials on hand in a commercial concern. An inventory process may be thought of as the counting and valuing of a group of items. This process may be applied to the valuing of liabilities as well as assets.

A number of methods are used for valuing policy reserves, but each is very detailed and time consuming. The reserve of a policy varies according to the face amount of insurance, plan of insurance, age of insured, and years the policy has been in force. Under one system for calculating policy reserves, amounts of insurance are summarized and multiplied by a factor for each plan, year, and age to determine the total reserve for a group of policies. However, the number of calculations required to value a 10-year plan of insurance might be as many as 600 (10 years × 60 ages). The values are also different for each mortality table and interest rate used in calculating premiums.

If reserve liabilities were recorded on the books, the closing of nominal accounts and their reopening for the subsequent accounting period would be delayed. With the advent of computers, the time required to value policy reserves and other policy liabilities has decreased, but several weeks may still be required in a typical life insurance company. In the meantime, accounting processes must continue. Therefore, most companies rely on working papers to prepare financial statements and do not record on the books assets and liabilities which must be inventoried.

The processes a company uses to close its books for the year just ended without fully recording its assets and liabilities are explained in other sections of this chapter.

Nonledger Assets and Nonledger Liabilities

Assets recorded on the books are called *ledger assets*. Most of the assets of a life insurance company are investment holdings such as bonds, stocks, mortgage loans, and real estate. These investments are recorded on the books when cash is disbursed in payment for them.

Assets not entered on the books are called *nonledger assets*. Income due and accrued on investments is an example of this type of asset. It is determined by an inventory process at the end of the year. Asset amounts determined in this manner are not usually entered on the books of a U.S. company. They are incorporated in the balance sheet pages and summary of operations through the use of working papers.

The excess of market value over book value of investments is another form of nonledger asset and will be discussed in the next section of this book in connection with admitted and nonadmitted assets.

Liabilities entered on the books are called *ledger liabilities*. Only certain liabilities are recorded on the books, such as amount deducted from an employee's paycheck for taxes or for a retirement fund. While these types of liabilities are recorded on the ledger, most liabilities are not. Even when a liability of a known and readily determinable amount is created, such as a policy death settlement, an entry is not usually made to record the liability.

Liabilities not entered on the books are called *nonledger* liabilities. Policy reserves are an example. They could be recorded on the books at the end of the accounting period by use of a process similar to that used in commercial accounting for recording inventories, but most U.S. companies do not record these changing liabilities on the books at any time.

The increase in policy reserve liability from one year-end to the next is treated as a *cost of operations*.

The term *nonledger assets* is used in the U.S. Annual Statement, but the term *nonledger liabilities* is not. Neither term is used in the Canadian Annual Statement.

Admitted and Nonadmitted Assets

Assets in a commercial concern are usually valued according to the *going-concern* concept. Briefly, this means that some assets which have little or no market value but have a value for producing future income are shown on the balance sheet at cost even when this may be higher than market value. A magazine publisher's subscription list, for example, may be recognized as having an asset value if money were spent to build it up and if repeat business could be expected from it. Such a list may have only a nominal market value, but it may properly be shown at its depreciated cost. As another example, furniture and equipment might be usable for years. It is, therefore, shown in the financial statement at its depreciated value, which still may be much higher than the amount that could be realized if it were sold to a used-equipment dealer.

The initial cost of each long-term asset is entered on the ledger of a commercial concern and gradually reduced (depreciated) over the years of expected use. Each year the depreciated value, or book value, is shown in the balance sheet as an asset.

Accounting in a commercial firm is concerned primarily with the needs of management and the stockholders and, secondarily, with the needs of creditors. Commercial accounting might be described as *profit-oriented*.

In a life insurance company, the interest of stockholders is secondary to that of policyowners who must have assurance of the solidity of the company. In fact, in a mutual life insurance company there are no stockholders. It follows, therefore, that more conservative methods of valuing assets are desirable. Insurance accounting might be described as *solvency-oriented*.

Life insurance company assets are valued on a modified liquidation-value concept. *Liquidation value* is market value, or if a market value is not readily available, it is an appraised value. If the market value of an asset is uncertain, usually no value is allowed. For example, no value is allowed for furniture and most equipment.

Some assets are valued on an amortized basis which usually is different from market value. Amortized value is obtained by periodically and systematically adjusting on the books the cost of an investment so that it becomes equal to the maturity value on the maturity date. For example, if a bond was purchased for $950 a year ago and it will mature three years from now for $1,000, the amortized value now is $962.50 (the cost plus one fourth of the difference between cost and maturity value). By adding one fourth each year to the book value, the book value will equal the maturity value on the maturity date.

An amount equal to each periodic adjustment in the asset account is either charged or credited to an appropriate income account. In the example, the $12.50 increase in the asset (debit to the asset account) is also credited to an income account. If the book value adjustment had been a decrease in the asset (credit to the asset account), a like amount would have been debited to an income account.

The example just given is simplified to facilitate an understanding of the basic process. A more detailed discussion of the amortization process and related entries is included in a later chapter.

Amortization is a modification of the liquidation concept because, on the maturity date, the amortized value is actually the market value. Prior to that date, the amortized value may be higher or lower than the market value. When the amortized value is higher, amortized value is clearly less conservative than liquidation or market value.

Asset values used in a life insurance balance sheet are referred to as *admitted asset values*. Admitted asset values may be defined as those values which are allowed by law or insurance department ruling to be shown on the Annual Statement balance sheet.

These regulations specify which bonds are eligible for valuation on an amortized basis. The admitted value of other bonds and for stocks is the market value as prescribed by governmental authority. Market values fluctuate from time to time and may vary considerably from book values.

To adjust book values to admitted values, a special asset exhibit is included in the U.S. Annual Statement blank. In this exhibit, book values of each of the major asset classifications are adjusted to the admitted values. (See pages 416 and 417.)

The portion of admitted asset value in excess of book value is described in this exhibit as *nonledger assets* because this portion of the admitted value is not reflected in an asset ledger account. For example, if the book value of a bond not eligible for amortization is $950 and the market value is $980, then the *nonledger* asset value relative to this bond is $30 ($980 − $950).

The portion of book value in excess of admitted value is described as *assets not admitted* or, more simply, *nonadmitted assets*. In the example just cited, if the market value had been $950 and the book value $980, the nonadmitted asset value relative to this bond would have been $30 ($980 − $950), and the admitted asset value would have been $950.

Nonadmitted assets fall into two broad classes: (1) assets of which a portion is admitted and the remainder is nonadmitted and (2) assets of which no portion of the value is admitted.

Most assets in the first class are investments which have a lower admitted value (usually market value) than the current book value, such as the bond just cited which had a market value of $950. Decreases and increases in surplus resulting from these changes in asset values are classified in both the U.S. and Canadian Annual Statements as capital gains and capital losses.

Most assets in the second class are not investments but are assets acquired in carrying out the normal process of doing business. Examples are furniture and equipment, and amounts advanced to agents against future commissions. The value of items of this type would be uncertain if a company became insolvent, so no part of these assets is admitted. The reduction in surplus that results from reducing asset values of this type to zero admitted values is treated as direct changes in surplus in the U.S. Statement (loss on nonadmitted assets), and not as an operating cost.

Ownership of nonadmitted assets is not necessarily a sign of weakness in a company. Many items that might be accepted at their full value in a commercial company are nonadmitted in a life insurance statement. Some, such as amounts advanced to agents, may be fully collectible, but they are nonadmitted primarily because they have no market value and for other reasons which are discussed in later parts of this book.

The use of an asset exhibit for adjusting values from ledger amounts to admitted amounts allows the cost or amortized value to remain on the books. Having this value on the books facilitates calculating gains or losses on the sale of assets and the income tax from these sales. No tax is payable on changes in market value, but only on the difference between sales price and cost. If amortized values are used, the gain is determined on the difference between sales price and amortized value at time of sale.

In the Canadian Annual Statement assets are shown at book value. Book values of these assets are, therefore, the admitted values. If the aggregate book value of stocks and any bonds not eligible for amortization is higher than the aggregate market value of these items as determined by Canadian authorities, it is necessary to either (1) reduce the book value of some items by crediting the appropriate asset account or (2) credit an *Investment Reserve* account in an amount equal to the excess book value. If an *Investment Reserve* account is used, its balance is shown in the balance sheet as a liability.

The offsetting portion of each entry is a debit to an account with a title such as *Stocks Written Down*. The exact account title is worded, of course, to fit the asset classification being adjusted. This account is treated as a change in surplus (capital gain or loss), not as an operating income or cost.

A typical entry to decrease the book value of stocks owned from $1,200 to $1,000 is:

Stocks Written Down.................... 200
    Stocks Owned...   200

The credit portion of the entry could, of course, have been a credit to an *Investment Reserve* account. Entries of this type are discussed more fully in a later chapter.

Since assets are shown in the Canadian balance sheet at book value, there is no need for an asset exhibit similar to that described in connection with the U.S. Annual Statement. Neither are the terms admitted assets, nonadmitted assets, and nonledger assets used. These terms, however, are useful to indicate the nature of certain assets and liabilities and are used frequently in the remainder of this book.

Assets of the type which are totally nonadmitted in the U.S. Annual Statement, such as furniture and equipment and amounts advanced to agents, are not shown in the Canadian Statement as assets. Instead, the cost of these two items are treated as expenses and are reported in the Revenue account.

Balance Account

The use of cash basis accounting results in an unusual ledger account which may be called a *Balance account*. This account might be considered a form of surplus account because nominal accounts may be closed into it at the end of the accounting period. It is not, however, a true surplus account of the type discussed earlier in connection with commercial accounting.

The Balance account might be considered a composite of all nonledger items (including surplus) and all nonadmitted assets. If nonledger and nonadmitted items were recorded on the ledger, this account would reflect a true surplus balance. In its usual form, however, the Balance account is simply a device for keeping the ledger and trial balance in balance at all times.

An example will demonstrate why this Balance account is necessary. Assume the accounting equation $(A = L + C)$ has values of $\$1,000 = \$850 + \$150$. We shall now subdivide the equation so that it covers both ledger and nonledger items. The letter L is used to represent ledger and NL to represent nonledger in each of the three parts. The equation then becomes:

$$LA + NLA = LL + NLL + LC + NLC$$

If values are assigned to each portion, the result might appear as follows:

$$\$850(LA) + \$150(NLA) = \$50(LL) + \$800(NLL) + \$60(LC) + \$90(NLC)$$

If the nonledger items are deleted, the equation becomes:

$$\$850 = \$50 + \$60$$

The equation is no longer in balance. If a ledger Balance account with a credit balance of $\$740$ is added, the equation will be in balance. The effect would have been similar if the equation had been subdivided further to include a nonadmitted asset. The ledger will remain in balance if nominal accounts are closed into the Balance account. The following example demonstrates this.

Assume $\$100$ in premiums is received. The Cash (debit) and Premium Income (credit) balances will each increase by this amount. An $\$85$ claim is then paid. The Cash balance will decrease by $\$85$ (credit), and the Claims account balance will increase by $\$85$ (debit). It is apparent that the asset cash is up by a net amount of $15 ($100 − $85). If we now close the two nominal accounts, Premium Income and Claims into the Balance account, its balance will also increase by $15 ($100 credit − $85 debit). When these transactions are posted to the accounts used in the previous example and the nominal accounts closed into the Balance account the equation becomes:

$$\$865\,(LA) = \$50\,(LL) + \$60\,(LC) + \$755\,(BA)$$

The ledger is still in balance by virtue of the nominal accounts being closed into the Balance account ("BA" in the equation).

Since nonledger items are not included in the typical life insurance company ledger, the trial balance is frequently referred to as an *incomplete trial balance*. It must be remembered, however, that the ledger and the trial balance must have equal debits and credits at all times.

Entries are made to the Balance account only at the end of the year as a part of the closing process. Some companies do not follow the closing process but start the new year with a Balance account that is equal to all ledger assets, less ledger liabilities and less ledger capital. The result is the same, but the closing process is a desirable accounting discipline and prevents overlooking an item.

If a company chose to do so, at the end of each accounting period it might record on the books the items which a typical life company would treat as nonledger items. Under these circumstances, an increase in a liability would be recorded as a cost or as a decrease in Surplus. The journal entry to record an increase in policy reserves would be:

Increase in Policy Reserves....................................50.00
    Policy Reserve Liability.................................   50.00

Conversely a decrease in a liability would be recorded as income or as an increase in Surplus.

An increase in a nonledger asset creates an increase in surplus. Entries are not made for increases in these assets, but an entry shows the effect on surplus clearly. The journal entry to record an increase in admitted value of a bond owned would be:

Bonds Owned...75.00
    Increase in Admitted Assets.............................   75.00

Increases and decreases in nonadmitted assets and nonledger assets are discussed in more detail in a later chapter.

Most Canadian companies record all assets and liabilities on the ledger at the end of the accounting period. If this is done, the nominal accounts showing increases and decreases in assets and liabilities are closed into the Surplus account at the end of the accounting period. The Surplus account would then show the true surplus of the company and a Balance account would not be used.

Other titles used for the Balance account are *Ledger Surplus, General Fund,* and *Net Ledger Assets.*

SUMMARY OF LIFE INSURANCE ACCOUNTING PRINCIPLES

Life insurance companies usually maintain ledger accounts on a cash basis at all times but prepare accrual basis statements.

Assets in a life insurance company are valued under a modified liquidation concept.

The only assets and liabilities recorded on a typical U.S. life insurance company ledger are those which arise from transactions involving cash.

Admitted asset values are those values which are allowed by law or insurance department ruling to be reported on the Annual Statement balance sheet.

Nonadmitted asset value is the excess of book value over admitted values.

There are two types of nonadmitted asset values: (1) book values that are partially nonadmitted (principally investments) and (2) book values that are entirely nonadmitted (assets acquired in carrying out the normal process of doing business).

The *Balance account* is a composite of all nonledger and nonadmitted values. It equals all ledger assets less ledger liabilities and ledger capital.

Amortized value is a book value arrived at by periodically and systematically adjusting the cost of an asset so that it will become equal to the maturity value on the maturity date.

QUESTIONS

1. In what two respects is life insurance accounting significantly different from commercial accounting? What causes these differences?

2. Name five types of financial reports or statements included in a life company's Annual Statement. What organization or organizations prescribe the U.S. Statement form? The Canadian forms? Why do regulatory authorities require these forms?

3. Give three reasons why life insurance companies maintain their ledgers on a strictly cash basis during the accounting period. In what ways would recording all liabilities complicate the accounting process?

4. Define ledger assets, nonledger assets, ledger liabilities, and nonledger liabilities. What principal characteristic of an asset or liability causes it to be treated as a ledger or as a nonledger item? What is done in a Canadian company if the aggregate market value of bonds and of stocks is higher than their respective aggregate book values?

5. In what respects do asset values under a *going-concern* concept differ from values under a *modified liquidation* concept? In what direction is each of these concepts-oriented? Give four types of assets that are

valued differently for balance sheet purposes under the modified liquidation concept and under the going-concern concept.

6. Define amortized value and depreciated value. What is the relationship of each to book value?

7. What are the two broad classes of nonadmitted assets found in the U.S. Annual Statement? Is a well-managed company likely to have some of each class? Why, or why not?

8. Why is a Balance account included in a typical life insurance company ledger? It is a composite of what type of balance sheet items? Why is it sometimes called ledger surplus? What is meant by an incomplete trial balance?

Chapter 9

Composition of the Annual Statement

It is important to understand how the various phases of insurance accounting fit together to provide a complete picture of a company's financial condition and an analysis of its past operations. To accomplish this, a general survey of insurance company financial statements is presented in this chapter. This chapter will also serve as a basic reference point for each of the specialized phases of insurance accounting which follow.

Brief discussions of the principal items on the balance sheet pages and the summary of operations are presented. The chapter also includes a comprehensive discussion of policy reserves, which are the most important liability items in a life insurance company balance sheet. Except for reserves, all of these items are considered in greater detail in later chapters. At this point, it is most important to observe how the value of a particular kind of asset or liability in the balance sheet affects surplus and how a particular type of transaction affects operating gains.

BALANCE SHEET

The purpose of the life insurance balance sheet is to show the degree of solvency of a company, that is, the amount of assets available to meet contingencies and all known liabilities. All assets and liabilities must be properly valued to measure solvency. The amount of assets available in excess of liabilities is the capital of the company, which is represented by the capital stock and surplus items shown on the balance sheet.

Assets always exceed liabilities plus capital stock unless the company is insolvent, a condition which rarely occurs. A commercial concern may continue to operate when it has a deficit. If such a condition exists in a life insurance company, its operation is taken over by regulatory authorities who act to protect the interests of policyowners.

The balance sheets in U.S. and Canadian Annual Statements are not labeled as such. In both Annual Statement forms, the first page that contains financial data is simply labeled *assets*. The next page in the U.S. Statement is labeled *liabilities, surplus and other funds*, and in the Canadian statement, *liabilities, capital and surplus*. All figures are shown on an accrual basis.

Asset Classifications and Schedules

Assets may be classified as:

1. Investments
2. Cash
3. Deferred, due, and accrued income
4. Miscellaneous

Investments are those assets which produce income in the form of interest, rent, and dividends. Most of this income is required to maintain policy reserves, which are increased each year by an interest rate specified in the policies. A wise investment policy should produce a maximum income with a minimum of risk.

Accounting for investments and income from them will be covered in the next chapter. At this point, it is useful to examine values used in the balance sheet presentation and to examine the effect of these values on the surplus of the company.

The major portion of a life insurance company's investment portfolio consists of bonds, mortgages, and other investments which promise payment of *fixed* amounts on specified dates. Investments of this type are desirable because claim settlements on life insurance policies are payable in *fixed* amounts of money. These investments are usually shown at book value in annual statements.

A small percentage of insurance company funds is invested in assets that are subject to market fluctuation such as corporate stock and real estate. Corporate stock usually produces a satisfactory rate of return, but most stock must be shown in the balance sheet of the U.S. Annual Statement at market value, which changes frequently. If the market value of a stock decreases or increases, the company's surplus decreases or increases by an equal amount.[1] Real estate is less subject to fluctuation in market value than stock, but much of the principal may be lost through depreciation or changing neighborhood conditions. Because of the haz-

---

[1] A method to limit the effect of this fluctuation through a special surplus classification is presented in the next chapter.

ards involved, the amount of investment in corporate stocks and real estate by a life insurance company is limited by law.

Bonds that are fully secured and not in default are usually valued for annual statement purposes at amortized values,[2] which are also current book values. Bonds not eligible for amortization, and common stocks, are valued at market prices on the statement date. In the United States, market values for use in Annual Statement preparation are prescribed by the National Association of Insurance Commissioners.[3]

Mortgage loans are admitted at book value unless the mortgage is delinquent as to interest and principal payments. Policy loans are admitted in the balance sheet at book value unless the amount of a particular loan exceeds the cash surrender value of the policy; this is rare, but it could occur because of error.

Real estate is normally admitted at its depreciated book value if this value is not greater than market value as determined by competent appraisers. It is not customary to increase book value of real estate or to claim an asset value on real estate in excess of the book value even though the appraised value may be higher.

Schedules on which bond, stock, mortgage, and real estate investment holdings are listed are included in the Annual Statement. These schedules show various values, changes in book values, and income received during the year. One schedule shows mortgages summarized by type of security, type of mortgage, and by state or province.

When cash is on deposit at interest in a bank, it is in reality an invested asset, but it is included with cash and other bank deposits in the balance sheet. A schedule in the U.S. Annual Statement blank shows balances in each bank at the end of each month, and the amount of interest received during the year on time deposits.

Deferred, due and accrued income consists of (1) investment income due and accrued and (2) deferred and uncollected premiums on policies in force. This second classification will be referred to as *premium assets* for convenience.

Investment income due and *investment income accrued* are assets and are normally admitted at full value in the balance sheet.

Deferred and *uncollected* premiums appear on the balance sheet. The

---

[2] Canadian companies registered with the Federal Department of Insurance may amortize only redeemable securities, not in default, issued or guaranteed by the government of Canada, the United Kingdom, or the United States. All others are valued at market as determined by the Federal Department of Insurance.

[3] In Canada, the market values used by companies registered by the Federal Department of Insurance are taken from a List of Securities prepared each year by the Federal Department. The list used by provincially incorporated companies that are not federally registered is prepared by the Standing Committee on Valuation of Securities of the Association of Superintendents of Insurance of the Provinces of Canada.

distinction between them is found in the relationship between the due date of a premium and the end of the calendar year.

Uncollected premiums are premiums which became due on or before December 31 but which had not been received on that date. These are also referred to as due premiums and outstanding premiums. *Deferred* premiums are those which will become due after December 31 but prior to the next anniversary of the policy. The following example illustrates the difference between uncollected and deferred premiums. Assume that a policy has an anniversary date of July 28, and monthly premiums are $10 each. On December 31, premiums had been paid through the October 28 installment. The gross uncollected premiums are $20 (November and December premiums at $10 each). The gross deferred premiums are $60 (January through June premiums in the subsequent year). Deferred and uncollected premiums are admitted at their *net premium* values on the U.S. balance sheet.

A *net premium* value is gross premium less the expense loading included in the premium. For example, if the expense loading is 20 percent of the gross premium, the net premium is 80 percent of the gross premium. Thus the net due premium value in the example is $16 ($20 gross due × 80 percent) and the net deferred premium value is $48 ($60 × 80 percent). The net deferred and uncollected premiums on the policy are $64 ($16 + 48). This is also the admitted asset value.

Health insurance[4] premiums due are admitted assets on a gross premium basis.

In the U.S. Statement, all income due and accrued is handled as a nonledger asset but a Canadian company might enter this income on the ledger at the end of the accounting period.

Miscellaneous assets, of course, includes all other assets. Most of these are nonadmitted.

Liability Classifications

The fact that most life insurance liabilities are nonledger items was mentioned earlier. Most of these liabilities relate to policies now in force, or which have terminated with a remaining liability, as in the case of death claims incurred but unpaid or settlement amounts left on deposit with the company. A small percentage of nonledger liabilities represent unpaid administrative costs.

Liabilities may be classified as follows:

---

[4] In this book the simple term *health insurance* is used to describe the class of business referred to in the U.S. Annual Statement as *accident and health insurance*. *Health insurance* is simpler and has been accepted by an industry-wide committee on terminology as adequate and as appropriately descriptive for various other terms used in the insurance business which include *accident and sickness, disability*, and *sickness*.

1. Policy reserves
2. Amounts held on deposit for policyowners and beneficiaries
3. Claims incurred but not yet paid
4. Dividends (to policyowners or stockholders) which have been allocated but are not yet payable
5. Accrued expenses
6. Unearned income
7. Amounts temporarily held for disposition
8. Miscellaneous liabilities
9. Special reserves which are considered as liabilities

Items 3 through 8 in this listing relate to income that will be earned and costs that will be paid in the following year or years. Income and cost-related liabilities are discussed very briefly at this time, with more complete discussion in later chapters. Policy reserves, however, are not discussed at a later point, so it is appropriate to closely examine this important liability.

Policy Reserves

The valuation of policy reserves in a life insurance company is done by actuaries rather than by insurance accountants. These reserves, therefore, are often called actuarial reserves.[5] Because of the importance of these reserves in the balance sheet, the student should have a general understanding of the valuation processes used. The reserve liability of a life insurance company is determined as of December 31 each year for Annual Statement purposes. Since policies are issued throughout the calendar year, it is convenient and reasonably accurate to assume that all policies are issued as of the middle of the calendar year, that is, June 30. Therefore, when the reserve liability is determined as of December 31, each policy may then be considered as having been in force, ½, 1½, 2½, etc., years, depending upon the calendar year in which the policy was issued. Thus, the reserve liability as of December 31 for each policy may be approximated by taking the average of the reserve at the beginning of the policy year (the initial reserve)[6] and the reserve at the end of the policy year (the terminal reserve). This average is known as the *mean reserve* and is expressed in the equation

$$\text{Mean Reserve} = \frac{(\text{Initial Reserve}) + (\text{Terminal Reserve})}{2}$$

The total reported for policy reserve liability in the Annual Statement is arrived at on the assumption that all premiums are paid annually and

---

[5] Policy reserves are referred to as actuarial reserves in the Canadian Statement.

[6] An initial reserve is the terminal reserve of the preceding year plus an annual net premium.

have been received by the company. However, many policy premiums are paid on a monthly, quarterly, or semiannual basis so that on December 31 a portion of the year's premium income may not have been received. Thus, using the mean reserve on the balance sheet as of December 31 would overstate reserve liability unless an adjustment were made. In the U.S. Annual Statement, this overstatement is adjusted by reporting as assets both the amount of net deferred premiums and the amount of net uncollected premiums. In the Canadian Annual Statement the amount of net deferred premiums is deducted from actuarial reserves and the amount of gross uncollected premiums less commissions and other costs of collection is reported as an asset. This amount is slightly different from net uncollected premiums.

Whether an item is treated as an asset or as a reduction in liability, the effect on surplus is the same. To illustrate, in the equation $A = L + C$, consider that assets are $100, liabilities $85, and capital $20, with liabilities overstated by $5 because of the assumption that all premiums have been received for a full year. This overstatement results in an understatement of surplus unless an adjustment is made. Under U.S. Statement procedures, this is accomplished by creating an asset amount for premiums deferred and uncollected, amounting to $5. The equation then becomes $105 = $85 + $20, correctly reflecting surplus. Under Canadian Statement procedures, liability is reduced by the amount of net deferred premiums so that the equation becomes $100 = $80 + $20. In either case, surplus (in the capital part of the equation) remains unchanged.

The amount of mean reserve used in industrial insurance is one half of the total of (1) the terminal reserve at the end of the previous year and (2) the terminal reserve at the end of the present year. The net premium is not included in the calculation because generally there are no annual premiums paid on this type of insurance. Correct reserve liability results, assuming that all premiums are paid to December 31. Thus there are no deferred premiums for industrial insurance. Uncollected premiums on industrial insurance are handled in the same manner as for ordinary insurance.

In group life insurance and group annuities, there may or may not be deferred premiums, depending upon payment frequency and procedures used in valuing reserve liabilities. Simple group policies are usually annually renewable term insurance contracts which have zero terminal and mean reserves. Unearned premiums (fractions applicable to the following year) may be treated as policy reserves. Uncollected group life premiums are treated as assets on a net premium basis.

Mean reserves may also be used in connection with Annual Statement valuation for health insurance, particularly with reference to policies which are guaranteed renewable or noncancellable.

Policy reserves are assembled in exhibits in the Annual Statement blank, and only the totals are entered on the liability page of the balance sheet. One exhibit shows reserves by (1) type of coverage (life insurance, annuity, supplementary contracts with life contingencies, etc.); (2) mortality table, interest rate, and valuation method used in calculating them, such as the Commissioners Reserve Valuation Method; and (3) line of business—ordinary insurance, industrial insurance, and group insurance. Reserves on reinsurance ceded are deducted so that the final total is net after reinsurance.

The liability for supplementary contracts which do not involve life contingencies is summarized in a special exhibit, and the total is shown on a separate line of the balance sheet. The exhibit for health insurance reserves in the U.S. Statement shows information in much less detail.

Amounts Held on Deposit

This liability classification covers amounts left with the company at interest. It includes amounts left in connection with death settlements, premiums paid sufficiently in advance that a discount has been allowed, and policy dividends left to accumulate at interest. For discussion purposes, supplemental contracts not involving life contingencies are included in this classification.

The liability for Annual Statement purposes of amounts on deposit is the amount as of the preceding policy anniversary plus estimated interest to the end of the year.

Claims Incurred but Not Yet Paid

The liability classification *claims incurred but not yet paid* includes all types of claims that must be settled. Claim liabilities are usually entered in the balance sheet for the full amount of benefit claimed, even if the amount is in dispute. A liability for claims not yet reported must be estimated on the basis of past experience and included.

Dividend Liabilities

This classification includes a liability for all policy dividends that have been declared by the board of directors, but which are not yet payable. Most companies also include an amount for dividends that will become payable in the following calendar year, whether or not already declared payable by the board. This is done on the assumption that policy dividends payable on the anniversary in the subsequent year should be paid out of surplus actually earned in the year covered by the statement.

The amount of policy dividend liability must be approximated. Usually, policy dividends are contingent upon certain conditions such as the policy being in force on its anniversary or premiums being paid to a specified date. While an actuary can calculate exactly the liability on policies currently in force, some dividends may never become payable because the required conditions have not been met.

In addition to the liability for policy dividends on participating business in force, stock companies must also establish a liability for cash dividends to stockholders, declared by the board, but not yet paid. The amount of stockholder dividends is an exact amount because once the dividend is declared by the board, there is no contingency regarding the amount of the liability. Because it is fixed in amount, some companies record this liability on the ledger, but both stockholder dividends and policy dividends are normally treated as nonledger liabilities.

Accrued Costs (Other than Claims)

This classification includes the liability for unpaid commissions; unpaid expenses such as utilities, printing bills, and salaries accrued; taxes; and any other costs accrued or fully incurred, except policy claims. Accrued costs are treated as nonledger liabilities.

Unearned Income

This liability classification includes (1) investment income received in advance and any portion of investment income that may be allocable to the following calendar year and (2) advance premiums. Advance premiums are those due in the following year, but which were paid before December 31. Some companies include premiums paid several years in advance, but these are usually included with "amounts held on deposit." Unearned premiums (the portion of premiums applicable to the following year) are not usually considered as unearned income but instead are treated as policy reserves. Unearned income amounts are treated as nonledger liabilities.

Amounts Temporarily Held for Disposition

This liability classification covers only two items on the liability page of the Annual Statement but represents most of the liabilities that are normally entered on the company's ledger, i.e., those which are the result of a cash transaction. The first Statement item is *amounts withheld or retained by company as agent or trustee*. This includes (1) deposits by mortgagors to pay future taxes and casualty insurance premiums (held by the company in what are known as escrow accounts) and (2) amounts withheld by payroll deduction. The second statement item is *remittances and items not allocated*. This includes amounts received and held in *suspense accounts*, a form of liability account for temporarily recording cash that for one reason or another cannot be immediately credited to the proper account. It might include payments being held until a new policy is issued, at which time they will be taken into premium income, or amounts being held pending approval of a request for reinstatement.

Miscellaneous Liabilities

This classification covers all remaining liabilities. Among these may be money borrowed plus accrued interest, adjustments in assets and liabilities due to foreign exchange rates, and bank overdrafts.

Special Reserves Classed as Liabilities

The life insurance business is a risk-taking business, and its earnings are subject to a considerable amount of fluctuation, depending upon economic conditions that affect its investments, and epidemics and wars that affect its claim costs. Companies establish special reserves so that in years of adverse experience some of the reserves held can be released to equalize costs. In years when experience is favorable, these reserves are replenished or increased.

Only one such reserve is required in the U.S. Annual Statement. This is known as the Mandatory Securities Valuation Reserve which is used to level out fluctuations in surplus which would otherwise result from unusual gains or losses in invested assets. It is discussed in more detail later in this chapter in connection with the surplus account and in Chapter 10.

Special reserves, established for a particular condition (such as a mortality contingency reserve) are usually shown as liabilities. A general contingency reserve is treated as a subdivision or an earmarking of surplus.

Capital and Surplus

The following discussion relates generally to surplus as shown in the U.S. Annual Statement. The descriptions of capital stock and surplus items also apply to Canadian companies, but surplus in the balance sheet of the Canadian Annual Statement is shown differently. In that statement, surplus is divided into an amount for stockholders (described as *surplus in shareholders fund*) and for policyowners (described as *surplus in insurance funds*).

Capital Stock

This item represents the par value of all shares of stock outstanding (i.e., sold to stockholders). The amount is usually carried in a ledger account. The title of this item in the U.S. Statement is *capital paid-up*, and in the Canadian Statement, *capital stock paid*.

On the liabilities page of the U.S. Statement, *surplus* is broken down into *contributed surplus, special surplus funds,* and *unassigned surplus*. Normally, when an insurance company is first organized, the capital stock is sold for several times the par value. An amount equal to the par value of the stock is credited to the *Capital Stock* account, and the balance received is credited to a *Contributed Surplus* account.

Life insurance companies rarely operate at a profit until they have been in business for several years because the cost of selling and issuing new business usually exceeds the premiums received. This excess cost and the fixed overhead must be paid from contributed surplus until the renewal premium volume reaches a sufficiently high level to pay expenses.[7] In most states it is illegal to pay cash dividends to stockholders from contributed surplus, although stock dividends may be paid from it.

Special surplus funds refers to reserves accumulated by some companies to be used when general contingencies occur. The establishing of these reserves is optional. They are discussed in a later chapter.

Unassigned surplus is all other surplus and arises from operating earnings as well as miscellaneous sources. All cash dividends must be, and stock dividends may be, paid from unassigned surplus.

SUMMARY OF OPERATIONS

All figures in the summary of operations are shown on an accrual basis. The summary is used to determine the surplus increase or decrease resulting from *life insurance operations* as opposed to the increase or decrease resulting from other sources. The net gain from operations thus determined is then reduced by (1) amounts paid out in dividends to policyholders and (2) federal income taxes in order to arrive at the final figure for *net gain* on the summary. Capital gains or losses are not a part of gain from operations.

The phrase net gain is used in the U.S. summary rather than the word profit because the term *profit* implies a gain made on behalf of owners of a profit-making business. While this is true of a stock company, it is not applicable to gains made from insurance operations in a mutual company which theoretically returns gains or earnings to its policyholder owners.

The income and cost items in the summary of operations may be broadly classified for discussion purposes as follows:

---

[7] The contributed surplus shown in the balance sheet is the amount paid in by stockholders less transfers to capital on account of stock dividends paid. If accumulated losses exceed accumulated earnings, the difference is shown as a negative amount in Unassigned Surplus.

INCOME:
  Income from insurance contracts
  Net investment income
COSTS:
  Policy benefits (including payments on settlement contracts)
  Increase in policy reserves
  Increase in loading
  Commissions
  General expenses
  Taxes
  Policy Dividends

Income from insurance contracts consists primarily of insurance premium income, annuity considerations, and policy proceeds retained under supplementary contracts.

Net income from investments consists of interest, dividends, and rent derived from invested assets, less depreciation on real estate and all costs of servicing and accounting for assets and income from such assets. It does not include gains or losses from the sale of invested assets.

It may not seem proper at first thought to group investment income with insurance income. However, it should be recalled that there is an interest element in policy reserves. This element contributes in part to the increase in policy reserves, which is an insurance cost. Since the interest element in policy reserves must be derived from investment income, it is logical to include investment income as a type of insurance income in the summary of operations.

Policy benefits consists of all types of contractual policy payments. It includes death claims, matured endowments, annuity payments, disability payments, surrender benefits, and payments on health insurance policies.

Increase in policy reserves includes increase in reserves, both those with and those without life contingencies. In U.S. companies, increase in deposit liabilities is included as a part of the increase in supplemental contract reserves without life contingencies.

Increase in loading is a special adjustment item used in the U.S. Statement in connection with increase in uncollected and deferred premiums. It is discussed in the chapter relating to premium accounting.

The other four classifications—*commissions, general expenses, taxes,* and *policy dividends*—are self-explanatory.

ANALYSIS OF OPERATIONS

Following the summary of operations in the Annual Statement, there is a supplementary report titled *analysis of operations by lines of business* in which the net gain is calculated for each of various lines of business. The equivalent Canadian report is called *analysis of revenue account by line of business*. The items in the two analyses are similar, but there are some differences in classifications for lines of business. The Canadian *analysis* shows the gains in each line of business separately for participating and for nonparticipating business. A few states now require companies to file one analysis of operations for participating business and another for nonparticipating business.

The analysis is helpful to management in determining sources of gains (or losses) from insurance operations. The net gain for each line and the combined gain is an indication of the efficiency of management. Comparison between companies based on figures shown for each line of business in the analysis may be helpful in locating weaknesses in insurance operations.

A line of business may be defined from an accounting standpoint as a segment of the insurance market which has a cost pattern distinctly different from that of other lines. There are differences in sales and servicing methods also, and it is these which create a distinctive cost pattern.

Lines of business can be classified as major lines and secondary lines each with subclassifications, or more simply, sublines. The following may be considered as being major lines of insurance:

1. Industrial
2. Ordinary
3. Group
4. Individual health

The expression "secondary lines" refers to lines of business which parallel the major or principal line in many respects but which have a distinctly separate cost pattern. An example is credit insurance, usually classed under group insurance but covering a distinct and separate portion of the group insurance market.

Sublines in the U.S. Statement are usually determined by the *types* of insurance covered, such as life insurance, health insurance, and annuities. For example, group insurance is divided into life insurance, health insurance, and annuities. Industrial insurance might be divided into life insurance and health insurance. Ordinary insurance might be divided into life insurance, individual annuities, accidental death benefits, and limited health insurance coverage provided by disability riders attached to the policies. Individual health insurance may be subdivided into classifications such as noncancellable and guaranteed renewable coverages.

Line of business classifications as just presented differ from the classifications used in the U.S. Annual Statement blank with respect to group insurance. In fact, there are inconsistencies in the blank. Instructions for Annual Statement preparation describe group life, group annuities, and group health insurance as each being major lines, but column headings in the analysis show group health insurance as a subdivision of the health line of business. Instructions refer to disability benefits and other sublines of ordinary insurance as being secondary lines.

It is preferable, therefore, to use the classifications described here to prevent confusion and to aid in understanding the nature of and subdivisions in the variations of major lines of business.

Most of the figures in the summary of operations and analysis of operations are taken from various exhibits in the Annual Statement blank, although a few are taken from supplementary working papers or other sources. These exhibits provide considerable detail on income and cost items. In a general sense, each item in the summary is a total of a number of account balances and nonledger items summarized in an exhibit or section of an exhibit, although there are several exceptions.[8]

Some exhibits, such as those relating to premium income and policy benefits, provide for showing the same distribution by line of business as is shown in the analysis. Exhibits covering expenses and taxes do not show this distribution, so these costs must be analyzed or assembled on separate working papers before entering them in the analysis. These two exhibits do, however, include a column for investment costs, which are deducted from investment income to produce a net investment income figure for the summary. This deduction is made in an exhibit relating to investment income.

All items in the summary and analysis (and in the balance sheet) are shown net of reinsurance. For example, if the accrual basis premium income is $100 million and the accrual basis reinsurance premiums paid are $3 million, the premium income is shown in these two reports as $97 million. Claims and policy reserve increases are also shown net of reinsurance. The amount of reinsurance deductions is shown separately in each exhibit.

Exhibits and details by lines of business are discussed in later chapters.

Surplus Account

In the accounting process, every business transaction must be recorded in terms of dollars received and dollars expended. These transactions may be summarized and analyzed to determine the causes for increases and decreases in surplus during the year. Analyzing these causes provides useful decision-making information to management.

Causes for surplus change in a life insurance company are not limited to gains from operations which result from insurance and investment income less insurance costs. There are several other sources of surplus change, which may be referred to as *direct changes in surplus*. These changes are shown in a statement of surplus in the annual statement forms.

---

[8] Many asset and liability items in the balance sheet are also taken from exhibits.

The U.S. surplus account and the Canadian reconciliation of surplus are presented in a reconciliation form which shows the surplus changes between the end of one year and the end of the next.

The principal sources of surplus change in a life insurance company are:

1. Net gains from operations
2. Capital gains and losses
3. Changes in the Mandatory Securities Valuation Reserve
4. Dividends paid to stockholders
5. Changes in nonadmitted assets and related items.
6. Special surplus adjustments
7. Changes in valuation basis of policy reserves

Items 3 and 5 are not found in the Canadian reconciliation for reasons explained in the following discussion.

Various exhibits and reports of the Annual Statement blank are used to summarize data relating to the surplus reconciliation.

Net gain from operations[9] is determined in the *summary of operations.* This summary has already been described. It is the equivalent of the income and expense statement of commercial accounting.

Capital gains and losses are gains and losses realized from the sale of invested assets and changes in the admitted value of invested assets. These gains or losses have a direct effect on surplus unless the change is offset by a change in the Mandatory Securities Valuation Reserve. Capital gains and losses are not treated as a part of investment earnings and are not, therefore, included in the summary as a part of insurance operations. They are treated as a source of gain (or loss) distinct from gains made from insurance operations.

The *Mandatory Securities Valuation Reserve* (MSVR) is a surplus reserve shown as a liability in the U.S. Annual Statement. It is designed to absorb fluctuations in statement values of securities held. A maximum reserve is established over a period of years in accordance with rules of the NAIC. Each year's contribution to this reserve is made up from two principal sources: (1) an amount equal to capital gains, less capital losses on bonds and stocks, and (2) amounts based on percentages of present investments in stocks and bonds.

When the MSVR is less than its maximum, a capital gain is offset by an equal increase in the MSVR. Otherwise, a capital gain results in an increase in surplus. Similarly, a capital loss is offset by an equal decrease in the MSVR. The percentage-of-securities portion of the contribution, item (2) above, is a transfer from surplus to the MSVR liability.

Once the maximum MSVR amount is reached, it is not increased

---

[9] The Canadian equivalent is: "balance carried to reconciliation of surplus" which is determined in the revenue account.

further. Thereafter, a capital gain results in a surplus increase. If the MSVR is reduced to zero because of prior losses, a capital loss will, of course, result in reduction of surplus. This reserve is described in more detail in the chapter on investment.

Dividends paid to stockholders is not an operating cost but is a distribution of surplus to *stockholders*. It is, therefore, shown in the surplus account as a direct decrease in surplus. Dividends paid to *policyowners* are not included in this reconciliation but are treated as an insurance cost and therefore are included in the summary of operations. This is done on the premise that policyowner dividends are actually premium adjustments and not distributions of surplus.

Changes in *nonadmitted assets and related items*[10] refers primarily to increases and decreases in the book value of assets used in, or created through, insurance operations, such as furniture and equipment. The amount of this item is taken from an exhibit in the U.S. Annual Statement which specifies the assets which are to be included under this classification. An increase in the book value of a nonadmitted asset decreases surplus. Similarly, a decrease in the value of these assets results in an increase in surplus. All of these nonadmitted asset items in the exhibit are related to insurance operations, but increases are not treated as insurance costs in the U.S. Annual Statement, nor are decreases treated as insurance income.

To illustrate the effect on surplus of not admitting these assets, assume the accounting equation is $1,000(A) = $650(L) + $350(C) and immediately thereafter $100 is spent for furniture. The Furniture account is debited and Cash is credited. A statement prepared at this point must not admit the $100 furniture asset, so the equation becomes $900(A) = $650(L) + $250(C). It was necessary to reduce capital (or more specifically, surplus) in order to keep the equation in balance.

Special surplus adjustments reflects the increase or decrease in special contingency reserves to prevent undue fluctuation in unassigned surplus in years of adverse experience. These reserves are established by transferring a portion of unassigned surplus, thereby decreasing unassigned surplus by the amount transferred.

The establishing of a reserve of this type might be done by a nonledger (memorandum) transaction, since such accounts are not carried on a life insurance ledger, but showing it as a ledger transaction facilitates understanding it. The entry for establishing a mortality contingency reserve would be:

Surplus..100,000
    Mortality Reserve.....................................   100,000

---

[10] This surplus change item is not found in the Canadian reconciliation of surplus. Most of the items equivalent to those included in the exhibit are treated as insurance expenses in the revenue account of the Canadian statement.

The debit portion of the entry decreases surplus and the credit portion establishes a reserve that will be treated as a liability in the balance sheet.

Change in valuation basis of policy reserves is an increase in policy reserves that is not properly an insurance operating cost. For example, a company may decide to value policy reserves on a more conservative basis than is required by law, i.e., at a greater amount. In such a case, the portion of reserve increase attributable to the change in valuation basis is not treated as an insurance cost, but as a direct deduction from surplus. This process of setting up additional policy reserves is known as *reserve strengthening*.

A more detailed consideration of the items in the balance sheet, the summary of operations, and other reports and reconciliations of the Annual Statement blanks is included in later chapters of this book.

SUMMARY OF LIFE INSURANCE ACCOUNTING FUNDAMENTALS

Deferred premiums are premiums which will become due after the end of the calendar year and prior to the next policy anniversary.

Uncollected, due, or *outstanding premiums* are those which became due prior to December 31 but which had not been received as of that date.

Net deferred premiums are gross deferred premiums less an expense loading. They constitute an adjustment to counterbalance overstated policy reserve liability.

A *mean reserve* is the reserve liability reported for a policy at the end of the calendar year, calculated by averaging the initial reserve and the terminal reserve.

Line of business refers to a segment of the insurance market which has a distinctive cost pattern. A line of business may be subdivided into secondary lines and further subdivided into sublines (usually by types of insurance).

Type of insurance is a basic form of insurance coverage, such as life insurance, health insurance, and annuities.

All figures in life insurance balance sheets and operating statements are shown net of reinsurance.

QUESTIONS

1. How is each major investment classification valued for Annual Statement purposes?

2. Briefly describe the principal liability classifications in the balance sheet. Which are ledger liabilities? Indicate which liability classifications relate to adjusting income and costs to the accrual basis.

3. In what way do the mean reserves of ordinary and industrial insurance differ? In what way do deferred premiums differ from due or uncol-

lected premiums? From advance premiums? In what respects do advance premiums and premium deposits differ?

4. What is meant by special surplus reserves? By assigned surplus? Contributed surplus? Surplus in shareholders fund? Surplus in insurance funds?

5. What two conditions create capital gains and losses? If a company has less than the maximum MSVR, how do capital gains affect surplus? Why?

6. How do Canadian companies handle the noninvestment items that are treated as nonadmitted assets in the U.S. statement? In general, what is the effect on surplus in each case? What is the effect on operating gain (or revenue)?

7. What is the distinction, if any, between the following expressions: (1) net gain from operations, (2) balance of revenue account, (3) net income, and (4) profit.

8. Why is net investment income treated as insurance income in a life insurance company statement?

9. Give examples of major lines and sublines of insurance and types of insurance.

Chapter 10

Accounting for Investments (Part One)

More than 95 percent of the assets of a typical life insurance company are investments. The investment function is, therefore, one of the most important functions of a life company. This importance is also reflected by the fact that more pages of Annual Statement blanks are devoted to investments than to any other aspect of a company's business.

Investments are made primarily for the benefit and protection of a company's policyowners. The rights of stockholders are important, but they are secondary. The responsibility to policyowners and the fixed dollar nature of a life insurance company's policy liabilities, as well as government regulation, determine the investment policy and to a considerable extent investment accounting processes.

Good investment practice requires that amounts invested (the principal) be conserved and that a reasonable return be earned on investments. This rate of return ideally should be in excess of that assumed by the actuaries when they calculated premium rates to be charged for insurance.

Life insurance company funds available for investment may be used to buy bonds, stocks, or real estate. These funds also may be used to make mortgage loans, policy loans, and collateral loans. Accounting for the principal of these six major types of investments and accounting for related investment income is discussed in this and in the next chapter.

Three principal aspects of accounting for investments are described here. These are (1) accounting for the income derived from investments, (2) accounting for purchases and sales of investments including capital gains and losses, and (3) presentation of investment accounting data in the Annual Statements.

The first two of these aspects and some phases of the third are

167

discussed in sections of this chapter devoted to accounting in connection with each of the six major investment classifications. The third aspect is discussed in separate U.S. and Canadian Annual Statement supplements in the next chapter. First, however, it is useful to consider the principles and methods of investment accounting that are common to all types of investments.

ACCOUNTING FOR INVESTMENT PRINCIPAL

When securities (bonds or stocks) are purchased or funds are loaned, the asset account for that particular type of investment is debited and the asset account Cash is credited. A typical entry is one recording the purchase of a $1,000 bond. It is:

Bonds Owned...	1,000.00	
Cash..		1,000.00

When investments are sold, capital gains or losses may be realized. These gains or losses are not included with operating income or costs but are treated as direct changes in surplus.

Capital gains and losses are described as *realized* and *unrealized*. A *realized capital gain* is the excess of sales price over cost (or amortized value, in the case of bonds eligible for amortization). This gain is described in the U.S. Annual Statement as *profit on sale or maturity*.[1] Note that "profit" is used here interchangeably with "gain." Note also that book value rather than actual cost is used to determine gain. This is logical on amortized securities because the book value at time of sale reflects changes due to amortization in past years. These changes were used to adjust income in those years and are not a part of the capital gain.

By similar reasoning, *realized capital loss* is the excess of book value over sale price at time of sale. A realized capital loss is described in U.S. Annual Statement as *loss on sale or maturity*.

The cost of a security (bond or stock) and the sale price recorded on the books is the net (after adjustment for expenses incurred, including commissions paid to a broker). If the purchase price of stock is $1,650 and the commission paid is $50, the cost recorded on the books is $1,700. If the sales price less commission is $1,800, the realized capital gain is $100 ($1,800 − $1,700).

Realized capital gains and losses are recorded in nominal accounts classified as capital gain and loss accounts. A typical entry to record the sale of a $1,000 par value bond for $975 when its book value is $960 is a debit to Cash for the $975 received, a credit to Bonds Owned for $960 to zero balance this account with reference to the bond sold, and a credit to

---

[1] Canadian Annual Statement presentation does not distinguish between realized and unrealized capital gains and losses.

Profit on Sale of Bonds for $15, the excess of sales price over book value. The entry is:

```
Cash..............................................................975.00
    Bonds Owned.......................................................    960.00
    Profit on Sale of Bonds...........................................     15.00
```

Other entries recording realized capital gains and losses are presented in other sections of this chapter as the particular asset is discussed.

Income entries are frequently required in connection with the purchase and sale of investments. These entries vary according to investment classification and are discussed with each of these classifications.

Increases in admitted value of invested assets owned as of the statement date are known as *unrealized capital gains,* and decreases in admitted values of invested assets are known as *unrealized capital losses.*

A control account is maintained in the general ledger for each investment classification, and a subsidiary ledger account is maintained for each specific investment. For example, a Bonds Owned account is included in the general ledger, and an account for each specific bond purchase is included in a subsidiary bond ledger.

Subsidiary ledger investment accounts are usually in card form. On each card, companies show the amount of each investment, which is referred to as the principal balance. Most companies also show debit and credit entries affecting the principal balance. The total of all subsidiary account balances always must be equal to the control account balance.

Much data not necessarily a part of a subsidiary ledger account is also recorded on subsidiary ledger cards. This data is different for each investment classification. In some respects, the data recorded also varies from company to company, but the essential data is very similar for all companies.

Income from investments is recorded in a separate column from the principal balance on each subsidiary ledger card. This income record is historical in nature and is not controlled by an income account in the general ledger in the same sense that a subsidiary ledger account is controlled.

ACCOUNTING FOR INVESTMENT INCOME

There are three principal types of investment income. These are (1) *interest* on bonds owned and loans made, (2) *dividends* on stocks, and (3) *rent* on real estate.

Entries for income received are quite simple: Cash is debited, and an income account is credited. A journal entry recording $100 of policy loan interest is:

```
Cash..............................................................100.00
    Policy Loan Interest..............................................    100.00
```

The process for adjusting investment income from the cash to accrual basis is much more complex because a number of related asset and liability amounts must be used. The student should now have a good understanding of how this process is accomplished, but it will be helpful to reexamine this process with particular reference to investment income.

Income on investments may be collected, earned, unearned, accrued, and due. *Collected income* is the amount actually received in cash during an accounting period. *Earned income* is the amount properly recorded as earned during an accounting period, whether received or not. *Unearned income* is that part of collected income which belongs in a later accounting period because it will not be earned until then. *Accrued income* is income earned from the date on which interest was last due up to the statement date. For example, interest paid quarterly may have been due and paid on November 1 and will become due again on February 1. As of December 31, interest for November and December is *accrued income*. It will be *due income* on February 1—the date on which it becomes receivable.

Each of these classifications applies to interest and to rent. Accrued and unearned income classifications usually do not apply to dividends. Cash dividends are payable on a specific date and do not accrue. When declared by the board of directors, they become liabilities of the declaring corporation and on the specified date become income to the stockholder. Dividends are never prepaid, so they cannot be treated as unearned income.

Accrual basis accounting attributes income and expenses to the period in which the income is *earned* or the expense *incurred*. The process for adjusting cash basis investment income to earned income (accrual basis) is as follows (illustrative amounts are inserted):

A. Income collected in this accounting period ($50,000 cash basis *income* from the ledger),
B. *Plus* unearned income from the end of the previous accounting period ($1,000 *liability* at the end of previous period),
C. *Less* unearned income at the end of this accounting period ($1,120 *liability* at the end of present period),
D. *Less* income due and accrued at the end of the previous accounting period ($500 *asset* at the end of the previous period),
E. *Plus* income due and accrued at the end of this accounting period ($625 *asset* at end of present period),
F. *Equals* income earned during this accounting period ($50,005 earned, or accrual basis, income).

Interest due and accrued (asset) and unearned interest (liability) amounts must be calculated for each individual investment and summarized prior to making adjusting entries. These asset and liability amounts for the current year are not reflected by account balances unless and until adjusting entries are recorded on the books. If a company chooses to record these entries, the account balances will, of course, remain on the ledger until removed or adjusted by another entry, usually at the end of the next year.

It was stressed earlier that adjusting entries for a life insurance company are usually made on working papers and not posted to the ledger. These entries are illustrated here, however, in the form of journal entries. Assume for this purpose that accrued income and unearned income are carried on the ledger. The reversal and reentry method will be used and the entries posted to T-accounts to demonstrate the ultimate effect on income, assets, and liabilities. The letters used to designate the steps of the adjusting process just described are again used to indicate the corresponding entry. No entry is required for step A because this amount is already on the ledger.

First, it is necessary to reverse the previous year's unearned income entry. This amount has now been earned and must be taken into income for the current year. This is accomplished by crediting Interest Income. A debit to Unearned Interest zero balances this liability account. The entry is:

```
B   Unearned Interest.................................1,000.00
        Interest Income......................................          1,000.00
```

It is also necessary to record the current year's unearned income liability and to decrease the current year's income by this amount. This is accomplished by crediting Unearned Interest and debiting Interest Income. The entry is:

```
C   Interest Income...................................1,120.00
        Unearned Interest....................................          1,120.00
```

It is necessary to reverse the previous year's due and accrued income entry. During the current year this amount was received and was credited to the Interest Income account at that time. Debiting Interest Income now in the amount of unearned interest at the beginning of the year removes the excess amount from the Interest Income account balance. A credit to Interest Due and Accrued zero balances this asset account. The entry is:

```
D   Interest Income...................................500.00
        Interest Due and Accrued.............................          500.00
```

It also is necessary to record the current year's due and accrued income as an asset and to take this amount into current year's income because it has been earned even though it has not been received. This is accomplished by debiting the Interest Due and Accrued account and crediting the Interest Income account. The entry is:

```
E   Interest Due and Accrued..........................625.00
        Interest Income......................................          625.00
```

If these entries are posted to T-accounts, the accounts appear as follows (the symbol # indicates beginning balances and letters indicate entries):

Interest Income (Income)		Interest Due and Accrued (Asset)		Unearned Interest (Liability)	
1,120 C	50,000 #	500 #	500 D	1,000 B	1,000 #
500 D	1,000 B	625 E			1,120 C
	625 E				
	50,005	*625*			*1,120*

The interest income for the year on the accrual basis is, therefore, $50,005, and at year-end accrued income (assets) is $625 and unearned income (liability) is $1,120.

BOND ACCOUNTING

Bonds are certificates of indebtedness issued by corporations and governmental authorities in which the issuer agrees to pay a certain amount on a specified date and in the meantime to pay interest to the owner of the bond. The amount of the bond is called the *principal* amount, the *par* value, the *face* value, or the *maturity* value. The settlement date is called the *maturity* date.

Most bonds have a par value of $1,000. The rate of interest, maturity date, and other information concerning the bond agreement are printed on the bond certificate. Interest is usually payable semiannually. Thus, the owner of a $1,000, 5 percent bond is entitled to receive $25 interest twice each year. The rate of interest specified in the bond contract is referred to as the *stated* rate.

Government bonds may be classified as general obligation bonds or special obligation bonds. General obligation bonds are secured by the general taxing power of the issuing governmental unit, and special obligation bonds are secured by revenue from a restricted source such as a toll bridge or a water system, or by a special tax source such as gasoline taxes or special property taxes.

Corporate bonds generally are secured by a mortgage on real estate (mortgage bonds), or by other stocks or bonds (collateral bonds), or by the general credit of the corporation (debenture bonds).

Bonds may be registered as to principal only or as to principal and interest; or, interest coupons may be attached to the bond certificate. The interest on registered bonds is paid by check to the registered owner of the bonds without any collection action on his part. Coupon bonds have interest coupons attached, one for each of the interest periods in the life of the bond. The proper coupon must be clipped and presented for payment to receive the interest on the due date. The holder of the bond usually gives the coupon to his bank for collection.

Accrued Bond Interest

Bonds are seldom purchased on the first day of an interest period. The buyer must, therefore, pay the seller for interest accrued up to the purchase date.

If a $1,000, 5 percent bond is purchased at par with $10 interest accrued at the purchase date, the entry is:

```
Bonds Owned..................................................1,000.00
Interest Income on Bonds...............................    10.00
    Cash....................................................              1,010.00
```

The debit to Interest Income on Bonds records a decrease in income. The reason for this debit becomes apparent several months later when a semiannual interest payment of $25 is received. A proper entry to record that interest is:

```
Cash...........................................................25.00
    Interest Income on Bonds.............................           25.00
```

If the interest for six months is $25 and the previous owner earned $10 of this amount, the remaining $15 ($25 − $10) is obviously the portion of the interest the new owner has earned. The debit to Interest Income on Bonds for $10 at the time the bond was purchased and the credit to that account for $25 when the interest payment is received results in a credit balance of $15, the correct amount of interest earned during the period.

Some life insurance companies debit such accrued interest to an account called Accrued Interest on Bonds Purchased so that a total can be quickly obtained for a footnote in the U.S. Annual Statement. However, the debit balance of this account must be combined with the credit balance of the Interest Income on Bonds account when entered in the investment income exhibit. Such combining is usually done on a work sheet.

Bond Discount and Premium

The annual interest paid on a bond is determined by multiplying the par value of the bond by the stated rate of interest. This fixed dollar amount of interest is payable to the owner, regardless of the actual price paid for the bond. If a price other than par is paid, the *actual* rate of interest (or return) earned on the amount paid will differ from the stated rate. This actual rate is called the *effective* rate or *yield*. The difference between cost and par value of a bond is known as *discount* if cost is lower than par, or *premium* if cost is higher than par.

The price paid for the bond determines the effective rate of interest on the bond. For example, if a 5 percent bond maturing in one year is purchased for $990, the purchaser will receive $60 on his $990 investment ($10 increase in value plus $50 interest). The effective rate or yield is, therefore, 6.06 percent ($60.00 ÷ $990.00).

When a bond is bought at a discount as in the example just given, the effective rate of interest or yield will be higher than the stated rate. Conversely, when a bond is bought at a premium the effective rate of interest will be lower than the stated rate.

Technically, the effective rate of interest determines the market price of a bond. The market price is determined by the rate of interest an investor is willing to accept for use of his money from the day he purchases the bond to the maturity date. The market value of a bond, therefore, is the *present value* of the amount due at maturity of the bond, discounted at the effective rate of interest, plus the *present value* of unmatured interest coupons, discounted at the same rate. Consider these two examples: (1) If a $1,000 4 percent 10-year bond is purchased to yield an effective rate of interest of 4¼ percent, the maturity value and coupons discounted at 4¼ percent will produce a market value of $979.81. (2) If a $1,000, 5 percent, 10-year bond is purchased to yield an effective rate of 4¼ percent, the maturity value and coupons discounted at 4¼ percent will produce a market value of $1,060.60.

When bonds are purchased they are recorded on the books at cost. The entry to record the purchase of $10,000 par value bonds at a $201.90 discount is a $9,798.10 debit to Bonds Owned and an equal credit to Cash. The entry is:

Bonds Owned..9,798.10
    Cash... 9,798.10

Each year an amortization entry is made to adjust the book value so that it equals the par value on the maturity date. *Amortization,* it will be recalled, is the accounting process by which the cost of an investment is periodically and systematically adjusted on the books so that it eventually equals the par value. The amortization process results in earned income (interest received plus or minus amortization) in each bond year equal to the book value times the effective rate. The amortization process is demonstrated in the following examples.

Assume the bonds purchased for $9,798.10 had a stated rate of 4 percent and were purchased on January 1 to yield an effective rate of 4¼ percent. Interest of $200 for a six months' period is received on June 30. The receipt of interest is recorded by a debit to Cash and a credit to the income account Interest Income on Bonds. The interest entry is:

Cash...200.00
    Interest Income on Bonds................................ 200.00

An amortization entry is also made as of June 30. The cost of the bonds, $9,798.10 times one half (for six months) the effective rate of 4¼ percent, is $208.21. An additional $8.21 ($208.21 − $200.00) must, therefore, be credited to the income account to reflect the earned amount. The equal debit is made to the Bonds Owned account to increase the book value. The entry is:

```
Bonds Owned.........................................................8.21
    Interest Income on Bonds...................................        8.21
```

This entry increases the Interest Income on Bonds to $208.21 for the six months and the book value of Bonds Owned to $9,806.31. At the end of the year, this $9,806.31 is multiplied by one half of 4¼ percent to give $208.38. The amortization entry at that time will be for $8.38 ($208.38 − $200.00). The process will be continued each six months until the book value of the bonds becomes equal to par value on the maturity date.

If a bond is purchased at a premium, the amortization entry is the reverse of that shown for bonds purchased at a discount. In this case the effective rate is lower than the stated rate, so the income account must be debited to decrease earned income and the asset account must be credited to reduce the asset amount.

In the example of a 10-year $1,000 bond with a 5 percent stated rate purchased for $1,060.60 to yield a 4¼ percent effective rate, the amortization amount for the first six months is $2.46 ($25.00 at the stated rate less $22.54 at the effective rate). The entry is:

```
Interest Income on Bonds.......................................2.46
    Bonds Owned.............................................        2.46
```

Suppose that rather than being held to maturity the bonds in the first illustration (purchased for $9,798.10) had been sold on September 30, nine months after they were purchased and that the sale price was $9,910.

Amortization is calculated to date of sale at the effective rate. During the period of ownership, the effective rate used for calculating amortization is not changed. The new purchaser may base his price on a different effective rate from that used by the seller. This is reasonable since the money market changes from day to day.

The new purchaser is required to pay the interest accrued since the last interest due date at the stated rate. This amount in the example is $100 (10,000 × 4 percent × ¼ year). Allowance is made for this accrued interest in calculating the amount of seller's amortization, which is $4.19 ($9,806.31 book value × 4¼ percent × ¼ year-$100). The entry is:

```
Bonds Owned.........................................................4.19
    Interest Income on Bonds...................................        4.19
```

When this entry is posted, the book value of bonds is $9,810.50 ($9,806.31 + $4.19). The asset account Bonds Owned must be credited by this amount to zero balance the Bonds Owned account with reference to the bonds being sold. The amount received from the purchaser is $10,010 ($9,910 price + $100 interest) and is debited to Cash. The

Interest Income on Bonds account is credited for the $100 interest received. The sales price is higher than the book value by $99.50 ($9,910.00 − $9,810.50). This is a realized capital gain and is credited to a capital gain account called *Profit on the Sale of Bonds.*

The complete entry is:

```
Cash.................................................10,010.00
    Bonds Owned......................................          9,810.50
    Interest Income on Bonds.........................           100.00
    Profit on the Sale of Bonds......................            99.50
```

If the sales price had been $9,600, there would have been a realized capital loss of $210.50 ($9,810.50 book value less $9,600). This amount would have been debited to a capital loss account called *Loss on the Sale of Bonds.* The credits to Bonds Owned and Interest Income on Bonds would have been the same, and the debit to Cash would have been $9,700 ($9,600 + $100).

If the bonds had been originally purchased at a premium, the amortization entry would, of course, have been a credit to Bonds Owned and a debit to Interest Income on Bonds. The method of calculating the gain or loss and recording the sale would have been the same as shown.

There is an alternate method of recording bonds purchased at a discount or premium. A separate account is established for the discount or the premium and the bond is carried in the books at par. Under this method, the entry for a bond purchased at $950 on the first day of an interest period is:

```
Bonds Owned.........................................1,000.00
    Discount on Bonds...............................            50.00
    Cash...........................................           950.00
```

The amortization entry is then:

```
Discount on Bonds...................................xxxx
    Interest Income on Bonds........................          xxxx
```

If the bonds are resold before maturity, the Discount on Bonds account is debited in the sale entry with an amount that will bring its balance to zero.

If a premium is paid, this amount is debited to a Premium on Bonds account at time of purchase. Amortization amounts are credited to this account and debited to Interest Income on Bonds.

The general ledger account Bonds Owned again is a control account. The subsididary ledger account contains all of the detail information about each bond issue owned, including the present premium and discount balances.

Figure 10–1 shows the type of information usually maintained on each bond in its subsidiary ledger account.

Figure 10–1. Ledger Sheet for Bonds or Stocks

SECURITIES RECORD

FORM NO. 6-229

PAR VALUE AND BOOK VALUE OWNED

ACCT'G DATE	PAR VALUE			BOOK VALUE		
	INCREASE	DECREASE	BALANCE	INCREASE	DECREASE	BALANCE

INTEREST AND DIVIDEND RECORD

DATE PAYABLE	DATE PAID	AMOUNT PAID	BAL. UNPAID	DATE PAYABLE	DATE DEPOSITED	DATE PAID	AMOUNT PAID	BAL. UNPAID

SECURITIES ACQUIRED (SCHEDULE D PART 3)

DATE ACQUIRED	NAME OF VENDOR	COST TO CO. EXCL. ACC. INT.	PAR VALUE OR NO. SHARES	PD. FOR ACC. INT.	COST PER $100	NET YIELD

NAME AND DESCRIPTION																	
CODE	RATE	MATURITY	JAN JULY	FEB AUG	MAR SEPT	APR OCT	MAY NOV	JUN DEC	RATING	1	2	3	4	5	6	INTEREST PAY. AT	

MO. INC. $	ADJ. $	ACC. INT. TO 12-31 $	ON

Amortization entries are entered as increases or decreases in the book value section. Stock dividends are entered on the reverse side. This is a manual record.

ACCOUNTING FOR STOCK OWNED

Shares of capital stock are units of ownership in a corporation. A stock certificate which indicates the number of shares owned is issued to each stockholder. A return on an investment in stock is generally in the form of cash dividends which are paid by check to the owner; occasionally dividends are paid in the form of additional shares of stock.

The two ordinary classes of capital stock are *common* and *preferred*. All corporations issue common stock which represents part ownership in the corporation. Preferred stock owners usually are guaranteed a specified dividend rate and have a prior right to dividends over common stockholders. They may also have prior rights to corporate assets in the event of liquidation. Usually preferred stockholders do not have the right to vote for directors and may be paid dividends at a lower rate than common stockholders, provided the rate paid is at least equal to the guaranteed rate.

Some stock has a par value. This is a stated amount that is printed on each stock certificate. The par value of all stock issued is carried as a credit balance in the Capital Stock account of the issuer. Stock issued by life insurance companies must by law have a par value.

A dividend may be expressed as a percentage of par, but this is not a common practice in the United States; it is more commonly expressed in dollars per share. Whether a particular issue of capital stock has a par value or no par value does not affect accounting for it on the books of the purchaser (stockholder), nor does it have any relationship to the market value of the stock.

The stockholder records his purchase of stock at cost. If an insurance company bought 100 shares of $10 par value stock of the XYZ Corporation for $89 per share, the transaction is recorded by debiting the cost to the asset account Stocks Owned and crediting the Cash account by an equal amount. The entry is:

Stocks Owned	8,900.00	
Cash		8,900.00

The entry for a $1 per share cash dividend on this stock is a debit to Cash and a credit to the income account, Dividends Received. The entry is:

Cash	100.00	
Dividends Received		100.00

The Stocks Owned account is a general ledger control account. A subsidiary ledger account is kept for each specific block of stock owned. The subsidiary account contains information similar to that shown in Figure 10–2. The market value per share of each stock owned on December 31 is noted in its subsidiary record to facilitate the preparation of the Annual Statement.

The number of shares of each stock owned is also noted on the subsidiary record. If a *stock dividend,* that is, a dividend in the form of additional stock of the issuing corporation rather than cash, is received, no journal entry is required. Indeed, since no change in total cost is involved, a journal entry could not be made. The number of shares received as a dividend, however, must be noted in the subsidiary account so that gains or losses may be calculated when the stock is sold.

Figure 10–2. Ledger Sheets for Stocks Owned

Form 291 STOCK LEDGER CARD

DESCRIPTION

PAR VALUE | PAID FOR ACCRUED DIVIDENDS

DATE	PURCHASER – VENDER	BOOK VALUE			NUMBER OF SHARES			Profit On Sale	Loss On Sale
		Dr.	Cr.	Balance	Dr.	Cr.	Balance		

Dividends are recorded on the reverse side. This is a manual record.

For example, if an insurance company owned 100 shares of XYZ Corporation stock, which cost $9,000, and XYZ declared a 50 percent stock dividend, the number of shares owned would increase to 150, but the cost would remain $9,000. The book value per share would drop from $90 to $60 ($9,000 ÷ 150). If any of this stock is sold, the gain or loss is the difference between the sales price and the adjusted cost, $60 per share.

Thus, if 50 shares of this stock are sold at $65 per share, the profit is $250 ($65 selling price – $60 cost per share × 50 shares). The entry to record the sale is a debit to Cash for $3,250 ($65 × 50 shares), a credit to

Stocks Owned for $3,000 ($60 cost × 50 shares), and a credit to a capital gain account for the realized gain of $250. The entry is:

Cash...	3,250.00	
Stocks Owned.......................................		3,000.00
Gain on Sale of Stock................................		250.00

If instead of the transaction just given, all 150 shares were sold at $70 per share, the entry would be:

Cash...	10,500.00	
Stocks Owned.......................................		9,000.00
Gain on Sale of Stock................................		1,500.00

If instead of either transaction given, all 150 shares were sold for $55 per share, there would have been a realized capital loss of $750 ($60 − $55 × 150 shares). The amount received would be $8,250 ($55 × 150). The entry is:

Cash...	8,250.00	
Loss on Sale of Stock................................	750.00	
Stocks Owned.......................................		9,000.00

If shares of stock are bought and sold at various times and at different market prices, the determination of cost, to be used in calculating gains or losses, is more complex than when only one purchase is involved. This determination may be made by any one of several methods which are not discussed here, since the accounting process is not affected by the method used.

If dividends have been declared but are not yet paid, the market price of the stock includes the unpaid dividend. When the dividend is received, the purchaser usually credits the Dividends Received account rather than the Stocks Owned account.

MANDATORY SECURITIES VALUATION RESERVE

It will be recalled that for Annual Statement purposes, stocks are valued at market value as determined by governmental authorities. These asset values fluctuate from time to time, causing surplus to fluctuate accordingly (since A = L + C at all times). Bonds not eligible for amortization are also subject to market fluctuations and have a similar effect on surplus. These changes in surplus are *unrealized* capital gains and losses. When bonds and stocks are sold there may be *realized* capital gains or losses.

For a life insurance company it is desirable to provide a cushion to protect surplus against changes in asset values due to market prices. This is accomplished in the U.S. Annual Statement by use of the Mandatory Securities Valuation Reserve, which will be hereafter referred to as the MSVR. This reserve is treated as a liability in the balance sheet. In the

Canadian Statement an *Investment Reserve Fund* may be used to perform a similar function, so it is useful to the Canadian student to understand the operation of the MSVR. The U.S. Reserve is mandatory, whereas the Canadian Fund is optional.

The National Association of Insurance Commissioners requires the MSVR primarily as a means of preventing undue surplus changes arising from fluctuation in the market value of securities owned. The MSVR also absorbs, within certain specified limits, fluctuations in surplus caused by increases and decreases arising out of *realized* capital gains and *realized* capital losses.

The change in the market value of stocks and bonds and the annual change in the MSVR are calculated on working papers but are not usually entered on a life company's ledger. However it is useful to illustrate the changes in the form of journal entries for the benefit of the student in order to clarify the effects of the changes on the accounting equation. An entry for an increase in the value of stocks is:

```
Stocks Owned.............................................1,000
     Unrealized Capital Gain on Stocks........................      1,000
```

The debit portion of the entry is an increase in an asset and the credit is an increase in surplus. If the value of stocks had decreased, the debit would have been to Unrealized Capital Loss on Stocks, reflecting a decrease in surplus, and the credit would have been to Stocks Owned.

The entry to absorb the unrealized capital gain in the MSVR is:

```
Increase in MSVR..........................................1,000
     MSVR.................................................      1,000
```

The debit portion of the entry is a decrease in surplus and the credit portion is an increase in liability (or reserve). If the MSVR had decreased, the debit would have been to the MSVR account and the credit to Decrease in MSVR.

Since the capital gain entry increased surplus by $1,000 and the MSVR entry decreased it by the same amount, there obviously is no net change in surplus. Conversely, there is no net change in surplus if the MSVR is decreased in an amount equal to a capital loss.

The amount of the MSVR each year consists of (1) the previous year's balance plus (2) capital gains less capital losses for the current year plus (3) an additional amount added each year in accordance with a formula.

A maximum amount is established for the MSVR. Until this maximum is reached, capital gains and losses are absorbed by the reserve so that they have no effect on surplus. After the maximum is reached, capital *gains* directly increase surplus and capital *losses* cause the reserve to decrease. If the MSVR balance becomes zero, subsequent capital *losses* would directly decrease surplus.

The maximum MSVR and annual additions to it are calculated by multiplying the admitted values of each of several different types of bonds or stocks by specified percentages. The exact method of calculation is complex and will not be presented here. It is interesting to note, however, some of the specified percentages that are used. The required annual addition to the MSVR on most bonds is one tenth of 1 percent of the admitted value of the bonds, and the maximum reserve for bonds is 2 percent of the admitted value. In the case of common stocks the annual addition is 1 percent and the maximum is $33\frac{1}{3}$ percent of the admitted value. The addition for preferred stocks in good standing is one quarter of 1 percent and the maximum is 5 percent of admitted value. There are several other classifications on which the annual addition is 0.5 percent or 1 percent with maximums of 10 percent or 20 percent of admitted values. In all instances the annual addition is 1/20 of the maximum except in the case of common stocks.

Although the MSVR absorbs surplus fluctuations arising from both bonds and stocks, it is more useful in connection with changes in the market value of common stocks, even though the proportion of insurance company funds invested in stocks is relatively small when compared to that invested in bonds. There are three reasons why this is so: (1) most bonds are eligible for amortization, and their values as presented in the Annual Statement are not, therefore, subject to market fluctuations; (2) the degree of rise and fall in market price is much greater for common stocks than for bonds or preferred stocks; and (3) while common stock holdings of most life insurance companies are a small percentage of total assets, they constitute a large percentage of surplus so that changes in market price could be the cause of substantial surplus changes.

Since U.S. life insurance companies must value common stocks at market for Annual Statement purposes, they must be concerned with unrealized gains or losses on stocks which they own. If no investment reserve were maintained, surplus would fluctuate widely and persons not familiar with this aspect of insurance company statements would assume incorrectly that these swings indicated instability. The protection afforded by the MSVR, therefore, is very important to companies that find it expedient to invest in common stocks.

Since there is no direct change in surplus because of change in market value of amortizable bonds and since most bondholdings are in this category, a lower percentage annual addition to the MSVR is required for bonds owned than for stocks owned. Some reserve is required, however, to absorb gains or losses when bonds are sold and to absorb changes in market value of nonamortizable bonds.

The MSVR is treated as a nonledger liability in the Annual Statement but under the liquidation theory might logically be considered a special surplus classification. This becomes apparent by examining the effect liquidation of a company's assets would have on the MSVR. Common stocks would be sold at market value, which is also the admitted value, so no loss would be suffered on stocks. If the market value of bonds was below the amortized value, some loss would result. This would be taken from the MSVR. The remainder of the MSVR would then become surplus.

Increases or decreases in the MSVR are shown in the surplus account of the Annual Statement as direct charges or credits to Surplus.

MORTGAGE LOANS

Life insurance companies invest heavily in real estate mortgage loans. There are several reasons for this. Life insurance contracts and mortgage loans both tend to be long term. Both are payable in fixed dollar amounts that do not fluctuate with the purchasing power of the dollar. The gross rate of return is usually higher on mortgage loans than on bonds because mortgage loans have relatively higher handling costs.

A real estate mortgage loan is secured by some specific piece of real estate, such as a house, farm, or office building. If the borrower fails to make the required periodic payments of interest and principal, to keep taxes on the property paid currently, or to maintain and insure the property adequately, the lender may foreclose. Foreclosure is a legal procedure by which the lender recovers the unpaid balance or gains title to the real estate if the borrower defaults in his obligation.

The same piece of real estate may be the security for more than one mortgage loan. The basic or major mortgage is called the first mortgage. The difference between the market value of the property and the mortgage loan outstanding is the owner's equity. If the owner's equity is large enough, a second mortgage loan may be made. Most states do not permit insurance companies to invest in second mortgages because a greater risk is involved. The holder of a first mortgage has a claim prior to any other. If the holder of the second mortgage is forced to foreclose the mortgage because the borrower does not make his agreed payments, he must assume the first mortgage to collect on his loan. A mortgage loan made directly by the seller of real estate is known as a *purchase money mortgage*.

Insurance laws generally prohibit first-mortgage loans in excess of 75 percent (in some states 66⅔ percent) of the value of the property, unless the loan is guaranteed by a governmental agency. These agencies, such as the U.S. Federal Housing Authority (FHA) and the Veterans Administration (VA), agree to purchase mortgage loans which the FHA insures or the VA guarantees, in the event of a default. Loans of this type are sometimes made up to 100 percent of the appraised value of the property. The private lender is protected by the government agency guarantee against loss and is presumably, therefore, willing to accept a somewhat lower rate of interest. Mortgage loans which are not insured or guaranteed by a government agency are called *conventional mortgage loans*.

Mortgages may be for any number of years, but on a government-backed loan the term is usually a multiple of 5 up to a maximum of 30 years. On conventional mortgages the term is generally for a shorter period.

The accounting process for mortgage loans in a life insurance company is similar to that used by other financial institutions making mortgage loans. The type of information recorded in connection with each loan is indicated by the subsidiary ledger card shown in Figure 10–3.

When a mortgage is made, an asset account Mortgage Loans is debited on the lender's books and Cash is credited. Usually there are closing costs which are paid by the borrower, but if any expenses are paid by the lender, a simple expense entry of the type discussed in an earlier chapter is used.

In addition the borrower may be required to pay an amount to the lender to be held *in escrow,* or trust, from which property taxes and hazard insurance premiums are paid when due. The amount held in escrow is credited to a ledger liability account in the books of the lending company. If an initial amount of $900 is required for escrow at the time the loan is made, the entry is:

```
Cash......................................................900.00
     Escrow Funds—Mortgages..............................      900.00
```

Escrow entries for each mortgage are posted on each mortgage loan record card to an escrow account. This is a subsidiary ledger account with a control account maintained in the general ledger for all escrow accounts.

The lender has no *legal* obligation to notify the borrower of the due dates of mortgage payments. Many mortgagees, however, send a notice for each payment due shortly before the due date. Another common method is to provide the borrower with a book of dated coupons, one for each payment due. If a payment is a few days late a penalty may be assessed. Penalty charges received may be credited either to Interest Income on Mortgages or to Miscellaneous Investment Income.

Most mortgage loans are repayable in monthly installments. The discussion of accounting for mortgage payments received is, therefore, based on the assumption that all payments are due monthly.

The payment made by the borrower each month includes interest, principal, and in many cases an amount to be placed in escrow. The borrower pays the same total amount to cover interest and principal each month. The portion of the payment applicable to interest is slightly smaller each month because the amount which is applied to principal reduces the loan, which in turn reduces the interest required for the next month. As the interest portion reduces, the portion applicable to principal correspondingly increases. The amount to be placed in escrow is the same

Figure 10–3. Mortgage Loan Ledger Card

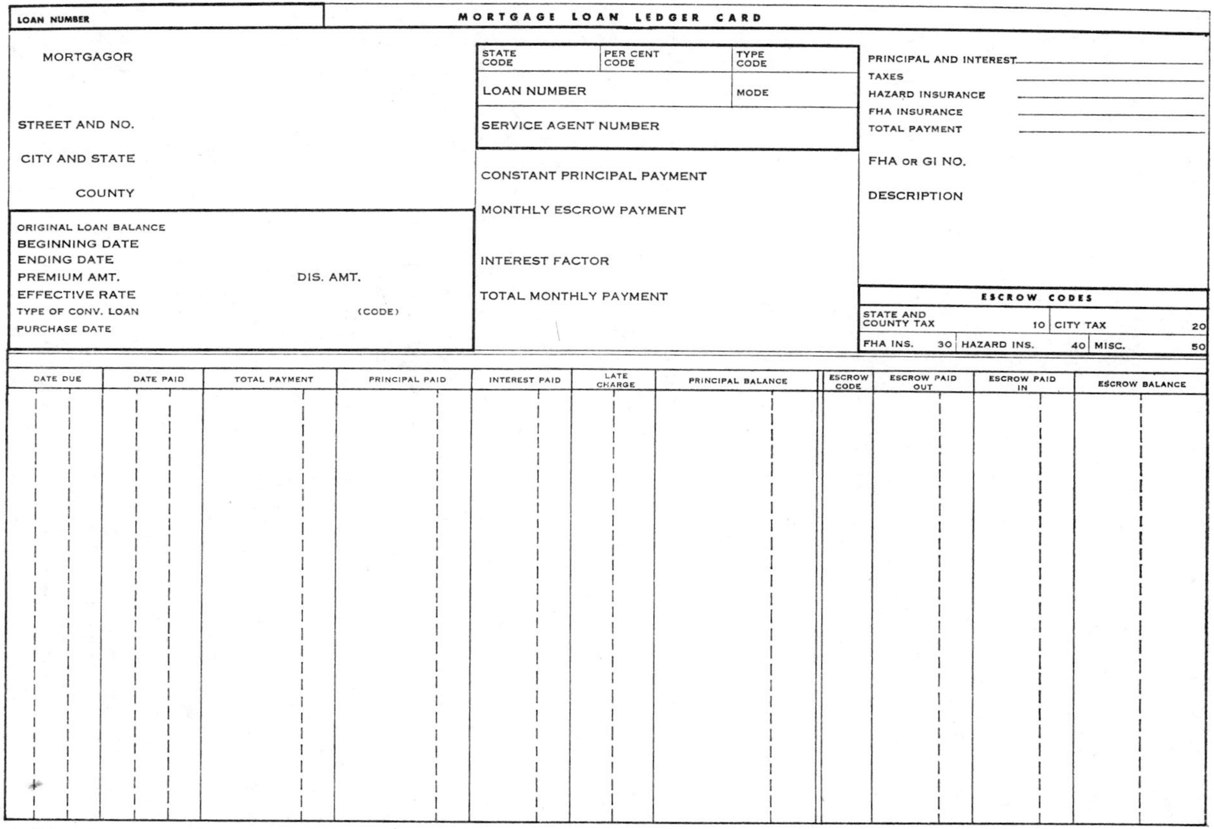
LOAN NUMBER

MORTGAGE LOAN LEDGER CARD

MORTGAGOR

STREET AND NO.

CITY AND STATE

COUNTY

ORIGINAL LOAN BALANCE
BEGINNING DATE
ENDING DATE
PREMIUM AMT. DIS. AMT.
EFFECTIVE RATE
TYPE OF CONV. LOAN (CODE)
PURCHASE DATE

STATE CODE	PER CENT CODE	TYPE CODE
LOAN NUMBER		MODE
SERVICE AGENT NUMBER		

CONSTANT PRINCIPAL PAYMENT

MONTHLY ESCROW PAYMENT

INTEREST FACTOR

TOTAL MONTHLY PAYMENT

PRINCIPAL AND INTEREST
TAXES
HAZARD INSURANCE
FHA INSURANCE
TOTAL PAYMENT

FHA OR GI NO.

DESCRIPTION

ESCROW CODES

STATE AND COUNTY TAX	10	CITY TAX	20		
FHA INS.	30	HAZARD INS.	40	MISC.	50

DATE DUE	DATE PAID	TOTAL PAYMENT	PRINCIPAL PAID	INTEREST PAID	LATE CHARGE	PRINCIPAL BALANCE	ESCROW CODE	ESCROW PAID OUT	ESCROW PAID IN	ESCROW BALANCE

Payments are journalized by using listings made with punched cards and then posted to this record by use of a Transfer-Posting Machine.

each month until changed because the taxes or insurance on the property have changed.

A $10,000, 6 percent, 20-year mortgage requires a monthly payment from the borrower (exclusive of escrow items) of $71.70. The interest income for the first month is $50 ($10,000 × 6 percent ÷ 12) which is credited to an income account. The remaining $21.70 reduces the loan balance. If the total required monthly payment is $80, the amount to be credited to the escrow account is $8.30 ($80.00 − $71.70). If a journal entry were made for the first monthly payment, it would be:

Cash	80.00	
Mortgage Loans		21.70
Interest Income on Mortgages		50.00
Escrow Funds—Mortgages		8.30

When taxes or insurance premiums are paid on the borrower's property, the escrow account is reduced by a debit entry equal to the amount paid. Cash is, of course, credited.

If a mortgaged property is sold to a third party before the mortgage is paid off and if the new owner *assumes* the mortgage, no journal entry is required on the lender's books. The subsidiary ledger account is changed to indicate the new owner, who is then liable for payments as they fall due.

A mortgage may be paid off prior to the end of its term, either by the original borrower or as part of the resale of the property. If, for example, the loan has a balance of $6,500, a credit entry of this amount is required to zero balance the Mortgage Loan account with reference to this particular loan. If the escrow account has a credit balance of $61, a debit entry is required to bring it to a zero balance. If interest accrued since the last monthly payment is $32, a credit entry is required to record this income. The borrower must pay $6,471 ($6,500 loan − $61 escrow + $32 accrued interest).

The entry to record the payoff of the mortgage is:

Cash	6,471.00	
Escrow Funds—Mortgages	61.00	
Mortgage Loans		6,500.00
Interest Income on Mortgages		32.00

Many mortgage loans made by insurance companies are made through real estate firms or mortgage brokers which then service the loans for a fee (usually a percentage of the unpaid balance, e.g., one half of one percent). These servicing firms are called *correspondents*, and their fees are debited to Mortgage Service Fees Paid, an expense account.

Mortgage brokers often make mortgage loans from their own funds and later sell the mortgages to an insurance company. The insurance company may pay an amount equal to the balance of the loan or it may buy the loan at a premium or a discount. The broker continues to service the loan. The borrower may be unaware of the sale because his payments continue to be made to the broker.

A premium paid for a mortgage is usually debited to an account which might be called *Unamortized Premiums on Mortgages.* A discount is usually credited to an account which might be called *Unamortized Discount on Mortgages.* Maintaining separate accounts for the premium and discount amounts permits recording the principal amount in the Mortgage Loan account. This is a desirable practice, since principal and interest payments are based on the balance of principal still unpaid by the mortgagor. Both premiums and discounts are amortized under the alternate method mentioned in connection with bond amortization, but a period shorter than the mortgage period is frequently used. The net book value (principal plus premium or less discount) is the mortgage loan amount shown in the balance sheet.

Once each year the amount to be amortized is determined. Any reduction in premium is, of course, credited to the Unamortized Premium on Mortgages account. Interest Income on Mortgages is debited, thereby decreasing interest earned on mortgages. A typical entry to amortize $1,000 of mortgage premiums is:

Interest Income on Mortgages............................1,000.00
    Unamortized Premium on Mortgages.................   1,000.00

The entry to amortize a discount is a debit to Unamortized Discount on Mortgages and a credit to Interest Income on Mortgages, thereby increasing interest income.

Some companies prefer to record the adjustment to income arising out of amortization of discount by using a subdivision of the Interest Income on Mortgages account. This is done to facilitate preparation of annual statements where the annual amortization must be shown in footnotes.

Occasionally, an insurance company must foreclose a mortgage. On the foreclosure date, the unpaid balance of the loan plus accrued interest and foreclosure costs are recorded as the value of a real estate asset acquired. The essence of the transaction is the conversion of the asset mortage loan into the asset real estate foreclosed.

The following example will illustrate some of the elements of a foreclosure. Assume that the loan balance is $7,290; the appraised value of the property is $10,000; interest has accrued to $710; legal fees of $300 have been incurred relative to the foreclosure.

The total of the loan balance plus accrued interest and costs is $8,300. This total, not the appraised value, becomes the book value of the real estate. The interest income account is credited to record the income, and Mortgage Suspense, a liability account, is credited to record foreclosure costs owed by the company. The entry is:

```
Real Estate Foreclosed...............................8,300.00
        Mortgage Loans.....................................    7,290.00
        Interest Income on Mortgages.......................     710.00
        Mortgage Suspense..................................     300.00
```

When the check in payment of the legal fees is issued, the entry to zero balance the Suspense account with reference to this particular liability is:

```
Mortgage Suspense.......................................300.00
        Cash...............................................     300.00
```

(Questions and problems relating to the two chapters on investment accounting will be found at the end of the next chapter.)

Chapter 11

Accounting for Investments (Part Two)

POLICY LOANS

Policy loans are not handled by the investment department even though these loans are, in fact, investments and interest received on them is treated as investment income. In contrast to other loans, policy loans do not have maturity dates. Systematic repayment plans are not required, and interest need not be paid if a policy has sufficient cash value to secure the loan plus interest. However, most companies bill for interest annually and many encourage systematic repayment of the principal.

Every ordinary life or endowment policy must have a policy loan provision. Policy conditions vary, but a policyowner usually may borrow any amount up to the maximum loan value of his policy. This value consists of the cash value of his policy and paid-up additions less existing indebtedness and interest. If there is an existing loan, it is usually repaid from the proceeds of the new loan. This procedure results in there being only one loan outstanding at any given time.

Loans are usually calculated so that interest will be payable on policy anniversaries. Some companies charge interest on policy loans at the end of the policy year, while others charge interest in advance. Interest charged in advance results in a higher effective rate than when interest is charged at the end of the year, assuming the same stated percent. The following calculations demonstrate the difference.

If 6 percent interest is payable in advance and if $100 cash is desired, a $106.38 loan must be made to produce $100 for the policyowner, the interest charged is $6.38 ($106.38 × 6 percent). The effective rate is, therefore, 6.38 percent ($6.38 ÷ $100). To pay off the loan on the due date requires $106.38.

If interest is payable at the end of the year, the loan amount is $100 and the interest is $6, the effective rate is 6 percent. To pay off the loan on the due date requires $106.

There are two common types of policy loans: conventional policy loans and automatic premium loans.

A *conventional policy loan* is made to the policyowner when he signs an agreement assigning his policy to the insurance company as security for the loan. Endorsement of the policy itself by the company, showing the assignment, may be required as a protection for banks and other loan sources to whom the policy might be offered as security for another loan.

Figure 11–1

RECORD OF LOAN

NO. _____

NAME _____

ANNIVERSARY
DATE _____

ADDRESS _____

DATE OF LOAN _____

| ACCTG. DATE | LOAN | | | INTEREST | |
	DEBIT	CREDIT	BALANCE	AMOUNT	PAID TO

This is a manually posted record.

An *automatic premium loan* (APL) is one which is made in accordance with policy provisions for automatically paying a delinquent premium at the end of its grace period. A special loan agreement is not required because the policyowner previously requested that the APL option in his policy be made effective.

There is a *Policy Loans* control account in the general ledger and an account in a subsidiary ledger for each individual loan. The subsidiary ledger may consist of a file of cards (Figure 11–1), or it may be included as a part of a magnetic record file such as a consolidated function master policy record file.

If a policy loan is made to produce $100 in cash for the policyowner, to pay a premium due of $20, and to pay six months' interest to the next policy anniversary at the rate of 6 percent per annum in advance ($3.72),[1] the journal entry is:

```
Policy Loans...............................................123.72
     Renewal Premiums...................................        20.00
     Interest on Policy Loans............................         3.72
     Cash...............................................       100.00
```

Three months later, the policyowner borrows another $100. The interest to the next policy anniversary on this additional amount is $1.52. The entry increases the Policy Loan account in the amount of the new loan, decreases the same account in the amount of the old loan, records interest income, and records the payment of cash. The entry is:

```
Policy Loans...............................................225.24
     Policy Loans......................................       123.72
     Interest on Policy Loans............................         1.52
     Cash...............................................       100.00
```

It is possible to debit Policy Loans just for the increase, but the method shown permits easier audit and control. If an automatic premium loan is applied, the debit may be made to a special loan account, Automatic Premium Loans.

Separate subsidiary ledger accounts may be maintained for a conventional policy loan and an automatic premium loan made to the same policyowner, or the two may be consolidated, since one interest billing is used to cover both.

A policy loan interest billing usually accompanies or is shown on the premium notice. Exceptions occur when premiums are being paid at some date other than the anniversary or when a policy is paid up.

The entry when policy loan interest is received is:

```
Cash......................................................xxxx
     Interest on Policy Loans............................       xxxx
```

---

[1] The method of calculating interest in advance is a mathematical exercise and not necessary in a study of accounting phases.

If policy loan interest payable at the end of the year is not paid when due and if the cash value is sufficient to cover it, interest is automatically added to the loan. Whenever a loan plus the unpaid interest to date becomes equal to or greater than the cash value of the policy, the policyowner must pay some or all of the interest due or his policy will be cancelled.

If interest has been paid in advance on a policy loan and the loan is paid off or reduced prior to the next interest date, the policyowner may be entitled to a refund for part of the interest he prepaid. This amount of refund can reduce the amount required to pay off the loan. For example, if a $200 loan on which 6 percent interest has been paid in advance is repaid three months before the next interest due date, the entry is:

Cash...	197.00	
Interest on Policy Loans...............................	3.00	
Policy Loans......................................		200.00

The debit to Interest on Policy Loans reduces the interest income to the correct amount for the period for which this loan was outstanding.

If the company does not collect interest in advance, the policyholder must pay the interest when he pays off the loan. When a $200, 6 percent policy loan is paid off three months before its next anniversary, the company must collect nine months' accrued interest in addition to principal. The entry is:

Cash...	209.00	
Interest on Policy Loans............................		9.00
Policy Loans......................................		200.00

The entries required to settle or charge off a policy loan on a policy which is terminated or placed on a nonforfeiture option are discussed in Chapter 17.

REAL ESTATE

The amount invested in real estate constitutes a very small percentage of the investments of most life insurance companies. Most companies own their home office buildings, some branch offices, and a limited amount of other real estate, e.g., that acquired through foreclosures of mortgage loans and not yet sold. Real estate accounting is a specialized subject; consequently, only general elements and entries are presented here.

The cost of real estate is recorded on the books as an asset. This cost includes the purchase price and any *acquisition* costs which include such items as legal fees connected with the purchase and title insurance premiums.

Separate accounts are used for the various types of expense related to ownership of the home office building. Other real estate may be operated for the insurance company by a real estate company which also does the bookkeeping. When this is done, the insurance company accounts are concerned only with the gross income from real estate and total expenses as reported by the operating company.

Property taxes are always an element in the purchase or sale of real estate, but they are recorded as an investment cost, except when property is acquired through foreclosure. Taxes are generally payable in advance at particular times during the year; and in buying or selling real estate, taxes are treated as accruing between tax payment dates. If a purchase occurs after the taxes are paid for the current tax period, the purchaser must reimburse the seller for taxes applicable to the remainder of the tax period.

A comparable situation exists where taxes are not paid in advance. For example, assume that real estate is purchased for $100,000; the title insurance premium is $1,000; legal fees are $1,500; an unpaid property tax for the year amounts to $1,200; and the asset value of $102,500 is debited to Real Estate Owned account. Of the $1,200 tax, $400 has accrued against the seller who must pay this amount to the purchaser or credit it against the purchase payment. On the purchaser's books, this amount is credited to the expense account, Real Estate Taxes Paid. The entry is:

```
Real Estate Owned................................102,500.00
    Real Estate Taxes Paid.........................         400.00
    Cash...........................................     102,100.00
```

After the property tax of $1,200 is paid later in the year and the entry to record the payment is posted, the debit balance of the account Real Estate Taxes Paid will be $800, the amount of taxes applicable to the part of the year the company owned the property. If the property taxes had been paid by the seller prior to the purchase date, Real Estate Taxes Paid would have been debited $800 on the purchase date and Cash would have been credited $103,300 to cover purchase price, acquisition costs, and taxes.

Property taxes paid on real estate obtained by foreclosure and held for resale are usually *capitalized*. This means they are added to the cost of the property. The entry is:

```
Real Estate Foreclosed...........................................xxxx
    Cash..............................................         xxxx
```

If capitalizing taxes brings the book value of the real estate to more than its appraised value in the U.S. Annual Statement, the excess is nonadmitted.[2]

When foreclosed property is sold, any amount received for prepaid taxes or paid for accrued taxes is added to or deducted from the sales price in determining capital gain or loss.

---

[2] A Canadian company must decrease or *write down* the book value, or credit an Investment Reserve account in the amount of excess.

If foreclosed property is rented to produce income, taxes paid are treated as a cost of operating the real estate and are not capitalized.

The cost of real estate (exclusive of land) used in the business or rented to others is amortized over the *useful economic life* of the property by the depreciation accounting process. At least once each year a depreciation entry is made as follows:

```
Depreciation on Real Estate.....................................xxxx
    Accumulated Depreciation on Real Estate.....................        xxxx
```

The credit is made to the Accumulated Depreciation account rather than to the Real Estate Owned account. As a result the original cost of the property remains on the books.

Real estate is admitted in the Annual Statement at the lower of book value or appraised value. Book value is the net of *real estate owned* minus *accumulated depreciation* and any encumbrances which may exist. *Depreciation on real estate* is classed as an investment expense item in Annual Statements and is deducted from gross investment income to determine net investment income.

Major improvements or major repairs which lengthen useful life or are necessary to make saleable real estate acquired through foreclosure may be debited to Real Estate Owned or to the Accumulated Depreciation account, according to the nature of the improvement or repair. If the value of the building is substantially increased by the improvement, such as building an addition, the Real Estate Owned account is debited. If the improvement constitutes a major repair, such as a new roof or new elevators, the Accumulated Depreciation account is customarily debited. The net book value shown in the Annual Statement is the same in either event.

If real estate is sold, the property account and the related accumulated depreciation account in the subsidiary ledger must both be closed. For example, if real estate is sold for $105,000, the cost was $100,000, and the depreciation accumulated to date is $15,000, then there is a realized capital gain of $20,000. The entry is:

```
Cash...........................................105,000.00
Accumulated Depreciation...........................  15,000.00
    Real Estate Owned.............................          100,000.00
    Profit on Sale of Real Estate.................           20,000.00
```

If the selling price had been $80,000, there would have been a $5,000 capital loss ($80,000 − $100,000 + $15,000). The debit to Cash would then be $80,000, and Loss on Sale of Real Estate would have been debited. If there are any selling costs, such as real estate commissions, they are deducted from the sales price in determining capital gain or loss.

Much data is required in the Annual Statement with reference to real estate owned, acquired, and in process of sale. In order to facilitate the preparation of this data, the real estate subsidiary ledger card must include a considerable amount of detail. A sample card is shown in Figure 11–2.

Figure 11–2. Real Estate Ledger Card

REAL ESTATE LEDGER CARD

CARD NO._____

TYPE_____
ADDRESS_____
_____
COST:
  LAND_____
  BUILDING_____
  TOTAL_____

DIMENSIONS:
  LOT_____
  BUILDING_____
  RATE OF DEPRECIATION_____
  MONTHLY RENT_____

REAL ESTATE NO._____
DATE OCCUPIED_____
VENDOR_____
LESSEE_____
LAND COST_____

BOOK BALANCE	DEPRECIATION		RENT			TOTAL RENT TO DATE	BOOK BALANCE	DEPRECIATION		RENT			TOTAL RENT TO DATE
	Amount	Quarter	Amount	Due Date	Date			Amount	Quarter	Amount	Due Date	Date	

This company maintains a record of income and depreciation as well as the current book value on this ledger account card. A separate card of the same size and type is posted to show a history of disbursements for each parcel of real estate. This is a manually posted record.

Mortgage loans against real estate owned are referred to in the Annual Statement as *encumbrances*. Most life insurance companies do not borrow against real estate since they usually have sufficient funds to invest without the need for borrowing. However, some small companies with a limited amount of assets may build or purchase a home office building or other investment real estate subject to a mortgage loan.

If the book value of real estate exceeds the appraised value, the excess must be nonadmitted in the U.S. Annual Statement or the book value reduced. Any reduction in the book value is debited to a capital loss account and credited to Real Estate Owned.

The entry to record income received for rent on real estate is a debit to Cash and a credit to Rental Income.

Most companies own their home office buildings. In such a case, a bookkeeping entry must be made periodically to charge an expense account for rent on space occupied and to credit Rental Income. This is necessary in order to show proper income on invested assets. The cost of rent is usually debited to a Rent Expense account.

OTHER INVESTMENTS

Collateral loans are short-term loans secured by bond or stock assets owned by the borrower. Life companies make few such loans. The accounting for these loans is similar to that for policy loans.

Most states permit a company to carry its EDP equipment as an admitted asset. The entries for the purchase, depreciation, and sale of this equipment are similar to those for real estate, except that no property tax entries are made at the time of purchase or sale.

GROSS AND NET INVESTMENT INCOME

Accrual basis income is shown for each of the major investment classifications in an exhibit in both the U.S. and Canadian Statements. The cash basis income is also shown in the U.S. Statement. The total investment income is described as the gross investment income (see Figure 11–3).

Net investment income is the gross investment income less investment costs. These costs include expenses for servicing and maintaining real estate and for taxes, licenses and fees on investments, and depreciation on real estate. In exhibits relating to expenses and taxes, special columns are included for showing the details of these investment costs. In the analysis of operations (or Canadian analysis of revenue account), *net* investment income is allocated to lines of business. If *gross* rather than *net* income were used, deductions for investment expenses, depreciation, and taxes would also have to be allocated by line of business.

U.S. ANNUAL STATEMENT ASPECTS

Market values of bonds and stocks as of December 31 are published each year by the NAIC. The book in which these values are shown includes many instructions about the valuation of assets and the rules for establishing and maintaining the MSVR. It also shows which bonds are eligible for amortization.

The *admitted* or statement value of a *bond* owned usually is its amortized value. Ordinarily only bonds in default or those with inadequate security are designated as unamortizable and are included in admitted assets at market value. Even though it is not the practice in U.S. companies to actually adjust the book value of bonds or stocks to market value, most subsidiary ledger account cards provide a space for noting the market value as of December 31 each year. This information is shown in the bond schedule included in the Annual Statement blank (Schedule D) which not only shows bonds and stocks owned but also acquisitions and sales during the year.

Schedule D data is used to determine security values that must be non-admitted (excess of book value over market value) and values that may be included as nonledger values (excess of market value over book value). The totals of these nonadmitted and nonledger values are then shown in the Annual Statement's asset exhibit where book values are adjusted to admitted values for the balance sheet.

Bonds owned are listed in Schedule D and subdivided by type of issuing organization as follows: (1) federal governments; (2) states, territories, and possessions; (3) political subdivisions of states, territories, and possessions; (4) revenue authorities and special assessment bonds sponsored by political entities; (5) railroads; (6) public utilities; and (7) industrial and miscellaneous sources.

Schedule D lists stocks owned by company and classifies them as (1) railroads; (2) public utilities; (3) banks, trust companies, and insurance companies; (4) savings and loan associations; and (5) industrial and miscellaneous.

Schedule D also provides space for reconciling the previous and current end-of-year bond and stock balances and shows the amounts of increases and decreases.

Common stocks are valued at market prices, but most preferred stocks in good standing are admitted at cost. Other preferred stocks are admitted at market values quoted by the NAIC. The local market value on December 31 may be used for stocks *not* listed by the NAIC, provided they meet certain standards.

Share certificates in solvent savings and loan associations are admitted at par value since they are practically the same as deposits. Income from such shares is treated as dividends in the Annual Statement.

Mortgage loans are normally admitted at book value for Annual Statement purposes. If, however, a loan exceeds the percentage of appraised value of real estate permitted by law, the excess is not admitted. When payments reduce the principal balance to the permitted percentage, the full balance is then admitted. Mortgages delinquent in payments and those in the process of foreclosure are also admitted at book value if this value does not exceed the maximum prescribed by law.

Mortgage loans are summarized in Schedule B according to type, geographic location, and status of payment, i.e., current, delinquent more than three months, and in process of foreclosure. Only extremely large mortgages are shown as separate items. Mortgage groupings in this schedule include: farm, nonfarm, purchase money, FHA insured, VA guaranteed, and conventional. A reconciliation is also included to show the increases and decreases in the mortgage account from the beginning of year to the end of the year.

Figure 11–3

ANNUAL STATEMENT FOR THE YEAR 1968

Form 1

The figures on this page do not include
Separate Account items, if any.

8

OF THE..COMPANY
(Write or stamp name of Company)

EXHIBIT 2—NET INVESTMENT INCOME
(Accrual Basis)

	DOLLARS	CENTS
1. Gross investment income (Exhibit 3, Col. 7, Line 10)		
2. Investment expenses (Exhibit 5, Col. 3, Line 13)		
3. Investment taxes, licenses and fees, excluding federal income taxes (Exhibit 6, Col. 3, Line 10) . . .		
4. Depreciation on real estate		
5.		
6. TOTAL (Lines 2 to 5 inclusive)		
7. NET INVESTMENT INCOME — Line 1 less Line 6 (to Item 4, Page 4)		
8. Ratio of net investment income to mean assets (see instructions)		%

YEAR OF INVESTMENT INTERROGATORIES

(To be completed by companies allocating Net Investment Income to line of business on page 5 by a year of investment method)

1. Has the material described in Interrogatories 2 and 3 below been previously submitted to the supervisory official of this jurisdiction? ANSWER..............

2. If the answer to Interrogatory 1 is no, attach a full description of the year of investment method used to allocate net investment income by line of business, including;
   (a) The method of classification of investments into categories;
   (b) The method of determination of the contribution of each line of business to each category of investments.

3. If the answer to Interrogatory 1 is no, is the method described in answer to Interrogatory 2 specifically authorized by the law or insurance supervisory official of the state or other jurisdiction under whose laws the company is organized? ANSWER..............

4. If the answer to Interrogatory 1 is yes,
   (a) as to what statement year was the material furnished?
      ANSWER..............
   (b) does the description then furnished remain a full description of the year of investment method currently used to allocate net investment income by line of business?
      ANSWER.............. If not, attach a full description of the method currently used.

EXHIBIT 3—GROSS INVESTMENT INCOME

| | Collected During Year (1) | CURRENT YEAR | | | | Previous Year (3)+(4)—(2)—(5) (6) | Earned During Year (1)—(2)+(3) +(4)—(5)—(6) (7) |
		Unearned (2)	Due (3)	Accrued (4)	Non-Admitted† (5)		
1. Interest on bonds . . *							
2.1 Dividends on preferred stocks . . . †							
2.2 Dividends on common stocks . . .							
3. Interest on mortgage loans . . . . ** ***							
4. Real estate income .							
5. Interest on premium notes, policy loans and liens .							
6. Interest on collateral loans							
7. Interest on bank deposits							
8. Other invested assets (Schedule BA) . . .							
9.							
9.1							
10. TOTALS . . .							

*Includes $..............accrual of discount less $..............amortization of premium and less $..............paid for accrued interest on purchases.

†Excludes $..............paid for accrued dividends on purchases.

**Includes $..............accrual of discount less $..............amortization of premium and less $..............paid for accrued interest on purchases.

***Includes $..............for company's occupancy of its own buildings; and excludes $..............interest on encumbrances.

†State bases of exclusions:

Bonds..............

Stocks..............

Mortgage loans..............

Real estate..............

Collateral loans..............

Bank deposits..............

Other invested assets..............

Policy loans are admitted at book value provided they do not exceed the cash values of the policies on which they were made. Any excess is nonadmitted. No schedule is included in the Annual Statement blank for policy loans.

Each item of real estate owned is described in Schedule A. Items acquired during the year are listed separately from those acquired previously. Each of these two groups are further subdivided into items (1) owned at the end of the year, (2) under contract of sale at the end of the year, and (3) sold during the year. Other portions of Schedule A show summaries of real estate owned by state and foreign country, a reconciliation of the 1–1 and 12–31 real estate account balances, and an analysis of book value of real estate acquired in satisfaction of debt.

The *ratio of net invested income to mean assets* in Exhibit 2 (see Figure 11–3) is calculated by dividing the amount of net investment income earned during the year by the mean admitted value of assets minus one half of the net earned investment income. This net rate is an indication of the soundness of investments and of the success of the investment department in obtaining an appropriate return from funds available. A rate higher than the industry average could suggest speculative and unsound investment, but more commonly it would indicate successful selection of high-return investments. This aspect is discussed more fully in a later chapter in connection with interpreting the analysis of operations.

Capital Gains and Losses Exhibit

Capital gains and losses are presented in a special capital gains and losses exhibit in the Annual Statement blank (see Figure 11–4). Although changes in book value of assets do not create capital gains or losses, one column in the exhibit is headed *Increase in Book Value* and another is headed *Decrease in Book Value.* These two columns together with amounts entered in the fifth column, *Change in Difference between Book and Admitted Values,* are required to determine net capital gains or losses for the year.

The need for including changes in book values in this exhibit becomes apparent when example entries are examined. Assume that stock carried on the books at $1,000 had an admitted asset value of $1 at the beginning of the year and an admitted asset value of $100 at the end of the year. This change in admitted values constitutes an unrealized capital gain of $99. However, it is not possible to obtain capital gains or losses on a mass basis by using the difference in totals of admitted values, because stock is purchased from time to time and new admitted values are constantly being added. If there is no change in book value during the year, the gains or losses can be obtained by using the difference in book and admitted at the beginning of the year (loss to date of $999 in the example) and subtracting

Figure 11–4

*EXHIBIT 4—CAPITAL GAINS AND LOSSES ON INVESTMENTS

	Increase in Book Value (1)	Profit on Sale or Maturity (2)	Decrease in Book Value (3)	Loss on Sale or Maturity (4)	Net Gain (+) or Loss (−) From Change in Difference Between Book and Admitted Values (5)	Net Gains (+) or Losses (−) (1)+(2)−(3)−(4)+(6) (6)
1. Bonds						
2.1 Preferred stocks						
2.2 Common stocks						
3. Mortgage loans						
4. Real estate			**			
5. Premium notes, policy loans and liens						
6. Collateral loans						
7. Cash and bank deposits						
8. Other invested assets (Schedule BA)						
9. Foreign exchange	X X X	X X X	X X X	X X X		
9.1						
10. TOTALS						

10.1 Less federal income taxes incurred on capital gains (show figure in Col. 6) . . . .

10.2 Balance to Surplus Account, Page 4 (show figure in Col. 6) . . . .

DISTRIBUTION OF LINE 10.2, COL. (6). (Attach statement or memorandum explaining basis of division.)

11. Net realized capital gains (+) or losses (−) on assets disposed of during the year $...............less $...............reflected in previous years' statements and less $...............federal income tax incurred on capital gains . . . .

12. Net unrealized capital gains (+) or losses (−) of the year . . . .

*Adjustments due to amortization to be reported in Exhibit 3.

**Excluding $...............depreciation on real estate included in Exhibit 2, Line 4.

the difference at the end of the year (a loss to date of $900 at the end of the year. The change in these differences for the year is a gain of $99).

If the book value is changed during the year, these differences will not produce the correct capital gain or loss. Assume, for example, the book value was written down during the year to $1, representing a recorded capital loss of $999. The change in differences is a gain of $1,098 (from a negative $999 to a positive $99). If this $1,098 gain is consolidated with the book loss of $999, it produces the correct net capital gain of $99.

A column is also included in the exhibit for realized capital gains (*Profit on Sale or Maturity*) and another for realized capital losses (*Loss on Sale or Maturity*).

The final column of the exhibit shows the net gain or loss from all sales and all changes in admitted values of the various investments. Note that federal income tax on capital gains is deducted from the net amount before the net gain is transferred to the Surplus account.

CANADIAN ANNUAL STATEMENT ASPECTS

The method of determining the value of bonds for the Canadian Annual Statement is similar to the U.S. method, but fewer bonds are eligible for amortization. Canadian and provincial bonds and those issued by the Treasury Department of the United States and government of the United Kingdom are valued on an amortized basis. All others are valued in accordance with market values on published lists prepared annually by the Standing Committee on Valuation of Securities of the Association of Superintendents of Insurance of the Provinces of Canada.

Canadian Annual Statements do not show purchases and sales of bonds and stocks, but Canadian life companies are required to file semiannual returns giving this information.

The value of stocks is determined more conservatively for the Canadian Statement than for the U.S. Statement. The book value is used in all instances, but the book value of any stock may not be increased except by specific approval of the Superintendent of Insurance of the Province in which the company has its head office.

If the aggregate book value of securities (bonds and stocks) exceeds their aggregate market value, Canadian companies must establish an investment reserve equal to the excess of book values over market values. This reserve may be a nonledger item. A memorandum adjusting entry to establish this reserve is a debit to Increase in Investment Reserves and a credit to Investment Reserve Funds. The latter item is included with liabilities in the Annual Statement. The debit item is shown as a decrease in surplus in the reconciliation of surplus.

Companies provincially incorporated and not federally registered need not establish the reserve in one year but must increase it each year by at least 20 percent of the aggregate book value over aggregate market value. Companies federally registered are required to establish the reserve by uniform increments over a period of three years.

Since the Canadian method of valuing stocks is more conservative than the U.S. method, there is less need in Canada for a counterpart to the Mandatory Securities Valuation Reserve. However, Canadian companies may elect to use the above mentioned Investment Reserve Fund in a manner which is equivalent to the MSVR.

Other investments such as mortgage loans, policy loans, and real estate are generally included in the statement at book value. Any investment in default or not amply secured may require an adjustment in book value. The same would be true of any item with a market value below the book value or real estate with an appraised value below the book value. Relatively few details are shown in schedules relating to mortgage loans and real estate.

The *investment income*, Exhibit 6 (see Figure 11–5), is the equivalent of Exhibits 2 and 3 of the U.S. Statement in which income items are itemized and totaled. From this total, related expenses, taxes, and depreciation are deducted to obtain the net investment income. Since adjustments to the accrual basis are not made in the annual statement blank, there are fewer columns; the principal one is for the income earned during the year. Columns are included to assemble income due and income accrued amounts at the end of the year. No column is included for unearned investment income, although there is a liability item in the balance sheet entitled *investment income received in advance*. There is a special exhibit (Exhibit 7) for calculating the net rate of investment income earned on cash and invested assets.

Capital Gains and Losses (Exhibit 8)

There are two principal differences between this exhibit and its equivalent in the U.S. blank: (1) there is no reference to admitted values because book values are used as admitted values in the statement and (2) the column headings are worded differently even though they have the same meaning. The expressions *writing-down* and *writing-up* are used rather than *increase* or *decrease in book value*. *Excess of sale price* and *deficiency of sale price* are used and generally have the same meanings as *profit* and *loss* (see Figure 11–5).

Although changes in the book value of invested assets have no effect on surplus in the U.S. Statement, this is not true in the Canadian Statement. Since the Canadian Statement does not provide for nonledger and nonadmitted assets, the book values are, in effect, the admitted values. There-

12

Figure 11-5. Canadian Statement Exhibits

....
(Name of Company)

EXHIBIT 6—INVESTMENT INCOME

	Earned during year (1)	Due at end of year (2)	Accrued at end of year (3)
	$	$	$
1. Interest on bonds			
2. Dividends on stocks			
3. Interest on mortgage loans			
4. Interest on agreements of sale of real estate			
5. Income from real estate, including $............... for Company's occupancy of its own buildings			
6. Interest on collateral loans			
7. Interest on policy loans			
8. Interest on bank deposits			
9. Interest on overdue premiums			
10.			
11.			
12.			
13. Totals: Gross investment income			
14. Investment expenses, including $............... real estate expenses			
15. Investment taxes, including $............... real estate taxes			
16. Regular annual depreciation of real estate			
17. Total: Investment expenses, investment taxes and regular annual depreciation of real estate			

1. Net investment income.. = I = $.................... (Exhibit 6, item 18)

2. Income-yielding assets (including cash), together with investment income due and accrued:

   (1) At beginning of year.. = A = $.................... (items..............., page 2, statement for previous year.)

   (2) At end of year... = B = $.................... (items..............., page 2, this statement)

3. Net rate of investment income earned $= \dfrac{2I}{A + B - I} =$ .... %

EXHIBIT 8—CAPITAL GAINS AND LOSSES ON INVESTMENTS

	Gains			Losses		Net gain (+) or net loss (−)
	Writing-up of book value	Recoveries	Excess of sale price or maturity value over book value	Writing-down of book value	Deficiency of sale price or maturity value under book value	
	$	$	$	$	$	$
1. Bonds....................................						
2. Stocks....................................						
3. Mortgage loans on real estate........						
4. Agreements of sale of real estate......						
5. Real estate owned, not under agreement of sale.....						
6. Collateral loans.........................						
7.						
8.						
9.						
10.						
11. Totals....................................						

fore, a change in book values in the Canadian Statement increases or decreases surplus by the amount of the increase or decrease.

A change in book value does not change unrealized gains to realized gains, but it does affect subsequent "gain or loss" entries. If stock is purchased for $1,000 and the book value is later reduced to $800, the capital gain and loss exhibit shows a $200 capital loss (write down) in the year the reduction is recorded. The entry is:

```
Stocks Written Down........................................200.00
    Stocks Owned........................................            200.00
```

If the stock is later sold for $1,100, a $300 capital gain (excess of sale price over book value) is shown in the exhibit. The entry in year of sale is:

```
Cash........................................1,100.00
    Stocks Owned........................................            800.00
    Excess, Sales Price versus Book Value..................            300.00
```

SUMMARY OF ACCOUNTING FOR LIFE INSURANCE COMPANY INVESTMENTS

A *control account* is maintained in the general ledger for each investment classification, and a *subsidiary ledger account* is maintained for each specific investment.

Accrual basis investment income (earned income) consists of investment income collected in the accounting period, adjusted for the increase or decrease in (1) unearned investment income, and (2) due and accrued investment income.

An *interest adjustment* is made when bonds are bought and sold.

A *bond premium* is the excess of cost over par value. The effective or yield rate of interest on bonds purchased at a premium is lower than the stated or coupon rate.

A *bond discount* is the excess of par value over cost. The effective or yield rate of interest on bonds purchased at a discount is higher than the stated or coupon rate.

Realized capital gain is the excess of sales price over cost or amortized value of an investment. *Unrealized capital gain* is an increase in the admitted values of an investment.

Realized capital loss is the excess of cost or amortized value over sales price of an investment. *Unrealized capital loss* is a decrease in the admitted value of an investment.

The *Mandatory Securities Valuation Reserve* is an amount set aside as a liability in the U.S. Annual Statement for the purpose of minimizing ill effects arising out of the fluctuations in surplus that would otherwise result from both realized and unrealized capital gains and losses on bonds and stocks.

Mortgage payments usually include three amounts: a reduction of principal, interest, and escrow. Escrow is an amount set aside in a liability account for payment of taxes and insurance premiums. Unpaid interest and taxes on a delinquent mortgage may be capitalized at the time it is foreclosed.

Real estate is recorded on the books at cost, which includes purchase price, title insurance, and legal fees. Depreciation entries on buildings owned must be made at least once annually. Major improvements or major repairs made to real estate which lengthen its useful life may be capitalized.

Offsetting rent income and rent expense entries must be made in connection with real estate occupied by the company.

QUESTIONS FOR CHAPTERS 10 AND 11

1. How are individual investment amounts reflected in the general ledger? In what respects do subsidiary investment records differ from simple ledger accounts?

2. Name two types of government bonds and three types of corporate bonds. What are two methods for paying interest on bonds? Name two classes of stock, two types of mortgage loans, and two types of policy loans.

3. What effect, if any, does par value have on (*a*) market prices? (*b*) on the accounts of a company that issues par-value stock? or (*c*) on the accounts of a company that buys it?

4. If the Mandatory Securities Valuation Reserve is well below the maximum amount, how do the following changes in value effect the MSVR: (*a*) Realized capital gain on bonds? (*b*) Realized capital gains on stocks? (*c*) Change in market value of amortizable bonds? (*d*) Change in market value of stocks? (*e*) Realized capital gain on real estate? and (*f*) Loss on the sale of amortizable bonds?

5. How would the changes in value in Question 4 affect the MSVR and surplus if the MSVR has reached (*a*) its maximum prior to these changes? (*b*) a zero amount?

6. What are the four types of first-mortgage loans? Are premiums and discounts on mortgage loans amortized over the mortgage period? Why is it desirable to record the original principal balance remaining unpaid in the mortgage loan account if a premium is paid for a mortgage?

7. If a mortgage is purchased at a discount, how is the discount entered on the books? How is it amortized?

8. Under what circumstances must a policyowner pay policy loan inter-

est to prevent cancellation of his policy? Under what circumstances are policy loans nonadmitted in the U.S. Annual Statement?

U.S. Annual Statement Questions

9. How are the various investment income items assembled for the U.S. summary of operations? How are capital gains and losses assembled for the surplus account of the Annual Statement? What exhibits and schedules in the U.S. Annual Statement show data on the various investment classifications?

10. How is the book value of stock adjusted to the admitted value (*a*) if the admitted value is less? (*b*) if the book value is less?

Canadian Annual Statement Questions

11. How is the value of stocks determined for the Canadian Annual Statement? What affect does market value have on the value used? What bonds are amortizable?

12. How are the various investment income items assembled for the revenue account? How are capital gains and losses assembled for the surplus reconciliation? What exhibits in the Canadian Annual Statement show data on the various investment classifications?

PROBLEMS FOR CHAPTERS 10 AND 11

1. Prepare journal entries, post to T-accounts, and prepare a trial balance showing the effect of the following entries. (This problem emphasizes investment accounting only, so insurance income and costs have been intentionally omitted.)

The trial balance on January 1 is as follows:

Cash	$155,000.00	
Bonds owned	11,500.00	
Stocks owned	1,450.00	
Mortgage loans	15,600.00	
Policy loans	8,333.00	
Foreclosed real estate	15,125.00	
Mortgage escrow		$ 586.00
Balance account		206,422.00
	$207,008.00	$207,008.00

a) On January 1, 100 shares of stock in XYZ Corporation are purchased for $59 per share. The par value is $10 per share.

b) On February 1 a policy loan is increased to pay a $25 premium, pay $95 in cash to the borrower, and pay interest of $11 on the old loan of $220.

c) On March 1 a cash dividend of $145 is received on stock owned on January 1.

d) A cash dividend of 50 cents per share and a stock dividend of 10 shares are also received from XYZ Corporation.

e) On April 1 a $1,000 revenue bond is purchased for $950. The interest dates are January 1 and July 1. The stated interest rate is 3 percent, and the effective rate is 4 percent. Accrued interest of $10 is paid.

f) On May 1, $250 is paid from the Mortgage Escrow account to pay insurance premiums.

g) On June 1 the company buys a home office building for $100,000. The title fee is $890, and accrued taxes to date are $1,100.

h) On June 15, $500 in bond interest is received.

i) On July 1, 55 shares of stock in XYZ Corporation are sold for $63 per share.

j) On July 1 semiannual interest of $15 is received on the revenue bond purchased in April.

k) On August 1 the company receives a cash dividend from XYZ Corporation of $1 per share. The company also receives mortgage payments totaling $1,500. Of this amount, one half is interest, $600 is to be applied to principal, and the remainder is escrow deposits.

l) On September 1 the company pays $275 from the escrow account for taxes on mortgaged property and it pays $300 for taxes on foreclosed real estate held for sale and $3,000 for taxes on the home office.

m) On October 1 the company sells all of the foreclosed real estate for $16,000. Sales commission is $960, and the buyer reimburses the company for $75 in incurred taxes.

n) On November 1 the company receives $500 in policy loan interest.

o) On December 1 the company makes a journal entry recording $6,000 for rent paid to itself for use of the home office building.

p) On December 31, the company makes an amortization entry for $6.33 in connection with the revenue bonds and a depreciation entry on the home office building in the amount of $1,500.

2. Determine accrual basis income on bonds, mortgages, real estate, and policy loans using the cash basis income from the trial balance in Problem 1 and the following asset and liability amounts:

	End of Year	Beginning of Year
Accrued interest on bonds	$ 48.00	$ 41.00
Accrued interest on mortgages	86.00	75.00
Accrued rent	600.00	0.00
Accrued interest on policy loans	42.00	35.00
Unearned interest on mortgages	10.00	16.00
Unearned interest on policy loans	272.00	211.00

Chapter 12

Premium Accounting— General

Premium income is the principal source of income of a life insurance company. It is appropriate, therefore, to discuss in considerable detail the accounting processes used to control and record this income.

Entries to record premium income are relatively simple, but the related processes for billing and accounting for premiums are quite intricate. This is so because—

1. Premiums must be controlled so that all premiums due are collected and recorded in a manner that will provide a clear history of payment.
2. Accounting for commissions payable to agents and premium taxes payable to states must be coordinated with accounting for premiums.
3. Annual Statement requirements pertaining to premiums, commissions, and premium taxes are quite complex.

PREMIUM ACCOUNTING SYSTEMS

The methods used to control and account for premiums and commissions vary according to the premium collection systems used. These systems may be classified for discussion purposes as individual, debit, and group. Under these systems the methods are generally described as collection by mail, collection by agent, and collection through employers. There are variations within each system, however, that would make these general descriptions inappropriate in some cases.

The *individual* premium system involves collection of one premium at a time by mail. It is usually applied to premiums in the ordinary, individual health, and annuity lines of insurance.

The *debit* premium system involves collecting premiums through agents who call at the homes of policyowners. The debit system was originally developed for use in connection with industrial insurance, but it is often used in connection with ordinary life and individual health insurance in those companies using the debit system.

The *group* system involves billing and collecting premiums on a number of insured persons through a common employer, trustee, or association. It is used primarily in connection with group life and health insurance and in connection with group annuities.

Each of these premium collection systems, together with related commission accounting processes, is described in subsequent chapters. First, however, it is desirable to understand the general phases of premium and commission accounting and the method of presenting this data in Annual Statements. This chapter is devoted, therefore, to premium matters which are common to all three systems, and the next chapter is devoted to general phases of commission accounting. Examples in these two chapters are based on ordinary insurance for convenience, but they also are generally applicable to other lines of business.

OBJECTIVES OF PREMIUM ACCOUNTING

The first step toward an understanding of premium accounting is an appreciation of the objectives of this important function.

The objectives of premium accounting are:

1. To provide a means of quickly determining at any time the date to which premiums have been paid. This date is required for most transactions with policyowners and is also required in connection with valuation of premium assets and premium liabilities at the end of each accounting period.

2. To control premiums currently payable, or about to become payable, so that (*a*) all premiums are properly billed when due; (*b*) no payment is applied against a currently due premium until all premiums outstanding have been accepted; *(c)* no premium is accepted after the expiration of the grace period, except under circumstances acceptable to the company; and (*d*) if a premium is not paid, the policy is terminated or changed from premium-paying status to one of the nonforfeiture option classifications.

3. To control premiums received so that (*a*) all amounts collected outside the home office are promptly remitted or deposited and reported to the home office, and (*b*) all premiums received at the home office are promptly accounted for, deposited, and recorded to the credit of the proper policy.

4. To establish audit trails to (*a*) the bank deposit in which a particular premium was included, (*b*) the journal entry in which that premium was included, (*c*) the policy record to which it was credited, and (*d*) to the commission payment made in connection with the receipt of the premium. The audit trail must be sufficiently complete to enable a state examiner or other auditor to begin from any one of the four points mentioned and trace the specific payment to the others without undue searching.

5. To record premium income accurately *(a)* by states and sometimes by cities and counties for the purpose of premium tax assessments, *(b)* by line of business, and *(c)* by participating and nonparticipating classifications.

The processes by which these objectives are achieved under each of the premium collection systems are covered in detail in subsequent chapters. Conditions that constitute legal payment of a premium are common to all three systems and will be discussed at this point.

PREMIUM CONDITIONS

Unlike many other businesses which bill for individual purchases, a life insurance company cannot legally enforce the collection of a premium. Since insurance premiums are payable in advance before the service is received by the purchaser, the service can be terminated if the payment is not made. The only penalty to the policyowner for nonpayment of a premium before the expiration of the grace period is termination of his insurance protection at the end of that period, subject to his rights under applicable nonforfeiture options. The provisions of reduced paid-up or extended insurance options constitute continued service (insurance protection), but on a modified basis.

If a policyowner fails to pay a premium within the grace period, he may still make application for reinstatement of the policy. He must pay the back premiums, plus interest, and submit certain required forms to the company, which may include a statement of insurability. A policyowner's request for reinstatement may be refused by the company and his money refunded if he is no longer insurable.

If the payment was made by mail, the postmark date is considered the date of payment; and in case of late payment, the envelope is usually retained as evidence of the date of payment.

In the case of ordinary insurance, many companies extend a liberal reinstatement offer for a limited time after the grace period. During this offer period, the only requirement for reinstatement may be that the insured be living on date of reinstatement. Payments made after the end of this period, however, are subject to the normal reinstatement requirements.

If a premium payment is made after the grace period, the company cashier must determine that the policy has been properly approved for reinstatement before the premium is credited to the policy. This approval is usually made by an underwriter.

Sometimes a policyowner sends a check for an amount slightly different from that actually due or he enters a different amount in the space for figures than he entered in the space for the written amount. In such a case, the payee (the insurance company) may make a correction on the face of the check, endorsing it to guarantee payment of the altered amount. With this procedure, the check will be cleared by the policyowner's bank for the correct amount of premium in a timely manner, without the delay and annoyance of correspondence or phone calls. There is rarely a dispute with a policyowner because of this practice. This procedure is not used, however, if the amount is in dispute.

A check presented by a policyowner may be returned by the bank on which it was drawn because there was insufficient funds in the policyowner's account, or for other reasons. Many companies merely deposit insufficient fund checks a second time. Often, by the time the check again reaches the policyowner's bank, the policyowner's account will have a balance large enough to cover the check.

Unless notice is given to the contrary, a policyowner's right to be credited for a premium is not forfeited when a check is not honored. To provide proper notice, premium notices or receipts usually include a provision to the effect that a check does not constitute premium payment until it has been honored by the depository on which it is drawn. Notice of dishonor can be given by written notice to the person who wrote the check within 24 hours after the payee learns that it has been dishonored.

If proper notice is not given, the rights of the company are limited to making collection on the check. In this event, the company cannot declare the policy lapsed even though it is unable to collect the amount of the check.

Premium notices are mailed to policyowners as a means of inducing them to make prompt payment. Once this is done, it becomes a legal obligation to continue mailing notices. Some states require proof by affidavit that premium notices were mailed a minimum number of days before premium due dates.

PREMIUM LIABILITIES

Before examining premium entries, it is desirable to examine the nature of the four principal premium liability classifications. These classifications are (1) advance premiums, (2) premium deposits, (3) unearned premiums, and (4) premium suspense.

An *advance premium* is a whole premium not yet due which has been recorded in a premium account prior to the statement date. For example, a premium due on January 2, which was credited to the premium income account prior to December 31, is an advance premium on December 31. Principally, this advance premium classification covers only premiums received in the normal course of business but may be applied to cover premiums paid several years in advance. The amount of advance premiums on the statement date is a liability and is used, along with the amount at the beginning of the period, to adjust premium income from the cash to accrual basis. "Advance premiums" is a nonledger liability.

Most companies allow a discount on premiums paid a year or more in advance. In the United States these premiums may be recorded in the premium account, in which case the present value on statement date is treated as advance premiums. However, most U.S. companies and all Canadian companies treat discounted premiums as premium deposits.

Premium deposits are amounts accepted by and left on deposit with the company for payment of future premiums. The amount received is credited to a special premium deposit account and not to a premium account. The deposit account is usually a ledger liability account, in which case premiums are transferred to the premium account and interest is added to the deposit account each year. Premium deposits are not used to adjust premium income from the cash to accrual basis.

Although most companies prefer to accept only discounted premiums as premium deposits, some companies accept regular contributions in amounts unrelated to the premium on a policy. This is done (1) to accumulate an emergency fund that can be used when the policyowner is otherwise short of funds, (2) to accumulate an additional amount that may be withdrawn at maturity, or (3) to establish a payment frequency or amount different from that available to the policyowner under usual payment methods.

The distinction between advance premiums and premium deposits is largely the manner in which amounts intended to pay future premiums are recorded. This distinction is apparent in the following example.

A policyowner pays two $100 premiums in December of the current year. The first of the two will be due in January of next year and is recorded in the premium account. On December 31, it is an advance premium. The second premium paid will not be due until a year later, so a $4 discount is allowed (one year's interest at 4 percent). This second payment of $96 may be recorded in the premium deposit account, in which case the $96 becomes a premium deposit. If the $96 had been credited to the premium account, it would have been an advance premium.

Unearned premium is the portion of a gross premium either due or received in the current year but applicable to the following year. For example, on December 31 a quarterly premium of $24 due on December 1 has an unearned premium liability of two months, or $16 ($24 × ⅔).

The term "unearned premiums" is applied usually to health insurance, not to life insurance or annuity business. Life insurance and annuity policy reserves are set up on the theory that an annual premium has been paid in advance. The net premium applicable to the next calendar year is included in the mean reserve. In health insurance, reserves are set up on a midterminal basis, which does not include premiums applicable to the following calendar year. It is necessary, therefore, to set up an additional liability for the portions of premiums that will be earned in that period.

In industrial insurance, mean reserves are usually calculated on a midterminal basis. Any weekly premium paid for a period extending into the following year might be considered an unearned gross premium, but it is usually treated as an advance premium. In connection with group life insurance, some companies calculate reserves as though they were unearned net premiums but show them in the annual statement as policy reserves. The distinction here between advance premiums and policy reserves lies in the fact that industrial unearned premiums are calculated on a gross premium basis, whereas group life insurance unearned premiums are calculated on a net premium basis.

A fourth premium liability is *premium suspense*. Premium suspense describes a ledger liability account used to record amounts intended as premiums but which cannot be accepted into income until a particular event occurs. For example, money may be credited to premium suspense, pending approval and issue of a policy.

PREMIUM ENTRIES

The basic entry for premiums collected is:

Cash...xxxx
   Premium Income... xxxx

The amount of premium received is credited to the Premium Income account regardless of the actual due date unless it is to be placed on deposit or held in suspense.

Premium entries are usually compound entries and may affect accounts other than premium income and cash. For example, the policyowner may also pay policy loan interest or deduct policy dividends when he makes his premium payment.

If the premium due is $100, loan interest due is $25, and a policy dividend of $11 is payable to the policyowner, the proper amount of the check will be $114 ($100 + $25 − $11), and the entry is:

Cash..114.00
Dividends Applied to Premium...............................11.00
   Premium Income.. 100.00
   Interest on Policy Loans.............................. 25.00

Most journal entries for premium payments cover many payments rather than only one as is shown in this example. A large number of premiums may be combined and listed so that only one journal entry need be made for the entire list. The greater the number of payments included in one entry, the greater the possibility of account variations in the composite entry. Such an entry might include credits for ordinary premium income in the first policy year, other credits for premium income in subsequent years, and still other credits for health insurance premiums and annuity considerations in first policy year and for subsequent policy years. There would, of course, be a debit to cash, and there could be other debits for dividends paid and for several other types of permissible deductions.

If a check is not honored by the bank on which it is drawn, the original premium entry must be reversed by means of a new entry. The Premium Income account is debited to reduce the premium income, and Cash is credited to correct the bank account.

The entry to reverse a $150 premium entry is:

```
Premium Income....................................150.00
    Cash...........................................         150.00
```

Notice that the entry is an exact reversal of the original premium payment entry. The Cash (or Bank) account and Premium Income account balances are reduced in the amount of the dishonored check. Entries which may have been made to other accounts at the time the check was received also are reversed.

Some companies prefer to delay reversing the premium entry until an effort has been made to collect on the check. If this is to be done, an entry must be made to correct the bank account. The entry requires a debit to an accounts receivable account known as Returned Checks (or similar title) and the credit to the Cash account. If the check is made good, the returned check entry is reversed. If a $150 check is not made good, the entry is:

```
Premium Income....................................150.00
    Returned Checks................................         150.00
```

This entry effectively removes the specific returned check item from the account by that title and reduces the premium income account balance to the amount prior to the first premium entry.

Amounts may be received which cannot be immediately credited to premium income. Since it is desirable to deposit the money immediately, a liability account Premium Suspense is created for that purpose and credited for the amount deposited. The entry to record a $200 amount placed in suspense is:

```
Cash..............................................200.00
    Premium Suspense...............................         200.00
```

When the reason for holding the premium is satisfied, the entry to apply the amount in suspense as an actual premium is:

```
Premium Suspense.........................................200.00
      Premium Income.......................................          200.00
```

Note that this entry clears the Premium Suspense account of the amount which had been placed in it, that is, the account is zero balanced with reference to this particular $200 item.

Premium deposit entries have some of the characteristics of suspense entries in that premium deposits are usually credited to ledger liability accounts and eventually must be cleared out when all amounts have been applied to premiums. However, the interest paid or allowed as a discount on these deposits introduces a new element.

If, for example, renewal premiums on an ordinary policy are $100 per year and are paid 10 years in advance for a discounted value of $843.53, the typical entry to record the amount received is:

```
Cash...................................................843.53
      Premium Deposits.....................................          743.53
      Premium Income.......................................          100.00
```

Note that the currently due premium is not credited to the premium deposit account (liability) but is credited directly to the Premium Income account (income).

To continue the example, one year later when the next premium becomes due, the $29.74 interest on the total principal (4 percent of $743.53), is entered as a debit to a cost account for Interest Paid on Policy and Contract Funds. The full amount of the premium due is credited to the Premium Income account, and the difference is debited to the Premium Deposit account. The typical entry to transfer a premium from the Premium Deposit account to the premium income account is:

```
Premium Deposits.........................................70.26
Interest Paid on Policy and Contract Funds...................29.74
      Premium Income.......................................          100.00
```

Each year the process is repeated until the amount held in the deposit account has been reduced to zero. Because of the interest allowed, the 10 premiums credited over the 10-year period will, of course, be more than the amount received.

Commissions are not normally paid on premium deposits until the due dates of the premiums occur because the policyowner may request that his deposits be returned to him, in which case the commission will not have been earned. Each year the commission account is debited for the amount of commission on the premium then due and the agent's account is credited. Thus, at the end of the 10th policy year the agent will have been credited with the same total commissions he would have received had the premiums been paid in cash year by year.

If a U.S. company chooses to credit the discounted amount of premium deposits to an income account at time of initial receipt, the annual entries can be eliminated.[1] However, such a procedure would complicate reporting the amount of interest credited to the deposit for federal tax purposes each year. Commissions would, presumably, be paid on the entire deposit at time of receipt. In such a case, the premium liability at the end of each year would be inventoried and included in the annual statement as advance premiums, a nonledger liability.

PREMIUM COLLECTION PROCESS AND CONTROL

Controlling premiums through billing, collecting, accounting, and recording operations is an especially intricate process. Absolute accuracy must be achieved if the goodwill of policyowners is to be retained and business conserved.

In commercial accounting, control of amounts due is accomplished by bookkeeping entries recording the amounts due which are then posted to accounts in the ledger. These amounts remain on the books until paid or deemed uncollectable. Since most life insurance companies keep books on a cash basis and since life insurance premiums are not debts, accounting and control of due items is normally accomplished outside of the formal accounting system.

A premium control process must insure that each premium due—

1. Is either paid
   a) In the amount billed, or
   b) On a modified but acceptable basis, or
2. If not paid, the policy records are changed from a premium-paying status to one indicating either:
   a) A nonforfeiture option is in effect, or
   b) The policy is terminated without value.

Premium control may be accomplished by two general types of accounting control. These are (1) item control and (2) dollar control.

Item Control

Item control is the use of records in a control file which are changed or removed one by one as each transaction occurs. No record is removed from the control file or changed until the final step in the process being controlled has been or is about to be completed. This method is used for handling individual premium payments in small companies and branch

---

[1] Canadian companies treat all premiums on which a discount is allowed as premium deposits.

offices of larger companies. It is also used along with dollar controls in large companies.

The principal control record in a premium collection process is usually a punched card which is referred to here as a *collection card*. Premium notice stubs and other types of records may be used, but punched cards are most frequently used, even when master files are on magnetic tapes or discs.

Collection cards are prepared concurrently with premium notices and are then used to prepare accounting entries and to post status records. The term collection card as used here means any record that is used to provide item control on due premiums and which is used also to list premium transactions. This record may be in card form or may be a part of a magnetic record file.

Each time a premium is paid, a collection card is removed from the control file and used to make a journal entry. If a premium is not paid by a certain date, the collection card is removed from the control file and used to list policies to be changed from an active premium-paying status to a lapsed or nonforfeiture status. The card is returned to the file until the change process is completed, and then it is removed. When the last card has been removed, there is assurance that all items have been paid or properly processed for termination of payment status.

When computers are used, item control may be achieved by the use of the master policy record. The paid-to-dates on the master file are periodically compared with current dates and special forms or lists printed out to trigger various phases of notice preparation and conservation activity or to change policies from a premium-paying to a nonpremium-paying status.

When the master file rather than a collection card file is used for item control, a simple input record may be prepared when each premium is paid. This record may be in the form of punched cards or paper tape, or may be a premium notice stub if an optical scanner is used. The computer then generates premium and commission transaction records automatically from the input and from commission schedules and other data stored on magnetic records.

Item control on a manual basis is reasonably effective if adequately supervised and if extreme care is used to insure that every card removed temporarily for change or correction is returned to the file. Individuals working on records may not be properly instructed or may be careless. They may inadvertently destroy a card, punch it incorrectly, return it to the wrong file, or otherwise destroy its usefulness as a control device. Machines may also malfunction, resulting in an incomplete report or erroneous totals. These difficulties in effective item control can be detected by use of dollar control. This method was discussed in connection with machine accounting (Chapter 6), but it will be useful to examine it as it applies to premium accounting transactions.

Dollar Control

Dollar control is a process for continuously maintaining a grand total on hundreds of separate amounts in a file while amounts are being added to and deleted from the file. A dollar control is established initially by adding all of the amounts to be controlled. The resulting total is updated periodically thereafter by adding new amounts being added to the file and subtracting amounts being deleted from the file.

Typical uses for dollar control are: (1) under the individual premium system, determining if all premiums due at a particular time have been billed; (2) under the weekly premium system, determining the amount of premiums due each week from an agent; and (3) under the group premium system, determining the amount of premium due each month from an employer.

Dollar control is most effective when changes are listed as they are made and when the individual amounts in the file are resummarized periodically to prove the accuracy of the updated total. If a discrepancy occurs, the change lists must be used to reconcile the beginning list with the resummarized list to identify the error and to correct it.

Dollar controls are especially effective and are inexpensively maintained when computers are used. Dollar controls are also frequently used in connection with unit record equipment. When manual accounting processes must be used, this method of control is too tedious and expensive to maintain.

Typical Premium Control Process

This book frequently refers to accounting processes used in an imaginary company, The Model Life Insurance Company. This is done to assist the student to understand the many phases of insurance accounting and to apply this knowledge to practical situations.

The accounting processes described are typical and are commonly used. They are not necessarily recommended for general use because the needs of one company vary from those of others.

The following is a typical process for maintaining a dollar control as used in individual premium accounting.

In The Model Life Insurance Company the master premium billing file is dollar controlled by totaling all premiums in a billing category, i.e., all premiums due on a particular date in a particular branch office, payable on a particular mode. As policies are issued, premium amounts of the new policies are added to the proper control total, and as policies lapse, their premium amounts are subtracted. As changes in collection office or mode occur, the premium amounts are deducted from one control total and added to another.

The dollar control total at Model Life Insurance Company on all policies in force with monthly premiums payable to Collection Office A on April 10 is $10,051. A policy is issued with a monthly premium of $25 which will be due on the 10th day of each month. Another policy on which a premium of $12 was due on April 10 is lapsed. A policyowner whose monthly premium of $9 was due on April 10 changes his premium to $100 payable annually. The new in-force control total for monthly premiums due on the 10th to Collection Office A, is calculated as follows:

Beginning total	$10,051.00
Add issues	25.00
Subtract lapses	−12.00
Subtract transfer to annual	− 9.00
Ending total	$10,055.00

When monthly premium notices are prepared for April 10, the total of premium amounts in them must agree with the in-force control total to prove there is a notice for every premium due on that date. This control total is then maintained for premiums due on April 10 of that year. The total is decreased for payments received, changes to other modes, transfers to other branch offices, and transfers to nonforfeiture or lapsed status, until the control total is reduced to zero. The zero balance proves that every premium due was paid or the policy was transferred to a lapsed or nonforfeiture status.

Dollar controls on premiums for policies in force at The Model Life Insurance Company are used to calculate deferred premiums at the end of the year. For example, the dollar control on all policies in force on December 31 payable on the monthly mode with a March anniversary month is $1,000. The gross deferred premium for those policies is $2,000 ($1,000 for January and $1,000 for February).

Due premiums on December 31 are calculated quickly from dollar controls on the due file. For example, on December 31, the dollar controls on premiums due in October but still unpaid add up to $100. The controls on premiums due in November but still unpaid add to $560, and the controls on premiums due in December but still unpaid add to $5,200. The total of gross due premiums at the end of the year, therefore, is $5,860 ($100 + $560 + $5,200).

U.S. ANNUAL STATEMENT ASPECTS

There are two major reports in the U.S. Annual Statement relating to premium income. These are the premium exhibit in which premiums are adjusted from the cash to the accrual basis and Schedule T in which the premiums collected during the year are shown by states. These are discussed in this section along with balance sheet items, including the unique process used to reduce gross premium assets to their admitted values.

Premium Exhibit

The premium exhibit is divided into two parts (see Figure 12–1). The first shows the premium adjustment process and is entitled "Premiums and Annuity Considerations (Gross, Less Reinsurance Ceded)." The second part shows the amount of reinsurance premiums deducted in Part 1. The second part also shows dividends applied toward payment of premiums during the year and commissions incurred.

Accrual basis premiums are calculated in the premium exhibit by treating both gross deferred and gross due premiums as accrued income in the sense discussed in connection with commercial accounting. Advance premiums are treated as unearned income in the same sense. Unearned life insurance premiums are not shown as such in the premium exhibit. However, unearned industrial and unearned health insurance premiums may be included with advance premiums.

Using life insurance terminology, accrual basis premiums are (1) collected premiums, (2) plus gross deferred and uncollected premiums at the end of the current year, (3) less gross deferred and uncollected premiums at the end of the previous year, (4) less advance premiums at the end of the current year, (5) plus advance premiums at the end of the previous year. An example of the calculation of accrual basis premium income is presented in the section of this chapter entitled "Increase in Loading."

Premiums for the first policy year are shown in the premium exhibit separately from single premiums and renewal premiums. This first-year information is useful to insurance departments in determining whether the rights of participating policyowners or of stockholders are being impaired by the payment of excessive commissions or other first-year costs in connection with new business.

In both the first-year and renewal sections of the exhibit, the amount of uncollected, deferred, and advance premiums at the end of the year are shown on separate lines. These amounts for the beginning of the year are combined into one line.

Only one line is required in the exhibit for single premiums because there are no due and advance premiums in connection with single premiums.

A column is included in the premium exhibit for each major line of business and for some sublines.

Column headings for all parts of the premium exhibit are the same as those in the analysis of operations, except that there is no column in this exhibit for supplementary contracts. Amounts held under supplementary contracts are the same on the accrual basis as they are on the cash basis, so no useful purpose would be served by including such a column. The totals by line of business are entered in the analysis of operations.

Schedule T

In the U.S. Annual Statement, this schedule shows the allocation of collected premiums (cash basis) by states and territories. The totals from this schedule must agree with the amount of collected premiums shown in the premium exhibit (Exhibit 1) and with the company's premium journals to prove that all premiums have been allocated and none omitted.

Columns are provided for life insurance premiums, health insurance premiums, and annuity considerations. Spaces are also provided for showing nontaxable premiums, such as premiums waived because of disability and portions of premiums that may be nontaxable in some states, such as dividends deducted from premiums.

State insurance departments refer to Schedule T to verify premiums reported to them in connection with premium taxes. The departments also require an affidavit as to the total premiums collected in their particular states, not only to doubly verify the amounts reported but also to certify the accuracy of any deductions or credits allowed by the states not provided for in Schedule T.

Periodically during the year premiums collected by mail must be tabulated by states from which they were received and reconciled with the related account totals in the general ledger to prove that all premiums have been tabulated and totaled. This must be done frequently to prevent an undue clerical burden at the year-end when premium taxes become payable and when Schedule T is prepared.

Companies which have regional collection offices often do the distribution by state in these offices, especially if collection office responsibilities overlap state lines. The premium totals for each state are reported to the home office where a state register of premiums is maintained for each line of business. At the end of the year, the totals of the various registers such as industrial, ordinary, and group are consolidated to produce the totals that are entered in Schedule T.

Increase in Loading

In the summary of operations and the analysis of operations there is an unusual item known as *increase in loading on and cost of collection in excess of loading on deferred and uncollected premiums*. This item represents a combination of two subitems: (1) *increase in loading on deferred and uncollected premiums* and (2) *cost of collection in excess of loading*

Figure 12–1. U.S. Premium and Commission Exhibit

Form 1   ANNUAL STATEMENT FOR THE YEAR 1968 OF THE.......................................

		TOTAL (1)	INDUSTRIAL LIFE (INCLUDING TOTAL AND PERMANENT DISABILITY AND ACCIDENTAL DEATH BENEFITS) (2)	ORDINARY	
				LIFE INSURANCE (3)	TOTAL AND PERMANENT DISABILITY (4)
PART 1—Premiums and Annuity Considerations (Gross, Less Reinsurance Ceded)					
FIRST YEAR (Other Than Single)					
	1. Uncollected				
	2. Deferred				
	3. Line 1 + Line 2				
	4. Advance				
	5. Line 3 — Line 4				
	6. Collected during year				
	7. Line 5 + Line 6				
	8. Previous year (uncollected + deferred — advance)				
	9. First year premiums and considerations Line 7 — Line 8				
	SINGLE				
	10. Single premiums and considerations . . .				
	RENEWAL				
	11. Uncollected				
	12. Deferred				
	13. Line 11 + Line 12				
	14. Advance				
	15. Line 13 — Line 14				
	16. Collected during year				
	17. Line 15 + Line 16				
	18. Previous year (uncollected + deferred — advance)				
	19. Renewal premiums and considerations Line 17 — Line 18				
	TOTAL				
	20. Total premiums and annuity considerations Lines 9, 10 and 19 (to agree with Item 1, Page 4)				
PART 2—Dividends Applied, Reinsurance Ceded and Commissions Incurred					
	DIVIDENDS APPLIED (Included in Part 1)				
	21. To pay renewal premiums (Exhibit 7, Line 1)				
	22. All other (Exhibit 7, Lines 2, 3 and 4) . .				
	REINSURANCE CEDED (Deducted in Part 1)				
	23. First year (other than single)				
	24. Single				
	25. Renewal				
	26. Total				
	COMMISSIONS INCURRED				
	27. First year (other than single)				
	28. Single				
	29. Renewal				
	30. Total (to agree with Item 21, Page 5) . .				

Note: In Part 1, the "CURRENT YEAR" label appears vertically beside lines 1–9 (FIRST YEAR) and beside lines 11–19 (RENEWAL).

....COMPANY
(Write or stamp name of Company)

EXHIBIT 1

The figures on this page do not include Separate Account items, if any.

ADDITIONAL ACCIDENTAL DEATH (5)	INDIVIDUAL ANNUITIES (6)	GROUP		ACCIDENT AND HEALTH		
		LIFE INSURANCE (7)	ANNUITIES (8)	GROUP (9)	OTHER (10)	
						1.
						2.
						3.
						4.
						5.
						6.
						7.
						8.
						9.
						10.
						11.
						12.
						13.
						14.
						15.
						16.
						17.
						18.
						19.
						20.
						21.
						22.
						23.
						24.
						25.
						26.
						27.
						28.
						29.
						30.

on deferred and uncollected premiums. For convenience, this item is referred to here more simply as *increase in loading.*

The gross amount of deferred and uncollected premiums is used to adjust premium income from the cash to the accrual basis for the summary of operations. The anticipated cost of collecting these premiums, including commissions to be paid on them, might be considered accrued expense. Therefore, the increase in this cost from one year-end to the next, or increase in loading if greater, is treated as an insurance cost in the summary of operations. However, on the liability page of the balance sheet, only the anticipated cost of collection in excess of loading is shown as accrued expense. The portion of this cost represented by loading is deducted from gross uncollected and deferred premiums, and the net amount is shown as an admitted asset.

An example, using adjusting entries, will clarify the adjusting process used to obtain the Increase in Loading. Assume that anticipated cost of collection does not exceed loading.

The following figures were used in adjusting from the cash to accrual basis premium income:

Premiums collected this year	$1,200.00
Less premiums in advance 12/31 this year	−45.00
Plus premiums in advance 12/31 last year	+15.00
Plus gross premiums deferred and uncollected 12/31 this year	+185.00
Less gross premiums deferred and uncollected 12/31 last year	−148.00
Premium income (accrual basis)	$1,207.00

Assume loading of $46.25 on premiums deferred and uncollected at the end of this year. The proper admitted asset value is then $138.75 ($185.00 − $46.25). Last year the corresponding loading was $37.00, and the net admitted asset value was $111.00 ($148.00 − $37.00).

If adjusting entries were made on working papers by use of the reversal and reentry method, the reversal of last year's gross deferred and uncollected premiums would be:

Premium Income	148.00	
Deferred and Uncollected Premiums		148.00

The entry to record the amount this year would be:

Deferred and Uncollected Premiums	185.00	
Premium Income		185.00

These entries result in the correct accrual basis premium income, but result in the deferred and uncollected premium asset being shown on a gross premium basis. At the end of the previous year, the gross deferred and uncollected premiums were reduced to the then admitted amount of $111.00 by an adjusting entry. The entry this year to reverse that adjustment is:

Deferred and Uncollected Premiums	37.00	
Increase in Loading		37.00

The entry to reduce the premium asset to the admitted amount at the end of the current year is:

```
Increase in Loading.........................................46.25
    Deferred and Uncollected Premiums........................        46.25
```

When posted to T-accounts, the Increase in Loading account will show a debit balance (or cost) of $9.25, and the balance in the asset account Deferred and Uncollected Premiums will be $138.75, which is the new admitted value.

If there had been accrued costs in excess of loading, similar adjustments would have been made to establish a liability for cost of collection in excess of loading.

Miscellaneous

In the U.S. Annual Statement unearned health insurance premiums may be included with advance premiums, in which case they are used to adjust premium income from the cash to the accrual basis. The exhibit for health insurance reserves includes a line for unearned premiums, so most companies treat them as policy reserves, not as advance premiums. Only in connection with health insurance are unearned premiums mentioned in the U.S. Annual Statement. They are included in an exhibit and on the liability page as a part of the item described as *aggregate reserve for accident and health policies.* This item is a nonledger liability.

Health insurance premiums due are admitted at the gross amount. Related commissions and estimated cost of collection are included with commission liabilities and are used to adjust commissions from the cash to the accrual basis.

Advance premiums and premium deposits are shown as separate liabilities in the balance sheet. If a discount was allowed when the premiums were received, the liability amount is the present value of future premiums on December 31.

Amounts held in suspense pending issue or reinstatement of a policy are ledger liabilities and are shown on the balance sheet under the title *remittances and items not allocated.* The Returned Check account, if one is used, is treated as a nonadmitted asset for balance sheet purposes.

CANADIAN ANNUAL STATEMENT ASPECTS

There are a number of exhibits in the Canadian Annual Statement relating to premium income and one relating to commissions.

Premium Exhibits

Accrual basis income figures only are shown in the Canadian premium exhibits. Neither cash basis figures nor adjustments from cash to accrual

Figure 12-2.   Canadian Premium and Commission Exhibits

EXHIBITS

.... *(Name of Company)* ....

	Insurances				
—	Ordinary		Group		Industrial
	Participating	Non-participating	Participating	Non-participating	
	$	$	$	$	$

EXHIBIT 1—INSURANCE PREMIUMS AND ANNUITY CONSIDERATIONS

	Participating	Non-participating	Participating	Non-participating	Industrial
1. Net of reinsurance ceded:					
(1) Single					
(2) First year					
(3) Renewal					
(4) Totals					
2. Reinsurance ceded:					
(1) Single					
(2) First year					
(3) Renewal					
(4) Totals					

EXHIBIT 2—COMMISSIONS ON INSURANCE PREMIUMS AND ANNUITY CONSIDERATIONS

	Participating	Non-participating	Participating	Non-participating	Industrial
Net of reinsurance ceded:					
1. Single					
2. First year					
3. Renewal					
4. Totals					

basis are included. Related premium asset and premium liability figures are shown in other exhibits.

Exhibit 1 is titled *Insurance Premiums and Annuity Considerations* (see Figure 12-2). Amounts are shown separately for first-year premiums, single premiums, and renewal premiums and are shown net of reinsurance ceded.

The premium exhibit is divided into two parts: the first shows the accrual basis premium income, net of reinsurance; the second part of the exhibit shows reinsurance premiums which were deducted in Part 1.

The column headings of Exhibit 1 show the same lines of business as the "Analysis of Revenue Account by Line of Business" but are arranged differently. Premiums relating to insurance are shown in the left portion of the exhibit and summarized into a total column for insurance. Annuity considerations are shown in the right portion and summarized

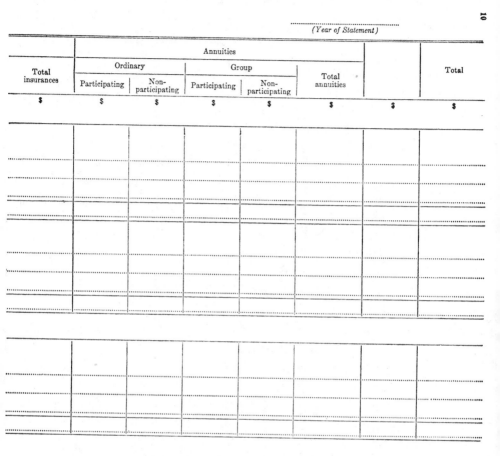

Total insurances	Annuities					Total annuities		Total
	Ordinary		Group					
	Participating	Non-participating	Participating	Non-participating				
$	$	$	$	$		$	$	$

(Year of Statement)

into a total column for annuities. The premium income totals for each line of business column become the premium income amounts shown in the "Analysis of Revenue Account by Line of Business."

Details relating to the premium asset for outstanding premiums at the end of the year are shown in Exhibit 12, which is titled *outstanding insurance premiums and annuity considerations*. Details relating to deferred premiums are shown in Exhibit 13, titled *deferred insurance premiums and annuity considerations* (see Figure 12–3).

The format of Exhibits 12 and 13 is substantially similar. Each has columns for showing first-year premiums, renewal premiums, and a total column. In addition, the exhibit for outstanding premiums has a column for single premiums. Each exhibit is divided into two sections, one for insurance premiums and the other for annuity considerations.

For balance sheet purposes, the gross outstanding premiums and annu-

Figure 12-3. Canadian Premium Asset Exhibits

....
(Name of Company)

....
(Year of Statement)

EXHIBIT 12—OUTSTANDING INSURANCE PREMIUMS AND ANNUITY CONSIDERATIONS

(net of reinsurance ceded)

	Single	First year	Renewal	Total
1. Insurances:	$	$	$	$
(1) Gross				
(2) Deduct commissions and estimated loss in collection				
(3) Net totals				
2. Annuities:				
(1) Gross				
(2) Deduct commissions and estimated loss in collection				
(3) Net totals				
3. Net totals: Insurances and annuities				

EXHIBIT 13—DEFERRED INSURANCE PREMIUMS AND ANNUITY CONSIDERATIONS

(net of reinsurance ceded)

	First year	Renewal	Total
1. Insurances:	$	$	$
(1) Gross			
(2) Deduct loading			
(3) Net totals			
2. Annuities:			
(1) Gross			
(2) Deduct loading			
(3) Net totals			
3. Net totals: Insurances and annuities			

ity considerations are reduced by the amount of commissions that will become payable, and estimated cost of collection that will be incurred when these premiums and annuity considerations are received. This reduction is shown in Exhibit 12. Only the net amount is allowable as an asset in the balance sheet, where it appears as *outstanding premiums and annuity considerations.*

The *gross* outstanding premium amount at the beginning and end of the year is used to adjust premium income to the revenue basis. The amount of *Estimated Commissions and Collection Charges* deducted from these premiums is an accrued expense, but is not treated as a liability in the balance sheet. It is treated as a negative asset and is offset or netted against outstanding premiums. For example, if Outstanding Premiums are $800 and the related commission and collection cost is $60, the amount shown as an asset under Outstanding Premiums is $740 ($800 − $60). This netting is shown in Exhibit 12. This accrued expense at the beginning and end of the year is used to adjust Commissions from the cash to the revenue basis. Health insurance due premiums are handled in the casualty blank in a similar manner.

In each section of the deferred premium exhibit, loading is deducted from the gross deferred premiums and annuity considerations to arrive at net deferred premiums and annuity considerations. These amounts are then deducted from the mean reserve liability at the end of Exhibit 15, which is titled *valuation summary.* The net amount from Exhibit 15 is the actuarial reserve shown on the liability page on the balance sheet. In effect, the net deferred premiums are treated as a reduction in reserve liability rather than as an asset. The effect on surplus is the same.

There is no need for an item in the revenue account equivalent to the *increase in loading* item of the U.S. summary of operations because net deferred premiums and annuity considerations are deducted from policy reserves and because the anticipated cost of commissions and estimated cost of collecting outstanding premiums are used to adjust commissions. In effect, the commission account is increased by the amount that would be shown in a U.S. Statement as *increase in loading on due premiums.*

Exhibits 12 and 13 do not show premiums by line of business. The gross amount of outstanding premiums and annuity considerations must be allocated by line of business on working papers to arrive at the premium income for Exhibit 1. Neither do the exhibits show these premiums and considerations by participating and nonparticipating insurance. They are shown separately, however, when used in the valuation summary.

Miscellaneous

Unearned premiums are calculated in connection with group life insurance and included with policy reserves. Unearned health insurance premiums are treated as premium liabilities in the casualty blank and are used to adjust health insurance premium income from the cash to the revenue basis.

Advance premiums are nonledger liabilities and are used to adjust premium income to the accrual basis. Advance premiums are shown on the liability page of the balance sheet as *insurance premiums and annuity considerations received in advance*. They are not shown in any exhibit.

Premium deposit liabilities are included with other amounts on deposit and shown as a part of the deposit liability in the balance sheet.

Premium suspense amounts are included on the liability page as a part of *amounts received but not yet allocated*.

A Returned Checks account balance is not an admissable asset. If such an account is used, its balance must be written off. This can be done by crediting the Returned Check account and debiting a premium account at the end of the year. The use of a Returned Check account has some advantages in controlling unpaid premiums, but a Canadian company might prefer to debit the Premium account each time a check is returned to minimize end-of-year problems.

The Canadian equivalent of Schedule T of the U.S. Annual Statement is Exhibit J (b) which is entitled *insurance premiums and annuity considerations (net of reinsurance ceded)*. Premiums are shown for each Canadian province with a single line for all *out of Canada* business. Premiums are shown by lines of business in this schedule. Premiums are not separated for participating and nonparticipating as they are in many other exhibits and reports. A similar exhibit is included in the casualty blank.

The method for assembling the figures by provinces is the same as that described for U.S. companies relative to states.

SUMMARY OF PREMIUM ACCOUNTING FUNDAMENTALS

An *advance premium* is a whole premium not yet due which has been recorded in a premium account prior to the statement date.

Premium deposits are amounts accepted by and left on deposit with the company for payment of future premiums.

Unearned premium is the portion of a gross premium *due* or received in the current year but applicable to the following year.

Premium suspense is a ledger liability account used for recording amounts until they can be credited to a premium account.

Dollar control is a process for continuously maintaining a grand total on hundreds of separate amounts in a file while amounts are being added to and deleted.

Item control is accomplished by use of a file from which records are removed as controlled transactions occur.

Inclusion of uncollected premiums on the asset page of the balance sheet at net premium values and at gross premium values in the premium income item of the summary of operations requires a special adjustment amount in the operating statement. This is shown as a separate item known as *increase in loading* in the U.S. Statement and is included with commissions in the Canadian Statement. Similar treatment to that used for due premiums is required in connection with deferred premiums in the U.S. Statement.

QUESTIONS

1. Describe each of the three principal premium collection systems. Name the lines of business with which they are commonly used.

2. What are the objectives to be achieved in properly accounting for premiums? Why is the process so much more complex than simply journalizing premiums as they are received? Why aren't premiums recorded on the journal as they become due?

3. If a payment is late, how does the company establish the fact that the premium was mailed within the grace period? If a check is not honored, describe two alternate ways of recording the transaction. What must the company do if it wishes to consider such a dishonored check as nonpayment of the premium?

4. What is the extent of a company's responsibility with reference to mailing premium notices? Is it acceptable practice to alter check amounts? If so, how is it done?

5. Describe each of the principal premium liabilities. What distinction, if any, exists between premium deposits and advance premiums as shown in U.S. Annual Statements? In the Canadian Statement? Which of these liabilities are normally used to adjust life premium income from the cash to accrual basis?

6. Describe a premium accounting system that uses both item and dollar control, explaining how each is adjusted when (*a*) a premium is paid, (*b*) a policy is lapsed, and (*c*) a premium is paid under a different mode than billed.

U.S. Question

7. How are premium assets shown in the balance sheet? In what way are they used to calculate accrual basis life premium income? Which premium liabilities are used to adjust premium income to the accrual basis? Is the increase in loading treated as an operating cost? Why? How is it calculated?

Canadian Question

8. How are deferred premiums and outstanding premium amounts incorporated in the balance sheet? Explain how each is used to adjust

premium income from the cash to accrual basis, if so used. How is cost of collecting outstanding premiums shown on the balance sheet? Which premium liabilities are used to adjust life premium income to the accrual basis? Why is there no *increase in loading* item in the revenue account?

PROBLEM

Make the journal entries for the transactions described below. Post them to T-accounts, prepare a trial balance, make adjusting entries, and prepare an adjusted trial balance. A balance account is used to eliminate unnecessary detail.

At the beginning of the year the trial balance is as follows:

Trial Balance

Cash	$ 9,750.00	
Policy loans	250.00	
Premium deposits		$ 140.00
Premium suspense		12.00
Balance account		9,848.00
	$10,000.00	$10,000.00

The chart of accounts shows accounts for Interest Paid on Policy and Contract Funds, Premium Income—Life, Premium Income—Health, Policy Loan Interest, and Dividends Applied to Premiums.

U.S. terminology is used to present the problem, but Canadian students should use Canadian methods in the solution.

a) On December 31 of the preceding year, advance life premiums were $105, unearned health insurance premiums were $58, gross due premiums were $78, gross deferred premiums were $273, and accrued policy loan interest was $3.

b) On January 1 a check was received to pay a $100 premium and $15 in policy loan interest due on December 15 of the previous year.

c) On January 15 a policy was issued and $12 in suspense was applied to pay the premium.

d) On February 1 a check was received to pay a $120 premium currently due, less $18 in policy dividends.

e) On February 15 a check to pay a $700 premium was received.

f) On February 16 check received on February 1 was returned by the bank.

g) On February 28 the February 1 check was made good with a money order.

h) On March 1 the sum of $450 was received to pay a currently due premium of $100, with the balance to be placed on premium deposit at 4 percent per annum.

i) On April 1 a $10 premium was applied from a premium deposit of $100. The interest is 4 percent per annum.

j) On May 1 an application for insurance was received and $15 was tendered as the first premium.

k) On May 10 the policy applied for on May 1 was issued.

l) On June 1 a $45 check was received to pay a health insurance premium.

m) On December 15 an agent submitted an application for a new policy and remitted $100 on a $200 annual premium.

n) On December 24 the check received on December 15 is returned by the bank unpaid. On the same day the company issues the policy C.O.D., and reverses the suspense entry.

o) At the end of the year advance premiums total $102, unearned health insurance premiums total $69, gross uncollected life premiums total $85, gross deferred premiums total $281, and accrued policy loan interest totals $5.

p) The loading and cost of collection in excess of loading are 20 percent of the gross deferred and uncollected premiums. The reversal and reentry method is recommended for making the adjustments.

Use of working papers with this problem will complicate the solution because more than two entries are required to adjust each premium account. It is suggested that T-accounts be used and that each nonledger asset item at the beginning of the year be recorded in an asset account. This can be done by debiting the proper asset account and crediting the Balance account. Nonledger liabilities required in the adjusting process should also be transferred from the Balance account. A credit to the liability account and a debit to the Balance account will accomplish this. Show the nonledger account balances in your adjusted trial balance along with the revised balance of the Balance account.

The object of this problem is to test your knowledge of (1) typical premium entries, (2) the process by which premium assets and premium liabilities are used to adjust premium income from the cash to accrual basis, and (3) the amounts shown in the balance sheet for each premium asset or liability. It is not necessary to prepare an operating statement or balance sheet for this purpose.

The total of the trial balance and the account balances in the adjusted trial balance are shown in the "Answer to Problem" to enable you to check your work.

Chapter 13

Accounting for Agents' Commissions

The amount of commissions payable to an agent in connection with the sale or servicing of a life insurance policy is dependent upon the amount of premiums received. Commission accounting processes must, therefore, be coordinated with premium accounting processes.

Different methods of computing commissions may be used for each line of insurance, but in all lines, commissions usually are specified as a percentage of premiums received by the company. A higher percentage is payable on premiums collected during the first policy year than on those collected in subsequent (renewal) years. In ordinary and industrial insurance, the first-year percentage also varies by plan of insurance. The percentage during renewal years may remain at one level for a period of years and varies little by plan of insurance.

Commissions may also be paid upon increase of insurance in force or other indication of increased production.

General agents, branch managers, and other sales supervisors may be paid a percentage of each premium collected on policies written by agents who work under their supervision. This type of commission is known as an overwriting or overriding commission. For convenience, these supervisory personnel will be referred to as overriding agents.

Commission calculations can be quite complex. Extreme care is required to make the correct calculation and to credit each commission to the proper agent.

OBJECTIVES OF COMMISSION ACCOUNTING

Commission accounting can best be understood in the light of its objectives. These are as follows:

1. To determine accurately the amount of commission payable on each premium received
2. To record and tabulate accurately commission amounts payable to, and premiums or other amounts due from, each agent so that periodic settlement may be made
3. To report earnings for each agent to tax authorities and forward all payroll and withholding taxes on those earnings
4. To establish an audit trail from the premium payment on which the commission was calculated, to the commission entry in the journal, and to the commission entry in the agent's account

COMMISSION RECORDS

Two primary records are used in connection with commission accounting for all lines of insurance other than debit system insurance. These two records are the commission statement and the agent's ledger account. They are frequently consolidated into a single record when electronic data processing equipment is used, but they are discussed here as separate records. Some companies call the agent's account a statement, so care is needed to distinguish between the two.

Commission statements (see Figure 13–1) are lists of commissions earned. These statements usually show the amount of commission earned on each premium received, the policy number, the amount of each premium, the month and year the premium was due, and the name of the insured. One of these statements is prepared for each agent. A separate statement may be prepared for each line of business, such as ordinary, group, individual annuities, individual health, and any convenient subdivision.

Notice in Figure 13–1 the following: (1) this particular statement covers only ordinary renewal commissions as indicated by the code 2 on the statement; (2) the first money column shows the premium received, the second column shows the agent's commissions, and the third shows the overriding commissions; and (3) totals are shown which can be posted to the agent's and general agent's accounts in a subsidiary ledger.

The *agent's account* is a combination of accounts receivable (when the agent owes the company) and accounts payable (when the company owes the agent). Both conditions may exist from time to time, but not simultaneously for any one agent. Many companies advance commissions (that is, make a loan) to a new agent during his early months under contract. During this period his account will have a debit balance like any other account receivable. Later, when the advances are repaid and the company owes commissions to the agent, his account will have a credit balance signifying an account payable (see Figure 13–2).

Commissions earned year-to-date are usually shown on the account

Figure 13-1. A Typical Commission Statement

ML THE MODEL LIFE INSURANCE COMPANY

DETAIL LISTING OF COMMISSIONS

Period Ending	Account Number	
0 1 / 3 1 / 6 9 Month / Day / Year	1 2 6 1 2 3	JOHN Q. AGENT

2

TYPE OF BUSINESS: 1 = ORDINARY 1st YEAR   2 = ORDINARY RENEWAL   3 = A & S

Due Date		Mode & Pr. Mo.	Policy Number	Name of Insured or Sal. Sav. No.	Plan Code	Premium Amount	Commission Amount	Commission Amount
Month	Day							
B	1 4	4 1	9 3 0 3 5	H A T A L I A F	A	1 7 7 6	1 7 8	8 9
1	1 4	D 1	9 3 0 3 6	S M Y O R K	A	1 6 6 6	1 6 7	8 3
1	1 4	D 1	9 3 0 4 9	C O S A N S O N	A	9 2 6	9 3	4 6
1	1 3	D 1	9 3 0 5 0	B W K I N G	A	8 4 1	8 4	4 2
1	1 3	D 1	9 3 0 5 1	C L W H I T E	A	9 0 1	9 0	4 5
1	1 2	D 1	9 3 3 5 6	D L W H I T E	A	8 5 6	8 6	4 3
1	0 6	D 1	9 3 4 5 6	C L F O R D	A	3 8 8 6	3 8 9	1 9 4
1	2 7	Q 1	9 3 5 2 7	M T B A R N E T	A	4 0 2 5	4 0 3	2 0 1
1	1 4	4 1	9 3 7 9 7	T C L E W I S	A	1 5 9 0	1 5 9	8 0
1	1 2	4 1	9 4 2 8 3	N L W A G O N E	A	9 2 0	9 2	4 6
J	2 5	A J	9 4 5 0 3	T E B E A T L E	A	3 6 4 0 0	3 6 4 0	1 8 2 0

51-020	TOTALS ⟶	5 3 7 8 7	5 3 8 1	2 6 8 9

This information will be reflected on your monthly summary statement (Form 71-027) by total only

form, but this is supplemental information and not a part of the account in a bookkeeping sense. This information is required for earnings reports to tax authorities and is included because it can easily be recorded and summarized whenever the ledger is posted. Companies with computers frequently include statistical information on the agent's account record because this information can be obtained economically from the same machine runs that produce or post each agent's account.

Agents' accounts are usually maintained in a subsidiary ledger, with a

Figure 13-2

THE MODEL LIFE INSURANCE COMPANY

FEB., 1969 SUMMARY STATEMENT OF AGENT'S ACCOUNT

AGENT JOHN Q. AGENT #111
AGENCY
ADDRESS

DATE	REFERENCE	PARTICULARS	FIRST YEAR PREMIUM	TRANSACTION AFFECTING YOUR COMMISSION ACCOUNT (EARNED-BLACK REVERSED)	TRANSACTION AFFECTING YOUR DUE ACCOUNT WITH THE COMPANY — DEBITS	— CREDITS	TOTAL CURRENT BALANCE	THIS YEAR'S EARNINGS TO DATE	PROOF (AGENT DISREGARD THIS COLUMN)
		BALANCES FORWARDED					275.38 $	1,624.75 CR	1,349.37 CR
FEB 3 65	11,773	JOHN Q. AGENT - ADVANCE.			300.00		575.38 $	1,624.75 CR	1,049.37 CR
FEB 10 65		J Q AGENT - CHG. SHORTAGE ON #104773 FOXWORTH			.46		575.84 $	1,624.75 CR	1,048.91 CR
FEB 14 65		J Q AGENT - CREDIT OVERAGE ON #102334 JONES				.27	575.57 $	1,624.75 CR	1,049.18 CR
FEB 28 65		J Q AGENT - CHG. CANCELLATION FEE ON #102345 BROWN			5.00		580.57 $	1,624.75 CR	1,044.18 CR
FEB 28 65		J Q AGENT - FEES RETAINED.			32.00		612.57 $	1,624.75 CR	1,012.18 CR
FEB 28 65		J Q AGENT - HEALTH INSURANCE COMM.		196.30		196.30	416.27 $	1,821.05 CR	1,404.78 CR
FEB 28 65		J Q AGENT - GROUP COMM.		84.62		84.62	331.65 $	1,905.67 CR	1,574.02 CR
FEB 28 65		J Q AGENT - RENEWAL COMM.		157.14		157.14	174.51 $	2,062.81 CR	1,888.30 CR
FEB 28 65		J Q AGENT - FIRST YEAR COMM.		574.81		574.81	400.30 CR	2,637.62 CR	3,037.92 CR
FEB 28 65		J Q AGENT - CHG. GROUP INSURANCE FOR FEB.			9.56		390.74 CR	2,637.62 CR	3,028.36 CR
FEB 28 65		J Q AGENT - CHG. AGENTS DEFERRED COMPENSATION PLAN			33.34		357.40 CR	2,637.62 CR	2,995.02 CR

PLEASE EXAMINE THIS STATEMENT CAREFULLY, IN ACCORDANCE WITH YOUR CONTRACT, UNLESS WITHIN 60 DAYS AFTER THE CLOSE OF THE PERIOD TO WHICH THIS STATEMENT RELATES, YOU NOTIFY US IN WRITING OF WHAT YOU BELIEVE TO BE AN ERROR, THIS STATEMENT WILL BE BINDING UPON YOU AS CORRECT.

BLACK DEBIT BALANCES ARE DUE COMPANY
RED CREDIT BALANCES ARE DUE AGENT

FORM 71-027

control account in the general ledger. Summary amounts from special journals are posted to a control account in the general ledger and must equal amounts posted in detail to accounts in the subsidiary ledger. If the posting to control and subsidiary accounts is done correctly, the balance in the control account will always be equal to the sum of the account balances in the subsidiary ledger.

The amount of commissions earned by an agent is debited to the Commissions Paid account and credited to the Agents' Ledger Control account in the general ledger. It is not necessary to post these accounts every day, but the transactions posted to the agent's account and control account in total must be identically the same transactions as those listed on the commission statements. For example, commissions payable to an agent may be listed on a commission statement once each month and the total of the statement posted to the agent's account at the same time. At least once each month the total of subsidiary ledger account balances must be proven equal to the control account balance.

The titles of commission accounts vary from company to company. Examples are Commissions Paid, Commissions Earned, Servicing Commissions, and Production Commissions. Account titles usually include the line of business, whether premiums are first-year, renewal or single, and whether the business is participating or nonparticipating.

Most insurance companies using only the debit system of collecting premiums do not use the type of account discussed here but use a commission system which is in some respects similar to a straight salary system. Systems of this type are discussed in the chapter relating to debit insurance.

In the discussion that follows, entries shown affect only the control account. To simplify illustrations, subsidiary ledger entries are not shown, but the student should remember that subsidiary ledger posting *is* required.

AGENT'S ACCOUNT ENTRIES

There are several types of accounting transactions that occur frequently in connection with an agent's account. These include crediting the agent with commissions earned, disbursing amounts payable to him less taxes and other deductions, and making special charges for services rendered or for premium adjustments.

Commission Entries

A simple entry to record commissions earned by an agent is a debit to the Commissions Paid account to record the cost and a credit to the

Agents' Ledger Control account to record the company's liability for the amount which has been earned and is now payable.

Commissions Paid. 100.00
    Agents' Ledger Control. 100.00

The crediting of earned commissions to an agent's subsidiary account provides a simple method of summarizing the commissions earned for tax purposes and provides an accounting control over amounts payable from time to time. Therefore, most companies use agents' accounts in connection with payment of commissions.

At times it may be necessary to refund a premium, particularly on a new policy. Upon refund, the original commission entry is reversed. The entry is a debit to the Agents' Ledger Control account and a credit to the Commissions Paid account.

The processes used to post commissions to an agent's account in the subsidiary ledger vary from company to company because of different machines available to prepare commission statements and post agents' accounts. It will be useful, however, to examine a typical process—that of The Model Life Insurance Company.

At Model Life, commission amounts and premiums are recorded daily on a machine-made list or register. The list shows the following data with reference to each premium received: the policy number, entry date, writing agent's number, general agent's (or overriding commission agent's) number, and the amount of commission and overriding commission payable on each premium. The premium and commission amounts are totaled and become the basis for a single journal entry for all commissions earned by all agents that day.

The policy number, date of entry, and premium amount recorded on the daily list provide an audit trail between policy record, premium amounts, and commission amounts shown on the daily lists and on the commission statements prepared later. The agent's number completes the audit trail to the agent's account.

Although commission totals at The Model Life Insurance Company are debited to the Commission Paid account and credited to the Agents' Ledger Control account in the general ledger daily, commission statements are not prepared until the end of the month. These commission statements consist of three parts: one copy is for the agent, one for the overriding agent, and one for the company. Overriding commissions are listed in a separate column on the same commission statement form, but the agent's copy is perforated so that he does not receive the portion showing overriding commissions. The copy prepared for the overriding agent is not perforated, so that it shows both amounts. At the end of each month, the commission totals from the daily lists recorded in the journal are verified and proven against the commissions listed on the statements. The total of each commission statement is then posted to each agent's account in the subsidiary ledger.

Payments to Agents

Whenever payments are made to an agent following the earnings entry on page 242, the journal entry is:

```
Agents' Ledger Control.....................................100.00
    Cash...................................................       100.00
```

After both the earnings entry and this payment entry are posted, the control account balance becomes zero with reference to the particular commissions involved, indicating that the agent has been paid the full amount earned. The combined effect of the two transactions is the recording of a $100 cost for commissions, a $100 decrease in the asset cash, and a complete historical record of the agent's earnings.

If a company advances money to an agent against future commissions or makes any other type of payment to an agent, the entry is the same as the payment entry just shown.

A company may choose to pay commissions without first recording them in an agent's account. An entry in such a case is:

```
Commissions Paid..........................................100.00
    Cash...................................................       100.00
```

In this case the company must maintain a supplemental earnings record for tax purposes.

Taxes on Commission Earnings

Withholding taxes must be deducted from the earnings of agents who are classed as employees. This includes most agents who sell insurance and collect premiums under the debit collection system. Most other agents are not employees in a legal sense but are independent contractors. The U.S. Internal Revenue Service does not require withholding of income taxes on agents who are independent contractors, but it does require deducting FICA (social security) taxes on earnings of full time agents.

The entry recording the commission payment just shown might have included a credit to a tax liability account for an amount deducted. If $5 in taxes had been deducted, there would have been a $5 credit to a liability account in the general ledger for amounts held for later payment to the U.S. Treasury. Such an account might be titled *FICA Taxes Withheld.* A credit to Cash in the amount of $95 would complete the entry.

Many companies charge the tax to the agent's account and pay him the credit balance remaining. A typical entry to record a tax in this manner is a debit to the control account to reflect a charge to the agent and a credit to the appropriate Taxes Withheld account in the general ledger.

The entry to record a deduction of $5 for FICA tax is:

Agents' Ledger Control..	5.00	
FICA Taxes Withheld..................................		5.00

The entry to record payment of the remaining commission would then be a debit to the control account for $95 and an equal credit to Cash. The $95 debit to the control account (and agent's account) would zero balance the account with reference to this commission. Entries for taxes are usually made only once monthly but may be made as frequently as commissions are settled.

Miscellaneous Charges

Life insurance companies provide most supplies and services to agents without cost, but for some items there is a small charge. Inasmuch as such a charge is equivalent to a payment to him, his account is debited. The amount due the company then becomes an amount receivable to the company if the agent's account had a zero balance at the time. If his account has a credit balance when a charge is made, the debit reduces the amount payable to him. The credit portion of the entry might be to an income account maintained for this purpose.

A typical entry for sale of advertising novelties to an agent is:

Agents' Ledger Control..	xxxx	
Income from Agents' Supplies..............................		xxxx

The Annual Statement does not provide for income accounts of this type. If such an account is used, its balance is netted against an appropriate expense account balance and the net (reduced) amount is entered in the Annual Statement.

Annual Statement expense exhibits include lines for *advertising* and for *agency allowances,* so accounts by these titles are included in the general ledger. When advertising novelties are purchased from a vendor, accounts representing either one of these two items might be debited to record the cost. Assume for the purpose of illustrating that the account debited is Advertising, and at the end of the year it had a $10,000 debit balance, and the Income from Agents' Supplies account had a $2,500 credit balance. The difference in balances, $7,500, would be shown in the Statement as advertising expense.

An alternate method is to credit the expense account when the supplies are sold to the agent rather than crediting an income account. The effect of the credit in either case is an increase in surplus.

Many companies also charge the agent cancellation fees for "not taken out" (often abbreviated to NTO) policies and make various other charges in connection with policies, such as charges for premium shortages. Cancellation charges are made because the cost of underwriting new applications is substantial, and assessing the agent for a part of the cost when a new policy is not accepted and paid for deters careless field underwriting. To the agent these charges are a cost of doing business, but to the company they provide income which partially offsets expenses incurred. The entry to record a cancellation charge is a debit to the Agents' Ledger Control account because the charge is an amount receivable (asset) and a credit entry to an appropriate income or expense account. A typical policy charge entry when an income account is used is:

```
Agents' Ledger Control.......................................5.00
     Cancellation Fees.........................................      5.00
```

There is no cancellation fees item in the Annual Statement blanks. If such an account is used, the balance is netted against Inspection Fees, reducing that expense account when entered in the Annual Statement. This is proper because the cancellation fees charged represent reclaimed underwriting costs. These costs include inspection fees and medical costs.

Remitting Nets

Remitting "nets" is a common expression in the life insurance business. It indicates that an agent who collected a *full* premium from a policy-owner has deducted his commission before remitting to the company. Thus, he forwards only the net amount due the company. This practice is principally used with individual insurance. An illustration of entries and of accounts affected by a transaction of this type will give a much better understanding of agents' accounts and of the relationship between premium entries and commission entries.

The purpose of a company accepting "nets" is to get the agent's commission to him immediately, but this practice creates some special problems. For example, if an application is declined by the company, the agent is obligated to return the full payment to the applicant. This includes the commission he retained. The company must have evidence that the full refund was made so that the company is released from liability on the policy. Consequently, many companies restrict the practice of accepting nets to policies where the initial premium is collected on delivery (C.O.D.). Some allow the agent to remit net on subsequent premiums in the first policy year because the commission is a substantial portion of the premium. Others do not permit it on any basis.

The practice of remitting nets is most often permitted in connection with a general agency that has an established office and a competent bookkeeper. It is seldom permitted in connection with premiums on policies written by an agent who is being advanced money against future commissions. Such an agent is said to be under financing or to be financed. An agent being financed is not permitted to remit nets, except in connection with insurance on the members of his family or himself. In this case if the application is declined, the company is obligated to return only the net amount remitted.

When an agent is permitted to remit nets, his account is charged (debited) with the amount retained and Cash is debited for the amount received. The Premium account is credited for the full premium. A typical entry for a $100 premium, on which the full commission of $35 was retained, is:

```
Cash.............................................65.00
Agents' Ledger Control...........................35.00
     Premium Income....................................    100.00
```

A commission entry is then made in which the agent's account is credited with the full commission. This entry records his earnings of $35 and causes his account to zero balance with reference to this particular commission. In effect, the commission was paid when the agent deducted it from his remittance.

The next example illustrates the procedure followed when the agent makes a mistake in the amount of commission retained and also illustrates the use of premium suspense.

An agent submitted an application and remitted nets in the amount of $60 to pay the first premium which he calculated as $100. The amount received was placed in Premium Suspense. The entry was:

```
Cash.............................................60.00
     Premium Suspense..................................    60.00
```

The entire premium is not credited to Premium Suspense because it is good practice to have a premium income entry made only once for the exact amount of the correct premium. This practice establishes a clear audit trail on the premium. It also simplifies the entry in those cases where additional amounts may be required.

If the correct nets had been remitted, the entry to record the premium when the policy was issued and clear Premium Suspense would have been:

```
Premium Suspense.................................60.00
Agents' Ledger Control...........................40.00
     Premium Income....................................    100.00
```

However, when the policy was issued, the correct premium was determined to be $102 and the correct commission, $40.80. The correct net amount should have been $61.20 ($102.00 — $40.80), or $1.20 more than was remitted. The entry to record the premium and apply the amount in suspense is:

```
Premium Suspense...........................................60.00
Agents' Ledger Control.....................................42.00
    Premium Income.......................................          102.00
```

Notice that the shortage in amount remitted is $42 ($102 — $60), which is charged to the agent's account since it is due the company. This is logical because it is the difference between the amount placed in the Premium Suspense account which must be cleared and the Premium Income credit which must reflect the correct premium. The commission entry is:

```
Commission Paid...........................................40.80
    Agents' Ledger Control...............................          40.80
```

Notice that this entry records the correct commission on the correct premium. This series of journal entries may be reflected in T-account form:

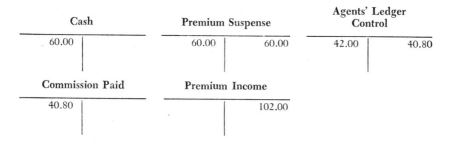

Notice that the Premium Suspense has been cleared out (zero balanced), that the Premiums and Commission balances are correct, and that the balance in agent's account (indicated by the control account) is a debit of $1.20. This is also correct because he was short $2 in premium but he was entitled to 40 percent commission (80 cents) on this portion of the premium. He still owes the difference of $1.20 ($2.00 — $0.80) to the company. When the agent collects the shortage in premium of $2, he must remit $1.20 to the company. When received, this amount will be debited to Cash and credited to his account, causing it to zero balance, thus indicating he has received his full commission and the company has received its full premium.

If the policy had been issued subject to premium collection on delivery and the agent had remitted $60 nets upon delivery, the first suspense entry would have been eliminated and the $60 debit in the next entry would have been to Cash instead of Premium Suspense. All other entries would have been the same as shown.

U.S. ANNUAL STATEMENT ASPECTS

Commissions are shown in Part 2 of the premium exhibit on an accrual basis only. The accrual basis and cash basis are frequently the same because commissions usually are either paid or promptly credited to an agent's account as premiums are received. However, there are exceptions which are noted in the following discussion of commission liabilities.

The liability page of the Annual Statement blank shows two items relating to commissions. The first is *commissions to agents due or accrued —life and annuity* $_____ *accident and health* $_____. Included in the amount reported on this line are nonledger commission liabilities. These might occur under two conditions: (1) commissions earned but not credited to the agent's account during the accounting period because they were based on a qualification that could not be determined until after the end of the accounting period, and (2) contingent commissions and agency bonuses partially accrued but not payable until a later date.

Included with contingent commissions are those which will become payable if health insurance premiums due are received. It will be recalled that these due premiums are assets on a gross premium basis. The establishment of a commission liability (and expense liability for cost of collection) has an effect on surplus similar to that accomplished by deducting loading and excess cost from gross life premiums due and uncollected, as described in the premium chapter.

Commissions due and accrued are used to adjust commissions from the cash to the accrual basis before the accrual basis figures are entered in the commission section of the premium exhibit.

The second commission liability item is *amounts held for agents' account (including* $_____ *agents' credit balances)*. Most companies include only agents' credit account balances on this line. These credit balances are not used to adjust Commissions Paid. The total of credit balances represents only a part of the Agents' Ledger Control account which is divided into two items when shown in the Annual Statement. One is the sum of control account debit balances, which is treated as a not admitted asset, and the other is the sum of credit balances, which is shown as a liability. This method of reporting agents' balances causes surplus to be reduced by an amount equal to the total of all debit balances. An example will clarify this process.

Assume that the following is a list of agents' account balances in an agents' subsidiary ledger at the end of the current year:

	Dr.	Cr.
John Doe	100	
Pete Smith	50	
Marion Brown		110
Total	150	110
Control account balance	40	

Note that the debit balances total $150 and the credit balance totals $110. Only the Agents' Ledger Control account balance is entered as a ledger asset in the asset exhibit of the U.S. Annual Statement. This amount is reentered in the not admitted assets column, with a zero in the admitted assets column. In the example, not admitting $40 reduces surplus by $40. The total amount of credit balances ($110) is shown on the liability page which thus causes an additional reduction in surplus equal to the $40 remainder of the debit balances.

In the U.S. Annual Statement there is an exhibit for showing the change during the year in assets which are not admitted in total (see Figure 20–4). In this exhibit, both the change in the Agents' Ledger Control account balance and the increase in the agents' credit balances are shown.

In determining debit balances for presentation in the Annual Statement, if a general agent is responsible for the debts of a subagent and the general agent has a credit balance, the two balances can be offset against each other to produce a net debit or net credit balance for the agency as a whole. This is logical since the amount payable to the general agent is owed by the company, and in the event of liquidation, the debit balance of the agent could be deducted from the amount payable to the general agent.

CANADIAN ANNUAL STATEMENT ASPECTS

The exhibit for commissions in the Canadian Statement is Exhibit 2 entitled *Commissions on Insurance Premiums and Annuity Considerations.* It is on a revenue or accrual basis and shows commissions by line of business and separately for participating and nonparticipating business. *Advances to Agents* are shown as an expense item rather than as an increase in nonadmitted assets, as in the U.S. Statement. The totals are shown in the Analysis of Revenue Account by Line of Business and a final total is shown in the Revenue account.

On the liability page of the Annual Statement, there is one item for agents' commission liabilities: *commissions on insurance premiums and annuity considerations, due and accrued.* Included in this item are credit balances on agents' accounts, commissions fully or partially accrued, and contingent commissions. The portion of this liability not already credited to agents' accounts is used to adjust commissions from the cash to the accrual basis.

SUMMARY OF COMMISSION ACCOUNTING FUNDAMENTALS

Commissions are usually payable to agents as a specified percentage of premiums *received,* but they may be payable on any basis that indicates increased production.

Agents' accounts are maintained in a subsidiary ledger with a control account in the general ledger.

Commissions may be listed on statements and only the totals posted to the agent's accounts.

Agents' debit balances refers to the total of all agents' accounts with a debit balance in the agents' subsidiary ledger. These balances are treated as not admitted assets. An increase in debit balances is treated as a direct decrease in surplus in the U.S. Annual Statement and as an insurance expense in the Canadian Annual Statement.

QUESTIONS

1. What are the objectives of a commission accounting system? Why must the system be closely coordinated with the premium collection system?
2. Name the two primary records used in connection with commission accounting and describe briefly the function of each.
3. Under what conditions is an agent's account an account receivable? When is it an account payable? How does the control account function? Why is it desirable to have an account rather than simply pay the agent from data on a commission list?
4. How are the following amounts shown in the Annual Statement: Income from supplies charged to agents? Income from cancellation fees charged?
5. What is meant by "remitting net"? Why is this practice used? When is it not desirable to permit it? What entries are made? In what way is the procedure on a premium paid with application different than when it is paid after the policy is issued?
6. What type of nonledger commission liabilities are shown in the Annual Statements? How is increase in debit balances shown in the U.S. Statement? In the Canadian Statement?

PROBLEM

Using a multicolumn premium journal and cash disbursements journal, make the premium and commission entries required in connection with the following transactions, and post the transactions to the general ledger and to individual agents' accounts. Then prepare a schedule of agents' balances and indicate how the debit and credit balances are presented in the Annual Statement of your country and what effect they have on surplus.

The premium journal has columns as follows: Debit Cash, Debit Commission, Debit General Ledger, Credit General Ledger, Account Identification, Credit Premium, Agent's Number, Credit Agents' Ledger, and Debit Dividends Applied.

The cash disbursements journal has columns as follows: Agent's Number, Debit Agents' Ledger, Credit Taxes Withheld, Debit General Ledger, and Credit Cash.

At the start of the month, the agents' account schedule and trial balance amounts were as follows:

Schedule Agents' Accounts
April 30, 19___

Agent	Dr.	Cr.
15..................	$ 10.00	
25..................		$ 569.00
35..................	1,300.00	
45..................		4,219.00
61..................		316.00
73..................	750.00	
79..................		2,635.00
	$2,060.00	$7,739.00
Difference...........		$5,679.00 Cr.

Trial Balance

Account	Dr.	Cr.
Cash........................	$ 10,000.00	
Bonds owned.................	100,000.00	
Premium income..............		$ 50,000.00
Income from agents' supplies....		1,200.00
Dividends applied.............	1,100.00	
Inspection fees...............	7,500.00	
Premium suspense............		15.00
Commissions.................	20,000.00	
Agents' ledger control.........		5,679.00
Balance account..............		81,706.00
	$138,600.00	$138,600.00

Transactions during the period are as follows:

a) May 1: Premium report received from branch office. Amounts received and commissions payable are as follows:

Report of Premiums

```
Premiums........................$1,069.00
Money with new applications:
   Mary Brown.........$18.00
   Joe Smith........... 28.50        46.50
Less dividends applied.............. −110.00
Cash received.....................$1,005.50
```

Commissions
Payable

```
Agent  5..........................$10.00
Agent  6.......................... 16.50
Agent 45.......................... 35.25
Agent 73.......................... 10.36
                                  $72.11
```

b) May 5: Checks were issued to agents as follows:

```
Agent 25.....................$  569.00
Agent 45..................... 1,000.00
Agent 61.....................   316.00
Agent 73.....................   100.00
Agent 79.....................   500.00
                            $2,485.00
```

c) May 6: Policy is issued on Mary Brown, whose application was received on May 1. Premium is $36, and commission for Agent 35 is $17.50.

d) May 7: Policy is issued on Joe Smith. Premium is $28.75, and commission for Agent 15 is $9.13.

e) May 15: Premium report received from branch office. Amounts received and commissions payable as follows:

Report of Premiums

```
Premiums..........................$2,316.00
Policy loan interest....................   110.00
Apps. and money received
   John Doe.................$ 16.00
   Marian Rush............. 110.00       126.00
Less dividends applied.................. −235.00
                                        $2,317.00
```

Commissions

```
Agent 25..............................$ 21.00
Agent 45.............................. 114.00
Agent 61..............................   5.00
Agent 73..............................  53.00
Agent 79.............................. 569.00
                                      $762.00
```

f) May 16: The underwriting department declined application on Carl Watson and ordered a refund of $15 received in April. Agent 79 is charged a $5 cancellation fee.

g) May 20: Checks are issued to agents as follows:

Agent 35	$ 300.00
Agent 45	1,000.00
Agent 73	100.00
Agent 79	500.00
	$1,900.00

h) May 23: Novelties to be used as sales aids are shipped to Agent 79. He is to be charged $25 for these aids.

i) May 31: Taxes on commissions earned during the month are charged to agents' accounts as follows:

Agent 5	$ 2.00
Agent 6	3.15
Agent 15	0.90
Agent 25	4.05
Agent 35	3.10
Agent 45	15.32
Agent 61	0.25
Agent 73	1.53
Agent 79	7.33
	$37.63

Chapter 14

Individual Premium and Commission Accounting

The individual premium system has been generally defined as one which involves collection of one premium at a time by mail. Other means of collection may be used, however, such as collection through banks or employers.

The individual system was originally the only premium system, debit and group systems being developed later to serve special markets for life insurance. The individual system is used most frequently in connection with ordinary life insurance, individual health insurance, and individual annuities, but also to a limited extent in other lines of business.

Accounting for individual premiums and for commissions on these premiums varies slightly from company to company. However, the legal conditions and the objectives of premium and commission accounting are generally the same in all companies and result in similar processes. This chapter presents typical situations in which the individual system is used. Discussion of accounting systems and sample entries shown relate to ordinary insurance, except as noted, but are generally applicable to health insurance and annuities. General references to insurance contracts or policies should be construed to include annuity contracts.

CHARACTERISTICS OF THE INDIVIDUAL SYSTEM

Under the individual system, a premium notice is usually mailed to the policyowner who then remits to the company. There are modifications of the system under which premium notices are eliminated, or where billings or payments are made on a group basis, but all other characteristics of the individual premium system are retained. These modifications are discussed later in the chapter, with the principal portion of the chapter devoted to individual mail billings and payments.

More types of records are required in the home office and branch office in connection with individual premium accounting than under either the debit or group systems. More detail is also included on the records, and more detailed accounting summaries are required. This is necessarily so because policyowners are allowed a great deal of flexibility in time and method of payment, and agents are usually paid under complex commissions systems.

Premium Payment Flexibility

Premiums fall due on every day of a month but a company may choose to omit the last three days when dating policies in order to prevent monthly premiums from falling due on nonexistent days in February. Some policyowners pay premiums before they are due, and others use the full grace period.

Individual premiums are usually paid by check because this is a reasonably safe and economical method for transmitting payments by mail. However, sometimes checks are not honored by the bank on which they are drawn. This results in correspondence and other special handling. Such a situation also requires procedures for reversing accounting entries and nullifying record postings.

The insured may be allowed the option of making payment on an annual, semiannual, quarterly, or monthly basis. These optional methods of payment are known as *modes*. Many companies allow the insured to change from one mode to another at his convenience, while others permit these changes only on dates that coincide with the anniversary. For example, if an anniversary falls in February and premiums are being paid monthly, some companies permit a change to quarterly mode only in February, May, August, or November.

Dividends may be allowed under options which are related to premium payment conditions, and policyowners are permitted to borrow against the cash values. As a result, methods used for billing, accounting for, and recording premiums must be coordinated with methods used to handle dividends, loan interest, and loan-principal repayments.

Cashiers receive individual premiums paid by policyowners and remit them to the home offices. Their work is periodically audited by a representative from the home office known as a field auditor. His responsibilities may include reviewing the accounting records to ascertain that they are being properly maintained, training new cashiers, and supervising cashiers and managers in connection with accounting and policy service activities.

Commission Systems

When selling insurance on which premiums are normally collected under individual premium systems, agents operate under a minimum of restrictions and a maximum of freedom in their sales activities. Commissions are paid only for results produced. To provide the necessary incentive to induce an agent to sell new policies and service old policies, commission schedules and systems must be quite complex.

Usually an agent who sells individual insurance is an independent contractor in a legal sense and is not an employee of the insurance company. He is regarded as self-employed and is compensated solely by commissions as set out in an agency contract. An agent is free to work as few or as many hours as he chooses and to select the time of day he works. He can devote all of his efforts to selling and none to servicing, if he so desires. Frequently he will represent more than one company, but most companies prohibit this in contracts designed for career agents.

The only time an agent may be restricted or controlled as to hours or direction of his activity is during his early training. During this period the company or supervising agent makes an investment in the new agent in the form of training and financing. A supplemental contract is usually placed in effect during this period to specify additional benefits he may receive and additional obligations placed on him.

The freedom granted to the agent under the individual premium system is possible because the policyowner need not deal with the agent after the sale. The policyowner can mail his payments to the company and can correspond directly with the home office or a branch office on all matters because the company keeps complete records on each policy.

Commissions are usually paid to an agent as long as he is under contract and his policyowners pay premiums. In many cases he also will continue to receive commissions for years after the agency contract terminates. Failure to service policies he has written carries with it no penalty other than a possibility of lapse, and resultant loss of commissions. However, most agents prefer to service their policyowners periodically, not only to conserve the business but also to maintain friendly relations which may lead to additional sales.

Commission schedules are tables in an agent's contract showing the percentage of each premium that is payable to him as a commission. These percentages vary by duration of policy. The commission rate (percent of premium) in the first policy year is higher than in renewal years and usually is slightly higher in the second and third policy years than in subsequent years. Ordinary insurance commission rates for the first policy year vary widely by plan of insurance but vary little by plan in renewal years. Renewal commissions in many companies are lower on special preferred-risk plans and some endowment policies. Commissions on first-year annuity considerations are a much smaller percentage than on ordinary insurance premiums but are still higher than annuity renewal considerations.

A typical commission scale for whole life insurance might be 55 percent, first year; 10 percent, second year; 7½ percent, third year; 5 percent, fourth through tenth years; and 2 percent, thereafter. The scale for a 20-year endowment might be 35 percent for first year and the same as whole life for subsequent years. Commission rates may be reduced or eliminated in renewal years if an agent fails to produce a certain volume of new business or if his contract is terminated within a specified period. Additional amounts based on premiums received, such as bonuses and expense allowances, may also be paid to him if he meets certain conditions.

Commissions paid to supervising agents (general agents, state agents, or branch managers) are usually a higher percentage of the premium than commissions paid to writing agents. A typical supervising agent's scale is 65 percent, first year; 15 percent, second year; 10 percent, third year; 7½ percent, fourth through tenth years; and 3 percent, thereafter. A typical commission on a single premium policy is 5 percent.

The difference between a supervising agent's scale and a writing agent's scale is the *overriding commission* on business written by the writing agent. For example, if the supervising agent's commission on a particular premium is 10 percent and his agent's commission is 7.5 percent, then 2.5 percent (10 percent − 7.5 percent) is the overriding commission payable on business written by the agent.

If a writing agent's commission is reduced or terminated, the overriding commission may be increased accordingly. In the example just cited, if the agent's contract had been terminated and commissions were not vested, the overriding commission would be 10 percent. The increase because of the termination (7½ percent in this case) is frequently referred to as *salvage commission*. Salvage commissions may be pledged to the company as security for agent loans or financing. Many companies do not pay salvage commissions but retain them to absorb costs incurred in connection with financing agents. Overriding commissions are calculated at the same time as writing commissions because of their interrelationship. Some branch managers are paid a percent of premiums without regard to the amount payable to a writing agent, in which case the calculation method is simplified.

In health insurance, there are fewer variations among plans than in ordinary life insurance. Commission rates on first-year premiums are usually higher than the rates on renewal premiums. Renewal rates often vary by policy duration. Some companies pay a higher percentage on the initial premium only and a level rate thereafter on both first-year and renewal premiums. This latter system was widely used in the early days of health insurance, but now it is used infrequently.

Many companies charge the policyowner a one-time charge called a *policy fee* that is added to the initial health insurance premium. All or the major portion of this fee may be retained by the agent as a commission. The fee must be reported to the company and entered on the books because premium taxes are payable on it and because the agent's earnings record must show the amount retained as a commission earned.

POLICY STATUS RECORDS

Policy *status* means the current state of a policy with respect to the date to which premiums have been paid, the amount of any policy loan outstanding, the date to which loan interest has been paid, the amount of dividends payable, the amount of dividend accumulations, the amount of paid-up insurance additions, the amount of the current cash value, the current amount of insurance in force, and the agent or agents currently entitled to receive commissions on premium payments. A status record must be consulted in all accounting situations, e.g., when accepting premium or interest payments, when a policyowner makes a claim or surrenders a policy, when making maturity payments or applying a nonforfeiture option in the event of lapse. It is also customary to check the status record when answering policyowner requests for current and accurate information.

When a computer is used, all of the data that affects accounting operations, as described for policy record cards, may be included on a master policy record file which is stored magnetically or on punched cards. A computer can then print-out policy data when desired on what is referred to as a *status print-out* or *status report*. This speeds service to policyowners and provides more complete and more accurate information than manual systems. This is so because of error controls programed into machine systems and because computer-stored files usually include some data, such as cash values, which are not included on policy record cards. A typical status print-out is illustrated in Figure 14–1.

Policy Record Card

The traditional record on which most status information is recorded is known as a *policy record card*. The importance of this card (Figure 14–2) has decreased in companies which use computers, and the card is no longer used in many home offices. These cards are still frequently used in branch offices and regional or local offices which collect premium and render other accounting services. A discussion of the uses of this card will facilitate an understanding of computer *status print-outs* which serve the same purposes as policy record cards.

In companies which use computers, policy record cards still may be

Figure 14-1. Typical Policy Status Print-Out

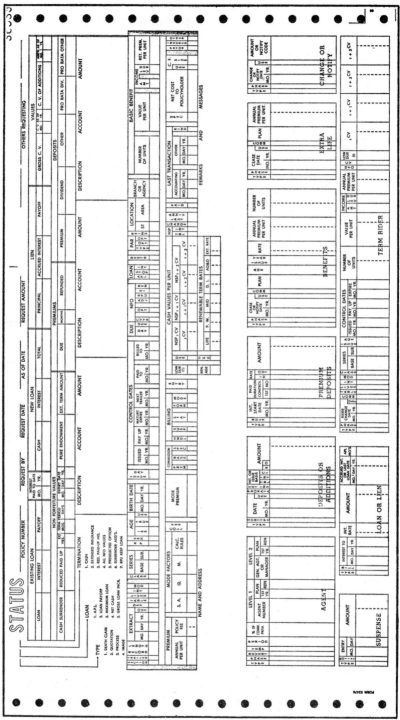

Figure 14–2.   A Typical Policy Record Card

Front

POLICY NO.	REG. DATE		NAME								
0 000 000	9-1-57		Upright, Abner (Mr)								
POLICY DATE	AMOUNT	AGE	ADDRESS								
9-1-57	10,000	35	1234 Main St.						SAMPLE		
PLAN			Indianapolis, Ind.								
OL-160			RENEWAL NOTICE TO								
RATING		DIV.OPT									
Std.		Par2									
BORN 8-25-1922 Ind. BRA				2	3	4	5	6	7	8	9	10
LIFE	A 264.70	S.A.	Q.	M.	OFFICE	100					
M.I.D.					AM-20	46					
W.P.D.					R.A. Jones						
D.I.					DM-20	4776					
					John Doe*						
PLAT EXTRA											
TOTAL	264.70										

STATE	PLAN	DIS.D.I.	TABLE	A.P.L.				
				Yes	WRITTEN 8-15-57	EXAM. RECD: 8-20-57	REINS. PURCHASED XXXX NO	
DATE LAPSED	DATE REINSTATED		OTHER POLICIES					
			POLICY NUMBER	STATUS 19		Abigail Upright, wife of insured		

FINAL TERMINATION-CAUSE AND DATE	PREMIUM NOTES OR POLICY LOANS				CHANGED FROM	DATE OF CHANGE
	KIND	AMOUNT	DATE MADE	DATE DUE		
						EFFECTIVE DATE

Back

8-3932C				PREMIUM PAYMENTS										DIVIDENDS/COUPONS					P.
POL. YEAR	CAL. YEAR	JAN.	FEB.	MARCH	APRIL	MAY	JUNE	JULY	AUG.	SEPT.	OCT.	NOV.	DEC.	CREDITED			SURRENDERED		D. NO. BU.
														DATE	AMOUNT	OPT.	ADDTNS OR ACCUM	DATE	AMOUNT
1																			1
2																			2
3																			3
4																			4
5																			5
6																			6
7																			7
8																			8
9																			9
10																			10
11																			11
12																			12
13																			13
14																			14
15																			15
16																			16
17																			17
18																			18
19																			19
20																			
21																			

LOAN DATA						OTHER PAYMENTS					
KIND	DATE	AMOUNT	KIND	DATE	AMOUNT	KIND	DATE	AMOUNT	KIND	DATE	AMOUNT

I 3

maintained as a supplementary file in order to record nonaccounting data and major status changes, such as beneficiary changes and date and cause of termination. This historical data may be needed after a policy lapses and is no longer carried in an active computer file.

Policy record cards are sometimes called *premium record cards* or *premium ledger cards,* but neither of these terms is technically correct. The cards are more than *premium* records since a great deal of status information recorded on them is not related to premiums. They are not ledger cards in an accounting sense because no debit or credit entries are posted to them nor do they provide an account balance. However, a similarity between policy record cards and ledger cards exists because dates and amounts of premium payments are *posted* to policy record cards even though they are not part of the formal books of account. The date recorded is the same as that of the journal entry; this provides an audit trail to the journal entry which recorded the cash received and also provides a historical record of premium transactions.

The following are items of accounting information generally found on policy record cards along with the principal use or uses of this information:

1. Policy number—for positive identification of all records
2. Policyowner's name and address—for premium billing and for correspondence
3. Amount of insurance—for reserve valuation, and calculation of premium changes, benefit payment, etc.
4. Policy anniversary date—for valuation, determining premium due dates, determining benefit settlements, and calculating nonforfeiture options
5. Plan of insurance—for valuation, determining benefit amounts, and calculating loan and nonforfeiture values
6. Benefit riders attached—for same reasons as plan of insurance
7. Amounts of premium and mode of premium—for valuation and premium billing
8. Substandard premium amounts, if any—for valuation and premium billing
9. Name of agent and agency receiving commissions on the policy—for commission accounting
10. Codes indicating commission schedules—for calculating commission amounts payable
11. Policy loan or premium notes outstanding against the policy—for loan accounting and determining policy settlement amounts
12. Dates of lapse and subsequent reinstatement—for applying incontestable clause in settlements and determining present status
13. Issue age of insured—for valuation, determining reinstatement requirements, calculating cash and loan values, and calculating other policy settlement amounts

Policy record cards include additional nonaccounting information as:

1. Insured's birth date, place of birth, and occupation—for positive identification of the insured person
2. A brief beneficiary designation or reference to a special settlement agreement—for policy settlement

3. Applicability of automatic premium loan provision in the event of lapse—for facilitating reinstatement and conservation activity

4. If reinsured, reinsurance identification (name of company), reinsurance number, and amount of reinsurance—for notifying reinsurance companies of lapses, reinstatements, and other policy changes

5. Whether the policy is participating or nonparticipating—for properly classifying premium income and coordinating dividend records

6. The numbers of other policies in force on the same life, or on which premiums are being paid by the particular policyowner—for making address changes and determining reinsurance requirements

A computer's status print-outs have some limitations when compared to policy record cards. These are:

1. *Lack of historical data.* Normally only the dates of *last* accounting and policy change transactions are shown so that tracing transactions requires consulting a number of records. However, error controls built into computer accounting systems minimize the need for historical data.

2. *Delay in producing the report.* Unless a computer is equipped with a mass storage device, status print-outs are not immediately available. Companies which use magnetic tape or punched cards for data storage normally produce status print-outs only once or twice daily.

3. Much data printed out is in coded form and thus is not meaningful to an individual not familiar with the codes.

Other Records

Many companies maintain policy loan records on special loan cards which are accounts in a subsidiary ledger. However, smaller companies frequently record policy loan balances on the policy record card and use it as a subsidiary ledger card.

Many companies maintain records of dividends paid and dividend accumulations on deposit on special dividend record cards. These cards become subsidiary ledger accounts for dividend accumulation balances if a control account is maintained on the ledger.

Many small companies maintain a history of dividend payments, dividend accumulations, and paid-up additions on the policy record card but do not use an account in the general ledger to control accumulation balances.

A file folder is prepared for each policy issued. The original application and underwriting papers and all major policy status changes are filed in this folder. Using a single folder for each policy enables anyone familiar with the company's systems to quickly answer inquiries about a policy. These folders and all other policy records are usually filed in policy number sequence.

Many policyowners fail to mention policy numbers when writing to the company or paying premiums. Since records are filed by policy number, it is necessary to maintain an alphabetic index file. This file usually consists of small card records containing the name of each insured along with his policy number and other policy data. These cards are prepared along with other policy records when policies are issued. If the premium payor and the insured are different persons, a card for each may be placed in the file.

PREMIUM BILLING AND CONTROL PROCESSES

It will be recalled that the objectives of premium accounting include the control of premiums from the date they become due until they are credited to the correct policies. It is appropriate, therefore, to examine typical processes involving billing for, and collection of, individual premiums by mail to learn how this control is achieved.

Processes used to control and account for individual premiums are very similar in all companies. However, forms and their titles vary from company to company. The form titles and definitions presented here are intended to facilitate understanding and not to describe precisely common practices. A comparison of these forms and processes with those used in a specific company will reveal many similarities and provide a broader understanding of this important aspect of individual premium accounting.

Premium Notices and Related Transaction Records

The premium notice is the principal form used in the billing process. It shows the policy number, amount of premium due, date due, the period covered by the premium, the name and address of the premium payor (imprinted on it in a position to use a window envelope), and may also include data relating to policy loan interest due, dividends which may be deducted, and payment instructions (Figure 14–3).

Attached to the notice is a *policyowner's stub* which contains some, but not necessarily all, of the optional data included on the premium notice. This stub usually carries wording which instructs the policyowner to return the stub with his payment; some companies request the premium notice be returned instead.

Other forms are frequently prepared which are mailed to policyowners and to agents at various stages in the premium collection process. These may be referred to by terms such as warning notice, agent's notice, lapse notice, etc., or collectively as follow-up notices.

A *remittance stub* is any stub, slip, or punched card used by collection offices in reporting premium payments to the home office. Each stub contains data similar to that on the premium notice and may contain data relating to agents' commissions. In companies where item control is maintained through a computer process, the functions of the remittance stub and collection card are frequently performed by a single punched card.

Figure 14-3. A Set of Typical Premium Notices and Stubs

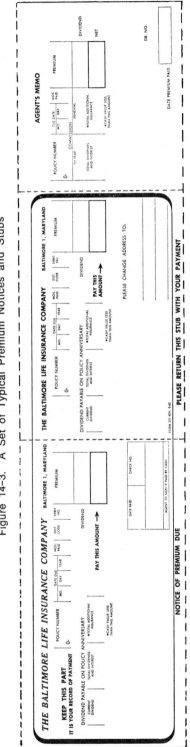

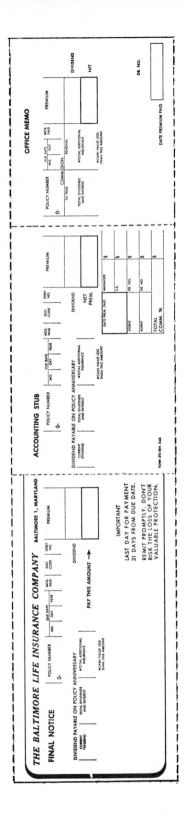

A *collection card* is one used by the home office to *control* each premium due and to make premium and commission accounting entries. After a premium is paid, the card may be stored in a historical file for making analyses of premiums received by states and for other purposes. This card is sometimes called an accounting card because it is used to make accounting entries. Some companies with computers use means other than collection cards to initiate accounting entries. Some use optical scanners which read data directly from remittance stubs; others use add punch or key punch equipment. The computer then combines this input data with stored data to produce a complete transaction record.

Preparing Notices and Related Accounting Records

Premium notices are usually prepared by unit record equipment or by computers (but a few companies use special addressing equipment) using data taken from a *master billing file*. This file may be defined as one which contains data that may be reproduced to create transaction records required for processing each premium payment.

When a computer is used, the function of a master billing file may be performed by a *master policy file*. A master policy file is a consolidated function file that serves many purposes other than premium billing.

Much of the data on premium billing records is in coded form in order to condense record size and to speed processing. Agents and states, for example, are coded numerically.

When unit record equipment or addressing equipment is used, premium notices are usually prepared a month in advance. Lapse, warning, and agents' notices, stubs, and punched cards used for premium and commission accounting may be prepared concurrently. Before mailing, notices are checked against the policy record cards to ascertain that a premium is due in each instance because: some policyowners may have paid in advance or by policy loan; premiums may be subject to waiver due to disability of the insured; changes may have been made in the policy between the date the notice was made and mailed. It is usually easier to reproduce the whole master billing file without regard to actual payment status and to destroy a few excess notices than it is to keep the file adjusted for current payment conditions.

Policy record cards, master billing records, and addressing plates (if used) are usually filed numerically under collection office, control month, and mode. The collection office grouping eliminates sorting of notices and stubs before they are transmitted to a collection office.

The *control month* is the first month in a calendar year in which a premium falls due. For example, January is the control month for all monthly premiums because the first monthly premium will fall due in January. Similarly, January is the control month for semiannual premiums falling due in January and July, February is the control month for those semi annual policies whose installments fall due in February and August, etc. Control month and mode together constitute a billing cycle. Filing by billing cycle facilitates premium notice checking.

Lists of notices may be prepared by machine to prove which notices were made. A date on the list or a small check mark in the due space of the policy record card is also a satisfactory method for indicating that a notice was made or mailed.

When computers are used, premium notice checking and use of a control month may be eliminated because the master policy file is always current. Premium notices and other billing forms and accounting records may, therefore, be prepared daily or as needed. Usually, a list of notices prepared is printed and filed as evidence that the notices were mailed.

Controlling Initial Premiums

If the initial premium on a new policy is paid with the application, it is often controlled by the use of a number printed on the *application* form and on the *receipt* given to the applicant. The agent records the amount paid on both the application and receipt. He then sends the application and payment to the branch or home office. A branch office cashier usually prepares another receipt in triplicate. One copy is a receipt for the agent, one serves as a remittance stub, and the third as a record for the branch office.

If any portion of an initial premium is unpaid at the time a policy is issued, an *initial premium invoice* is used. Occasions when such an invoice is necessary are as follows: (1) no part of the premium was collected with the application, or (2) the premium collected with the application was miscalculated, or (3) the policy was issued substandard with an additional amount due for the extra premium, or (4) there is delay in the underwriting process and the agent may be required to collect more than one monthly premium.

This invoice is prepared with three or four copies. When the amount due is collected by the agent, the original is used as a receipt for the new policyowner, one copy serves as a remittance stub, one as a record for the branch office, and the fourth, if made, as a receipt for the agent.

Controlling Suspense Accounts

Suspense accounts are used in connection with amounts received on new applications prior to the date the policy is issued and in connection with amounts submitted with applications for reinstatement. Amounts placed in suspense (credits to a suspense account) are controlled in a manner similar to that used to control a subsidiary ledger. This is necessary to prevent overlooking amounts that should be credited to a premium account later on when a policy is issued or a deposit is refunded to an applicant when his application is not accepted.

A typical procedure is to record each suspense amount on a special control register which is kept in balance with the suspense control account in the general ledger. Alternate methods are to record the suspense amount on a slip, manual card, or punched card. Since there is only one credit entry for each item and one debit entry when it is cleared, separate subsidiary ledger accounts are not required.

The dates of entries to the Suspense account and a reference number are noted on the register or card to provide an audit trail. At the end of each month the items outstanding are reconciled to the account balance in a manner very similar to the reconciliation of a bank account. Any items pending for 30 days or longer are then investigated and cleared if possible.

PROCESSING INDIVIDUAL PREMIUM PAYMENTS

Good financial control requires that as few people handle cash as conditions permit and that premium payments be deposited in the bank frequently and with a minimum of delay. To minimize the cost of handling payments, machine processes must be utilized to the maximum practical extent. Such processes vary from company to company depending on the types of records and equipment used and whether premiums are paid through branch offices or directly to the home office.

Most premium amounts received by a life insurance company are paid in the amount billed. These can be handled easily and quickly by use of machine-made records, stubs, or other documents. However, the many conditions affecting individual premiums also require many manually prepared documents and special control processes.

The most commonly encountered premium-related transactions other than paid-as-billed payments are errors in check amounts, payment on a mode different from that billed, receipt of amounts paid in connection with applications for insurance, receipt of amounts due on initial premiums after policies are issued, receipt of a premium tendered on a policy which has lapsed, and payments received to cover returned checks.

The student of insurance accounting should understand how the objectives of premium and commission accounting are achieved under the various payment situations. These processes differ among companies, but a typical process is presented in the following sections of this chapter to illustrate methods of handling some of these situations.

Payment Handling in the Branch Office

At the time premium notices are prepared at Model Life Insurance Company, two punched cards are made for each due premium. One is designed to serve as a remittance stub and the other as a collection card. Remittance and collection cards are also prepared for policy loan interest due and for dividends to be deducted from premiums.

A list of premiums due, interest due, and dividends payable is also prepared for each branch office. The purpose of this list is to provide an item control so that the cashier may trace any remittance card removed from the file. The total of the list is also used by the home office to establish a dollar control on premiums due from the branch office. The remittance cards along with a copy of the list are sent to each branch office. The collection cards are retained in the home office in a due premium file for control and accounting purposes.

Premium notices are mailed by the home office directly to policyowners together with a reply envelope addressed to the branch office. The notice instructs the policyowner to pay at the designated office, and to return the policyowner's stub with the payment. All follow-up notices (except one) are mailed to the branch office where, if premiums have not been received on or before the appropriate dates, they may be verified against payment records and mailed to policyowners. After the expiration of the grace period, a special notice is mailed to the policyowner by the home office, extending the grace period fifteen days if the insured is living. This is done to alert the policyowner in case his payment failed to reach the home office, and as a conservation device.

When a premium amount is received, the cashier pulls the proper remittance card and verifies the accuracy of the payment, that it was paid within the grace period, and that no interim premiums were overlooked. If the payment is acceptable in all respects, the amount paid, medium of payment (such as check or cash), and date of payment are noted on the policyowner's stub, and placed with other payments ready for deposit and reporting to the home office. Payment data recorded on the policyowner's stub will be used later to post policy record cards and then retained as a historical record. If the policyowner fails to return his stub, a policyowner's stub is prepared manually.

When a premium is paid on a mode different from that billed, the machine-made remittance card is pulled from the file and a revised remittance stub is prepared manually in duplicate. Payment data is recorded on the copy which is thereafter used as a policyowner stub (branch office record). The original remittance card is voided, the new original of the new remittance slip attached, and both are placed with items ready for deposit and reporting to the home office.

When money is received for which there are no prepared cards, such as money paid with a new application, or a reinstatement, a receipt is prepared in quadruplicate. The original is the receipt for the payment received. One copy is attached to the related papers (such as the application), one is used as a remittance stub and the remaining copy is retained as a branch office record.

Model Life Insurance Company does not deposit a check for a premium submitted after the extension of the grace period expires. Courts have frequently ruled that depositing a delinquent payment automatically reinstates a policy unless there is a clear agreement to the contrary. Many companies do deposit reinstatement checks and use a special receipt which limits the company's liability in connection with the payment.

Depositing and Remitting Premiums to the Home Office

Once each day, the cashier in the branch office of Model Life Insurance Company prepares a bank deposit and a *Summary Remittance Report* (Figure 14–4). This report is made up in the form of a journal entry, but with less detail than is used in a home office entry. The amount of deposit is entered as a debit to Cash. Premium income, policy loan interest, payments on loans, returned checks, and amounts to be applied on initial premiums are entered as credits. Dividends deducted from premiums are shown as debits. Home office copies of returned check notices, premium reversal slips, and checks to be applied to reinstatements and new applications are itemized in a special section of the report.

The report shown in Figure 14–4 is a combination Summary Remittance Report and Cash Payment Report. In this case, it is called a *Branch Service Office Report*. The center portion serves as a check register for cash payments the branch office is permitted to make, but the remainder pertains to remittance reporting.

The top center portion is a remittance summary. Notice that Item 3 is total premiums, Item 4 is over and under, Item 5 is interest on policy loans and delinquent premiums, and Item 6 covers dividends (and coupons) deducted from premiums. Most of these items are "paid as billed" and reported to the home office by use of remittance punched cards. Items not represented by cards, such as over and under and interest on delinquent premiums, are reported on individual slips from which cards will be punched.

Amounts received but not billed are itemized in sections around the outside of the report. Included are amounts received on new applications and on reinstatements, checks for premiums where policies are being changed from mail pay to Automatic Bank Check, payroll deduction amounts, advance premiums, amounts paid other than billed, and special amounts paid where policies are being reissued, converted, or otherwise changed. All of these items require some action by the home office before the money can be credited to a premium account. They will, therefore, be credited to suspense accounts temporarily. These suspense items are summarized on the

BRANCH SERVICE OFFICE REPORT

THE MODEL LIFE INSURANCE COMPANY
FORT WAYNE, INDIANA

ORIGINAL COPY
FORM 1458-B.O 1-66

SUSPENSE

COMPANY CODE / POLICY NUMBER / B.S.O. #	CR DATE	SUSPENSE AMOUNT DEBIT	SUSPENSE AMOUNT CREDIT	MEMORANDUM
				BANK SUMMARY SUSPENSE
				COLLECTIONS NOT PAID AS BILLED
				REISSUES/CONVERSIONS
				REINSTATEMENTS
				ABC
				PRD-PENSION TRUST
				PAID IN ADVANCE (DISC.)
				POLICY LOAN TRANSACTIONS(F1458-L.B.O.)
TOTALS				ENTER IN REPORT SUMMARY - Line 1

REPORT SUMMARY

		DEBIT	CREDIT
1. SUSPENSE	(HOME OFFICE ACCOUNT #150)		
2. AGENTS LEDGER	(ATTACH FORM 928)		
3. TOTAL PREMIUMS			
4. OVER & UNDER			
5. INTEREST ON	LOAN		
	PREMIUM		
6. DIVIDENDS & COUPONS	CURRENT		
7. MISCELLANEOUS			
CO. CODE-POLICY NO.	ACCOUNT / H.O. ACCT. NO.		
8. GRAND TOTALS			

CHECKS ISSUED

CHECK NUMBER	AMOUNT	CO. CODE-POL. NO.	CHECK NUMBER	AMOUNT	CO. CODE-POL. NO.
			BAL. FORWARD		
SUB-TOTAL			TOTAL		

DATE ______ B.S.O. ______ MANAGER ______

COLLECTIONS NOT PAID AS BILLED

CO. CODE – POLICY NO.	CHG HP	SUSPENSE CR.
SUSPENSE		

DATE ______ B.S.O. ______

REISSUES/CONVERSIONS

CO. CODE–POLICY NUMBER	SUSPENSE CR.
SUSPENSE	

DATE ______ B.S.O. ______

REINSTATEMENTS (FORMS 330 & 8023)

SUSPENSE

DATE ______ B.S.O. ______

A B C (FORM 1748)

SUSPENSE

DATE ______ B.S.O. ______

PRD PENSION TRUST (FORMS 1748, 3238, 8132)

SUSPENSE

DATE ______ B.S.O. ______

PAID IN ADVANCE (DISC.) (FORM 1748)

SUSPENSE

DATE ______ B.S.O. ______

BANK SUMMARY

DEPOSIT	
MINUS CHECKS	
SUB-TOTAL	
MINUS BANK CHARGES	
SUSPENSE	

DATE ______ B.S.O. ______

Figure 14–4. A Typical Summary Remittance Report

left side of the report and the total entered as item 1 in the report summary section.

Charges and credits to agents for supplies and premium adjustments are recorded as item 2, with the details shown on a separate report.

Returned checks, premium reversals, payments on policy loan principal, and other miscellaneous debits and credits are itemized at the bottom of the report summary section.

The small report at the bottom right hand corner consolidates the remittance portion with the payment portion and shows the net change in the bank account. "Suspense" is used to indicate the net change that will be credited to the *Branch Office Suspense* account in the home office while the report is being audited.

The deposit and reporting process in Model Life Insurance Company follows these steps: policyowner stubs and receipts to be retained are separated from all items serving as remittance stubs. These stubs are sorted into the following groupings to facilitate work in the home office—renewal premiums, initial premiums on new applications, other first-year premiums, any policy loan interest billed on a separate notice, and miscellaneous items. Health insurance premiums and annuity considerations are sorted into similar groupings. The amount in each group is summarized and the adding machine tapes attached to the Summary Remittance Report.

A duplicate deposit ticket is attached to the Summary Remittance Report and mailed to the home office along with copies of all remittance stubs, checks pending reinstatement, and all other accounting slips, and cards. The policyowner's stubs and one copy each of forms prepared in the branch office are retained in the branch office for historical reference and for posting payments to policy record cards.

Processing Payments in the Home Office

When the Summary Remittance Report and other payment forms are received by the home office of Model Life Insurance Company, an entry is made debiting the bank account and crediting a branch office suspense account or accounts for the amount deposited. This entry brings the bank account balance up to date. A day or several days may be required to audit the report before the premium and related entries can be recorded.

A typical entry to record a Summary Remittance Report is:

```
ABC Bank.............................................xxx
    Branch Office Suspense............................      xxx
```

Punched cards are selected from the file, new cards are punched where changes have occurred, and the cards are used to prepare machine listings called *Premium Audit Reports.* These reports show premiums paid, dividends deducted from premiums, interest received on policy loans, reductions in policy loans, and other amounts deposited. Status records are automatically up-dated in this process.

At the end of each day, the totals from all Premium Audit Reports are summarized and used to make a single composite premium entry. The proper premium, loan principal, loan interest, and suspense accounts are debited and credited so that the entry is in balance. A composite entry of this type is illustrated in the next section of this chapter.

The collection cards are then used to calculate commissions and to prepare a daily commission listing, from which a single commission entry is made for the entire day's transactions. This consists of a debit to the proper commission accounts and a credit to the Agents' Ledger Control account. The cards are then set aside to be held for preparation of commission statements, and for premium tax analysis.

If premiums are paid directly to the home office, many of the processes are similar to those used in branch offices but some steps can be eliminated.

PREMIUM ACCOUNTS AND ENTRIES IN INDIVIDUAL PREMIUM SYSTEMS

Account Titles

If a company writes more than one line of business, income and cost account titles must distinguish between accounts with similar titles in different lines of business. The entries in examples in this chapter relate to ordinary life insurance, since the greatest variety of premium conditions are found with ordinary. Entries relating to other lines of business are similar. In the case of annuities, the word *consideration* is substituted for the word *premium.*

In the U.S. Annual Statement, disability and accidental death benefits, which are provided by riders attached to life policies, are treated as sublines of ordinary insurance. Separate premium accounts usually are not established for these sublines because these premiums are billed and collected as an integral part of the policy premiums. To break premiums down into component elements would considerably increase the complexity of the accounting processes, so they are usually approximated

Figure 14–5

PREMIUM AUDIT REPORT

Branch Office No. _533_   Date _10-16-68_ Page _16_

Policy No.	Name	Account	Amount	Date Due	Mos. Paid	Transaction
123450	DOE, JOHN	204.1	10.10	10-1-68	1	PREM. DUE LIFE R
123450	DOE, JOHN	204.1	.10-			PREM. SHORT
123450	DOE, JOHN	884.0	45.00			POL. LOAN PRINC.
123450	DOE, JOHN	815.0	5.16	10-5-68	12	POL. LOAN INT.
123450	DOE, JOHN	233.1	5.69-			DIV. APPLIED
N8058	DARLINGTON, R.	292.0	15.69			NEW BUSN. SUSP.
089642	JONES, A.B.	989.1	56.84-			RETURNED CHECK
184639	DOOLEY, A.C.	989.1	17.85			RET. CK. REV.
184640	DOOLEY, AVA	201.1	13.64	10-11-68	6	PREM DUE LIFE F
153215	BENNET, JOE	252.0	.27			POSTAGE, OVERAGE
153215	BENNET, JOE	204.1	150.58	10-16-68	3	PREM. DUE LIFE R.
H43862	SMITH BEN	506.1	84.32	10-7-68	12	PREM. DUE HEA F
H43863	SMITH, ALICE	506.1	59.62	10-7-68	12	PREM. DUE HEA F
164392	LOWRY, JOHN	201.1	14.65	10-10-68	1	PREM. INVOICE LIFE F
173241	ZWICKNAGEL, J.	204.1	16.85	1-15-68	12	PREM. ADVANCE LIFE R
173242	ZWICKNAGEL, J.	204.1	11.64	10-15-68	12	PREM. DUE LIFE R

Totals This Report:

CREDIT	Prems. Life F.	Prems. Hea.F.	Annuity Cons.F.	Pol. Loan Cr.	Postage	Oth. Suspense
	5,861.21	1,286.51	2,187.39	116.42	5.63	11.64
	Prems. Life R.	Prems. Hea. R.	Annuity Cons.R.	Ret. Check	New Bus. Susp.	Pol. Loan Int.
	15,362.81	4,381.63	8,432.19	568.43	569.34	111.64
DR	Divs. App. Li.		Misc. Coll. Exp.	Ret. Check	New Bus. Susp.	Net Deposit
	1,689.43		16.32	56.84	186.44	36,945.76

once each year from the total premiums collected. With the advent of computers there has been a trend toward more detailed account analysis, including use of separate accounts for sublines of insurance.

Income and costs in connection with individual health insurance are shown by sublines in the health insurance exhibit of the U.S. Annual

Statement and in the casualty insurance statement of Canadian companies. In health insurance these coverages are usually written under a separate policy form for each subline rather than by a rider to a policy, as in the case of ordinary insurance. As a result, separate ledger accounts for each subline can be maintained with ease. If health insurance benefits under one subline are provided by attaching a rider to a base policy which is classified under another subline, the premiums might be recorded under the base policy and the appropriate portion for the other subline extracted later by approximate methods. Each company must use the account arrangement that best fits its needs.

First-year premiums, renewal premiums, and single premiums for ordinary insurance, health insurance, and annuities must be shown separately in the premium exhibits of the U.S. and Canadian Annual Statement forms. Therefore, separate premium accounts are maintained for each of these classifications within each of these major lines of business. An appropriate descriptive word or words is included in the account title.

Premium Entries

When the Premium Audit Report is reconciled to the amount of cash received, a composite journal entry is prepared. A simplified but typical entry of this type is:

Branch Office Suspense...............................	1,518.94	
Dividends Applied to Premium.........................	58.69	
Suspense—First Year—Ordinary.....................		100.00
Premiums—First Year—Ordinary....................		102.00
Premiums—Renewal—Health.......................		40.00
Premiums—Renewal—Ordinary.....................		1,316.80
Interest—Policy Loans—Ordinary..................		15.73
Postage...		3.10

Typically the account Branch Office Suspense is credited when a report is received. The debit of the present journal entry, therefore, zero balances this suspense account with reference to this particular Summary Remittance Report. The Suspense—First Year—Ordinary account represents amounts received on new applications, which is held as a liability until policies are issued. Notice that the account title is more specific than Premium Suspense as used in the previous chapter.

If any amount paid by the branch office is different from that due, it can be adjusted in the entry by (1) debiting a Collection Expense account for underpayment, (2) crediting Postage for an overpayment, (3) crediting a suspense account for amounts to be refunded by check, or (4) debit or credit an Overage and Shortage account.

If the suspense account method is used to adjust premiums, a later transaction is required when the refund check is written. The proper suspense account is debited to zero balance it with reference to the item, and the bank or cash account is credited in the amount of the check written. Both amounts must, of course, be the same.

If stamps are used to refund overpayments, a credit to the Postage account reduces postage expense, which otherwise would have been inflated by the cost of stamps used for this purpose.

The audit report may also serve as a source for historical data and for policy status data when such status is not otherwise immediately available.

CONTROLLING, CALCULATING, AND ACCOUNTING FOR COMMISSIONS

Commission processes can be quite complex because of the many variations that usually occur in agency contracts within a company, the different commission rates payable within a contract, the variable conditions of premium payment, and because many subaccounts are used to indicate line of business and first-year, renewal, or single premiums.

Commissions are payable only on premiums actually received. To properly record the correct commission cost, commission entries must be made in the accounting cycle in which premium entries are made. Controls are required to insure that commissions are credited in all instances where they are due.

SPECIAL MONTHLY PAYMENT SYSTEMS

For many years most ordinary life and annuity premiums were paid annually. When monthly payment plans became common for purchase of homes, automobiles, and other modern conveniences, monthly payments for life insurance also came into vogue. Today, it is the most popular mode of premium payment.

Methods for remitting premiums have been developed that are more economical to the company than direct mail because they eliminate billing for each premium payment. Such methods benefit the policyholder through reduced premiums and better service. These are: (1) preauthorized checks, (2) postdated checks, (3) government allotment, and (4) salary allotment. Under each of these methods, the insurance company allows the insured a lower premium rate than that charged for regular monthly mail payment.

Preauthorized Checks (PAC)

This plan for monthly premium payments is also known by such names as Bank-A-Matic, Automatic Bank Check, and many others. Each company tries to give a distinctive name to its own PAC plan. All are basically the same.

The preauthorized check is similar in appearance to a regular check but it bears the printed name of the payor instead of a signature. Also imprinted are the payor's bank account number, policy number, a reference to a premium due date, and a reminder to the bank that an authorization is on file. When the check is honored by the bank, it constitutes a receipt for the itemized premiums.

Under the preauthorized check system, an arrangement is made in advance by the policyholder, the insurance company, and a bank under which (1) the policyowner authorizes the insurance company to draw a check against his account each month for the premium; (2) the policyowner authorizes his bank to honor the checks as drawn; and (3) the company files an indemnity agreement with the bank to protect the bank from liability resulting from errors, if any, which might be made by the bank or the insurance company. Without the indemnity agreement, a bank could be held liable for a death claim if through oversight it caused a policy to lapse by not honoring a preauthorized check when funds were available in the customer's account. It could also be liable for an improper charge if it paid such a check after the customer had withdrawn his authorization.

Preauthorized checks are prepared by the home office periodically near the dates on which premiums fall due. Collection cards may be prepared at the same time or several days in advance. Lapse notices and other follow-up notices and stubs are not required. After the collection cards are pulled and balanced to the amount of preauthorized checks to be deposited, the process is the same as it would be had the premium been remitted by mail. Premium collections under a preauthorized check system are usually centralized in large regional collection offices or at the home office to effect maximum economy in writing and *handling* checks on a mass production basis.

Advantages of this method to the company include (1) the cost of mailing and handling premium and lapse notices is eliminated, (2) premiums are received as they fall due so that money is available at an earlier date for investment (many policyowners would otherwise pay during their grace period), and (3) greater clerical efficiency is achieved because peaks and valleys in work flow are avoided.

Although preauthorized checks are usually deposited by the home office, they may be deposited by branch offices. This would be advantageous because it is easier for the company (through the agent) to contact the policyowner and the bank on dishonored checks.

Postdated Checks

Under the postdated check system, the policyowner gives the company 12 signed checks once each year—one dated for each of the next 12 months. These 12 monthly predated checks are prepared in advance by machine on each policy anniversary and mailed to the policyowner who may either sign them or substitute his own check forms.

This method may be used instead of the preauthorized checks if a bank does not permit use of the preauthorized check system, or if the policyowner has a special checking account of a type that requires use of a specific check form. A few life insurance companies use this method exclusively in preference to the preauthorized check system. The advantages to the company and policyowner are similar to those under the preauthorized check system.

Government Allotment

Members of the armed forces are permitted to have premiums deducted from their pay each month and sent directly to the home office of any insurance company. The government will send individual checks to the company for each policy or will send one check covering a number of servicemen, together with a list of premiums being paid. When the plan is first established, it frequently is difficult to coordinate the allotment dates with premium dates because approximately two months pass between the date the serviceman requests an allotment and the date the first allotment check is received. To be certain that a check is forthcoming, most companies require certification by an armed services finance officer that the allotment has been requested. When the policyholder is released from military service, there is again difficulty in coordinating payments with due dates. In order to conserve policies during the period immediately after termination of military service, liberal reinstatement privileges are usually extended.

The benefits to the company are similar to those under the preauthorized check system except that a peak work load occurs early in the month as a result of the government offices mailing all checks at one time. After the collection card is pulled, the accounting process is the same as that for any other premium.

SALARY ALLOTMENT

Many employers agree to deduct life insurance premiums from the paychecks of employees who have authorized such action and to remit the premiums directly to the insurance company. A minimum number of employees usually must agree to pay not less than a minimum amount of premiums under the plan. Such a minimum might be five employees and $70 total premiums per payment. This system is known by various names, such as salary savings, salary deduction, payroll deduction, and salary allotment insurance.

The system is used to collect ordinary life insurance premiums and health insurance premiums. When used for health insurance, it is generally known as franchise health insurance and a special agreement is included in the policies guaranteeing that premiums will not be increased or policies cancelled individually. The entire group may be cancelled, however. In this respect, franchise policies are similar to group health insurance. Methods of accounting for franchise health insurance are the same as those used for ordinary insurance.

Premiums on any plan of ordinary or health insurance may be collected under the salary allotment method. There is no restriction as to the number of agents or the dates when policies may be added to the system.

One consolidated billing, which shows all of the premiums due from a single employer, is prepared each month and mailed to the employer. The employer is expected to remit all of the premiums on the listing, unless an employee cancels his salary allotment authorization, leaves his employment, etc. The advantages of this system to the company and policyowners are the same as those under the preauthorized check system.

REINSURANCE PREMIUMS

Life insurance companies establish limits on the amounts of insurance risk they are willing to carry on one life. A limit of this type is referred to as *retention*. A company will accept applications for amounts larger than its retention and purchase reinsurance from other life insurance companies to cover the excess. For example, if a company has a retention limit of $100,000, it will reinsure all amounts on an applicant in excess of $100,000. Purchasing reinsurance is also referred to as *ceding risks or ceding reinsurance*. The two common methods of reinsuring are known as yearly renewable term reinsurance and coinsurance.

When the yearly renewable term method is used, reinsurance premiums are paid on the net risk portion of the amount reinsured. *Net risk* is the difference between the death benefit and the terminal reserve of a particular policy year. For example, if a $100,000 policy is written and the retention is $60,000, then $40,000 is reinsured. If the terminal reserve on a face amount of $40,000 is $1,000 at the end of the first year and $3,000 at the end of the second year, the net risk reinsured the first year is $39,000, and the net risk reinsured the second year is $37,000.

The premium payable by the ceding company to the reinsurance company is the yearly renewable term rate per $1,000 of insurance times the net risk. It is obvious, therefore, that life reinsurance premiums vary from year to year, the amount depending upon the attained age of the insured person and the current amount of net risk. Life insurance yearly renewable term premium rates increase each year as the attained age of the insured person increases, but net risk usually decreases because the terminal reserve increases. Accidental death and disability premiums are less in the first year than in renewal years but remain level after the first year.

When policies are coinsured, a share of the total policy is reinsured. The ceding company's premiums on coinsured policies are based on the premiums charged the insured less dividends and specified expense allowances. These allowances are higher in the first year because of higher commissions to agents, underwriting costs, and issue costs.

Accounting for reinsurance premiums paid is a relatively simple process. A monthly billing is received from the reinsurer showing first-year premiums in one section, renewal premiums in another, with reinsurance premiums for disability and accidental death benefits shown in separate columns on the billing statement. Premiums on reinsurance are usually paid annually in advance, but other payment plans are available.

The typical reinsurance billing statement covers all of the annual premiums due during a particular anniversary month. If the reinsured policy is in force on the anniversary, the full reinsurance premium for the year is paid. In the event of termination of a reinsured policy between anniversaries, the unearned reinsurance premium is claimed from the reinsurer.

Since reinsurance billing statements show rider benefit premiums separately from life premiums, it is practical to maintain separate ledger accounts for each even though separate ledger accounts are not maintained in connection with premiums received from policyowners. A typical entry for reinsurance premiums paid might be:

Reinsurance Premiums Paid—Life, First Year............	569.13	
Reinsurance Premiums Paid—A.D.B., First Year..........	67.75	
Reinsurance Premiums Paid—Disability, First Year........	45.10	
Reinsurance Premiums Paid—Life, Renewal.............	10,569.34	
Reinsurance Premiums Paid—A.D.B., Renewal...........	683.75	
Reinsurance Premiums Paid—Disability, Renewal.........	481.99	
Cash..		12,417.06

Each time the reinsurer is notified that a principal policy has been placed, it supplies the ceding company with a reinsurance record card. This card shows the amounts due for five or more years, and other pertinent information about the insured person and the amount of reinsurance. It is customary to post these cards by showing a date paid after the amount of premium. This simplifies the procedure for claiming a refund if the principal policy lapses and provides a control to insure that all premiums payable have actually been paid. This is a particularly important step in controlling payment of new premiums which may be billed a month or more after the premium on the principal policy is received.

The only control process required in connection with reinsurance premiums for renewal years is checking the reinsurance billing against status records to determine that policies are still in force.

YEAR-END PROCESSES

The method of calculating the *net uncollected and deferred premiums and gross advance premiums* was discussed in Chapter 12, as was the method of consolidating premium collections by states for preparation of Schedule T in the Annual Statement. The following section presents briefly how these figures are inventoried and summarized for individual premiums.

Once collection cards have been used to prepare premium lists for journalizing and the dates of transactions have been recorded in them, they become historical records. These cards can be sorted and analyzed for calculating premium taxes and preparing reports on completed accounting transactions. Many companies keep transaction histories on magnetic tapes even though they may have used cards in the daily accounting process.

The most common process for summarizing individual premiums for Schedule T[1] is to sort premium transaction records by state at the end of every month. However, this may be done daily if a computer is used, bringing totals up-to-date each time. State totals are reconciled to account balances in the general ledger to prove that every premium has been classified by state.

Similar processes may be used for determining the amount of taxable premiums collected in cities or counties where premiums are taxed by cities or counties. Where branch offices are maintained, these amounts may be summarized from Summary Remittance Reports or other supplementary records.

If a dollar control is kept on the billing file by anniversary month, as well as billing cycle, deferred premiums can be calculated very quickly by use of these dollar controls. Deferred premiums are tabulated separately for each line of business and separately for first-year and renewal premiums.

Due premiums are calculated by adding all of the outstanding collection cards in the due-premium file in the home office, or by adding totals if a dollar control on due premiums is maintained. Due premiums are tabulated separately for each line of business and separately for first-year and renewal premiums.

Advance premiums are inventoried either by (1) examining the premium status records and summarizing amounts of premium paid but not yet due, or (2) selecting premium accounting transaction records proc-

---

[1] Exhibit J(b) in the Canadian Statement.

essed for payment prior to December 31 which show a due date in the following year. Advance premiums are totaled separately for first-year and for renewal premiums.

If premiums paid more than a year in advance are credited to the Premium Income account, the totals of those not yet due are usually tabulated from supplemental records and multiplied by discount factors.

Since reinsurance premiums are normally paid annually in advance, but after the due date of premiums on the principal policies, there are no deferred or advance premiums at the end of the year. Due premiums are calculated by adding any unpaid reinsurance statements and any reinsurance premiums not yet billed on new policies which have been paid for. Reinsurance premiums due are deducted from direct premiums to determine the amount of due premiums, both gross and net, shown in the Annual Statement.

Since commissions are recorded in an agent's account in the same accounting cycle in which the premiums were received, the liability for unpaid commissions is usually reflected in the account balances of the agents' subsidiary ledger. Other commission liabilities may be estimated and included as nonledger liabilities as discussed in the previous chapter.

No insurance accounting fundamentals were introduced in this chapter. Therefore a summary is omitted.

QUESTIONS

1. Why must records used in accounting for individual premiums and commissions be more detailed than those used for other types of premiums?

2. What factors cause commission schedules used in connection with individual insurance to be quite complex? When might an agent's hours or activity be controlled? Commission schedules and systems are designed to induce an agent to perform what two functions? What are overriding commissions? How is the amount of each such commission determined? What is meant by salvage commissions?

3. Name 10 items of accounting data usually recorded on policy record cards and status print-outs. Name three items of nonaccounting data frequently recorded on premium cards but not on status print-outs. Name three advantages of status print-outs over premium record cards and three possible disadvantages. When do policy record cards and status print-outs function as subsidiary ledger records? What other two types of basic records are required for a policy? Describe the function of each.

4. What are two common functions for each of the following records as described by the authors? (*a*) policyowner's stub, (*b*) remittance

stub, and (*c*) collection card; what methods can be used to eliminate the need for a collection card?

5. What is the difference between a master billing file and master policy file? When are premium notices usually prepared if a computer is available? If unit record equipment is used? If addressing equipment is used? Why may checking of notices be eliminated if they are prepared on a computer?

6. How are initial premiums controlled if they are paid with application and if they are paid when a policy is delivered in (1) the field, (2) the branch office, (3) the home office? What control does the home office use to prevent oversights in crediting initial premiums to a new policy?

7. Name at least six types of payments which a branch office might receive other than paid as billed and describe a process that might be used to insure that all records are changed and entries made in connection with each transaction.

8. What method might a company use to remind a policyowner that his premium has not been received in the home office? What two methods might a company use to refund an overpayment of premium? What would the bookkeeping entry be at time of refund in either case? What two methods might be used if there is an underpayment? Is an entry required in either event? If not, why not? How may a premium audit report be adjusted for a shortage?

9. How might a premium audit report be adjusted for a shortage? What processes are used, and entries made, to adjust overages and shortages with policyowners?

10. List six circumstances under which a home office might credit Suspense accounts in connection with processing a branch office report.

11. What are the principal characteristics of the following systems for collection of premiums: (1) preauthorized checks? (2) postdated checks? (3) government allotment? (4) salary allotment? What are the advantages of each for the company and for the policyowner? What particular problem does the government allotment system present? What does the word "franchise" mean when applied to health insurance?

12. What is retention? Net risk? What two factors cause life reinsurance premiums to vary from year to year? What factors, if any, cause reinsurance premiums for accidental death and disability insurance to change? What two factors cause coinsurance premiums to change? Why might a company use separate accounts for accidental death and disability reinsurance premiums when it does not use them for direct premiums? If a reinsured policy lapses between policy anniversaries,

how is the unearned premium adjusted? Why are there no deferred or advance premiums on reinsurance?

13. In crediting commissions, is it desirable to post the Agents' Ledger Control account daily? Is it necessary? How frequently *must* the subsidiary ledger be posted? How can commissions be controlled to be sure each one is credited to an agent?

14. What are two methods for determining advance premium liabilities at the end of the year in connection with individual premium policies? How can dollar controls be used to determine due and deferred premiums?

Chapter 15

Debit Insurance Accounting

The principal characteristic of the *debit system* of collecting and accounting for insurance premiums is the fact that an agent personally calls at the home or place of business or employment of each policyowner and collects premiums due. The system was originally developed to serve industrial workers who paid life insurance premiums weekly. For many years the terms *industrial insurance, weekly premium insurance,* and *debit insurance* were synonymous.

There is a trend away from weekly premium insurance. Many companies, including the two largest life insurance companies in the world, were built on industrial insurance, but no longer sell weekly premium insurance. These companies continue to service old weekly premium policies but debit collection systems are now also used for collecting *monthly* premiums in the ordinary and health insurance lines of business.

As applied to the premium collection system, the term *debit* derives from the fact that the agent is charged (debited) in a *memorandum* account with the total premium due each week, or each month, on policies assigned to him. The group of policies on which premiums are due weekly are referred to as a weekly debit. Those on which premiums are due monthly are referred to as a monthly debit. The word debit also means the geographical area in which assigned policyowners live.

The amount of each individual weekly or monthly premium collected is relatively small, sometimes as little as 5 cents per week or 25 cents per month. When a whole family is insured, the amount due may still be only a few dollars. However, moderately large premiums may also be collected under the system.

Because of the typically small size of these premiums, the cost of collecting them must be held to a minimum. To keep down these costs and at the same time to control premiums due and cash received, it is necessary to use accounting techniques which are designed for mass data handling. Methods used in this chapter are based upon weekly premium debits but are equally applicable to monthly premium debits, except where otherwise noted.

AGENCY ACCOUNTING FUNCTIONS

Premiums are usually paid to the debit agent in cash which is turned over to a field office cashier for deposit. The agent and the field office cashier are, therefore, each involved in the accounting for debit insurance premiums. Each field office has at least one cashier who receives premiums collected by agents and does a number of other accounting tasks.

Field offices in a company selling debit insurance are usually referred to as *district offices*. A district is a geographical area and may be all or part of a city. The district office is under the direction of a *district manager* who supervises one or more *staff managers*. Each staff manager supervises from four to six agents. The titles *district manager* and *staff manager* used in this chapter are not used in all companies but equivalent functions are found in every district office. The district manager is responsible for all of the sales and premium collection activities in his district but is not directly involved in accounting functions.

The Debit Agent

Each agent collects premiums, handles claims, and sells new policies. In his premium collection activities, the debit agent is directly concerned with two types of basic accounting records: the *premium receipt book* and the *route collection book*.

Each new policyowner is given a premium receipt book (Figure 15–1), which serves as his notice of premiums due and as his receipt for premiums paid. Separate but similar books are used for weekly premium and monthly premium policies.

All policies in one family are usually listed on the first page of each receipt book showing policy numbers, names of insured persons, and the amount of each premium. Premium amounts are totaled to give one weekly, or one monthly, premium for all policies in the family. Subsequent pages of the receipt book provide one line for every due date over a period of many weeks or months. Only one entry is required to receipt all premiums collected from the family.

The agent carries with him a *route collection book* (Figure 15–2)

Figure 15–1.   Weekly Premium Receipt Book

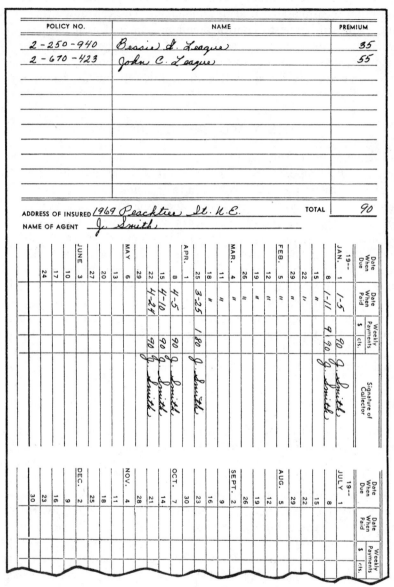

which has a page for each family on his debit, arranged in the same order as the agent makes his calls. Each time he receives a payment and records it in a receipt book, he also records it in this route book.

The route book and the receipt book are very important source

Figure 15-2.   Route or Collection Book Page Weekly Premiums

New Book D. L. P.	Overage	Type	Premium Total	No. Pols.	GE	Branch No.	Debit	Group No.

Wk. | Yr.								
17,69		WKLY	90	2		132	560	661

Policy No.	Name of Insured	Age	Prem.	Issue Date Mo. Day Yr.	Amount	Plan	Date Lapsed or Trans.	To Debit
2-250-940	BESSIE G LEAGUE	48	35	011540	322	140		
2-670-423	JOHN C LEAGUE	23	55	042141	1000	241		

(Premium Payer; Address; Premium For:; Wks/Mo.; Group to be Collected Next)

JAN 1969 FEB 1969 MAR 1969 APR 1969 MAY 1969 JUN 1969
JUL 1969 AUG 1969 SEP 1969 OCT 1969 NOV 1969 DEC 1969
JAN 1970 FEB 1970 MAR 1970 APR 1970 MAY 1970 JUN 1970
JUL 1970 AUG 1970 SEP 1970 OCT 1970 NOV 1970 DEC 1970

documents and usually are the only records of premium status that show actual dates of payments. These records share the characteristic, unusual for accounting source documents, of being outside the company offices and outside the direct control of the company.

The Staff Manager

The staff manager performs certain audit functions in connection with the supervision of agents on his staff, such as occasionally verifying the accuracy of weekly reports of collections made by agents and verifying entries in policyowner receipt books against those in the agents' route books. The latter verification is made at least once in each quarter of the year when the staff manager accompanies the agent on his debit. As premiums are collected, the manager makes the premium entries in the receipt books and route book. Any discrepancy is immediately apparent to him. The value of this practice as a control on cash paid by policyowners is very great. If the staff manager finds, for example, that the dates in the route book and those in the receipt book do not agree, it indicates that the agent (1) has been careless in posting his records or turning in cash received, (2) may not have been turning in all collections received, or (3) has been paying premiums out of his pocket and allowing policies to run beyond the grace period. The latter practice is especially undesirable because a debit agent's commission is based partially on the business in force on his debit. These and many other undesirable practices may be detected by a staff manager audit.

District Office Cashiers

The district office cashier has a key role in the debit insurance accounting process. The cashier's duties include receiving premium collections from agents, depositing these collections in the bank, reporting collections to the home office, calculating commissions, and assembling payroll data. Often the cashier also prepares payroll checks and in some companies may even issue claim checks.

The cashier ordinarily deposits premium receipts daily and prepares, among other reports, a *District Office Summary Report* which is a consolidation of the agents' weekly premium reports. This report is equivalent to the Ordinary Summary Report discussed in the chapter on individual premium accounting systems.

CONTROL OF DEBIT COLLECTION

The two basic control systems for debit premium collections are called the *advance and arrears system* and the *cash* or *field accounting system*. The former is the traditional and still the more common system. The latter is simpler for the agent, but it is virtually restricted to companies with computers.

Advance and Arrears System

Under this premium control system a debit agent is charged with all premiums due on his debit and is credited with all premiums collected. However, an agent does not collect exactly the amount of premiums charged to him. He may miss some policyowners on his calls and may collect some premiums not yet due. As a result, at the end of each week some premiums are overdue or in *arrears*. Others are paid in *advance*. Thus the name for this traditional premium control system.

The advance and arrears system is based on two separate *dollar-control* figures. The first is a dollar control on premiums in force. It is maintained on a form known as a *Life and Lapse Register*, or more simply as a *Life Register*. The second is a dollar control on premiums due, which is referred to as the *agent's account*. The agent's account is fundamental to the advance and arrears system and is discussed first.

Agent's Account. A debit agent's account might be described either as a memorandum premium settlement account or as a dollar control on premiums due. It is *not* a subsidiary ledger account. No entries are made in the company's journals when amounts are charged or credited to a debit agent's account.

At the beginning of each week there is a balance in the account carried forward from the previous week. This balance is the difference between the total arrears and the total advance premiums at the end of the previous week. These two totals are also called *gross arrears* and *gross advance* premiums. Their difference is called *net arrears* when gross arrears exceed the gross advance, and is called *net advance* when the gross advance exceeds the gross arrears.

The agent's "account" shown on the right side of an agent's weekly settlement report (Figure 15–3) is clearly not in standard account form. It is a reconciliation form, of a type used to reconcile a beginning balance with an ending balance.

Figure 15–3

SUMMARY OF REGISTER CHANGES

Total of Life Register (Debit this Week) (1)					
	LIFE AND ACCIDENT PREMIUM	POLICIES	HOSPITAL PREMIUM	CHARGES	CREDITS
Issued (Cr. Agent)	150	1		xx xx	xx xx
Revived (Cr. Agent)	3.00	1		Arrs 21.00	Adv
Lapsed (Dr. Agent)	10.00		1,000	Adv	Arrs 50.00
Increase (Cr. Agent)				xx xx	xx xx
Decrease (Dr. Agent)	550			xx xx	xx xx
Issued (Personal)				xx xx	xx xx
Revived (By)				Arrs	Adv
Trans. to this Debit				Arrs	Adv
Issued By				xx xx	xx xx
				xx xx	xx xx
Lapsed By *Death*	1.50			Adv 1.50	Arrs
				Adv	Arrs
				Adv	Arrs
Trans. from this Debit	.50			Adv	Arrs 1.00
Net Increase				(2) 2250	(3) 51.00
Net Decrease	750			For Week	For'd For Year
Previous Debit	350.00			Net Increase	
Present Debit	342.50			Net Decrease	

THE MODEL LIFE INSURANCE COMPANY
Agent's Weekly Report & Account

Debit No. _____
Mr. _____ Agent
(Name must be printed)
City _____

District _____
Dist. Mgr. _____
Staff Mgr. _____
Week Beginning Monday, _____ 196 ___

AGENT'S ACCOUNT

DEBITS			CREDITS		
Net Arrears last Report	28	00	Net Adv. Pay last Report		0
Debit this Week (Item 1)	342	50	Collection	284	50
Charges to Acct.	22	50	Credits to Acct.	57	00
Debit Note from H. O.	0		Credit Note from H. O.		
Extra } Policy Charge) No.					
Net Adv. Pay (Gross Adv.) Less Arrs.)	0		Net Arrears (Gross Arrs. Less Adv.)	57	50
Total	393	00	Total	393	00
EXPENSE (attach receipt)			REMITTANCE		
			TOTAL EXPENSE		
Postage			Credit Sheet		
Exchange & M.O. Fees			List Checks and Money Orders Below. Give Names of Signers		
Telephone					
Utilities					
Supplies					
Janitor Service					
P. O. Box Rent					
Other Expense					
			TOTAL (Must be Same as Collection Above)		
Total Expense carried forward			Gross Arrs.		%

I certify that I have personally checked the summary of this account with the Agent's collection book and find that the amount of cash collected and entered therein has been correctly reported, and that all policies lapsable under the Company's rules have been reported to the Home Office on lapsed schedules.

Signed _____
Dist. Manager—Staff Mgr.—Spec. Agt.

I certify that the total amount collected is reported herewith and that it represents cash actually collected from policy-holders on my debit and from no other source.

_____ Agent
Street Address _____

[1] The information in the agent's account is taken from the recapitulation at the left, which was taken from the premium register.

All debits and credits are shown on a reconciliation form in the same manner as in an ordinary bookkeeping account *except the ending balance,* which is shown on the opposite side, i.e., a debit balance is shown on the credit side and a credit balance is shown on the debit side. The total of the debit side of a reconciliation form then will be equal to the total of the credit side. An example will clarify the differences between a standard account form and the reconciliation form usually used to control a debit agent's collections.

Assume the beginning balance is a debit of $28.00, the agent is charged with $314.00 in premiums due, and credited with $284.50 collected. The account forms and reconciliation form showing this data appear as follows:

	Account Form		Reconciliation Form	
	Dr.	Cr.	Dr.	Cr.
Beginning balance	28.00		28.00	
Amount due	314.00		314.00	
Amount received		284.50		284.50
Ending balance	57.50			57.50
Total			342.00	342.00

Notice that only the ending balance is placed differently, and that the two sides of the reconciliation form are in balance. In the following week, the $57.50 balance will become a beginning debit balance on the reconciliation form for that week.

In Figure 15–3 the net arrears at the beginning of the period (beginning balance) is a debit amount of $28.00. This net arrears amount is the difference between a gross arrears of $100.00 and a gross advance of $72.00. Gross amounts are not shown on this reconciliation, because the use of a net amount is simpler. A few companies show gross advance and gross arrears in the agent's account so that supervisors can quickly determine the collection status of a particular debit.

Each week the agent's account is charged with the premiums due that week on his debit. This figure is taken from the in-force premium figure shown on the life register for his debit. The account is also charged with and credited with adjustments to the control total maintained on due premiums. These adjustments arise from the following sources.

1. Premiums previously charged and no longer due. These consist primarily of arrears on policies now being removed from the in-force register because of lapse, termination, or transfer. A credit to the account relieves the agent of charges made for premiums while the policies were considered in force.

2. Advance premiums on policies transferred to the agent's debit. A credit to the account offsets charges for premiums that will be made to his

account in subsequent weeks when these policies will be treated as in force on his debit.

3. Arrears on policies being reinstated and arrears on policies transferred to his debit. A debit to the agent's account makes him responsible for collecting and turning in these premiums.

4. Advance premiums on policies terminated or transferred from the agent's debit. A debit entry to the agent's account offsets premium collection credits allowed on these policies in prior weeks. These credits were reflected in his account balance at the beginning of the period.

The agent's account is then credited with the premiums collected and turned into the company. After all charges and credits are recorded in the account, the new account balance is the net arrears or net advance at the end of the week. This is also the beginning balance for the following week.

The agent's account was referred to as a form of dollar control. It is useful to examine the account shown in Figure 15–3 in this respect. Additions (debits) and deductions (credits) appear in dollar control format as follows:

Beginning balance	$ 28.00
Due premiums this week	342.50
Other additions	22.50
Total due	$393.00
Less collections	284.50
Less other credits	51.00
New balance	$ 57.50

The new balance is a net arrears of $57.50, which would be a debit balance if it were shown in account format. Entering these amounts on a T-account form will allow one to prove these facts.

If an error has been made in the amount of collections turned in by an agent, or if he has incorrectly recorded the date to which a premium is paid, the balance of his account will not agree with the amount of arrears and advance premiums shown in his route book. To detect these errors, it is necessary for the agent to periodically "call his account."

Calling the Account. This is a procedure by which an agent lists and summarizes all arrears premiums and all advance premiums with a view to reconciling his net arrears, or net advance, to his account balance. The process is very similar, in many respects, to a bank reconciliation process.

A form used to call a weekly debit account is shown in Figure 15–4. The following terms are commonly used in connection with debit insurance and are used in the following discussion:

The term *date-last-paid* (DLP) means the *due date* of the last premium paid. It does *not* mean the actual date of receipt of a premium payment. On a weekly premium policy, the DLP is one week earlier than the paid-to-date. For example, if a weekly premium due on December 14 was collected on December 16, the DLP is December 14 until another premium is received and the premium paid-to-date is December 21. In the case

Figure 15–4. Typical Weekly Call Sheet

FORM 11-072 (R 3-66)	COASTAL STATES LIFE INSURANCE COMPANY	SCHEDULE OF WEEKLY PREMIUM AND MONTHLY DEBIT INSURANCE ADVANCES AND ARREARS

WEEKLY PREMIUM DEBIT

PREMIUMS IN ARREARS

4 WEEKS		3 WEEKS	2 WEEKS		1 WEEK		1 WEEK	2 WEEKS
C.B. PAGE / PREM.		C.B. PAGE / PREM.	C.B. PAGE / PREM.	C.B. PAGE / PREM.	C.B. PAGE / PREM.	C.D. PAGE / PREM.	C.B. PAGE / PREM.	C.D. PAGE / PREM.
0110	9.24	0010 90	0010 1.05	0160 2.98		0125 3.00		0035 2.10
0240	2.40	0020 1.19	0140 2.05	0280 1.01				0520 .85
0320	1.10	0030 57	0180 1.14	0290 2.33				
0330	1.52	0250 1.99	0170 74	0350 1.15				
0370	63	0310 96	0210 1.99	0360 68				
0430	77	0340 1.25	0300 71	0410 1.84				
		0390 1.85	0305 90	0460 2.34				
		0440 1.05	0380 1.99	0540 68				
		0480 41	0430 2.82					
		0490 35	0450 65					
			0470 43					
			0510 66					

9.76								
1		2	3					

8 WEEKS AND OVER IN ARREARS

C.B. PAGE	NO. OF WKS.	PREM.	AMOUNT OF ARREARS	EXPLANATION
0140	5	70	3.60	
0230	5	62	3.40	

6.90		9.08	15.20		14.92		3.00	2.96
4		5	6	7	8	9	10	11	12	13

of monthly debit insurance, the DLP is frequently referred to as a month-last-paid or MLP. If the MLP is December, this means the premium due in December has been paid. Premiums are said to be paid to *even date* when all premiums due have been collected and no premiums are paid in advance.

Calling the agent's account should uncover any intentional or unintentional errors both in the route book entries, which were recorded on the call sheet, and in the amounts of cash turned in. Errors are indicated when the account call discloses that the net arrears (or net advance) fails to equal the balance of the agent's account. In a sense, calling the account establishes the amount an agent should turn in to the district office cashier. To determine his settlement, he enters all known debits and credits in his account. The excess of debits over credits is the amount of collections.

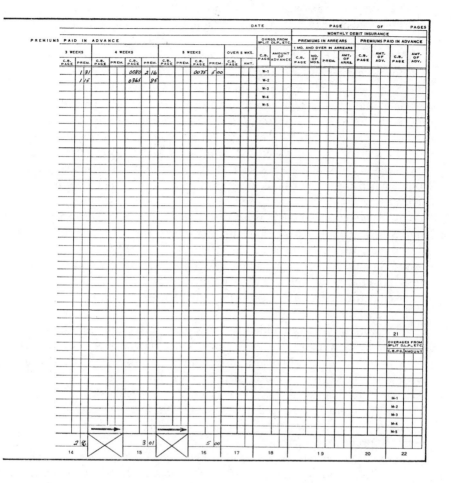

Assume that an agent is responsible for a $300 debit and that his net arrears were $11 at the end of the previous week. His call sheet shows $12 in net arrears at the end of this week. He made change from personal funds during the week and becomes confused as to the amount of premium collections. To determine the amount collected, he enters the debits and credits in his premium settlement account. The account appears as follows:

Debit Agent's Account

	Dr.	Cr.
Beginning net arrears	11.00	
Debit	300.00	
Ending net arrears		12.00
Collections		
	311.00	

The difference between debits and credits is $299, the amount of collections he must turn in. When this amount is entered in the credit side of the account, it is in balance.

If the agent enters his actual collections and his account does not balance, it is apparent an error has occurred in posting his route book or in calling his account. The amount of the error is the difference between the debit and credit side of the account reconciliation. An error should, of course, be found and corrected, but it is not necessary to do this immediately, if the agent is willing to settle his account on the basis of the call sheet. An error in a call sheet will be offset and, therefore, automatically corrected in the following week's call. An error in the route book will be found when the receipt book is again posted for the policy payment in error.

Life Register. Although primarily a dollar-control register on premiums in force on a debit, it is also the source for advance and arrears adjustments to an agent's accounts when policies are added to or taken from his debit. In some companies the register is used to record commissions credited to agents and if a policy lapses to record commissions reversed before these commissions are fully earned.

The traditional life register consisted of one set of pages on which policies were listed when added to the weekly debit and another set on which policies were listed when they were removed from the weekly debit. Totals to date of the add portion and totals to date of the deduct portion of the register were carried forward from week to week. The difference in these totals was the amount of the weekly debit. The two parts of the register were filed in a single binder, and registers for weekly premium business were usually maintained separately from those for monthly premium business.

With the advent of computers, there has been a trend toward combining additions and deductions and monthly and weekly premium business on the same pages. Separate totals are used, of course, for weekly debit and monthly debit amounts. Computers make it possible to print on these registers numerous other totals that are useful to company management. As a result, life registers have become increasingly complex and the data recorded has become less standardized among companies.

Every week a new register page is prepared for each debit. All of the data required to adjust the agent's account on policies moving in and out of the debit are listed and amounts are subtotaled for each type of change. The total premium in force for the previous week is brought forward and adjusted for the changes in the current week to obtain a new debit (premiums in-force) total. Eventually, the number of change pages become so numerous that it becomes difficult to find a particular policy to determine if it is still in force. It then becomes necessary to relist all of the policies on a debit.

A copy of each life register is retained in the home office of the company. Other copies are usually prepared for the agent and the district office. Life registers frequently are the only historical records available on a debit insurance policy. This is so because the agent destroys his old route book page on an active policy whenever a new page is required. On a lapsed policy, he destroys the page when he decides that the policy will not be reinstated. He destroys old life registers when relisted registers are received and found to be correct.

A closer examination of the life register is useful to obtain a better understanding of its use in supplying many of the figures required in the agent's account. A life register page in a simplified form is shown in Figure 15–5 with specimen changes recorded to illustrate its function and typical data.

A large amount of important data on each policy is recorded on a life register. This data may include the policy number, policy date of issue, a code for the insurance plan, the amount of insurance, age of the insured, the insured's name, a code indicating the type of transaction (such as issue, revival, lapse, etc.), and the amount of premium being either added or subtracted from the in-force premiums of the debit.

There is also a transfer column on this life register to show the district

Figure 15–5

FORM NO. 14-007

COASTAL STATES LIFE INSURANCE COMPANY — PREMIUM REGISTER

DEBIT	DIST.	A & S BENEFIT	NUMBER OF POLICIES IN FORCE	NAME OF AGENT	T I A N	PREMIUMS IN FORCE	HOSP. PREMIUM	WEEK OF (NO. DAY YR)
129	15	850 00	700	John Doe		350 00	57 15	12 23 8

DATE ISSUED (MO. DAY YR.)	PLAN	POLICY NUMBER	AMOUNT OF INSURANCE	AGE	NAME	T R A N	PAGE IN COLL BOOK	PREMIUM	TRANSFER (DEBIT DIST.)	D.L.P. (NO. DAY YR)	ADVANCE OR ARREARS
12 23 68	359	65510013	890	36	A. B. Cable	1	15	1 50 / 1 50*			
5 13 62	821	62241389	1 500	56	B. C. Doge	2	47	3 00 / 3 00*		11 04 8	21 00 / 21 00*
7 25 58	833	58305681	500	38	C. D. Edwards	5	17	2 00		11 18 8	10 00 CR
9 13 59	834	59414215	625	39	D. E. Fine	5	65	1 80		11 18 8	9 00 CR
12 05 62	162	62481382	932	47	E. F. Goal	5	143	6 20 / 10 00 CR		11 18 8	31 00 CR / 50 00 CR
10 06 53	162	53408167	832	58	F. G. Hart	E	74	1 50 / 1 50 CR		12 30 8	1 50 / 1 50*
11 05 58	162	58445831	321	28	G. H. Iral	4	59	50 / 50 CR		12 09 8	1 00 CR / 1 00 CR

DEBIT	DIST.	TOTAL A & S BENEFIT	TOTAL NO. OF POLICIES IN FORCE	TRAN. CODE — 1 OR A - ISSUE 2 OR B - REVIVAL 3 OR C - TRANSFER TO 4 OR D - TRANSFER FROM 5 OR E - LAPSE — HOME OFFICE	PAGE NO.	TOTAL PREMIUMS IN FORCE	TOTAL HOSP. PREMIUM	* - ITEM #2 CR - ITEM #3
		850 00	697	HOME OFFICE		342 50	57 15	28 50 CR

and debit number from which, or to which, a policy is being transferred. The DLP column is used to show the DLP on policies when adjustments are required in the agent's account for advances and arrears. Finally, there is a column for the amount of advance and arrears being charged or credited during the week of the register page.

The register illustrated includes only weekly premium amounts. A column for agent's collection book page number is provided for the convenience of the agent. A similar register is required for monthly debit premiums. Columns are included for commission adjustments, as previously mentioned, and data might have been included on ordinary and health insurance policies serviced by the debit agent.

The first transaction shown is an issue, as indicated by the transaction code. Premiums on new issues are due on the date of issue so no arrears or advance premium adjustments are required. All due dates on weekly premium policies fall on Mondays. This is done so that all premiums each week will be due on the same day of the week, and so that the agent can be charged only once per week for premiums due on his debit. Due dates on monthly premium policies usually fall on the first of the month, but some companies may use several dates within a month.

The next policy is a revival. The DLP indicates that seven weeks of premiums are due. The arrears to be charged to the agent, as shown on the register, is $21. ($3 per week times seven weeks.) This charge balances or offsets the credit for collections of $21 included in the amounts turned into the cashier.

The next three policies on the register are listed as being lapsed. The grace period on weekly debit insurance is four weeks rather than one month as is the case with ordinary insurance. The policies listed were reported for lapse in the fifth week as indicated by the DLP. Therefore, the arrears to be credited to the agent on all of the lapses are five weeks' premiums totaling $50.

The next policy is being removed from the debit because of death of the insured. The premium was $1.50 per week and was paid one week in advance. This advance amount was reflected in the agent's account balance at the beginning of the week as a gross advance. The charge in the current week offsets the advance premium credit in the beginning account balance. This advance premium will be paid to the beneficiary in a company check in settlement of the claim.

The last item on the register is a transfer from the agent's debit. The DLP indicates there are two weeks' premiums in arrears. This arrears amount was a part of the net debit balance in the agent's account at the beginning of the week. The credit shown on the register in the current week for these two weeks' arrears relieves the agent of the charge which was included in his beginning account balance.

All amounts used in the agent's settlement account shown in Figure

15–4 were taken from the life register shown in Figure 15–5. Notice how each total is entered in the account. In Figure 15–4, the net arrears at the end of the week are $57.50 (arrears $118.50, advance $61). The agent's account call sheet (Figure 15–3) shows how the agent reached this result.

Cash Premium Accounting System

This is a system under which the agent reports to the home office the exact amount collected on each policy. The company then updates the in-force policy records and prepares a list of premiums due in the next premium reporting period, including premiums overdue. The use of this system frees the agent from much accounting detail and allows him more time for sales and servicing activity.

This system is usually called the *field accounting system*. This is a poor term since less premium accounting is done in the field when this system is used than with the advance and arrears system. *Cash accounting system* is a more appropriate term because the agent must account only for cash collected.

This system is not widely used because time delays in transmitting data to the home office and back to the agent are critical and an enormous amount of detail handling is transferred to the home office. Computers can be used very effectively with this system, but much human intervention is still necessary. An agent's settlement account is not required under the cash accounting system.

Each week, or perhaps biweekly, the company prepares a *collection list* for each agent. This list, sometimes called a collection card, shows all the premiums due in a particular week, arranged by page number in the route book which is in route sequence. The agent records each collected premium in the policyowner's receipt book, his own route book, and on the collection list. At the end of the period he turns in a copy of the completed collection card to the district office, which then sends it to the home office.

The collection card (Figure 15–6) lists many policies and has spaces for collections to be entered manually. Both weekly and monthly premiums are listed. In lieu of the collection card, a company may use a set of individual punched cards, one for each family unit.

When the collection cards are returned to the home office, the amount received on each family unit is entered in the computer and the DLP is automatically advanced. A new set of collection cards is then prepared by the computer.

Premium registers are not required with the cash accounting system, but they may be used for commission calculations, production statistics, and other purposes.

Figure 15–6

AGENT'S REPORT OF DEBIT COLLECTIONS

FOLIO	DISTRICT	DEBIT	PAGE NO
246	642	204	01

MEMORANDUM 1	WEEKS OR MONTHS PAST DUE 2	PREMIUM 3	FOLIO DLP 4	PARTIAL PAY (HOME OFFICE USE ONLY) 5	FAMILY GROUP NUMBER 6 ROUTE NUMBER	CODE & SPLIT DLP 6	NO LAPSE CODE 7	AMOUNT COLLECTED 8	LINE NO. 9	INTERIM COLLECTIONS * 10
	3	.98	243		0010	6			01	
	2	1.05	244		0015	6			02	
	M2	17.12	209		0020	1			03	
	3	1.13	243		0020	6			04	
	3	.38	243		0030	6			05	'
	M2	4.84	209		0040	1			06	
		3.93	247		0050	6			07	
		1.10	306		0060	6			08	
	M2	2.12	209		0070	1			09	
		.14	305		0090	6			10	
	2	2.05	244	1.41	0100	6			11	
	4	3.82	242	.02	0110	6			12	
		2.79	211		0120	1			13	
		.75	249		0120	6			14	
	M1	4.60	210		0130	1			15	
	2	1.14	244		0130	6			16	
	M1	5.82	210		0140	1			17	
	5	.70	241		0140	6			18	
		2.10	211		0150	1			19	
		.48	250		0150	6			20	
	1	2.98	245		0160	6			21	
	2	.74	244		0170	6			22	
		.90	246		0180	6			23	
		.30	248		0190	6			24	
	M2	8.73	209		0200	1			25	
	M1	7.74	210		0210	1			26	
	2	1.99	244		0210	6			27	
		.28	253		0220	6			28	
	5	.68	241		0220	7			29	
		.15	248		0230	6			30	
	4	2.40	242		0240	6			31	
	3	1.39	243		0250	6			32	
	M1	6.10	210		0260	1			33	
		2.51	246		0260	6			34	
		1.04	246		0270	6			35	
	1	1.01	245		0280	6			36	

*USE ONLY FOR COLLECTIONS MADE AFTER SETTLEMENTS.
BRING FORWARD THESE ENTRIES TO YOUR NEXT FORM 50.   TOTAL

FORM 50 REV. 12-62

ACCOUNTING RECORDS

Debit insurance companies maintain a minimum of records on policies. The original application and policy change papers are the basic sources of data. These are usually filed in numerical order in boxes. File folders are rarely used in order to minimize expense, and since the agent answers most questions in person, there is a minimum of correspondence. Alphabetical index cards are not usually prepared.

Other policy records are the receipt book, route book, and life registers previously discussed. The only other record in the home office is a magnetic or punched card type of master policy record which is used to prepare life registers or collection cards, to make reserve valuations, and to supply current status information, except DLP.

Master Policy Record

The basic source of information for preparing the life register or collection cards on debit policies is the master policy record, which is maintained in a master policy file in the home office. These records are filed in numerical sequence under debit and district and may be maintained on punched cards, magnetic tape, magnetic discs, or on-line mass storage.

As policies are issued or revived, the master policy record for each is placed in its proper position in the master file. Policy records on terminated policies are removed from the master file and transfers are reidentified by the new debit and refiled. When an agent reports a change, the new status is recorded in the master file.

When the advance and arrears system is used, lapsed debit insurance policy records are removed from the debit file immediately after lapse, pending possible reinstatement. This is done because the agent's account must be credited for the arrears and he must not be permitted to collect back premiums without a proper reinstatement.

Controlling transfer of policy records to the nonforfeiture file is accomplished by a process similar to that described for ordinary policies. It is, of course, necessary to transfer them temporarily to a lapsed file unless a computer is programed to immediately calculate nonforfeiture values, in which case they may be transferred directly to the nonforfeiture file.

ORDINARY PREMIUM COLLECTIONS ON THE DEBIT

Most combination companies (those which write both mail pay ordinary and debit insurance) use the size of monthly premium to distinguish between *monthly debit insurance* and *regular monthly ordinary*. Fifteen dollars may be a typical dividing figure. Usually the debit agent is not encouraged to make collections of regular ordinary premiums. He is, however, informed of pending lapse of these policies, so that he may conserve his business.

If debit agents are permitted to make regular ordinary life insurance collections, the accounting control system may be similar to either the cash accounting system or the method described in Chapter 14 for individual premiums.

COMMISSION PAYMENT SYSTEMS

The two common debit insurance commission systems are (1) the *times* commission system and (2) the *commission and conservation* or "C and C" system. To best understand these systems, it is useful to examine some of the purposes of sound debit commission plans.

A good debit insurance commission plan should meet the following specifications:

1. Provide an incentive to the agent to acquire new business
2. Compensate the agent for collecting premiums and servicing policies
3. Reward the agent for having good persistency or penalize him for lapses
4. Produce relatively level earnings for the agent from week to week

Commissions paid for the writing of new business are known as writing commissions or first-year commissions. To provide adequate inducement to write new business, these commissions must be many times greater in amount than the premiums collected for the first week or month of a new policy. This need becomes quite apparent if the conditions involved in starting a new debit are examined.

If an agent is assigned to start building a debit, and he has no other duties, he might write as much as $5 per week in new premiums. A man capable of doing this must be paid at least $125 per week, which is 25 times his first week's collection. Good agents earn much more than this, but this example illustrates the point.

In order for the company to recover its initial outlay for new business commissions, the major part of the new business must be conserved (kept in force). Conservation involves the agent collecting premiums as they become due, "reselling" policies when they are about to lapse, and encouraging the reinstatement of policies after they lapse.

A debit agent is paid a *collection commission* for collecting premiums and servicing policies. This commission is usually a percentage of each premium collected, including both first-year and renewal premiums. This percentage varies considerably among companies and is usually higher for collecting weekly premiums than for collecting monthly premiums. The percent might be as low as 5 percent or as high as 25 percent of the premiums collected.

A collection commission usually does not provide sufficient incentive to induce an agent to resell and reinstate policies when he can earn a great deal more by selling new business. An adequate incentive is supplied if the writing commission is based on increase in debit size. In this case the agent might receive $25 for writing $1 in new premiums if he has no lapses but might receive nothing for $1 of new premiums if he did have policy lapses.

If writing commissions are payable on a basis other than increase in premiums, first-year commissions are usually reversed on early lapses and a special conservation commission is paid for good persistency. Methods of calculating conservation commissions vary greatly among companies and are quite complex.

Times Commission System

Under this system the agent is paid for new business at a stated multiple of the dollar increase in his debit. For example, if a contract provides for paying writing commissions of 25 times, the agent is paid $25 for every dollar his debit increases because of his efforts. The number of times payable usually does not vary by plan of insurance within a company, but there may be a difference between life and health insurance, and there is a difference between weekly premium and monthly premium debit insurance.

Under the times system, commissions are paid only on the increase in debit size, i.e., on premiums added less premiums on policies reported as lapsed that week. A reinstatement has a commission value equal to a new application with the same amount of premium. In calculating the net increase in debit for commission purposes, the agent is charged with a decrease if a policy lapses or if a policyowner exercises a nonforfeiture option. He is not charged with decreases resulting from transfers out of his debit, nor is he credited for an increase when a policy is transferred into his debit. Most companies do not charge him with automatic decreases such as death claims, policies paid up in full, and matured endowments. If an agent writes or reinstates $2 of premium and loses $1 in old premiums on account of a death or maturity, he is paid for a $2 increase in debit.

The times system is commonly used by smaller companies but is found in a few large companies as well. It is the original commission system used for industrial insurance. The principal advantage of the times system is that it provides both an incentive to the agent to write new business and an incentive for him to conserve old business. However, it works an undue hardship on an agent when old policies terminate for reasons beyond the agent's control, such as adverse economic conditions and strikes.

A collection commission is always paid for collecting premiums under the times system. A conservation commission might also be paid as a bonus for good persistency; i.e. for success in conserving business in force.

Commission and Conservation System

Under this system the agent is paid a full first-year's commission at the time the policy is issued and the first premium paid. This commission is calculated as a percent of an annualized premium.

An *annualized premium* is the policy premium times the number of premiums due in one year. For example, the annualized premium on a policy with a $1 weekly premium is $52 and for a policy with a $4 monthly premium it is $48. When this type of commission contract is used, the commission percent frequently varies by plan of insurance.

Under the C and C system, a typical commission might be 40 percent of the annualized first-year premium. If the policy lapses in the first year, all or a part of this commission is reversed. Commission adjustments may be made on life registers.

Conservation commissions are usually paid under the C and C system. A penalty is also assessed when agents write business on former policy-owners whose policies have been lapsed less than a certain period, typically three to six months. The penalty is usually a reduction in the writing commission paid on the replacement policy.

As in the case of the times system, a collection commission is paid on both first-year and renewal premiums.

Debit Commission Leveling Plans

Commission leveling plans are designed to provide the agent with a relatively stable weekly income despite fluctuations in his new business earnings. They are applied primarily to writing commissions but are also frequently used to level conservation, collection, and other types of commissions.

A leveling plan is particularly important for debit agents because these agents must have earnings each week sufficient to pay fixed living expenses. Under a pure commission plan, without a leveling aspect, the agent might earn several times his needs in some weeks and too little in other weeks. In those weeks with too little income, an otherwise honest agent might be tempted to improperly report collections or to resort to unsound debit practices in order to temporarily keep his income from decreasing. Leveling is especially helpful when there are seasonal and local short-term economic fluctuations and strikes which may make writing new business unusually difficult during a short period of time.

Commission leveling plans vary considerably from company to company. Only the more common plans are discussed to give an idea of how leveling is accomplished. The more common plans are (1) the reserve plan, (2) the fiscal or calendar quarter plan, and (3) the floating quarter plan.

Under the *reserve* plan, all commissions on new business are credited to a memorandum account known as a reserve. This reserve serves as a basis for disbursing new business commissions. A percentage of the reserve (10 percent might be typical) is paid to the agent each week. The amount paid is debited to the reserve account.

An example will clarify the process. Assume that an agent's reserve is $900 and that his commissions credited to the account for the week are $100. If he is paid 10 percent of the reserve each week, he will receive $100. When the payment is debited to his reserve, the balance is again $900. One week later he is credited with writing commissions of $200. The amount paid that week is $110. When this payment is debited to his reserve, the balance becomes $990 ($900 + $200 − $110). The following week his writing commissions are $50, so the amount paid is $104 (10 percent of $990 + $50). His reserve balance becomes $936 ($990 + $50 − $104).

Notice in the example that the agent's earnings increased in a good week and decreased in a less productive week. However, in all weeks they were near the agent's average weekly earnings.

When a new agent is employed under the reserve commission system, companies either credit the reserve with a lump sum so that the prescribed weekly percent pays a living wage, or they pay the agent a subsidy or salary until his reserve account is built up to an amount that will pay him a greater weekly earning.

The *fiscal-quarter* system is one under which all of an agent's commissions to be leveled are accumulated until the end of a calendar quarter and then paid at the rate of $\frac{1}{13}$ each week during the subsequent quarter. A new agent is paid a salary until a full quarter's commissions are credited to him.

The *floating quarter* method is similar in principal to the reserve plan except $\frac{1}{13}$ of accumulated commissions is paid each week. During the agent's first 13 weeks, his account might be credited with a lump sum or he might be paid a salary until after the 13th week.

HOME OFFICE ACCOUNTING PROCESSES

Each week the field office cashier prepares a District Office Summary Report in which all of the agent's weekly settlement reports are summarized. The bank deposits made by the district office cashier must agree with the total deposits shown on this summary report.

In some districts, agents are authorized to pay specified expenses and to deduct them from settlements for premiums collected. To account for

Figure 15–7

THE MODEL LIFE INSURANCE COMPANY

DISTRICT SUMMARY AND RECEIPTS

District Name_____

State No._____District No._____

Week of_____

DISTRICT SUMMARY CREDITS				DISTRICT SUMMARY RECEIPTS DUE COMPANY			
H. O. A/C No.	Account	For Dist. Use	For H. O. Use Only	H. O. A/C No.	Account	For Dist. Use	For H. O. Use Only
5000	Branch Office Exp.			5100	Ref. of Salary (Gross Amt.)		
6700	Real Estate Exp.				Name:		
				4001	Ref. of Coll. Comm. (Gross Amt.)		
5100	Salary				Name:		
4001	Coll. Comm.				Name:		
4002	N. B. Comm.				Name:		
4003	Bonus			4002	Ref. of N. B. Comm. (Gross Amt.)		
5300	Travel Allowance				Name:		
					Name:		
3000	Accident and Health Claims			4003	Refund of Bonus		
3002	Hospital Claims				Name:		
3003	Non-Can Claims				Name:		
					Name:		
9664	Life Claims				Name:		
				5300	Ref. of Travel Exp.		
9661	Group Disability Claims				Name:		
				9125	State Tax		
				9150	City Tax		
				7500	F. O. A. B.		
				9100	Withholding Tax		
8904	Agents Deficiency			9420	Pension Fund		
Name:							
9510	Office Pays —			9600	Collections		
				1000	Lien Collections		
3030	Ind'l cash Dividends Paid to Policyholders						
9506	Due Mgr. Prev. Rept.			9506	Due Co. Prev. Rept.		
	Sub Total				Sub Total		
8650-39	Bal. Due Company			9506	Bal. Due Manager		
	GRAND TOTAL				GRAND TOTAL		

253 Rev. 12/66

This district summary constitutes a voucher that may be used as the source of a journal entry and posted directly to the general ledger.

these expenses, space is provided on the agent's settlement report (see Figure 15–3). Expenses deducted and money turned in must equal premiums collected as shown by the settlement account portion of the report.

The district office usually has a petty cash and/or limited bank account for paying expenses. These disbursements and the expenses and premiums shown by agents' settlement accounts are consolidated and entered on the District Summary Report.

In the home office, weekly reports from the district offices are audited and may be consolidated into a company-wide summary for the entire debit premium operation. This summary report may be used as the source for a journal entry. An alternate method is to enter data from each report (Figure 15–7) directly in the general ledger rather than summarizing them first. A computer can then be used to prepare desired home office accounting summaries.

The audit trail is clear under either method of entering district reports in the company's general ledger. The home office summary shows the date, district, and amounts from each district report. The district report shows the date, agent, and amount from each agent's report. The audit trail from each agent's report to the policyholder's receipt book is through the dates, page numbers, policy numbers, and amounts of payments in the agent's route book.

Entries for disbursements made from the home office, such as claims paid, may be posted to the ledger weekly, as are the summary reports. This practice tends to match income and disbursements on a weekly basis and avoids difficulties of comparing four and five-week months.

No formal journal entries are made for commissions paid to agents until the commission check is issued. A journal entry for the payment of a debit agent's commission might be

```
New Business Commission Paid—Industrial....................100.00
    Income Tax Withheld.....................................          8.00
    FICA Taxes Withheld.....................................          3.25
    Cash....................................................         88.75
```

An agent's earnings statement form is presented in Figure 15–8.

Figure 15–8

THE MODEL LIFE INSURANCE COMPANY

EARNINGS STATEMENT

DIST.	DEBIT	EMPLOYEE NUMBER	SUPERVISION COMMISSION	FIRST YEAR OVERRIDING	FIRST YEAR COMMISSION	FINANCING PAYMENT	SERV. COMM.	CONSV. COMM.	GROSS EARNINGS	EXPENSE	WITHHOLDING		F.I.C.A.	CHECK NUMBER	CHECK DATE		
											FEDERAL	STATE			MO.	DAY	YR.

		SALARY SAVINGS	LICENSE	XMAS SAVINGS		STOCK	GROUP INSURANCE	RED RESERVE	MISC.	SURETY	NET PAY
KEEP THIS STATEMENT FOR YOUR RECORDS											

DETACH THIS STATEMENT BEFORE CASHING CHECK

YEAR-END MATTERS

District reports each week show all premiums in arrears and all advance premiums at the end of the last week of the year. It is a simple matter to add these to obtain the due (arrears) and advance premiums for annual statement.

If the first day of January falls on any day other than Monday, a portion of premiums paid to even date are advance premiums. For example, if January first falls on Wednesday, the policies with a December 30 DLP (date-last-paid) are paid five days in advance to January 6. This fractional week's premiums is usually added to other advance premiums to obtain the total advance premiums for the Annual Statement. It is logical that, if the following full week's advance premium is to be considered as advance premiums, then a fraction of a week's premium should be treated in like manner.

First-year and renewal debit insurance premiums are shown together in the renewal premium section of the premium exhibit.

Premiums by state for entry in Schedule T are summarized from District Summary Reports. If a district covers parts of two states, the district office may be required to submit a supplementary report by state.

QUESTIONS

1. What does the word *debit* in debit life insurance mean? How did this word originate? What was the origin of the term *industrial* insurance?

2. Why are mass accounting techniques used in connection with debit premiums? What roles do the district manager, staff manager, and cashier have in the premium accounting function?

3. Describe a premium receipt book and tell how it is used. How many receipt books are usually used if four people in a family are insured under six different policies? What if some are insured under monthly premium policies?

4. Describe a route collection book. How is it related to the premium receipt book? What is unique about these books as accounting source documents?

5. Describe the advance and arrears system of debit premium collection and indicate how the life register is used in calculating the weekly settlement due from an agent. What is meant by gross advance, gross arrears, net advance, and net arrears premiums?

6. Explain carefully the procedure for "calling" an agent's account. What purposes does this procedure serve? What is the effect of an error in calling the account? How is it corrected?

7. What is the difference between these accounting-related forms: ledger account? dollar control? reconciliation? Why is a reconciliation form preferable to an account form for an agent's account?

8. What are two important uses of the life register? What important accounting data must be included on it? What other accounting data is frequently included? How is the DLP used on a life register?

9. What do the terms *date last paid, month last paid,* and *even date* mean in debit insurance?

10. How does the cash accounting system of debit premium collection differ from the advance and arrears system? What other name is used for this system? Why would an agent prefer the system? Why hasn't it been widely adopted?

11. What in-force debit records are maintained in the home office? How are premiums reported to the home office under the advance and arrears system and under the cash accounting system?

12. Give four requisites or specifications for a sound debit agent's commission system? Why are they important?

13. What are the two common debit insurance commission systems? Explain in detail how each of these systems works and how each fulfills the requisites for a good debit commission system?

14. What is the purpose of a commission leveling plan? Tell how two of the standard leveling plans accomplishes this purpose.

15. Outline the audit trail from the premium receipt book to the home office summary report.

Chapter 16

Group Premium and Commission Accounting Systems

The principal characteristic of the group system for collecting and accounting for insurance premiums is that one company or organization, which is the policyowner, is billed for and pays monthly premiums for the insurance on a group of insured persons. This system, as its name suggests, is applied primarily to various types and forms of group insurance. The salary deduction method of collecting ordinary life and health insurance premiums might, however, be considered a variation of the group system.

Originally the group premium system was applied only to group life insurance. The monthly billing consisted of a simple list of premiums which showed the amount due on each insured and the total amount due. Over the years, group policies have been developed which provide all types of benefits sold by life insurance companies. Likewise, group premium systems have been adapted to serve the expanded market, to fit many special situations, and to satisfy the individual desires or needs of each policyowner served.

Group insurance is the most inexpensive method of providing insurance protection. There are three reasons for the lower cost of group insurance: (1) intense competition among companies keeps premium rates low; (2) one policyowner pays all premiums for many insured persons, substantially reducing the service cost per dollar of premium collected; and (3) commission rates paid for selling and servicing group insurance are much lower than for any other major line of insurance.

Each insurer strives to capture an ever greater share of the group market. This intense competition has resulted in better, as well as less expensive, coverages for the public. Many innovations in group coverages have also resulted. In a number of companies, however, low premiums have resulted in operating losses from this type of insurance.

To write new groups and retain present group insurance in force, companies must have available (1) a large variety of coverages, (2) several methods of billing premiums and servicing policies, (3) very low premium rates, (4) competitive schedules of commissions for agents and insurance brokers, and (5) a staff of well-trained specialists to assist brokers and agents.

Many phases of accounting for group premiums and commissions are presented in this chapter. Accounting for group annuity considerations is not discussed because this is a highly specialized area and is subject to many variations. Several other specialized group coverages are not discussed for similar reasons.

GROUP MARKETS AND COVERAGES

Group insurance coverages may be classified in a number of ways. One classification method is by the special portion of the group market served. The principal market classification is *employee group* in which employers are usually the policyowners and the employees are the insured persons. Other market classifications are *association group, creditor group,* and *credit union group.*

Several types of group insurance coverages or benefits may be included in a policy designed to serve any one of the market classifications. These are:

1. Group term life insurance
2. Group health insurance
3. Group annuities (or pensions)

Permanent types of life insurance, known as group permanent and group ordinary, may also be included in an employee group policy, but these special coverages are not widely sold and are not discussed in this book.

Before the special phases of each line of group insurance are discussed, it is useful to examine those aspects of group insurance which are common to all of these lines.

STANDARD GROUP CHARACTERISTICS

Points of similarity in group insurance lines include the following: one policy covers many insureds, certificates of insurance are issued to each insured person, the amount of an individual's insurance is determined by a formula, the premium rate is lower than for comparable individual policies, and mass billing is used.

A master policy, which contains all of the provisions of coverage, is issued to the employer or sponsoring organization. Provisions usually include (1) a description of the coverages, (2) amounts of coverage available to each insured person within several classifications, (3) the conditions under which the person or persons to be insured under a particular classification becomes eligible for coverage, and (4) the conditions of premium payment.

The requirements for eligibility and the formulae used for determining amounts of coverage for each insured person depend upon the provisions of the master policy. Methods frequently used for determining eligibility and amounts of coverage are discussed in connection with each of the lines of group insurance.

Usually no evidence of insurability is required from an individual. Evidence may be required, however, in groups involving fewer than 25 persons, on individuals who apply for coverage after the period of automatic eligibility, and in those cases where less than a specified percentage of eligible applicants apply for coverage.

When eligibility requirements are satisfied on large group cases, a standard or average group insurance premium is adequate to pay all claims. However, in the case of small groups there is a chance that one or two highly substandard persons might apply for insurance, in which case a standard premium on the few persons applying would not be adequate to cover the total risk. In such a case, the group cannot be accepted at standard rates, or may not be acceptable for insurance at any rates. In order to determine the insurability of a small group as a whole, evidence of insurability may be required from all applicants. Usually the entire group is either accepted or rejected. Evidence of insurability is required from applicants who apply after the initial period of eligibility to prevent adverse selection.

Each insured person in a group is issued an individual certificate of coverage which shows (1) the insurance protection furnished, (2) the beneficiary, and (3) conversion privileges, if any, in the event of termination.

Premiums charged the employer for coverages vary by amounts of coverage provided, but usually do not vary by age of the insured. There are exceptions in case of group annuities and the several forms of "permanent" group life coverage. Premium rates are not usually guaranteed for more than a year at a time.

In accounting and policy service matters, the insurance company deals with only one other party, the policyowner. These transactions include premium billing, premium collection, adding insureds, deleting insureds, changing premiums when required, and settling claims. In the case of large groups, the policyowner may pay claims subject to reimbursement by the insurance company or may draw drafts on the insurance company. The draft procedure is discussed in Chapter 18. A more common procedure, however, is for the policyowner to forward the claim papers to the insurer. The claim payment check is sent directly to the payee which in the case of health insurance may be a hospital or doctor. A copy usually is sent to the policyowner.

Group insurance policies have a grace period for the payment of premiums. If the coverage is terminated without first notifying the insurance company, the policyowner must pay the premiums to date of termination, including premiums for the grace period. Group is the only type of insurance where premiums for coverage in the grace period can be collected by legal means. This requirement is necessary because of the small margin of profit for the company in group insurance premiums. Claims which occur during the grace period must be paid by the company, so the company is entitled to the premium for that period.

EMPLOYEE GROUP

The type of group insurance which is most familiar to the public is *employee group*. It is also known as *employer group*. In the insurance industry, a policy covering more than 25 employees of an employer is usually classed as *true group* and a policy covering less than 25 employees is classed as *baby group* or small group. Some states do not permit insuring fewer than 25 lives under a group policy.

Union and trustee groups are variations of employee group. Under these forms, a number of employers pay premiums to a union or to a trustee, who is the policyowner and is responsible to the company for all premiums due. One of the principal uses for this form is to provide group insurance for individuals who work for a number of employers, as do union carpenters, bricklayers, electricians, etc. Laws relating to union and trustee groups and provisions in the policies are slightly different from those relating to employee groups, but the procedures for handling premiums and claims are very similar.

Employee Contributions

An employer is required to remit to the insurance company the entire premium for all persons insured under a policy. However, the employer may require that insured employees contribute a portion of the premium. Employees' dependents may also be insured, and the employer may require a greater contribution on the dependents' coverage.

If the employer pays the total premium, the insurance is called *noncon-*

tributory group. All full-time employees who meet the requirements for coverage must then be enrolled. No employee may be excluded because of bad health. If the employees contribute a portion of each premium, the insurance is called *contributory group,* and at least 75 percent of the eligible employees must be enrolled. In a few states, this enrollment percentage requirement may be slightly lower. Group insurance issued to labor unions and to trustees may also be contributory or noncontributory and is subject to the same participation requirements as employee group.

Employee Classification

The amount of insurance and premium payable in employee group is determined by each employee's classification within the group, which, in turn, is determined by conditions of employment. These conditions include (1) amount of annual earnings, (2) years of service, and (3) title or degree of supervisory responsibility.

The following is a sample schedule of benefits and premiums based on annual salary brackets:

Class	Description	Life Insurance	Hospital Room and Board Daily	Surgical	Weekly Disability Income	Monthly Premium
I......	Earnings to $7,000	$10,000	$30	$400	$ 50	$12.78
II......	Earnings $7,000 to $12,000	15,000	36	500	100	22.74
III......	Earnings above $12,000	20,000	42	600	150	32.70

An employee must accept or reject insurance on the basis of the benefits offered in his classification only. If this requirement did not exist, all those in bad health would probably select the largest benefits available, and the usual group premiums would be inadequate. Within each employee classification, premiums and benefits are the same for each insured employee; but if coverage is included for dependents, premiums may vary by the number of dependents covered.

During the policy year, the total monthly premium billed to and paid by the policyowner each month changes only because of insured employees and dependents being added or deleted. This is so because premium rates are usually guaranteed for one year at a time. The life insurance portion of a group premium is recalculated annually from a schedule included in the policy showing annual term premiums by attained ages of insured persons. Prior to each anniversary date, the amount of insurance of each insured is multiplied by the premium for his attained age, and the result is averaged to determine a premium per thousand dollars of insurance. The resulting rate per $1,000 is then charged in the ensuing policy year on all life insurance coverage provided by the policy. The same rate is charged for life insurance on new applicants added to the policy during the year regardless of the applicant's attained age.

In effect, the life insurance rate at each attained age is guaranteed indefinitely. Occasionally, however, life rates are reduced through premium rate credits if the company has satisfactory claim experience on the group, or directly reduced if new mortality tables for calculating premiums are adopted.

The health insurance portion of group premiums may be changed on every anniversary date, the amount of increase varying according to the experience of the particular group or the experience of the insurance company with all similar coverages. In a particular group, however, companies try to hold health insurance rate changes to once in each two or three years.

Premium rates in a company's rate book for group health insurance covering medical expenses incurred increase from year to year. This is so because cost of hospitalization and other medical care is increasing rapidly and steadily, and because each year the public tends to seek hospital care more frequently than in the past years. The health insurance premium rate for each insured employee is the same throughout a policy year but may vary among classifications as the extent of coverage varies.

Premiums on baby group, both life and health, are usually slightly higher than those on large groups.

Premiums on employee group insurance policies are ordinarily paid on a monthly basis. Premiums on other modes are permitted.

Accounting Records

Four types of records are usually found in any company writing employer group insurance. These are (1) an enrollment card or application (Figure 16–1), on each insured employee, (2) a master record on each insured person, (3) a master record for each group, and (4) an in-force premium register.

The *enrollment card* is usually 4 × 6 inches in size and provides a space for employee's name, the amount of his contribution, the name of his beneficiary, and a limited amount of employment information or other information relative to his classification and benefits. It is signed by the applicant to indicate his desire to be covered. One copy is returned to the employer when the group certificate is issued. Taking applications on a new group is frequently referred to as enrolling the group.

An employee master record may be a punched register card or mag-

Figure 16–1. Group Enrollment Card

ML THE MODEL LIFE INSURANCE COMPANY
GROUP ENROLLMENT CARD

PLEASE TYPE OR PRINT—PRESS FIRMLY
(DO NOT DETACH COPY OR REMOVE CARBON)

EMPLOYEE'S LAST NAME	FIRST	MIDDLE	GROUP NUMBER	CERTIFICATE NO.
BENEFICIARY'S LAST NAME	FIRST (Given Name)	MIDDLE	RELATIONSHIP TO EMPLOYEE	
EMPLOYER			FOR OFFICE USE ONLY	

EMPLOYEE'S OCCUPATION	DATE OF BIRTH	H.O. USE

DATE EMPLOYED	BASE EARNINGS (Check One)	MARITAL STATUS	RACE	SEX
BADGE or CLOCK No.	$ ______ ☐ WEEKLY ☐ MONTHLY ☐ YEARLY	PLANT OR DEPT.		

CLASS NO.	EFFECTIVE DATE	Employee Contrib.

COMPLETE THIS SECTION IF DEPENDENTS INSURANCE IS PROVIDED UNDER POLICY(IES)

How many "Eligible Dependents" have you: Spouse? Yes ☐ No ☐

Number of Children? ______

Do you desire to insure such Eligible Dependents? Yes ☐ No ☐

(The definition of an "Eligible Dependent" may be obtained from your Employer or The Model Life Insurance Co.

I hereby apply for the amount(s) and form(s) of Group Insurance for which I am or may become eligible under the group policy(ies) issued to my Employer by The Model Life Insurance Company, and authorize the deductions from my earnings (if contributory) of the amount required to cover my share of the premiums.

DATE SIGNED ______ X ______
SIGNATURE OF EMPLOYEE

netic record which includes the name of the insured, his birthdate, the amount of, and code for, each benefit applied for, the monthly premiums for each, and the total premium. This record is used to list additions to, or deductions from, the group each month, and it may be used for billing. It is also used on the anniversary to recalculate the average life premium rate.

The master record for the group may consist of two manual record cards, in which case one is a premium history card and the other a master coverage record showing important data on the group as a whole. Many companies with computers have eliminated the premium history card in favor of periodic reports showing cumulative premiums and claims. Even with computers, a manual master record is usually maintained to provide basic coverage data.

Two manual type premium history cards are shown in Figure 16–2. These cards have a space for premium, claim, and commission histories. The function of a group premium history card will be discussed more completely in the sections dealing with premium entries, experience refunds, and commission calculation.

Figure 16–2

PREMIUM RECORD CARD – GROUP INSURANCE

☐ Simplified
☒ Standard
☐ Self-Accounting

For Commission Instructions

Regular Brokers enter D/S separate for Life & A&H

Regular Override D/S to:

Policy Number GL897-GA%897	Effective Date 5-17-65	Renewal Date 5-17	Prem. Payable M	Contrib. or Non-Contrib. Contrib.	State Georgia

Name BCP Company

Address 1764 Industrial Blvd., Atlanta, Georgia

Type of Industry   Agent J.M. Shawnee 15843

A. T. Mills – 7983 Stf. Mgr.
L. R. James – Dist. Mgr.

Remarks   Group Office Atlanta   Manager & District L. R. James Atlanta 843

PREMIUMS / COMMISSIONS

Date Due	Amount Due Life	A & H	Amount Paid Life	A & H	Date Paid	Balance Life	A & H	Policy Yr. to Date Life	A & H	Agent Life	A & H	Manager Life	A & H	Date Paid	Policy Yr. to Date Life	A & H
5-17	14.75 DepLife		14.36 DepLife			-11								6.26	19.50	72.26
5-17	68.14	286.78	63.63	289.03	6-19	-49	-2.25	77.99	289.03	19.50	72.26			7-10	39.89	147.82
6-17	14.14 DepLife		15.02 DepLife			-88								7-24	59.09	218.95
	62.65	284.53	66.54	302.22	6-26	-389	17.69	158.55	591.25	20.39	75.56			9-25	79.00	294.29

PREMIUM CARD

Group X Y Z Corporation   Agent(s) John Doe

Address Anytown, U.S.A.   Branch Office

Policy No. GL-1111-SD   Policy Year 1st.   Effective Date Dec. 1, 1963

Level Commission (Life) $ 10.00 (Casualty) $20.00

Code Amt. Code Amt. Code Amt. Code Amt.

Basis (Depends on Commission Agreement)

		9-25	99.95	373.49
		12-11	121.71	440.16
		12-11	143.47	506.52
		2-19	165.23	572.88
		2-19	186.99	639.24

Date Due	Date Received	PREMIUMS Life	Casualty	COMMISSIONS (Life)	(Casualty)	Death Claims
12-1-63	12-10-63	$ 100.00	$ 200.00	$ 10.00	$ 20.00	

EXAMPLES OF GROUP PREMIUM HISTORY CARDS

[1] The small card is simple and self-explanatory. It has a space for death claim information. The word casualty is synonymous to health when used in group insurance.

[2] The large card provides more statistical information along with accounting information. The top portion of each premium space is for dependent coverage. Overpayments or underpayments are entered in the "Balance" column and adjusted on the following month's billing, automatically adjusting the new "Due" amount. Premiums are accumulated in the "Year to Date" column for commission calculations which are figured on the accumulated premium. Commissions paid each month are the increase in the "Year to Date" commissions shown.

The *in-force premium register* provides dollar control on premiums in force and due each month and is used to verify the accuracy of billings. In some cases the register change sheets are a part of the billing.

EMPLOYER GROUP BILLING

Group premium invoices are usually prepared in triplicate. The original and one copy are sent to the policyowner with instructions to return one copy with the payment. Changes in the group are frequently written on the copy returned. The third copy remains in the home office as a control medium. Follow-up notices may be prepared from this copy if payment is not received before the end of the grace period.

There are three common billing systems (each with several variations) used in connection with employee group insurance. These are:

Figure 16–3.   Group List Billing

| | STATEMENT OF PREMIUM DUE | **SEP 27 1969** | WILL PAY PREMIUM TO | **OCT 27 1969** |

THE MINNESOTA MUTUAL LIFE INSURANCE COMPANY
GROUP DEPARTMENT
SAINT PAUL, MINNESOTA, 55101

POLICY NUMBER **9915**

A. B. C. COMPANY

LIVES AND VOLUME LAST STATEMENT	23 LIVES			198 000	198 000	PREMIUM				ADJUSTMENTS	
NAME	CHANGES	INS AGE	CLASS	LIFE INSURANCE	ACCIDENTAL DEATH AND DISMEMBERMENT	LIFE INSURANCE	ACCIDENTAL DEATH AND DISMEMBERMENT	DEPENDENT COVERAGE	TOTAL BEFORE ADJUSTMENTS	PREMIUM	NO MOS
10000 ANDERSON KENNETH L	ADN 070869	50	B	10 000	10 000	8 50	70		9 20	18 40	2
10251 BOONE CLYDE D		39	B	10 000	10 000	8 50	70		9 20		
13161 CASON EDWARD B		37	B	10 000	10 000	8 50	70		9 20		
18201 DEWITT WILLIAM D		42	A	15 000	15 000	12 75	1 05		13 80		
20392 EASTWOOD CARR L		69	AX	7 500	7 500	6 38	53		6 91		
23201 ELDER ALEX R		33	A	15 000	15 000	12 75	1 05		13 80		
23421 ELLSWORTH JESSE W		53	A	15 000	15 000	12 75	1 05		13 80		
25181 ESTES BURNETT R		45	A	15 000	15 000	12 75	1 05		13 80		
25981 EVERETT CLARENCE H		36	A	15 000	15 000	12 75	1 05		13 80		
33181 GUNTER ROY E		53	C	5 000	5 000	4 25	35		4 60		
34042 HOLLADAY JOE T		57	C	5 000	5 000	4 25	35		4 60		
37881 HUDGINS WILLIAM A		73	CX	2 500	2 500	2 13	18		2 31		
45764 JANICEK MELBA JO		31	D	3 000	3 000	2 55	21		2 76		
52661 LINDSAY RONALD E		28	C	5 000	5 000	4 25	35		4 60		
52783 LITTLE WILLIE ALLEN	TRM 070869	35	C	5 000	5 000					9 20-	2
53281 LORANCE E A		46	D	3 000	3 000	2 55	21		2 76		
54592 MARCUSSEN ERNEST J		59	A	15 000	15 000	12 75	1 05		13 80		
57501 MITCHELL BOYD E		43	C	5 000	5 000	4 25	35		4 60		
69553 PAYNE LLOYD E		63	CX	2 500	2 500	2 13	18		2 31		
73751 REED LESLIE E		40	B	10 000	10 000	8 50	70		9 20		
77012 SANDERS SHIRLEY T		36	D	3 000	3 000	2 55	21		2 76		
79123 SIMMONS KENNETH H		40	A	15 000	15 000	12 75	1 05		13 80		
79921 SMITH AARON D		64	DX	1 500	1 500	1 28	11		1 39		
95321 WOODARD WILLIAM R		46	A	15 000	15 000	12 75	1 05		13 80		
IN FORCE	23 LIVES			203 000	203 000	172 57	14 23		186 80	9 20	

A. B. C. COMPANY
123 MAIN STREET
ANYWHERE, U. S. A.

PREMIUM	$ 186.80
ADJUSTMENT	$ 9.20
PLEASE PAY THIS AMOUNT	➤ $ 196.00

CHANGE CODES
ADV—ADDITION   CNG—CHANGE IN CLASS   DTC—DEATH CLAIM
RNS—REINSTATEMENT   TRM—TERMINATION   DBL—DISABILITY CLAIM

F. 1200 REV 12-64

| M | 091564 | 102764 | 072764 | *** |

1. List billing
2. Summary billing
3. Self-administered billing

The *list billing* (Figure 16–3) is often used for groups involving up to 100 employees, but it may be used for any size group. Each insured person's name and premium is printed on a list billing and the total premium determined. Some companies show the amount of each employee's contribution for the convenience of the employer in contributory plans. With a large group, a list billing is very bulky and awkward to handle, so a summary billing frequently is used.

A *summary billing* shows the number of insureds and premiums due in each classification instead of the amount due for each insured. The premium rate for each particular classification is multiplied by the amount of insurance or number insured in that classification, and the results summarized to obtain a final total (see Figure 16–4).

With summary billing it is necessary to maintain a life register on in-force business. This register may be similar to the life register de-

Figure 16-4. Group Summary Billing

CONNECTICUT GENERAL LIFE INSURANCE COMPANY to insure proper credit
Hartford, Connecticut 06115

please use the enclosed envelope and premium payment card when sending your remittance.

Account Number 90000
Bill Division

JOHN DOE CO.   01
4049 GENESEE ST.
BUFFALO, N. Y.   JOHN DOE CO.   05P
ATT: MR. JOHN DOE   4048 GENESEE ST.
                                  229000001   02
GROUP ACCOUNTS ADMINISTRATION

CLASS	COVERAGE	Policy Code	NUMBER OF EMPLOYEES AND AMOUNT OF INSURANCE						Rate Basis	Rate	Premium	Premium Adjustments
			Totals Shown on Previous Statement		Net Change Since Previous Statement		Present Totals					
			Employees	INSURANCE	Employees	INSURANCE	Employees	INSURANCE				
1	100	01	12	90,000.00	1	4,000.00	13	94,000.00	1	.600	56.40	
1	200	02	12	90,000.00	1	4,000.00	13	94,000.00	1	.060	5.64	
1	300	03	12	545.00	1	35.00	13	580.00	3	.570	33.06	
1	400	04	12		1		13		4	4.621	60.07	
1	700	04	10		1		11		4	12.768	140.45	10.20
2	101	01	2	20,000.00			2	20,000.00	1			

COVERAGE

000-099 EMPLOYEE INSURANCE
100-199 LIFE
200-299 DEATH & DISMEMBERMENT
300-399 DISABILITY INCOME
400-499 EMPLOYEE MEDICAL CARE
500-599 SINGLE DEPENDENT MEDICAL CARE
600-699 MULTIPLE DEPENDENTS MEDICAL CARE
700-799 COMPOSITE DEPENDENTS MEDICAL CARE

SPECIFIC IDENTIFICATION OF COVERAGE CODES
IS OUTLINED IN YOUR ADMINISTRATION MANUAL.

*POLICY NUMBER IS DERIVED
BY AFFIXING POLICY CODE
TO ACCOUNT NUMBER.

**RATE BASIS
1. PER $1000
2. PER $100
3. PER $10
4. PER EMPLOYEE
5. OTHER

Previous Balance
305.82

Payments

Amount Due 611.64
Date Due 08 18

GF 128d-DP

Both life and health insurance are billed on this form. Additions and terminations are listed on a different form

scribed in connection with debit premium accounting in which premiums (or merely the number insured in each class) are brought forward each month. This register may simply be a listing of insured persons added and deleted each month with a dollar control amount carried forward from month to month. Some companies include the additions and deletions on the billing form. Once each year the register cards are listed so the policyowner may reconcile the items on the list to the totals on the in-force register (dollar-control total).

In some very large employer groups, a policyowner may prefer to do the bulk of the record keeping in exchange for a slightly lower premium rate. The employer, for example, may prepare his own premium statement in much the same manner as with summary billing form. This type of billing is called a *self-administered billing* or *self-billing*. The employer keeps a complete set of records, issues certificates, and then reports only totals to the company. A minimum of records are maintained by the insurance company.

In some cases, claims are also paid by the employer, who is then reimbursed by the company. These cases are known as self-administered groups. All self-administered groups are subject to periodic audits to verify the accuracy of premium payments and to review claims to confirm that claim settlements were properly figured.

PREMIUM REPORTS AND ENTRIES

The method of accounting for and journalizing premiums on group insurance policies is very similar to that used for individual policies. Differences result from the fact that amounts due and amounts received constantly change due to employee turnover. Changes are usually marked on the copy of the list billing which is returned with premium payment. If a summary billing is used, a register showing the changes is prepared by the policyowner and returned along with a corrected summary. Master records are updated, the in-force register is adjusted, and a machine-readable *transaction record* is prepared and used to make a list of premiums paid for journal-entry purposes. If there is an overpayment or an underpayment of premium, an appropriate adjustment is made in the present month and in the next billing.

The company may maintain separate ledger accounts to record premium income from the several types or sublines of group insurance (such as hospital, disability, or accident insurance). If so, a separate in-force premium amount for each account is updated and included in the transaction record used for premium accounting purposes. An analysis made through use of premium and claim accounts is helpful in comparing premiums received with claims paid for the purpose of testing the adequacy of premium rates.

When the premiums listed are proven correct and balanced against the total cash received, a single journal entry is made for all transactions recorded on the list. Assume the premium due on May 17 and recorded on the premium record card in Figure 16–2 was the only premium received on June 19. The entry to record the payment is:

```
Cash......................................................367.02
    Premiums—Group Life..................................          77.99
    Premiums—Group Health...............................         289.03
```

If the company maintains separate accounts for first year and renewal premiums,[1] an appropriate abbreviation to indicate this fact is included in the account title. If the company maintains accounts for types or subtypes of insurance within the group line, a word indicating the subtype would also be included.

---

[1] Canadian statements require showing first-year group premiums separately from renewal premiums.

GROUP COMMISSIONS

Most large group cases are sold through insurance brokers who submit bids to employers upon request. Premiums are reduced to an absolute minimum, and commissions also are frequently reduced below normal scales to permit low premium quotations. Medium and small group cases are frequently sold by full-time agents of insurance companies without bidding, in which case premium and commission rates may be slightly higher. Group specialists often assist in the submitting of bids and in enrolling employees. These specialists are usually full-time salaried employees of the insurance company. A small bonus or commission is sometimes paid to these specialists as a sales incentive.

Group insurance commission rates are calculated on a sliding scale under which both first-year and renewal commission percentages become smaller as the amount of annual premium increases. Most group commission schedules provide for a higher percentage of premiums in the first policy year than in renewal years. A typical first-year scale specifies commissions of 20 percent on the first $5,000 of premiums received. This scale decreases in steps until only one half of 1 percent is payable on all premiums over $250,000 per year. A typical renewal commission scale provides a maximum of 5 percent and gradually decreases in steps until only $\frac{1}{10}$ of 1 percent is payable on premiums in excess of $250,000. The sliding scale presents special computation problems.

The following illustration demonstrates the method of calculating the commissions on a group case where the premiums are exactly $1,500 per month or $18,000 for the first year (rounded figures are used for simplicity). Assume the commission schedule calls for a commission of 20 percent on the first $5,000 in premiums, 15 percent on the next $5,000, and 12½ percent on the next $10,000.

During the first through the third months, the full 20 percent commission is payable because premiums for these three months at $1,500 per month are $4,500 (less than the $5,000 total of the first "step"). Each month the commissions are $300 ($1,500 × 20 percent).

In the fourth month, the accumulated premiums year-to-date becomes $6,000. Commissions on the first $500 of the $1,500 payment are 20 percent, since $500 is required to bring the premiums to the $5,000 accumulation point. Commissions on the remaining $1,000 are payable at 15 percent. The commission for the fourth month, therefore, is $250 ($500 × 20 percent + $1,000 × 15 percent).

During the fifth and sixth months the accumulated premiums increase to $9,000, and the commission rate is 15 percent. In the seventh month the commission rate is 15 percent on the first $1,000 and is 12½ percent on the next $500. The commission that month is $212.50. Thereafter the commission is 12½ percent per month. These commission calculations for the entire year are shown in table form in Figure 16–5.

In order to level out the commissions payable to an agent each month, many companies use an estimated but level percent to calculate the amount of commissions. Commissions are paid at this rate on each premium until the end of the policy year at which time they are calculated precisely and adjusted to the correct amount for the year.

Other companies pay first-year and renewal commission rates that are level throughout the year. The rate is less, of course, for large groups. Most companies do not pay first-year commissions on additions to groups after the policy has been in force one year. However, there are exceptions.

Figure 16–5. Group Commissions

Month	Accumulated Premium	Premiums at Applicable Percent	Commission Percent	Commissions
1, 2, 3	$0 to $4,500	$1,500 per month	20	$300 per month
4	$6,000	First $500	20	$100 plus
		Next $1,000	15	$150
5 and 6	$6,000 to 9,000	$1,500 per month	15	$225 per month
7	$10,500	First $1,000	15	$150 plus
		Next $500	12½	$62.50
8–12	$10,500 to $18,000	$1,500 per month	12½	$187.50 per month

The methods used for crediting and disbursing group commissions to agents vary widely among companies, and even within companies when there are several types of agency contracts in use.

If the agent is a broker and the company has no social security or withholding tax obligations, the debit entry may be to the appropriate group commission account and the credit to cash when the check is issued. For a full-time agent, the company must make deductions from checks for tax purposes. The preferred method under these circumstances is to first credit the commission earned to the Agents' Ledger Control account (debiting Commissions Paid) and then when payment is made, debit the amount paid to this control account and credit Cash. The control account portion of each entry is, of course, posted to the agent's account in a subsidiary ledger.

An entry to record the commissions on the first month's premium recorded on the premium record card in Figure 16–2 is:

```
Commissions Paid—Group Life . . . . . . . . . . . . . . . . . . . . . . . . . . . . . . . . .19.50
Commissions Paid—Group Health . . . . . . . . . . . . . . . . . . . . . . . . . . . . . .72.26
    Agents' Ledger Control (or Cash) . . . . . . . . . . . . . . . . . . . . . . . . . .     91.76
```

If a company maintains separate ledger accounts for first-year premiums, it will also maintain separate accounts for first-year commissions.

In that case the commission account titles include appropriate designations.

Note that the commissions (25 percent) recorded on the large card in Figure 16–2 are calculated not on the amount due but on the amount *recorded as paid*, and that they are accumulated on a policy-year-to-date basis. The accumulated commission data is useful in verifying commission calculations, determining the profitability of a case, and might also be used for reporting income earned by agents to governmental authorities.

Experience Refunds

Many group policies provide for *experience refunds*. An experience refund is a credit against premiums which is allowed when claims and other costs during a period are less than those anticipated in the premiums charged. In the case of large groups, the experience refund calculation is based on the experience of that particular policyowner. Group insurance is unique in that it is the only line of insurance coverage in which premium rates charged a particular policyowner are adjusted downward as a result of favorable claim experience of that policyowner. In the case of small and medium sized groups, an experience refund is frequently based on the experience of a number of groups of similar size.

There are various methods of accounting for experience refunds. The most common is to deduct the amount of refund from the current billing and to credit the net amount received to the appropriate premium accounts. If, for example, a health insurance premium due is $1,000 and the policyowner is granted a $50 experience refund credit, the entry to record the net amount of premium received is:

Cash	950.00	
Premiums—Group Health		950.00

The dividend account is not debited for the $50 because the adjustment is not a dividend declared by the board of directors but is a premium reduction guaranteed through a formula included in the master policy. An Experience Refund account may be debited on the books. If this is done, this account balance is combined with the appropriate premium income account balance to produce a net amount for entry in the premium exhibits of the Annual Statement.

Mutual companies may declare dividends on group policies in addition to allowing experience refunds. If the $50 paid actually had been a dividend, the entry would have been similar to that used when dividends are deducted from ordinary premiums. The only difference is a change of line of business in the account title. The entry is:

Cash	950.00	
Dividends Applied to Premium—Group	50.00	
Premiums—Group Health		1,000.00

ASSOCIATION GROUP

Association or franchise group describes a special type of term life insurance and a special type of health insurance. The policyowner is an "association," and the individuals insured are members of the association. The insured persons usually pay the entire premium. This form of group insurance cannot be issued under the laws of some states. Frequently individual policies are issued rather than a group policy with certificates.

Association group has many of the characteristics of individual insurance, some of assessment insurance, and some of group insurance. Premiums are subject to change annually as in the case of group insurance. The amount of premium payable or the amount of insurance under a certificate frequently is based on the attained age of the insured. Usually the association consists of individuals with a common occupation or profession. The amount of insurance, classifications, and eligibility are frequently determined by factors other than conditions of employment. For example, eligibility may be determined by the attained age of the insured or other factor. Evidence of insurability is frequently required, and premiums may vary by broad age brackets. The insured person must accept or reject the amount available within his classification.

Premium experience refunds are not provided for in the usual association group policy. First-year commissions rates are paid on approximately the same level as small employer groups without regard to the size of the case. Billing, premium accounting records, and commissions are usually handled by methods similar to those used for employer group. These procedures may be modified to meet the demands of the association if the association is sufficiently large to warrant special consideration.

CREDITOR AND CREDIT UNION GROUP INSURANCE

Under creditor group insurance a bank, finance company, or other lending institution is the policyowner and the debtors of the institution are the insured persons. The amount of insurance is determined by the amount of indebtedness up to a stated limit. A credit union is the policyowner in the case of credit union group and the depositors of the credit union are the insured persons. The amount of insurance is determined by the amount in the depositor's account, and is also limited to a stated maximum, such as $1,000. A beneficiary is named.

Premium rates for creditor and credit union groups are subject to change periodically, but companies make such changes infrequently. Experience refund provisions may be included in these policies when a large number of persons are insured.

Creditor group insurance is also known as *debtor group* and as *credit insurance*. It is issued under two principal plans. These are known as the *outstanding balance* plan and the *single premium* plan.

Outstanding Balance Plan

Under the *outstanding balance* plan, the policyowner issues certificates of coverage to all debtors in a specific class or account. An example of such an account might be all automobile loan debtors. Collateral loans are not usually covered because they are larger in amount and because persons who borrow on stocks and bonds are less interested in insurance than persons who borrow small amounts.

All debtors under an insured account are charged the same interest rate which *includes* a small charge for insurance. No evidence of insurability is required, and usually all borrowers are covered regardless of health or age. The insurance company does not know the names of the insureds unless a claim is filed. A beneficiary is not named because the death benefit is used to pay off indebtedness, and the amount of insurance is always equal to the indebtedness.

Premiums are paid by the policyowner at a stated monthly rate per $1,000 of outstanding balance in the insured loan accounts. The rates for this coverage are quite low, being between one half and three quarters of 1 percent per annum of the loan balances covered.

Usually only life insurance coverage is provided under creditor insurance group, although disability insurance coverage might be provided.

Single Premium Plan

Under the *single premium* plan of creditor insurance, the policyowner issues certificates of coverage to all individuals willing to pay the necessary premium. A specific amount of insurance and period of coverage are usually named in each certificate. Some evidence of insurability may be required because the debtor has the right to accept or reject coverage. Applicants at some ages might not be covered, or might be required to pay a higher premium rate.

Premium rates under single premium credit insurance are somewhat higher than under the outstanding balance plan. There are no premium billing problems because the policyowner sends a check to the insurance company along with copies of certificates issued. An employee of the lending institution might be paid a commission on this type of insurance. If so, he may remit nets. Commissions are usually higher than on the outstanding balance plan, but commissions on both the outstanding balance type and on credit union group are usually much lower than for employee group. A beneficiary might be named because an amount could become payable to a beneficiary if a loan were paid off prior to the expiry date of the group insurance. Most single premium credit insurance policies provide life insurance coverages only, but some also provide disability health insurance coverage.

YEAR-END MATTERS

The valuation reserve on group term life and single premium credit life insurance consists only of the unearned net life premiums, which is a relatively small amount. Policy reserves on group permanent, group ordinary, and group annuities may be quite large in amount. These reserves are usually calculated on a midterminal reserve basis, but they may be calculated by use of ordinary insurance mean reserves, in which case deferred premiums must also be calculated. It will be recalled that deferred premiums are, in effect, a reserve adjustment and are used only with ordinary insurance mean reserves. Most companies selling group insurance do not show group insurance deferred premiums in their annual statements.

Due premiums on each type of group insurance are easily calculated at the end of each year by adding all premium notices or records due and unpaid. On self-administered employee groups and credit insurance cases it is usually necessary to estimate due premiums. These are adjusted to net premium amounts and reported in the Annual Statement as described in Chapter 12.

Unearned life insurance net premiums are shown as policy reserves. Unearned health insurance gross premiums may be shown in the U.S. Annual Statement as either advance premiums or as health insurance reserves. There is a special line in the U.S. Annual Statement's health insurance reserve and claim exhibit (Exhibit 9) which indicates that the preferred treatment is to show unearned health insurance premiums as health insurance reserves.

When unearned premiums are shown as policy reserves, they are not, of course, used to adjust premium income from the cash to the accrual basis in the premium exhibit of the U.S. Annual Statement. If they are shown as advance premiums, they would be so used.

An estimated commission liability must be calculated on all due health premiums. This is included with other commissions due and accrued in the Annual Statement.

A reserve for future experience refunds on group life insurance must be estimated at the end of each year and included as a special item on the liability page of the U.S. Annual Statement.[2] Reserves for experience refunds on health insurance are shown as health insurance reserves. These reserves should not be treated as a dividend liability.

First-year group insurance premiums need not be separated from re-

---

[2] Experience refunds are not mentioned in the Canadian life blank but are included with provision for dividends on the liability page of the casualty blank.

newal premiums in the premium exhibit of the U.S. Annual Statement.[3] Many companies, however, choose to make the separation. Whether or not a premium is first year or renewal is determined by the issue date of the policy. Dates of certificates issued after the policy date are disregarded for this purpose.

State distribution of premiums for premium tax purposes is handled in much the same manner as ordinary insurance.

QUESTIONS

1. Why is group insurance the most economical type of insurance? To obtain its share of the group insurance markets, what features must a company have available?

2. What are the more common group markets? What types of group insurance are usually sold in each? Who are the policyowners and insured persons under the lines of group insurance designed to serve each market?

3. When is evidence of insurability required in connection with individuals applying for coverage under a group contract? What factors determine how much insurance each person may apply for?

4. What are the rights of the insurance company if an employer does not pay a premium in the grace period but the company has paid a claim to an employee during that period?

5. How frequently may the average premiums for group life be changed? Group health? How is the new premium for each determined?

6. What is meant by *contributory* and *noncontributory* when these terms are used in connection with group insurance? What classifications of group insurance are found within the employer market? How are the coverage classifications in employer group determined?

7. What are the more common records used in connection with employer group and how is each used? What are the three most common types of billing and how are they used? What is the advantage of each? How does an employer report terminations under each of the three types of billing?

8. Describe briefly a premium accounting record and give the steps from its inception to the point where a journal entry is made. How are group premium account titles determined?

9. Under what conditions might an experience refund be calculated? How is the refund shown in the Annual Statement in connection with

---

[3] First-year group *life* insurance premiums are shown separately in the Canadian life blank but not in the casualty insurance blank.

premiums collected and premium or reserve liabilities? Are dividends paid on group insurance?

10. How does association group differ from employer group in the following respects: (1) premiums payable by insured person? (2) level of premiums and commissions? and (3) evidence of insurability required?

11. What are the differences between outstanding balance and single premium credit insurance? Why might the premiums for outstanding balance type be lower? How is the liability for single premium life insurance determined for Annual Statement purposes?

12. Who is insured under credit union insurance? Does the company know the names of the insured persons?

13. In what two ways may unearned group life and health premiums be handled in the U.S. Annual Statement? Which is the preferred method in U.S. companies?

Chapter 17

Policy Benefit Settlements

More than three fourths of the income of all U.S. and Canadian life insurance companies are assigned to meet current and future obligations to policyowners. These obligations include payment of policy and supplementary contract benefits and the establishment of policy reserves.

For discussion purposes, policy and contract benefits may be divided into four general classifications: (1) policy dividend settlements, (2) nonforfeiture settlements, (3) claim settlements, and (4) annuity and supplemental contract payments. The first two are discussed in this chapter along with matters related to, or common to, all types of benefit payments and optional settlements. The latter two are discussed in Chapter 18.

In general, the objectives of proper accounting for policy settlements are:

1. To issue a check, or make a settlement entry, only upon *proper* authorization
2. To maintain a historical record of all policy benefit payments
3. To provide an audit trail from disbursement authorization to general ledger account and policy record
4. To provide data from which unpaid policy liabilities may be calculated for Annual Statement purposes

Good accounting procedure requires as a security measure that someone outside the accounting area authorize every disbursement. This is especially important in handling policy payments because many are very large in amount.

Histories of policy disbursements of all types must be maintained for governmental reporting, statistical analysis, and answering inquiries from policyowners. The latter need is especially important if the principal policy or contract remains in force after a payment is made. Analysis of claim statistics is useful in determining adequate rates to be charged for insurance coverages in the future. Although such analysis is not an accounting function, claim accounting systems must be designed to facilitate statistical studies.

Methods of achieving accounting objectives are somewhat different for each benefit classification. These methods are, therefore, discussed with each classification. Accounting for policyowner money left on deposit is presented next as a preliminary to the study of other phases of policy benefit accounting.

AMOUNTS LEFT ON DEPOSIT WITH THE COMPANY

There are three principal deposit classifications. These are (1) premium deposits, (2) proceeds of policies and contracts without life contingencies, and (3) dividend accumulations.

The first classification, *premium deposits,* was discussed in Chapter 12. Entries shown were based on the assumption that this liability is recorded in the general ledger, which is the practice in most U.S. and Canadian life companies. The second and third classifications are treated in both U.S. and Canadian Annual Statement blanks as nonledger liabilities, even though these items are frequently recorded as ledger liabilities. Processes used for accounting for liabilities on a nonledger basis are different from those used when liabilities are maintained on a ledger basis.

It will be recalled that a life insurance company does not usually record policy liabilities on the ledger and ordinarily makes no entry on the books until a cash amount is either received or paid out. These facts are characteristic of the nonledger process. Other characteristics include the following: (1) amounts received are usually treated as income even though a liability may be created in an equal amount, (2) amounts paid out are usually treated as insurance costs even though a liability is reduced in an equal amount and (3) increases in nonledger liabilities are treated as insurance costs. In case of amounts on deposit with the company, interest added to the deposits usually is not recorded on the books as an interest cost but is added to the deposit liability. It then becomes a part of the *increase in liability* cost.

In order to clarify the difference between ledger and nonledger liability processes, each will be illustrated, using the same amounts.

Ledger Liability Process

Assume the company has assets of $100,000 and capital (surplus) of $100,000. The accounting equation is in balance. On June 30 the company accepts a $10,000 deposit to be disbursed in annual installments of $1,000 each plus interest at the rate of 4 percent per annum. The entry to record the receipt of this amount is a debit to Cash and a credit to a ledger liability account, Deposit Liability, for $10,000.

It will be recalled that in the case of premium deposits, an item is included in the U.S. Annual Statement called *interest paid on policy and contract funds.* When liabilities are carried on the ledger, the interest account must be debited when the liability account is credited to record interest added to the deposit amount.

(Alternatively an accrued liability account, such as Accrued Interest, might be credited. If handled in this manner the balance in the account must be added to the principal deposit when entered on the liability page.)

At the end of the year, one half of a year's interest is accrued, so the liability at that time is $10,200 ($10,000 principal plus $200 accrued interest). An adjusting entry to record the $200 interest cost and an equal increase in liability is:

```
Interest Paid on Deposits.....................................200.00
     Deposit Liability........................................          200.00
```

After the entry is recorded and the interest account is closed into surplus, account balances appear as follows:

```
          Cash...................$110,000.00
          Deposit liability...........           $ 10,200.00
          Surplus.................                 99,800.00
              Total..............$110,000.00     $110,000.00
```

Note that the surplus decreased by the amount of interest accrued.

On June 30 of the following year, $1,000 of the principal plus $400 interest is paid out. The entry is:

```
Interest Paid on Deposits................................. 200.00
Deposit Liability.........................................1,200.00
     Cash.........................................              1,400.00
```

Since $200 of interest had already been credited to the liability account at the end of the previous year, it is proper to debit the interest account only for the additional $200 accrued. The $1,200 debit to Deposit Liability reduces this account balance to $9,000.

At the end of the year the accrued interest on the remaining $9,000 of principal is $180 ($9,000 × 4 percent × ½) and another adjusting entry is made to record this interest cost and to increase the liability accordingly.

After these entries are posted, account balances would appear as follows:

```
          Cash....................$108,600.00
          Interest Paid on Deposits....    380.00
          Deposit Liability..........           $ 9,180.00
          Surplus.................                 99,800.00
              Total..............$108,980.00     $108,980.00
```

When the interest account is closed, surplus decreases to $99,420.

Notice the following facts in connection with the transactions just presented. (1) Surplus decreased each year by the amount of interest cost incurred during the year. In the second year this was $380 ($200 for the first half-year and $180 for the second half). (2) The liability at the end of the first year is $10,200, and at the end of the second year it is $9,180. These figures are used in the nonledger liability illustration which follows. (3) The amount of interest credited to deposits is reflected as a separate item in the trial balance, but the amount deposited, the amount paid out, and the increase in liability are not shown as separate items.

The Nonledger Liability Process

If this process is used, the first entry is a debit to Cash and a credit to an income account, Deposits Received, for $10,000. This causes surplus to increase by $10,000.

At the end of the year the liability with accrued interest is $10,200 as in the previous illustration. However, since it is a nonledger liability, it is recorded on working papers as follows:

```
Increase in Deposit Liability............................10,200.00
    Deposit Liability.................................              10,200.00
```

The account Increase in Deposit Liability is an insurance cost item which causes surplus to decrease.

After the entries are posted an adjusted trial balance would appear as follows:

```
Cash...................$110,000.00
Deposit Liability..........                $ 10,200.00
Surplus...................                  100,000.00
Increase in Deposit Liabilities   10,200.00
Deposits Received.........                   10,000.00
          Total..............$120,200.00    $120,200.00
```

Note that there is an income item for deposits received and a cost item for the increase in liability, but no item showing interest credited. After the two nominal accounts *Increase in Deposit Liability* and *Deposits Received* are closed, the post-closing trial balance is exactly as illustrated in the ledger liability illustration.

The net effect of the income and cost entries on surplus is a decrease of $200, which is exactly the amount of interest credited to the deposit in the ledger liability illustration.

In the second year when $1,000 of principal plus $400 of interest is paid out, the entry is:

```
Deposits Paid Out.......................................1,400.00
    Cash...........................................              1,400.00
```

Deposits Paid Out is an insurance cost account which causes surplus to decrease. Note that an interest paid account is not debited and that the total payment is debited to the one cost account.

At the end of the second year the liability is $9,180. The reversal and reentry method for making adjustments is used here since it is desirable to record this end-of-year liability in total.

The entry to reverse the previous year's adjustment is:

```
Deposit Liability.......................................10,200.00
    Increase in Deposit Liability.......................          10,200.00
```

The entry to record the current year's liability is:

```
Increase in Deposit Liability............................9,180.00
    Deposit Liability.....................................          9,180.00
```

After these entries are posted, the Increase in Deposit Liability account has a credit balance of $1,020, reflecting a decrease in liability. The title of the account is changed to indicate the decrease and the adjusted trial balance appears as follows:

```
Cash...................$108,600.00
Deposit Liabilities.........          $  9,180.00
Surplus...................          99,800.00
Deposit Paid Out..........  1,400.00
Decrease in Deposit Liability          1,020.00
        Total..............$110,000.00   $110,000.00
```

Note again that there is no account indicating interest paid or credited to deposits, but there is an item showing the amount paid out, which includes interest, and an account classified as an insurance cost item to show the decrease in deposit liability.

After closing the two nominal accounts into surplus, the post-closing trial balance at the end of the second year appears exactly as in the ledger liability illustration. Surplus during the year decreased exactly by the $380 interest incurred. Under both methods, the effect on surplus is identical even though there are differences in the manner of recording income, disbursements, end-of-year liabilities, and the increase in liabilities.

A comparison of the presentation of deposits in the U.S. and Canadian Statements will provide a better understanding of deposit accounting. Annual Statement treatment is, therefore, discussed here even though Annual Statement aspects of other life insurance topics are usually presented in supplements to the chapters.

In the U.S. summary of operations, there are three items relating to proceeds of contracts and dividend accumulations. Amounts placed on deposit are referred to as *consideration for supplementary contracts without life contingencies and dividend accumulations*. Amounts paid out are referred to as *payments on supplementary contracts* (etc.). Increase in deposit liability is referred to as *increase in reserves for* (etc.). It is apparently the intention of the blank that these deposit amounts are to be handled on a nonledger basis.

In the revenue account of the Canadian Statement there is only one item relating to amounts placed on deposit. This is described as *interest credited to amounts on deposit with the company*. Since this single item reflects the net change in surplus on account of deposits, it is not necessary to include *considerations, payments,* and *reserve increases,* as in the U.S. blank. However, these amounts are shown in a separate deposit exhibit where amounts received and paid out are simply titled *deposits* and *withdrawals*. It is apparent that a nonledger basis is also intended by the Canadian blank as indicated by the *deposit* and *withdrawal* items, and by the fact that these items are used to reconcile the beginning deposit liability with the ending liability.

Interest credited is also shown as a source of increased liability in the deposit exhibit. *Interest credited* is equivalent to the three items of the U.S. Statement, i.e., *increase in reserves, considerations,* and *payments*. The figures used in the first-year nonledger example demonstrate this fact: Increase in deposit liability $10,200 (a cost), less deposits received of $10,000 (income), equals $200 net cost for *interest credited*.

Interest credited to individual deposits must be reported to the U.S. government each year for income tax purposes. To obtain a control amount on the ledger for interest credited to deposits and paid in cash, many U.S. and Canadian companies record deposits as ledger liabilities. If this is done, supplemental records must be maintained to obtain amounts deposited and withdrawn for Annual Statement purposes each year. An alternative method is to subdivide the Payments on . . . account, adding an account for interest paid and offsetting accounts for interest credited.

POLICY DIVIDENDS

An extra charge, intended as a cushion against adverse claim experience, is included in premiums for participating insurance. The extra charge is rarely if ever needed and, therefore, would result in a greater gain from operations and would become surplus, unless paid out as policy dividends. When it becomes apparent the extra premium charge will not be needed, the board of directors declares a policy dividend to return the excess charge to policyowners. This action is based on the recommendation of the company's actuary, who prepares an estimate of the total amount of dividends he believes should be paid and suggests a schedule for calculating each dividend.

The dividend schedule shows an amount per $1,000 of insurance for each plan, year of policy duration, and issue age. The appropriate dividend per $1,000 is then multiplied by the amount of insurance in force under each policy. Sometimes separate schedules are prepared for policies above and below a certain face value, such as $10,000.

The total amount of dividends payable cannot be precisely determined at the time of declaration, as is possible for dividends on capital stock. This is so because the payment of a dividend on a particular policy is contingent upon the policy being in force on its anniversary date; some policies will lapse prior to that date. Others that were not in force on the declaration date will be reinstated and will be entitled to the usual anniversary dividend.

Policy dividends on ordinary insurance and most other lines of business are usually declared once each year and are usually payable on each policy anniversary after the first. Dividends on industrial policies may be payable on a specific date, such as January 1. Since they must be declared before this date, a contingency exists on them also. Some companies have policies on which dividends are declared less frequently than annually, for example, on every fifth anniversary of the policy. These are known as deferred dividend policies.

Dividend Payment Options

Policy dividends may be paid or applied under one or more of the following options: (1) paid in cash, (2) applied to reduce the current premium due on the policy,[1] (3) left with the company at interest, (4) applied to purchase paid-up additions[2] to the policy, and (5) applied to purchase one-year term insurance. The fifth option is less common than the other four and the insurance provided is frequently limited to an amount not in excess of the cash value of the policy. Any remaining portion of the dividend may be applied to another option.

Variations on the basic options are often available. For example, under a variation of the fourth option dividends may be used to shorten the premium-paying period or the endowment period of a policy. This is done by applying the dividends to increase the reserve value of the policy until it becomes equal to a net single premium for a paid-up policy. Under a variation of the third option, dividend accumulations may be applied to make the policy fully paid-up when they, plus the policy reserve, become equal to a net single premium.

Dividend Records

Dividend amounts are relatively small when compared to premium amounts and must, therefore, be calculated and processed as economically

---

[1] The Canadian Annual Statement shows a *reduction of premiums* option. This refers to a rarely used option not discussed; it does not refer to option 2. Dividends applied in payment of premiums are reported as paid in cash.

[2] The Canadian term is *bonus additions* for options 4 and 5.

as possible. Dividends are calculated on a mass basis through use of dividend schedules at least once annually. Entries to record the payment of dividends are also made on a mass basis whenever practical, but are made more frequently than annually.

A notice is mailed to policyowners when each dividend becomes payable. If the dividend is to be applied to pay premiums, the amount to be deducted from the premium is shown on the premium notice. If it is to be paid in cash, the pertinent data is shown on the check stub. If the dividend is applied under other options, special dividend notices are usually prepared. Some companies enter dividend data on the premium notice stub that is retained by the policyowner showing the dividend payable, the amount of insurance purchased under the option, if any, and the total amount accumulated under an option, to date.

In every life insurance company selling participating insurance there is a master dividend record for each participating policy. The types of data usually included and the use of each type are:

1. Dividend calculation data which includes plan, issue age, amount and duration of the policy—for computing the dividend payable each year.
2. Dividend payment data which includes policy number, name of policyowner, dividend option elected, amount of dividend, and amount of paid-up addition available—for preparing checks, accounting entries, and dividend notices to the policyowner.
3. Balances being held under each option—for policy status and liability determination.
4. History of dividends paid or applied under each option—used for audit trail and policyowner inquiries.

Dividend records usually are not subsidiary ledger accounts and thus do not have a control account in the general ledger. Such a control could, of course, be maintained for dividend deposit balances.

Shortly before the date when a dividend becomes payable, the master dividend record is used to produce the dividend notice and to produce a current dividend transaction record. This transaction record is used to make a register or list for accounting purposes. One entry is made for an entire list. The amount of each entry is the total dollar amount of all dividends being applied under the particular option. After a dividend is paid or applied under an option, the master dividend record is updated.

As each list is prepared, the transaction records are saved to provide a detailed history of dividend transactions. This file is used later to (1) prepare summaries of dividend transactions by state and province for annual statement purposes, (2) prepare listings by policy numbers and branch office for tracing dividend disbursements in case an insured should question whether he received a dividend, (3) facilitate audits by supervisory authorities, and (4) report interest credited for income tax purposes.

DIVIDEND ENTRIES

Accounting problems and procedures for policy dividends differ from those discussed in earlier chapters for dividends on capital stock. No journal entry is made for policy dividends at the time they are declared, but a nonledger liability is created in the amount of estimated dividends payable. Journal entries are made for policy dividends when they are paid in cash or when they are applied under an option. These entries may be made daily, but may be made less often to more efficiently utilize data processing equipment in preparing checks, notices, and lists. A separate account is used for each option.

Dividends Paid in Cash

The journal entry to record dividends paid in cash is a debit to Policy Dividends Paid which is an insurance cost account and a credit to Cash.

Terminal policy dividends are paid by some companies. A terminal dividend may be a substantial extra dividend or a pro rata dividend covering the period between the last anniversary date and the termination date. When a policy matures, becomes a final claim, or is surrendered, these terminal dividends are payable in cash.

If a policy is lapsed and placed under a nonforfeiture option, the terminal dividend may be used to increase the values applied under the option. Entries for these dividend settlements are made as a part of the policy settlement entry and are covered in other sections of this and the following chapter.

Dividends Applied to Pay Premiums

Journal entries for dividends applied to pay premiums due were shown in Chapter 14. These entries are made daily as the premiums are recorded. If a dividend applied to pay a premium is greater than the premium, as may happen in connection with a monthly premium, the difference is paid in cash and the cash portion of the payment is recorded as for a cash dividend. Each journal list should indicate a partial dividend paid or applied in order to provide a clear audit trail.

If the policy lapses while a dividend is being held to be applied under this option, the dividend is usually applied under a nonforfeiture option in the same manner as a cash dividend.

Other Entries

When current dividends are applied under the deposit option, it is common practice at the same time to add interest accrued on previous deposits since the last anniversary date. Many companies make the entry on the anniversary date that the dividend becomes payable, provided premiums are paid to that date. Others do so when the premium payment is received. A typical entry to record dividends left to accumulate is:

Dividends Left on Deposit...xxxx
    Dividend Deposits Received..................................   xxxx

The entry to record $3,000 in dividends applied to buy $5,000 worth of paid-up additions (PUA) is:

Dividends to Purchase PUA.............................3,000.00
    Single Premiums for Paid-Up Additions................   3,000.00

Note that the credit is to a premium account. Premiums for paid-up additions and other options which provide insurance are usually recorded in separate single premium accounts on the ledger because such premiums are exempt from premium tax in most states and all Canadian provinces. This is proper since tax was paid on the full policy premium, and the additional insurance is a benefit provided by that premium. The entry for dividends applied to shorten the premium-paying period is:

Dividends to Shorten Premium Period...........................xxxx
    Single Premiums to Shorten Premium Period...................   xxxx

A similar entry is used to record a shortening of an endowment period or to buy one-year term insurance. In the latter case, an appropriate account title might be *Renewal Premiums to Purchase Term Additions*.

Entries to provide additional insurance are frequently made on the anniversary without regard to whether the premium then due is paid. If a policy lapses after a dividend is applied, there is no need to reverse the entry or to make another in connection with the dividend. This is so because entries to use dividends under nonforfeiture options are substantially the same as the entries illustrated. Policyowners who request options that provide additional insurance are less likely to change options than those who choose the cash and deposit options. The entry can be delayed, of course, and made as a part of the nonforfeiture option entry.

DISBURSEMENT OF DIVIDENDS HELD UNDER AN OPTION

There are a number of circumstances under which dividends applied under an option must be paid out. These include (1) withdrawal of dividend accumulations by the policyowner, (2) surrender of paid-up additions for their cash surrender value, and (3) termination of the policy by surrender, death, or as a paid matured endowment.

Entries for the payment of accumulated dividends held under an option or of the cash surrender values of paid-up additions are made daily since they involve Cash, which must always be current. The transaction must be recorded so that an audit trail from the payment to the dividend record is maintained. The balance in the master file dividend record must also be concurrently adjusted to reflect the revised balance. If the policy terminates, the master dividend record for that policy must also be placed in a terminated status to prevent generation of further dividend transactions.

The entry for paying out dividend accumulations is:

```
Dividend Deposits Paid........................................xxxx
    Cash.....................................................      xxxx
```

Dividend Deposits Paid is an insurance cost account. It is not a ledger liability account since dividend deposits are usually a nonledger liability. Interest accrued on the accumulations is added to the amount paid, increasing the amount of the entry. The only difference between this entry and the one shown in the section on "Amounts Left on Deposit with the Company" is a slight change in title to indicate that the amount paid relates to dividends.

If dividend accumulations are used to shorten the premium period of a policy, the entry is:

```
Dividend Deposits............................................xxxx
    Single Premiums to Shorten Premium Period..................      xxxx
```

Entries for dividend accumulations paid in connection with a death claim or matured endowment are presented in the next chapter.

The entry recording the surrender of $500 in paid-up additions on which the cash value is $300 is:

```
Surrenders Paid (or Surrenders Paid on PUA)..................300.00
    Cash.....................................................      300.00
```

Surrenders Paid is an insurance cost account. In the event of death, the amount paid is the face value of the paid-up additions. Entries for these payments are presented in the next chapter.

NONFORFEITURE OPTIONS

When a policy lapses, the basic contract is terminated, except for such rights as the policyowner has under nonforfeiture options. If a policyowner has previously elected the automatic premium loan privilege and if the loan value is greater than the amount of premium due plus interest, technically the policy is not lapsed. The loan is automatically applied to keep the policy in force. Nonforfeiture options are (1) cash surrender, (2) reduced paid-up insurance, and (3) extended term insurance.

Cash Surrenders

When a policy is surrendered for cash, the entry is the same as when the cash surrender value of PUA is paid out—debit Surrenders Paid and credit Cash. The debit to the Surrenders Paid account records a decrease in surplus. However, a change in the nonledger liability for policy reserves occurs simultaneously. The net effect of the transaction on surplus is very small because the decrease in surplus caused by the surrender is offset by an increase in surplus caused by a reserve released. The phrase *reserve released* means that a policy reserve, previously established in connection with an in-force policy, is no longer required. If the reserve released is $3,400 and the surrender value paid is $3,200, the net effect is an increase in surplus of $200.

Since policy reserves are nonledger liabilities, no bookkeeping entry is made in connection with reserves released. The effect of the decrease in liability occurs automatically when reserve liabilities are calculated at the end of the accounting period.

If there are paid-up additions on a policy being surrendered, the cash value of these additions is added to the surrender value of the policy. Again a reserve of a nearly equal amount is released.

If there are dividend accumulations on deposit, the amount of the check payable is increased accordingly. The Dividend Deposits Paid account is debited in the same manner as though these deposits were being paid out independently of the surrender.

If a policy loan is outstanding on the policy, the amount of the loan plus accrued interest (if any) to the date of lapse must be deducted from the settlement, and the cash payment reduced accordingly. The Policy Loans account is credited to zero balance this account with reference to this particular loan, and the Policy Loan Interest account is credited for accrued interest or debited for advance interest being refunded.

If terminal dividends are payable, they are also added to the settlement and the Policy Dividends Paid account debited. Current dividends are paid out prior to the lapse date so they are not ordinarily included with policy surrender payments.

If the cash value of an ordinary policy is $3,200, the cash value of $100 in paid-up additions is $60, dividend accumulations are $532.30, and a $2,000 policy loan is outstanding with $10 in interest paid in advance, the amount payable is calculated as follows:

```
Cash surrender value, policy............$3,200.00
Cash surrender value, PUA.............    60.00
Dividend deposits.....................   532.30
Loan interest refund..................    10.00
        Total........................$3,802.30
    Less Loan........................ 2,000.00
        Net payable...................$1,802.30
```

The entry is:

```
Surrenders Paid—Ordinary..............................3,260.00
Dividend Deposits Paid.................................  532.30
Policy Loan Interest—Ordinary.........................   10.00
    Policy Loans—Ordinary.............................            2,000.00
    Cash.............................................            1,802.30
```

Note that the debit to Surrenders Paid—Ordinary includes the cash value of paid-up additions.

Reduced Paid-Up and Extended Term Insurance

Applying a nonforfeiture option constitutes a settlement of the net cash value, but instead of receiving cash, the policyowner receives an equivalent value in the form of paid-up term (extended) insurance, paid-up whole life, or paid-up endowment insurance. If the net cash value of the active policy is $2,100, the reserve under the revised coverage is also $2,100.

When a policy is to be continued under one of these options and there are no dividend accumulations or loans outstanding, no accounting entry is required. The transaction is simply a transfer of reserve liability from one policy classification (premium paying) to another (paid-up insurance). Bookkeeping entries are required only if there are dividend accumulations on deposit at time of lapse or if a policy loan is outstanding.

If an ordinary policy has a $200 cash value, dividend accumulations total $25, there is a policy loan outstanding of $75, and interest of $3.75 was due on the policy loan at time of lapse, the entry is:

```
Dividend Deposits Paid.....................................25.00
Surrenders Paid—Ordinary...................................53.75
    Policy Loans—Ordinary.................................            75.00
    Policy Loans Interest—Ordinary........................             3.75
```

Note that the *Surrenders Paid—Ordinary* account was debited only with that part of the cash value required to liquidate the loan, plus interest due, less dividend accumulations, or with a net amount of $53.75 ($75.00 + $3.75 − $25.00).

Concurrently with the entries for nonforfeiture transactions, the following record changes take place: (1) the in-force policy record is removed from the file; (2) the paid-up insurance record is established; and (3) item or dollar control on due premiums, if any, is adjusted to indicate the premium is no longer due.

When policies are reinstated, entries which were made at time of lapse are reversed. Accounts are debited in the same amount as was credited at time of lapse, and accounts are credited in the same amounts as was debited at time of lapse.

U.S. ANNUAL STATEMENT ASPECTS

There are five items on the liability page of the U.S. Annual Statement which include dividend liabilities:

1. The liability for paid-up additions is included as a part of the life insurance policy reserves. It is not shown as a separate item on either the liability page or in the policy reserve exhibit.

2. The liability for dividend accumulations is shown as a separate item on the liability page. It is calculated by totaling the dividend deposit amounts on the master records. These show the liability as of each policy anniversary. The total is then increased for accrued interest to December 31. The combined liability for dividend accumulations and accrued interest is included in the exhibit for supplementary contracts not involving life contingencies (see Figure 18–6).

3. *Policyholders' dividends due and unpaid* is also a separate item on the liability page. It covers dividends which have become payable but which have not yet been paid or applied to an option. This item primarily covers policy dividends to be applied toward the payment of premiums, although dividends under other options might be included. Since some premiums are unpaid by the policyowners at the end of the year, any policy dividends contingent upon payment of those premiums will be unpaid by the company.

4. *Provision for policyholders' dividends payable in following calendar year—estimated amounts* is another separate item on the liability page. It covers all dividends which have been declared and which will become payable if the policies are in force on their anniversaries during the following year. It is customary to include a full year's liability for dividends, even though the dividends for a part of the following year have not yet been declared. Establishing a liability for dividends not yet declared is an optional practice in most states and provinces.

5. Estimated liability for deferred dividend policies is still another separate item on the liability page. Companies with deferred dividend policies usually set up a liability for a portion of the deferred dividend each year, even though it is not yet payable. For example, if the deferred dividends are payable on every fifth anniversary, a fifth of the anticipated

Figure 17-1. U.S. Dividend Exhibit

EXHIBIT 7—DIVIDENDS TO POLICYHOLDERS

	LIFE	ACCIDENT AND HEALTH
1. Applied to pay renewal premiums		
2. Applied to shorten the endowment or premium-paying period		
3. Applied to provide paid-up additions		
4. Applied to provide paid-up annuities		
5. TOTAL LINES 1-4		
6. Paid in cash		
7. Left on deposit with the company		
8.		
9. TOTAL LINES 5-8		
10. Amount due and unpaid (Item 6, Page 3)		
11. Provision for annual dividend policies, including $_____ terminal dividends (Item 7, Page 3, in part)		
12. Provision for deferred dividend policies (Item 7, Page 3, in part)		
13. TOTAL LINES 10-12		
14. Line 13 of previous year		
15. TOTAL DIVIDENDS TO POLICYHOLDERS (Lines 9+13—14)		
	(To Item 29, Page 4)	(To Item 30, Page 4)

Figure 17–2.　Canadian Dividend Exhibit

EXHIBITS

....
(*Name of Company*)

—	Insurances				
	Ordinary		Group		Industrial
	Participating	Non-participating	Participating	Non-participating	
	$	$	$	$	$

~~~~~~

EXHIBIT 3—DIVIDENDS TO POLICYHOLDERS

Net of reinsurance ceded:					
1. Paid or payable in cash....................					
2. Left with the Company at interest........					
3. Applied as single premiums—					
(1) to purchase bonus additions..............					
(2) to purchase premium reductions..........					
(3) to shorten endowment or premium-paying period					
4.　　　Totals....................					

dividend on each policy is added to this liability each year until the dividend is paid.

Increases in dividend liabilities from one year-end to the next are included in the summary of operations as follows:

1. The increase from beginning of year balance to end of year balance for (*a*) policyholders' dividends due and unpaid, (*b*) dividends payable in the following year, and (*c*) amount held for deferred dividend policies are all included in the dividend exhibit (Exhibit 7) where cash basis figures are adjusted to the accrual basis. The adjusted amount (line 15, Figure 17–1) is included in the Exhibit 7 total that is carried to the summary of operations as *Dividends to life policyholders*.

2. The increase in dividend accumulations is included on the line entitled "Increase in reserve for supplementary contracts without life contingencies and for dividend accumulations."

3. The increase in reserve on paid-up additions is included with the increase in life insurance policy reserves.

Schedule T of the U.S. Annual Statement requires that dividends used to reduce premiums be reported along with premium income by states. However, some states allow all policy dividends as deductions from premiums for premium tax purposes.

A special report for each state in which the Annual Statement is filed requires that all dividends applied to policies on residents of that state be

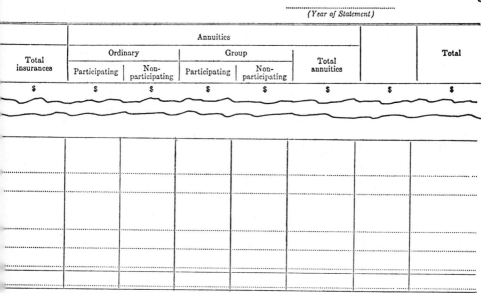

Total insurances	Annuities					Total annuities		Total
	Ordinary		Group					
	Participating	Non-participating	Participating	Non-participating				
$	$	$	$	$		$	$	$

shown by dividend option and by major line of insurance. This distribution by state can be made from the dividend transaction records.

CANADIAN ANNUAL STATEMENT ASPECTS

The dividend exhibit of the Canadian Statement is entitled *dividends to policyholders* (see Figure 17–2). The column headings are the lines of business shown in the "Analysis of Revenue Account by Line of Business," but they are rearranged to provide separate subtotals for insurance business and annuities. The term *bonus additions* on line 3(1) has the same meaning as the expression *paid-up additions* of the U.S. Statement. Dividends applied to pay renewal premiums are included with dividends paid in cash.

Dividend liabilities in the Canadian Statement are similar to and are reported in much the same manner as in the U.S. Statement. More specifically, these are shown as follows:

1. Reserves on paid-up additions are included with policy reserves.
2. Liability for dividend accumulations is not shown separately but is included as a part of *amounts on deposit with the company*.
3. *Dividends to policyholders, due but unpaid . . .* is a separate item on the liability page.

Figure 17-3. Canadian Deposit Exhibit

EXHIBIT 11—AMOUNTS ON DEPOSIT WITH THE COMPANY

pertaining to insurance and annuity contracts and including interest accumulations

A. MOVEMENT IN THE ACCOUNT DURING THE YEAR

	Proceeds of contracts	Dividends	Amounts on deposit to pay future premiums	Other	Total
1. Liability, 31 December 19	$	$	$	$	$
2. Deposits					
3.					
4. Interest credited					
DEDUCT:					
5. Withdrawals					
6.					
7. Net increase in liability					
8. Liability, 31 December 19					

B. CLASSIFICATION OF LIABILITY AT THE END OF THE YEAR, BY GUARANTEED INTEREST RATE

1. Guaranteed interest rate:

.... %						
....						
....						
....						
....						
....						
....						
Totals........						

2.

4. Dividends to policyholders (other than deferred dividends) payable in the following year is also a separate item on the liability page.
5. The sum of amounts set aside for dividends on deferred dividend policies is another separately reported liability.

Increases in dividend liabilities are included in the revenue account as follows:

1. The increase in paid-up addition reserves is shown as a part of the increase in life insurance policy reserves.
2. Increase in dividend accumulations is handled as an integral part of amounts on deposit. Only the interest credited to deposits is treated as an insurance cost.
3. The increase in policyholder dividends due and unpaid is used to adjust *dividends to policyholders* from the cash to the accrual basis.
4. Increase in liability for dividends payable in the following year and provision for accrued profits to policyholders are combined and shown in the revenue account as *increase in provision for dividends and accrued profits to policyholders.*

Amounts left on deposit are assembled in the deposit exhibit (Figure 17–3) and entered on the liability page of the balance sheet as *amounts on deposit with the Company, pertaining to insurance and annuity contracts and including interest accumulations.* This exhibit consists of two parts: the first shows causes for increases and decreases in a reconciliation of liability from one year-end to the next; the second itemizes the liability at the end of the year by guaranteed interest rates such as 4 percent, $4\frac{1}{2}$ percent, etc.

The only item in this exhibit that affects operating gains or losses is *interest credited* on deposit items, which is entered as a cost in the revenue account. All other increases in the deposit liability have an equivalent increase in assets and do not, therefore, affect surplus. Likewise, decreases in the liability have an equal decrease in assets.

SUMMARY OF LIFE INSURANCE DEPOSIT, DIVIDEND AND NONFORFEITURE ACCOUNTING FUNDAMENTALS

Deposits are maintained on a nonledger basis in most life insurance companies. A change in a nonledger liability is treated as an income or insurance cost item. If deposits are handled as ledger liabilities, supplemental records are required to show amounts received and paid out.

Policy dividends are recorded as insurance costs when they are paid or applied under an option. Cost accounts and offsetting income accounts are used to record dividends left with the company under an option. When dividends are applied to purchase additional insurance, premium accounts are credited.

At the end of each policy year the change in estimated dividend liabilities is used to adjust, from the cash to the accrual basis, the amount reported as policyholder dividends paid.

When a policy is placed on a nonforfeiture option, entries are made only for cash disbursed, policy loans paid off, or policy dividend deposits applied to increase nonforfeiture option amounts. No entry is made to record net cash values applied to purchase insurance under the option.

QUESTIONS

1. What are the objectives in properly accounting for policy settlements?
2. If deposit liabilities are handled on a nonledger basis, what accounts and nonledger income or cost items are used in the U.S. and Canadian Annual Statements to record changes in the liability? What are the three principal deposit liability classifications?
3. Why should policy dividends be declared by the board of directors when the actuary determines dividend schedules? What type of entries are made, if any, and what liabilities created when policy dividends are declared? Is this different from liabilities created when stock dividends are declared? Is so, why?
4. Name four conditions under which policy dividends are applied to buy insurance.
5. What are five types of data found on a master dividend record and indicate which are used when (1) a dividend is calculated, (2) a dividend is paid or applied, (3) a dividend notice is prepared, and (4) a policyowner makes an inquiry? Why are dividend entries made on a summary basis?
6. The journal entry for dividends left with the company is said to reflect a purely internal transfer. What does this mean?
7. What are five dividend liability classifications? Explain the nature of each. How are the changes in these liabilities shown in the U.S. or the Canadian Annual Statements?

PROBLEMS

1. Make traditional summary entries, if any are required, to record dividends applied, and for accrued interest if applicable, under the following transactions. In connection with each entry, give the most important items of data that are normally included on lists of supporting detail prepared in connection with such entries.

a) Dividends paid in cash......................$10,500.00
b) Dividends left on deposit.................... 15,000.00
c) Interest accrued on deposits................. 11,600.00
d) Dividends applied to buy PUA............... 5,150.00
e) Dividend deposits withdrawn................ 768.00
f) Dividends applied to insurance options........ 348.00
g) Surrender of $500 of PUA for cash........... 310.00

2. Make the traditional journal entries for the following nonforfeiture transactions:

a) Policy is surrendered for $2,000 cash value. There are dividend accumulations on the records amounting to $532 as of the last anniversary. Interest of $5.10 has accrued since that date.

b) A policy is placed on the reduced paid-up insurance option. The cash value is $1,000, and there are paid-up additions of $100 credited to the policy. These have a cash value of $50. There is a policy loan of $600 on which interest of $16 has accrued.

3. What effect do the transactions in Problem 2 have on surplus if the reserve on the first policy is $2,100 and the reserve on the second policy and paid-up additions is $1,150. Show the steps in your calculation.

Chapter 18

Claim and Contract Settlement

Claims are defined as policy benefit amounts payable in accordance with insuring clauses in life and health insurance policies. *Contract payments* are defined as payments on annuities and supplementary contracts. Each claim must be examined carefully and approved by a qualified person before money is paid because the amounts of these payments often are quite large. Many claim payments involve thousands of dollars.

The responsibility for authorizing payments and accounting entries in connection with claim settlements is assigned to a claim approver. He is a specialist in investigating claims and is thoroughly familiar with various policy and contract provisions. He may also have legal training. Joint participation by this approver and the accountant in making settlements provides an element of security to the company and is a most efficient process.

Journal entries for claim settlements are made when a claim is approved. If a check is issued, the entry is made in connection with the issuance of the check. If the proceeds are left with the company under a settlement option, the entry is made as soon as the amounts and conditions of the settlement contract are established.

In most companies no entry is made prior to the approval date of the claim even though the company may have known the exact amount payable for some time. This is consistent with the practice of life insurance companies of omitting most liabilities from the ledger. However, many Canadian companies do establish a ledger liability when notice of claim is received. These companies might also simultaneously establish a ledger asset for amounts due from reinsurance companies.

A claim payment entry is very simple if no policy loans, premiums, or

349

dividend values are outstanding. The entry is a debit to an insurance cost account identifying the type of claim being paid, such as Death Claims Paid—Group, and a credit to Cash.

If an insured person dies by accident while insured under an accidental death rider, the amount of accidental death benefit payable is debited to a separate account. This is done to provide appropriate information for the Annual Statement on accidental death benefits paid.

Accounting controls and records are required for calculating claim liability amounts at the end of each year and for controlling claim payments made in installments. These controls vary according to claim classifications and are, therefore, discussed after these classifications. The two principal claim classifications are life insurance claims (which includes matured endowments) and health insurance claims.

DEATH CLAIMS

The amount of the debit in a death claim entry is the death benefit payable, usually the face amount of the policy. If the settlement is adjusted because of an error in the issue age, suicide within two years, or for any other reason, the amount of the entry is the adjusted amount. For example, if an insured commits suicide soon after paying $150 as a first premium and the policy provides that the company's liability in such a case shall be limited to an amount equal to the premiums paid, the entry is:

```
Death Claims Paid—Ordinary............................150.00
    Cash.................................................          150.00
```

If a contestable claim is declined because of misrepresentation or fraud in applying for the policy, the policy is deemed to be void from the beginning. In such a case a refund of all premiums must be made. The entry is treated not as a claim disbursement but as a premium refund:

```
Premiums—First-Year Ordinary...............................xxxx
    Cash.................................................          xxxx
```

Sometimes a company may feel that the insured obtained the policy by misrepresenting the state of his health when applying for the policy but wishes to avoid a lawsuit. The company may then make a compromise settlement. The entry to record a $2,000 check paid in settlement of a $5,000 claim is:

```
Death Claims Paid—Ordinary............................2,000.00
    Cash.................................................          2,000.00
```

Policy loans outstanding plus any interest due are deducted from a death settlement. Currently payable dividends, dividend accumulations, and loan interest prepaid are added to the settlement amount.

Assume that a policyowner insured under a $10,000 ordinary insurance policy died in an automobile accident and that his policy provided for an accidental death benefit equal to the face amount. His dividend accumulations with interest to date of death were $532.30. There was a loan against his policy on date of death in the amount of $2,000, on which $10 interest was paid in advance.

A compound entry to record this settlement is:

```
Death Claims Paid—Ordinary...........................10,000.00
Accidental Death Claims Paid—Ordinary.................10,000.00
Dividend Deposits Paid...............................    532.30
Policy Loan Interest.................................     10.00
     Policy Loans....................................              2,000.00
     Cash............................................             18,542.30
```

If a company normally collects interest after it is earned, there might have been an interest amount due the company on date of death and the Policy Loan Interest account would have been credited instead of debited and the credit to Cash adjusted accordingly.

If a part of the proceeds is left with the company under a supplementary contract, an income account is credited for the portion of the settlement to be applied under the settlement option, e.g., Consideration for Supplementary Contracts with Life Contingencies (WLC) or Consideration for Supplementary Contracts without Life Contingencies (WOLC),[1] according to the circumstances of the case. The initials shown will be used hereafter to shorten these titles. *Settlement contracts* will be used as a general term to cover both. The difference between WLC and WOLC is explained in another section of this chapter.

If in the example just given the company agreed to pay cash in the amount of $10,542.30 and to hold the remaining portion of the settlement to provide a monthly income for 10 years certain and life thereafter, the entry is:

```
Death Claims Paid—Ordinary...........................10,000.00
Accidental Death Claims Paid—Ordinary.................10,000.00
Dividend Accumulations Paid..........................    532.30
Policy Loan Interest.................................     10.00
     Policy Loans....................................              2,000.00
     Consideration for Supplementary Contracts WLC......           8,000.00
     Cash............................................             10,542.30
```

If a premium was due and unpaid at the time of death and while the policy was in the grace period, the claim payment entry must include a credit to premium income. The credit to Cash is, of course, reduced by the amount of the premium due. The full mode premium due is usually deducted, but some companies deduct only a pro rata fractional premium.

---

[1] Canadian titles would typically be *Considerations for Settlement Annuities* and *Proceeds Left on Deposit.* Settlement annuities include amounts without life contingencies if the proceeds are payable in installments.

For example, if a quarterly premium is due, many companies deduct a quarterly premium. Others deduct only one third of this amount to pay a monthly premium for the grace period.

If premiums were paid beyond the date of death, many companies refund the portion of the premium paid beyond date of death. The premium account is debited in the amount of refund, and the cash payable is increased accordingly.

The amount of any paid-up additions is simply added to the death claim amount in the entry and to the amount of the check. A separate claim account is not needed for the paid-up additions, but some companies may use a separate account to better control changes in paid-up addition records.

Assume that a $5,000 ordinary insurance death claim was incurred while the policy was in the grace period. An age adjustment reduced the amount payable to $4,750. The policy had paid-up additions of $100. A terminal cash dividend of $50 is payable, and the current monthly premium due at time of death was $15. The entry is:

Death Claims Paid—Ordinary	4,850.00	
Dividends Paid	50.00	
Premiums—Renewal Ordinary		15.00
Cash		4,885.00

Amounts debited to the Death Claims Paid account result in a decrease in surplus. However, policy reserves are released when the policy becomes a claim, so that the effect on surplus is less than the amount paid. If the reserve released on both the policy and the paid-up addition had been $2,170 in the example just cited, the claim would have reduced surplus by $2,680 ($4,850 − $2,170).

The premium credit in the entry has a minimal effect on surplus. This credit would be offset by a reduction in the nonledger asset for net due premiums. The gain from the loading on the premium may be offset by commissions payable to agents. No entries are made for changes in nonledger assets (due premiums) and nonledger liabilities (policy reserves). The effect of these changes on surplus occurs at the end of the accounting period when the nonledger items are valued.

Payment of an accidental death claim reduces surplus almost to the full extent of the claim because reserves released on accidental death claims are very small. Reserves released on paid-up life additions average nearly 50 percent of the claim amount. Policy reserves released on an average industrial insurance death claim may be nearly as large a percentage of each claim paid as those released on an ordinary insurance claim. Group insurance certificates are usually term insurance with very little or no reserve released at death of the insured person. Therefore, a group claim has a greater impact on surplus than either industrial or ordinary claims of the same size.

MATURED ENDOWMENTS

When an endowment policy reaches maturity, the entry is the same as for a death claim except that the account debited to record the claim payment is a Matured Endowments Paid account. Assume that a $10,000 face amount ordinary insurance policy has matured and a policy dividend of $113 was payable on the maturity date. There are also $532.30 in dividend accumulations and $800 of paid-up additions. A $5,320 policy loan is outstanding against the policy, and interest of $116 is due. The entry for the settlement is:

```
Matured Endowments Paid—Ordinary.....................10,800.00
Policy Dividends Paid—Ordinary.........................   113.00
Dividend Accumulations Paid............................   532.30
     Policy Loans.......................................              5,320.00
     Policy Loan Interest...............................                116.00
     Cash...............................................              6,009.30
```

Surplus is not affected by a matured endowment settlement. This is so because the combined reserve of the policy and paid-up additions on the maturity date is exactly equal to the endowment amount of the policy. As in the case of a death claim, this reserve is released when the payment is made.

Many companies sell policies which provide a series of small annual endowments payable to policyowners. These annual endowments frequently are in the form of coupons attached to policies, and may be applied under the same options as dividends. When these endowment amounts are paid or left to accumulate at interest, a matured endowment account is debited. When they are applied to purchase additional insurance, no entry is required because the reserve is merely transferred from one form of insurance to another. Many companies do make entries, however, in order to provide statistical data on these transactions.

HEALTH INSURANCE CLAIMS

The term *health insurance* as used in this book covers the type of insurance referred to in the U.S. Annual Statement as *accident and health insurance* and in the Canadian Casualty Insurance Annual Statement as *accident and sickness insurance.*

Health insurance policies state the conditions under which the company may refuse to accept further premiums, thereby cancelling the coverage. These renewability conditions are (1) renewable at the option of the company, (2) guaranteed renewable, (3) collectively renewable, (4) guaranteed renewable and noncancellable.

In guaranteed renewable policies the company cannot refuse to continue insurance but may increase premium rates. Collectively renewable was described in an earlier chapter as franchise insurance. On this insurance, the company can increase premium rates or refuse to renew policies only if this is done on an entire franchise (group of policyowners). In guaranteed renewable noncancellable policies the company cannot cancel insurance, refuse to renew, or increase premium rates.

U.S. companies are required to show individual health insurance premiums in the Annual Statement by each of these and several other less common renewability classifications. Premiums for accident-only coverages are also shown separately. Ledger accounts are therefore, usually maintained for claims paid within each of the renewability classifications and within each of the three principal health insurance classifications: disability claims, medical expense claims, and indemnity claims. Accounts may be further subdivided. For example, medical expense benefits may be subdivided into hospital benefits, surgical benefits, etc.

Disability claims are those under which amounts are paid for loss of income or policy premiums are waived while the insured person is unable to work because of illness or accident. Medical expense claims are those under which amounts are paid to reimburse the insured for hospital, surgical, and other medical costs actually incurred. Indemnity claims are lump sum payments made for loss of life and for loss of arms, legs, eyes, and other important body members.

Most health insurance is sold either as individual insurance or as group insurance, but some is also sold under the debit insurance system, in which case benefits are usually lower than under typical individual health insurance coverage.

The accounting entries for health insurance claims are very similar to entries for life insurance policy claims. The processes for controlling claim payments are somewhat different, however, because the policy usually remains in force after a claim is paid.

Disability Claims

When an insured person becomes disabled as defined by the provisions of a health insurance policy, or disability rider of a life insurance policy, he becomes eligible for a series of payments that will continue until he recovers, dies, or until the policy benefit limit is reached. As a result, a large claim reserve liability is automatically created in connection with his disability. This reserve is the present value of all amounts that will become payable while the insured is disabled, as determined in accordance with morbidity tables and interest rates used by the company for this purpose. Reserves of this type frequently are called *disabled life* reserves as distinguished from *active life* reserves, a term applied to reserves not related to claims.

Morbidity tables show the probability of disability or sickness and the probability of its continuing over various periods of time. The longer a disability claim exists, the longer it is likely to continue into the future, unless limited by policy provisions. For example, at age 45 a disability which has existed for one year is likely to continue for three additional years, whereas a disability that has existed for two years is likely to continue for four additional years. It follows that the reserve liability for a disability claim continues to *increase* with the passage of time even though claim payments are regularly being made. This increase continues until near the end of the maximum time period provided in the policy after which point the reserve liability begins to decrease.

When an insured person recovers from a disability and is able to return to work, the disabled life reserve is released. Some insureds recover early and thereby release reserves, while others continue to be disabled for periods even longer than expected and more reserves will be required. As a result, total reserves on a large number of disabled persons are relatively stable. No entry is made to record changes in disability claim reserve liabilities.

A claim approver is responsible for determining that the insured is still disabled before each payment is made. He may investigate the claim only once a year if recovery seems unlikely.

A typical entry for a $400 monthly disability payment is:

```
Disability Claims Paid—Ordinary...........................400.00
    Cash...............................................      400.00
```

Ordinary insurance premiums waived because of the disability of an insured person are claims against the disability subline of business and premium income to the life insurance line of business. Premiums applicable to supplemental coverages, such as premiums for accidental death benefits, are also waived by the disability waiver provision. The amount of the entry is the amount of the gross premium waived. The disability premium, technically, should not be included in the premium waived, but some companies include it for convenience.

A typical entry to record the waiver of $110 life insurance and $5 accidental death premium in a U.S. life company[2] is:

```
Premiums Waived—Disability—Ordinary.................. ..115.00
    Premiums Renewal—Ordinary..........................      115.00
```

The premium record must be posted as though the premium had been paid in cash, but the premium taxes and commissions are not payable since the premium was not actually received by the company. Some companies use a special income account to facilitate premium tax reporting.

---

[2] Canadian companies are not required to make entries for premiums waived due to disability because the Annual Statement excludes these amounts from premium income. However, there is a disability exhibit where this information is shown. A company might, therefore, prefer to make entries and then offset these two nominal accounts against each other when the Statement is prepared.

In the case of health insurance provided by an individual policy, no entry is required for waiver because both the income and disbursement are in the same line of business. Many companies, however, do make such an entry to facilitate claim studies. A typical entry for health insurance waiver would be the same as for ordinary, with only a change of line of business in the account titles.

Medical Expense Claims

Medical expense insurance is usually referred to as hospital insurance. This is a misnomer because these policies provide several different types of medical coverages. These are known as basic coverages and are designed to pay for cost of hospital room and board, miscellaneous hospital expense, surgical expense, and cost of limited medical care. A limit for each coverage may be stated in the policy in terms of days or amounts.

Major medical insurance is a form of medical expense insurance. This title implies a very high overall maximum limit on all covered expenses rather than limits by types of expense. However, some limits for particular types of expense are included within the maximum limit. The maximum may be as high as $10,000 or $15,000 for a single illness within a calendar year or policy year. Normally these policies pay less than the total costs incurred by the insured person. For example, on a $1,000 hospital care bill, the first $50 and 20 percent of the remainder may not be covered. The amount paid would then be $760 ($1,000 − $50 − $190). By having a portion of the medical expense borne by the insured, he is encouraged to avoid unnecessary costs; this permits a lower premium charge.

Medical expense claims (including those under major medical policies) normally do not result in a continuing claim liability over months and years as do disability policies. Therefore, the amount of claim liability created at the time of claim is not as great as in the case of a disability claim. The liability begins on the date the claim is incurred, and this date is determined by the policy wording and the circumstances.

Hospitals frequently require assignment of hospital claim benefits before the insured is released from the hospital. Surgeons, likewise, may require that surgical benefits be assigned to pay the surgical fee. As a result, many claims are paid to someone other than the insured.

A typical journal entry recording a medical expense claim on a group insurance policy would show a debit to Hospital Benefits Paid—Group. For recording a payment to a surgeon, the debit would be to Surgical Claims Paid—Group. No specific reserve is released when a hospital claim is paid, so the payment entry decreases surplus in the amount of payment.

Indemnity Claims

Entries for these claims are very simple, since they are incurred in an amount specified in the policy. In case of accidental death, the amount might be over $100,000. The entry is a debit to a claim account describing the type of claim and a credit to Cash for the same amount. Usually the decrease in surplus resulting from paying such a claim is almost the full claim amount since policy reserves are very small on riders or policies that provide these benefits.

REINSURANCE BENEFIT ENTRIES

No claim file is considered closed until the reinsurance in connection with that claim has been collected from the reinsurance company. However, no entry is made for reinsurance receivable until the claim check is received from the reinsurance company. Each reinsurance claim in connection with ordinary insurance is usually paid individually. Reinsurance on group life insurance or health insurance may be either settled individually or once each month. A typical entry when the reimbursement check is received from the reinsurance company is:

```
Cash.................................................................xxxx
    Reinsurance Benefits Received—Ordinary Life................    xxxx
    Reinsurance Benefits Received—Accidental Death.............    xxxx
```

In the case of coinsurance, the amount of the credit entry for the ordinary life portion of the reinsurance is the face amount reinsured. If the reinsurance is yearly renewable term, the reserve on the reinsured portion of the principal policy is deducted from the face amount of the reinsurance, with the debit to Cash adjusted accordingly. The accounts credited are, of course, income accounts.

CLAIM RECORDS AND CONTROLS

Claim disbursements may be classified by their effect on policy status. Classifications of this type are useful in discussing claim accounting records and control processes and the effect a particular type of claim has on the company's liability. These classifications are: (1) single claim payments that terminate the policy liability, as in the case of death claims or matured endowments; (2) single claim payments that do not terminate the policy, such as medical expense claims; and (3) continuous periodic payments made after the filing of a single original claim, such as installments under supplementary contracts or disability income payments. Payments under the latter classification may be terminated by death or special compromise settlements.

The settlement on a particular policy might involve both the first and third classifications. For example, a death claim might be settled by issuing a supplemental contract, in which case the initial claim settlement would fall under the first classification and the payments under the supplemental contract under the third.

Upon receipt at the home office of notice that a claim has occurred, the policy records are assembled and an entry is made in a *claim register.* The purposes are:

1. To control the processing of claims from the time the first notice is received until payment is made and reinsurance, if any, is collected.
2. To enable the company to determine the liability for *claims incurred but not yet paid* at the end of the year for entry in the Annual Statement.

The pertinent policy information and all currently available information about the claim are entered in the register. Major steps in processing the claim are entered in the register as they occur (see Figure 18–1). If the claim is not valid because of misrepresentation or fraud in obtaining the policy, the facts are recorded in the claim register. In case of death claims, if an amount different from the face of the policy is payable as a result of a suicide clause, age correction, or for any other reason, these facts are also entered in the register.

In the case of claims which do not cause the policy to terminate, it is customary to assign a separate claim number to each claim. This number provides an audit trail from the claim register to the policy record, to the claim papers, and to the disbursement check.

When claim numbers are assigned, it is customary to establish a separate file folder for each claim to prevent undue cluttering of the principal policy file folder since there may be many claims on a single policy. Claim papers are not normally needed after a claim is paid. Keeping them in a separate claim file, therefore, also facilitates operation of record destruction programs.

Payments on claims of a continuing nature are usually recorded on a manual record card or a sheet in the principal file folder. This historical record is useful as a reference when later claims are received, the amount of which may be affected by the amount of previous payments.

In the case of disability claims, it is desirable to maintain a control to indicate when the next payment is payable or when the next premium is to be waived. A simple record showing payment data satisfactorily serves this purpose.

Many companies do not use claim numbers or claim control records if a claim terminates the policy, as happens with a death claim. In these cases, all proof papers and other records related to the claim and the disbursement are filed in the principal file for the particular policy. If

Figure 18-1. Claim Registers

DEATH CLAIM REGISTER

Claim Number	Policy No.	Cert. No.	NAME OF INSURED	State	Effective Date of Policy	Age at Issue	Date Notice Received	Date of Death	Amount of Policy and Reinsurance	Prem. Ded.	Indebtedness Ded.	Adj. in Age	Net Amount Paid	Date Paid	Cause of Death	
1																1
2																2
3																3
4																4
5																5
6																6
7																7

INDIVIDUAL ACCIDENT AND HEALTH CLAIM REGISTER

CLAIMANT'S NAME	DATE AND PLACE OF BIRTH				OCCUPATION (Omit Duties)	RESIDENCE (City and State Only)	DATE	SYMBOL	CLAIM NUMBER	POLICY NUMBER	D or C	DISPOSITION - DATE
	MO.	DAY	YR.	PLACE								
1.												
2.												
3.												
4.												
5.												
6.												
7.												
8.												
9.												
10.												
11.												
12.												
13.												
14.												
15.												
16.												
17.												
18.												
19.												

proceeds are left with the company for later disbursement, a new file and record ordinarily are prepared under a new contract number.

The recipient usually wants to know how the amount he receives in payment of his claim was determined. There are two methods for providing this information. Probably the more common method is to give the policyowner a copy of the voucher which authorizes the preparation of the check (see Figure 18–2). These vouchers can be worded so that they

Figure 18–2. Claim Voucher

CLAIM #	POLICY #	CERT. #	R & S	E or D	STATE & TERR.	M	WID	HMD	SURG	MO. & YR. INCRD.	CLAIM TYPE

CODE   BENEFITS PAYABLE

LIFE A. D. & D. DISABILITY
- ____ LIFE BENEFITS
- ____ A. D. & D. BENEFITS
- ____ DISABILITY BENEFITS
  - FROM_____ TO _____
  - LESS _____ DAYS

HOSPITAL
- ____ ROOM_____ DAYS CONFINED @ $_____
- ____ ROOM_____ DAYS CONFINED @ $_____
- ____ HOSPITAL MISC. – CONFINED
- ____ HOSPITAL MISC. – NOT CONFINED
- ____ MATERNITY CONFINEMENT

DOCTORS
- ____ SURGERY
- ____ # _____TRANSFUSIONS @ $_____
- ____ MEDICAL BENEFITS
- _____MEDICAL CALLS @ $_____

OTHER
- ____ DIAGNOSTIC LAB & X-RAY
- ____ POLIO
- ____ DREAD DISEASE
- ____ MAJOR MEDICAL
- ____ EMERGENCY FIRST AID

TOTAL PAYABLE $_____

FORM NO. 62-048 (R5-64)

FILE COPY

are, in effect, form letters to the payee. The second method is for the check to be issued with the explanation on a detachable stub.

A few companies issue drafts in payment of claims. These drafts are similar in appearance to checks, but they are not automatically charged by the bank against the company's bank account. Instead, the bank notifies the company each day of drafts received, and after approval, the company issues a check to the bank in the amount of the drafts or allows the bank to charge the company's account. The bank sends a charge notice to serve as the basis for an entry in the books and for use in bank statement reconciliation.

The draft system expedites claim payment. Drafts may be drawn in regional service offices, in large group policyowners' offices, or may be prepared in the claim department at the home office. A copy of each draft is then sent to the insurance company accounting officer. At the same time, claim papers are sent to the claim department if the drafts have not originated there. A draft drawn improperly or drawn to pay an amount not properly payable may be refused by the insurance company.

The entry need not be made when the draft is originally prepared, but an entry must be made when the check is written or the bank charge is recorded. The appropriate claim accounts are debited, and Cash is credited.

Punched cards prepared from the vouchers, check copies, or draft copies are often used in claims accounting to prepare lists from which journal entries are made. These listings should include the check or draft number; the policy or claim number; the payee; date of the check or draft; its amount; accounts and amounts debited and accounts and amounts credited. The listing, of course, includes separate totals for each account to be debited or credited.

After accuracy has been verified, the appropriate totals are entered at least once each day in a journal. In some companies the lists replace the journal, and summary entries are posted directly from list to ledger. Listings used as journals or listings providing details for journal entries should be bound in chronological order to provide an audit trail and to be used for reconciling the bank account.

CLAIM LIABILITIES

The liabilities for unpaid claims included in a life insurance company's balance sheet are nonledger liabilities. The amount payable on claims being investigated can be approximated quite accurately at the end of each year by examining the claim registers and totaling unpaid claims. However, estimates are made of other claim liabilities which have been incurred but have not been reported to the company. These estimates must be made carefully because large amounts may be involved and because every dollar of claim liability reduces the company's surplus.

Claim settlements frequently are not made until many months after they are incurred. Reasons for this delay include the following: (1) Time is required to investigate and determine that a claim is covered by the policy. (This is particularly true in the case of a contested claim or in the case of a restricted coverage such as accidental death coverage.) (2) There may be difficulty in determining the proper payee or in ascertaining the amount payable. (3) An insured person may not file a claim for some time after the claim is first incurred, particularly in the case of a disability claim. (4) Releases from state inheritance or federal estate tax offices may be required.

The date a claim is incurred determines whether or not a claim liability should be set up. The incurred date determines the beginning of liability even though the insured may wait months before filing his claim. This date varies according to the type of claim. In the case of health insurance, unless the policy provides otherwise, a claim may be incurred on the day the disability first manifests itself if the policy was in force on that date. If a medical expense policy provides that it must be in force when the insured enters the hospital, the claim is incurred on date of entry.

Many disability policies provide that payments will not start until after the disability has continued for six months. In such a case, there are two significant dates: (1) date when actual disablement began and (2) date when the waiting period is satisfied. On the first date a contingent liability of an indefinite amount is created. On the second date a definite liability is established equal to the present value of future payments.

In the case of a death claim, a claim liability is incurred the minute the insured dies; at this point, the beneficiary owns the proceeds.

Liabilities for unpaid claims are divided into four parts for inclusion in the Annual Statements: (1) claims in the course of settlement, (2) due and unpaid claims, (3) incurred but unreported claims, and (4) resisted claims. There are two additional types of claim liabilities which occur only in connection with health insurance claims. These are (1) present value of amounts not yet due on claims, and (2) reserve for future contingent benefits. These are called *claim reserves* and are not treated as unpaid claims. They are treated as health insurance reserves on the liability page of the U.S. Annual Statement.[3]

Claims in the course of settlement are those claims on which notice has been received by the company and which are being investigated. This amount is easily calculated by examining claim registers and claim files. The full amount claimed is usually set up as a liability even though a claim has not yet been approved.

Due and unpaid claims are those claims which have been approved by

---

[3] The Canadian treatment is discussed in the last section of this chapter.

the company but which have not been paid because of delays in the disbursement routine, delays in arranging settlement contracts, clarification of beneficiary rights, and other factors that do not affect the amount of the liability.

Only the amount that would have been payable prior to the end of the accounting period is included. For example, if in December the insured became disabled as defined by policy provisions, only the December payment is included as an unpaid claim. The present value of future payments are treated as claim reserves.

Incurred but unreported claims are those claims which were incurred in the accounting period, but which had not been reported to the company on the date of the Annual Statement. Companies rarely complete the Statement until some days have elapsed in the new year, so some of this claim liability can be determined by reviewing entries made in the claim registers in the new year.

The liability for unreported death claims is the estimated difference between the face amount of each claim and the reserve that will be released to surplus when the claim is paid. Estimates must be used since the company does not know which insured persons died, nor the size or number of policies affected. Estimates must be based on analysis of claims paid in the past with allowance made for increased insurance in force and other changing conditions.

Resisted claims are those on which the company has refused payment for various reasons but on which there is a possibility of liability. Included in this classification are claims for benefits not clearly covered by a policy and claims on which lawsuits are pending against the company. If a lawsuit has been filed, the full amount claimed is usually included in this claim liability classification. This liability can be determined by examining claim registers.

Present value of amounts not yet due on claims is an amount set aside as a reserve for future payments on claims currently being paid in installments, as in the case of disability waiver and income coverages. In the case of disability income and disability waiver insurance provided by riders attached to life policies, this reserve is described in the reserve exhibit of the U.S. Annual Statement as reserves on disabled lives.

Reserve for future contingent benefits is an amount established as a reserve for deferred maternity benefits and for any other claims which may have already been incurred, but which may be contingent upon a future event or circumstances beyond the company's control. Some companies treat deferred maternity benefits as an unearned premium liability (on the assumption that a portion of the premium paid is set aside for these claims).[4] The effect on operating gains is the same in either instance.

---

[4] In the Canadian Casualty Statement deferred maternity benefits are treated as unearned premiums.

CLAIM RATIOS

A *claim ratio* is the percentage relationship between premiums and claims during the same period of time. For example, a 90 percent claim ratio for a year means that claims are 90 percent of premiums received during the year.

Claim ratios are especially useful to life insurance company management in determining whether risks are being adequately underwritten and if premium rates for a particular coverage are in line with the cost of providing insurance protection. The trend in claim ratios is especially significant in industrial insurance where much of the underwriting is done by field personnel and in group health insurance where incurred claim ratios approach 90 percent and where medical costs increase from year to year. An understanding of claim ratios will also give the student a special insight into the significance of accrual basis accounting as opposed to cash basis accounting.

Claim ratios can be calculated on a cash basis or on an incurred basis. A *cash ratio* is the percentage of claims paid to premiums received during the same period. An *incurred ratio* is the percentage of claims incurred to premiums earned during the same period.

Calculating Claim Ratios

A cash ratio can be readily calculated from ledger account balances or by analyzing accounting transaction records. Cash claim ratios are reasonably satisfactory for measuring claim experience with reference to a particular block of policies, provided the claim and premium volumes are fairly constant. Cash ratios can be distorted when the volume of claims and premiums are changing or when they do not cover precisely the same period of time. Incurred ratios are more reliable but are more difficult to calculate.

The amount of claims *incurred* during a period is (1) claims *paid* during the period, (2) less *claims unpaid at beginning* of the period, (3) plus *claims unpaid at end* of period. The incurred ratio is more meaningful when claim reserves are included as a part of the unpaid claims.

The amount of premiums *earned* during a period is (1) premiums *collected* during the period, (2) less the increase, or plus the decrease, in *unearned* premiums and premiums paid in advance, (3) plus the increase, or less the decrease, in due premiums.

The relationship between cash basis and accrual basis income and cost can be depicted in table form as follows:

Premiums		Claims	
Collected......................	$100,000	Paid........................	$40,000
Unearned and advance, start......	+4,000	Unpaid, start.................	−10,000
Unearned and advance, end.......	−6,000	Unpaid, end..................	+20,000
Due, start.....................	−10,000		
Due, end......................	+15,000		
Premiums earned..............	$103,000	Claims incurred..............	$50,000

The cash ratio is 40 percent ($40,000/$100,000) and the incurred ratio is 48.5 percent ($50,000/$103,000), a significant difference.

Other Observations concerning Cash and Incurred Ratios

The average stay in the hospital is about seven days, and claimants do not submit claim forms until they are dismissed or many days after that date. If a claimant enters the hospital on or near the last day of the month, it is virtually impossible for him to file his claim and be paid during the month in which the claim is incurred. Few health insurance claims are filed within seven days of the time they are incurred, and some may not be filed for 30, 60, or even 90 days. It is obvious, therefore, that there will be a difference between the amount incurred and the amount paid.

If a group policy is terminated, the cash ratio will not catch up to the incurred ratio until several months after the last claim is paid. Where there is deferred maternity coverage or a large major medical claim, this last claim payment could be more than a year after termination of the policy.

In the case of disability income insurance, under which claims can run for months and even years, the incurred claim ratio, to be meaningful, must include an adjustment for the present value of future benefits (amounts not yet due). To obtain an incurred claim figure, these liability amounts at the beginning of the period are subtracted from the claims paid and these liabilities at the end of the period are added.

Where there are claim reserves, as in the case of disability insurance, the incurred ratio is the most meaningful, but it provides only an approximate estimate as to the adequacy of underwriting and premiums charged. This is true because claim reserves used in calculating the amount of claims incurred are necessarily approximations. Morbidity tables are used to determine these reserves, but the actual experience over a period of time might vary considerably from that reflected by the tables.

Where policy reserves of a significant amount are required on an in-force policy, cash and accrual ratios may be used to indicate trends, but they are not completely reliable unless many factors are considered. For example, on paid-up policies, no premiums are received after the policy becomes paid up, but claims are incurred each year. Reserves released on these claims are substantial and partially offset the claim costs recorded on the ledger. Claim amounts paid on paid-up policies must, therefore, be excluded in figuring a ratio on premium-paying policies, or special adjustments must be made in the figures to compensate for surplus changes created by the claims.

Use of Claim Ratios

Cash claim ratios are frequently used in connection with industrial insurance. Premiums are all payable on the same mode, and the amount received each month or year remains fairly constant. Similarly, claims are fairly uniform in amount with very little change in the liability for incurred but unpaid claims between the end of one period and the end of the next.

In addition to indicating trends and giving an approximate idea as to the adequacy of premiums charged for a benefit, cash ratios are also useful in testing the adequacy of field underwriting in a region or district. This is possible if the ratio of a district is compared with the company ratio.

An incurred claim ratio can be used to test the apparent adequacy of a premium rate where no policy reserves are involved or where the policy reserves are not a significant amount. This test is particularly useful for testing group medical expense insurance rates where rates must be adjusted from time to time because costs are continually increasing.

Assume, for example, that 7 percent of the premium on a group insurance case is required for commissions and service costs. Another 2 percent is required for premium taxes, and 3 percent is required to cover the cost of home office servicing and processing of claims. Since costs total 12 percent, an incurred claim ratio in excess of 88 percent will leave no margin for profit or in the case of a mutual company no means for building up surplus to serve as a risk cushion. If the incurred claim ratio is 90 percent, it is obvious that the premium rate is deficient by 2 percent.

There are ways of testing the adequacy of rates when reserves are involved, but these tests are made by actuaries and are not presented here.

SUPPLEMENTARY CONTRACTS AND ANNUITIES

A supplementary contract is one issued to replace a life insurance contract that is terminated by death, maturity, or surrender in those cases where some or all of the policy benefits are to be held by the company and paid to beneficiaries under a type of settlement other than lump sum. Although the term *supplementary contract* is used in the U.S. Annual Statement blank, these contracts actually are more in the nature of substitute or settlement contracts than supplementary. They are contracts substituted for the initial policy in settling the claim after it has been approved.

Supplementary Contracts WOLC

This designation includes proceeds held at interest and proceeds to be disbursed in a series of installments if the amount of each installment and the period are fixed, such as $100 per month for 10 years. It does not include contracts where payment of any installment is contingent upon a payee being alive at time of payment. Some supplementary contracts provide for payments of a series of installments for a period certain and life thereafter. Payments are thus guaranteed to the payee or his contingent beneficiary for the "certain" period. Many companies classify the certain period payments as WOLC and the payments thereafter as WLC. Thus, at the time such a supplementary contract is established, part of the proceeds are credited to *Considerations for Supplementary Contracts WOLC* and the remainder credited to *Considerations for Supplementary Contracts WLC.*

An interest rate is guaranteed in connection with settlement contracts. This rate is usually lower than that actually paid on settlement contracts WOLC. For example, interest may be guaranteed at 3 percent per annum but credited to proceeds at the rate of 4 percent per annum. Some companies pay a slightly higher rate when the proceeds cannot be withdrawn by the beneficiary or contract holder. For example, 4 percent may be paid on withdrawable deposits but 4¼ percent if not withdrawable.

Entries when a company receives considerations for supplementary contracts were shown in the claims section of this chapter and in Chapter 17. An entry recording amounts paid to a beneficiary is a simple debit to an account indicating the type of payment, such as Paid on Supplemental Contracts WOLC and a credit to Cash. If more than the guaranteed interest is paid, a few companies prefer to debit the excess interest to Dividends Paid on Supplemental Contracts WOLC.

Supplemental Contracts WLC

This title includes settlement contracts where the proceeds are payable during the life of the payee. When a payment is made, the account debited would normally be titled Paid on Supplementary Contracts WLC. If any interest in excess of the guaranteed amount is paid, it too is debited to the account shown, unless debited to a dividend account. It is less common to pay extra interest under contracts with life contingencies than under contracts without life contingencies because mortality of annuitants (those receiving periodic installments) is such that many companies would suffer losses on these life contingency contracts if they did not retain this interest.

Annuities

The word *annuity* means, technically, a series of annual payments. It is used, however, to mean more frequent periodic payments. As used in the U.S. Annual Statement it means any contract purchased primarily to provide retirement income, with little or no life insurance coverage included. Annuities usually involve life contingencies, but in the Canadian Annual Statement the term *settlement annuity* is used whether or not life contingencies are involved. The cost account debited when recording payments made on life annuities is typically *Annuity Payments*. Dividends paid on annuities are debited to an appropriate dividend account.

Records and Payment Control

A supplementary contract is usually given a number which is different from that of the policy which was terminated and a new set of records is prepared, using the new number. A register is usually maintained in which the initial information on supplementary contracts is recorded. This register is a control device which enables the actuary or accountant to determine which supplementary contracts are outstanding and, therefore, which ones should be valued as a liability for Annual Statement purposes (see Figure 18–3).

An annuity payment record is very similar to a settlement contract record. These records usually do not show an outstanding balance, but they do describe the contract and payments made or to be made. The record shows the amount of each installment, payee, the payment dates, and period of installments. Usually a balance is maintained only when settlement proceeds are left on deposit at interest, subject to withdrawal.

Most companies use manual records for supplemental contracts because the quantity involved is relatively small. Manual records provide a space for each payment. However, a system of automatic disbursements may be set up for annuities and settlement contract payments to assure the issuance of a proper check on the due date of each installment.

It is important to know that the payee is living when checks are issued. If a payee dies, the proper contingent payee must be substituted. Frequently, the face of the check and the endorsement space on the back contain language to invalidate the check if the payee is not living or does not personally endorse it.

Liability for Supplementary Contracts

At the end of each year, the valuation of liability assumes that all amounts payable prior to the end of the year have been disbursed. If, in fact, there were any outstanding amounts due but not paid, they are

Figure 18–3. Supplemental Contract Records

COMPANY "A"

Policy or DC No. 123456   Memo To:

Payee's Name and Address

Mrs. Mary Doe
111 N. Kane St.
Urbana, Illinois

No.	Date Issued	Amt.	Date Paid	No.	Date Issued	Amt.	Date Paid
1	3-2-62	$100.00	3-1-63				

Policy No. 15321 & 20789

Claim No. 54321

Insured   John Doe

Method of Payment $100.00 a mo.
through 11-2-69 and $71.44
on December 2, 1969

Excess Interest

	1		
	2		
	3		

Effective Date 3-2-62

| | 4 | | |
| | 5 | | |

Excess Interest   Date 3-2-62   Rate 1%

| | 6 | | |
| | 7 | | |

Amount Deposited $8,532.00   Tax Stamp

Code No. 53-5-893-543   Follow-up Dates

Company "B" (back)

Contract No. 123456   How Payable Mo.

Account No.

Year	62	63				
Jan.						
Feb.						
Mar.	3-2					
Apr.	4-1					
May						
Jun.						
Jul.						
Aug.						
Sep.						
Oct.						
Nov.						
Dec.						
Year						
Jan.						
Feb.						
Mar.						
Apr.						
May						
Jun.						
Jul.						
Aug.						
Sep.						
Oct.						
Nov.						
Dec.						
Remarks:						

Company "C"

Mrs. Mary Doe   Monthly   2nd
111 N. Kane St.
Urbana, Illinois $100.00

SUPP. CONT. Pol. 123456, DC-54321: Proceeds of $8,532.00
to be paid in 93 monthly installments of $100.00 each.
First installment to be paid as of March 2, 1962, with
final $100.00 payment to be made on November 2, 1969 and
$71.44 to be paid on December 2, 1969.

2½%   #2211   Final $100.00 on
11-2-69 plus a
payment of $71.44 on
12-2-69

JAN. FEB. MAR. APR. MAY JUNE JULY AUG. SEPT. OCT. NOV. DEC.

Company B (Front)

Cont. No.	Name Mrs. Mary Doe	Address 111 Kane St. Urbana, Illinois	State Ill.
123456			

Code   53   5   893   543

Kind of Contract   Supp. 10 Yr. & Life

		Inv. x	Not. Inv. x	Age 54	Sex F	Birth Date 5-23 14	Claim Nos. 54321

Par   Yes   Consideration 8,532.00   Guar. 2½   Interest From 3-2-62   Name of Insured John Doe   Policy Nos. 15321 & 20789

From Insure   Annuity   First Payment Due 3-2-62   Pyts. Guar. $100.00   On 2nd day each month

x   Final Payment Date 11-2-69   Exc. Int. $4.32

D.C. x   Mat.   Surr.   Final Payment Amt. 71.44

Selected by   Annual Payment

Ins.   Bene.   Other

x

Remarks:

The supplemental contract records of three companies are shown. Note that Companies A and B post the history of payments to the card. Company C retains a copy of the check in the case file for historical purposes.

included with the claim liability. A bookkeeping entry is not made at the end of the year in connection with the liability or the increase in reserves for settlement contracts and annuities. This increase is treated as a non-ledger insurance cost, except as previously mentioned in connection with all Canadian deposits and U.S. premium deposits.

U.S. ANNUAL STATEMENT ASPECTS

The Annual Statement blank contains two policy claim exhibits in which the claims data are assembled for the *summary of operations*,

Figure 18–4

Form 1   ANNUAL STATEMENT FOR THE YEAR 1968 OF THE.............................

EXHIBIT 11—POLICY AND CONTRACT CLAIMS

PART 1—Liability End of Current Year

	TOTAL (1)	INDUSTRIAL LIFE (INCLUDING TOTAL AND PERMANENT DISABILITY AND ACCIDENTAL DEATH BENEFITS) (2)	ORDINARY		
			LIFE INSURANCE (3)	TOTAL AND PERMANENT DISABILITY (4)	ADDITIONAL ACCIDENTAL DEATH (5)
1. Due and unpaid					
2. In course of settlement:					
2.1 Resisted				†	
2.2 Other.				†	
3. Incurred but unreported (less reinsurance ceded) .				†	
4. Total					
5. Less: reinsurance ceded on reported claims (Schedule S)					
6. NET LIABILITY (Column 1 to Item 4, Page 3)		*	**		

*Including matured endowments unpaid amounting to $............................. **Including matured endowments unpaid amounting to $.............................
†Include only portion of liability applicable to assumed "accrued" disability benefits. Reserve for unaccrued benefits for Ordinary Total and Permanent Disability $.............
and for Group Accident and Health $.............................. and Other Accident and Health $.............................. are included in Item 2, Page 3 (see Exhibit 9, Section B).

PART 2—Incurred During the Year

	TOTAL (1)	INDUSTRIAL LIFE (INCLUDING TOTAL AND PERMANENT DISABILITY AND ACCIDENTAL DEATH BENEFITS) (2)*	ORDINARY		
			LIFE INSURANCE (3)**	TOTAL AND PERMANENT DISABILITY (4)	ADDITIONAL ACCIDENTAL DEATH (5)
1. Settlements during the year					
2. Deduct reinsurance ceded					
3. Net settlements (Line 1 minus Line 2)	†				
4. Net liability December 31, current year from Part 1					
5. Amounts recoverable from reinsurers December 31, previous year					
6. Line 3 plus Line 4 plus Line 5					
7. Net liability December 31, previous year					
8. Amounts recoverable from reinsurers December 31, current year (Schedule S)					
9. Line 7 plus Line 8					
10. NET INCURRED BENEFITS (Line 6 minus Line 9).					

*Including matured endowments amounting to $.......................in Line 1 and $.......................in Line 10.
**Including matured endowments amounting to $.......................in Line 1 and $.......................in Line 10.
†Equals sum of Lines 16.1, 16.2, 17 and 22, Exhibit 12. Includes $.......................premiums waived under total and permanent disability benefits.

analysis of operations, and balance sheet pages. One relates to all claims and is referred to here as the general claim exhibit. The other refers to health insurance claims only.

The general claim exhibit is divided into two parts (see Figure 18–4) with columns that coincide with those in the analysis of operation.

Lines in the first part of the general claim exhibit are provided to show the total liability by the following types: (1) due and unpaid, (2) in course of settlement, (3) resisted, and (4) incurred but unreported (less reinsurance). These can be referred to collectively as incurred and unpaid claims. The type of claim (such as death claim, matured endowment,

....COMPANY

(rite or stamp name of Company)

The figures on this page do not include Separate Account items, if any.

| | | GROUP | | ACCIDENT AND HEALTH | | |
INDIVIDUAL ANNUITIES (6)	SUPPLEMENTARY CONTRACTS (7)	LIFE INSURANCE (8)	ANNUITIES (9)	GROUP (10)	OTHER (11)	
		†		XXX	XXX	
		†		†	†	
		†		†	†	

and Group Life Total and Permanent Disability $.................................. are included in Item 1, Page 3 (see Exhibit 8, Section F);

| | | GROUP | | ACCIDENT AND HEALTH | | |
NDIVIDUAL NNUITIES (6)	SUPPLEMENTARY CONTRACTS (7)	LIFE INSURANCE (8)	ANNUITIES (9)	GROUP (10)	OTHER (11)	

etc.) is not shown in this exhibit since the column headings provide an approximate classification by type of claims. Matured endowments are included with death claims, but the amounts of matured endowments, both cash basis and accrual basis, are shown in footnotes.

Part 2 of this exhibit shows amounts, including reinsurance benefits, used to arrive at *net incurred claims.* This net amount is subdivided by type of claim when entered in the summary of operations and analysis of operations even though it is not subdivided in the general claim exhibit.

There are two claim reserve liabilities included in a special health insurance reserve exhibit (see Figure 18–5), which also consists of two parts: "A. Active Life Reserve" and "B. Claim Reserve." Columns are included for group health insurance reserves and for various renewability classifications.

The first item in the first part of this exhibit, *unearned premium reserve,* is usually treated as a policy reserve. When treated in this manner, it is not used to adjust premium income from a cash to accrual basis. Unearned premiums may, however, be included with advance premiums in the premium exhibit, in which case they are used to adjust premium income.

The second item, *additional reserves,* is similar to a life reserve in that it is a reserve on an in-force policy and constitutes a portion of the premiums set aside to pay claims that may be incurred in future years. It may also be described as the present value of future claims as predicted by a morbidity table less the present value of future premiums. The word "additional" in this case means "in addition to unearned premiums." The third item in Part A is *reserve for future contingent benefits.* This item is also included in Part B, thereby giving a company the option of treating it as an adjustment of either premiums or claims. The fourth item, *reserve for rate credits,* was discussed in connection with group insurance. Rate credits usually are not allowed on individual health insurance policies.

On the liability page of the Annual Statement, the total liabilities for unpaid life insurance claims is entered on a separate line from unpaid health insurance claims. Unpaid settlement contract installments and unpaid disability benefits provided by life policies are included with the life insurance claim liability.

There is a special health insurance exhibit (Schedule H) in the Annual Statement blank in which premiums, claims, and other insurance costs are adjusted from the cash to the incurred basis. A company can then arrive at (1) incurred claim ratios and other significant percentages and (2) a gain described as "gain from underwriting after dividends." This gain is the result of deducting incurred claims, expenses, and taxes from earned premiums. Investment income is ignored for this purpose. The *increase in present value of future benefits* and *increase in reserve for future contin-*

Figure 18-5. U.S. Health Insurance Reserve Exhibit

EXHIBIT 9—AGGREGATE RESERVE FOR ACCIDENT AND HEALTH POLICIES

	Total (1)	Group Accident and Health (2)	Other Individual Policies					
			Collectively Renewable (3)	Non-Cancellable (4)	Guaranteed Renewable (5)	Non-Renewable for Stated Reasons Only (6)	Other Accident Only (7)	All Other (8)
A. Active Life Reserve								
1. Unearned premium reserve								
2. Additional reserves*		XXXX					XXXX	XXXX
3. Reserve for future contingent benefits (deferred maternity and other similar benefits)								
4. Reserve for rate credits								
5. Total (Gross)								
6. Reinsurance ceded								
7. Total (Net)								
B. Claim Reserve								
1. Present value of amounts not yet due on claims**								
2. Reserve for future contingent benefits (deferred maternity and other similar benefits)								
3.								
4. Total (Gross)								
5. Reinsurance ceded								
6. Total (Net)								
C. GRAND TOTAL (Net) (to Item 2, Page 3)								

*Attach statement as to valuation standard used in calculating this reserve, specifying reserve bases, interest rates and methods.
**Includes reserves for unreported claims. Accrued benefits on incurred but unaccrued benefits should be reported in Exhibit 11, Part 1, Lines 2.2 and 3.

gent benefits are treated as a part of claim costs in arriving at *losses incurred in the current year* as shown in this exhibit. However, as previously noted, the increase in reserve for future contingent benefits may be used to adjust premiums rather than claims.

Health insurance claims and premiums, both individual and group, must be reported to each state semiannually on an incurred basis for each principal plan of health insurance in force. This report is made on a form separate from the Annual Statement.

The Annual Statement blank filed in each state requires data on claims incurred and paid in that state, by type of renewability clause, and by method of settlement, such as paid-in-full, resisted, etc. Because of the information required for the many claims exhibits and schedules in the Annual Statement, it is necessary that each company keep a statistical record of each claim paid during the year and to reconcile the total shown on the records to the general ledger accounts. It is also necessary to separately value incurred but unpaid claim liabilities for each state, and to determine an incurred total for each state in which the company is licensed.

The liability for supplementary contracts with life contingencies is assembled in Exhibit 8 of the Annual Statement, which covers reserves on life policies. Therefore, the reserves on supplementary contracts WLC become a part of the life reserve on the liability page of the Annual Statement.

The reserves for supplementary contracts without life contingencies and the liability for dividends left with the company to accumulate at interest are shown in Exhibit 10 (see Figure 18–6) with a separate line for each valuation rate and the rate guaranteed in the contract. Companies are permitted to value these supplementary contracts and dividend deposits on an interest rate other than that specified in the contract if it produces a greater liability amount; the rate used is usually the guaranteed rate plus the excess interest rate. The column headed *Amounts Left on Deposit* covers only policy proceeds left on deposit, not premiums left on deposit.

CANADIAN ANNUAL STATEMENT ASPECTS

There are two items in the revenue account that relate to policy disbursement. These are (1) *claims incurred under insurance and annuity contracts* . . . and (2) *payments under settlement annuities.*

Claims figures are assembled in two claim exhibits. The first (see Figure 18–7) bears the same title as the first revenue account item listed above, namely, Claims Incurred Under Insurance and Annuity Contracts. The other claims exhibit shows the claim liability amounts at the end of the year for the items in the first claims exhibit. It is referred to here as the claim liability exhibit. Column headings in these two claim exhibits are the

Figure 18–6. Exhibit for U.S. Supplemental Contracts WOLC, and Deposits

EXHIBIT 10—SUPPLEMENTARY CONTRACTS WITHOUT LIFE CONTINGENCIES AND DIVIDEND ACCUMULATIONS

	VALUATION RATE (1)	CONTRACT RATE OR RATES ‡ (2)	SUPPLEMENTARY CONTRACTS WITHOUT LIFE CONTINGENCIES			DIVIDEND ACCUMULATIONS (6)
			PRESENT VALUE OF AMOUNTS NOT YET DUE (3)	AMOUNTS LEFT ON DEPOSIT (4)	TOTALS (5)	
1.						
2.						
3.						
4.						
5.						
6.						
7.	TOTALS (as per Items 3 and 5, Page 3) . .					

‡Show contract rate or rates corresponding to each valuation rate.

Figure 18–7.   Canadian Claim Exhibits

(Name of Company)

—	Insurances				
	Ordinary		Group		Industrial
	Participating	Non-participating	Participating	Non-participating	
	$	$	$	$	$

EXHIBIT 4—CLAIMS INCURRED UNDER INSURANCE AND ANNUITY CONTRACTS

1. Net of reinsurance ceded:

(1) Death claims					
(2) Accidental death claims					
(3) Disability claims					
(4) Matured endowments					
(5) Annuity payments					
(6) Surrender values					
(7)					
(8) Totals					

2. Reinsurance ceded

EXHIBIT 5—OUTSTANDING CLAIMS UNDER INSURANCE AND ANNUITY CONTRACTS, INCLUDING PROVISION FOR UNREPORTED DEATH CLAIMS

1. Net of reinsurance ceded:

(1) Death claims					
(2) Accidental death claims					
(3) Disability claims					
(4) Matured endowments					
(5) Annuity payments					
(6) Surrender values					
(7)					
(8) Provision for unreported death claims					
(9) Totals					

2. Due from other companies on reinsured contracts for claims paid

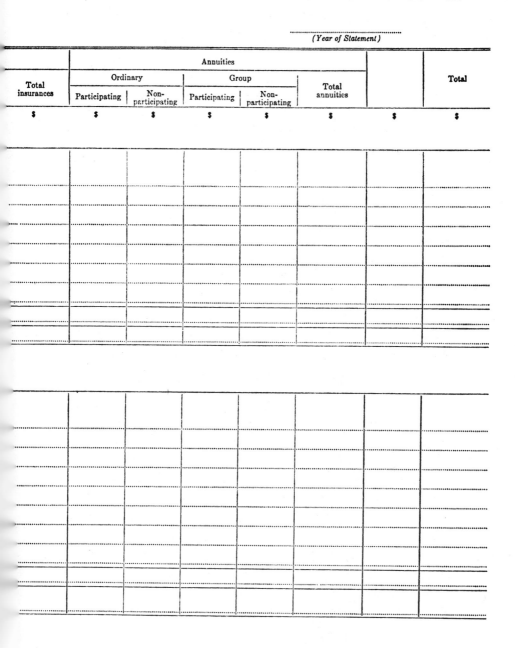

	Annuities						Total
Total insurances	Ordinary		Group		Total annuities		
	Participating	Non-participating	Participating	Non-participating			
$	$	$	$	$	$	$	$

same as those in the "Analysis of Revenue Account by Line of Business," except that they are rearranged to provide a subtotal for insurance coverages and a subtotal for annuities.

The claim liability exhibit (Exhibit 5) includes a separate item entitled *provision for unreported death claims;* unreported claims of all types are reported here. *Surrender values* paid are treated as claims rather than as a separate cost item as in the U.S. blank. Both claim exhibits provide a line for reinsurance amounts. Claims incurred are shown net of reinsurance in the revenue account. Amounts due on account of reinsured policies are not deducted from the liability for outstanding claims, but are shown as an asset item in the balance sheet.

There is a schedule (Schedule L) provided for claims resisted or compromised during the year. One column shows claims remaining unsettled at the end of the year. There are also supplemental exhibits for accidental death benefits (Exhibit H) and disability benefits (Exhibit I). These latter exhibits show premiums earned as well as claims incurred in order to facilitate analyzing claim experience.

In the Canadian casualty blank, the increase in unearned health insurance premiums and "additional reserves" (all except claim reserves) are used to determine incurred premiums. These "additional reserves" are the same as those described in connection with the U.S. Statement. The liability for deferred maternity benefits is included with unearned premiums.

Health insurance claim liabilities are reported as a single item in the claim liability exhibit of the casualty blank. The present value of installments on disability claims is shown separately in a footnote to the exhibit and is included as a part of the total claim liability on the liability page. The change in this claim liability is used to determine the amount of incurred health insurance claims.

The *settlement annuities* of the Canadian statement consist of all supplementary contracts involving life contingencies and those supplementary contracts not involving life contingencies where there is an agreement to pay the proceeds in installments. Agreements that do not provide for installments are included under *amounts on deposit with company as proceeds of contracts.*

Considerations for settlement annuities and *payments on settlement annuities* are included in the analysis of revenue account with the income and disbursements of the line of business under which the annuity originated. As a result, any profit or loss from these annuities is included with that for the line of business under which the settlement annuity originated. The liabilities in connection with settlement annuities are included in the valuation summary and included with the *actuarial reserve for insurance and annuity contracts in force* reported on the liability page of the balance sheet.

SUMMARY OF LIFE INSURANCE CLAIM ACCOUNTING

Claims are recorded as insurance costs when they are paid or applied under a settlement option. Claim payments may result in reducing surplus in a lesser amount than the claim amount because reserves are released.

If claim settlements are to be retained by the company to be disbursed under a settlement contract, a debit entry is made to a claim account to record the cost and a credit entry is made to an income account in an equal amount to record income. Claim liabilities are treated as nonledger liabilities by U.S. companies. The liability for unpaid claims includes, besides known claims unpaid, an estimate for unreported claims and the full amount of resisted, but unsettled, claims.

QUESTIONS

1. Why is there a strong human element in the payment of claims? In what areas must a claim approver be qualified?
2. Show what account or accounts are debited, and for what amounts, when settlement is made on a $5,000 policy and the following conditions exist:
   a) Insured died accidentally while insured under accidental death coverage.
   b) Insured died of suicide after paying $150 in premiums for one year. Policy has a two-year suicide clause.
   c) Insured died of suicide after paying $150 premiums for one year, but the company found the insured made a material misrepresentation as to the condition of his health when applying for the policy.
   d) Policy matures with $500 in paid-up additions.
3. State the effect on the company's surplus under the following circumstances:
   a) Insured dies and has a $2,500 policy which had reserves of $500.
   b) Insured dies and has $100 of paid-up life additions with reserves of $50.
   c) Matured endowment for $2,500 with paid-up additions of $150 is paid.
   d) Matured endowment for $2,500 with dividend accumulations of $225 is paid.
   e) Insured becomes permanently disabled and is to be paid $400 per month for one year. (Ignore interest and morbidity.)
4. Give the three principal health insurance claim classifications; and with reference to a $100 payment, select the following statement most descriptive of the effect of each payment on the company's surplus:

(*a*) little or no decrease, (*b*) decrease equal to payment, (*c*) decrease approximately equal to payment.

5. Why are claim registers used? What are five items of information usually recorded on a claim register? Why are claim numbers used? When might separate claim folders be used and when are they not really needed? What methods are used to show an insured person how the amounts included in his check were determined? Name six items of data that should be included on a claim check register.

6. What are the four principal unpaid claim liabilities? Describe each briefly. What are the two health insurance claim reserves that are treated as health insurance reserves in the U.S. Annual Statement? How are they treated in the Canadian Statement? Describe each briefly. What determines the date a claim is actually incurred?

7. What is the difference between a cash and an incurred claim ratio? When is a cash ratio satisfactory as a measure of premium rates? When is an incurred ratio better? When is neither completely satisfactory?

8. What is the difference between supplementary contracts with life contingencies and those without? What is difference between Canadian settlement annuities and U.S. supplementary contracts WLC?

9. Why are new numbers assigned to supplementary contracts? What protective methods may a company use to assure itself that the proper payee endorses and cashes checks?

U.S. Students Only

10. Name two nonclaim health insurance reserves which are presented as active life policy reserves? What claim liability classifications are used to adjust claims paid from the cash to accrual basis? Why must incurred but unpaid claims be calculated by states?

Canadian Students Only

11. What are two types of claim liabilities shown in the life blank? Are resisted claims included? In the casualty blank is the liability for deferred maternity benefits used to determine premiums earned or incurred claims? Is the present value of disability benefits included as a claim liability or policy reserve?

12. What is the difference between settlement annuities and supplementary contracts with life contingencies? Since a separate column is not provided for settlement annuities in the analysis of revenue account, in which column or columns are the settlement annuity income and cost items included?

PROBLEMS

1. Make the traditional compound entry for a death claim under an ordinary insurance policy if the following conditions exist:
a) Face amount $5,000, age corrected amount $4,750.
b) Policy loan $1,800 with $20 interest in advance.
c) Paid up additions $100, cash value $60.
d) Dividend accumulations, $269 plus $15.50 accrued interest since the last policy anniversary.
e) Quarterly premium due of $69. Company policy is to deduct full amount.

2. Make the traditional entry for a matured endowment under an ordinary insurance policy with the following conditions:
a) Face amount $3,000.
b) Policy loan of $950 with $21 interest due.
c) Paid up additions $116.
d) Settlement agreement has been arranged to leave proceeds with company to be paid $100 per month until proceeds and interest are exhausted.
What difference, if any, would there be in the entry if the proceeds are left with the company to be disbursed in equal installments for life with 10 years certain?

3. Make the entry for the following conditions, if any is required. If none is required, so indicate and explain why.
a) Disability income payment made for $400.
b) Medical expense payment to hospital $250.
c) Medical expense payment to doctor $400.
d) A premium of $100 is waived on a life insurance policy due to disability (U.S. method).
e) A premium of $100 is waived on a health insurance policy due to disability.
f) Claim is paid for $2,000 as an indemnity for loss of an arm.
g) Check is received for $48,916 reinsurance benefit on a life policy reinsured.

4. Give entry for $110 guaranteed interest paid on a supplementary contract WOLC plus $25 of additional interest.

5. Give entry for $225 paid on a life annuity plus $15 of additional interest.

Chapter 19

Expense and Taxes

Profits in any company, whether life insurance, manufacturing, retail sales, service to the public, or any other type of business, result in large part from proper control of expenses. Additional profits can be realized, of course, from increased income, but only if expenses and other costs of doing business are controlled.

In the life insurance business, there is relatively little that company management can do to control claim, commission, or tax costs. When a claim is incurred in accordance with policy provisions, it must be paid. When a premium is received, commissions specified in an agency contract must be paid. Taxes are levied by government authority and also must be paid. The only control possible on claims, commissions, and taxes is vigilance and care to prevent overpayment. Operating expenses, therefore, are the only major disbursements over which management can have meaningful control. In this area management has a very great and serious responsibility.

Accounting for expenses in a life insurance company is centered around the prime objective of preventing excessive expenditures. A second objective is to maintain an audit trail from the approval of an expenditure to the presentation of the expense item in the Annual Statement. A third objective, relative only to supplies and fixed assets, is to maintain adequate records for calculating depreciation expense and for determining the amount of liability at the end of the year in connection with orders placed.

Many officers and employees of a company have authority for approving expenses. Each person with such authority is usually restricted as to the type of expenses and the amounts he may approve. Wide dispersal of approval authority is considered desirable because the person most familiar with the need is also in the best position to control the expense. There is a tendency, however, to become careless in examining the need for expenses. To prevent this carelessness, management ordinarily requires reports which analyze expenses by (1) persons responsible for incurring the expense, (2) type of expense, and (3) insurance functions. These reports enable management to recognize and eliminate unnecessary expenses and to reward individuals who conscientiously control expenses.

This chapter is concerned with the accounting entries for expense payments and with processes required to control expenses. Accounting for purchase of supplies and fixed assets is also discussed briefly because these purchases are frequently treated as expense items by life insurance companies. Entries for tax payments and related processes are very similar to those used in connection with expenses, so they are also discussed in this chapter.

ACCOUNTING ENTRIES AND PAYMENT CONTROL

Life insurance companies must have money available at all times to pay claims promptly. Usually money is also available to pay expenses promptly.

A check in payment of an expense is not issued until an authorized person approves that particular expenditure. This approval is usually provided through the use of a form called a check requisition or check voucher. In the case of purchases, payment may be authorized by approving an invoice from the vendor. In the case of salaries, rent, and other periodic payments, a single directive may be used to authorize a series of checks.

A formal check requisition system is essential to good disbursement control. The use of such a requisition places responsibility on the person who requests or authorizes issuance of the check. This person is, or should be, familiar with the reason for the expenditure and should be qualified to determine just which expense account should be debited.

A check requisition shows the amount of the check to be issued, the name of the payee, the purpose of the payment, account numbers to be debited, the signature or initials of the person requisitioning the check, and the date of the requisition. Check requisitions are frequently numbered, in which case they may be used as a source for recording the disbursement in the journal. The preferred method is to use a copy of the check to prepare the accounting entry.

Each time a check is issued to pay an expense, an entry is made debiting an expense account and crediting Cash. It is not the practice of insurance companies to credit an Accounts Payable account when expenses are incurred or when supplies or equipment are received.

Expense entries were discussed in Chapter 3 and subsequent chapters. Special types of expense entries are presented here, together with payment control processes.

Payments for Salaries and Related Taxes

Salaries usually represent more than half of the total expenses shown in the Annual Statement expense exhibit. Salary payments, therefore, justify considerable study and analysis to determine the effectiveness of these important expenditures. To facilitate analyzing costs, numerous salary accounts are maintained in general ledgers. In fact, companies using computers frequently maintain a separate salary account for each department or other responsibility area.

Journal entries to record salary expense are compound entries because a number of accounts must be credited to record deductions for employee benefit plans and for various taxes. An entry to record the payment of a salary to an employee who has earned $100 regular salary and $10 for overtime, and who has typical deductions is:

```
Salaries and Wages Paid—Home Office..........................110.00
    Withheld for Income Tax.................................        8.56
    FICA Tax Withheld......................................        4.84
    Group Insurance Premiums Withheld......................        3.45
    Charitable Contributions Withheld......................        1.00
    Cash...................................................       92.15
```

Note that in the example the entire amount earned is debited to a salary account. A separate salary account for overtime is sometimes used so that overtime can be shown separately in expense control reports.

When disbursement of money withheld is made, the entry is a debit to the proper liability account for the full amount paid. When an additional amount is paid by the company, the company issues one check to cover the amount withheld plus the company's share. For example if $1,000 FICA taxes have been withheld, an additional $1,000 is payable by the company and the entry is:

```
FICA Taxes Withheld.................................1,000.00
FICA Taxes Paid....................................1,000.00
    Cash...........................................           2,000.00
```

FICA Taxes Paid is a tax expense account.

No requisition is required for a salary payment other than a time card or supervisor's report on attendance.

Purchase of Supplies, Furniture, and Equipment

In the Canadian Statement both *supplies* and *furniture and equipment* are treated as expense items. In the U.S. Annual Statement these items may be treated either as expenses or as assets. If treated as assets, they must be nonadmitted on the balance sheet. Computer equipment is an exception and may be treated as an asset in both countries, subject to some limitations. Supplies for the purpose of this discussion includes printed forms purchased from outside sources and does not include printing done by a company-owned printing plant.

The asset method of handling supplies was discussed in the "Prepaid Expense" section of Chapter 3, and the asset method of handling fixed assets was discussed in the "Fixed Assets" section of Chapter 5. Through the adjustment process, this method spreads the cost of the items to operations over the useful life of the assets. The expense method merely involves making a debit entry to an expense account when these items are purchased which means that the whole amount is charged as an operating expense in the year of purchase.

For many years, most U.S. life insurance companies used the expense method for recording and accounting for furniture and equipment because these items were not admitted to the balance sheet in the Annual Statement. The decrease in surplus caused by the purchase is the same under either method, and the expense process is simpler. There is a trend now toward the use of the asset method because federal income tax provisions do not permit the entire cost of the furniture and equipment to be charged off in one year when calculating expense for income tax reporting. Companies which treat furniture and equipment as an expense must use supplemental furniture and equipment records for preparing federal income tax returns.

Purchases of supplies, furniture, and equipment must be controlled carefully to prevent double payments and to prevent payment for incorrect or improper billings. Such payments are possible because phases of the purchase routine are usually handled by three or more separate departments. These items are usually ordered by a purchasing department, received by a supply department, and the invoices are paid by an accounting department. Special forms are used to facilitate the control of payments. A typical process (and the forms used) is described in the following section for the Model Life Insurance Company.

When an order is placed the purchasing department makes up a purchase order in triplicate. One copy is retained by the purchasing department, one is given to the vendor, and one is sent to the supply department. A purchase order shows an identification number, the name of the vendor, the quantity ordered, the price, and special instructions.

The vendor is requested to show the purchase order number on its invoice. In addition to the invoice, vendors typically use (1) a shipping document that is often called a *shipping ticket* and (2) a *statement* rendered monthly.

When items ordered are received by the shipping department, the shipping document is checked against a copy of the purchase order to determine that all items ordered have been received. A record is made for any items not received. The shipping ticket is marked to show quantities received and is then transmitted to the purchasing department, which holds the shipping ticket until the invoice is received.

When the invoice is received from the vendor, the purchasing department verifies (1) the quantities invoiced against those received as indicated by the shipping ticket, (2) the quantities and prices of items invoiced against the quantities and prices of items ordered as indicated by the purchase order, and (3) approves the invoice for payment if all quantities and prices are correct. At the same time, the items and quantities received are noted on the copy of the purchase order in order to prevent payment for duplicate shipments or duplicate invoices. The approved invoice is then sent to the accounting department to be held until a statement is received.

When the monthly statement is received, the accounting department compares approved invoices against it. Payment is not made for missing invoices. This avoids paying for shipments not accepted and for invoices in dispute. Some companies make immediate payment from approved invoices and do not wait for a statement. Payment requisitions are not required because approved copies of invoices serve this purpose. Invoices prepared by vendors provide more assurance of a proper requisition than does an internally prepared form.

The entry to record payment for supplies is a debit to an appropriate account, such as Supplies, and a credit to Cash. The entry is the same whether supplies are treated as assets or expenses. A similar entry, except for account title, is made when furniture or equipment is purchased. When the expense account method is used for recording supplies or furniture and equipment purchased, these expense accounts are closed into the Balance account at the end of the year.

Agents' Balances Charged Off

The business of life insurance is becoming more complex each year, and a considerable amount of time is required to train a new agent. Circumstances require most companies to either advance to a new agent a certain amount per week or month as a loan or pay him a salary while he is in training in order to make a commission job in the life insurance business more attractive. Without financial assistance, a new agent would either have to live on his prior personal savings or borrow from an outside source during his training period. Few prospective agents could afford to, or would be willing to, support themselves fully during this time. Debit insurance companies pay a salary while the agent is being trained, in which case it is not necessary to advance money. Amounts advanced to an agent create a debit balance in his account.

When a sound loan of this type is made, it will either be repaid out of commissions earned by the agent or if the agent is terminated the loan will be assumed by a general agent. There are times, however, when agents' debit balances become uncollectible. In a U.S. company, the entry to record an agent's balance deemed uncollectible is a debit to Agents' Balances Charged Off and a credit to the Agents' Ledger Control account (to zero balance this account with reference to the particular agent's account). The agent's account in the agents' subsidiary ledger is also credited to zero balance it.

LIABILITY FOR EXPENSES AND TAXES

Expense liabilities may be classified into three types:

1. Liability incurred on the date the merchandise is ordered or the contract for purchase signed
2. Liability incurred subsequent to the order date, such as when merchandise is received
3. Continually accruing expenses on which some portion of a cost is incurred each day

Liability Incurred at Time of Order

Items that fall in this category include printed brochures and supplies carrying the company's name, which would have no value to any other person or company. Also included are medical examination fees, inspection report fees, and any item purchased under contract where the specifications are such that the order may not be cancelled by the company once it is placed. This category does not necessarily include the cost of continuous forms that are scheduled for delivery at some date considerably after the first of the year because such orders can usually be cancelled up to a short time before delivery.

A considerable amount of judgment must be used in determining this type of liability. It is necessary to review the unfilled purchase order to pick out the approximate cost of all items ordered but not yet received. Medical examinations and inspection reports are ordered by agents, so this portion of the liability must be estimated by less exact methods. Reasonably accurate estimates can be made shortly after the first of the year by reviewing charges made for these services during the first few days of the new year.

Liability Incurred Subsequent to the Order Date

The principal items falling in this category are furniture and equipment. The company does not enter the cost of these items in its books until the check has been made in payment of the purchase. No liability is incurred for furniture and equipment unless it is delivered and in use before the end of the year. If it is in use and not yet paid for, the full cost of furniture or equipment must be shown as a liability.

Insurance department licenses and fees and real estate taxes are usually incurred on a certain date. Unless that date is passed, there is no liability. Such tax items are usually paid promptly so there is seldom a remaining liability at the end of the calendar year.

Continually Accruing Expenses

The largest and most important expense liability is for services received for which the company is liable and taxes incurred for a period prior to December 31. Most of the expense items and many of the tax items fall in this category. Salaries and wages are usually partially incurred at the time the statement is prepared, creating a liability for the portion incurred but unpaid. There also may be an existing liability for contributions to employees' plans, for professional and service fees, for utility services used, and for a number of investment expenses. Premium taxes, FICA taxes, and income taxes are of this type. Most of these liabilities must be calculated separately.

Adjusting Expenses and Taxes

Prepaid expenses are not used in calculating accrual basis expenses. Neither are they included in the balance sheet as assets because few such items have a recoverable value in event of liquidation.

To adjust paid expenses from a cash to accrual basis, it is necessary only to add the accrued expenses (expenses payable) at the end of the current year and subtract accrued expenses at the end of the previous year. To illustrate, assume that expenses paid are $1,000 and unpaid expenses at the end of the current year are $150, and at the end of the previous year they were $100. The entries on *working papers* (presented here in journal form) to accomplish this adjustment are:

```
Expenses...................................................150.00
    Accrued Expense........................................              150.00
Accrued Expense............................................100.00
    Expenses...............................................              100.00
```

The first entry records this year's liability for accrued expense and the second removes that of last year. The two together produce the required adjusted incurred expense amount of $1,050 ($1,000 + $150 − $100). The same process is used for adjusting taxes paid from the cash to accrual basis.

EXPENSE REPORTING

The volume and variety of expense accounts found in a typical life insurance general ledger are very great. The accounts are not limited to those required to prepare annual statements. Many are included to obtain more meaningful data for management.

Each expense payment must be classified and debited to the proper account. At the end of each month, quarter, or year, account balances are arranged in various groups and then listed on reports and summarized so that they may be studied, interpreted, and compared with similar reports for other periods. These balances must also be summarized in particular ways for presentation in the Annual Statement.

There are three principal ways of classifying, grouping, and summarizing expenses for management interpretation and control. These are by (1) type of expense, (2) responsibility area, and (3) function.

Type of expense refers to the nature of the expense. Examples of types of expense are rents, salaries, advertising, travel, and depreciation. Most expenses are presented by type in the expense exhibit of the Annual Statement, but a few are presented on a functional basis.

Responsibility area is an operational unit under the supervision of one person responsible for controlling costs in that area. An operational unit might be a large department or it might be any work unit which consists of at least one supervisor and his employees.

Functional reporting involves showing expenses according to functions performed such as issuing policies, paying claims, and selling. Reporting expenses by line of business constitutes a broad functional classification. If, however, each line is the responsibility of a different executive, the line of business might be considered a responsibility classification.

Some illustrations will help clarify various aspects of expense reports. Assume that the salary accounts in the general ledger of a particular company have the following balances:

Salaries, agency supervision	$240,000
Salaries, other first-year ordinary	180,000
Salaries, renewal ordinary	100,000
Salaries, data processing	50,000
Salaries, investment	60,000
Total	$630,000

Accounts listed in this manner to provide a total Salary Expense constitute a report by type of expense.

Salaries, Other First-Year Ordinary in the example might consist of $100,000 relative to underwriting activities and $80,000 for supervisory and clerical salaries paid in connection with the issue of policies. A simple example of a responsibility report made to the issue department supervisor and showing the amount of salaries and other expenses paid through his department might appear as follows:

```
Salaries.......................................$80,000
Printing and stationery...........................  5,000
    Total Issue Department Costs.................$85,000
```

If a functional cost report showing ordinary insurance policy issue costs in the same company is prepared, it might show:

```
Issue department costs..........................$ 85,000
Data processing department costs.................  10,000
Premium accounting department costs.............   3,000
File department costs...........................   2,000
    Total Issue Costs...........................$100,000
```

Note in the examples that it was necessary to analyze entries to the Salaries, Other First-Year Ordinary account to obtain responsibility reports because this account included salaries of two departments. It was necessary to allocate a part of the costs of three other departments to the issue function to prepare the functional cost report because each department did parts of the issue functions as well as parts of other functions.

RESPONSIBILITY REPORTS

There are various forms of expense responsibility reports. The simplest is an itemization of expenses paid in an operational unit of a company during a specific period of time. Another is a comparison of these expenses in one period with those of an earlier period. Still a third is a comparison of these expenses with a prior budget estimate of expenses and may include the amount of variance from the prediction and cause for the variance.

Budgeting is a control system in which expenditures are planned for each operational unit of a business and compared periodically with actual expenses. The predicted expenses are also called budgeted amounts or budgeted expenses. The purpose of a budget is to induce executives to control expenses and other costs.

A budget, if properly used, has distinct advantages over other forms of responsibility reports for controlling expenses because (1) the person who authorizes each expenditure normally participates in the planning, thereby committing himself to a certain figure; and (2) budgeted amounts are based on anticipated work volumes and not on past volumes which may have been much lower.

Responsibility areas are referred to as *expense centers* or *cost centers* in many companies. The latter term is not used here to avoid confusion with *cost centers* as used in connection with functional cost reports.

The form of the budget (see Figure 19–1) varies considerably among companies, but the basic feature of comparing budgeted amounts against actual amounts is the same. In many budgets there are four or more column headings: (1) budgeted for month; (2) actual for month; (3)

Figure 19–1. Typical Budget

EXPENSE CLASSIFICATIONS (H.O. Departmental) A-598 (Rev. 2-66) Ptd. in U.S.A.

MONY

PAGE NO. 48

DEPT. or DIV. _Department "A"_ TAB. DIV. CODE 325

AS OF _April 30_ 19 --

EXPENSE ACCOUNT NUMBER	CLASSIFICATION	19__ ANNUAL BUDGET	19 MOS. ACTUAL	UNEXPENDED BALANCE	BUDGET SAVINGS OR DEFICITS (-)
	DISAB.				
00100	Salaries (over grade 13) (0)	175,000	59,000	116,000	0
00200	Salaries (under grade 13) (1,500)	847,000	282,300	564,700	10,000
00300	Salaries – Differential Pay				
	Total Salaries	1,022,000	341,300	680,700	10,000
	(Dis. & Ins. Pay't. to Employees)	(5,000)	(5,000)	0	
	(Replacements at Lower Salaries)	(2,000)	(2,000)	0	
	(Replacements at Higher Salaries)				
	(Promotional Increases)				
	(Vacancies & Absences)	(15,500)	(15,000)	0	
00500	Extended & Overtime ($6,448 & under)	7,000	5,000	2,000	500
01000	Supper & Luncheon Allowance	500	400	100	
	Total Overtime and Supper Allowance	7,500	5,400	2,100	500
03300	Association Membership – Indiv.	600	300	300	100
02500	Credit & Other Reports				
01710	Equipment – Rentals				
01740	Equipment – Repairs	100	0	100	
01750	Equipment – Maintenance				
01770	Equipment – Allowances & Sales				
01780	Equipment Not Capitalized	400	500	-100	-100
02450	Meetings – Other Organizations	7,000	2,300	4,700	300
02460	Company Meetings	1,500	500	1,000	500
	PRINTING & STATIONERY:				
01400	Printed Forms & Corres. Papers	6,000	1,800	4,200	
01410	Printed Forms – Field				
01420	Office Supplies	3,000	1,500	1,500	-500
01430	Company Publications	2,500	900	1,600	100
01900	Photostats, Photographs, etc.	300	0	300	
01800	Rent, H.O. Occupancy	47,000	14,000	33,000	
03400	Rent, Outside of H.O.				
02900	Subscriptions – Books & Periodicals	1,500	400	1,100	100
01600	Telegraph	200	100	100	
01610	Telephone – Long Distance	900	300	600	-100
	TRAVELING EXPENSES:				
02300	Regular	22,000	3,500	18,500	
02310	Other				
02400	Expense Agents Visiting H.O.				
02410	Expense Home Office Visitors				
02800	Express & Freight	100	0	100	
02810	Moving Household Effects				
	Total – Express & Freight	100	0	100	
02100	Meals – Business Conferences	2,500	1,000	1,500	500
03000	Fees & Expenses – Various Services	3,000	1,200	1,800	200
03100	Unclassified Admin. Expenses	200	100	100	
	TOTAL OTHER EXPENSES	106,300	33,800	72,500	1,600
	TOTAL EXPENSE	1,128,300	375,100	753,200	11,600
	EQUIPMENT PURCHASES:				
01720	Replacements	300	200	100	
01730	Additional	1,500	1,100	400	100

budgeted, year to date; and (4) actual, year to date. A fifth column is frequently included to show variations from the budgeted amounts on the year-to-date basis.

Actual data are obtained from ledger account balances or by sorting and summarizing transaction records. To accomplish this sorting, responsibility area codes are placed in each disbursement transaction record at the time the check is written.

An *interim statement* is any form of financial statement prepared at a time other than at the end of the accounting year.

If a company budgets its premium income and predicts claims, policy reserves, and uncontrollable disbursements, budget reports can be combined to produce an interim statement. Figure 19–2 presents a variation of a budget which includes income and which, therefore, also constitutes an interim statement. Nonledger items such as reserve increases and increase in net due and deferred premiums are usually estimated for interim statements, but many companies with computers calculate these items accurately.

Budget Supervision

To be most effective, a budget must be under the control of a budget officer, frequently assisted by a budget committee. The supervisor of each operational unit must also be heavily involved in making estimates concerning volume of business to be handled by his unit and costs for personnel, space, and other facilities that will be required. Since salaries and overtime comprise more than 50 percent of a typical company's total expenses, the forecast for these items must be made with particular care.

The chief executive may also require that major expenditures be anticipated and submitted to the executive committee or a budget committee of the company for approval prior to their being included in the budget. The budget officer is responsible for keeping the predictions realistic and for coordinating all expenditures so that the total amount planned for all responsibility areas will not exceed the funds available to pay expenses. The budget process also requires review throughout the year by unit supervisors and by the budget officer or committee as to reasons a supervisor is not staying within his budgeted amounts. A wise chief executive will not hold his supervisors and officers to the exact prediction but will require an explanation of differences.

Budget Procedures

The *Budget Manual*, LOMA, July, 1961, included this paragraph:

The existence of a budget does not necessarily imply control; it is a dynamic tool of operation and must not be allowed to degenerate into a summary of

Figure 19–2. Typical Interim Statement and Budget

	One Twelfth Annual Budget	Totals	Budget Year to Date	Actual Totals Year to Date
BUDGET REPORT				
FIRST-YEAR LIFE		DATE:		
Premium income				
Coupon dividend applied				
Total premiums received				
Increase in due and deferred premiums				
Total premiums				
Death claims paid				
Increase in pending claims				
Total claims				
Balance				
First-year reserve				
Balance for expenses				
Commissions				
Production expense				
Claim expense				
Legal claim expense				
Medical fees				
Inspection fees				
M.I.B.				
Salaries				
Furniture and fixture repairs				
Home office travel				
Rent				
Furniture and fixture purchases				
Printing and stationery				
Books and periodicals				
Postage, telephone, and telegraph				
Insurance				
I.B.M.				
General office maintenance				
Premium tax				
Pension cost				
Total				
General overhead				
Total				
Increase in premium tax liabilities				
Total expenses				
Gain from first-year life				

historical facts. To be effective, budget procedures must be continually reviewed, and results must be most critically analyzed at a level high enough to impress management with the need for responsible budget preparation and with the obligation to operate within budget limits.

There are no rules which tell just what expenses should be included in a budget. *It is important, however, that only controllable expenses be included in the budget for which one officer or unit supervisor is responsible.* He can then take pride in controlling those expenses and staying within his estimates. If two or more people have the authority to make expenditures included in one budget, neither will feel responsible nor exercise proper control. Alternatively, if expenses outside the control of a particular unit supervisor are included in his budget, his feeling of responsibility for expense control will be lessened. Budgets can be operated, however, at several levels of responsibility. For example, several budgets for lesser operational units under one department head can be consolidated into a single budget for the department.

Budget predictions are usually prepared near the end of each year preceding the one to which they are to apply. Forecasts are made of the increased work volume that will be done in the budgeted responsibility area. Current salary schedules and current expense schedules are modified to provide for the anticipated work load, and a determination is made as to a reasonable amount for each type of expenditure. Estimates of expenses may be based on data supplied by the budget officer but are determined by the supervisor affected and approved by the budget committee or other committee serving this function.

It is usually unwise to change a budget during the year merely because the actual figures are somewhat different from the predicted figures. Most deviations can be analyzed adequately by comparing actual expenses versus anticipated expenses and work units performed versus work units anticipated. However, no budget should be so inflexible that it cannot be adjusted to reflect important deviations from original assumptions when these deviations are the result of unforeseen contingencies.

Amounts entered in the *actual* column of a budget are usually entered on a cash basis because most controllable expenses are paid as they are incurred. It is not usual to adjust a budget for unpaid expenses because the cost of calculating them is considerable, and the amounts do not vary materially from period to period.

FUNCTIONAL COST ANALYSIS

Functional cost analysis involves examining costs of performing a function, or process, of a major line of business and relating this cost to a unit of measurement of work. *Functional unit cost* is defined as the total cost of operations necessary to perform a specific function divided by the number of units of work processed within that function. Functional unit costs are expressed in dollars and cents per unit. For example, it might be said that it costs $150 to put on the books a new policy having a $100 annual premium.

Representatives of the life insurance industry through LOMA have developed a set of guidelines which member companies may use in determining functional unit costs. Annually LOMA's Intercompany Financial Comparison Committee makes functional unit cost studies of insurance and investment functions. The following list includes a few of the functions analyzed and some of the units of measure used. The letter *M* means $1,000. Notice that most of the functions are determined by at least two units of measure.

Function	Units of Measure
Selling expense	Per policy issued and paid for; per M of new business
Selection expense	Per policy issued and paid for; per M of new business
Issue expense	Per policy issued and paid for; per M of new business
Total initial expense (sum of preceding items)	Per policy issued and paid for; per M of new business
Premium collections	Per premium collected; per M of business in force
Commission processing	Per $100 of commissions credited
Claims processing	Per termination by death; per M of business in force
Mortgage loans	Per $100 of mean investment in mortgage loans
Policy loans	Per $100 of mean investment in policy loans

Use of Functional Costs

Unit costs are used to measure efficiency and to identify areas where costs are too high. If unit costs are compared with those of other companies from year to year, it is possible to determine the trend generally and where better planning or better control may be needed.

Unit costs may also be used in connection with calculating premium rates to help an actuary more accurately determine the amount of money required to put a new policy on the books of the company. He can determine also in renewal years how much it costs to service each policy and how much it costs to collect each dollar of premium. From this information, he can calculate premium rates high enough to pay the costs of servicing policies, and provide a reasonable margin for safety and profit or policy dividends, yet low enough to be competitive.

Through the use of unit costs, management can better determine the amount of new business it can afford to write. This is particularly true in small companies where actuaries may not be available for extensive analysis of insurance operations. The need for first-year cost information is especially important in a company selling ordinary life insurance because it costs much more than the first-year premium income to sell, underwrite, and issue an ordinary life insurance policy. Without adequate cost information, a new company might be misled into believing that its premium rates are inadequate since first-year costs would exceed the first-year premiums and produce a loss.

Conversely, if a company with a large amount of renewal premium income is not writing new business, much less cost is incurred, and the company would very likely show a substantial operating gain. The company might be misled into believing that premium rates are too high and reduce them (or increase dividends). The lower premium rates would stimulate new business at an inadequate rate which could never return to surplus the amount required to sell, underwrite, and issue the policies.

Calculating Functional Costs

Functional costs can be calculated by using figures obtained from the *actual* column of responsibility reports.

The cost of a function may overlap several responsibility areas. For example, the cost for issuing policies usually is not confined to the expenses of the issue department. Expenses from other responsibility areas such as a part of the cost of the file department and of the data processing unit must be included to obtain the complete functional cost.

Expenses such as rent, printing, and stationery may be allocated to responsibility areas as a percentage of salaries. This percentage is obtained by dividing the cost of these items by the total salaries of the persons incurring the expense. These costs, along with salaries, may then be reallocated to cost centers in accordance with the volume of work performed on each function within each responsibility area. If adequate production records are not available, work sampling techniques may be used to estimate the volume.

PRESENTATION OF EXPENSES AND TAXES IN ANNUAL STATEMENTS

Expenses and taxes are presented in the Canadian Life Annual Statement blank in much the same manner as in the U.S. Annual Statement. Annual Statement phases of expenses and tax items are, therefore, discussed as a unit, with footnotes and a brief supplement devoted to Canadian differences.

The expense and tax exhibits of the U.S. and Canadian Annual Statements have a single column for life insurance. Thus, expenses for group life, ordinary life, annuities, and industrial life are shown on a consolidated basis. In the U.S. exhibits,[1] there is also a single column for health insurance and a separate column for investment expenses and investment taxes. Investment amounts are segregated from insurance amounts to facilitate calculating the *net* investment income before allocating it to lines of business.

Allocation of Expenses to Major Lines of Business

It will be recalled that total incurred expenses and total incurred taxes are shown for each line of business in the analysis of operations. Since the exhibits for summarizing expenses and taxes do not include columns for lines of business, such allocations must be made on working papers. Annual Statement instructions for allocating expenses are quite comprehensive.

Some expenses can be allocated directly to the appropriate line of business by maintaining separate general ledger accounts for each type of expense within each major line of business. Premium taxes can be charged directly to a line of business because premiums must be reported by line of business to each state. Many other expenses, such as cafeteria expense and payroll taxes, must be allocated periodically by formula, such as a percent of total employees or percent of total salaries. In some cases, allocation might be made first to responsibility areas and then reallocated to lines of business in accordance with work volume for each line of business within the responsibility areas.

It usually is not practical to use a set of expense and tax accounts for sublines of business, such as disability, accidental death benefits, and supplementary contracts. Expenses and taxes should be allocated to sublines of insurance by the same methods as are used in major lines to the extent practicable. In small companies these items might be first allocated to major lines on a reasonably exact basis and then reallocated to sublines in proportion to premium income and claim costs.

Since investment functions do not overlap insurance functions to any significant extent, most investment expenses can easily be segregated by the use of separate investment expense accounts.

If the company is functionally organized, i.e., with only one sales organization, one underwriting department, one claim department, and one premium collection and policy service department, the expense allocation to line of business must be based on special studies.

General expenses, such as the president's salary, and many other expenses can be allocated to lines of business by use of the same techniques used in allocating by function. Salaries of supervisors and executives can be

---

[1] The exhibits in the Canadian casualty blank for health insurance expenses and taxes do not include a separate column for investment expenses.

Figure 19-3. U.S. Expense and Tax Exhibits

Form 1
The figures on this page do not include
Separate Account items, if any.
OF THE.................

(Write or stamp name of Company)

.................COMPANY

ANNUAL STATEMENT FOR THE YEAR 1968

EXHIBIT 5—GENERAL EXPENSES

| | INSURANCE | | INVESTMENT | TOTAL |
	LIFE (1)	ACCIDENT AND HEALTH (2)	(3)	(4)
1. Rent				
2. Salaries and wages				
3.11 *Contributions for benefit plans for employees				
3.12 *Contributions for benefit plans for agents				
3.21 Payments to employees under non-funded benefit programs				
3.22 Payments to agents under non-funded benefit programs				
3.31 Other employee welfare				
3.32 Other agent welfare				
3.4				
4.1 Legal fees and expenses				
4.2 Medical examination fees				
4.3 Inspection report fees				
4.4 Fees of public accountants and consulting actuaries .				
4.5 Expense of investigation and settlement of policy claims .				
4.6				
5.1 Traveling expenses				
5.2 Advertising				
5.3 Postage, express, telegraph and telephone .				
5.4 Printing and stationery				
5.5 Cost or depreciation of furniture and equipment .				
5.6 Rental of equipment				
5.7				
6.1 Books and periodicals				
6.2 Bureau and association dues				
6.3 Insurance, except on real estate . .				
6.4 Miscellaneous losses				
6.5 Collection and bank service charges .				
6.6 Sundry general expenses				
6.7 Group service and administration fees .				
6.8				

7.1 Agency expense allowance . . . .
7.2 Agents' balances charged off (less $_____recovered)
7.3 Agency conferences other than local meetings . . . .
8.1
8.2
9.1 Real estate expenses . . . .
9.2 Investment expenses not included elsewhere . . . .
9.3
10. GENERAL EXPENSES PAID . . . .
11. General expenses unpaid December 31, current year . .
12. General expenses unpaid December 31, previous year . .
13. General expenses incurred during year (10+11—12) . .

(To Line 2, Exhibit 2)   (To Item 23, Page 4)   (To Line 27, Exhibit 12)

A. Compensation to agents on a plan other than commissions, included in Col. (1): First year $_____, Renewal $
B. Agency supervision, except Home Office, included in Col. (1): Line 2 $_____, Line 5.1 $_____, Line ____ $_____, All other lines $
C. Branch office expenses other than those in A and B included in Col. (1): Line 1 $_____, Line 2 $_____,

*These items include $_____on account of prior service.

EXHIBIT 6—TAXES, LICENSES AND FEES (EXCLUDING FEDERAL INCOME TAXES)

	INSURANCE		INVESTMENT	TOTAL
	LIFE (1)	ACCIDENT AND HEALTH (2)	(3)	(4)
1. Real estate taxes				
2. State insurance department licenses and fees . . .				
3. State taxes on premiums				
4. Other state taxes, incl. $_____ Social Security				
5. U. S. Social Security taxes				
6. All other taxes				
7. TAXES, LICENSES AND FEES PAID				
8. Taxes, licenses and fees unpaid December 31, current year.				(To Line 28.1, Exhibit 12)
9. Taxes, licenses and fees unpaid December 31, previous year				
10. Taxes, licenses and fees incurred during year (7+8—9). .				
	(To Item 24, Page 4)		(To Line 3, Exhibit 2)	

NOTE: Canadian and other foreign taxes are included appropriately in Lines 1, 2, 3, 4 and 6.

allocated to lines of business in proportion to the salaries paid to subordinate employees in each line.

Rent is generally charged to a department, first on the basis of the amount of space occupied and then allocated to line of business in the same proportion as salaries paid are allocated. Many expenses, such as telephone, postage, etc., can be charged to departments on the basis of actual usage and then allocated by line of business on a salary basis or by a special study. Certain indices, such as premium volume, number of policies in force, or amount of insurance in force, are used as a basis of allocation only if no better method is available.

The direct cost of entering a new line of business is normally charged entirely to that line, even though expenses are incurred before any premium income is realized.

The U.S. Annual Statement instructions provide:

> Each company shall employ those principles and methods that will reasonably reflect the actual incidence of cost by line of business. The relative time spent, the extent of usage and the varying volume of work performed for each line of business shall be considered in distributing cost to major lines of business and, to the extent practicable, to secondary lines.[2] The costs of any unit of activity in performing work for one line of business and only incidentally for other lines may be allocated entirely to the single line of business.

The instructions also suggest methods that may be used to allocate each expense and tax item. These methods are of importance to the insurance accountant but they are, generally, outside the scope of this book.

TYPES OF EXPENSES

One or more accounts are maintained in the general ledger for each item in the expense exhibit (see Figures 19–3 and 19–4). Those expenses which are incurred in connection with service functions, operated as a convenience and not as a direct part of the insurance operations, are shown by function. Those shown by function include the cost of operating (1) a company-owned printing plant; (2) a lunch facility; (3) facilities for employees such as infirmary, recreation club, etc.; and (4) real estate. For example, salaries, rent, and other expenses of operating a print shop are shown as *Printing and Stationery*.

Expenses as shown in the Annual Statement expense exhibits may be divided into several broad categories: (1) rents; (2) salaries, wages, and allowances; (3) employees' and agents' welfare; (4) professional service fees and expenses; (5) investment expenses; and (6) miscellaneous expenses.

---

[2] Secondary lines refers to subline classifications as used in this book.

Rent

Rent expense includes all rent paid by the company for home office and branch office space and the cost of utilities and building maintenance. If a company owns its own home office and branch office buildings, a reasonable rent amount for this space must be included here. Rent for the advertising, legal, and medical departments are included in the *rent* item because these services are essential to operating an insurance company. Rent for cafeteria and other functionally reported expenses are included elsewhere. A separate ledger account is usually maintained for branch office rent because this information must be shown as a footnote to the U.S. expense exhibit.[3]

Salaries and Wages

This item covers all direct salaries paid in connection with insurance and investment functions. It also includes fees and other compensation paid to directors, agency compensation other than commissions, and salaries paid in advertising, legal, and medical departments. Separate ledger accounts are usually maintained for salaries paid to agents and salaries paid for agency supervision, other than those paid to home office supervisors. This data must be shown in a footnote to the U.S. expense exhibit.

Employee Benefits

There are five categories of employee benefits: (1) contributions for benefit plans for employees, (2) contributions for benefit plans for agents, (3) payments for employees under nonfunded benefit programs, (4) payment for agents under nonfunded benefit programs, and (5) other employee and agent welfare.

The first two items include contributions paid by the company toward permanent plans, such as pension, total and permanent disability benefits, group insurance benefits, medical, surgical, or other self-administered or trusteed plans under which benefits are payable to the employees on a systematic basis. The word *plan* in this instance means a formal contract which sets out the benefits payable. If the company makes payments either to active employees or retired employees directly from company funds without benefit of a formal plan, these payments are shown as *payments to employees* (or agents) *under nonfunded benefit programs.*[4]

---

[3] A separate line is provided in the Canadian exhibit.

[4] The Canadian expense exhibit does not require separation by funded and non-funded plans. There is one item called *contributions to pension and insurance plans for employees,* and a similar item for *agents.*

Figure 19–4. Canadian Expense Exhibit

....
(Name of Company)

....
(Year of Statement)

13

EXHIBIT 9—GENERAL AND INVESTMENT EXPENSES

	Incurred during year (1)	Due and accrued at end of year (2)	Amount incurred charged as investment expenses (3)
	$	$	$
Rent			
1. Head office rents			
2. Branch office rents			
3.			
4. Total rent			
Salaries, Wages, and Allowances			
5. Head office employees salaries and wages			
6. Branch office employees salaries and wages			
7. Managers and agents salaries			
8. Directors fees			
9. Agents expense allowances			
10. Advances to agents			
11.			
12. Total salaries, wages, and allowances			
Employees and Agents Welfare			
13. Contributions to pension and insurance plans for employees			
14. Contributions to pension and insurance plans for agents			
15. Unemployment insurance contributions			
16. Cafeteria expenses			
17.			
18.			
19.			
20.			
21. Total employees and agents welfare			

Professional and Service Fees and Expenses

22. Legal fees and expenses.
23. Medical examination fees.
24. Inspection report fees.
25. Auditors fees.
26.

27.   Total professional and service fees and expenses.

Miscellaneous Expenses

28. Advertising.
29. Agency conventions.
30. Books and periodicals.
31. Bureau and association dues.
32. Collection and bank charges.
33. Commissions on mortgages.
34. Custody of securities.
35. Insurance, except on real estate.
36. Postage, telegraph, telephone, express.
37. Printing and stationery.
38. Office furniture.
39. Rental of equipment.
40. Travelling expenses, head office.
41. Travelling expenses, branch office.
42.
43.
44.
45.
46.
47.
48.

49.   Total miscellaneous expenses.

Real Estate Expenses, excluding Taxes

50.
51.
52.

53.   Total real estate expenses, excluding taxes.

54.   Grand totals.

55. Less investment expenses.

56.   Total general expenses (i.e., excluding investment expenses).

Other employee and agent welfare covers the cost of meals to employees,[5] contributions by the company to employee associations or clubs, expense and maintenance of recreation grounds, payments to employees and agents in military service, and the expense of periodical medical or dental examinations and other medical dispensary, convalescent home, or sanitarium treatment for employees or agents. Rent, salaries, and other expenses paid in connection with a lunch facility, infirmary, and other employee benefits are included in this item.

Meal and cafeteria expense for employees is included on a net cost basis (expenses less income) and is usually shown on a separate fill-in line if the amount is large. A separate set of books may be established for the operation of a cafeteria or lunch room or several accounts may be maintained in the general ledger relative to its operation.

Professional Service Fees and Expenses

This group of items includes (1) legal fees and expenses, (2) medical examination fees, (3) inspection report fees, (4) fees of public accountants and consulting actuaries, and (5) expense of investigating and settling policy claims. *Salaries* paid to lawyers, doctors, accountants, and actuaries for any of these services are included with salaries.

Legal fees and expenses includes court costs, penalties, and all fees or retainers for legal services or expenses in connection with matters before administrative or legislative bodies, and any other outside legal expense incurred. It does not include legal salaries, legal expenses for settling policy claims, and legal expenses incurred in connection with real estate transactions where the fees are included in the cost of such investments. These items are, of course, included elsewhere.

Medical examination fees includes amounts paid to medical examiners in connection with new business, reinstatements, policy changes, and applications for employment. Fees paid to doctors for "welfare" of agents and employees are included elsewhere.

Inspection report fees includes all fees paid for inspection reports, whether obtained in connection with new business, reinstatements, policy changes, or applications for employment, and includes any services furnished by impairment bureaus. Assessments by or membership dues in impairment bureaus and inspection reports for investigation of policy claims are included elsewhere.

Fees of public accountants and consulting actuaries covers only payments to independent professional practitioners for services to the company on a fee basis. It does not include fees charged by state insurance departments. These are properly shown under the *tax* category.

---

[5] The Canadian exhibit has a separate *cafeteria expense* item. Other staff benefits paid under other than a contractual plan are shown on a fill-in line.

Expense of investigation and settlement of policy claims includes investigation and settlement costs, both legal and nonlegal, paid to persons other than company employees in connection with claims.

Miscellaneous Expenses

The items discussed in the following paragraphs do not fall into broad categories and are, therefore, classed as miscellaneous expenses.

Traveling expenses, one of the principal items in the miscellaneous category, covers travel expense of all salaried employees and agents. These expenses include rooms, meals, transportation, cost of telephone, telegraph, and postage charges incurred while traveling, amounts allowed employees for the use of their own cars on company business, and maintenance, depreciation, and operating expenses of company-owned automobiles. Cost of travel of home office employees going to agency conferences at company expense is included elsewhere. There are usually a number of travel expense accounts in the general ledger, all of which are summarized into a single item in the expense exhibit with the amount of branch office travel shown in a footnote.

Advertising covers all types of outside advertising, such as radio, newspaper, television and billboards, and the cost of all promotional materials such as calendars, blotters, wallets, advertising novelties, prospective mailing lists, and fees and expenses for advertising agencies. Advertising does not include the cost of educational materials, which may be promotional in effect, help wanted advertising, advertising in connection with investments, or salaries and expenses of the advertising department.

Advertising required by law, regulation, or governmental ruling is not normally included. This type of advertising is treated as a tax item. However, if the advertisement is considerably more expensive than that required by law, the excess cost is included in advertising.

Postage, express, telegraph, and telephone is self-explanatory. It includes the direct cost of the types of services named.

Printing and stationery includes cost of printing policy forms, home office and branch office forms, educational pamphlets, and the annual report to policyowners and stockholders. It does not include the cost of printing promotional and advertising material. If the company operates a printing department, the cost of printing department salaries and rent, heat, lights, printing supplies, depreciation of printing equipment, and any other costs of the department are included here.

Cost or depreciation of furniture and equipment[6] includes the purchase price of equipment if the cost is treated as an expense item. Otherwise,

---

[6] In the Canadian statement the equivalent item is *office furniture*. The cost of furniture and equipment is shown as an expense here in the year of purchase.

this item includes only one year's charge for depreciation. Depreciation of equipment used in maintenance of the home office building is not included here but is included with real estate expenses. Depreciation of printing equipment, cafeteria equipment, and company-owned automobiles also are included elsewhere.

Rental of equipment covers the rental cost of data processing equipment. Insurance companies rarely rent other types of equipment if it can be purchased.

Books and periodicals covers the cost of books and subscriptions for periodicals and the cost of legal, tax, and other informational services.

Bureau and association dues includes dues of associations to which the company belongs and dues paid for employees or agents in insurance and professional organizations. It does not include contributions for scientific, disease prevention, or other activity directly pertaining to the welfare of policyowners and the public. These latter items are shown on a fill-in line as *gifts and donations* or included with *sundry general expenses*.

Insurance, except on real estate includes all premiums paid for casualty insurance except life reinsurance and premiums paid in connection with real estate; the latter are included under *real estate expenses*.

Miscellaneous losses would include losses which are uninsured by casualty and workmens' compensation policies.

Collection and bank service charges covers collection charges made by banks and deducted from the amount of checks and drafts deposited by the company. Foreign exchange losses on funds transferred in or out of the country are not included here.

Sundry general expenses is a consolidated total of a number of the lesser ledger expense account balances which may include not only general expenses but many miscellaneous insurance and agency expenses as well. The U.S. Annual Statement instructions provide that *sundry general expenses* shall include direct expense of local agency meetings, luncheons, and dinners; tabulating service rendered by outside organizations;[7] expense allowances on reinsurance assumed (except for any portion representing commissions and premium taxes); and amounts paid to other insurers for expenses of jointly underwritten group contracts. Other expenses which are properly included in *sundry general expenses* are stockholders' expenses paid other than to a company employee, employment fees, and fees paid to management consultants.

In the U.S. Statement this item must not include any individual expense which represents more than 25 percent of the total. Any individual expense items in excess of 25 percent are shown under a specific subheading. For example, if these general expense items total $100,000 and gifts and donations represent $26,000 of this amount, then *gifts and donations* is shown as a separate item, and *sundry general expenses* is shown as $74,000.

---

[7] In the Canadian expense exhibit this is included with *rental of equipment*.

Group Service and Administration Fees

It will be recalled that some group insurance policyowners are self-billing and also pay claims. A company may allow an employer a small reduction in premiums for rendering such service. The amount allowed in such a case is debited to an expense account, the balance of which is included in group service and administration fees. This item does not include commissions paid to agents or brokers in connection with servicing group insurance.

Agency Conferences Other Than Local Meetings

Most life insurance companies conduct agency conferences, both for the training of the agency forces and also as a reward for outstanding production. Cost of banquets and meals, rental of meeting room, hotel expense, and travel expense of personnel attending the meetings are included in this item. Expenses of home office representatives, whose expenses would be normally charged to an agency or home office travel expense account, are included here when the travel relates to an agency conference.

Agency Expense Allowance

When a new general agency or a branch office is established, the company frequently provides a specific allowance for the purchase of furniture in the branch office, for office rent, utilities, and other expenses over and above commissions or salaries to be paid to employees. All such expenditures are included in the item, *agency expense allowance.*[8]

Agents' Balances Charged Off

This item was discussed in an earlier section of this chapter.

Real Estate Expenses

There is a single line in the expense exhibit for real estate expenses. This is a functional expense item and includes servicing costs of all real estate owned, including the home office building. Included are salaries paid to employees who service and rent such properties, legal fees, cost of repairs, maintenance service, and any other real estate cost except taxes.

The purpose of this item is to permit calculation of the net earnings from real estate separately from the earnings on other investments.

---

[8] This item and *advances to agents* are included under a section entitled salaries, wages, and allowances in the Canadian expense exhibit.

Knowledge of the extent of these earnings is useful to investment managers because real estate is generally more expensive to service than other investments. Separate accounts are usually maintained on the ledger for each type of real estate cost. Care is necessary in connection with allocating real estate expenses because a portion of the salaries of people servicing other investments may also be chargeable to real estate.

Investment Expenses Not Included Elsewhere

This item covers all investment costs not specifically included elsewhere, such as: fees paid to nonsalaried investment counsel, fees paid to custodian of securities, and fees paid to trustees other than those paid in connection with real estate.

TAXES, LICENSES, AND FEES

The titles to the various lines of U.S. and Canadian tax exhibits may be seen by examining Figures 19–4 and 19–5.

Real estate taxes includes primarily those taxes directly assessed against property owned. A portion of social security taxes on employees who service real estate should be included to be consistent with the manner of handling *real estate expenses* as a functional item.

State insurance department licenses and fees includes any annual license fees paid for the company and for any of the agents of the company. It also includes the cost of examination by state insurance departments.

State taxes on premiums includes premium taxes and any state taxes based on policy reserves if these are in lieu of premium taxes. Any adjustments for premium taxes allowed on reinsurance ceded or assumed is deducted to show the net cost for premium taxes.

Other state taxes, including social security, includes taxes paid to the state in connection with the Unemployment Compensation Act and assessments of state industrial or other boards for operating expenses and benefits to sick or unemployed persons. Also included in this item are advertising required by law, regulation, or ruling (except in connection with investments), and state sales taxes, if the company segregates sales taxes from the cost of purchases.

No line is included in the U.S. tax exhibit for federal income tax because this tax is shown elsewhere. Any portion of the tax that results from capital gains is deducted from realized capital gains in the capital gain and loss exhibit. The remainder is shown as a special deduction in the summary of operations where operating gains (net income) is shown both before and after federal income taxes. Since liability for income tax attaches to the year just completed, it must be determined after all other portions of the summary of operations have been completed.

U.S. social security taxes includes taxes paid in connection with FICA provisions and the federal unemployment compensation excise tax.[9] Another line in the tax exhibit covers all other taxes, including taxes paid other governments, municipal license taxes, municipal sales taxes, and any licenses or taxes not otherwise classified. There is no line for reporting federal withholding taxes on employee wages because these amounts are liabilities. The same reasoning applies to any amount of the FICA tax deducted from employees' salaries and held by the company. However, the additional FICA tax paid by the company is a tax to the company.

Liabilities for Expenses and Taxes

There may be a liability at the end of the year for virtually every one of the items in the expense and tax exhibits. These items are inventoried separately and included in one grand total at the bottom of the proper exhibit of the U.S. Statement.[10] When the cash basis total is adjusted for the liabilities at the beginning and the end of the year, the result is the incurred total.

CANADIAN ANNUAL STATEMENT ASPECTS

The expense exhibit of the Canadian Statement is Exhibit 9 and is entitled, *general and investment expenses.* (See Figure 19–4.) The items are almost identical to those in the expense exhibit of the U.S. Statement, except that there are a few additional items which include (1) advances to agents, (2) directors' fees, (3) cafeteria expenses, (4) auditors' fees, (5) commissions on mortgages, and (6) custody of securities. These items have been discussed or are largely self-explanatory. The last item covers fees of depositories in which securities are placed for safekeeping and related trustee fees.

The tax exhibit is No. 10. (See Figure 19–5.) There is a separate item for reporting the cost of governmental supervision and examination, itemized into "Dominion, Provincial, and Other." As can be seen from column captions, all items in the two exhibits are shown on an incurred (accrual) basis rather than a cash basis. The first column is a total column and shows the combined incurred insurance and investment amounts. The second column shows the composite liability at the end of the year for each item. The third column shows investment amounts included in the first column.

Since health insurance income and expenses are not included in the

---

[9] In Canada, unemployment insurance contributions assessed by governmental authority are included in the expense exhibit instead of the tax exhibit.

[10] In the Canadian expense and tax exhibits the liability for each type of expense item at the end of the current year is shown in a separate column.

14

Figure 19–5. Canadian Tax Exhibit

....
(Name of Company)

....
(Year of Statement)

EXHIBIT 10—TAXES, LICENCES, AND FEES

	Incurred during year (1) $	Due and accrued at end of year (2) $	Amount incurred charged as investment taxes (3) $
1. Premium taxes: (1) Provincial			
(2) Other			
Total premium taxes			
2. Income taxes: (1) Dominion			
(2) Provincial			
(3) Other			
Total income taxes			
3. Supervision and examination: (1) Dominion			
(2) Provincial			
(3) Other			
Total supervision and examination			
4. Licences and fees: (1) Provincial			
(2) Other			
Total licences and fees			
5. Real estate taxes			
6. Other taxes			
7. Grand totals			
8. Less investment taxes			
9. Total taxes, licences, and fees, excluding investment taxes			

statement, there is no column for this purpose. Similar expense items are shown for health insurance in the casualty blank. Amounts incurred by line of business are determined on working papers and allocated to each line in the *analysis of revenue account by line of business.*

SUMMARY OF EXPENSE ACCOUNTING FUNDAMENTALS

Type of expense refers to the nature of an expense, such as salaries, rent, etc.

Responsibility reports are reports of expenses incurred in an operating unit under the supervision of one individual. *Budgets* are a form of responsibility report, and budget reports compare actual expenses to estimates of expenses.

Interim statements are operating statements which include income as well as costs and which are prepared at times other than at the end of the accounting period. The figures may be for one responsibility area, for a broad operational area, or for the whole company. Assets and liabilities may also be included.

In an accounting sense, a *function* is an activity performed for a specific purpose. Examples are selling policies and underwriting. *Functional unit cost* is the cost of performing one measurable unit of work in a functional cost center or area.

QUESTIONS

1. Why is control of expenses more important than control of other operating statement items? Why are many officers and employees given authority for authorizing expenditures? What methods can be used to provide management control of expenses?
2. What office forms are used for authorizing disbursements? Why is an approved invoice preferable to other methods of authorizing expenditures for supplies? Why are special records required in connection with purchases? What forms are used by a typical purchasing department and a typical vendor?
3. Why are salary entries always composite entries? Why might a company desire to use a large number of salary accounts? Why might a company use separate overtime accounts?
4. Compare the advantages of the expense and asset methods of accounting for supplies and fixed assets. What is the effect on surplus in the year of purchase under each method when the cost of furniture purchased is $1,000? What is the effect on operating gains in that year under each method if depreciation cost for tax purposes is $50?
5. Why is it usually necessary to finance new agents? Under what

conditions are loans to agents usually repaid? Under what conditions are they charged off as an expense?

6. What are the three types of expense liability? Give examples of each. How are prepaid expenses handled in preparing balance sheets and operating statements? Why?

7. What is meant by type of expense, responsibility area, and function? Why might a company desire to prepare a summary of expenses under each of these general classifications?

8. Describe several types of responsibility reports. Which is most effective in controlling expenses. Why?

9. What are the principal characteristics of a budget report? Why is a budget officer necessary for effectively administering a budget? When should a budget be adjusted? Under what condition might several budgets be consolidated into a single budget for a broad area of responsibility?

10. Define *function* and give several examples of insurance functions. What are three ways functional costs may be used? What might comparison of functional costs with those of other companies indicate?

11. What three processes might a company use to allocate expenses by line of business? Why might it be undesirable to use premium income as a basis for allocation? When might this method be satisfactory? Why is it simpler to allocate expenses to the investment department?

12. What are several items shown in annual statements on a functional basis? What do most of these items have in common? How are salaries paid to doctors and lawyers shown in the expense exhibit? How are fees paid to doctors and lawyers in connection with settlement of claims shown?

13. Which of the following items are included as advertising in the expense exhibit? (*a*) educational pamphlets, (*b*) balance sheets published in newspapers when required by law, (*c*) general newspaper advertising, (*d*) salary of the director of advertising, (*e*) fees paid to an advertising agency, (*f*) pencils carrying the company's imprint, and (*g*) sales brochures used by agents.

U.S. Students Only

14. Where are income taxes shown in the U.S. Annual Statement? Name several other taxes a life company must pay.

Canadian Students Only

15. Where are income taxes shown in the Canadian Annual Statement? Name several other taxes a life insurance company must pay.

PROBLEM

1. Using the salary report shown on page 389 and the costs and other data listed below determine the unit cost of collecting a renewal life insurance premium. Assume that there are no departments in the company other than those shown in connection with the following salary list:

a) Depreciation of equipment—renewal ordinary, $10,000.
b) Depreciation of equipment—computer department, $25,000.
c) Printing and stationery—renewal ordinary, $5,000.
d) Employee benefits—all departments, $63,000.
e) Postage—renewal ordinary, $650.
f) Rent—all departments, $31,500.
g) Ten percent of computer time was used preparing notices and processing 200,000 premium payments.

2. Make entries as follows:

a) Salary paid $200, less deductions of $20 for income tax withholding, group insurance premium of $12, and FICA tax of $10.
b) Group insurance premium of $1,000 paid. One fourth of this amount is in a liability account as a result of payroll deductions.
c) Agent's debit balance of $50 is charged off.

Chapter 20

Special U.S. Annual Statement Exhibits and Reports

There are several exhibits in the U.S. Annual Statement of a type which do not appear in the Canadian Annual Statement. These exhibits, the analysis of operations by line of business, and several "wrap-up" phases of the U.S. Annual Statement are presented in this chapter.

ASSET EXHIBIT (EXHIBIT 13)

This exhibit was introduced in Chapter 8 and is simply titled "assets." Its purpose is to eliminate a need that would otherwise exist for making bookkeeping entries to adjust book values of assets to admitted values for balance sheet purposes. The use of an exhibit in lieu of entries permits retaining either the cost or amortized value of investments on the ledger. This cost or value is required to calculate realized capital gains or losses when invested assets are sold. The asset exhibit is coordinated with the reconciliation of ledger assets which is discussed in the next section of this chapter. The fourth column heading in the asset exhibit is *Net Admitted Assets*, but the word *net* is not used in this chapter because *admitted assets* alone is adequate.

The items in this asset exhibit and the amounts in its Admitted Assets column are the same as those shown on the asset page of the balance sheet, except for one figure. The exception is an insert amount on the balance sheet asset page described as "cash and invested assets $_____ (Items 1–10)." This insert amount is used to calculate the net rate of investment income earned on cash and invested assets. Cash is included since it is available for investment.

The process for arriving at the amount of admitted assets can be expressed in the form of an equation: Ledger Assets + Non-Ledger Assets − Assets Not Admitted = Admitted Assets. This process can be demonstrated by use of two simple examples.

Assume that two blocks of stock are carried on the ledger at $1,000 each and that the first block of stock had a market value of $1,500 and the second block had a market value of $10 at the end of the year. Assume also that the market value is the admitted value.

The $2,000 book value for the two items is entered on a single line in the Ledger Assets column of the asset exhibit. The $500 excess of market over book value on the first block of stock is entered in the Non-Ledger Assets column. The $990 excess of book value over the $10 market value on the second block of stock is entered in the Assets Not Admitted column. The $1,510 result of the equation ($2,000 + $500 − $990) is entered in the Admitted Assets column.

Non-Ledger Assets

The following are the principal asset values which are entered in the Non-Ledger Assets column of the asset exhibit.

1. Excess of market over book value of bonds not eligible for amortization
2. Excess of market over book value of common stocks
3. Due and accrued investment income
4. Amounts recoverable from reinsurers
5. Premiums and annuity considerations deferred and uncollected

All but "4" has been adequately discussed earlier.

Amounts recoverable from reinsurers includes amounts due on claims which have been paid. Amounts that will become due from a reinsurer when a pending claim is settled are not shown here but are deducted from the liability for unpaid claims in the appropriate claim exhibit.

Life insurance premiums and annuity considerations deferred and un-collected are entered in the Non-Ledger Assets column on a net premium basis. Note in Figure 20–1 that the loading deducted from the gross deferred and uncollected premiums is shown in the item description column. The gross amount of premiums and considerations deferred and uncollected can be reconstructed by adding the loading to the net premium amount. It will be recalled that the gross amount appears in the premium exhibit.

Due premiums on health insurance are shown on a gross premium basis. There are no deferred premiums for this type of insurance.

Figure 20–1. U.S. Asset Exhibit

ANNUAL STATEMENT FOR THE YEAR 1968

Form 1

Except for Items 25A and 26, the figures on this page do not include Separate Account items, if any.

OF THE .... **COMPANY**

(Write or stamp name of Company)

14

EXHIBIT 13—ASSETS

	Ledger Assets (1)	Non-Ledger Assets (2)	Assets Not Admitted (3)	Net Admitted Assets (4)
1. Bonds				
2. Stocks:				
2.1 Preferred stocks				
2.2 Common stocks				
3. Mortgage loans on real estate:				
3.1 First liens				
3.2 Other than first liens . . .				
4. Real estate (less $_____ encumbrances):				
4.1 Properties occupied by the company . .				
4.2 Properties acquired in satisfaction of debt				
4.3 Investment real estate				
5. Policy loans				
6. Premium notes (including $_____ for first year premiums)				
7. Collateral loans				
8. Cash and bank deposits:				
8.1 Cash in company's office				
8.2 Deposits in banks and trust companies (Schedule E)				
9. Other invested assets				
10. Amounts recoverable from reinsurers . . .				
11. Agents' balances (debit $_____ credit $_____)				
12. Other assets (give items and amounts):				
12.1				
12.2 Bills receivable				Ø
12.3 Furniture and equipment				Ø
12.4 Cash advanced to or in hands of officers or agents				Ø
12.5 Loans on personal security, endorsed or not . .				Ø
12.6				Ø

13.

14.

15.

16.

17. Life insurance premiums and annuity considerations deferred and uncollected on in force Dec. 31st of current year (less premiums on reinsurance ceded):

   17.1 Industrial uncollected (excluding $............ loading) . . . . . .

   17.2 Ordinary deferred and uncollected—New business (excluding $............ loading) . . . .

   17.3 Ordinary deferred and uncollected—Renewal (excluding $............ loading) . . . .

   17.4 Group life deferred and uncollected (excluding $............ loading) . . . .

   17.5 Group annuity deferred and uncollected (excluding $............ loading) . . . .

   17.6   Total (to Col. 2) . . . . . .

18. Accident and health premiums due and unpaid . . . . . .

19. Investment income due and accrued . . . . . .

20. Net adjustment in assets and liabilities due to foreign exchange rates . . . .

21.

22.

23.

24.

25.

25A. Separate Account Business (see Separate Account Statement)

26.   Totals . . . .

Figure 20-2. U.S. Annual Statement Liability Page

ANNUAL STATEMENT FOR THE YEAR 1968

Form 1
Except for Items 28A, 26, 27, 29, 30 and 31, the
figures on this page do not include Separate
Account items. (See page ___)

OF THE _____ COMPANY

(Write or stamp name of Company)

LIABILITIES, SURPLUS AND OTHER FUNDS

	DOLLARS	CENTS
1. Aggregate reserve for life policies and contracts (Exhibit 8)		
2. Aggregate reserve for accident and health policies (Exhibit 9)		
3. Supplementary contracts without life contingencies (Exhibit 10, Col. 5)		
4. Policy and contract claims (Exhibit 11, Part 1)		
4.1 Life		
4.2 Accident and Health		
5. Policyholders' dividend accumulations (Exhibit 10, Col. 6)		
6. Policyholders' dividends due and unpaid		
7. Provision for policyholders' dividends payable in following calendar year—estimated amounts:		
7.1 Apportioned for payment to _____, 19___ . . . . $		
7.2 Not yet apportioned		
8. Amount provisionally held for deferred dividend policies not included in Item 7		
9. Premiums and annuity considerations received in advance less $ _____ discount; including $ _____ accident and health premiums		
10. Liability for premium deposit funds		
11. Policy and contract liabilities not included elsewhere:		
11.1 Surrender values on cancelled policies		
11.2 Provision for experience rating refunds		
11.3 _____		
12. _____		
13. Commissions to agents due or accrued—Life and Annuity $ _____ Accident and Health $ _____		
14. General expenses due or accrued (Exhibit 5, Line 11)		
15. Taxes, licenses and fees due or accrued, excluding federal income taxes (Exhibit 6, Line 8)		
15A. Federal income taxes due or accrued (including $ _____ on capital gains)		

16. "Cost of collection" on premiums and annuity considerations deferred and uncollected in excess of total
loading thereon . . . .

17. Unearned investment income (Exhibit 3, Col. 2) . . . .

18. Amounts withheld or retained by company as agent or trustee . . . .

19. Amounts held for agents' account (including $................ agents' credit balances) . . . .

20. Remittances and items not allocated . . . .

21. Net adjustment in assets and liabilities due to foreign exchange rates . . . .

22. Liability for benefits for employees and agents if not included above . . . .

23. Borrowed money $................ and interest thereon $................ . . . .

24. Dividends to stockholders declared and unpaid . . . .

25. Miscellaneous liabilities (give items and amounts)

    25.1 Mandatory securities valuation reserve . . . .

    25.2 . . . .

    25.3 . . . .

    25.4 . . . .

    25.5 . . . .

    25.6 . . . .

    25.7 . . . .

    25.8 . . . .

    25.9 . . . .

25A. Separate Account Business (see Separate Account Statement) . . . .

26.   TOTAL LIABILITIES (Except Capital) . . . .

27. Special surplus funds:

    27.1 . . . . $................

    27.2 . . . .

    27.3 . . . . $................

28. Capital paid-up . . . . $................

29A. Gross paid in and contributed surplus . . . . $................

29B. Unassigned surplus . . . .

29C. Total of Items 29A and 29B . . . .

30. Total of Items 27, 28 and 29C . . . .

31.   TOTAL . . . .

Assets Not Admitted

Not admitted values in connection with investments have been discussed in Chapters 10 and 11. Other not admitted items are discussed in connection with an exhibit covering the change in not admitted assets (Exhibit 14) which is presented in a later section of this chapter.

Item 25A on the asset page refers to *separate account business.* This line and line 25A on the liability page are used by companies selling variable annuities and other business where assets and related income are accounted for separately from insurance assets and income. These lines are used to incorporate the assets and liabilities of the separate accounts into the company balance sheet.

LIABILITIES

Most of the items on the liability page (see Figure 20–2) are nonledger liabilities which have already been discussed. It is suggested that the student examine Figure 20–2 and then review Chapter 9 and the various U.S. Statement supplements with reference to any item which may not be clearly understood.

Item 21, *net adjustment in assets and liabilities due to foreign exchange rates,* is used only by companies doing foreign business. Values of foreign money in terms of U.S. money change from time to time. Use of this item permits an overall adjustment to show equivalent U.S. values without the need for special bookkeeping entries.

RECONCILIATION OF LEDGER ASSETS (EXHIBIT 12)

This exhibit virtually forces the use of cash basis accounting by U.S. life insurance companies. Although this exhibit is not very useful from a management viewpoint, it does serve an audit function for supervisory authorities. Other purposes are (1) to provide an audit trail from the cash basis figures in the trial balance to the cash basis figures used in the various exhibits and (2) to prove that all figures in the trial balance (except the balance account) have been entered either as a receipt or as a disbursement in this exhibit, or as a ledger asset in the asset exhibit.

The formula used in the reconciliation of ledger assets can be expressed in the form of a reconciliation equation: *Ledger assets* at the beginning of the year, plus *receipts*, less *disbursements*, equals *ledger assets* at the end of the year.

The phrase *increases in ledger assets* is used in this exhibit rather than the word *receipts*. The phrase *decreases in ledger assets* is used rather than the word *disbursements*. An early version of the Annual Statement (prior to 1951) used the words *income* and *disbursements*. The word *income* in commercial accounting normally implies an accrual basis concept, and the word was deemed inappropriate in connection with this exhibit. The words *receipts* and *disbursements* are, in fact, more descriptive of the nature of these items in a life insurance company (see Figure 20–3). As used in this equation, *receipts* means (1) cash basis income (including realized capital gains), (2) increases in *book* value of assets, and (3) increases in *ledger* liabilities. *Disbursements* means (1) cash basis costs (including realized capital losses), (2) decreases in *book* value of assets, and (3) decreases in *ledger* liabilities.

It should be noted that increases in ledger liabilities and increases in book value of ledger assets are treated as receipts, and decreases in ledger liabilities and decreases in book value of ledger assets are treated as disbursements. This is consistent with the nonledger liability concept discussed in Chapter 17 in connection with deposits. Several example entries will clarify this effect.

If book value of bonds is written up by $1,000, the entry is:

Bonds Owned...	1,000.00	
Increase in Book Value of Bonds......................		1,000.00

The credit portion of the entry is obviously a surplus increase item which also reflects an increase in ledger assets. It must be included in the reconciliation equation to show increase in ledger assets.

If $1,000 is received to be placed on deposit for the payment of future premiums, the entry is:

Cash...	1,000.00	
Premium Deposits.....................................		1,000.00

The credit in this case is to a ledger liability account. This credit is equal to the increase in Cash, which is a ledger asset. It is apparent, therefore, that an increase in a ledger liability also reflects an increase in ledger assets (Cash) and must be included as a receipt item in the reconciliation equation. It should be equally apparent that a decrease in a ledger liability reflects a decrease in a ledger asset and must be included as a disbursement item in the reconciliation.

Increases and decreases in ledger liabilities are usually summarized and entered in the reconciliation exhibit on a net increase or net decrease basis. This entry is made on a fill-in line because no line is included for this purpose.

All cash basis account balances from the trial balance other than asset account balances are consolidated into broad classification totals before being entered in this exhibit. Most of these totals are obtained from other exhibits.

The last section of the exhibit is headed *reconciliation between years.* In it, the difference between receipts and disbursements during the year is added to or subtracted from the total ledger assets at the beginning of the year thus arriving at the total of ledger assets at the end of the year. If

Figure 20–3

13

ANNUAL STATEMENT FOR THE YEAR 1968

Form 1 for Items 14A, 15, 27A and 38–41, the figures on this page do not include Separate Account Items, if any.

.... COMPANY
OF THE ....

(Write or stamp name of Company)

EXHIBIT 12—RECONCILIATION OF LEDGER ASSETS

INCREASES IN LEDGER ASSETS

	DOLLARS	CENTS
1. Premiums on life policies and annuity considerations (see Exhibit 1, Part 1)		
2. Accident and health cash premiums, including $............policy, membership and other fees		
3. Consideration for supplementary contracts with life contingencies		
4. Consideration for supplementary contracts without life contingencies including $............disability		
5. Dividends left with the Company to accumulate at interest		
6. Gross investment income (Exhibit 3, Col. 1, Line 10)		
7. Increase of paid-up capital during the year		
8. From other sources (give items and amounts):		
8.1		
8.2		
8.3		
9. Borrowed money gross $............, less amount repaid $............		
10.		
11.		
12.		
13. From sale or maturity of ledger assets (Exhibit 4, Column 2)		
14. By adjustment in book value of ledger assets (Exhibit 4, Column 1)		
14A. Separate Account Business (see Separate Account Statement)		
15. TOTAL INCREASES IN LEDGER ASSETS		

DECREASES IN LEDGER ASSETS

	DOLLARS	CENTS
16. Policy and contract claims (Exhibit 11, Part 2):		
16.1 Life		
16.2 Accident and health		
17. For annuities with life contingencies, excluding payments on supplementary contracts (including cash refund payments)		
18. Premium notes and liens voided by lapse, less $............restorations		
19. Surrender values		
19A. Group conversions		
19B. Interest on policy or contract funds		
20. Dividends to policyholders:		

20.1   Life insurance and annuities (Exhibit 7) . . . .

20.2   Accident and health (Exhibit 7) . . . .

21.   TOTAL PAID POLICYHOLDERS . . . .

22.   Paid for claims on supplementary contracts:

  22.1 With life contingencies . . . .

  22.2 Without life contingencies . . . .

23.   Dividends and interest thereon held on deposit disbursed during the year . . . .

24.   . . . .

25.   . . . .

26.   Commissions to agents (less commissions on reinsurance):

  26.1 Life insurance and annuities (including $..............commuted commissions) . . . .

  26.2 Accident and health (including $.............. commuted commissions)

  26.3 Policy, membership and other fees retained by agents . . . .

27.   General expenses (Exhibit 5, Line 10) . . . .

28.1   Taxes, licenses and fees, excluding federal income taxes (Exhibit 6, Line 7) . . . . .

28.2   Federal income taxes (including $.............. on capital gains) . . . . .

29.   Decrease of paid-up capital during the year . . . .

30.   Paid stockholders for dividends (cash $.............. stock $..............) . . . .

31.   Borrowed money repaid gross $.............. less amount borrowed $.............. . . . .

32.   Interest on borrowed money . . . .

33.   . . . .

34.   . . . .

35.   . . . .

36.   From sale or maturity of ledger assets (Exhibit 4, Column 4) . . . .

37.   By adjustment in book value of ledger assets (Exhibit 4, Column 3 and Exhibit 2, Line 4) . . . .

37A. Separate Account Business (see Separate Account Statement) . . . . . .

38.   TOTAL DECREASES IN LEDGER ASSETS . . . .

RECONCILIATION BETWEEN YEARS

39.   Amount of ledger assets December 31st of previous year . . . .

40.   Increase (+) or decrease (−) in ledger assets during the year (Line 15 minus Line 38) . . . .

41.   TOTAL = LEDGER ASSETS DECEMBER 31st OF CURRENT YEAR . . . . . .

total receipts are greater than total disbursements, the net increase (or difference) is added to the total ledger assets at the end of the previous year to obtain *ledger assets December 31 of current year.* If total disbursements are greater than receipts, the net decrease is subtracted.

Reconciliation Process

The reconciliation exhibit, as was mentioned earlier, has more or less forced companies to continue using cash basis accounting and to omit most liabilities from the ledger. The Balance account is partially a result of this unusual reconciliation. These facts can be more readily understood in the following illustrations. In the first illustration, it is assumed that no liabilities and no capital accounts are carried on the ledger.

Since only asset accounts are included in the ledger, it is necessary to establish a Balance account and record in it an amount equal to all ledger assets in order to start the year with the ledger in balance.

Assume that the beginning ledger asset total was $10,000 cash and the Balance account balance was, of course, $10,000. The following entries were made during the year:

(1)

Cash...	1,200.00	
Premium Income.....................................		1,200.00

(2)

Death Claim Paid......................................	1,000.00	
Cash...		1,000.00

(3)

Salaries Paid...	100.00	
Withholding Tax.....................................		10.00
Cash...		90.00

(4)

Cash...	5.00	
Premium Deposits Received...........................		5.00

After the entries are posted to the ledger, the trial balance would appear as follows:

			Account Classification
Cash........................	$10,115		LA
Death claim paid.................	1,000		D
Salaries paid....................	100		D
Premium income.................		$ 1,200	R
Withholding tax.................		10	R
Premium deposits received.........		5	R
Balance account.................		10,000	L
Total.....................	$11,215	$11,215	

Code Key
LA = ledger asset
D = *disbursement* in the reconciliation equation
R = *receipt* in the reconciliation equation
L = liability

If all receipts and all disbursements are consolidated into one amount each, the reconciliation equation reflects the following amounts (the subscript "0" in the term LA_0 represents the balance at the beginning of the year, and subscript "1" in LA_1 reflects the balance at the end of the year):

$$\$10,000\ (LA_0) + \$1,215\ (R) - \$1,100\ (D) = \$10,115\ (LA_1)$$

Note that the balance of the Balance account was ignored in the equation and did not change during the year.

Now, assume the same beginning asset amount and the same transactions, but that the Withholding Tax and Premium Deposit accounts are treated as ledger liabilities. The purpose of this illustration is to prove that reconciliation can be accomplished only by treating increases in ledger liabilities as receipts.

After the entries are posted, the trial balance appears exactly as before, but the $10 and $5 credit items are classified as liabilities instead of as *receipts* in the equation. If the receipts and disbursements are each consolidated into one amount and the liabilities ignored, the reconciliation equation is as follows:

$$\$10,000\ (LA_0) + \$1,200\ (R) - \$1,100\ (D) = \$10,100\ (LA_1)$$

Obviously reconciliation was not achieved because the equation indicates ledger assets are $10,100, not $10,115, the correct amount. Only by treating the increase in deposits ($5) and the increase in withholding tax ($10) as receipts, can reconciliation be accomplished. The reconciliation equation in Exhibit 12 provides control against overlooking items or incorrectly entering them in the statement blank.

Relationship of Balance Account to Reconciliation of Ledger Assets

The balance of the *Balance* account for the beginning of each year can be obtained by closing nominal accounts into the *Balance* account at the end of the previous year. To demonstrate, assume the withholding tax liability and premium deposit liability are carried as ledger liabilities and that all nominal account balances shown in the trial balance on page 424 are closed into the Balance account.

A compound entry is used to reduce the steps required. The entry is as follows:

Premium Income.	1,200	
Death Claim Paid.		1,000
Salaries Paid.		100
Balance Account.		100

The post-closing trial balance is:

Cash.	$10,115	
Premiums on deposit.		5
Withholding tax.		10
Balance account.		10,100

The $5 deposit liability and the $10 withholding tax liability remain on the ledger, and the accounting equation is in balance.

To determine the amount to be shown in the reconciliation in connection with ledger liability changes, the liabilities at the beginning of the year are deducted from the ledger liabilities at the end of the year. The increase in the illustration is $15 ($15 at end of year less 0 at beginning). This increase is shown in the equation as a receipt.

(Posting the above entries to T-accounts will assist the student in following the transactions. It might also be helpful to repeat the transactions in a second year starting from the balances at the end of he first year, and then prove the accuracy of the work by use of the reconciliation equation.)

Nothing is accomplished in a U.S. company by recording so-called nonledger and not admitted items in the ledger other than more nearly conforming to methods used in commercial accounting. The reconciliation equation in Exhibit 12 provides control against overlooking items or incorrectly entering them in the statement blank.

Description of Items in the Reconciliation of Ledger Assets

A comparison between items in the reconciliation of ledger assets with those in the summary of operations and analysis (page 434) shows that most of these items are very similar. The main differences are (1) amounts are shown on a cash basis in the reconciliation as opposed to an accrual basis in the summary and (2) all sources of surplus change reflected in account balances are included in the reconciliation, while only operating income and cost items are included in the summary of operations. Other differences include the following:

In the receipts section of the reconciliation, *dividends left with the company to accumulate at interest* is shown separately from *considerations for supplementary contracts without life contingencies . . . ,* whereas they are combined in the *summary*.

There is a line in the reconciliation, but not in the summary, for *increase of paid-up capital during the year*. This item is, in effect, an increase in a liability account (amounts owed to stockholders).

When a dividend is paid to stockholders in the form of additional shares of stock, a bookkeeping entry is made to reflect a dividend paid from the Surplus account and an offsetting income item to reflect an increase in capital stock outstanding. The entry is:

Dividend Paid Stockholders...xxxx
  Increase of Paid-Up Capital................................   xxxx

Since an increase in a liability account (or capital account) is treated as a receipt in the reconciliation, this *Increase* account balance is entered in the receipts section. The *dividend paid stockholders* account balance is, of course, entered in the disbursement section, thereby producing an off-setting effect.

In the receipts section there is also a line for profit *from sale or maturity of ledger assets* and for increases *by adjustment in book value of ledger assets.* These amounts are taken from ledger account balances and are nonoperating changes in surplus (capital gains).

In the disbursement section of the reconciliation, most policy benefit items are consolidated to a greater extent than in the summary of operations. *Premium notes and liens voided by lapse . . .* is an exception. It is a minor item and is shown as a separate item in the reconciliation. It is included with *surrenders* in the summary. Capital losses are also shown.

Lines are included in the reconciliation for *decrease of paid-up capital during the year* and *borrowed money repaid. . . . .* These represent decreases in liabilities.

ANALYSIS OF NONADMITTED ASSETS AND RELATED ITEMS (EXHIBIT 14)

This exhibit shows a recapitulation of increases and decreases in the book value of assets which are nonadmitted in total. These assets are those which are used in, or created through, insurance operations. No investments are included. The net increase or decrease from this exhibit is shown in the Surplus account of the Annual Statement blank as a direct change in surplus.

It will be recalled that changes in the admitted value of assets directly increase or decrease surplus. Similarly, changes in the book value during the year increase or decrease surplus at the end of the year when the book value is nonadmitted.

The effect on surplus of totally nonadmitting an asset can be demonstrated with a simple example. Assume that cash on hand is $3,000, there are no liabilities, surplus is $3,000, and furniture is purchased for $1,000. The entry to record the purchase is:

```
Furniture and Equipment.......................................1,000
    Cash.................................................        1,000
```

When this entry is posted, Cash is reduced by $1,000 to $2,000, the Furniture and Equipment account balance becomes $1,000, and Surplus account remains at $3,000. In the asset exhibit, the Furniture and Equipment balance is not admitted. This reduces surplus by the amount nonadmitted, since the accounting equation, $A = L + C$, must be in balance at all times. The balance sheet then shows assets of $2,000 and surplus of $2,000.

Items shown in this analysis may be divided into three general classes for discussion purposes: (1) prepaid expenses, (2) company's stock owned, and (3) loans and amounts receivable not adequately secured. These groups of items will be discussed in this order rather than in the order shown in this analysis (see Figure 20–4).

Prepaid Expenses

This covers items which may be treated either as insurance expenses or as nonadmitted assets. Included are furniture, equipment, inventories of supplies, and commuted commissions of sales agents.

If *furniture and equipment* is carried on the ledger as an asset, the full amount must be nonadmitted, and the resulting change in surplus is reflected in this exhibit. If purchases are treated as expenses, the cost is not shown in this exhibit.

The item *supplies, stationery, printed matter* is usually treated as an expense in the year of purchase. However, such expenses may be capitalized, in which case they are shown on a fill-in line of the asset exhibit (Exhibit 13). This amount must be nonadmitted, and the change in surplus from one year-end to the next is recorded in Exhibit 14.

Commuted commissions describes the present value of amounts paid to agents in lieu of commissions that would otherwise be payable in future years. Agents who terminate their services with a company are sometimes willing to sell their future commissions to the company at a substantial discount. This cost may be recorded as an asset and decreased annually to spread the commission cost over the years in which it would otherwise have been payable. The entry each year is a debit to a commission expense account and a credit to an asset account such as *Commuted Commissions*.

Company's Stock Owned

A life insurance company might purchase some of its own stock for various reasons, but the cost entered in the ledger as an asset must be nonadmitted. The reason for nonadmitting this item is based on the modified liquidation concept for valuing life insurance assets. In the event a company is liquidated, creditors, including policyowners, would have a prior right to the assets. Stockholders would be entitled to assets, only after all other obligations were settled. At that time stock of the company might have little or no value. The book value of this stock, therefore, must be nonadmitted and the resulting surplus change reflected in this exhibit.

Loans and Amounts Receivable Not Adequately Secured

Most miscellaneous assets of a life insurance company come under this general classification.

Figure 20-4

EXHIBIT 14—ANALYSIS OF NON-ADMITTED ASSETS AND RELATED ITEMS
(Excluding Investment Adjustments Not Listed)

	End of Previous Year (1)	End of Current Year (2)	Changes for Year Increase (−) or Decrease (+) (3)
27. Company's stock owned			X X X X
28. Loans on company's stock			
29. Supplies, stationery, printed matter . . .			
30. Furniture and equipment			
31. Commuted commissions			X X X X X
32. Agents' balances (net)			
33. Cash advanced to or in the hands of officers or agents.			
34. Loans on personal security endorsed or not . .			
35. Bills receivable			
36. Premium notes, etc., in excess of net value and other policy liabilities on individual policies			X X X X
37. Accident and health premiums due and unpaid . .			
38. Other assets not admitted (itemize)			
38.1 _____			
38.2 _____			
38.3 _____			
39. Agents' credit balances (Page 3, Item 19 inside) . .	X X X X	X X X X X	
40. Total Change (Col. 3)*	X X X X	X X X X X	

*(Carry to Item 40, Page 4 if (+), or to Item 47, Page 4 if (−))

Loans on company's stock represents loans made against the value of company stock. Because the value of the stock is not acceptable as an admitted asset, the loan is unsecured for balance sheet purposes and must be nonadmitted.

Agents' balances (net) describes the balance in the control account in the general ledger relating to individual accounts with agents. *Agents' credit balances* is also an item in this *analysis*. The change in control account balance and the change in credit balance equal the change in agents' debit balances. This effect was described in detail in Chapter 13.

Cash advanced to or in the hands of officers or agents represents amounts which the company has placed at the disposal of agents or officers for the purpose of carrying on necessary daily activities. An example is advances against travel expenses to be incurred by these persons. These advances are not sufficiently secured to be admitted assets.

Loans on personal security endorsed or not is a minor item because life insurance companies do not normally make loans on personal security. If these loans are made they must be nonadmitted.

Bills receivable represents small amounts due from outside sources. They are unsecured so they, also, are nonadmitted.

Premium notes, etc., in excess of net value and other policy liabilities on individual policies represents amounts receivable on notes given by a policyowner in payment of premiums. Some companies permit agents to accept notes in payment of premiums, and the company may agree to buy these notes from the agent under some conditions. When a note is taken in connection with a premium, it is usually for a premium in the first policy year when the policy has no cash value to support a policy loan. In cases where a premium note is secured by sufficient cash value in the policy, it is acceptable as an admitted asset. However, most such notes are not secured and must, therefore, be nonadmitted.

Accident and health premiums due and unpaid covers premiums that must be nonadmitted because of time limitations. For example, individual health premiums admitted are limited to one premium. All other due premiums and any due premium which became due prior to October 1 must be nonadmitted.

SURPLUS ACCOUNT

The so-called surplus account in the U.S. Annual Statement blank is in fact a reconciliation which shows the changes in surplus between one year-end and the next (see Figure 20–5).

The amounts in this reconciliation are presented in two columns. The surplus balance of the previous year and increases in surplus are entered in the first column. Decreases in surplus and the balance at the end of the current year are entered in the second. The totals of the two columns

Figure 20–5

SURPLUS ACCOUNT

	DOLLARS	CENTS		DOLLARS	CENTS
34. Special surplus funds December 31, previous year			43. Dividends to stockholders		
35A. Gross paid in and contributed surplus December 31, previous year			44.		
35B. Unassigned surplus December 31, previous year			44A.		
36.			44B.		
36A.			45. Net capital losses (Exhibit 4, Line 10.2)		
36B.			46. Increase in reserve on account of change in valuation basis		
37. Net gain (from Item 33)			47. Net loss from non-admitted and related items (Exhibit 14, Col. 3, Line 40)		
38. Net capital gains (Exhibit 4, Line 10.2)			48. Increase in mandatory securities valuation reserve		
39. Surplus paid in			48A. Decrease in surplus of Separate Account Business (see Separate Account Statement)		
40. Net gain from non-admitted and related items (Exhibit 14, Col. 3, Line 40)			49. Special surplus funds December 31, current year (Item 27, Page 3)		
41. Decrease in mandatory securities valuation reserve			50A. Gross paid in and contributed surplus December 31, current year (Item 29A, Page 3)		
41A. Increase in surplus of Separate Account Business (see Separate Account Statement)			50B. Unassigned surplus December 31, current year (Item 29B, Page 3)		
42. TOTAL			51. TOTAL		

must be equal to prove that all sources of surplus change have been included. A reconciliation form of this type was discussed in Chapter 15 in connection with a debit agent's account.

Each change item is shown on a net basis in this reconciliation. For example, if capital gains exceed capital losses, the difference is shown as an increase in surplus and the line for capital losses is left blank. If capital losses are greater, the difference is shown as a decrease in surplus.

All items in this reconciliation have been previously discussed. It is suggested that the student examine them and review pertinent discussions in previous chapters.

ANALYSIS OF OPERATIONS

The nature of the *analysis of operations by lines of business* and the method of allocating expenses and other costs for entry in this analysis have been discussed in earlier chapters. In the following discussion, this report will be referred to as the analysis, and the summary of operations will be referred to as the summary. This section is devoted to completing an examination of the structure of the analysis, including several items not previously discussed (see Figure 20–6).

The total column of the analysis is almost identical to the only column of the summary. The only difference between the two is that premiums on life insurance and health insurance are shown separately in the summary but are combined into one item in the analysis. Therefore, the student should assume that discussion of items in the analysis also applies to items in the summary unless otherwise noted.

Although this analysis includes all of the information shown in the summary, the latter is included in the Annual Statement blank for the convenience of individuals outside the life insurance business who are not interested in details by line of business. The many columns of the analysis can be confusing to one who has only a limited knowledge of life insurance.

Items in the analysis and summary are grouped by (1) income; (2) policy costs; (3) all other insurance costs, commissions, expenses, and transfers; (4) policy dividends; and (5) federal income taxes incurred. Policy costs include policy benefits paid to policyowners and reserve increases. A subtotal is shown on policy costs, and a final total is shown after deducting all other insurance costs, commissions, expenses, and transfers. Net gain is then determined before deducting dividends to policyowners. It is again determined after deducting these dividends, and finally determined after deducting federal income taxes incurred.

Column headings generally indicate the type of income and costs to be shown in each, but there are some elements of the supplementary contract income and cost items that warrant additional discussion.

Supplementary Contracts

There is a column (Column 7) in the analysis for supplementary contracts. Line titles which refer to supplementary contracts without life contingencies also refer to dividend accumulations. These accumulation amounts are entered in the column for the line of business under which the dividend originated, whereas income, costs, and reserve increases on supplementary contracts, both with and without life contingencies, are shown in the supplementary contract column.

It will be recalled that an entry is made on the books when a policy benefit payment is to be held by the company under a settlement contract. The debit entry is the same as that for a claim disbursement, but the credit is to a *Considerations for Supplementary Contracts,* an income account. This debit to an insurance cost account and credit to an income account constitutes a transfer of funds from the insurance line of business to a supplementary contract subline of business. The method described permits determining the gain or loss on supplemental contracts separately from those on life insurance contracts.

Among the insurance cost items of the *analysis,* there is one for increase in reserves on contracts with life contingencies. This describes the increase in both policy reserves and increase in supplementary contract reserves with life contingencies. The increase in policy reserves is entered in the column for the proper line of business, and the increase in supplementary contract reserves with life contingencies is entered in the supplementary contract column.

Insurance Cost and Expense Items

The nature of all items in the insurance cost section of the *analysis* have been discussed in previous chapters. These costs consist of claims and reserve increases. All of these cost amounts are obtained from exhibits except the following:

The *increase in policy reserves* is calculated simply by taking the difference between the corresponding liabilities at the end of the previous year and the end of the current year. The *increase in loading on deferred and uncollected premiums* is calculated on working papers as explained in Chapter 12.

Cash surrender values are entered on the books as they are paid. Usually the cash basis cash surrender figure is the same as the accrual basis figure, so no exhibit is required. The same is true of payments on dividend accumulations. Since a reserve of an equal amount is released when these payments are made, no adjustment is required to obtain accrual basis amounts.

Figure 20–6

(Write or stamp name of Company)

ANALYSIS OF OPERATIONS BY LINES OF BUSINESS
(Gain and Loss Exhibit)

	TOTAL (1)	INDUSTRIAL LIFE (INCLUDING TOTAL AND PERMANENT DISABILITY AND ACCIDENTAL DEATH BENEFITS) (2)	LIFE INSURANCE (3)	TOTAL AND PERMANENT DISABILITY (4)
1. Premiums and annuity considerations (Exhibit 1, Part 1) . .				
2. Considerations for supplementary contracts with life contingencies.			X X X	X X
3. Considerations for supplementary contracts without life contingencies and dividend accumulations				
4. Net investment income (Exhibit 2).				
5.				
6.				
7. TOTAL				
8. Death benefits.				X X
9. Matured endowments				X X
10. Annuity benefits			X X X	X X
11. Disability benefits			X X X	
12. Surrender benefits				X X
12A. Group conversions				
12B. Transfers on account of group package policies and contracts.	X X X	X X X	X X X	X X
13. Benefits under accident and health policies		X X X	X X X	X X
14. Interest on policy or contract funds				
15. Payments on supplementary contracts with life contingencies.			X X X	X X
16. Payments on supplementary contracts without life contingencies and of dividend accumulations				
17. Increase in aggregate reserve for policies and contracts with life contingencies.				
18. Increase in reserves for supplementary contracts without life contingencies and for dividend accumulations				
19. Increase in reserves for accident and health policies				
19A.				
20. SUBTOTAL (Items 8 to 19A)				
21. Commissions on premiums and annuity considerations . . .				
22.				
23. General insurance expenses (Exhibit 5, Cols. 1 and 2, Line 13).				
24. Insurance taxes, licenses and fees, excluding federal income taxes (Exhibit 6, Cols. 1 and 2, Line 10)				
25. Increase in loading on and cost of collection in excess of loading on deferred and uncollected premiums				
26.				
27. TOTAL (Items 20 to 26)				
28. Net gain from operations before dividends to policyholders and federal income taxes and excluding capital gains and losses (Item 7 minus Item 27)				
29. Dividends to life policyholders (Exhibit 7)				
30. Dividends on accident and health policies (Exhibit 7) . . .		X X X	X X X	X X
31. Increase in amounts provisionally held for deferred dividend policies.				
32. TOTAL (Items 29 to 31)				
32A. Net gain from operations after dividends to policyholders and before federal income taxes, excluding capital gains and losses (Item 28 minus Item 32)				
32B. Federal income taxes incurred (excluding tax on capital gains).				
33. Net gain from operations after dividends to policyholders and federal income taxes (excluding tax on capital gains) and excluding capital gains and losses (Item 32A minus Item 32B).				

The item *group conversions* is used to transfer reserves from the group insurance column to columns for other lines of business. A cost is shown in the group insurance column, and a negative amount is shown on the same line in the column for the line of business receiving the reserve. The amount in the total column is usually zero or a very nominal amount.

This item results from conversion privileges in group policies which

The figures on this page do not include Separate Account items, if any.

	ORDINARY			GROUP		ACCIDENT AND HEALTH	
	Additional Accidental Death (5)	Individual Annuities (6)	Supplementary Contracts (7)	Life Insurance (8)	Annuities (9)	Group (10)	Other (11)
			X X X				
	X X	X X X				X X X	X X X
		X X X			X X X	X X X	X X X
	X X	X X X			X X X	X X X	X X X
	X X			x x x		X X X	X X X
	X X					X X X	X X X
	X X	X X X			X X X	X X X	X X X
	X X	X X X			X X X		
	X X	X X X	X X X				x x x
	X X	X X X	X X X	x x x	x x x		
	X X	X X X				x x x	x x x
						X X X	X X X
	X X	X X X	X X X	X X X	X X X		
						X X X	X X X

provide that an insured person may apply for an individual policy at standard premium rates when he becomes ineligible to continue his insurance under the group policy. Many individuals who exercise the privilege are substandard risks who would not otherwise be eligible for insurance. The conversion privilege creates claim costs in the line of business under which the individual policy is issued which were not contemplated in the premium calculations for that line. To correct this inequity, policy reserves sufficient to absorb the extra claim costs must be transferred from the group insurance line to the line of business under which the converted policy is issued. *Transfers on account of group package policies and contracts* is a similar but minor item. It usually is used to transfer premium credits between group life and group health insurance. *Interest on policy or contract funds . . .* is also a minor item and was discussed in the claims chapter.

INTERPRETING THE ANALYSIS OF OPERATIONS

Although management should prepare many other internal accounting and statistical reports upon which to base decisions, the figures in this analysis indicate the areas of the company's operations which most need attention, i.e., those which reflect lower gains from operations than in preceding years and those which show losses or show less gain than should be expected, considering the volume of premium income and share of net investment income allocated to each line.

Stockholders do not normally see the official Annual Statement, but many of the figures shown in the annual reports which they do receive are extracted from the Annual Statement. These reports are frequently the only data investors and policyowners receive as to the company's progress. Much information included in these reports relate to gains made in each of the lines of business as reflected in the analysis of operations. Stockbrokers and various special reporting firms also make extracts from Annual Statements and supply them to insurance agents and financial institutions which rely upon them in serving the public.

The analysis is of interest to supervisory authorities who are concerned if a company is losing surplus each year, or if its operating gains are not sufficient to pay dividends to policyowners in amounts that should reasonably be expected. Data is this analysis serves to limit the areas that must be examined to determine the cause or probable cause of low operating gains and whether there is likely to be future impairment of surplus.

While the analysis is very helpful to management in locating weaknesses in insurance operations, much additional information is required to interpret the figures shown accurately. This is true because—

1. Investment income and expense items are allocated to lines of business by methods which may vary between companies.
2. Figures by lines of insurance may be substantially influenced by consolidating several secondary lines of insurance which have cost patterns widely divergent from the basic lines for which columns are provided.
3. Costs of new business usually exceed first-year income derived from

it, so that a large volume of new business in a particular line of business results in lower net gain than when there is a moderate amount of new business.

4. The amount of operating gain for a line of business is affected by the amount of capital and surplus and by the percent of net investment income earned on invested assets.

The third and fourth reasons cited can also have a substantial effect on the gain from operations for the company as a whole as shown in the summary of operations.

Allocation of Investment Income

Net investment income is distributed to lines of business in the analysis of operations. Interest earned on policy loans, premium notes, and other types of policy indebtedness, less related expenses, is distributed directly to the lines of business which produced the interest. Other net investment income is distributed by use of one of the three following methods: (1) mean of policy reserves and liabilities, (2) mean funds, or (3) investment generation method.

Under the *mean of policy reserves and liabilities* method, net investment income, less policy loan interest, is distributed to lines of business in accordance with the mean of policy reserves and liabilities for each line of business. The phrase "policy reserves and liabilities" covers all interest-bearing liabilities such as policy reserves and various deposits, and may include other policy liabilities such as claim liabilities and advance premiums. It does not include nonpolicy liabilities such as unpaid expenses.

The following example illustrates the "mean of policy reserves and liability" method. Only two lines of insurance are included to keep the illustration simple. Net investment income is $4,500,000. Of this amount $200,000 is policy loan interest from the ordinary line of business and $300,000 is policy loan interest from the annuity line of business. The remaining $4,000,000 of net investment income is distributed to ordinary life insurance and annuities in accordance with the mean of policy reserves and liabilities. These mean amounts are calculated as follows:

	Policy Reserves and Liabilities	Policy Loans	Net Amount
Ordinary insurance:			
Beginning of year	$55,000,000	$3,000,000	$52,000,000
End of year	58,000,000	4,000,000	54,000,000
Mean net amount			53,000,000
Annuities:			
Beginning of year	50,000,000	5,000,000	45,000,000
End of year	55,000,000	6,000,000	49,000,000
Mean net amount			47,000,000

The ordinary insurance mean policy reserves and liabilities are 53 percent of the total ($53/$100). Therefore, $2,120,000 of investment income ($4,000,000 × 53 percent) is allocated to ordinary insurance. The net policy loan interest of $200,000 is added to make a total of $2,320,000 investment income allocated to the ordinary line of insurance. The remainder of the investment income ($4,000,000 × 47 percent) plus $300,000 of policy loan interest is allocated to the annuity line of business.

Under this method, no portion of the surplus is included in the base for allocation. The stockholder's equity is disregarded, and no part of investment income is treated as belonging to stockholders. Canadian Annual Statement instructions and forms discourage the use of this method and encourage the use of the mean fund method. Refinements of the mean fund method are also commonly used in the United States.

The *mean funds* method of allocating net investment income is similar to the mean policy reserve and liability method, except that funds constitute a broader base for allocation. A "fund" as used here consists of interest-bearing policy liabilities and reserves, contingency reserves, and the accumulated surplus of a line of business. The only assets attributed to a particular fund are policy loans.

Under the mean fund method as used by Canadian companies, the shareholders' equity, including "shareholders' surplus," and reserves for staff retirement plans are treated as separate "funds." Current liabilities such as unpaid claims and advance premiums are not included in the funds. Capital gains and losses, as well as investment income, are distributed to the funds in the Annual Statement blank. Canadian methods are more fully discussed in Chapter 21.

In U.S. companies using the mean fund method, capital gains and losses are not distributed to lines of business in the analysis of operations but are included in determining the amount of surplus in each fund. Stockholders' equity and retirement plans are not treated as funds, so that all investment income is allocated to lines of business.

The *investment generation* method is a refinement of the fund method. Under it, each investment is attributed to a particular fund and the investment income derived from the investment is allocated to the corresponding fund.

A common variation of the investment generation method used by many companies, particularly those selling participating annuities, is known as the investment-year method. Under this method, investments are earmarked by year of purchase. Investment income from investments made during each purchase year is allocated to funds in accordance with the increase in each fund each year. To illustrate, assume a company has four classes of funds, A, B, C, and D. The amount of the funds in 1968 and the increases in 1969 and 1970 are as follows:

Fund	A	B	C	D	Total
End of 1968.................$4,000	$10,000	$ 6,000	$3,000	$23,000
Increase 1969................. 1,000	2,000	4,000	3,000	10,000
End of 1969................. 5,000	12,000	10,000	6,000	33,000
Increase 1970................. 2,000	3,000	4,000	4,000	13,000

Assume further than investments made in 1969 produce net investment income during that year of $300. This income is allocated $30 to Fund A ($1,000/$10,000 × $300), $60 to Fund B ($2,000/$10,000 × $300), etc. In 1970, the net investment income on the $10,000 of investments made in 1969 was $600. Of this amount, $60 is allocated to Fund A ($1,000/$10,000 × $600), $120 is allocated to Fund B ($2,000/$10,000 × $600), etc. In 1970, $13,000 of new investments are made to equal the increase in funds during that year. The 1970 earnings on the 1970 investments are allocated to Fund A on the basis of $2,000 increase in fund, to Fund B on the basis of $3,000, etc.

Under the investment-year method capital gains and losses, both realized and unrealized, usually are allocated to funds. Additions to the mandatory security valuation reserve in U.S. companies usually are not deducted from capital gains and losses. Some investment income, such as home office rent, policy loans, and all investment expenses are allocated to funds without regard to the year of investment.

Distribution of Income and Expense Items by Lines of Business

Many major income and cost items can easily be classified by line of business through use of a set of ledger accounts for each line, but other items must be distributed by less exact methods. The most important of these other items are net investment income and general expenses. The effects of methods used to distribute investment income are examined first.

Investment income distributed to lines of insurance includes some interest in excess of that required in actuarial calculations. Hereafter, for convenience, *net investment income* may be referred to as *interest earned*, and the difference between *interest earned* and *interest required* will be referred to as *excess* interest. The word "excess" in this use does not mean excessive. Without this interest, many companies would show an operating loss.

Excess interest is derived from two sources. These are (1) invested assets in excess of liabilities on which interest is required and (2) difference in rate of interest earned and the rate required for policy reserves and other liabilities. For example, in The XYZ Life Insurance Company (see page 440), if interest earned is 4.2 percent, invested assets are $179 million and policy reserves and other interest-bearing liabilities are $150 million, then there are $29 million ($179 − $150) of invested assets in excess of liabilities on which interest is required. These assets in excess of reserves are, in general, equal to the capital stock and surplus. There are some liabilities not requiring interest, and current assets other than investments, that do not earn interest, but these are not significant in amount. The assets in excess of reserves at XYZ Life produce $1,218,000 of excess interest ($29 million × 4.2 percent). There are also $150 million of assets producing 1.2 percent (4.2 percent − 3 percent) or $1.8 million of excess interest ($150 million × 1.2 percent).

Excess interest is allocated to lines of business along with the required interest in the analysis of operations. Under the fund allocation method some of the surplus is classed as shareholders' surplus, and a proportionate share of the total investment income is allocated to it. This would seem to be proper treatment in a U.S. stock company that sells both participating insurance and nonparticipating insurance. However, the Annual Statement blank makes no provision for allocating to stockholders a share of investment earnings.

Methods used to allocate investment income can substantially affect the operating gains shown for a line of business. This effect can be demonstrated by using figures from The XYZ Life Insurance Company. Those assets and liabilities which are general in nature and do not relate to specific lines of business are designated as NA, meaning "Not Applicable" in Figure 20–7.

All figures are millions of dollars; none are percentages. Of the $7.52 investment income earned, only $4.10 is required for reserves, leaving $3.42 of excess interest to be included in the allocation. All assets and

Figure 20–7

THE XYZ LIFE INSURANCE COMPANY

Balance Sheet
December 31, 19—

Item	Group	Ordinary	Total
Invested assets	NA	NA	179.0
Nonledger and miscellaneous assets	2.0	3.0	5.0
Total Assets	NA	NA	184.0
Policy reserves	12.0	113.0	125.0
Claim liabilities	2.0	2.0	4.0
All other liabilities	NA	25.0	25.0
Mandatory Securities Valuation Reserve	NA	NA	5.0
Capital	NA	NA	4.5
Surplus	5.0	16.5	21.5
Total Liabilities, Capital, and Surplus	NA	NA	184.0

Selected Items from Analysis of Operations

	Group	Ordinary	Total
Premium income	16.00	15.00	31.00
Claims incurred	12.00	3.00	15.00
Interest required for reserves	0.30	3.80	4.10
Net investment income allocated to lines of business	0.89	6.63	7.52
Operating gains	0.40	1.15	1.55

liabilities are mean amounts. The balance sheet is complete, but only selected items from the analysis of operations are shown. Only two lines of insurance are shown to keep the illustration as simple as possible.

The fund allocation method was used to produce the amount of net investment income allocated to the group and ordinary lines of insurance. It was calculated as follows:

Item	Group	Ordinary
Reserves............................	12.0	113.0
Other liabilities.....................	0.0	25.0
Surplus.............................	8.0	12.0
Total........................	20.0	150.0
Percent of total.....................	11.8%	88.2%
Percent times $7.52 million...........	$0.89	$6.63

Allocation under the mean liability method would have produced approximately $600,000 investment income for the group line of insurance and $6.92 million for ordinary. This was arrived at as follows:

Item	Group	Ordinary
Reserves............................	12.0	113.00
Other liabilities.....................	0.0	25.00
Total........................	12.0	138.00
Percent of total.....................	8%	92%
Percent times $7.52 million...........	$0.60	$6.92

The mean of policy reserves and liabilities method would have reduced the investment income of the group line of business as shown in the analysis of operations by $290,000 ($890,000 by the mean fund method less $600,000 by the mean liability method). As a result, the operating gains of the group line of business would have been reduced from $400,000 to $110,000 ($400,000 − $290,000). Use of the investment generation method might also have resulted in a substantial difference.

Although companies use different methods for allocating net investment income, each company should determine and consistently use a suitable formula. Otherwise comparisons between years, which should be useful to management as a basis for decisions, are misleading and less useful.

Allocation of expenses by line of business also requires a considerable amount of care and discretion to create equity between lines of business. If a clerk works in a department that services one line of business, his salary can be easily charged to the proper line. But how should such items as the salary of the cafeteria manager, cost of office supplies, advertising, and branch office expenses be charged?

A branch office may service several lines of business. The manager, cashier, and other employees service each line in accordance with need. Any method of distributing salary and rent precisely between lines in such an office is usually too expensive to be practical but various work sampling and other techniques may be used. Such methods are approximate but sufficient if the allocation is done carefully.

Effect of Consolidating Income and Costs by Sublines

Under each major line classification there are a number of specialized insurance lines which have been developed over the years to serve the needs of the public. These were classified in this book as secondary lines. For example, in group insurance there are such classifications as group permanent, debtor group, and association group. Each of these secondary classifications may have sublines such as life insurance and health insurance. Each of these secondary lines and sublines may have widely varying cost patterns from those of the basic line and when consolidated with the basic line may not be comparable with figures of other companies unless many behind-the-scene facts are known. The effect of consolidating sublines can be seen by consolidating the two major lines of The XYZ Life Insurance Company, using the figures shown on page 440.

The claim rate for group insurance is 75 percent of the premium ($12/$16). The claim rate for ordinary insurance is 20 percent ($3/$15). By consolidating the two, the rate becomes 48.4 percent ($15/$31), a substantially different percentage than either of the two calculated separately. The new figure is relatively meaningless for comparisons between companies. Of course, ordinary would not be combined with group in an Annual Statement form, but the results of merging the experience of a secondary line with that of a principal (or major) line could be similarly misleading.

Effect of New Business on Operating Gains

Ordinary insurance net premiums and policy reserves can be calculated so as to provide a greater loading for payment of expenses in the first year. A greater first-year loading is justified because selling expenses, issuing expenses, and underwriting expenses are costs incurred in the first year only and agents' commissions for the first policy year are higher. Any higher loading in premiums in the first year is used to pay these new business expenses. Even so, the new business expenses in most lines of business usually exceed this loading.

Some companies choose to set up "net level premium reserves" which means that the first-year loading is the same as loading for renewal years; the first-year excess of expenses over loading is aggravated for such companies, resulting in a greater "strain on surplus" from new business.

If ordinary insurance costs $1.50 to sell, underwrite, and issue for every

$1 of new business premium received, it follows that surplus will decrease by 50 percent of the new premium received plus the cost of claims paid and reserves required. To recover this extra cost, actuaries calculate the gross premiums so that loading in later years will be sufficient to return to surplus any costs in excess of income incurred in the first policy year.

First-year costs in excess of first-year premiums may be considered as "borrowed" from surplus. The surplus borrowed to pay for the new business does not come from the Surplus account directly but from the current year's gain, thereby causing a decrease in operating gains. The greater the volume of new business written, the lower the operating gain.

New business losses are not separated from renewal gains in the analysis of operations. Therefore, it is not apparent from figures in the analysis that new business costs in excess of first-year premiums have decreased the gain from operations on old business.

The effect of new business costs on *operating* gain is demonstrated by again using figures from The XYZ Life Insurance Company financial statements shown on page 440.

In the group insurance line, assume that selling, issuing, and underwriting costs were 34 percent of first-year premium income. No extra loading is allowed in group insurance premiums to pay these first-year costs. Claims and other first-year costs were 90 percent of premiums received. These combined costs caused a decrease in surplus (or loss) of 24 percent of the first-year premiums (34 percent + 90 percent − 100 percent of first-year premiums). Renewal costs were 98 percent of the renewal premium. Investment income allocated was $0.67 million.

In the following table the effect on surplus is demonstrated when 10 percent of $16 million total premium income is first-year premium income and when 20 percent is first-year premium.

Illustration showing the effect of a large volume of new business on operating gains:

THE XYZ LIFE INSURANCE COMPANY
Group Insurance Department
(000 Omitted)

	Assuming 10% of Premiums Received Are First-Year Premiums	*Assuming 20% of Premiums Received Are First-Year Premiums*
First-year premiums	$ 1,600	$ 3,200
Renewal premiums	14,400	12,800
Investment income allocated	670	670
Total Income	$16,670	$16,670
All first-year costs including claims and reserves (124 percent of premiums)	1,984	3,968
All renewal costs (98 percent of renewal premiums)	14,112	12,544
Net Gain	$ 574	$ 158

It is apparent from this illustration that the gain of $574,000 was reduced to $158,000 when a greater volume of new business was written, yet the management of the group insurance department was equally efficient under both assumptions. The $574,000 would have been a satisfactory gain although it was slightly less than 4 percent of premium income, but the $158,000 gain would have been considered unsatisfactory by a person who did not know just how the condition was created.

It is readily apparent from this illustration that the volume of new business written must be taken into consideration in examining the results shown by the analysis. The effect of new business on surplus as shown in the illustration applies to all lines of business.

Instructions for preparing the premium exhibit of the Annual Statement do not require separation of first-year premiums for group insurance and industrial insurance, but they do require the separation for ordinary insurance. Ordinary insurance has a greater cost difference between first year and renewal years than do most other lines. Where this separation is required, the amount of first-year premiums can be used to approximate the efficiency of a particular operation.

Effect of Capital and Surplus and Investment Effectiveness on Operating Gains

The effect that methods of allocating interest earned have on *operating gains* shown for each line of business in the analysis has been noted. It should be apparent that the greater the amount of capital and surplus, the greater the operating gain for each line. This fact can be made more apparent by noting the effect a larger surplus would have had on the operating gains of The XYZ Life Insurance Company.

In XYZ Life, if capital and surplus had been $30 million instead of $25 million, the invested assets would have been $5 million greater. The rate of *interest earned* was 4.2 percent. Therefore, an additional $210,000 ($5 million × 4.2 percent) of *excess interest* would have been earned, which would have increased income and operating gains by that amount. Since this amount must also be allocated among lines of insurance, the operating gains for each line is also increased. A person not familiar with insurance accounting might interpret the additional $210,000 operating gain as the result of efficient operations rather than as an earning attributable to the amount of the capital and surplus.

If the rate of interest earned on invested assets increases, the operating gain shown in the analysis for each line of business will also increase. This can be seen by examining the effect of a higher rate of return in The XYZ Life Insurance Company.

If the net investment income rate had been 4.5 percent instead of 4.2 percent, the interest earned, as shown by the summary, would have been

$537,000 more ($179 million invested assets times 0.3 of 1 percent). This figure would have increased operating gains by one third. This gain would have been a result of effective investment management, but might be interpreted by many as reflecting effective management in the group and ordinary lines.

The investment department might have a policy of investing a portion of the company's surplus in stocks of a type which produce small dividends, but substantial capital gains. This policy would have the effect of reducing net interest earned, thereby reducing operating gains, but would substantially increase surplus of the company through capital gains. This policy also would have the effect of reducing operating gains for each line of business.

Value of the Analysis of Operations

When sufficient care is used in interpreting the analysis, it becomes the most valuable report in the Annual Statement for management and is a very important report for policyowners, stockholders, and supervisory authorities.

SCHEDULE H—ACCIDENT AND HEALTH EXHIBIT

This isolated schedule in the Annual Statement relates to both group and individual health insurance.

Most other exhibits are designed to provide details for the balance sheet and summary of operations, but *Schedule H* is a report for analyzing losses and expenses in relation to premiums earned on the subclassifications of health insurance. Columns are included for showing each item by sublines of health insurance.

The first part is a statistical analysis of premiums in force and need not be discussed here. The second portion is titled *analysis of underwriting operations* and is presented in a format similar to that of the analysis of operations by lines of business, but with significant differences. Instead of arriving at a gain from operations, it arrives at a gain from underwriting. This gain does not include an allocation of investment income and is, therefore, a different figure from operating gains.

Health insurance premiums are adjusted in this exhibit to obtain premiums earned, the same as shown in the premium exhibit. The company has the option of showing increase in advance premiums and increase in active life reserves as separate items here or combining them with advance premiums in this exhibit and in the premium exhibit. Claims, commissions, expenses, and taxes are deducted in this exhibit from the premium earned to arrive at the underwriting gain.

Health insurance claims are described in this exhibit as *incurred claims*.

The increase in claim reserves is shown as a separate item, but it is used to obtain the amount of incurred claims. Incurred claims ratios and other cost ratios are shown in this exhibit.

QUESTIONS

1. What are two principle advantages of using an asset exhibit rather than ledger entries to adjust book values of assets to admitted values? What equation is expressed in this exhibit? How is loading on deferred and uncollected premiums shown? If an investment is carried on the books at $5,000 and the admitted value is $6,000, what is the difference called? If the admitted value is $3,000, what is the difference called?

2. What is the reconciliation of ledger assets equation? What two purposes does this reconciliation serve? Which of the following are treated as receipts and which as disbursements in this reconciliation?

   a) Increase in book value of stocks
   b) Decrease in ledger liabilities
   c) Increase in paid-up capital
   d) Premium deposits received
   e) Increase in ledger liabilities
   f) Profit on sale of stock
   g) Borrowed money repaid

3. What is the effect on surplus when $500 worth of furniture is purchased by a life insurance company? If the purchase is recorded as an asset, what is the name of the exhibit in which this change is calculated? Why must company stock owned be nonadmitted? Why might a company wish to show unused office supplies as an asset? Why are funds in the hands of company officers nonadmitted?

4. In what column of the analysis of operations are the following items shown?

   a) Ordinary insurance dividends left on deposit
   b) Death proceeds left on deposit at interest
   c) Death proceeds applied to provide an income for life
   d) Reserve transfers in connection with group life conversions
   e) Ordinary insurance premium deposits received
   f) Disability benefits paid

5. What is meant by mean funds and investment generation method as used in connection with allocation of investment income? What two sources produce excess interest? What effect does this interest have on the operating gains of a line of business as shown in the analysis of operations? Why is it impractical to compare the operating costs for group insurance shown in the analysis of operations of one company

with that of another company serving a different segment of the group insurance market?

PROBLEMS

1. Prepare a trial balance and show the amounts in a reconciliation equation if a company begins the year with $12,000 cash and no other assets; there is a $100 ledger liability for withholding taxes; and during the year the following transactions take place:

a) Furniture is purchased for $1,000. It is recorded as an asset. At the end of the year a depreciation entry is made charging $50 of the cost to depreciation expense.

b) Salaries of $500 are paid after deducting $115 in withholding taxes.

c) Taxes withheld of $100 are paid to the government along with $25 tax expense.

d) Premium income of $1,500 is received.

2. Determine the amount of increase in gains from operations in the industrial line of business if a company improves its net investment income by 1/10 of 1 percent and the following conditions exist:

	Beginning of Year	End of Year
Invested assets...................	$100,000	$110,000
Policy reserves, industrial...........	50,000	52,000
Policy reserves, ordinary............	30,000	35,000
Other assets......................	1,000	1,500
Noninterest-bearing liabilities........	5,000	6,000
Capital and surplus................	14,000	15,500

Investment income is allocated on the basis of mean policy reserves.

Chapter 21

Special Canadian Annual Statement Reports

A number of differences between U.S. and Canadian life insurance Annual Statement forms have been discussed in earlier chapters, but discussion of a major phase of the Canadian Statement has been reserved for this chapter. This phase is generally described as *fund accounting*. This chapter is also concerned with several "wrap-up" phases of the Canadian Annual Statement, but it is devoted primarily to discussing fund accounting and the related exhibits and financial reports of the Annual Statement blank.

All asset and liability items, other than Items 15 and 19, on the liability page of the Canadian Annual Statement have been discussed in previous chapters. Item 15 on the liability page is related to bank overdrafts, and Item 19 to pension and insurance funds. Overdrafts rarely occur in a life company, so this item usually has a zero amount. The fund item is discussed in this chapter. The two balance sheet pages are shown in Figures 21–1 and 21–2. It is suggested that the student examine each item, and if any are not understood, review the pertinent Annual Statement sections of previous chapters.

FUND ACCOUNTING

In Canada, most life insurance companies, both stock and mutual, write participating and nonparticipating business. The interests of the participating policyowners are protected by a legal requirement that separate funds be maintained for (1) participating business, (2) nonparticipating business, and (3) the shareholders' equity in the company.

448

The process used to account for and allocate revenue to the various funds in Canadian companies is referred to as *fund accounting*. A *fund*, as used in the Canadian Annual Statement, may be defined as all liabilities and surplus held for a particular purpose or particular group of persons. For example, the participating fund consists of all major participating insurance liabilities and surplus held for participating policyowners.

Assets are not segregated by funds. Fund accounting is comparable to an accounting arrangement for a group of companies, each with its own liabilities and surplus, but joined together in a common investment program. All interest-bearing liabilities (including policy reserves and amounts on deposit) and dividends payable in the following year are included in one of the funds. Capital stock outstanding is included in a separate fund, the shareholders' fund. Large common liabilities or reserves set aside, such as *investment reserve fund* and various retirement funds, are each treated as separate funds.

Miscellaneous liability items (primarily current liabilities on which interest is not required) are not included in a fund but are treated as general liabilities called *Amounts Owing by the Company*, or more simply, *Amounts Owing*. Included under this classification are all advance premiums and unearned investment income; all incurred but unpaid costs, including unpaid claims; and most ledger liabilities. An instruction in a report referred to here as the *Summary of Funds* specifies which items on the liability page are to be classified as *Amounts Owing*.

To effectively segregate surplus belonging to each fund, it is necessary to account for all income, costs, and net income by fund. Net investment earnings and capital gains (or losses) from assets are allocated to each fund on an equitable basis. Expenses and other costs are allocated on an exact basis whenever possible. When direct allocation is impractical, expenses and costs are apportioned by methods that produce equitable results. Each company is required to describe these methods in the statement blank.

Amounts may be transferred between funds under certain conditions, but Canadian law places restrictions on the amounts of surplus that may be transferred from insurance funds to the shareholders' fund in any year. These special statutory requirements result in a need for a considerable amount of accounting information by funds. This need is served by the following financial reports which are included in the Canadian Annual Statement blank: (1) *Analysis of Revenue Account by Fund* in which income, insurance cost, and expense items are analyzed by fund; (2) *Summary of Funds and Amounts Owing by the Company*, in which the various liability, capital, and surplus amounts in the balance sheet at the end of the year are classified by fund or as *Amounts Owing;* and (3) *Reconciliation of Funds*, which shows the amount of change in fund

Figure 21-1. Canadian Asset Page

....
(Name of Company)

....
(Year of Statement)

I. ASSETS

(at book values)

1. Bonds owned by the Company (Schedule A, page 25).. $ ....

2. Stocks owned by the Company (Schedule B, page 26).. ....

3. Mortgage loans on real estate (Schedule C, page 27).. ....

4. Agreements of sale of real estate (Schedule D, page 27).. ....

5. Real estate owned by the Company not under agreement of sale, less encumbrances (Schedule E, page 28).. ....

6. Collateral loans (Schedule F, page 29).. ....

7. Policy loans.. ....

8. Guaranteed investment certificates (give details below).. ....

9. Cash (Schedule G, page 30).. ....

10. ....

11. ....

12. ....

13. ....

14. Investment income, due and accrued (Exhibit 6, page 12)..

15. Outstanding insurance premiums and annuity considerations (Exhibit 12, page 15)..

16. Amounts due from other companies on reinsured contracts for claims paid (Exhibit 5, page 11)..

17. ....

18. ....

19. ....

20. ....

21. ....

22. ....

23. ....

24.   Total Assets.. $

Figure 21-2.   Canadian Liability Page

....
(Name of Company)

....
(Year of Statement)

II. LIABILITIES, CAPITAL, AND SURPLUS

1. Actuarial reserve for insurance and annuity contracts in force (Valuation Summary, Exhibit 15, page 17).. $ ....

2. Outstanding claims under insurance and annuity contracts, including provision for unreported death claims (Exhibit 5, page 11)..

3. Outstanding payments under settlement annuities ....

4. Amounts on deposit with the Company, pertaining to insurance and annuity contracts and including interest accumulations (Exhibit 11, page 14)..

5. Insurance premiums and annuity considerations, received in advance..

6. Dividends to policyholders, due but unpaid..

7. Other policy and contract liabilities, not included above..

8. Provision for dividends to policyholders (other than deferred dividends) payable in the year following the date of account..

9. Provision for accrued profits to policyholders, not included above (give details):

    ....

    ....

    ....

10. Taxes, licences, and fees, due and accrued (Exhibit 10, page 14)..

11. Commissions on insurance premiums and annuity considerations, due and accrued..

12. General and investment expenses, due and accrued (Exhibit 9, page 13)..

13. Investment income, received in advance..

14. Borrowed money and interest thereon, due and accrued..

17. Amounts received but not yet allocated..

18. Miscellaneous liabilities (give details):

19. Staff pension and insurance funds (give details):

20. Special reserves or funds, not included above (give details):

21.   Total Liabilities.. $

22. Capital stock paid...

23. Surplus in shareholders fund..

24. Surplus in insurance fund..

25.   Grand Total... $

liabilities and the sources of change in surplus of each fund during the
year. The second report hereafter will be referred to as simply *Summary
of Funds*.

Reports relating to fund accounting include sufficient detail so that an
audit trail is clearly established from the source of change to the resulting
surplus or liability amount in each fund. It is not in keeping with the
objectives of this book to explain in detail the accounting steps required
to produce these special reports. It is useful, however, for the student to
know the purpose of these reports and to understand the items included in
them.

The following are the funds for which columns are included in the
Analysis of Revenue Account by Fund and *Reconciliation of Funds:*

Participating fund
Nonparticipating fund
Shareholders' fund
Investment reserve fund
Employees' pension fund
Agents' pension fund

Three additional columns are provided in these two financial reports
for any other funds that may be maintained by a company. The participating fund and nonparticipating fund are referred to as *insurance funds.*
Health insurance is not included because health insurance data is reported
in the casualty blank. Assets of the casualty lines are accounted for
separately from those held in connection with life insurance funds.

Before the analysis and reconciliation related to funds are examined, it
is desirable to understand the method of classifying liabilities and surplus
by funds. Therefore, it is appropriate first to look at the *Summary of
Funds and Amounts Owing by the Company* (see Figure 21–3).

Summary of Funds and Amounts Owing by the Company

This is the title of a report which attributes all of the liability, capital,
and surplus items to a fund classification or to *Amounts Owing by the
Company*. The final total is shown as *total assets*. This appears to be a
misnomer unless the student recalls that in the accounting equation total
assets must be equal to the total of all liabilities and capital, or $A = L + C$.
If the total of the liabilities, capital, and surplus shown in this report is the
same as that for total assets as shown by the balance sheet, it is obvious
that every liability and capital item must have been included.

The first item in this summary is titled *insurance funds*. Under this title
the liability items in the two insurance funds (participating and nonparticipating) are listed. A column is included for each of these two insurance

funds, along with a total column. The liability items listed under insurance funds are:

1. Actuarial reserve
2. Amounts on deposit with the company
3. Provision for dividends and accrued profits to policyholders

The first two of these items have been discussed earlier. The third covers the liability for (1) policy dividends that will become payable in the following year, including deferred dividends then payable and (2) additional dividend or surplus profits set aside for payment of annual or deferred dividends in other than the following year. Dividends currently payable to policyowners but not yet paid are not considered a fund liability but are treated as Amounts Owing by the Company.

Lines are provided in this summary for special reserves including portions of surplus set aside within each of the insurance funds to meet future mortality and other cost contingencies. Provision for group experience refunds not yet due are included here.

There is a surplus item in this summary for each of the two insurance funds. The amounts shown are the surplus balances at the end of the year. These insurance surplus amounts are held in their respective insurance funds for the protection of policyholders. Surplus in insurance funds does not become shareholders' surplus until transferred by order of the board of directors.

Below the liabilities and surplus amounts related to insurance funds, there are two amounts representing the *shareholders' fund*. These are *capital* and *surplus* in the shareholders' fund. Dividends to shareholders are paid only from this surplus. Surplus set aside each year for shareholders includes an allocation from investment earnings and from capital gains less capital losses during the year. The surplus in the summary is shown after transfers between insurance funds.

One fund, the *investment reserve fund*, is similar in many respects to the Mandatory Securities Valuation Reserve of the U.S. statement. Invested assets are not classified by funds, so this investment reserve liability belongs, in a sense, to all funds. As a matter of convenience it is handled as a separate and distinct fund. Fill-in lines are provided for liabilities of "Other Funds."

Surplus and liabilities may be transferred between funds under certain conditions. Any surplus transferred or investment income allocated to a fund other than an insurance or shareholders' fund becomes a liability to the company as a whole. For example, if $1,000 is transferred from the company's surplus to the employees' pension fund, it is thereafter a liability to the company in much the same manner as a declared dividend becomes a liability. Funds of this type do not have surplus as such and are shown as liabilities in this summary.

Figure 21-3

(Name of Company)

(Year of Statement)

VII. SUMMARY OF FUNDS AND AMOUNTS OWING BY THE COMPANY

	Participating Fund	Non-participating Fund	Total
1. Insurance Funds:			
(1) Actuarial reserve	$	$	$
(2) Amounts on deposit with the Company			
(3) Provision for dividends and accrued profits to policy-holders			
(4) Special reserves:			
(5)			
(6) Surplus			
(7) Total insurance funds, 31 December 19	$	$	$
2. Shareholders Fund:			
(1) Capital		$	$
(2) Surplus			
3. Investment Reserve Fund			
4. Employees Pension Fund			
5. Agents Pension Fund			

7.   Total funds...........$

8.   Amounts owing by the Company (page 3, items 2, 3, 5, 6, 7, 10 to 18)...........$

9.   Total funds and amounts owing...........

10. Total assets...........$

	Participating Fund	Non-participating Fund
11. Insurance Funds, 31 December of previous year:		
(1) Actuarial reserve	$	$
(2) Amounts on deposit with the Company		
(3) Provision for dividends and accrued profits to policy-holders		
(4) Special reserves:		
(5)		
(6) Surplus		
(7) Total insurance funds	$	$
12. Shareholders Fund, 31 December of previous year:		
(1) Capital		$
(2) Surplus		

This Summary of Funds includes a supplement which shows insurance funds at the end of the previous year so that changes in liabilities and increases in surplus in the Reconciliation of Funds can be easily traced to the Analysis of Revenue Account by Funds. Other funds and amounts owing are not shown in this supplement.

Reconciliation of Funds

This report shows the amount of change in each liability and the source of change in surplus for each fund during the year.

In order to make clear the principles of fund accounting, a simplified Reconciliation of Funds for The XYZ Life Insurance Company of Canada is presented in succeeding sections. Only participating (par) and nonparticipating (nonpar) insurance funds and a shareholders' fund are used to keep the illustration as simple as possible. A Canadian company licensed in the U.S. might depend upon working papers and not enter adjusting and closing entries to the ledger, but the use of the adjusting entry method facilitates discussion and is used here.

Nominal account balances in the illustration are closed into Revenue accounts for each fund. Liability items are normally nonledger items but are included in the trial balance to simplify the illustration. Increases in fund liabilities are treated as insurance costs.

The adjusted trial balance is as follows:

THE XYZ LIFE INSURANCE COMPANY OF CANADA
Condensed Adjusted Trial Balance
December 31, 19__

	Debit	Credit
Assets	$100,000	
Actuarial reserve, par		$ 35,000
Actuarial reserve, nonpar		22,000
Amounts owing by company		5,000
Capital		10,000
Surplus, par		16,000
Surplus, nonpar		6,000
Surplus, shareholders		1,000
Income, par		17,000
Income, nonpar		6,000
Disbursements, par	7,000	
Disbursements, nonpar	2,000	
Capital gains		3,000
Increase in actuarial reserves, par	7,000	
Increase in actuarial reserves, nonpar	2,500	
Revenue account, par		
Revenue account, nonpar		
Dividends to policyowners	2,000	
Dividends to shareholders	500	
Total	$121,000	$121,000

Assume that at the start of the year the Summary of Funds and Amounts Owing by the Company was as follows:

	Participating Fund	Nonpartici- pating Fund	Shareholders' Fund	Total
Fund liabilities	$28,000	$19,500		$47,500
Surplus in insurance funds	16,000	6,000		22,000
Capital in shareholders' fund			$10,000	10,000
Surplus in shareholders' fund			1,000	1,000
Total Funds	$44,000	$25,500	$11,000	$80,500
Amounts Owing by the Company				4,000
Total Assets				$84,500

Investment income is omitted to keep the illustration simple. If investment income were included, it would be allocated to funds in much the same manner as capital gains are allocated in the following illustration.

Normally investment income and capital gains are allocated to funds on the basis of the mean of funds at the beginning and end of the year. To simplify the illustration, capital gains are allocated here on the basis of fund amounts at the beginning of the year. The participating fund represented 54.7 percent ($44,000 ÷ $80,500), the nonparticipating fund represented 31.6 percent ($25,500 ÷ $80,500), and the shareholders' fund represented 13.7 percent ($11,000 ÷ $80,500) of the total fund amounts.

The company had $3,000 in capital gains which are allocated $1,641 to the participating fund ($3,000 × 54.7 percent), $948 to the nonparticipating fund ($3,000 × 31.6 percent), and $411 to the shareholders' fund ($3,000 × 13.7 percent).

The closing entries are as follows:

(1)

Income—Par	17,000	
Income—Nonpar	6,000	
Revenue Account—Par		17,000
Revenue Account—Nonpar		6,000

(This entry closes the income accounts into the Revenue account.)

(2)

Revenue Account—Par	16,000	
Revenue Account—Nonpar	4,500	
Increase in Actuarial Reserve—Par		7,000
Increase in Actuarial Reserve—Nonpar		2,500
Dividends to Policyholders—Par		2,000
Disbursements—Par		7,000
Disbursements—Nonpar		2,000

(This entry closes the cost accounts into Revenue. Dividends to policyowners is closed only into the participating fund Revenue account.)

(3)

```
Revenue Account—Par........................................1,000
Revenue Account—Nonpar...................................1,500
    Surplus—Par...........................................          1,000
    Surplus—Nonpar........................................          1,500
```

(This entry closes the Revenue accounts into the Surplus accounts increasing the Surplus accounts by the amount of gain reflected in the Revenue accounts.)

(4)

```
Capital Gains.............................................3,000
    Surplus—Par...........................................          1,641
    Surplus—Nonpar........................................            948
    Surplus—Shareholders..................................            411
```

(This entry closes the Capital Gains account into each Surplus account in the ratio of each fund to total funds. If other funds were held, a portion of these capital gains might have been apportioned to them also. Note that this transaction does not affect the Revenue account.)

(5)

```
Surplus—Par..............................................300
Surplus—Nonpar...........................................600
    Surplus—Shareholders..................................            900
```

(This entry transfers surplus from insurance funds to shareholders funds, as permitted by law and as ordered by the board of directors.)

(6)

```
Surplus—Shareholders.....................................500
    Dividends to Shareholders—Par.........................            500
```

(This entry closes the Dividends to Shareholders account. All nominal accounts have been closed out, and the ledger is ready for the following year.)

Posting these entries to T-accounts will aid in following the discussion.

After these entries have been posted, the post-closing trial balance appears as follows:

THE XYZ LIFE INSURANCE COMPANY OF CANADA
Post-Closing Trial Balance
December 31, 19—

Assets..............................	$100,000	
Actuarial reserve, par...............		$ 35,000
Actuarial reserve, nonpar............		22,000
Surplus, par.........................		18,341
Surplus, nonpar......................		7,848
Capital..............................		10,000
Surplus, shareholders................		1,811
Amounts owing........................		5,000
Total...............................	$100,000	$100,000

The Summary of Funds and Amounts Owing by the Company at the end of the year appears as follows:

	Par Fund	Nonpar Fund	Shareholders' Fund	Total
Actuarial reserves....................	$35,000	$22,000		$ 57,000
Surplus in insurance funds..............	18,341	7,848		26,189
Capital in shareholders' fund...........			$10,000	10,000
Surplus in shareholders' fund...........			1,811	1,811
Total Funds....................	$53,341	$29,848	$11,811	$ 95,000
Amounts owing the company...........				5,000
Total Assets....................				$100,000

Notice that the Summary of Funds and Amounts Owing is simply a rearrangement of the liability column of the post-closing trial balance and the total, of course, is equal to the total assets.

The amounts in each of these funds can be reconciled from one year-end to the next by showing the changes in liability and surplus in each fund during the year. The reconciliation in the example of The XYZ Life Insurance Company of Canada would be:

THE XYZ LIFE INSURANCE COMPANY OF CANADA
Reconciliation of Funds

	Par	Nonpar	Shareholders	Total
1. Funds December 31, 19___ (last year)..	$44,000	$25,500	$11,000	$80,500
2. Balance from Revenue account........	1,000	1,500		2,500
3. Increase in actuarial reserve..........	7,000	2,500		9,500
4. Capital gains......................	1,641	948	411	3,000
5. Transfer of surplus to shareholders' fund.............................	−300	−600	900	00
6. Dividends to shareholders...........			−500	−500
7. Funds December 31, 19___(this year)...	$53,341	$29,848	$11,811	$95,000

If the student posts the closing entries to T-accounts, it should be easy to identify each of the above items. Note that the total is the same as the total funds shown in the Summary of Funds.

It is evident from the example that the Reconciliation of Funds maintains an audit trail from changes in liabilities in the Revenue Account to the new liabilities in the balance sheet and from the changes in surplus shown in the reconciliation of surplus to the surplus balances shown in the balance sheet.

There are more items and more funds in the Reconciliation of Funds (see Figure 21–4) than were used in the illustration. The reconciliation process is the same, however. Note that a column is included for each of the commonly used funds.

Items in this reconciliation which relate to increases in liabilities are:

1. Normal increase in actuarial reserve
2. Increase in staff pension and insurance funds

Figure 21–4

VI. RECONCILIATION OF FUNDS

—	Participating Fund	Non-participating Fund	Shareholders Fund	Investment Reserve Fund
	$	$	$	$
1. Funds, 31 December 19				
2. Balances carried from Analysis of Revenue Account				
3. Normal increase in actuarial reserve				
4. Increase in staff pension and insurance funds				
5. Net increase in amounts on deposit				
6. Increase in provision for dividends and accrued profits to policy-holders				
7. Net capital gain on investments				
8. Transfers of surplus from other funds				
9.				
10.				
11.				
12. Totals (items 2 to 11)				
13. Net capital loss on investments				
14. Transfers of surplus to Shareholders Fund				
15. Transfers of surplus to other funds (give details below)				
16. Dividends to shareholders				
17.				
18.				
19.				
20. Totals (Items 13 to 19)				
21. Funds, 31 December 19				

3. Net increase in amounts on deposit
4. Increase in provision for dividends and accrued profits to policy-holders

These increase-in-liability items relate to liability classifications discussed in connection with the Summary of Funds and Amounts Owing by the Company. These increase-in-liability items also appear in the Analysis of Revenue Account by Fund.

Employees Pension Fund	Agents Pension Fund				Total
$	$	$	$	$	$

(Name of Company)

(Year of Statement)

Items in this reconciliation which relate to surplus changes are:

Balances carried from Analysis of Revenue Account
Net capital gain (or losses) on investments
Transfers of surplus to shareholders' fund
Transfers of surplus from other funds

Net capital loss on investments
Transfers of surplus to other funds
Dividends to shareholders

The items related to transfer of surplus provide a clear audit trail between surplus balances in the participating, nonparticipating, and shareholders' funds. Periodically, surplus may be transferred from the nonparticipating fund to the shareholders' fund, and under some conditions and limitations, it may also be transferred from the participating fund to the shareholders' fund. These and any other surplus transfers permitted by statute are entered on the appropriate descriptive lines.

If $1,000 surplus is transferred from the participating fund and $3,000 is transferred from the nonparticipating fund to surplus in the shareholders' fund, the entry is a debit to each of the insurance surplus accounts to reflect a decrease in each and a credit to the Shareholders' Surplus to reflect an increase in this account.

The entry is:

```
Surplus, Par.............................................1,000.00
Surplus, Nonpar..........................................3,000.00
    Surplus, Shareholders................................           4,000.00
```

RECONCILIATION OF SURPLUS

This is the title of the surplus statement in the Canadian Annual Statement blank. The method of reconciling surplus changes between calendar years is essentially the same as in the U.S. statement (see Figure 20–3). There are differences in terminology, however, which are as follows:

Canadian Statement	U.S. Statement
Reconciliation of surplus	Surplus account
Surplus in shareholders fund	Unassigned surplus
Surplus in insurance funds	Unassigned surplus
Balance carried from Revenue account (+ or −)	Net gain from operations
Net capital gain (or loss) on investments	Net capital gains (or losses)
Increase (or decrease) in special reserves	(Optional—fill-in lines)
Special increase in actuarial reserve (i.e., increase due to change in valuation bases only)	Increase in reserve on account of change in valuation basis
Dividends to shareholders	Dividends to stockholders

The Canadian *reconciliation of surplus* does not show items similar to the increases and decreases in *Mandatory Securities Valuation Reserve* and to changes in value of *nonadmitted assets and related items* of the U.S. Statement. The item equivalent to the *unassigned surplus* of the U.S. Statement is divided into *surplus in shareholders fund* and *surplus in insurance funds* in the Canadian reconciliation of surplus.

Figure 21-5

IV. RECONCILIATION OF SURPLUS

26. Surplus, 31 December 19 :

    (1) In shareholders fund............$..............

    (2) In insurance funds.....................

27. Balance carried from Revenue Account (+ or −)...........

28. Net capital gain on investments (Exhibit 8, page 12)...........

29. Decrease in special reserves (give details):

30. ....

31. ....

32. ....

33. Total............$..............

34. Net capital loss on investments (Exhibit 8, page 12)..............$

35. Increase in special reserves (give details):

36. ....

37. Special increase in actuarial reserve (i.e., increase due to change in valuation bases only) (Exhibit 16, page 18)............

38. Dividends to shareholders...........

39. Surplus, 31 December 19 :

    (1) In shareholders fund............$

    (2) In insurance funds............

40. Total............$

REVENUE ACCOUNT AND RELATED ANALYSES

Much of this book has been based on accounting relative to the U.S. Annual Statement. It is useful, therefore, to make some comparisons between U.S. and Canadian statements of operations. These Canadian statements are the Revenue Account, the Analysis of Revenue Account by Line of Business, and the Analysis of Revenue Account by Fund.

Principal differences between the Canadian and U.S. operating statements are found in (1) the columnar arrangement of the analyses, (2) terminology used, (3) method of handling settlement contracts and deposits, and (4) provision in the Canadian statements for separate pension and insurance funds. These differences and presentation of items in the two analyses are discussed in this section in order to bring all parts into focus.

Columnar Arrangement

The items on each line of the three Canadian operating statements are nearly identical. A transfer item appears in the two analyses that does not appear in the Revenue Account, and three items pertaining to pension and insurance funds appear in the analysis by fund and in the Revenue Account that do not appear in the analysis by line of business.

The *Analysis of Revenue Account by Line of Business* is arranged so as to facilitate fund accounting. There are two sets of columns: one for participating lines of business and one for nonparticipating lines of business. In each set there is a column for ordinary insurance, individual annuities, group life insurance, group annuities, industrial insurance, and a total column.

In the *Analysis of Revenue Account by Fund* there is a column for Participating Insurance Fund and another for a Nonparticipating Fund. There are also columns for seven other funds and a total column.

The amounts in the Total Participating Insurance column of the Analysis of Revenue Account by Line of Business (Figure 21–6) are entered in the Participating Insurance Fund column of the analysis by fund (Figure 21–8). Amounts in the Total Nonparticipating Insurance column of the Analysis of Revenue Account by Line of Business are entered in the Nonparticipating Fund column of the analysis by fund. In turn, amounts in the total column of the Analysis of Revenue Account by Fund are entered in the only column of the Revenue Account (Figure 21–7).

No column or columns are included for health insurance. Income and costs of total and permanent disability insurance and accidental death insurance are not shown separately but are included in the figures for ordinary insurance. Figures for settlement contracts are included in the column for the line of business under which they originated.

Terminology Differences

Items in the Canadian Revenue Account (see Figure 21–7) which are very similar to those of the U.S. summary of operations but which involve a difference in terminology are listed below. Other differences, including some related to these items, are noted in the later discussion.

Canadian Statement	U.S. Statement
Insurance premiums and annuity considerations	Premiums and annuity considerations
Considerations for settlement annuities	Consideration for supplementary contracts with and without life contingencies
Net investment income	Net investment income
Claims incurred under insurance and annuity contracts, other than under settlement annuities	Death benefits, matured endowments, annuity benefits, disability benefits, surrender benefits
Payments under settlement annuities	Payments on supplementary contracts with and without life contingencies
Interfund transfers to meet liabilities transferred	Group conversions and transfers on account of group package policies and contracts
Normal increase in actuarial reserve	Increase in aggregate reserve for policies and contracts with life contingencies
Interest paid on claims, borrowed money, etc.	Interest paid on policy and contract funds (and fill-in line)
Taxes, licenses, and fees, excluding investment taxes	Taxes, licenses, and fees
Commissions on insurance premiums and annuity considerations	Commissions on premiums and annuity considerations
General expenses (i.e., excluding investment expenses)	General insurance expenses
Dividends to policyholders	Dividends to life policyholders
Increase in provision for dividends and accrued profits to policyowners	Increase in amounts provisionally held for deferred dividend policies
Balance carried to reconciliation of surplus	Net gain from operations after dividends to policyowners and excluding capital gains and losses

Settlement Contracts and Amounts on Deposit

In the Canadian operating statements, contracts involving life contingencies and those providing for payment of proceeds in installments, even

Figure 21-6

VIII. ANALYSIS OF REVENUE ACCOUNT BY LINE OF BUSINESS

	Participating			
	Ordinary		Group	
—	Insurance	Annuity	Insurance	Annuity
	$	$	$	$
1. Insurance premiums and annuity considerations				
2. Considerations for settlement annuities				
3. Net investment income				
4.				
5.				
6.				
7.				
8. Inter-fund transfers to meet liabilities transferred				
9. Totals (items 1 to 8)				
10 Claims incurred under insurance and annuity contracts, other than under settlement annuities				
11. Payments under settlement annuities				
12. Normal increase in actuarial reserve				
13.				
14. Interest credited to amounts on deposit				
15. Interest paid on claims, borrowed money, etc.				
16. Taxes, licences, and fees, excluding investment taxes				
17. Commissions on insurance premiums and annuity considerations				
18. General expenses (i.e., excluding investment expenses)				
19.				
20.				
21.				
22.				
23. Dividends to policyholders				
24. Increase in provision for dividends and accrued profits to policyholders				
25. Totals (items 10 to 24)				
26. Balances				

Industrial	Total	Non-participating					Total
		Ordinary		Group		Industrial	
		Insurance	Annuity	Insurance	Annuity		
$	$	$	$	$	$	$	$

(Name of Company)

(Year of Statement)

Figure 21-7

.... (Year of Statement)

III. REVENUE ACCOUNT

1. Insurance premiums and annuity considerations (Exhibit 1, page 10)... $............

2. Considerations for settlement annuities.. ....

3. Investment income, less $............... investment expenses, investment taxes and annual depreciation of real estate (Exhibit 6, page 12)... ....

4. Contributions to staff pension and insurance funds, including $............... by staff................................ ....

5. ....

6. ....

7. ....

8.   Total (items 1 to 7)... $............

9. Claims incurred under insurance and annuity contracts, other than under settlement annuities (Exhibit 4, page 11)... $............

10. Payments under settlement annuities.. ....

11. Normal increase in actuarial reserve (i.e., excluding increase due to change in valuation bases)............. ....

12. Increase in staff pension and insurance funds................................

13. Interest credited to amounts on deposit with the Company (Exhibit 11, page 14).........

14. Interest paid on claims, borrowed money, etc.................................

15. Taxes, licences, and fees, excluding investment taxes (Exhibit 10, page 14)...........

16. Commissions on insurance premiums and annuity considerations (Exhibit 2, page 10)......

17. General expenses (i.e., excluding investment expenses) (Exhibit 9, page 13)............

18. Payments from staff pension and insurance funds..............................

19. ....

20. ....

21. ....

22. Dividends to policyholders (Exhibit 3, page 10)..............................

23. Increase in provision for dividends and accrued profits to policyholders.........

24.   Total (items 9 to 23)................................ $

25. Balance carried to Reconciliation of Surplus................................ $

though no life contingencies are involved, are described as *settlement annuities*. Contract proceeds held on deposit are classified as *amounts on deposit*.

Lines are provided in the three operating statements for *considerations for*, and *payments on, settlement annuities*. The increase in reserves for settlement annuities is a part of the *increase in actuarial reserve* in the Revenue account and is entered in columns for the line of business under which the settlement annuity originated.

Amounts on deposit are shown in the deposit exhibit (Exhibit 11) which is titled *amounts on deposit with the company pertaining to insurance and annuity contracts and including interest accumulations*. This title is also used to describe the liability in the balance sheet. This deposit exhibit was discussed in Chapter 17.

There is only one item in the Canadian operating statements which refers to amounts on deposit. This is a cost item described as *interest credited to amounts on deposit*. There is no *considerations for payments on*, or *increase in reserve* items for deposits similar to those related to settlement annuities in the Canadian statement or to supplemental contracts not involving life contingencies as in the U.S. *summary of operations*. The interest credited to the deposits is shown as a cost under the line of business through which the deposit originated.

Pension and Insurance Funds

Columns are provided in the Analysis of Revenue Account by Fund for an employees' pension fund. If there is only one formal pension plan covering both employees and agents, a column heading is changed to read "Staff Pension Fund" or similar wording, and all amounts are entered in the one column.

There are three items in the Revenue Account and the analysis by fund which refer to staff pension and insurance funds. These are: (1) *contributions to staff pension and insurance funds*, (2) *increase in staff pension and in insurance funds*, and (3) *payments from staff pension and insurance funds*. Interest allocated to these funds from the net investment income of the company is shown on the investment income line of the analysis by fund.

The word *insurance* in connection with these items refers only to insurance plans accounted for separately from the company's regular insurance plans. If the plan is funded by a standard policy form also available to the public, the premiums, claims, and reserve increases are usually included with the appropriate life insurance funds.

Investment income allocated to staff funds is shown as income for each fund and is also included in the total liability for each fund and becomes a part of the *increase in staff pension and insurance funds*. As a result, the net income (or *balance in the Revenue Account*) in these staff fund columns is always zero. The following example shows why this is so.

Assume the following circumstances:

```
Liability at beginning of year.......................$1,000
Interest allocated................................    50
Contributions to fund.............................   400
Payments from fund............................  -200
Liability at end of year.........................$1,250
```

The increase in reserves is $250 ($1,250 at end of year less $1,000 at beginning of year). These transactions reassembled into Revenue Account format appear as follows:

```
Contributions to fund.............................  $400
Investment income................................    50
Payments from fund..............................  -200
Increase in fund..................................  -250
Balance in the revenue account.....................  $ 00
```

A separate surplus item is not shown for staff funds on the liability page of the balance sheet, as is done for insurance and shareholders funds, because all amounts credited to pension or insurance funds become a general liability of the company. These liabilities are shown on separate lines of the liability page of the balance sheet.

Interfund Transfers

One item that appears in the two analyses of the Revenue Account but not in the Revenue Account itself is *Interfund transfers to meet liabilities transferred.* This item is intended primarily for transferring policy reserves between the participating and nonparticipating lines of business. It may also be used to show reserves transferred between the ordinary and group insurance lines in connection with group conversions.[1] When a transfer occurs, the net difference is always zero, so there is no amount to extend into the total column or to the Revenue Account. The need for such an item can be made apparent with an example.

In The XYZ Life Insurance Company of Canada, assume that policy reserve liabilities of $2,000 are transferred from the participating fund to the nonparticipating fund. All other figures are taken from the example on page 458.

Before the transfer is made, the increase in liabilities in the par fund is

---

[1] This item is similar to the group conversion item included in the U.S. analysis of operations.

Figure 21–8

V. ANALYSIS OF REVENUE ACCOUNT BY FUND

—	Participating Fund	Non-participating Fund	Shareholders Fund	Investment Reserve Fund
	$	$	$	$
1. Insurance premiums and annuity considerations...........				
2. Considerations for settlement annuities...........				
3. Net investment income...........				
4. Contributions to staff pension and insurance funds...........				
5.				
6.				
7.				
8. Inter-fund transfers to meet liabilities transferred...........				
9. Totals (items 1 to 8)...........				
10. Claims incurred under insurance and annuity contracts, other than under settlement annuities...........				
11. Payments under settlement annuities...........				
12. Normal increase in actuarial reserve...........				
13. Increase in staff pension and insurance funds...........				
14. Interest credited to amounts on deposit...........				
15. Interest paid on claims, borrowed money, etc...........				
16. Taxes, licences, and fees, excluding investment taxes...........				
17. Commissions on insurance premiums and annuity considerations.				
18. General expenses (i.e., excluding investment expenses)...........				
19. Payments from staff pension and insurance funds...........				
20.				
21.				
22.				
23. Dividends to policyholders...........				
24. Increase in provision for dividends and accrued profits to policyholders...........				
25. Totals (items 10 to 24)...........				
26. Balances carried to Reconciliation of Funds...........				

$7,000 and the increase in liabilities in the nonpar fund is $2,500. These are the true costs in the two funds for liability increases, and these costs should not be affected by a transfer in liabilities.

After the transfer in liabilities, however, the par fund liability becomes $33,000 ($35,000 before transfer less $2,000), and the nonpar fund liability

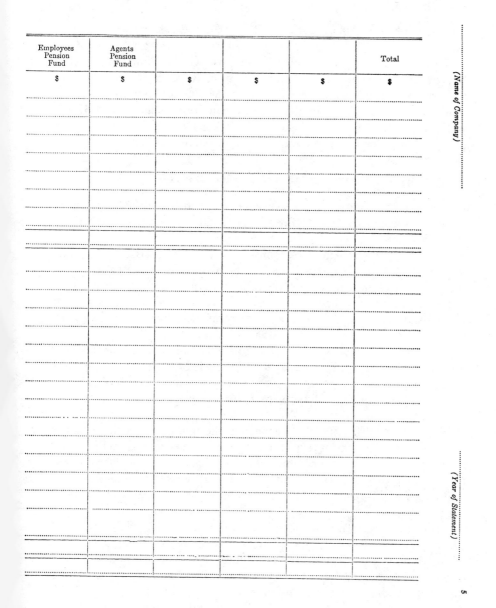

Employees Pension Fund	Agents Pension Fund				Total
$	$	$	$	$	$

(Name of Company)

(Year of Statement)

5

becomes $24,000 ($22,000 + $2,000). The increase in the par liability has obviously been reduced to $5,000 ($33,000 end of year − $28,000 beginning of year) and the increase in the nonpar liability has been increased to $4,500 ($24,000 end of year less $19,500 beginning of year).

In order that true cost may be reflected in the proper fund, an entry is made on working papers (and books, if consistent with company practice). The entry is:

Transfer of Reserves—Par.....................................2,000
    Transfer of Reserves—Nonpar.............................   2,000

These items are then included in the cost section of the Analysis of Revenue Account by Fund and the Analysis of Revenue Account by Line of Business. The normal reserve increase of $7,000 in the nonparticipating fund is thus reflected by two items: (1) the net reserve increase of $5,000, and (2) the debit reserve transfer of $2,000. Similar logic applies to the nonpar fund, except that the transfer is a negative $2,000.

Other Items in the Revenue Account and the Analyses

Most of the figures in the Revenue Account and the Analysis of Revenue Account by Line of Business are totals carried from the various exhibits in the Annual Statement blank.

Figures are entered in the exhibits on a revenue basis initially. Cash basis figures and adjustments from a cash basis to a revenue basis are not shown. As a result, it is not possible to trace Cash account balances in the ledger to the revenue basis items in the Revenue Account. However, if accounts are adjusted to the revenue basis on the ledger, an audit trail is complete from ledger to annual statement blank.

There are columns in the exhibits related to premiums, commissions, claims, and dividends to policyowners for each line and subline of business shown in the analysis by line of business. Separate total columns are also provided in these exhibits for participating and nonparticipating lines of business.

Net investment income is determined in the Investment Income exhibit by deducting investment expenses, investment taxes, and depreciation from the gross investment income. The net investment income is allocated to funds in the analysis by funds; and that which was allocated to insurance funds is reallocated to lines of business in the analysis by lines of business.

Since columns are not included in the expense and tax exhibits to show allocation of these two costs by line of business, working papers are required to make expense and tax allocations. The method used for allocating income and expenses must be reported on a page of the annual statement blank provided for this purpose.

The expense exhibit, it will be recalled, includes a line for advances to agents and another for office furniture (which includes equipment). It is not possible to capitalize and spread these costs over a period of years as may be done in the U.S. Statement. Data processing equipment, however, is an exception. It may be carried as asset and depreciated over a five year period.

All income, cost, and liability items involving reinsurance are shown in exhibits as net of reinsurance ceded. The reinsurance amount is also shown in each exhibit as a supplemental item of information. No reinsurance amounts, therefore, appear in the Revenue Account or the Analysis of Revenue Account by Line of Business.

A Canadian student who has not read Chapter 20 should now read the section of that chapter entitled "Interpreting the Analysis of Operations," paying particular attention to the portion relating to allocation of investment income. Material in that section is applicable to the Canadian Analysis of Revenue Account by Line of Business except where otherwise noted.

QUESTIONS

1. Why are separate funds maintained in a Canadian life insurance company? What balance sheet items are considered to be a part of the participating insurance fund? How are current liabilities classified in fund accounting?

2. How does the Analysis of Revenue Account by Fund enter into the audit trail from the Analysis of Revenue Account by Line of Business to the Revenue Account proper? What item appears in the Revenue Account with reference to amounts on deposit with the company? In what column of the Analysis by Line of Business is this amount (or amounts) shown? How does this differ from the U.S. method?

3. What items are shown in the Revenue Account that do not appear in the Analysis by Line of Business? What do these items have in common? What item appears in the two analyses of the Revenue Account, but does not appear in the Revenue Account proper? How is it used?

4. If the Analysis of the Revenue Account is used to measure the relative efficiency of a line of insurance in two companies, what three additional facts should be considered to interpret the figures correctly? What effects might these facts have on the operating gains of each line of business and the company as a whole?

5. Although Annual Statement instructions specify items to be included as *amounts owing*, what two characteristics generally determine these items? Give five items on the liability page classed as *amounts owing*, and five items that are classed as *fund* amounts. Since the annual statement blank makes provision for many funds, why does it provide for only three surplus items?

PROBLEM

Prepare a brief fund report of each of the following types:

1. Analysis of Revenue Account by Fund
2. Reconciliation of Funds
3. Summary of Funds and Amounts Owing by the Company

Assume that the following funds are affected: participating fund, nonparticipating fund, shareholders' fund, and staff pension fund. The investment income is to be allocated 35 percent to par, 50 percent to nonpar, 5 percent to staff pension fund, and 10 percent to shareholders' surplus. The beginning actuarial reserves are $78,000 (par) and $122,000 (nonpar).

The adjusted trial balance at the end of the year has been consolidated on working papers into the following amounts

Investment income.........................		$ 12,000
Premium income—par......................		35,000
Premium income—nonpar...................		42,000
Considerations for settlement annuities—nonpar..		4,000
Contributions to staff pension funds............		3,500
Claims paid—par.........................	$ 10,000	
Claims paid—nonpar......................	9,000	
Expenses paid—par.......................	6,000	
Expenses paid—nonpar....................	3,000	
Premiums due............................	1,500	
Investment income due and accrued...........	2,000	
Investments owned........................	338,000	
Increase in actuarial reserve—par............	22,000	
Increase in actuarial reserve—nonpar.........	28,000	
Payment from staff pension fund.............	1,500	
Dividends to policyowners..................	1,000	
Dividends to shareholders..................	1,500	
Claims unpaid............................		7,000
Actuarial reserve—par.....................		100,000
Actuarial reserve—nonpar..................		150,000
Capital..................................		10,000
Surplus—par.............................		20,000
Surplus—nonpar..........................		14,000
Staff pension fund........................		15,000
Shareholders' surplus......................		11,000
Nonpar surplus transfer out.................	4,000	
Shareholders' surplus transfer in.............		4,000
	$427,500	$427,500

It is suggested that closing entries be prepared first and posted to T-accounts to clarify the process before entering the data in report form. Columnar paper of four columns, one for each fund, should be used for the analysis and reconciliation. Omit the total column. On the summary use three columns, one for each insurance fund and one for totals of insurance funds and all other amounts. Remember the increase in the staff pension fund is the amount required to zero balance the staff pension fund column in the Analysis of Revenue Account.

Glossary

Account. Record of financial transactions by classification. This record shows the date and amount of each transaction and a reference to the original entry in the firm's books.

Account, clearing. Account for transferring amounts from one journal to another, or for transferring amounts between departments within a company. This type of account should have a zero balance at the end of each accounting period (month, year, etc.).

Account, control. Account in the general ledger representing the net sum of a related group of individual account balances in a subsidiary ledger.

Accounts, nominal. Accounts which represent a subdivision of the Surplus account and which are closed into the Surplus account at the end of the fiscal period, i.e., income and expense accounts.

Accounts, real. Accounts which are not closed at the end of the fiscal period, i.e., the asset, liability, and surplus accounts.

Accounting. The art of analyzing, recording, classifying, summarizing, interpreting, and reporting the financial activities of a business firm or other organization.

Accrual basis accounting. (Sometimes referred to as revenue basis accounting.) Accounting system in which income and expense items are adjusted to the amounts earned or incurred during the period, as contrasted with the cash basis which recognizes income only when collected and expenses only when paid.

Accumulations. Amounts left on deposit with a life insurance company at interest. Interest is added to the principal each year.

Adjusted trial balance. List of account balances after adjusting entries have been posted, with debit and credit balances separately totaled. The purpose of the adjusted trial balance is to prove that the ledger is in balance after recording the adjustments.

Adjusting entries. Entries made at the end of an accounting period to adjust account balances from the cash basis to the accrual basis.

Advance and arrears system. A method of controlling premiums collected by debit insurance agents under which the agent is charged each week or month with all premiums due on the debit, plus premiums paid in advance, less premiums past due.

Allocate. Apportion or distribute amounts to several selected areas.

Amortization. Accounting process of periodically and systematically adjusting the premium paid for, or discount allowed on, an investment so that on the maturity date the net book value becomes equal to the maturity value. The opposite debit or credit is charged or credited to an appropriate investment income account. Amortization also means a systematic reduction of a debt, such as a mortgage loan.

Analysis of operations by lines of business. A report included in the U.S. Annual Statement blank which shows operating gains in each of several lines of business, with a total column for all lines.

Asset. Anything of value owned by a business.

Asset, admitted. Asset value permissible for Annual Statement purposes as determined by regulatory authorities.

Asset, book value. Amount of asset as shown in a ledger account balance, usually the cost adjusted for depreciation, amortization, or payments on principal; not necessarily the same as market value.

Assets, fixed. Property of a relatively permanent nature (useful life of more than one year) used in the operations of the business and acquired primarily for use rather than resale.

Assets, nonledger. Asset values not recorded on an insurance company ledger during the accounting period. Includes, among others, due and accrued income, and admitted value of assets in excess of book value.

Asset, not admitted (or nonadmitted). An asset not acceptable for inclusion on the balance sheet in a life insurance Annual Statement, according to government regulations. Includes, among others, supplies, inventories, office furniture, etc.

Audit. A verification of the accuracy of the financial statements of a company and an examination of the entire accounting process in detail.

Audit trail. Detail included in recording an accounting transaction so that an auditor or other person can trace that transaction either from its origin through the original book entry to any subsidiary ledger or general ledger account to which it was posted or from the ledger posting back to the original entry.

Balance account. Special account found in life insurance ledgers. The account is used to absorb the difference between the total of ledger assets and total of ledger liabilities at the beginning of the accounting period. This account may also be known as Net Ledger Assets, Ledger Assets, General Fund, and Ledger Surplus.

Balance of an account. Difference between the total debits and total credits in an account at any particular time.

Balance sheet. A statement of the financial condition of a business on a specific date. Assets, liabilities, and capital items are listed on this statement.

Bookkeeping. Process for recording financial transactions. Double-entry bookkeeping is recording transactions consisting of two equal parts known as debits and credits.

Bookkeeping machine. Machine designed to perform bookkeeping processes. This machine has the ability to record dates, descriptive or explanatory information, dollar amounts, and the ability to add or subtract several columns of figures as they are entered.

Byte. A group of adjacent binary digits which are treated as a unit; eight binary digits plus what is called a *parity-bit;* may represent one alphabetic or special character, or two decimal digits.

Calculator. (1) Unit record machine capable of making arithmetical calculations and punching the results in a card. (2) Desk type machine used for multiplication, division, addition, and subtraction.

Capital gain. Increase in the admitted value of an asset, or the profit from the sale of an asset. The former is an unrealized capital gain, and the latter is a realized capital gain.

Capital loss. Decrease in the admitted value of an asset, or the loss from the sale of an asset. The former is an unrealized capital loss, and the latter is a realized capital loss.

Capitalize. To record an expense as an asset.

Cash accounting system. The accounting system used in connection with debit insurance under which the agent is charged with premiums collected, as compared with the advance and arrears system where the agent is charged with premiums due.

Cash basis accounting. An accounting method under which transactions are recognized and recorded only when cash is received or disbursed.

Central processor. Main unit of a computer. This unit is capable of storing programs and other data until needed, making calculations and comparisons, manipulating data as instructed by an internally stored program, and controlling other data processing machines.

Chart of accounts. List of accounts in the general ledger, with code numbers assigned to each account by classifications and subclassifications. Often the accounts are listed in the order in which they appear on the financial statements of the business.

Check digit. Extra character, or digit, used in connection with an identification number, such as a policy number. This character permits a computer to determine whether the identification number was correctly entered.

Closing the books. Process of closing nominal accounts directly or indirectly into the Surplus account or Balance account at the end of the fiscal period. *Closing Entries* are general journal entries made for this purpose.

Collator. Punched card machine capable of merging two decks of cards in the same sequence, selecting or matching common information in each deck of cards, and sequence-checking cards to determine that they are in the desired sequence.

Compound entry. Journal entry consisting of more than a single debit and/or credit; total debits and credits must be equal.

Computer. Set of interconnected data processing machines which use electronic circuits and magnetism for computing, processing, storing, and printing data.

Console. Machine attached on line to a computer to provide manual operator control.

Consolidated function record. Record containing all accounting and statistical data about a single account, such as a policy, or an agent.

Credit. (1) Entry to the right side of an account, or the portion of a journal entry that will be posted to the right side of an account. (2) Eligibility to borrow money or purchase goods without immediate cash payment.

Data processing equipment. Any equipment that processes data. Commonly used to describe machines which process accounting and statistical data to produce a complete report periodically, such as an agent's commission statement, insurance-in-force report, etc.

Debit. An entry to the left side of an account, or the portion of a journal entry that will be posted to the left side of an account.

Debit insurance. Any insurance on which weekly or monthly premiums are collected by an agent at the home or place of business of the insured. It may include industrial, ordinary, health, and even group insurance.

Deferred premiums. Premiums not yet due but which will become due after the end of the calendar year and prior to the next policy anniversary. *Net* deferred premiums are equal to gross deferred premiums less the expense loading.

Deficit. A deficiency in amount; a debit balance in Surplus.

Depreciation. Process of wearing out and/or becoming obsolete through passage of time. *Depreciation expense* is the cost of the depreciation on fixed assets, usually allocated periodically.

Depreciation, accumulated. The amount of depreciation which has been charged as an expense over the period a fixed asset has been owned. This amount is reflected in an account with a credit balance, and the related fixed asset account continues to show the original cost. (See Asset, book value.)

Depreciation process. Technique or method used to spread the cost of a fixed asset over the years of its useful life.

Direct access. Ability of a computer to answer inquiries for data on a random basis and to store data in an on-line storage device.

Discount, bonds. Excess of the face amount of a bond over its cost.

Discount, premiums. Amount of interest allowed a policyowner when he pays premiums in advance.

Dividends, cash. Distribution of corporate earnings to stockholders in the form of cash.

Dividends, policy. Return of a portion of the premium charged for participating insurance, representing the difference between the premium paid and the actual cost of furnishing insurance protection.

Dividends, stock. Distribution of corporate earnings to stockholders in the form of additional shares of stock.

Exhibit. Supplementary report in an Annual Statement showing greater detail of income, expense, or balance sheet items than is practical in the summary of operations or balance sheet.

Expense. Value disbursed or consumed in the normal course of business and which decreases the surplus of the company; a cost for service or supplies purchased as distinguished from cost of merchandise or raw material.

Expense, accrued. Liability for expense incurred during a period but which is not payable until a future date.

Expense, incurred. Expense applicable to a period which has passed, or an expense which has become payable.

Expense, prepaid. In commercial accounting: An expense which has been paid and recorded but not yet fully incurred. In life insurance accounting, expenses are usually treated as operating costs in the year paid; if prepaid expenses are recorded as assets they are treated as not admitted assets.

Field. (1) Portion of a magnetic record, or a column or group of columns on a punched card, used to record a particular item of data, such as a policy number, or amount of insurance. (2) Reference to insurance company operations "outside" of the home office, e.g., agency force.

Field accounting system. See Cash accounting system.

File. Any set of records, including those maintained on punched cards, magnetic tapes, and magnetic discs.

File, master. Set of records from which supplementary records are reproduced; serves as a principal data source about a particular set of records.

File, summary. Set of totals, usually totals of various types of transactions which have occurred.

Fiscal period. The accounting period during which the books remain open. Usually one year; may not coincide with calendar year.

Fixed assets. See Assets, fixed.

Folio. Page number. In a ledger account it indicates the number of the journal page from which data has been posted; on a journal page it indicates the number of the ledger page to which data has been posted.

Fund analysis. General expression used to describe the Analysis of Revenue Account by Fund which appears in the Canadian Annual Statement. This report shows the income and expenses relating to participating and nonparticipating funds, and any other special funds maintained for the benefit of agents, employees, or shareholders.

Imprest system. System under which a predetermined amount is set up in a special fund, such as Petty Cash, for the payment of small bills. Appropriate expense accounts are debited when the fund is replenished for amounts paid out.

Income. Value received or earned in the normal course of business and which increases the surplus of the company.

Income, accrued. Income that has been earned but which has not yet been received. It may include income not yet due.

Income and expense statement. Financial statement showing the income and expenses of a business firm during a stated period and the resulting gain or loss. Also known as profit and loss statement, revenue and expense statement, and summary of operations.

Income and expense summary. An account used to summarize income and expense account balances, all of which are closed into it. The balance of this account reflects net income which is then closed into the Surplus account. This account is sometimes called the Profit and Loss Summary.

Income, earned. Income applicable to a period of time which has passed.

Income, gross. Full amounts received.

Income, net. Gross income less all costs, expenses, and taxes.

Income, unearned. Income received and recorded which is applicable to a later accounting period. It is a liability on the balance sheet. Also known as deferred credits or deferred income.

Interpreter. Machine that reads data from a punched card and prints it on the card for visual processing.

Inventory process. Counting and valuing items for recording as of a specific date. This process may be used to calculate both asset and liability (e.g., policy reserve) amounts.

Journal. A book of original entry recording financial transactions chronologically, in terms of equal debit and credit amounts.

Journal, general. Simplest form of journal, providing separate amount columns for the debit and credit portions of each entry.

Journal, special. Journal in which frequently used accounts are assigned separate columns thus permitting summarized posting to those accounts in the general ledger.

Ledger. A set of accounts to which journal entries are posted.

Ledger, general. Principal ledger of a business firm. It includes accounts representing all assets, liabilities, and all capital accounts. During the accounting period it also includes all nominal accounts. It must be in balance (debit balances equal to credit balances) at all times.

Ledger, subsidiary. Set of accounts outside of the general ledger, which are represented in the general ledger by a single control account.

Liability. Debt or amount owed which may or may not be immediately payable. (See Reserves.)

Liability, nonledger. Liabilities of a life insurance company that are not entered in the ledger, such as policy reserves, unearned income, and accrued expense.

Loading. Amount added to a net premium to cover expenses and taxes; difference between gross and net premiums.

Loss, net. The amount of loss resulting when costs and expenses exceed income.

Machine language. (1) Systematic pattern of holes or magnetized spots which machines can read. (2) Symbols and numbers which tell a computer what functions to perform.

Machine readable. Recorded in such a way that a machine can recognize and process the record automatically.

Magnetic tape. Continuous ribbon of plastic or mylar material coated with a substance which can be magnetized in tiny spots known as bits.

Mark-sensing machine. Unit record machine capable of reading graphite pencil marks placed on a card and automatically punching into the card the data indicated by the marks.

Memory. Internal storage capacity of the central processor of a computer.

Mode of payment. Frequency of premium payment, such as annually, quarterly, monthly, weekly.

Morbidity reserve. Amount carried for future claims on health insurance policies.

Morbidity tables. Chart showing statistics and other numerical data on illness.

Off line. An expression to indicate that a machine is being operated in conjunction with a computer without being connected to the central processor.

On Line. An expression used to indicate that the operation of a machine is connected to and under the control of the central processor of a computer.

Overriding commission. An insurance commission paid to a general agent over and above a commission paid to his sales agent.

Paid-up additions. Additional units of paid-up life insurance purchased by policy dividends.

Participating insurance. Insurance on which policy dividends are payable.

Post. Enter a financial transaction from a journal to an account in a ledger.

Premium, bond. Excess of the cost of a bond over its face amount.

Premiums, advance. Premiums collected and entered to the premium account but due in a later accounting period. Does not include unearned premiums, or premiums recorded in a special premium deposit account.

Premiums, deferred. See Deferred premiums.

Premiums, net. Actuarially calculated premiums which do not include a loading for expenses.

Premiums, uncollected. Premiums due or past due on policies. Also known as Due Premiums and Outstanding Premiums.

Premiums, unearned. Fractions of premiums applicable to the following accounting period.

Profit and loss statement. See Income and expense statement.

Profit and loss summary. See Income and expense summary.

Profit, gross. Income from sales, less cost of merchandise, before expenses and taxes are deducted to obtain net profit.

Profit, net. Gross income, less all costs, expenses, and taxes.

Program language. Simplified instructions for telling a computer what steps to perform. Must be interpreted into machine language automatically by the computer before the program can be used.

Random access. See direct access.

Ratio. Relationship of one item to another, such as 4 to 1 or 25 percent of a total.

Reconciliation. Process for determining and identifying items that have caused changes in an account between two dates.

Reconciliation, bank. A process for locating differences between the balance shown on a bank statement and the ledger account balance shown on a company's books for that bank.

Reconciliation of surplus. Title of an exhibit in the Canadian Annual Statement which shows the increases and decreases in surplus between the end of one year and the end of the next. It is the equivalent of the surplus account of the U.S. Statement.

Record, consolidated function. See Consolidated function record.

Record, detail. See Transaction record.

Record, historical. Record of a financial or statistical transaction, including the date and amount of a transaction which has taken place.

Reproducer. Unit record machine which can duplicate all or any part of a deck of punched cards.

Reserve. Any amount needed for future payments, including reserves required by law and those held voluntarily. A reserve is a liability item and may be of a long-term nature, such as life insurance policy reserves, or may be short-term, such as contingency reserves held for claim payment or investment fluctuation.

Reserve, actuarial. Policy reserve calculated by mathematical formula; in financial statements usually refers to the mean reserve.

Reserve, initial. Policy reserve at the beginning of a policy year. In the ordinary classification of life insurance, it is equal to the terminal reserve for a policy at the end of the preceding policy year plus the net annual premium for the current policy year.

Reserve, mean. (1) Policy reserve amount equal to the average of the initial reserve and the terminal reserve for a given policy year. (2) Reserve amount generally used to value liability of insurance policies for Annual Statement purposes.

Reserve, policy. Amount of liability which a life insurance company is required by law to carry on its balance sheet in order to show ability to pay all future claims on its policies.

Reserve, terminal. Reserve amount on a policy at the end of a given policy year.

Responsibility area. Department or other organizational unit under the supervision of a single person.

Revenue account. Portion of the Canadian Annual Statement that is the equivalent of the summary of operations of the U.S. Statement.

Revenue basis. See Accrual basis.

Schedule. Listing of items with a summary which supports an item shown on the balance sheet or summary of operations.

Shareholder. See Stockholder.

Status print-out. Sheet printed by a computer showing the status of a life insurance policy or other record, such as an agent's record.

Stockholder. Part owner of a corporation; rights of such ownership is represented by shares of stock.

Summary of operations. Statement of income and charges against income that appears in the U.S. Annual Statement. It is the equivalent of income and expense statement of commercial accounting or Revenue Account of the Canadian Annual Statement.

Summary punch. Unit record machine which automatically punches into new cards identification and summarized data received from another machine.

Surplus. Ownership value in excess of capital stock; includes earnings retained in the business and amounts set aside for special contingencies.

Surplus account. (1) Title of the exhibit in U.S. Annual Statement which reconciles the surplus at the beginning of the year and surplus at the end of the year. (2) An account in the general ledger which shows surplus.

Surplus, contributed. Amount paid to a company for its capital stock in excess of the par value of the stock.

Surplus, unassigned. Surplus available for payment of dividends or any other purpose determined by the board of directors.

Suspense account. Liability account to which amounts are temporarily credited if the proper account is unknown or if certain conditions must be met before money received can be taken into income.

Tape drive. Machine connected to the central processor of a computer which reads coded data from, and enters it on, magnetic or paper tape.

Transaction record. A record used to control a transaction from the pending stage through the accounting phase. It may be used as a historical record after the transaction is recorded. Also known as a detail record.

Trial balance. List of all account balances in ledger on a particular day. All debit balances are shown in one column and totaled, and all credit balances are shown in another and totaled. The totals must be equal.

Trial balance, after-closing (or post-closing). Trial balance made after all nominal accounts have been closed at the end of fiscal period.

Unit record equipment. Data processing equipment which processes a fixed length record, usually a punched card.

Value, admitted. See Asset, admitted.

Value, amortized. Present net book value of an investment which is being amortized; cost of an investment adjusted for amortization to date.

Value, book. Current amount as reflected in a ledger account.

Value, nonadmitted or not admitted. See Asset, not admitted.

Value, salvage. The amount that is expected to be realized on a fixed asset when it is traded in or sold at the end of its useful life.

Verifier. Unit record machine that permits an operator to detect errors in punched cards or paper tape by repeating the typing operations of a keypunch operator.

Vested. Owned unconditionally; not contingent. When used with commissions, a commission payable to an agent after his contract is terminated.

Word. In computer usage, a group of digits or characters that are handled as a unit in data manipulation; may be fixed or variable in length, according to the design of the computer involved.

488   *Accounting—for Life Insurance Companies*

Working paper. A multicolumned form used to facilitate preparation (1) of adjusting and closing entries before recording them on the books, and (2) the three principal financial statements (income and expense statement, surplus statement, and balance sheet). Also known as a *work sheet.*

Update. Adjust a record to show a more current status.

Answers to Problems

CHAPTER 2

Trial Balance

Cash	$ 7,350	
Autos Owned	4,200	
Accounts Receivable	300	
Notes Payable		$ 1,500
Capital Stock		10,000
Fee Income		500
Salary Expense	150	
	$12,000	$12,000

CHAPTER 3

SERVICE INC.
Income and Expense Statement
For the Month of March, 19—

Service income	$ 1,120.00	
Interest income	23.50	
Total Income		$ 1,143.50
Salary expense	$ 671.00	
Insurance expense	10.00	
Rent expense	100.00	
Total Expense		781.00
Net Income		$ 362.50

Post-Closing Trial Balance

Cash	$10,450.00	
Notes receivable	450.00	
Prepaid insurance	45.00	
Accrued interest	1.50	
Accounts payable		$ 211.00
Accrued salary		346.00
Accrued rent		37.00
Prepaid service income		515.00
Capital		500.00
Surplus		9,337.50
	$10,946.50	$10,946.50

CHAPTER 4

ABC SERVICE INC.
Working Paper
For Year Ending December 31, 19—

Account	Adjusted Trial Balance Dr.	Adjusted Trial Balance Cr.	Income and Expense Dr.	Income and Expense Cr.	Surplus Dr.	Surplus Cr.	Balance Sheet Dr.	Balance Sheet Cr.
Cash	7,000.00						7,000.00	
Accounts Receivable	2,100.00						2,100.00	
Inventory	4,000.00		4,000.00	6,500.00			6,500.00	
Notes Receivable	1,500.00						1,500.00	
Office Supplies on Hand	500.00						500.00	
Unexpired Insurance	500.00						500.00	
Interest Income Due and Accrued	150.00						150.00	
Accounts Payable		250.00						250.00
Notes Payable		1,000.00						1,000.00
Accrued Salaries Payable		400.00						400.00
Accrued Rent Payable		300.00						300.00
Unearned Service Income		1,200.00						1,200.00
Interest Expense Accrued		34.00						34.00
Sales		25,000.00		25,000.00				
Service Income		5,900.00		5,900.00				
Interest Income		150.00		150.00				
Purchases	15,000.00		15,000.00					
Rent Expense	1,244.00		1,244.00					
Salary Expense	7,500.00		7,500.00					
Dividends Paid	300.00				300.00			
Capital		1,000.00						1,000.00
Surplus		5,294.00				5,294.00		
Office Supplies Used	200.00		200.00					
Insurance Expense	517.00		517.00					
Interest Expense	17.00		17.00					
	40,528.00	40,528.00	28,478.00	37,550.00	300.00			
Net Income			9,072.00			9,072.00		
			37,550.00	37,550.00	14,066.00	14,366.00		
Surplus								14,066.00

CHAPTER 5

Problem 1

	Outstanding Checks	Deposits-in-Transit
	$110	$69.20
	14	
	22	
	$146	

Reconciliation

Bank balance..................	$1,050.00	Cash balance..................	$994.40
Deposits-in-transit............	+ 69.20	Co. error, check 104	− 18.00
Outstanding checks..........	− 146.00	Service charge	− 3.20
Adjusted bank balance........	$ 973.20	Adjusted book balance..........	$973.20

Required Entries

```
Bank Service Charges.......................................  3.20
Rent.......................................................18.00
  Cash.....................................................         21.20
```

Problem 2

Schedule of Agents' Balances

No.	
3............	$ 9.00
16..........	10.49
25..........	5.36
42..........	6.85
	$31.70

Trial Balance

Acct.	Dr.	Cr.
Cash........................	1,235.04	
Agents ledger...............		31.70
Premium income.............		247.60
Commissions.................	21.71	
Surplus.....................		977.45
	1,256.75	1,256.75

CHAPTERS 10 AND 11

Problem 1.

Trial Balance, December 31, 19—

Cash	$ 65,775.00	
Bonds owned	12,456.33	
Stocks owned	4,400.00	
Policy loans	8,464.00	
Mortgage loans	15,000.00	
Real estate owned—home office	100,890.00	
Accrued depreciation—home office		$ 1,500.00
Escrow funds—mortgages		211.00
Balance account		206,422.00
Ren. premiums		25.00
Interest income on bonds		511.33
Dividends received		250.00
Interest on policy loans		511.00
Interest income on mortgages		750.00
Rental income		6,000.00
Taxes on real estate	1,900.00	
Depreciation on real estate—home office	1,500.00	
Gain on sale of stock		515.00
Loss on sale of real estate	310.00	
Rent expense	6,000.00	
	$216,695.33	$216,695.33

Problem 2. *Accrual basis income:*

Interest income on bonds	$	518.33
Interest income on mortgages		767.00
Rental income		6,600.00
Interest on policy loans		457.00

CHAPTER 12

The total of trial balance columns is $11,449. The adjusted trial balances are as follows:

	United States Dr.	United States Cr.	Canadian Dr.	Canadian Cr.
Cash........................	$11,177.00		$11,177.00	
Policy loans...................	250.00		250.00	
Premium deposits...............		484.00		484.00
Balance account................		10,026.80		9,750.40
Premium income—life...........		1,075.00		1,067.00
Premium income—health.........		45.00		34.00
Policy loan interest.............		17.00		17.00
Dividends applied to premiums......	18.00		18.00	
Accrued policy loan interest........	5.00		5.00	
Interest paid on policy and contract funds.......................	4.00		4.00	
Net uncollected premiums.........	68.00		68.00	
Net deferred premiums............	224.80			
Commissions....................				1.40
Increase in loading..............	3.00			
Unearned premiums—health.......				69.00
Advance premiums—life..........		102.00		102.00
	$11,749.80	$11,749.80	$11,523.40	$11,523.40

U.S. Comment: Unearned health insurance premiums and premium deposits are *not* used to adjust premium income to the accrual basis.

Canadian Comment: The debit balance for commissions is the increase in cost of collecting outstanding premiums.

Deferred premiums, premium deposits, and premium suspense are *not* used to adjust the premium income to the revenue basis.

CHAPTER 13

Schedule of Agents' Accounts
May 31, 19__

Agent	Dr.	Cr.
5...................		$ 8.00
6...................		13.35
15...................$	2.02	
25...................		16.95
35...................	1,603.60	
45...................		2,352.93
61...................		4.75
73...................	888.17	
79...................		2,166.67
	$2,493.79	$4,562.65
Difference..............		$2,068.86

Trial Balance

Account	Dr.	Cr.
Cash.....................$	8,922.50	
Bonds....................	100,000.00	
Premium income............		$ 53,449.75
Income agents supp...........		1,225.00
Dividends applied............	1,445.00	
Inspection fees..............	7,495.00	
Premium suspense...........		126.00
Commissions................	20,860.74	
Agents' ledger control........		2,068.86
Balance account.............		81,706.00
Policy loan interest..........		110.00
Taxes withheld..............		37.63
	$138,723.24	$138,723.24

In the U.S. Annual Statement the Agents' Ledger Control account balance, if a debit, is not admitted. A liability is entered on the balance sheet in the amount of credit balances. The effect on surplus is a $433.79 decrease for the year, equal to the increase in debit balances.

In the Canadian Annual Statement, the Agents' Ledger Control account is zero balanced. Increase in debit balances is treated as an expense, Advances to Agents. Credit balances are included with other commission liabilities.

CHAPTER 17

1. *a*) Policy Dividends Paid.........................10,500.00
Cash.....................................   10,500.00

Items included on a summary list would include check number, date, payee, amount of dividend, and policy number.

b) Dividends Left on Deposit........................15,000.00
Dividend Deposits Received..................   15,000.00

Summary list would include date, dividend amount, interest credited, and policy number.

c) No entry under traditional (nonledger) method.

d) Dividends to Purchase PUA...................... 5,150.00
Single Premium for PUA....................   5,150.00

Summary list would include date of entry, amount of current PUA, amount of dividend applied, and policy number.

e) Dividend Deposits Paid.......................... 768.00
Cash.....................................   768.00

Summary list would include check number, date of entry, payee, amount paid, and policy number.

f) Dividends to Insurance Options.................... 348.00
Single Premiums for Insurance Dividend Options   348.00

Summary list would include date of entry, amount of dividend applied, and policy number.

g) Surrenders Paid—Ordinary...................... 310.00
Cash.....................................   310.00

Summary list would include check number, date of entry, payee, amount paid, and policy number.

2. *a*) Surrenders Paid—Ordinary..................... 2,000.00
Dividend Deposits Paid........................ 537.10
Cash.....................................   2,537.10

b) Surrenders Paid—Ordinary..................... 616.00
Policy Loan..............................   600.00
Policy Loan Interest.......................   16.00

3. *a*) Since reserve on first policy was $2,100 when it was surrendered for $2,000, surplus will increase by $100. Surplus does not change as a result of paying out accumulations, a nonledger liability amount. In effect the surplus decrease from the debit to Dividend Deposits Paid is offset by an equal surplus increase resulting from the decrease in liability.

b) Surplus increases by $100, the difference between the reserve released and the amount paid ($1,150 − $1,050).

CHAPTER 18

1. Death Claims Paid—Ordinary.........................4,850.00
Dividend Deposits Paid.............................. 284.50
Policy Loan Interest................................. 20.00
    Premiums—Renewal Ordinary.....................   69.00
    Policy Loans.....................................   1,800.00
    Cash..   3,285.50

2. Matured Endowment...............................3,116.00
    Policy Loan......................................   950.00
    Interest Income..................................   21.00
    Considerations for Supplementary Contracts WOLC..   2,145.00

If proceeds left for life with 10 years certain, the $2,145 amount would have been credited to *Considerations for Supplementary Contracts WLC* or divided into two parts, one to WOLC and the other to WLC.

3. *a*) Disability Claims Paid......................... 400.00
        Cash.....................................   400.00
    b) Hospital Benefits Paid......................... 250.00
        Cash.....................................   250.00

    c) Same as (*b*) except for amount.

    d) Premiums Waived—Disability Ordinary........... 100.00
        Premiums—Renewal Ordinary..............   100.00

    e) No entry because the premium and claim are in the same line of business.

    f) Indemnity Claims Paid........................ 2,000.00
        Cash.....................................   2,000.00
    g) Cash.......................................48,916.00
        Reinsurance Benefits Received—Ordinary Life.   48,916.00

4. Paid on Supplementary Contracts WOLC............. 135.00
    Cash..   135.00

(It would be equally correct to debit $110 Paid on Supplementary Contracts WOLC and $25 to Dividends Paid on Supplementary Contracts WOLC in a U.S. company.)

5. Annuity Benefits Paid....................................225.00
Dividends Paid on Annuities............................. 15.00
    Cash...   240.00

CHAPTER 19

1. Sixty-seven cents.

2. *a*) Salaries Paid....................................200.00
　　　　Withheld for Income Tax.................... 　　20.00
　　　　Group Insurance Premiums Withheld........... 　　12.00
　　　　FICA Tax Withheld......................... 　　10.00
　　　　Cash...................................... 　158.00

　　b) Group Insurance Premium Paid....................750.00
　　　　Group Insurance Premium Withheld................250.00
　　　　Cash...................................... 　1,000.00

　　c) Agents' Balances Charged Off..................... 50.00
　　　　Agents' Ledger Control..................... 　50.00

CHAPTER 20

1. Trial balance total $13,515, reconciliation equation $12,000 (LA_0) + $1,515 (R) − $575 (D) = $12,940 (LA_1).

2. $64.13. Process for solving: mean invested assets, $105,000. Mean policy reserves: industrial, $51,000; ordinary, $32,500. Interest at $\frac{1}{10}$ of 1 percent = $105. Allocated 51/83.5 to industrial.

CHAPTER 21

(1) *Analysis of Revenue Account by Fund*

	Participating Fund	Nonparticipating Fund	Shareholders' Fund	Staff Pension Fund
Premium income	$ 35,000	$ 42,000		
Investment income	4,200	6,000	$ 1,200	$ 600
Consideration for settlement annuity		4,000		
Contribution to staff pension funds				3,500
Total	$ 39,200	$ 52,000	$ 1,200	$ 4,100
Claims	$ 10,000	$ 9,000		
Increase in actuarial reserve	22,000	28,000		
Increase in staff pension funds				$ 2,600
Expenses	6,000	3,000		
Payments from staff pension funds				1,500
Dividends to policyowners	1,000			
	$ 39,000	$ 40,000	0	$ 4,100
Balance to Revenue Account	$ 200	$ 12,000	$ 1,200	0

(2) *Reconciliation of Funds*

	Participating Funds	Nonparticipating Funds	Shareholders' Funds	Staff Pension Fund
Funds, December 31, beginning	$ 98,000	$136,000	$11,000	$15,000
Balances from analysis of revenue acct	200	12,000	1,200	0
Normal increase in actuarial reserve	22,000	28,000		
Increase in staff pension funds				2,600
Total	$120,200	$176,000	$12,200	$17,600
Transfer of surplus to shareholders fund		−4,000	+4,000	
Dividends to shareholders			−1,500	
Total	$ 0	−4,000	$ 2,500	$ 0
Funds, December 31 ending	$120,200	$172,000	$14,700	$17,600

(3) *Summary of Funds and Amounts Owing*

	Participating Fund	Nonparticipating Fund	Total
Actuarial reserve	$100,000	$150,000	$250,000
Surplus	20,200	22,000	42,200
Total Insurance Funds	$120,200	$172,000	$292,200
Shareholders' funds:			
Capital			10,000
Surplus			14,700
Staff pension fund			17,600
Amounts Owing by Company			7,000
			$341,500

Index

A

Accident insurance; *see* Health insurance
Accidental death rider, 350, 352
Account payable, 11
Account receivable, 11, 50
Accounting
  accrual basis of, 39
  analyzing transactions, 10–11
  basic formal unit of, 11–18; *see also*
    Accounts
  basic terminology of, 8
  business uses of, 2–3
  cash basis of, 39, 139–41, 148
  corporate, 7
  cycle, 23
  defined, 8
  functions of, 3–6
  fundamentals of general, 7 ff.; *see also*
    specific topics
  life, defined, 135; *see also* Life
    accounting
  life insurance companies; *see* Life ac-
    counting
  machine methods, 99 ff.; *see also* Ma-
    chine accounting
  personal uses of, 1–2
  profit-oriented, 143
  revenue basis, 39
  solvency-oriented, 143
  steps in process of, 23
  surplus, changes in, 27 ff.
  time elements in, 38–39
  usefulness of knowledge of, 1–3
Accounting by exception, 118
Accounting controls, 115; *see also specific*
    topics
  machine accounting, 115–16
Accounting cycle, 23
Accounting equation, 8–10
  capital element of, changes in, 27 ff.
  changes in elements of, 10–11
  subdivision of elements of, 11–18; *see*
    also Accounts

Accounting machines; *see* Machine ac-
    counting
Accounting period, 38
  adjustments at end of, 39 ff.; *see also*
    Adjusting entries
Accounts; *see also specific account*
  asset, 12
  balance of, 15
  capital, 12
  capital stock, 16, 27
  chart of, 88–90
    machine accounting, 106–7
    Model Life Insurance Company il-
      lustration, 93–98
  code numbers for, 88–89
    machine accounting, 106–7
    Model Life Insurance Company il-
      lustration of, 93–98
  credit balance of, 15
  credits, 12, 13, 24–25
  debit balance of, 15
  debits, 12, 13, 24–25
  defined, 11, 24
  essential feature of, 12
  folio references, 12
  illustration of use of, 13–18
  journal entries for, 18–20
  ledger of, 18
  liability, 12
  nominal, 32–33
  posting to, 18–20
  recording of, form of, 12
  skeleton form of, 12–13
  standard form of, 12
  T-account, 12–13
  trial balance of, 20
Accounts receivable
  control account, 85–87
  schedule, 86–87
  subsidiary ledger, 85–87
Accrual basis accounting, 39, 47
Accrued bond interest, 173
Accrued costs (other than claims), 157

Accrued expense
  adjusting entries for, 44–47, 65
  defined, 44
Accrued income, 152, 170
  adjusting entries for, 43–44, 47, 65
  defined, 43
Accumulated depreciation account, 74, 89
Adjusted balance method of making adjusting entries, 65–66
Adjusting entries
  accrued expense, 44–47
  accrued income, 43–44, 47
  adjusted balance method of making, 65–66; *see also* Working papers
  cash basis to accrual basis, 39–47
  expense liability, 388–90
  function of, 39–40
  investment income from cash to accrual basis, 170–72
  need for, 39–40
  posting of, 46
  prepaid expense, 41–42, 47
  reversal and reentry method of making, 65, 67–68; *see also* Working papers
  unearned income, 40–41, 47
  working papers, 61–70; *see also* Working papers
Administrative decisions, accounting as basis for, 3–4
Admitted asset values, 144, 148
Advance and arrears system of premium control, 288
  agent's account, 288–94
  calling of, 291–94
  life register, 288, 294–97
Advance premiums, 213–14, 233, 280–81
  discounts on, 214
Advertising expenses, 405
Agency accounting functions in debit insurance accounting, 285–88
Agency conferences, 407
Agency expense allowance, 407
Agent's account, 238–40, 250
  advance and arrears system of premium control, 288–94
  calling the account, 291–94
  cancellation fees for "not taken out" policies, 245
  commission entries, 241–43
  debit balances, 250
  entries for, 241–48
  miscellaneous charges, 244–45
  payments to agents, 243
  remitting nets, 245–48
  taxes on commission earnings, 243–44
Agents' balances charged off, 386–87

Agents' commissions; *see* Commissions
Amortized value
  assets, 144, 148
  bonds, 152
Amounts held on deposit, 156, 328, 346
  interest credited to, 328–32
  ledger liability process, 328–30, 346
  nonledger liability process, 330–32, 346
Amounts temporarily held for disposition, 157–58
Analysis of business transactions, 10–11
Analysis of functional unit costs, 394–96
Analysis of operations, 160–65, 432–36
  interpretation of, 436–45
  value of, 445
Annual report, 137
Annual statement
  allocation of investment income, 437–39
  amounts receivable, 428, 430
  analysis of nonadmitted assets and related items, 427–30
  analysis of operations, 160–65, 432–36
  interpretation of, 436–45
  value of, 445
  asset exhibit, 414–20
  balance sheet, 150–59; *see also* Balance sheet
  capital gains and losses exhibit, 200–202
  claim liabilities, inclusion of, 362–63
  claims and claim settlements, 370–74
  commissions indicated on, 248–50
  company's stock owned, 428
  composition of, 150 ff.
  consolidating income and costs by sublines, effect of, 442
  distribution of income and expense items by lines of business, 439–42
  dividend liabilities, 340–43
  exhibits in, 162
  expenses, preparation of, 396–99
  forms required for, 137–38
  group conversion, 434–36
  health insurance exhibit, 445–46
  insurance costs, 433–36
  investments indicated on, 196–200
  liabilities, 420
  loans, 428, 430
  nonadmitted assets, 420, 427–30
  nonledger assets, 415
  operating gains
    capital, surplus and investment effectiveness, effect of, 444–45
    new business, effect of, 442–44
  policy dividends, 340–43
  premium income aspects, 221–27, 233–34

Annual statement—*Cont.*
  prepaid expenses, 428
  reconciliation of ledger assets exhibit,
      420–26
    description of items in, 426–27
    entries for, 421
    process, 424–25
    relationship of balance account to,
        425–26
  schedule T, 280
  standardization of life accounting prac-
      tices by, 135–37
  summary of operations, 159–65; *see
      also* Summary of operations
  supplementary contracts, 433
  surplus account, 430–32
  taxes, presentation of, 396–97
  terminology differences with Canadian
      annual statement, 467
Annualized premium, 302
Annuities, 327, 368
  payment control, 368
  records of, 368
Answers to problems, 489 ff.
Armed forces members, government al-
    lotment for premium payment, 277
Assets, 8, 24; *see also specific type*
  accounts for, 12
  admitted, 144, 148
  amortized valuation of, 144, 148
  annual statement exhibit, 414–20
  classification of, 151–53
  going-concern valuation of, 142–43
  ledger, 142
  liquidation valuation of, 143, 148
  nonadmitted, 144–46, 148, 420, 427–30
  nonledger, 142, 144, 415
Association Annual Statement, 138
Association group insurance, 309, 322
Audit trail, 117–18
Automatic Bank Check, 275
Automatic premium loan (APL), 191

B

Balance account, 146–48
  relationship to reconciliation of ledger
      assets, 425–26
Balance sheet, 9, 24
  account form, 9 n
  asset classifications, 151–53
  form of, 151
  liability classifications, 153–59
  purpose of, 150–51
  report form, 9 n, 22–23
  supporting schedules, 152
  trial balance used in preparation of,
      21–23

Bank statement reconciliations, 78–82
Benefits of policies, settlement of; *see*
    Policy benefit settlements
Blue Statement, 138
Bond accounting, 168–76
  amortization; *see* Bond discount and
      premium
  annual statement form for, 196–203
Bond discount and premium, 173–77, 206
Bond valuation, 152
Book value, 74
Bookkeeping cycle, 23 n
Bookkeeping machines; *see* Conven-
    tional bookkeeping machines
Books and periodicals, cost of, 406
Branch office premium handling, 267–69
Budgets, 390–94, 411
Bureau and association dues, 406
Business ownership forms, 7
Business uses of accounting, 2–3

C

Calculators, 127
Calendar year versus fiscal year, 38
Canadian annual statement aspects; *see*
    Canadian life insurance accounting
Canadian life insurance accounting
  amounts on deposit, 467, 472
  analysis of revenue account by line of
      business, 161
  annual statement aspects of; *see spe-
      cific topics under this heading*
  annual statement form required, 137–
      38
  annual statement reports, 448 ff.
  asset page, 450–51
  bond valuation, 202
  capital gains and losses exhibit, 203,
      206
  claims and claim settlements, 374–78
  commissions on insurance premiums
      and annuity considerations, 249–50
  dividend liabilities, 343–46
  entries for claim settlements, 349
  expense exhibits, 409–11
  expenses, presentation of, 396, 402–3
  fund accounting, 448–64
  furniture and equipment cost, 73 n
  insurance funds, 472–73
  interfund transfers, 473–76
  investment income, 203–5
  investment reserve account, 145
  investment reserve fund, 181
  investments shown on annual state-
      ment, 202–6
  liability page, 451–52
  pension funds, 472–73

Canadian life insurance acounting—*Cont.*
  policy dividends, 343–46
  premium income exhibits on annual
    statement, 227–33
  reconciliation of funds, 458–64
  reconciliation of surplus, 139, 464–65
  revenue account, 30 n, 139, 466–77
    related analyses, 466–77
  settlement contracts, 467, 472
  stock valuation, 202–3
  summary of funds and amounts owing
    by the company, 454–58
  surplus in insurance funds, 158
  surplus, reconciliation of, 464–65
  surplus in shareholders fund, 158
  tax exhibit, 409–11
  taxes, presentation of, 396, 402–3
  terminology differences with United
    States annual statement, 467
Capital, 8, 24
  accounts for, 12
Capital gains and losses, 163
  exhibit on annual statement, 200–202
  investment principal, 168
Capital stock, balance sheet treatment of,
    158–59
Capital stock account, 16, 27
Capital stock ownership, 178–80
  annual statement form, 197–206
Cash, 152
  aspects of handling, 76
  bank statement reconciliations, 77–81,
    89; *see also* Bank statement recon-
    ciliations
    alternate form of, 81–82
  imprest system for petty cash, 76–77,
    89
Cash accounting system for debit in-
    surance, 297–99
Cash basis accounting, 39, 47
Cash basis life accounting, 139–42, 148
Cash ratios, 364–65
Cash surrender of policy, 338–39
Cashiers, 268, 285, 288
Character, 105
Chart of accounts, 88–90
  machine accounting, 106–7
  model, 93–98
Check digit, 107
Claim accounting; *see* Claim settlements;
    Claim liabilities; Claims *and related
    topics*
Claim approver, 349
Claim liabilities, 156, 361–63, 379
Claim ratios, 364–66
Claim register, 358–59
Claim reserves, 362–63, 372–78

Claim settlements, 327, 379
  accounting procedures, 358–61
  annual statement aspects of, 370–78
  classifications of, 357
  delay in making, reasons for, 362
  drafts issued in payment of, 361
  expense of, 405
  journal entries for, 349–56
  payment methods, 360–61
  records of, 358–61
  register entry, 358–59
  voucher authorizing payment, 360
Claim voucher, 360
Claims, 379
  accidental death rider, 350, 352
  accounting controls and records, 350,
    357–61
  annual statement aspects of, 370–74
  coinsurance benefit entries, 357
  course of settlement, 362
  death, 350–52
  defined, 349
  disability, 354–56
  disbursements classifications, 357
  due and unpaid, 362–63
  endowment policies, maturity of, 353
  health insurance, 353–57
  incurred but not yet paid, 156
  incurred but unreported, 363
  indemnity, 357
  liabilities for, 361–63
  matured endowments, 353
  medical expense, 356
  payment entries, 349–50
  records, 357–61
  reinsurance benefit entries, 357
  resisted, 363
Closing the books
  defined, 33
  objectives of, 33
  steps in, review of, 36–37
  time for, 33
Closing entries
  defined, 33
  illustration of, 33–35
Code number system, 88–89
  machine accounting, 106–7
  Model Life Insurance Company illus-
    tration of, 93–98
Coinsurance benefit entries, 357
Collateral loans, 196
Collators, 127
Collected income, 170
Collection and bank service charges, 406
Collection card, 219, 265, 280, 297
Collection list, 297
Commercial accounting; *see* Accounting
    and related topics

Commission and conservation system, 301, 302
Commission schedules, 256–57
Commission statement, 238–39, 250
Commissions
  accounting for, 237 ff.
  agent's account, 238–40, 250
    entries for, 241–48; *see also* Agent's account
  annual statement aspects, 248–50
  basis for amount payable as, 237, 250
  debit insurance systems, 300–303
  group insurance, 319–21; *see also* Group commissions
  individual premium accounting, 256–58, 275, 281
  methods used to control and account for, 210–11
  objectives of accounting for, 237–38
  overriding or overwriting, 237
  percentage payable as, 237, 250
  premium deposits, 217–18
  records of, 238–41
  statement of, 238–39, 250
  taxes on, 243–44
Common stock, 178; *see also* Capital stock ownership
Compound entries, 34
Computer systems, 105, 128; *see also* Computers
  audit trail requirements, 117
  equipment, 130–32
Computers, 100, 105
  central processor, 129
  functions of, 128–32
  language of, 129
  magnetic tape, use of, 130
  mass storage devices, 132–33
  memory of, 105, 129
  physical characteristics of, 128–29
  programs for, 129–30
  records, 105
  status print-out or report, 258
    limitations of, 262
Consideration for supplementary contracts
  with life contingencies (WCL), 351, 362
  without life contingencies (WOLC), 351, 367
Consolidated function file, 114
Consolidated function record, 105, 114
Consulting actuaries' fees, 404
Contract payments defined, 349
Contributed surplus, 159
Controls, 116

Control accounts, 85–87, 90
  advantage of, 87
  types of, 87
Control month, 265
Convention Blank, 138
Conventional bookkeeping machines, 100–103
  functions of, 120–23
  payroll check processing by, 120–23
Conventional mortgage loans, 183–84
Conventional policy loans, 190
Corporate bonds, 172
Corporate stock, investment in, 151–52
Corporation
  accounting for, 7
  defined, 7
Cost of operations, 142
Credit
  accounting as basis for determination of, 4–5
  accounting records required for, 2–3
Credit balance, 15
Credit insurance, 161; *see also* Creditor group insurance
Credit union group insurance, 309
  defined, 322
Creditor group insurance, 309
  defined, 322
  outstanding balance plan of issuance, 323
  plans for issuance of, 323–24
  single premium plan of issuance, 323–24
Crossfooting in conventional bookkeeping machines, 101

D

Data
  character to represent, 105
  defined, 103
  machine readable nature of, 103
  storage of, 106; *see also* Input media *and* Storage of data
Data coding, 106–7
Data processing equipment; *see* Repetitive-data processing equipment
Date payable, 38
Death claims, 350–52
  date payment starts, 362
  unreported, 363
Debit agent, 284–87
Debit balance, 15
Debit commission leveling plans, 302–3
  fiscal-quarter system, 303
  floating quarter method, 303
  reserve plan, 303

Debit insurance accounting, 284 ff.
  advance and arrears system for control, 88–97
  agency accounting functions, 285–88
  agent's earnings statement form, 305
  agent's report of collections, 298
  cash premium accounting system for control, 297–99
  cashiers, 285, 288
  commission payment systems, 300–303
    commission and conservation system, 302
    leveling plans, 302–3
    times commission system, 301–2
  control of debit collection, systems for, 288–99
  debit agent, 284–87
  defined, 210–11
  district manager, 285
  district offices, 285
  field accounting system, 297–99
  home office processes, 303–5
  master policy record, 299
  monthly premium collection by, 284
  ordinary premium collections, 299–300
  premium receipt book, 285–86
  principal characteristic of, 284
  records required, 298–99
  route collection book, 285–87
  staff managers, 285, 287–88
  techniques for mass data handling, 285
  weekly premium collection by, 284
  year-end matters, 306
Debtor group insurance, 322
Deferred income, 152
Deferred premiums, 152–53, 165
Deficit defined, 37
Definitions; see specific terms
Depreciation
  accounts for, 74
  real estate, 194, 207
  salvage or scrap value estimate, 73–74, 89
Depreciation base, 73, 89
Depreciation entries, 74–76, 89
Depreciation expense, 73, 89
  closing of account for, 74
  furniture and equipment, 405–6
  straight-line method of calculation, 73
Depreciation process, 73
Detail file, 114
Disability claims, 354–56, 362
Discounts
  advance premiums, 214
  bond, 173–77, 206
  mortgage loan, 187
District manager, 285

District offices, 285
  summary report, 288
District summary and receipts, 304
Dividend liabilities, 156–57
Dividends paid to policyholders; see Policy dividends
Dividends paid to stockholders, 32, 46, 164, 169–70
Dollar control, 116
  individual premium accounting, 280
  premium income, 220–21, 233
Dollar signs, use of, 31
Double-entry bookkeeping, 13, 23
  advantages of, 13, 23
Due, meaning attributed to, 38
Due and unpaid claims, 362–63
Due income, 152, 170
Due premiums, 165, 280
  group insurance, 324

E

Earned income, 170
Efficiency, accounting as means of measuring, 5
Electric accounting machines, 105
Electronic data processing; see Computers and Computer systems
Electronic data processing equipment, 105
  investment in, 196
Employee benefits, 401, 404
Employee group insurance, 311–15
Employer group insurance, 309; see also Employee group insurance
Endowment policies, maturity of, 353
Escrow entries for mortgage loans, 184, 186, 207
Expense accounts, 29–30, 46
Expense transactions, 28–31
  defined, 46
Expenses, 27, 382 ff.
  accounting entries for, 382–87
  agency, 407
  agents' balances charged off, 386–87
  allocation to major lines of business, 397, 400
  annual statement aspects, 396–97, 433–36
  approval of, 382–83
  budgeting, 390–94, 411; see also Budgets
  bureau and association dues, 406
  claim settlements, 405
  classification of, 389
  collection and bank service charges, 406
  consolidation by sublines of business, 442

Expenses—*Cont.*
control of, 382–87
defined, 17
depreciation of furniture and equipment, 405–6
distribution by lines of business, 439, 441–42
employee benefits, 401, 404
entries, 383–87
functional cost analysis, 394–96, 411; *see also* Functional costs
functional reporting, 389
furniture and equipment, 384–86
group service and administration fees, 407
investment costs, 408
legal fees and expenses, 404
liability for, 387–89, 409
objectives of accounting for, 382
real estate, 407–8
rental of equipment, 406
reporting of, 389–90
requisition for check for payment of, 383
responsibility area, 389, 391
responsibility reports, 390–94, 411
salaries, 384, 401
supplies, 384–86
tax, 384; *see also* Taxes
types of, 389, 400–408, 411
Experience refunds, 321
Express charges, 405
Extended term insurance, 339–40

F

Fee income account, 33–34
Field accounting system for premium control, 297–99
Files of records, 106, 113–15
Financial aspects of a business, 2
Fiscal period, 38
calendar year distinguished, 38
Fixed assets, 72–76, 89
Folio references, 12
Foreclosure, 183
Franchise insurance, 354
Fraud, accounting system as protection against, 5
Functional costs, 394–96, 411
Functional unit cost; *see* Functional costs
Functions of accounting, 3–6
Functions of machine accounting, 120 ff.; *see also specific machines*
Funds for further protection of policyowners, capital section of balance sheet, 22

Furniture and equipment, 72–73
accounting for purchase of, 384–86
depreciation cost, 405–6
rental costs, 406

G

Gain on disposal of fixed assets, 75–76
Gang-punching of cards, 126–27
General contingency reserve, 158
General fund, 148
General journal, 18 n, 19, 82
disadvantage of, 82
General ledgers, 85
Gifts and donations, 406
Glossary of terms, 479–88; *see also specific terms*
Going-concern concept, 142–43
Government allotment for premium payment, 277
Government bonds, 172
Government regulation
annual statement form, 137
reason for, 136
Grace period
failure to pay premium within, 212
group insurance, 311
Gross profit on sales, 51–53
Group commissions
calculation of rates of, 319–21
experience refunds, 321
Group conversion, 434–36
Group insurance, 161, 308–11; *see also* Employee group insurance *and* Group premium accounting
policy reserves, 155
service and administration fees, 407
unearned premiums, 215
Group premium accounting, 308 ff.; *see also* Group insurance
billing methods, 315–18
claim payment by employer, 318
defined, 211
due premiums, 324
employer group billing, 315–18
entries, 318
list billing, 316
policy reserves, 324
principal characteristic of, 308
reports, 318
self-administered billing or self-billing, 316, 317
summary billing, 316–17
transaction record, 318
unearned premiums, 324
year-end matters, 324–25

H

Hash totals, 116
Health insurance
  accounting and control of, 354
  annual statement, 138, 227, 445–46
  collectively renewable, 353–54
  individual, 161
  individual premium accounting,
    257–58
  policy fee, 258
  policy reserves, 155–56
  premium rates, increases in, 353–54
  premiums, 153
  renewability conditions, 353
  salary allotment for premium pay-
    ment, 278
  unearned premiums, 215
  waiver of premiums, 356
Home office accounting processes for
  debit insurance, 303–5
Home office buildings, 195–96
Hospital insurance, 356

I

Imprest system for petty cash, 76–77, 89
Income, 27
  consolidation by sublines of business,
    442
  defined, 17
  distribution by lines of business, 439–
    41
  premiums as source of; *see* Premium
    income
Income accounts, 29–30, 46
Income and expense statement, 30
  illustration, 31
Income and expense summary, 33, 46
Income from insurance contracts, 160
Income statement, 30
Income taxes
  accounting system as source of infor-
    mation for, 5–6
  preparation of personal returns, 1
Income transactions, 28–31
  defined, 46
Incurred ratios, 364–66
Indemnity claims, 357
Individual premium accounting, 254 ff.
  account titles, 272–74
  advance premiums, 280–81
  branch office handling of payments,
    268–69
  cashiers' work in, 255
  characteristics of system of, 254–58
  collection card, 265, 280

Individual premium accounting—*Cont.*
  computer status print-out or report,
    258
    limitations of, 262
  control month, 266
  control processes, 263–67
  defined, 210–11
  dividend records, 262
  dollar control, 280
  due premiums, 280
  file folder for each policy, 263
  flexibility in premium payment, 255
  government allotment for payment,
    277
  health insurance, 257–58
  home office handling of payments,
    269–72
  initial premiums, 266–67
  master files, 265
  modes of payment, 255
  monthly payment systems, 275–78
  optional methods of payment, 255
  policyholder's stub, 263
  postdated checks for payment, 276–77
  preauthorized check for payment,
    275–76
  premium audit report, 273
  premium entries, 274–75
  premium notices, 263–65
  processing payments of premiums,
    267–68
    branch office handling, 268–69
    home office handling, 269–72
  reinsurance premiums, 278–81
  remittance stub, 265
  salary allotment for payment, 277–78
  salvage commission, 257
  schedule T on annual statement, 280
  suspense accounts, control of, 267
  taxable premiums, determination of
    amount of, 280
  year-end processes, 280–81
Industrial insurance, 161, 284
  unearned premiums, 215
Initial premium invoice, 266–67
Input, 106
Input media, 106–7
  magnetic tape, 106, 112–13
  punched cards, 104–6, 108–10
  punched paper tape, 106, 111–12
Inspection report fees, 404
Insurance accounting; *see* Life accounting
Insurance costs and expenses, 139, 406,
  433–36
Interest adjustment, 206
Interest on bonds and loans, 169–72

Interest credited to amounts on deposit, 328-32
Interest on policy loans, 191-92
Interim statement, 392-93, 411
Interpreters, 126
Inventory, 51-52, 70
  adjusting entries for, 68-70
  beginning, 51, 70
  cost method of valuation, 51
  ending, 51, 70
  taking of, 52
  valuing of, 51
Inventory account, entries in, 53-54
Investigation expense, 405
Investment costs, 408
Investment generation, 438-39
Investment income
  accounting for, 169-72, 196
  accrual basis, 206
  accrued, 152, 170
  adjustment from cash to accrual basis, 170-72
  allocation of, 437-39
  annual statement form, 198-99
  collected, 170
  due, 152, 170
  earned, 170
  gross, 196
  investment generation method of allocation, 437, 438-39
  mean funds method of allocation, 437, 438
  net, 196
  types of, 169
  unearned, 170
Investment principal
  accounting for, 168-69
  capital gains and losses on, 168
  control account, 169, 206
  entry for purchase of, 168
  income entries, 169
  realized capital gains and losses, 168, 181, 206
  subsidiary ledger accounts, 169, 206
  unrealized capital gains and losses, 169, 180, 206
Investments, 151-52
  accounting for, 167 ff.; *see also specific topics*
  bond accounting, 172-77
  capital gains and losses exhibit on annual statement, 200-202
  collateral loans, 196
  electronic data processing equipment, 196
  importance of, 167
  income, accounting for; *see* Investment income

Investments—*Cont.*
  Mandatory Securities Valuation Reserve, 180-83
  mortgage loans, 183-88
  net income from, 160
  personal problems of, 1-2
  policy loans, 189-92
  principal, accounting for; *see* Investment principal
  purpose of, 167
  rate of return requirement, 167
  real estate, 192-96
  stock owned, accounting for, 178-80
  types of, 167
Item control, 116
  premium income, 218-20, 233

J

Journal entry, 18
Journals
  defined, 18, 25
  form of, 19
  general, 18 n, 19, 82
  ledger folio column, 19
  posting of entries from, 18-20
  special, 82-85, 89

K

Key punch machines, 124-25

L

Ledger, 18, 25
  general, 85
  posting to, 18-20
  subsidiary, 85, 87, 90
Ledger assets, 142
  reconciliation of, 420-26
    description of items in, 426-27
    entries for, 421
    process of, 424-25
    relationship of balance account to, 425-26
Ledger cards
  bonds, 177
  mortgage loans, 185
  payroll, 121
  real estate, 195
  stocks, 177, 179
Ledger folio column, 19
Ledger liabilities, 142
Ledger liability process, 328-30, 346
Ledger surplus, 148
Legal fees and expenses, 404
Leveling plans; *see* Debit commission leveling plans

Liabilities, 8, 24; *see also specific type*
  accounts for, 12
  annual statement, 420
  balance sheet classification of, 153–59
  ledger, 142
  nonledger, 142
License expense account, 34
Licenses and fees of insurance departments, 408
Life accounting; *see also specific topics*
  characteristics of, 136–37
  commercial accounting distinguished, 135, 138–48
  defined, 135
  standardization of practices, 135–36
  variances in practices among companies, 135–36
Life insurance accounting; *see* Life accounting
Life register, 288, 294–97
Line of business
  classification of, 161, 165
  defined, 161, 165
  major, 161
  secondary, 161, 165
Liquidation value, 143, 148
Loans; *see* Mortgage loans *and* Policy loans
Loss on disposal of fixed assets, 75–76; *see also* Capital gains and losses
Losses, expense of, 406

M

Machine accounting, 99; *see also specific types*
  accounting controls, 115–16
  advantages of, 100
  central processor, 105
  check digit, 107
  computer systems, 100, 105
  consolidated function record, 105
  conventional bookkeeping machines, 100–103
  data coding, 106–7
  disadvantages of, 100
  electronic data processing equipment, 105
  functions of, 120 ff.; *see also specific machine*
  input, 106
  input media; *see* Input media
  memory for storage of data, 105
  off line, 106
  on line, 106
  output, 106
  punched card machines, 105
  punched paper tape, 106
  record, 105

Machine accounting—*Cont.*
  registers, use of, 116
  repetitive-data processing equipment, 100, 103–4
  storage, 106–7
    direct access, 106
    mass, 106, 132–33
    media for; *see* Input media
  terminology used in, 104–7; *see also specific term*
  types of, 100
  unit record equipment, 100, 104–5
Machine language, 129
Magnetic discs, 106
Magnetic Ink Character Recognition (MICR), 106
Magnetic tape, 106, 112–13, 130
Major medical insurance, 356
Managerial responsibilities, accounting knowledge necessary for, 2
Mandatory Securities Valuation Reserve (MSVR), 158, 163–64
  accounting for, 180–83, 206
  amount of, maximum and additions to, 181–82, 206
  function of, 180–81
Mark reading machines, 127–28
Market price valuation, 152
Mass storage devices, 106, 132–33
Master billing file, 265
Master files, 113–14
Master policy file, 265
Master policy record, 299
Master record defined, 113
Maternity benefits, deferred, 363
Matured endowments, 353
Mean of policy reserves and liabilities, 437–38
Mean funds, 438
Mean reserve, 154–55, 165
Medical examination fees, 404
Medical expense claims, 356
Merchandise operations, 49, 70
Miscellaneous assets, 153
Miscellaneous expenses, 405–7
Miscellaneous liabilities, 158
Mortality table, 156
Mortgage brokers, 186–87
Mortgage loans, 152, 183–88, 207
  annual statement form, 197
Mutual life insurance company ledger, surplus account in, 27

N

Net deferred premiums, 165
Net gain, 58
Net gain from insurance operations, 139, 159

Net income, 46, 58
  defined, 31
Net ledger assets, 148
Net loss, 46, 58
  defined, 31
Net premium value, 153
Net worth, 8, 24
New business, effect on operating gains, 442–44
Nominal accounts, 32–33, 46
Nonadmitted assets
  annual statement, 420, 427–30
  changes in, analysis of, 164
  values, 144–46, 148
Nonforfeiture settlements, 327, 337–38, 347
  cash surrender, 338–39
  extended term insurance, 339–40
  reduced paid-up insurance, 339–40
Nonledger assets, 142, 144
  annual statement, 415
Nonledger liabilities, 142, 146, 156–57
Nonledger liability process, 330–32, 346
Note collections, 79
Note payable, 11, 17–18
Notice to policyholders
  policy dividends, 334
  premium income, 213

O

Operating gains, 159, 163
  capital, surplus and investment effectiveness, effect of, 444–45
  new business, effect of, 442–44
Operating statement, 138
Optical character recognition (OCR), 106
Optical scanner, 131–32
Ordinary insurance, 161
Output, 106
Outstanding premiums, 165
Overriding agents, 237
Overriding commission, 257

P

Par value
  bond, 172
  stock, 178
Partnership, 7
Payroll checks, bookkeeping machine processing of, 120–23
Payroll deduction plan, 277
Period earned, 38
Period incurred, 38–39
Personal uses of accounting, 1–2
Petty cash, imprest system for, 76–77, 89
Petty cash box, 77
Petty cash fund, 89

Petty cash voucher, 77
Plug boards, 123
Policy benefit settlements, 160
  amounts left on deposit with company, 328–32, 346
  analysis of claim statistics, 328
  authorization of disbursements, 327
  classification of benefits, 327
  nonforfeiture options; *see* Nonforfeiture settlements
  objectives of proper accounting for, 327
Policy dividends, 160, 164, 332–38
  additional insurance provided for, 336
  annual statement form for, 340–43
  application to pay premiums, 335
  cash payment of, 335
  disbursement when held under option, 336–37
  entries for, 335–38
  liability, 156–57, 340–46
Policy loans, 152, 189–92
  accounting for, 189–92
  annual statement form, 200
  interest on, 191–92
  records kept of, 190, 262
Policy record cards, 258–62
Policy reserves, 136, 154–56
  balance sheet treatment of, 154–56
  change in valuation basis of, 165
  group insurance, 324
  health insurance, 155–56
  increase in, 160
  mean reserve, 154–55, 165
  valuation, 141, 154
Policy status
  defined, 258
  records of, 258–63
Policyholders' stub, 263
Postage expenses, 405
Postdated checks for premium payment, 276–77
Posting, 18–20, 90
  adjusting entries, 46
  disadvantage of, 82
Preauthorized check for premium payment (PAC), 275–76
Preferred stock, 178
Premium audit report, 273
Premium collection process and control, 218–21, 233
Premium deposits, 213–14, 217, 233, 328
  commissions on, 217–18
Premium income
  accounting for, 210 ff.
  advance premiums, 213–14, 233
  allocation by states and territories in annual statement, 223

Premium income—*Cont.*
  annual statement aspects of, 221–27,
    233–34
  collection card for, 219
  complexity of billing and accounting
    problems, 210, 218
  conditions of payment of, 212–13
  control processes, 218–21, 233; *see also*
    specific premium accounting topic
  debit premium system, 210–11, 284 ff.;
    see also Debit insurance accounting
  dishonor of check given in payment
    of, 213, 216
  dollar control, 220–21, 233
  enforceability of collection of, 212
  entries for collection of, 215–18
  exhibits on annual statement, 222–25
  grace period expiration for payment
    of, 212
  group premium accounting, 210–11,
    308 ff.; *see also* Group premium
    accounting
  increase in loading, 223, 226–27, 234
  individual premium system, 210–11,
    254 ff.; *see also* Individual premium
    accounting
  insufficient funds to cover check for,
    213
  item control, 218–20, 233
  late payment of, 212–13
  liabilities for payment of, 213–15
  methods used to control and account
    for, 210–11
  nonpayment by policyholder, 212
  notice to policyholders, 213
  objectives of accounting for, 211–12
  postmark date as evidence of date of
    payment, 212
  premium deposits, 213–14, 217, 233
    commissions on, 217–18
  premium suspense, 213, 215, 233
  schedule T on annual statement, 223
  unearned premiums, 213–15, 233
  wrong amount paid as, 213
Premium ledger cards, 261
Premium notices, 213, 263–64
  preparation of, 265
Premium receipt book, 285–86
Premium record cards, 260
Premium suspense, 213, 215, 233
Premiums
  bond, 173–77, 206
  mortgage loan, 187
Prepaid expenses, 428
  adjusting entries for, 41–42, 47, 65–66
  defined, 41
Printing and stationery costs, 405

Problems at end of each chapter, answers
    to, 489 ff.
Professional service fees and expenses,
    404–5
Profit defined, 28
Profit on sale or maturity, 168
Profit and loss statement, 30
Profit and loss summary, 33 n
Programer language, 129
Programing of computers, 129–30
Property taxes, 193, 408
Public accountants' fees, 404
Punched card machines, 105
Punched cards, 104–10
Punched paper tape, 106, 111–12
  defined, 111
Purchase money mortgage, 183
Purchases, 50–51, 70

R

Random access devices, 132
Ratio of net invested income to mean
    assets, 200
Ratios, claim, 364–66
Real accounts, 46
Real estate, 192–96
  annual statement form, 200
  expenses in connection with, 407–8
  home office buildings, 195–96
  investment in, 151–52, 192–96
  mortgage loans on; *see* Mortgage loans
  rental on; *see* Rent on real estate
  taxes on; *see* Property taxes
Real time capability, 132
Realized capital gains and losses, 168,
    181, 206
Reconciliation of bank account; *see*
    Bank statement reconciliations
Reconciliation of ledger assets, 140–41
Record files; *see* Files of records
Reduced paid-up insurance, 339–40
Registered bonds, 172–73
Reinstatement of policy
  approval of, 213
  offer for, 212
  request for, 212
Reinsurance benefit entries, 357
Reinsurance premiums, 278–81
Remittance stub, 263
Remittances and items not allocated,
    157–58
Remitting nets, 245–48
Rent on real estate, 169–70
Rent expense, 401
  account for, 34
  allocation to major lines of business,
    400
Rent income account, 66–68

Rental of equipment, 406
Repetitive-data processing equipment
defined, 103
punched cards used in, 108
uses made of, 103–4
Reproducers, 126–27
Reserve for depreciation account, 74
Reserve strengthening, 165
Resisted claims, 363
Responsibility reports, 390–94, 411
Retained earnings, 16 n
Revenue and expense statement, 30
Revenue statement, 30
Reversal and reentry method of making
adjusting entries, 65, 67–68
Route collection book, 285–87

S

Salary allotment for premium payment,
277–78
Salary allotment insurance, 277
Salary deduction plan, 277
Salary expense, 384, 401
account for, 34
allocation to major lines of business,
397, 400
Salary savings plan, 277
Sales, 49–50, 70
cost of, 50–51
gross profit on, 51–53
net profit on, 53
Sales journal, 82–83
Salvage commission, 257
Salvage or scrap value, estimation of,
73–74, 89
Schedules on balance sheet, 152
Service fee income, 30
Settlement contracts, 351
Settlements of policy benefits; see Policy
benefit settlements
Share certificates on annual statement
form, 197
Shareholders; see Stockholders
Simple entries, 34
Single-entry bookkeeping, 24
Single proprietorship, 7
Social security taxes; see Taxes
Sorters, 125–26
Source of information, accounting
system as, 2, 5–6
Special journals, 82–85, 87, 89, 90
Special reserves, 158
Special surplus adjustments, 164
Special surplus funds, 159
Staff manager, 285, 287–88
Statement of financial condition, 9
Statement of income and expense, 46
Statement of surplus, 37–38

Status file, 113–14
Status print-out, 258–62
Stock dividend, 179
Stock life insurance company ledger,
capital stock account in, 27
Stock ownership; see Capital stock own-
ership
Stockholders, 8
dividends to; see Dividends paid to
stockholders
Stockholders' equity, 8
Storage of data, 106–7, 132–33
media for; see Input media
Straight-line depreciation, 73
Subsidiary ledgers, 85, 90
advantage of, 87
Suicide, 350
Summary of operations, 30–31, 139, 159–
60
Summary file, 114–15
Summary punch machines, 127
Summary Remittance Report, 269–70
Sundry general expenses, 406
Supplementary contracts, 327, 368–70
annual statement, 433
considerations with life contingencies,
351, 367
considerations without life contingencies, 351, 367
defined, 366
liability for, 368, 370
Surplus, 10, 16 n, 158–59
accounting for changes in, 27 ff.
statement of, 37–38
Surplus account, 27–28, 46, 139
analysis of changes in, 162–65
annual statement, 430–32
balance account as form of, 146
transfer of surplus changes to, 28
Suspense accounts, 158
control of, 266

T

T-accounts, 12–13
Tabulators, 123–24
Taxes, 160
allocation to major lines of business,
397
annual statement aspects, 396–99
commission earnings, 243–44
entries for payment of, 384
liability for, 388, 409
property; see Property taxes
social security, 408–9
Telephone and telegraph charges, 405
Time elements in accounting, 38–39
Times commission system, 301–2
Transaction file, 114

Transaction record defined, 114
Traveling expense, 405
Trial balance, 20–23, 25
   adjusted, 46
   after-closing, 35–36, 47
   balance sheet preparation from, 21–23
   function of, 20
   incomplete, 147
Trustee group insurance, 311
Type of insurance coverage, 156, 165
Types of insurance, 161, 165

U

Unassigned surplus, 159
Uncollected premiums, 152–53, 165
Unearned income, 157, 170
   adjusting entries for, 40–41, 47, 66
   defined, 40
Unearned premiums, 213–15, 233
   group insurance, 324
   health insurance, 227, 232–33
Union group insurance, 311
Unit costs; *see* Functional costs
Unit record equipment, 100, 104–5, 123–28
United States annual statement aspects; *see* Annual statement *or other related topics*

United States life insurance companies; *see* Annual statement *or other specific topics*
Unrealized capital gains and losses, 169, 180, 206

V

Valuation
   assets
      amortization, 144, 148
      going-concern, 142–43
      liquidation, 143, 148
   bonds, 152
   investments, 151
   policy reserves, 141, 154
Verifiers, 126

W

Wages; *see* Salary expense
Weekly premium insurance, 284
Working papers, 54–55, 70
   adjusting entries in, 61–68, 70
   defined, 54–55
   form illustrated, 55
   function of, 56
   preparation of, 56–61

This book has been set in 10 and 9 point Janson, leaded 2 points. Chapter numbers are in 16 point Helvetica Regular and chapter titles are in 24 point Helvetica Medium. The size of the type page is 27 x 45½ picas.